BEFORE THE BAUHAUS

Before the Bauhaus reevaluates the political, architectural, and artistic cultures of pre–World War I Germany. Every bit as contradictory and conflict-ridden as the German Second Reich itself, the world of architects, craftsmen, and applied-arts "artists" was in no way immune to the expansionist, imperialist, and capitalist struggles that transformed Germany in the quarter-century leading up to the First World War. In this study, John V. Maciuika brings together architectural and design history, political history, social history, and cultural geography. He substantially revises our understanding of the roots of the Bauhaus and, by extension, the historical roots of twentieth-century German architecture and design. At the same time, his book also sheds new light on hotly contested debates pertaining to the history of pre–World War I Germany: namely, questions involving the "modernity" or "anti-modernity" of the German Second Empire, the character and effectiveness of the government administration, and the role played by the nation's most important architects, members of the rising bourgeois class, in challenging the traditional aristocracy at the top of the new German economic and social order.

John V. Maciuika is assistant professor of art and architectural history at the City University of New York, Baruch College, and the City University of New York Graduate Center program in art history. A recipient of fellowships from the Alexander von Humbolt Foundation, the Graham Foundation, the NEH, and the DAAD, he has contributed to *Centropa*, *Design Issues*, and *German Studies Review*. He was the winner of the Year 2000 Research Article Prize from the German Studies Association of North America.

MODERN ARCHITECTURE AND CULTURAL IDENTITY

Series Editor:

Richard Etlin, *University of Maryland, College Park*

Advisory Board:

Steven Mansbach, *University of Maryland, College Park*
Narciso Menocal, *University of Wisconsin, Madison*
Andrew Saint, *Cambridge University*
Gwendolyn Wright, *Columbia University*

Modern Architecture and Cultural Identity will comprise monographic studies of important movements and buildings by European and American architects created roughly between 1850 and 1950. Unlike the first histories of modernism, which stressed the international aspects of modern architecture, recent scholarship has attempted to clarify the delicate balance achieved by architects working in a modernist idiom who maintained, nonetheless, a strong allegiance to their cultural roots. This series has been developed in response to this trend and will explore the complex interplay among modern identity and local, regional, national, and related cultural traditions.

Books published in the Series:

The Civic Architecture of Paul Cret, Elizabeth Grossman
The English Garden and National Identity, Anne Helmreich
The Modern American House, Sandy Isenstadt
Erich Mendelsohn and the Architecture of German Modernism, Kathleen James
*National Romanticism and Modern Architecture in Germany
and the Scandinavian Countries*, Barbara Miller Lane
Art Nouveau and the Social Vision of Modern Living, Amy Ogata
Arts and Crafts in Late Imperial Russia, Wendy Salmond
The Chicago Tribune Tower Competition, Katherine Solomonson

Before the Bauhaus

ARCHITECTURE, POLITICS, AND THE GERMAN STATE, 1890–1920 ಎ

John V. Maciuika

City University of New York, Baruch College and Graduate Center

CAMBRIDGE
UNIVERSITY PRESS

CAMBRIDGE UNIVERSITY PRESS
Cambridge, New York, Melbourne, Madrid, Cape Town, Singapore, São Paulo, Delhi

Cambridge University Press
32 Avenue of the Americas, New York, NY 10013-2473, USA

www.cambridge.org
Information on this title: www.cambridge.org/9780521728225

First published 2005
First paperback edition 2008

Printed in the United States of America

A catalog record for this publication is available from the British Library.

Library of Congress Cataloging in Publication Data

Maciuika, John V.
  Before the Bauhaus : architecture, politics and the German state, 1890–1920 /
John V. Maciuika.
    p. cm.
  Includes bibliographical references and index.
  ISBN 0-521-79004-2 (hardback)
  1. Architecture – Germany – 20th century. 2. Architecture – Germany – 19th century.
3. Architecture and state – Germany – History. 4. Bauhaus. I. Title.
NA1068.M33   2005
720'.943'0941 – dc22   2004018644

ISBN 978-0-521-79004-8 hardback
ISBN 978-0-521-72822-5 paperback

CONTENTS ॐ

v

LIST OF ILLUSTRATIONS ॐ

LIST OF ABBREVIATIONS ꕤ

BAGP	Bauhaus Archives, Gropius Papers
BAK	*Blätter für Architektur und Kunsthandwerk*
BArch	Bundesarchiv (Federal Archives–Berlin)
BDI	Bund der Industriellen (Association of Industrialists)
BWAZ	Bau- und Wohnungsaufsichtsamt Zehlendorf (Zehlendorf Building Office)
CdB	*Centralblatt der Bauverwaltung* (Construction Administration Gazette)
CDI	Centralverband Deutscher Industrieller (Central Association of German Industrialists)
DK	*Dekorative Kunst*
DKuD	*Deutsche Kunst und Dekoration*
DWB	Deutscher Werkbund
GCS	Garden City Society (Deutsche Gartenstadt-Gesellschaft)
GNM-ABK	Germanisches Nationalmuseum Nürnberg, Abteilung Bildende Kunst (Germanic National Museum Nuremberg, Fine Arts Section)
GStA PK	Geheimes Staatsarchiv Preussischer Kulturbesitz (Prussian State Archives)
HW	*Hohe Warte*
JDWB	*Jahrbuch des Deutschen Werkbundes*
KgBl	*Kunstgewerbeblatt*
KKH	*Kunst und Kunsthandwerk*
KW	*Kunstwart*
LAB	Landesarchiv Berlin (Berlin City and State Archive)
MB	*Moderne Bauformen*
MDWB	*Mitteilungen des Deutschen Werkbundes*
ND	*Neudeutsche Bauzeitung*
NMWA	Nachlass Muthesius im Werkbund-Archiv (Muthesius Estate in Werkbund Archives, Berlin)
ThHStA	Thüringisches Hauptstaatsarchiv
UdK	Archiv der Universität der Künste-Berlin (Berlin University of the Arts-Archives)
VB	*Verwaltungsbericht* (*Jahresbericht des Königlich Preussisches Ministerium für Handel und Gewerbe*)

ACKNOWLEDGMENTS ꙮ

This book is an effort to combine German architectural history and German history in a manner that sheds new light on debates involving the Wilhelmine era (1871–1918). It has benefited from the support of countless institutions as well as individuals, and it is a pleasure to thank them here. The incomparable and generous Alexander von Humboldt Foundation provided support in the form of two academic-year research grants: a postdoctoral Federal Chancellor's Fellowship in 1998–99, and a Faculty Research Fellowship in 2001–02. The German Academic Exchange Service (DAAD) also provided thirteen months of grant support in the 1995–96 academic year for research at the dissertation stage, enabling initial archival discoveries at the Prussian State Archives that laid important foundations for the present book.

Generous summer grant support for writing and research also came from the University of Virginia School of Architecture, Office of the Dean, in the summer of 2004, the University of Virginia Office of the Vice Provost for Research in the summer of 2003, and the National Endowment for the Humanities in the summer of 2001. I am also grateful for the generosity of the Graham Foundation for Advanced Studies in the Visual Arts, which funded the acquisition and reproduction of the illustrations in this book.

The Yale University Department of History kindly hosted a semester of academic research leave in the spring of 2004, which greatly eased the final stages of manuscript editing and illustration gathering. The Institute for Architectural History and Theory at the University of the Arts in Berlin, Germany, provided a supportive research base during the 1995–96 and 2001–02 academic years. The Institute for Regional Planning and Urban Development (IRS) in Berlin-Erkner offered similarly kind support by serving as my institutional host for the 1998–99 academic year. Thanks are also due to the helpful staffs at the archives listed in the bibliography at the end of this book, and among those to whom special thanks are due here are Reinhart Strecke and Charlotte Krause of the Prussian State Archives in Berlin-Dahlem, Angelika Thiekötter and Gabrielle Ganser of the Berlin Werkbund Archive, Sabine Hartmann of the Bauhaus Archive in Berlin, Andreas Matschenz of the Berlin State Archive (Landesarchiv), and Martina Wagner of the Federal Archives in Berlin-Lichterfelde.

The individuals who helped with various aspects of this book are far more numerous than it is possible to thank here, but I would be remiss if I did not at least express thanks to the following: Michael Bollé, Adelheid Rasche, Kathleen James-Chakraborty, Peter Gerlach, Stefan Muthesius, Gert Gröning, Werner Oechslin, Kevin Repp, Hinrich Seeba, Barry Bergdoll, Laurent Stalder, Stanford Anderson, Tilmann Buddensieg, Andrew Saint, Alan Crawford, Martin Jay, Dell Upton, Vera Muthesius, Ákos Moravánszky, Richard Etlin, Beatrice Rehl, Alon Confino, Paul Betts, Gerald Feldman, Gerald Kleinfeld, Konrad Jarausch, William Morrish, Todd Presner, Greg Castillo, Irina Hasnas Pascal, Markus Erbach, Roswitha Breckner, Meghen Quinn, Peter Heynert, Uwe Schneider, Fedor Roth, Anatol Gottfryd, Magdalena Droste, Beth Rader, Vera Heitmann, and the late Wolfgang Muthesius.

I would also like to thank students who participated in several University of Virginia graduate seminars that contributed to this book, including "The Bauhaus and the Twentieth-Century Modern Movement" and "Modern Architecture in German-Speaking Central Europe." I am grateful for outstanding research assistance to UVA graduate students Astrid Liverman, Jennifer Reut, and Pia Panella, for drawing assistance to Burak Erdim and Joseph Corridore, for help with indexing to Heather McMahon, and for typing assistance to Patty DeCourcy and the late Betty Leake. Special thanks for professional support as well as unending kindness and hospitality in Berlin are also due to Michael Bollé and Heidi Rasche, Markus Erbach, and Lothar Fehn-Krestas and Angelika Fehn-Krestas, who all helped make Berlin into a warm, welcoming second home – even under the blanketing grey skies and occasional Siberian blasts of three Berlin winters. For their hospitality in Munich and Vienna I am also indebted to Georg Raffelt, Susan Wiener, and Christian Witt-Dörring.

My hosts Michael Bollé at the UdK-Berlin and Peter Gerlach at the IRS-Erkner were especially kind to demonstrate faith in this project at its earliest phases, enabling me to obtain critical support from their own and other German institutions. Norbert Huse of the Munich Technical University remains a particular and early inspiration for advising me in my predoctoral days that "especially when writing about German architectural history between 1900 and 1914, it is critical to remember that major transformations were occurring virtually from year to year, and that these changes had significant effects on how architects chose to work and act in each subsequent year."

The valuable assistance of all of these people, and many more who could not be named, has made this book possible, while any errors appearing in it are my own. Lastly I would like to thank my family for their enduring support, understanding, and love through thick and thin. It is to them that I dedicate this book.

❧ INTRODUCTION

THE POLITICS OF DESIGN REFORM IN THE GERMAN *KAISERREICH* ❧

THE BAUHAUS AND WILHELMINE-ERA ARCHITECTURAL CULTURE

Progressive architectural currents in Weimar Germany could never have resembled those of the Wilhelmine era, any more than the Weimar Republic (1919–33) could have resembled the Wilhelmine Empire (1871–1918). The Weimar Republic, which emerged from the ashes of a shattering military defeat, existed in stark contrast to the Prusso-German *Kaiserreich*, which rose following a string of intoxicating military victories that galvanized Germans to accept forced unification at the hands of Prussia. Yet if the "great divide" of World War I separated the *Kaiserreich* from Weimar Germany, there were nonetheless important attributes of Wilhelmine politics, culture, and society that survived the war to shape the conditions of Weimar Germany, often in unexpected ways.

Walter Gropius's Bauhaus is a classic example of an institution that, in 1919, grew out of the post-war era's unique circumstances while remaining heir to important pre-war innovations in German art, architecture, and the applied arts. Twentieth-century Germany's best-known educational institution for the applied arts, fine arts, and architecture, the Bauhaus continues to be celebrated, reexamined, and criticized by a seemingly uninterrupted flow of literature about the school, its founding director, and an all-star faculty comprised of such luminaries as Wassily Kandinsky, Paul Klee, Johannes Itten, Laszlo Moholy-Nagy, Lyonel Feininger, and many others.[1]

The Thuringian state initially founded the "State Bauhaus in Weimar" (*Staatliches Bauhaus Weimar*) in 1919 for the purpose of reviving the crafts.[2] As the thirty-five-year-old Walter Gropius wrote when he sought budget approval from Thuringian state authorities in 1919, the Bauhaus would promote

1. Henry van de Velde, renovation of Grand Ducal School of Fine Arts, Weimar, 1904 and 1911 general view (altered) (Courtesy of the Fiske Kimball Fine Arts Library Image Collection, University of Virginia)

"a proliferation of the crafts and industry in the state of Weimar as a result of the re-molding of the schools in accordance with a craft-oriented, practical approach."[3] An ambitious school director whom the Belgian artist Henry van de Velde had recommended as his successor, Gropius successfully combined the Weimar Academy of Art and what remained of van de Velde's Weimar School of Applied Arts into a single institution (Figs. 1–3). The school quickly broadened its mission to promote a radical fusion of the fine arts, the decorative arts, architecture, and industrial design. The Bauhaus's innovative introductory course, developed initially by Johannes Itten, together with the school's production of numerous formally innovative industrial prototypes, seemed to leave many aspects of Wilhelmine applied-arts teaching and practice far behind.

From its beginning in 1919, the school met with considerable resistance from nationalist forces who saw the Bauhaus as a menace to traditional German culture. Constantly embattled, underfunded, and forced to leave the cities of Weimar, Dessau, and later Berlin, the school functioned as a kind of crucible for Germany's avant-garde. The Bauhaus drew strength from its affiliations and affinities to such peer European movements as Russian Constructivism, Dada, Surrealism, and the Dutch De Stijl movement – precisely the influences that conservative nationalists, and later Hitler's National Socialists, saw as such a threat to native

2. Henry van de Velde, Grand Ducal School of Applied Arts, Weimar, general view (altered) (*Kunstgewerbeblatt* 22, N.F., 1911)

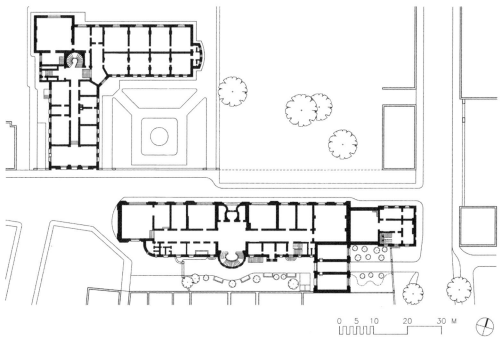

3. Site plan and building plans of Grand Ducal Schools of Fine and Applied Arts, Weimar, 1911 (Drawing by Joe Corridore after L. Walter)

German traditions. Aided in part by exhibitions and publicity received after the emigration of Gropius, Moholy-Nagy, Josef Albers, and Ludwig Mies van der Rohe to the United States, the Bauhaus's reputation achieved mythical status, towering over all other modern German schools of design. The dizzying number of historical reinterpretations of the Bauhaus that have accumulated since its dissolution in 1933 have, in fact, functioned as a veritable index of Western cultural trends and preoccupations ever since.[4]

The continuing popular and scholarly success of the Bauhaus "industry" has also done much to shape the historiography of German architecture and design prior to the First World War. The Bauhaus's dramatic historical trajectory alone was enough to confer an aura of uniqueness to the school that Gropius's tireless efforts at promotion helped reinforce.[5] This apparent uniqueness, however, belies important pre-war precedents that were of a foundational nature for the evolution of twentieth-century German architecture and design. For although the Bauhaus arose under the drastically altered conditions of the Weimar Republic, it was merely the best-known example among countless private and state applied-arts institutions that, for the past several decades, had been coming to grips with a powerful upsurge in German industrialization, rapid commercial development, and the growth of a sophisticated capitalist consumer culture. As much as the Bauhaus and its first director did to publicize fresh approaches to the applied arts and, later, architectural education, the school was advancing a spirit of innovation and experimentation pioneered by many Wilhelmine schools.

The southwest German kingdom of Württemberg, for example, erected a studio art building in Stuttgart in 1907 in order to attract leading artists to the state who would simultaneously teach in the Stuttgart School of Applied Arts (Fig. 4). The architect Bernhard Pankok, director of the local applied-arts school, designed a concrete and glass building as remarkable for its time as the series of changes made by the state of Württemberg to reorganize and strengthen the relationships between architecture, the applied and fine arts, and light manufacturing industries.[6]

Elsewhere, and as early as 1902, fresh approaches to the fine and applied arts could be seen at the Debschitz school in Munich, the Royal School of Art and Applied Arts in Breslau (under the architect Hans Poelzig), the Royal School of Applied Arts in Berlin (under the artist Bruno Paul), the Dusseldorf School of Applied Arts (under the artist and architect Peter Behrens), and many other schools. Not only did these schools pioneer new levels of experimental collaboration between artists, architects, and craftsmen, but they instituted one of the educational features that would become a cornerstone of Bauhaus pedagogy: the instructional workshop (Figs. 5 and 6). Originally inspired by British Arts and Crafts practitioners' principled, "hands-on" return to design training based on the practical mastery of materials and constructional principles, the instructional

4. Bernhard Pankok, atelier building for the Württemberg Association for the Friends of Art, Stuttgart, 1907, view of north side (*Deutsche Kunst und Dekoration* 20, 1907) (destroyed in World War II)

workshop lay at the heart of Germany's early-twentieth-century Applied Arts movement, or *Kunstgewerbebewegung*. Like the Bauhaus later on, this movement regarded architecture and the applied arts as inseparable.[7]

Instructional workshop-based applied-arts training reached particular heights during the Wilhelmine era at Hans Poelzig's Royal School of Art and Applied Arts in Breslau beginning in 1903. As the Bauhaus would do sixteen years later, Poelzig's school modified the fine-arts curriculum of an art academy and fused it with the instructional workshop program of an applied-arts school. Moreover, Poelzig's faculty taught a synthesis of the fine and applied arts in workshops geared explicitly toward architectural production (Fig. 7; see also Figs. 42–43 in Chapter 3). Indeed, Poelzig's emphasis on individual creativity and unification of the arts under the banner of architecture prompted the German architectural historian Hartmut Frank to characterize the pre-war Breslau academy as a "Bauhaus before the Bauhaus."[8]

Changes to the crafts in Second Empire Germany were of foundational importance to the subsequent evolution of architecture and the design fields in twentieth-century Germany. Similar to Britain, where early industrialization spurred an Arts and Crafts movement several decades earlier than Germany, the crafts' importance rested on a twin base. First, the crafts still represented a livelihood for millions.[9] Though threatened by rising mass production and

5. Crefeld School of Crafts and Applied Arts, instructional workshop for lithography and print-making, 1910 (*Grundsätze der Handwerker- und Kunstgewerbeschule Crefeld*, Crefeld, 1911)

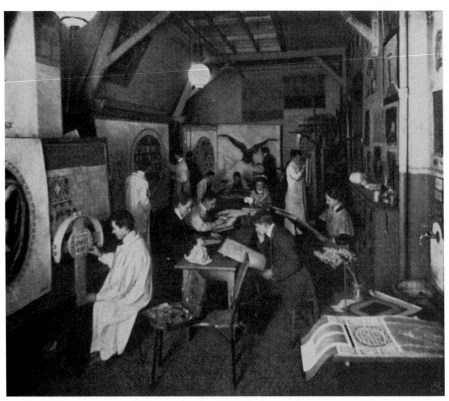

6. Crefeld School of Crafts and Applied Arts, instructional workshop for decorative painting, 1910 (*Grundsätze der Handwerker- und Kunstgewerbeschule Crefeld*, Crefeld, 1911)

7. Hans Poelzig with students and faculty of the Royal Art and Applied Arts School in Breslau, model home for the Breslau Applied Arts Exhibition of 1904, view of hall and dining room (Karl Masner, *Das Einfamilienhaus des Kunstgewerbevereins*, Berlin, 1905)

industrial concentration, this branch of the economy still saw the production of a huge variety of wares by individual artisans skilled in metalwork, cabinetry and furniture-making, bookbinding and leatherworking, ceramics, and other "practical" or "applied" arts (Fig. 8).[10] Second, the crafts represented an avenue for artistic expression and potential cultural reform – particularly among that class of highly trained artists, architects, and craftsmen who saw in the arts, crafts, and industry new ways of coming to grips with the social transformations and unsettling effects of industrial production. During the 1890s, when reform-minded applied artists began designing furnishings, room interiors, and eventually entire buildings in the form of fully integrated, harmonious "total works of art" (a *Gesamtkunstwerk*), architecture began to regain its reputation as what the nineteenth-century art critic John Ruskin had referred to as "the Mother of all the Arts." This provided many Wilhelmine architects and artists with another reason to regard crafts reform and architectural reform as virtually inseparable.

THE ART EDUCATION MOVEMENT, THE WERKBUND, AND WILHELMINE GERMAN REGIONALISM

All of Germany's important pre-war developments in the applied arts, in turn, evolved out of a particular matrix of Wilhelmine historical conditions – circumstances that enabled twentieth-century artists, architects, and applied artists to take on new roles in modern German society in the first place. On one hand, Wilhelmine imperial and state institutions pursued expansive commercial, industrial, and export policies consonant with larger German ambitions to compete with the world's leading imperial and economic powers on an equal footing. On the other hand, and riding a wave of economic expansion that began in the mid-1890s, artists, architects, and applied artists identified emerging areas of industrial growth, commercial expansion, and private consumption as legitimate domains of cultural production. In a development symbolic of the Wilhelmine era's remarkable economic growth and attendant opportunities for cultural experimentation, many of the most celebrated architects active in Germany between the late 1890s and 1918 – Peter Behrens, Richard Riemerschmid, Bruno Paul, and the Belgian Henry van de Velde among them – were professional painters who gravitated to the applied arts and architecture without ever having received even one semester of formal architectural education.

Among educated, artistically inclined turn-of-the-century Germans, the Wilhelmine artist, broadly conceived, would "spiritualize," "harmonize," and otherwise help overcome the adverse effects of industrialization, urbanization, and mass production through constant but varying invocations of German *Kultur*.[11] The Deutscher Werkbund, the design association dedicated since its creation in 1907 to harmonizing German culture and spiritualizing German work, became the epicenter of artists' efforts to recast German products, and indeed all manifestations of German growth, as symbols of a renewed twentieth-century German culture. Whether in factory architecture, domestic appliances and furnishings, luxury ocean liners and naval officers' quarters, or commercial advertising, Werkbund artists strove to become the lead organizers of a "tasteful," accomplished, and economically competitive German output. The architect Fritz Schumacher stated the Werkbund's ambitions clearly in his keynote address at the organization's founding meeting in Munich in 1907: "It is high time that Germany learned to comprehend the artist no longer as someone who pursues his dilettantish interests (*Liebhaberei*) more or less harmlessly, but as someone in whom there resides one of the most powerful forces for the ennoblement of German production. And through the ennoblement of this production, [the artist] ennobles the whole inner life of the nation, which in turn will enable this nation to be victorious in the competition of the peoples."[12]

Earlier developments in Wilhelmine artistic attitudes underpinned this ambitious mobilization of artists for the improvement of German production. Among the most important of these was the wide-ranging, diffuse, but powerful

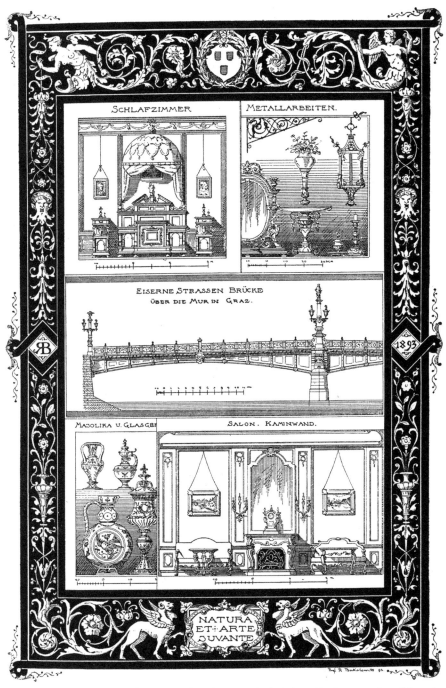

8. Rudolf Bakalowits, catalog entry in *German Applied-Arts Draftsmen*, 1893 (*Deutsche Kunstgewerbe-Zeichner: Ein Addressbuch Deutscher Künstler die sich mit Entwerfen kunstgewerblicher Gegenstände befassen*, Leipzig, 1893)

Movement for Artistic Education (*Kunsterziehungbewegung*), propagated during the 1890s by such cultural critics as Julius Langbehn, Ferdinand Avenarius, and Alfred Lichtwark. Each in their own way, these writers sought to influence German attitudes toward mass production, the proliferation of consumer goods, and home furnishings and decoration. Adherents of the Art Education movement located the source for united Germany's cultural redemption in the arts, which were seen as an antidote to a nineteenth century dominated by the development of science, instrumental reason, industrialization, and commercialization.[13]

Accomplished journalists and celebrated art critics such as Ferdinand Avenarius, Julius Meier-Graefe, and Alexander Koch led the movement in their respective journals *Kunstwart*, *Dekorative Kunst*, and *Deutsche Kunst und Dekoration*. Joined by Alfred Lichtwark, director of the Hamburg Museum of Art; Ludwig Pallat, an educational reformer in the Prussian Ministry of Culture; Peter Jessen of the Arts and Crafts Museum in Berlin; the Prussian architect and civil servant Hermann Muthesius; the Saxon artist and architect Paul Schultze-Naumburg; and the wealthy art patron and reformer Karl Ernst Osthaus, the various members of the Art Education movement embarked on an aggressive campaign to educate public taste in the fine arts and applied arts. By the early 1900s, the movement grew well beyond the readership of the new artistic journals to include museums such as the Museum of Art in Hamburg, the Folkwang Museum operated by Osthaus in Hagen, and various local schools of applied arts.[14]

Particularly successful authors such as Konrad Lange and Julius Langbehn adapted the theme of artistic education in programs to renew German culture and reground German "character" amid the widespread upheavals of German industrial expansion.[15] Langbehn exemplified the Art Education movement's sinister side: his immensely popular *Rembrandt as Educator* (*Rembrandt als Erzieher*) of 1890 sparked a reemergence of Volkish ideology in which adherents identified with their "Germanness" through an array of irrationalist notions. Among these were a belief in the importance of German blood, German soil, and racial purity as sources of national identity, which combined with antirationalism, antiurbanism, and an emphasis on aesthetic politics (*Kunstpolitik*) as an agent for the restoration of a collective, mystical German soul.[16] If Langbehn's calls for German racial purification and leadership by an "invisible emperor" foreshadowed the darkest mutations of Nazism's technologized Volkish thought in the second quarter of the twentieth century, then the nature-loving turn-of-the-century "Wandering Bird Group" (*Wandervogelgruppe*), along with the original, utopian incarnation of the German Garden City Society, represented a more hopeful, positive, opposite Volkish extreme.[17]

A similar diversity characterized Wilhelmine Germany's cultural and political geography. The Swiss architect Charles-Edouard Jeanneret (known as "Le Corbusier" after 1920), an avid student of Germany's applied-arts movement before the First World War, noted aptly in 1912 that the Wilhelmine Empire could

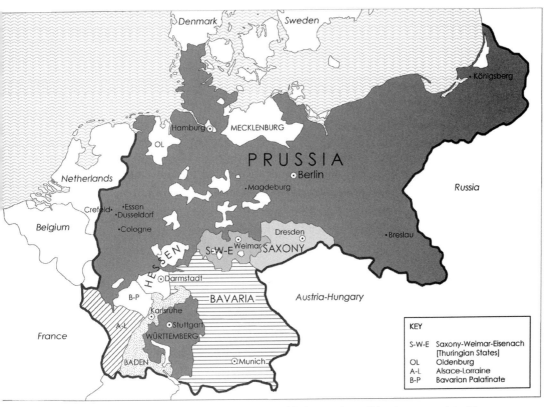

9. Map of German Second Empire, 1871–1918, highlighting selected kingdoms, grand duchies, capitals, and cities (Drawing by Joe Corridore)

perhaps best be understood as "many countries in one large country – Prussia, Bavaria, Württemberg, Saxony, etc."[18] Jeanneret's first book, a commissioned work entitled *A Study of the Decorative Arts Movement in Germany* (*Étude sur le mouvement d'art décoratif en Allemagne*), emphasized the strongly regional character of applied-arts developments in such cities as Berlin, Munich, Stuttgart, and Dresden. Germany's regionalism, Jeanneret argued, accounted for the diversity of appearance and variety of approaches to the German applied arts; this diversity divided the German movement and "deprived it of the unified character that one sees in Vienna."[19]

Without doubt, regional identity remained strong in Germany after unification in 1871. This might well have been expected in an Empire in which four separate kings continued to rule in the respective kingdoms of Prussia, Bavaria, Saxony, and Württemberg, with Prussia's king simultaneously reigning as German Emperor. Beyond these kingdoms, five grand duchies, thirteen duchies and principalities, and three "free cities" filled out the complex and radically asymmetrical political map of the Second Reich (Fig. 9).[20] Rivalries lingered, reflecting a combination of local pride in the "homeland" (*Heimat*) and an unwillingness to relinquish too much influence to the dominant state of Prussia, many of whose state ministries doubled as Imperial ministries.[21] The federal constitution, which made the areas of culture and education the responsibility of individual state governments, helped preserve a measure of state autonomy while feeding a lingering sense of competition among the federated states.[22] It also meant that the internal dynamics of design reform were influenced by the character of individual royal houses and regional governments, a fact not lost on Jeanneret during his extensive study tour and employment with Peter Behrens in Berlin in 1910–11.[23]

Regardless of how historians refer to the Germany of 1871–1918 – as Prusso-Germany, the German Second Empire, or the *Kaiserreich* – scholars are still confronting the political, religious, cultural, and regional diversity of a country whose rulers had, in 1871, at last agreed to consider themselves part of a unified "Germany."[24] For all the deserving attention that the *Kaiserreich* continues to receive from historians of Germany, however, historians of architecture and design are only just beginning to discover the complexity and richness of developments in architecture and the applied arts during this extraordinary time.[25] If debates concerning pre–World War I German architecture have not been as lively, differentiated, and sustained as those that have taken place among historians of Wilhelmine Germany for the past fifty years, then there are signs that this may be changing. To date, important studies from the 1960s, 1970s, and 1980s by Julius Posener, Joan Campbell, and John Heskett laid the groundwork for understanding major developments in architecture and the applied arts during the Wilhelmine era.[26] More recent works by Matthew Jeffries, Frederic Schwartz, and Barbara Miller Lane have added to these classic studies.[27] These books have been particularly helpful in illuminating, in much more nuanced fashion, the intellectual, cultural, and sociological bases of the Deutscher Werkbund, the preeminent Wilhelmine national association of progressive artists, architects, craftsmen, manufacturers, cultural critics, and government officials that convened in 1907. However, and as this book argues, it is the precise way in which the thoughts and actions of key figures in the Werkbund were conditioned by their links to different Wilhelmine state institutions that has yet to be adequately explained. Such an investigation not only reveals new ways of understanding Werkbund leaders like Friedrich Naumann, Hermann Muthesius, Ernst Jäckh, Karl Ernst Osthaus, and Henry van de Velde; it also sheds new light on the ways that specific government ministries – which were anything but acquiescent agents of an undifferentiated and functional "bureaucracy" – competed, struggled, and often improvised their way toward efforts at effective intervention in Wilhelmine German society, the economy, and culture.[28] Seen from this standpoint, new material forms in architecture and the applied arts were not simple reflections of changing design sensibilities; they also presented a record of ambitions and struggles among various, often competing institutions in the private as well as governmental spheres.

WILHELMINE GERMAN HISTORY AND GERMAN DESIGN HISTORY: A PRODUCTIVE CONVERSATION

This book proceeds on the assumption that valuable lessons for both the fields of German history and German architectural history may be contained in an investigation of material that crosses over the customary boundaries of these two disciplines. Many of the most significant developments in Wilhelmine design reform, in fact, came about in part as a result of efforts on the part of Wilhelmine politicians, civil servants, and government ministries pursuing particular policy goals. Standard accounts of the Werkbund's rise, however, tell us otherwise. For example, in much Werkbund literature the figure of the pastor, social activist, and influential politician Friedrich Naumann is frequently cited as the originating spirit and chief political voice of the Werkbund. However, this interpretation – apart from relying on anecdotal information from Naumann protegés, such as Theodor Heuss – greatly oversimplifies the political interests, ministerial influences, and private initiatives that coalesced in the Werkbund's formation.[29] Moreover, and as the historian Matthew Jeffries has shown, historians of architecture and design have a long-standing habit of misunderstanding Naumann's political motivations and misidentifying his political affiliations, which, after all, fueled the charismatic politician's impassioned arguments.[30]

Similarly, other figures in the Werkbund leadership, namely the Prussian architect and career civil servant Hermann Muthesius, are usually treated as influential, but nonpolitical Werkbund members. Although Muthesius is justly remembered for contributions to Wilhelmine architecture and for prolific writings on architectural questions, an ever-expanding literature on the architect continues to ignore his design-related civil service career with both the Prussian Ministry of Commerce and Trade and the Ministry of Public Works.[31] This career produced major transformations in the Prussian Commerce Ministry's extensive system of applied-arts education beginning in 1903, helped establish the organizational principles and design philosophy of the Deutscher Werkbund between 1907 and 1914, and exceeded in duration Muthesius's twenty-two years of private architectural practice in Berlin by more than a decade.

Symptomatic of entirely separate treatments of the Wilhelmine era by historians and architectural historians, the quasi-public nature of the Deutscher Werkbund has never been adequately addressed. To be sure, at the very time of its formation in 1907, the Deutscher Werkbund did much to emphasize its private character as a national design association composed of artists, craftsmen, architects, cultural critics, and light manufacturers. Likewise, scholars have certainly acknowledged the central roles that men like Hermann Muthesius, Friedrich Naumann, and the government advisor Ernst Jäckh played in the Werkbund. However, their roles as servants of particular ministries, administrations, and political ideologies have largely been ignored by analyses that, because of their grounding in architectural culture and design historiography, place an understandable but sometimes too-exclusive emphasis on the development of form, questions of style, or changing modes of representation. The irony of such architectural historical treatments is that men like Naumann, Muthesius, and Jäckh often had multiple professional affiliations that underscored the inherent inseparability of many Wilhelmine design reforms from the particular social, economic, and political contexts in which these men operated. Whether interpreted directly as "politics," or as forms of extra-governmental "anti-politics" as recently analyzed by the historian Kevin Repp, the activities of the Deutscher Werkbund before the First World War were more closely connected than previously thought to myriad efforts by private individuals, government ministries, political parties, and industrial and commercial interest groups.[32] These different interests, in turn, wished to place the applied arts and architecture in the service of promoting compelling – if also competing – visions of a twentieth-century German national culture and global economy.

Like the Wilhelmine Empire's numerous political parties and expanding industrial and commercial pressure groups, the Werkbund leadership was constantly having to define the growing organization's identity in relation to fast-paced changes in the German economy and political landscape. From its formation in 1907 to its near-dissolution following the notorious debates over the "making of industrial types" (*Typisierung*) in July 1914, the Werkbund contained within it leaders whose intellectual orientations, aesthetic priorities, and political affiliations greatly affected their attitudes toward the purpose and function of the Werkbund association. In recent scholarship, Frederick Schwartz has been particularly insightful in his analysis of the Werkbund's intellectual debates and their effect on the relationship of "form and economy under the conditions of capitalism." However, the Werkbund itself was divided in ways that resembled divisions evident in national politics, and this, the present study suggests, was by no means an accident. It is only by understanding the ways that different state, party, and bureaucratic interests exerted influence over various political figures, architects, and artists in the Werkbund that this organization can be understood for what it was: a microcosm, within the design world and finished goods industries, of the Wilhelmine Empire's own conflicting political forces and fractured efforts to overcome competing policy impulses. Even though the Werkbund's conflicts played out through discussions about design, production, and commercial policy, these fields in turn were intimately linked with broader, intense conflicts over domestic- and foreign-policy directions that came to a head especially between the years 1912 and the outbreak of war in August 1914. Without looking closely at this political context, the Werkbund's origins, development, and defining conflicts threaten to remain divorced from the turbulent historical forces that enveloped the Wilhelmine Empire in the darkening pre-war years.

THE POLITICS OF THE *MITTELSTAND* IN THE REFORM OF THE APPLIED ARTS AND ARCHITECTURE

If, as historians of Wilhelmine Germany maintain, the era was rife with change, then social and political organization were two areas in which Germany's transformations were most evident. In the social arena, evolving concepts of class contrasted with the lingering category of pre-modern German "estates" (*Stände*). No term better reflected this collision of traditional with modern categories than the word *Mittelstand*.[33] Used first in isolated instances in the late eighteenth century and traditionally associated during the nineteenth century with artisans, shopkeepers, and other independently employed "pre-industrial" tradespeople, the term *Mittelstand* denoted a diffuse group of small producers understood to be distinct from both the working class and the *Bürgertum*, or Germany's bourgeoisie.[34]

Policies affecting crafts practitioners and other members of the *Mittelstand*, known as *Mittelstandpolitik*, have deep roots as well as important implications for this study. As early as the 1840s, politicians made clear their awareness of the impact that industrialization was having on the *Handwerkerstand*, that preindustrial "estate" of crafts workers whose small, independent artisanal enterprises were most in danger from rising factory competition. The Prussian aristocrat, politician, and eventual founder of Second Empire Germany Otto von Bismarck voiced one of the signature concerns that drove Prussian social policy and, at times, police policy through the First World War.[35] Bismarck warned of the processes by which factory production was transforming independent, self-sufficient craftsmen from otherwise loyal citizens into an increasingly alienated working class susceptible to socialism and revolution. "The factories enrich the individual," Bismarck affirmed in a speech to the Prussian Diet in 1849, "but [they] also furnish us with a mass of proletarians who, through their poor nourishment and insecure existence, present a danger to the state; the independent craftspeople (*Handwerkerstand*), by contrast, represent the core of the middle estate (*Mittelstand*), a group whose existence is essential to the life of the state."[36] Reforming the crafts in politically viable ways was by no means a simple issue of design or taste during Germany's accelerated nineteenth-century industrialization: It was, for leaders like Bismarck, an issue of maintaining economic viability for an endangered estate-class (*Stand*), which, if mishandled, could tip the balance toward a revolution of the existing political, social, and economic order.[37]

Over the course of the nineteenth century, the traditional or "old" *Mittelstand* of small producers was joined by a "new" *Mittelstand* of white-collar clerks, secretaries, and office workers in business and civil service, adding to the complexity of this overdetermined German term. As the historian Shulamit Volkov has shown, individual members of the *Mittelstand* frequently joined together in groups to defend their interests against rising concentrations of economic power in commerce and industry.[38] In the crafts, important *Mittelstand* groups we encounter in this book include the Dusseldorf *Semperbund* and the Association for the Economic Interests of the Crafts (*Fachverband für die wirtschaftlichen Interessen des Kunstgewerbes*). Alternatively, some members of the *Mittelstand* sought ways to advance or even rise above their station. Gustav Schmoller, a prominent nineteenth-century member of the historical school of German economists, explicitly advocated the clearer delineation of steps for career advancement in turn-of-the-century public and private organizations to aid members of the economically threatened *Mittelstand*. This strategy, he argued, would enhance the sense among members of this group that there existed rules and expectations in Germany's rapidly changing economic system that, if fulfilled, would improve *Mittelstand* employees' status and well-being.[39] When Prussian Commerce Minister Theodor Möller, a Westphalian industrialist and National Liberal politician, appointed the architect Hermann Muthesius to advise his ministry in the reform of its arts, crafts, and trades schools in 1903, he claimed to be doing so out of just such an impulse: Amid the turbulence of rapid German industrialization and commercial growth, Möller wished to offer artisans and other struggling workers "ladders" for social advance, "an opportunity," as he also put it, "to work themselves up from out of the swamp in which they sit."[40]

Late-nineteenth-century conservative politicians courted the diffuse and divided *Mittelstand* by depicting them as the bedrock of German society in a dawning era of German mass politics. The Socialist Party, officially banned for twelve years until the repeal of Bismarck's "socialist laws" in 1890, forced competing political parties to adjust their tactics when socialists recruited waves of *Mittelstand* and working-class supporters by pioneering mass political organization in the closing decade of the nineteenth century.[41] The National Liberal and Center parties, meanwhile, debated the question of how best to attract the *Mittelstand* and working-class vote by developing various approaches to *Sammlungspolitik*, a Bismarckian politics of conservative coalition building revived at the turn of the century by Prussian Finance Minister Johannes von Miquel in an effort to broker compromises between different groups and their competing demands.[42]

HERMANN MUTHESIUS AND PRUSSIAN COMMERCIAL POLICIES TOWARD THE APPLIED ARTS

The architect and Prussian civil servant Hermann Muthesius, a bridge figure between the architecture, applied-arts, and government policy spheres in this study, typifies the hybrid nature of various Wilhelmine German reformers and their activities. Muthesius is not alone in combining government and private work. Figures like the journalist and Imperial Foreign Office adviser Ernst Jäckh or the

Heilbronn silver manufacturer, city councilman, and Werkbund president Peter Bruckmann did as well. But only by understanding the interpenetrating nature of Muthesius's work for the Prusso-German government, his publishing activities, his private architectural practice, and his prominent role in the Deutscher Werkbund can the full impact of this architect on early-twentieth-century German design culture be appreciated.

Born in 1861 in the tiny village of Gross-Neuhausen in the central German grand duchy of Saxony-Weimar-Eisenach, Muthesius was raised in a respectable German family that, in its rural context, was on the threshold of crossing over from the "old" trades *Mittelstand* to the German *Bürgertum*, or (upper-) middle class.[43] Muthesius's father, a master mason who owned a small contracting business for building and monument construction, trained him in a complete two-and-one-half-year mason's apprenticeship beginning when he was fourteen years old. In addition to learning the trades of stone cutting and bricklaying, Muthesius gained firsthand knowledge of drafting, elementary design principles, and the techniques of various other building and interior finishing trades.[44]

At the same time, Muthesius revealed himself to be an extremely promising and unusually hard-working student in the local *Realschule*, the nonclassical *Mittelstand* counterpart to the classical, elite *Gymnasium* in Germany's strictly hierarchical education system.[45] Exemplary performance from an early age brought him first to the attention of a local minister who tutored Muthesius in music, Latin, French, and German, while teaching him to become an accomplished performer on the church organ. Muthesius was, in effect, mentored by a Protestant minister who, recognizing his talents, energy, and dedicated study habits, would enable Muthesius to rise from rural *Mittelstand* roots into the urbane upper-middle class. This process assumed great social significance in nineteenth-century Germany generally by opening the way for many to become part of Germany's educated upper-middle class (*gebildetes Bürgertum*, or *Bildungsbürgertum*). Long before Ernst Troeltsch and Max Weber analyzed the influence of Protestantism on the development of capitalism and modern German culture, Emil Klein observed in 1876 (when Muthesius was fifteen years old) that German evangelical ministers were placing particular emphasis on fashioning an educated middle class as the "actual bearers of culture" in Wilhelmine Germany.[46]

After Muthesius passed his secondary examinations with distinction, his tutor brought him to the attention of Grand Duke Carl Alexander of Sachsen-Weimar. The Grand Duke became a great supporter of Muthesius and later helped him to obtain his first architectural commission, a project for a German evangelical church in Tokyo.[47] Muthesius's preparatory training and performance in Thuringia enabled him to complete one year of philosophy and art history studies at the Friedrich Wilhelm University in Berlin in 1882–83, at which point he moved on to complete the four-year architecture program at the nearby Charlottenburg Technical University in April 1887. By December of the same year, Muthesius passed examinations that qualified him to be named an entry-level royal government architect. This was the respectable job of a government employee (*Angestellte*), but not yet the privileged post of an official civil servant (*Staatsbeamter*).[48]

As a freshly minted government employee with high aspirations, Muthesius easily moved beyond the ranks of Germany's white-collar "new" *Mittelstand* to become a member of the *Bildungsbürgertum*, the educated upper-middle class. Working to gain the favor of the Prussian state, which had a long tradition of supporting architects and engineers in their efforts to develop private practices outside of their government posts, Muthesius ensured that he would have a generous, lifelong employer as well as a direct link to the officials in Berlin who were his first private architectural patrons.

Muthesius's place in the Prussian state bureaucracy is of paramount importance, not least because it is the area most overlooked by architectural historians and scholars in general. The Prussian tradition of efficient organization and well-educated bureaucratic authority provided more than simply a basis for Prussian military success in the 1860s or for the unification of Germany in 1871. In contrast to the progress of industrialization and bureaucratization in Anglo-Saxon lands, Prussian bureaucratization and centralization predated the first phase of Prussian industrialization that had begun in the 1830s. For this reason, a culture of centralized bureaucratic authority also indelibly shaped the ideology of the new *Mittelstand*. As the historian Jürgen Kocka has shown, state employment, along with state-influenced power arrangements in large industrial enterprises, encouraged civil employees in the Wilhelmine era to identify with a conservative hierarchy that opposed socialism and independent workers' movements in general.[49]

Muthesius was no exception to this line of thinking. Although he would emerge as one of the premier reformers of Wilhelmine architecture and design, Muthesius never departed from a pronounced top-down mentality of social and organizational change; indeed, his writings and government reform activities did much to further it. At the same time, Muthesius fashioned himself as a member of a new, educated class of modern *Bürgers* who, far from appearing as the new arrivals from the *Mittelstand* that they actually were, sought to represent themselves as the rightful heirs to German cultural traditions and as the vanguard of modern German leadership. Herein lies an important reason for Muthesius's attraction to England, an attraction he shared with many Germans: beginning in the 1860s, England's Queen Anne and Arts and Crafts movements revealed the capacity of architects to press historical revivalism into the service of legitimating the institutions, businesses, and dwellings of the growing urban bourgeoisie.[50] Earlier in the nineteenth century, as Prussia struggled to modernize, Karl Friedrich Schinkel, Prussia's leading government architect, adapted the classical and Gothic styles to what the architectural historian Barry Bergdoll has called "an architecture for Prussia." In 1896, exactly seventy years after the Prussian Commerce Ministry sent Schinkel on an extended study tour of England to learn from the architecture of the more established nation and empire, the ministry assigned Muthesius to the German Embassy in London to report further on a broad array of English developments.[51] Where Schinkel's British travels lasted some four months, Muthesius remained in London to report to the German government for nearly seven years, from October 1896 until June 1903.

During his stay in England, Muthesius came to champion a tradition-conscious yet objective, "realist" principle of *Sachlichkeit* as the core of a new philosophy for modern German design. In advancing his arguments, Muthesius thrust himself well above his origins in a practical German nonclassical *Realschule* education and technical university architectural training. Tellingly, it was common practice for the faculty and privileged students of the classical *Gymnasium* and university system to denigrate Germany's late-nineteenth-century *Realschulen* – with their lack of emphasis on Latin, Greek, and the classical ideal and their focus instead on math, the natural sciences, and modern languages – as "schools of useful junk" (*Nützlichkeitskramschulen*). Muthesius's efforts to shift the emphasis, and indeed the entire direction, of Wilhelmine architecture and design education were intimately bound up with Wilhelmine educational divisions and social transformations for, as the historian Fritz Ringer has noted, by the late nineteenth century "the conflict between classicism and modernism in secondary education had assumed the character of a class war."[52]

Acutely sensitive to the idealist, classical biases of *Gymnasium* and university education, Muthesius condensed the views of such contemporaries as Otto Wagner, Karl Neumann, and Richard Streiter into a well-received sixty-five-page essay called *Style-Architecture and Building-Art* (*Stilarchitektur und Baukunst*) in 1902. In it he argued that aristocratic traditions and the elitist character of the university establishment had little relevance to modern German life.[53] Adopting but subtly modifying the rhetoric of education and personal cultivation (*Bildung*) used by university elites and the *Bildungsbürgertum*, he advocated an alternative vision for modern German society that was based not on unreflective evocations of the historical styles favored by those trained in traditional academies and universities, but on practical, workshop-based design principles and a cultural outlook informed by *Sachlichkeit*. This realist, objective turn has particular resonance in the context of strident late-nineteenth-century German social prejudices and class tensions: Rising as he did from *Mittelstand* origins into the *Bildungsbürgertum*, Muthesius sought to revolutionize modern German design culture by realizing the very values that privileged defenders of mandarin academic traditions held most in contempt.[54]

THE APPLIED ARTS IN THE GOVERNMENT ADMINISTRATIVE CONTEXT

In addition to changes in applied-arts practice that came from within the design professions, developments in the government's administration of the German economy had an enormous effect on the evolution of the crafts and the fate of design reforms in the two decades before the First World War. Following German unification, economic affairs, it was widely anticipated, would soon come to be administered at the Reich level. The kingdom of Bavaria, for example, dissolved its Ministry of Commerce and Trade in 1871; its south German neighbor, Baden, followed Bavaria's lead in 1881.[55] These and other states simply took it for granted that a Reich Ministry of Commerce and Trade was in the offing, believing, as Chancellor Bismarck would later pronounce, that the "Prussian Commerce Ministry is in the long run a political impossibility, just as is one from Mecklenburg or Saxony."[56] But powerful leaders in the Prussian state administration – whose bureaucracy predated that of the Reich by well over a century – did not see things this way. Their successful resistance to Bismarck, and the survival of the Prussian Commerce Ministry, was a deciding factor in determining ultimate responsibility for design reforms affecting dozens of state crafts schools.

Elements of the large, entrenched Prussian bureaucracy mounted particularly stiff resistance to the imposition of many features of an Imperial German administration in the first two decades of the Second Empire. In what the historian Hans Goldschmidt has aptly described as "the Reich and Prussia in a battle for supremacy," competing agendas at the Imperial and state levels produced awkward, sometimes unpredictable administrative results.[57] In addition to conflicts with the new Imperial government, the formidable Prussian administration was beset with its own inner tensions. Prussia divided jurisdiction over the applied arts, for example, between the so-called Ministry of Education, Culture, and Medicinal Affairs (hereafter referred to as the Ministry of Culture) and the Ministry of Commerce and Trade. The battles between Prussia's Ministry of Culture and its Ministry of Commerce produced an uncomfortable "administrative dualism."[58] This dualism reflected, in fact, tensions immanent in the applied arts themselves. On the one hand "art," or an aesthetic component, informed crafts production from the point of view of design; on the other, the resulting applied-arts objects (such as furniture or domestic housewares) served simultaneously as consumer products and so contributed significantly to Germany's increasing commercial output.[59]

Following the orders of a Prussian commission appointed to resolve decades of conflict between the two ministries over this issue in 1884, the Ministry of Culture retained jurisdiction over the School of Applied Arts in Berlin and the School of Art and Applied Arts in Breslau. These were the institutions seen to be most closely associated with the state's educational and artistic mission. The Commerce Ministry, by contrast, viewed crafts and product design through the lens of commerce and the trades (*Handel und Gewerbe*), which tended to subordinate artistic elements of the crafts to economic considerations. The Commerce Ministry regained control of the arts, crafts, and trades education system in 1884 after arguing that schools and crafts industries alike were dangerously out of touch with epochal changes affecting nineteenth-century manufacturing and production

techniques. As evidence the ministry pointed to poor German showings throughout the late nineteenth century at world's exhibitions, which had drawn ridicule
from foreign and German observers alike. In the world's exhibitions in Paris in
1855 and 1867, in London in 1862, in Vienna in 1873, and in Philadelphia in
1876, German applied-arts goods were roundly criticized for their "technical
backwardness, aesthetic inferiority, and economic worthlessness."[60] In response,
and beginning with the restoration of the schools to its control, the Commerce
Ministry ordered that the schools be considered "an inseparable part of the national economic policy."[61]

After separate battles involving the Prussian Commerce Ministry and Chancellor Bismarck, the former emerged in the 1880s as the de facto trade ministry
for the whole German Empire.[62] The Prussian Commerce Ministry thus sought
actively to influence growth in all sectors of the German Reich's economy, from
agriculture and heavy industry to commercial trade and the individual arts, crafts,
and trades. Policy measures affecting applied-arts education had particular importance for pre–World War I innovations in architecture and design, and as such
are a major focus of this study.

Although it represented only one economic sector among many, the applied
arts were of particular interest to the ministry because German manufacturing and exports of finished goods had long been on the rise.[63] As Chapters 2
and 3 discuss in detail, the Commerce Ministry relied heavily on the writings
and recommendations of Hermann Muthesius to give direction to policies with
implications for applied-arts industries and design education across Prussia. Although the ministry had no technical constitutional authority to make policy for
the entire Reich, surviving archival evidence suggests that the Commerce Ministry both anticipated and helped precipitate the events that led to the founding
of the Werkbund in an effort to encourage organization of the applied arts at
the national level. As a private, national design association, the Werkbund could
promote design and economic policies throughout the entire Reich in ways that
Commerce Ministry officials had previously only been able to do within Prussia.
Moreover, and as Commerce Ministry fiascos like the "Hibernia Affair" of 1905
demonstrated, the Prusso-German government had increasingly to rely on measures other than direct state intervention in the increasingly cartellized and complex industrial economy; for the purpose of economic advance in the applied-arts
and finished-goods industries, organizations like the Werkbund offered the advantage of furthering economic development from within the private sector.[64]

Overlooked connections between Wilhelmine Germany's turn-of-the-century
Applied Arts movement, state cultural and economic development policies, and
the growth of the Deutscher Werkbund are the main focus of this book. To this
end, Chapter 1 begins by inquiring into the early stirrings of the Applied-Arts
movement in the states and locations where its emergence, beginning in the early
1890s, was most prominent. In particular, this chapter surveys the interaction
of private and state forces through accomplishments in such important central

and southern German states as Bavaria, Hessen, Saxony-Weimar-Eisenach, Württemberg, and Saxony (Fig. 9). The Prussian state, of course, made efforts in this area as well. Because of its sheer size and dominant role in German affairs – Prussia covered two-thirds of German territory and contained two-thirds of its population – its main accomplishments are investigated in two parts.[65] Chapter 2 details the efforts made by the Prussian Ministries of Commerce and Public Works to learn from a broad array of British achievements by sending the architect Hermann Muthesius to report on technical, economic, architectural, and applied-arts topics from the German Embassy in London between 1896 and 1903. Chapter 3 examines substantial measures taken by the Prussian Ministry of Commerce and the Ministry of Culture to reform the Prussian system of applied-arts education following Muthesius's return to Berlin in summer 1903.

Prussia's emphasis on placing design in the service of a fast-growing industrial and commercial economy coincided with the kingdom of Saxony's avid promotion of its own applied-arts industries and practitioners. The Third German Applied Arts Exhibition of 1906 in Dresden, the subject of Chapter 4, made Saxony into an important catalyst for the growing German Applied Arts movement's efforts to organize along national and no longer just regional or state lines. With these regional efforts at applied-arts reform as background, Chapter 4 reinterprets the Dresden applied-arts exhibition and the subsequent formation of the Deutscher Werkbund as products of combined private, state, and semipublic initiatives.

Chapter 5 explores the Berlin-based private architectural practice that Hermann Muthesius opened when he returned to Berlin from London in 1903. It uncovers links between Muthesius's domestic architectural reform agenda, the architectural "battleground" that was turn-of-the-century suburban development in Berlin, and the state officials, commercial and industrial magnates, and artists whom the architect cultivated as his client base. The analysis of Muthesius's house designs furnishes new insights into his promotion of a modern German bourgeois culture (*bürgerliche Kultur*) among such clients as Commerce Ministry officials Hermann von Seefeld, Gustav von Velsen, and Heinrich Neuhaus; the industrialists Heinrich Soetbeer and Fritz Gugenheim; the department store owner Hermann Freudenberg; and others who proved instrumental to Deutscher Werkbund and Prussian Commerce Ministry successes in the areas of export development and the advancement of a modern German commercial culture. Muthesius explicitly promoted his suburban country houses as the architectural symbols of an emerging "spiritual aristocracy" (*geistige Aristokratie*) and as a new German bourgeois leadership class.

Chapter 6 analyzes the expansion of political, social, and artistic networks in the Werkbund and the German Garden City movement, a closely related reform-minded organization. The "cultural fault lines" running through the German Garden City movement and its epicenter at Dresden-Hellerau are shown to be of a piece with tensions building in the Deutscher Werkbund, particularly with the approach of the First Werkbund Exhibition in Cologne in summer 1914.

Chapter 7 demonstrates the close connections between Germany's growing national political tensions of 1912–14 and the dramatic shift in direction undertaken by the leadership faction dominant in the Werkbund at this time. Policies directed at commercial growth, colonial expansion, and the calculated avoidance of a seemingly intractable domestic political situation were, it turns out, powerful contributors to Werkbund Vice President Hermann Muthesius's move to redirect the organization's membership toward the design and production of standardized "types" in applied arts and architectural design. The notorious "showdown" between Muthesius and the Belgian artist Henry van de Velde between July 3 and July 5, 1914, at the Werkbund conference in Cologne – which features as an early climax in virtually all standard histories of twentieth-century European architecture and design – emerges in quite a different historical light as a result of this analysis. The "Werkbund debate" of July 1914, it turns out, was only superficially a debate between factions favoring the conflicting agendas of "standardization" (*Typisierung* – really, the "making of types"), as forcefully advocated by Muthesius, and artistic "individualism," as defended by van de Velde.[66] After state policies and the behavior of such key members of the Werkbund leadership as Muthesius, Ernst Jäckh, Friedrich Naumann, and Peter Bruckmann are factored in, the dominant theme to emerge from the contentious Werkbund conference in summer 1914 turns out to be the willingness of the Reich government and Werkbund leaders to subordinate the design association to concrete German international and imperialist policy imperatives, and to make it the linchpin of a comprehensive new commercial strategy to be guided by the Prussian Commerce Ministry, the Imperial Ministry of the Interior, the Foreign Office, and the Colonial Office.

Interfering with this new agenda before it could even get off the ground, of course, were the protracted and disastrous events of the First World War. Walter Gropius, a sergeant-major with a Prussian Hussars regiment and a particularly animated, behind-the-scenes defender of artistic prerogatives during the 1914 Werkbund debacle, emerged as a charismatic, reform-minded school director at the Weimar Bauhaus in 1919. Stung from having narrowly avoided being blocked from participating in the Werkbund Exhibition of 1914 in Cologne by Muthesius and dominant governmental, commercial, and industrial interests, the young architect now found, in the directorship of the Bauhaus, an opportunity to react to the abuses under which he felt he had labored and that he, Henry van de Velde, and Karl Ernst Osthaus had so vigorously opposed in 1914.

Certainly the most prominent result of the architect's ambitions, the Bauhaus in its early and especially middle, more industrially oriented phases would profit from ideas promulgated by Muthesius and other leading Wilhelmine-era figures. However, and with perhaps good reason, as we shall see, Gropius would never acknowledge any debts to prior Wilhelmine state policies; nor would he ever mention Muthesius's name or role in the development of early-twentieth-century design thinking regarding the development of crafts-influenced industrial design prototypes. The obfuscation or outright suppression of this part of Gropius's

Wilhelmine past, its key players, and sophisticated design culture played a crucial role in the architect's "self-fashioning" throughout his career; not insignificantly, it also influenced subsequent accounts of twentieth-century modern architecture that various Gropius supporters – from Nikolaus Pevsner to Sigfried Giedion – released to epoch-making acclaim.[67] From the Bauhaus's early guild-inspired, crafts-oriented Expressionist phase to its reorientation toward industry and technology in 1922–23, Gropius would practice techniques of promoting his school and approach that effectively declared a kind of *Stunde Null*, or "zero hour," in the developmental history of twentieth-century German architecture and design. Never much of a fan of history in the teaching of architecture, Gropius would ensure that much of what had happened in the Wilhelmine era, "before the Bauhaus," would remain obscured for the remainder of the architect's long and productive career in Germany, England, and the United States.

CHAPTER ONE

DESIGN REFORM IN GERMANY'S CENTRAL AND SOUTHERN STATES, 1890–1914 ∞

In Germany's Second Reich, two main national events concentrated the energies of early-twentieth-century reformers on the attainment of an affirmative, modern German "artistic culture." The first was the Third German Applied Arts Exhibition, held in Dresden during summer 1906. The second, which emerged out of the Dresden exhibition a year later, was the formation of the private, national association of artists, craftsmen, architects, and manufacturers known as the Deutscher Werkbund. Typically cast as the starting points of twentieth-century modern German architecture and design, the Dresden Exhibition and formation of the Werkbund were, in fact, the culmination of numerous complex reform developments that began gathering steam in the late 1890s. The diversity of views in the Deutscher Werkbund is due not only to the organization's embrace of artists, manufacturers, craftsmen, architects, and government officials; equally important is the fact that many of the attitudes and philosophies that members brought to the Werkbund were the product of reforms experienced within local cultural contexts in Bavaria, Hessen, Württemberg, Saxony-Weimar-Eisenach, Saxony, and so on.

The leading states and personalities examined here collectively represent, if not a coherent movement, then a series of gradually expanding circles of progressive artists, architects, museum directors, craftsmen, entrepreneurs, and critics.[1] Emerging in each of the German states under circumstances influenced to a greater or lesser degree by government policies at various levels, these circles began increasingly to touch and overlap through the network of exhibitions, new arts journals, artists' associations, and schools that sought consciously to promote a "new movement," especially after around 1900. Its diverse adherents shared a belief in the search for new modes of making and expression among applied artists and architects. At the same time, local politics and regional characteristics conditioned the attitudes of the growing movement's participants in a number of ways. The local character of developments in numerous states helps account for the diversity of opinion that arose later, and particularly after 1907, as the Werkbund sought to organize a huge array of dispersed, local practitioners along more coherent national lines.

This is not an exhaustive survey of applied-arts developments in each German state and principality – only an analysis of several of the most active states in the quarter century preceding the First World War. These include Bavaria, Hessen, Württemberg, Saxony-Weimar-Eisenach, and Saxony. Although Bavarian policies did not support progressive applied-arts developments as explicitly as those in the other states, it was, because of the vibrant artistic culture of Munich, nevertheless a pioneering locus for innovation. Moreover, larger states, such as the kingdoms of Württemberg and Saxony, tended to advance policies that linked the applied arts to industry, whereas smaller grand duchies – in this case Hessen and Saxony-Weimar-Eisenach – promoted visions of applied-arts reform more closely aligned with older notions of German culture (*Kultur*). Whereas this chapter concentrates on developments in Germany's central and southern states, those that follow examine Prussia and events such as the Third German Applied Arts Exhibition in Dresden of 1906 and the formation of the Werkbund in 1907, which led the Applied Arts movement to take on its national character.

MUNICH: CRADLE OF THE GERMAN SECESSION AND APPLIED ARTS MOVEMENT

Munich, capital of Bavaria, Germany's second-largest kingdom, was the first German city to show evidence of consequential reforms affecting the applied arts and architecture.[2] Throughout the nineteenth century, Bavaria's Wittelsbach dynasty had played a major part in cultivating Munich as an artistic and cultural center. This helped attract artists to the city even after King Ludwig II, known as "Mad Ludwig," turned against the sponsorship of the arts in Munich following Richard Wagner's scandalous departure from the city in 1876. After Ludwig's tragic death by drowning in 1886, the generous flow of royal funds for the arts abated, though the city continued to derive great benefit from the energies of its sizable artists' population.[3]

A center for realist painting that had begun to challenge established academic thinking in the 1880s, Munich had also earned a reputation as an applied-arts center with the success of locally produced neo-Renaissance furnishings at the First German Applied Arts Exhibition of 1876.[4] An ongoing search for styles appropriate to Germany's new sense of nationhood brought baroque and rococo styles to prominence at the Second German Applied Arts Exhibition of 1888, also held in Munich. By the early 1890s, fashion trends had shifted again: English Arts and Crafts movement products had risen sufficiently in their popularity that they overshadowed German historicist styles. *The Studio*, launched in 1893 as the main journal of the Arts and Crafts movement, gained leading British practitioners like William Morris, C. R. Ashbee, and M. H. Baillie Scott international attention, and the impact of the journal on artists and architects in Munich was no exception.[5] As Hermann Muthesius observed in 1899, "Today, decoration in the English manner is the ideal even for the most narrow-minded commoner (*Spiessbürger*); English today is the 'newest thing.'"[6]

By the mid-1890s, leading Munich artists like Hermann Obrist, Otto Eckmann, and Richard Riemerschmid made their first forays into designing ceramics and glassware, following trends in England, Belgium, and France. They were reacting in seemingly equal parts to the pomp of official, ceremonial art from the academies, the dominance of historical fashions at the Munich exhibitions, and the challenge posed by the success of movements like the British Arts and Crafts and the Belgian Art Nouveau. Like the individualistic, romantic paintings of the Munich Secession, comprised of seventy-eight artists who withdrew from the Munich Artists' Association in 1893, new applied-arts works favored naturalistic lines, bright colors, and rejection of ornamentation based on academic historical styles. Coinciding with these artists' early efforts was the debut of four internationally oriented arts journals in Munich during this decade: *Pan*, launched in 1895, *Jugend* (Youth) and *Simplicissimus*, both begun in 1896, and *Dekorative Kunst* (Decorative Art), founded in 1897. *Jugend* prompted the name for the *Jugendstil*, Germany's version of Art Nouveau. These liberal-minded journals aimed at Germany's growing urban bourgeoisie, a population that benefited from the economic upswing of the mid-1890s.

Like Riemerschmid, Obrist, and Eckmann, many of the most innovative applied artists working in Munich during the 1890s – Bernhard Pankok, Peter Behrens, Theo Schmuz-Baudiss, Fritz Erler, and Wilhelm von Debschitz, among others – were originally trained as painters and illustrators.[7] Munich-trained artists were well aware of divisions within Munich's art establishment, which was dominated by the Academy of Arts and the Artists' Association. Defenders of a historical, "national" style of painting – among them such influential academy members as Karl Theodor von Piloty and Wilhelm von Kaulbach – had been contending with younger backers of French-influenced realist, landscape, and plein-air painting since the 1870s. By the time of the Munich Secession in 1893, many younger artists were calling not only for artistic independence from traditional rules guiding composition, use of color, and choice of subjects and themes, but also for a more expressive, personal art that responded to the unique conditions of modern German life.[8]

Much as naturalistic themes provided an alternative source of inspiration to painters protesting against historical tradition, nature also inspired many experimental forms in the applied arts. Along with Hector Guimard in France, Belgian artists Victor Horta and Henry van de Velde responded to the challenging

10. August Endell, Photo Atelier Elvira, Munich, 1898, view of street façade (destroyed in World War II) (Foto-Marburg/Art Resource, NY)

writings of the nineteenth-century French architect and theorist Eugène-Emmanuel Viollet-le-Duc by incorporating floral metalwork and vegetative lines into buildings, furniture, and other objects of everyday use. The Munich-based artist August Endell realized the city's best-known building in this mode, the Elvira Photo Studio, in 1897 (Fig. 10). Anita Augspurg and Sophia Goudstikker, a pair of radical feminists and photographers, commissioned the building and were likely drawn, as Endell was, to the influential Swiss artist and Munich resident Hermann Obrist. Obrist had led the way in experimenting with many of the abstract, dynamic, naturalistic forms that found their way into Endell's façade and interior.[9]

In the same year, and in a similar effort to participate in trends evident in England and on the continent, the Munich Secessionists successfully campaigned to have two small rooms set aside at the annual Arts Exhibition in Munich's Glass Palace in 1897. As the Bavarian Applied Arts Association wrote in a circular appealing to artists for project submissions, the desire was not simply for works that paid homage to "Our Fathers' Works" (Unserer Väter Werke), a reference to the motto and neo-Renaissance displays of the association's 1876 exhibition. Rather, and because "the French and especially the English command a not insignificant lead" in the applied arts, the association explicitly requested works that "grow out of present conditions" and "reflect the character, ideals, and needs of their time."[10] In support of the association, state organizers permitted the Secession's applied artists to show furniture and applied-arts objects in interiors designed by architects sympathetic to the new direction.[11]

The architects Theodor Fischer and Martin Dülfer, former classmates at the Munich Technical University in the 1880s, designed the two Secession rooms in cooperation with the artists Richard Riemerschmid and Fritz Erler (Fig. 11). Fischer and Dülfer derived the modest interiors from the wood-paneled forms of a typical late-nineteenth-century bourgeois Bavarian room, or *Stube*; within were the personally expressive, *Jugendstil* murals by Riemerschmid and Erler, wall hangings, curtains, and stucco friezes by Otto Eckmann and August Endell, furniture pieces by Hermann Obrist and Hans Eduard van Berlepsch-Valendas, and

11. Theodor Fischer and Martin Dülfer, exhibition room for applied arts, Seventh International Art Exhibition, in Glass Palace, Munich, 1897, interior view (*Kunst und Kunsthandwerk* 47, 1897–98)

various applied-arts works by other artists. Although the Secessionists' naturalistic forms set their pieces apart, the familiar wood panelling, wooden furniture, and displays of domestic objects maintained a link with more typical Bavarian interiors. The scarcity of financial resources prevented the room from being conceived as a "total work of art" (*Gesamtkunstwerk*), and the Secessionists each worked with skilled producers at considerable personal sacrifice. This fortified their assertion of one of the applied artists' cardinal principles: that their applied-arts works were every bit the equal of the fine-arts works on display in the rest of the Glass Palace exhibition. When Henry van de Velde, Bruno Paul, and Bernhard Pankok exhibited in an expanded applied-arts section of the Glass Palace Arts Exhibition in 1899, the Secession could rightly claim to have attained its goal of combining all fields of artistic expression, the fine as well as the applied arts, working in concert with architecture.[12]

Despite these auspicious beginnings, the Secession artists' showings at Munich Arts Exhibitions failed to attract broader support from official circles in Munich and Bavaria. Applied artists seeking greater exposure and commissions were compelled to organize along private lines. Riemerschmid, Paul, and Pankok united together in 1898 and, inspired by William Morris's *News from Nowhere* and the founding of Morris's legendary firm some thirty-five years earlier, formed Munich's United Workshops for Art in Handcraft (*Vereinigten Werkstätten für Kunst im Handwerk*). The United Workshops were Germany's first organized professional artists' workshop to follow a British Arts and Crafts precedent. They proved highly successful and supported more than a dozen Secession artists in their efforts to design furniture and applied-arts goods for a small but growing bourgeois clientele. Among the workshops' early artistic collaborators were Hermann Obrist, Peter Behrens, the painter Franz August Otto Krüger, and Paul Schultze-Naumburg.[13] To support the enterprise several of these artists also founded the nonprofit Association for Applied Arts (*Vereinigung für angewandte Kunst e.V.*) in 1903. Led by the ceramics artist Julius Jacob Scharvogel and also known under the name the Munich Association (*Münchener Bund*), this organization popularized its artists' works, sought official commissions, and helped to organize exhibitions.[14]

Also acting on private initiative, the Munich-based artists Hermann Obrist and Wilhelm von Debschitz opened an alternative school to provide a fresh nonacademic approach to artistic and applied-arts training. Obrist and Debschitz called their school the Instructional and Trials Workshops for Applied and Fine Arts (*Lehr- und Versuchs-Ateliers für angewandte und freie Kunst*). The school's cumbersome name took pains to express precisely its founders' antiacademic, practice-oriented pedagogical program.[15] Obrist first outlined ideas for a new kind of workshop-based educational institution in a lecture during fall 1900, and the school opened its doors January 1902. The Swiss-born Obrist, who had studied in the late 1880s in Scotland, mixed the type of workshop training he encountered

among British Arts and Crafts practitioners with his own highly personal, naturalistic approach to sculpture, drawing, and embroidery. After Obrist departed
from the school in 1904 because of increasingly debilitating deafness, the school
became commonly known as the "Debschitzschule."[16]

Wilhelm von Debschitz missed no opportunity to promote the school's instructional workshops as the perfect solution for "all those who were dissatisfied
with other methods of learning."[17] The school's best-known student was the
painter Ernst Ludwig Kirchner; Paul Klee briefly taught painting at the school
in 1908. More than simply an homage to British Arts and Crafts practices, Obrist's
and Debschitz's embrace of workshop instruction also reflected the shift of some
Wilhelmine applied artists away from what has been described as the "decorative"
phase of the early and mid-1890s to the "tectonic" or "constructive" phase that
began toward the turn of the century.[18] A significant precedent emerging some
seventeen years prior to the Bauhaus's vaunted experimental fine- and applied-
arts curriculum of 1919, the Debschitz School grounded students in basic fine-
arts principles through drawing and instruction in rules governing form, line,
and color. Only with mastery of these basic teachings were students considered
prepared to work in what was later referred to as the "tectonic approach": the
practical study of materials and construction methods in workshops for wood,
metal, ceramics, and textiles. Learning in these "trial and instructional workshops" represented the heart of the "constructive approach." Beginning in 1903,
the school held annual exhibitions of student-designed products, the sale of which
supplemented meager state funds until the First World War. Offering "individual, free, creative development of every talent under experienced guidance," the
school functioned with an experimental energy that would prompt Obrist at a
later point to recall nostalgically, "the Zeitgeist was stirring here."[19]

THE MUNICH ARCHITECTURAL SCENE AND THE PROSPECTS
FOR STATE SUPPORT

The critical mass of artists and applied artists in Munich during the 1890s
seemed, for a time, to bode well for a continued expansion of opportunities
for its leading practitioners. As the largest arts association in the nation with
some 4,500 members, the Bavarian Art Association presided over Germany's
leading artistic center. Excitement over the expanding Applied Arts movement
in Munich inspired some of its adherents, like the architect and city planner
Theodor Fischer, to design on a large scale. Fischer had proven his mettle as
Munich's first city planner from 1893 to 1901, combining attention to existing
property lines, economic and demographic conditions, and local topography in
plans for new suburban districts such as Laim, Schwabing, and Giesing. Fischer's
quiet and serious demeanor belied the architect's ultimately romantic disposition.

Devoted to the idea of blending new architecture and urban forms into the historic landscape, Fischer took cues from local topography, historic land-use patterns, and even farmers' cart paths for his layout of roads and new districts in the expanding Bavarian capital.[20]

Typical of Fischer's search for a historically contextual German urban design idiom was his effort to marry architectural, cultural, artistic, and economic goals in the "Kohleninsel" project of 1899 (Fig. 12). The Kohleninsel, the name of an island at the center of Munich's Isar River, had served as the site of the Second German Applied Arts Exhibition in 1888. Planning a proud Bavarian homage to this national event, Fischer now sought to develop the island with permanent buildings for an exhibition commemorating the fiftieth anniversary of the Bavarian Applied Arts Association (*Kunstgewerbeverein*), the original sponsor of the 1888 exhibition. In consultation with the association, Fischer designed an idealized town square based on the forms and building types of medieval Bavarian towns. In Fischer's scheme, the stone buildings of this quaint island townscape would live on past the projected applied-arts exhibition to anchor a new "applied-arts center" near the heart of Munich. Fischer's detailed program called for a school, a museum, abundant space for crafts workshops, apartments, shops, and other supporting services for Bavaria's crafts and trades. In their prospectus Fischer and the Applied Arts Association argued that only the existence of such a complex would "enable Munich's crafts producers to maintain their outstanding position in the German economy in the face of the increasing demands of coming times."[21]

Bavarian authorities, whose support for the Secession and for progressive thinking in the applied arts had always been lukewarm at best, refused to underwrite the Kohleninsel project. The city government withheld its support as well, continuing to do so even after Fischer, who remained committed to the applied-arts center concept, presented increasingly scaled-down versions of the design over coming years. In the end, and in what the architectural historian Winfried Nerdinger has interpreted as a slap at Fischer and his supporters, city authorities selected Fischer's rival and enemy, the architect Gabriel von Seidl, to design a large, neoclassical complex on the island site. Completed in 1904, it housed the Deutsches Museum, Bavaria's proud state interpretation of Germany's educational, cultural, and scientific achievements.[22]

The city's rejection of the Kohleninsel project came as a blow to Fischer, particularly following his years of loyal service as Munich's leading planner of new districts and public buildings. The architect was likely not alone in interpreting the Kohleninsel debacle as a bad omen for Bavarian state support of applied-arts reform initiatives, for try as they might, practitioners of the self-proclaimed "new movement" could only secure isolated, piecemeal Bavarian state sponsorship.[23] For example, Richard Riemerschmid and Peter Behrens persuaded the director of the Bavarian Trades Museum (*Gewerbemuseum*) in Nuremberg, Theodor von Kramer, to hire them as instructors for decorative arts master classes at the museum in 1901. However, when Behrens presented the Bavarian Ministry

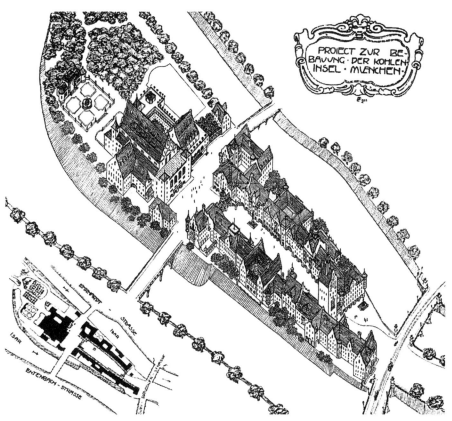

12. Theodor Fischer, project for a new applied-arts center on Kohleninsel Island, 1899–1902, Munich, bird's-eye view with site plan (*Dekorative Kunst* 5, 1902)

of Culture with a plan for new decorative arts curricula at the Munich and Nuremberg art academies, he was flatly rejected. In its review, the ministry ridiculed "the so-called modern style in the applied arts" as an arbitrary, "passing style" (*Stilerscheinung*), too "inartistic" and "disrespectful toward historical tradition" to deserve incorporation into the curriculum of state arts academies.[24]

Munich-based artists fared considerably better in international exhibitions, despite the government authorities' apparent ambivalence to the role the emerging Applied Arts movement should play in representing Germany at such events as the World's Exhibition in Paris in 1900. Eager to express national pride, economic success, and expanding influence abroad, German exhibitions most often reflected a two-pronged effort to compete with Germany's main rival, the French, who were still regarded with envy as culturally superior, if no longer seen as a military threat after 1870–71. Thus, and as John Heskett has shown, official bombast in large, ceremonial exhibition rooms coexisted with smaller, less-conspicuous applied-arts interiors in tune with contemporary international trends. The exhibition in Paris in 1900 was typical: two established architects, Karl Hoffacker of Berlin and Emmanuel Seidl of Munich, designed the exhibition pavilion and official ceremonial room. Hoffacker's monumental entrance court featured armored knights on horseback flanking a raised, heavily ornamented entrance gate. Beyond it, Seidl's ceremonial hall featured the same abundant neo-Renaissance ornamentation that the architect had used a dozen years earlier in his pavilion for the German Applied Arts Exhibition of 1888.[25] Toward the back of Seidl's pavilion, smaller rooms showcased interiors by the United Workshops for Art in Handicraft: a smoking room by Bernhard Pankok, a "room for a lover of art" by Richard Riemerschmid, and a hunting room by Bruno Paul, all of which featured crafted wood interiors and inventive *Jugendstil* ornamentation integrated with more familiar Bavarian domestic furnishings. Riemerschmid, in particular, was interested in bringing together modern considerations of craft quality with furniture designs that were *volkstümlich* (of the people) and respectful of south German traditions.[26] Riemerschmid would continue to pursue this direction in furniture design that led, a few years later, to the development of "machined furniture" (*Maschinenmöbel*) for his brother-in-law, the craftsman Karl Schmidt, who operated the successful entrepreneurial Dresden Workshops for Art in Handicraft.

With the lack of programmatic support from the Bavarian government or the royal house in the early years of the twentieth century, it soon became clear that only private, well-organized applied-arts enterprises such as the United Workshops or the Debschitz School could sustain themselves in Bavaria. In the absence of larger scale Bavarian initiatives, artists and architects began pursuing opportunities in Germany's other fast-growing urban centers. The progressive arts journal *Deutsche Kunst und Dekoration* recorded the extent of the "artistic migration out of Munich," particularly between 1897 and 1902. August Endell and Otto Eckmann were among those departing for Berlin, where Endell opened a private practice and Eckmann accepted a teaching post at Berlin's Royal Applied Arts School (*Königliche Kunstgewerbeschule*), affiliated with the Berlin Museum of Applied Arts. Theodor Fischer left in 1901 for a professorship in architecture and city planning at the Technical University in nearby Stuttgart, the capital of Württemberg. Otto Krüger and Bernhard Pankok left for Stuttgart as well, taking respective positions as director and instructor at the Stuttgart School of the Applied Arts. Richard Riemerschmid elected to stay in Munich, continuing to collaborate with the flourishing United Workshops while operating a private architectural practice. Peter Behrens left Bavaria for Darmstadt, the capital of Hessen, in 1899, greatly enlarging the scope of his creative activities at the Grand Duke Ernst Ludwig's new Darmstadt Artists' Colony. Three other Munich-based artists – Ludwig Habich, Patriz Huber, and Paul Bürck – also moved to the Darmstadt colony in a drain of talent that aroused a degree of resentment on the part of artists who remained in Munich.[27] They appeared to have reason to envy the conditions being offered to the artists in Hessen: Darmstadt was in the process of assembling the largest officially sponsored experimental arts colony in Wilhelmine Germany. Munich's loss appeared to be Darmstadt's gain.

THE DARMSTADT ARTISTS' COLONY: FEUDAL PATRONAGE FOR AN ARTISTIC NEW AGE

The Darmstadt Artists' Colony (*Künstlerkolonie*) arose from a blend of local aristocratic patronage, bourgeois artistic progressivism, and mutually reinforcing private and state initiatives. Formed by decree in spring 1899 by the youthful Grand Duke Ernst Ludwig of Hessen, the colony was intended to transform the Grand Ducal Hessian capital from a sleepy, middle-sized town of some 72,000 inhabitants into a leading center for applied-arts production – and, by extension, into a center of modern German culture.[28] Throughout its fifteen-year existence, however, the Darmstadt experiment was an artists' colony in name only. Unlike truly voluntary associations of artists at the late-nineteenth-century colonies of Worpswede, Sylt, or Hiddensee, the Darmstadt Artists' Colony was exclusively the product of policies initiated by the grand duke and the Hessian state government. Promoting a progressive image for German architecture and applied arts on the one hand, the colony relied on grand ducal patronage and functioned as an updated variant of feudal artistic workshops on the other. The subject of great contemporary as well as subsequent critical attention, the colony operated at a scale that stands out among early-twentieth-century German efforts to recruit leading artists for local economic development and increased cultural prestige.[29] These efforts produced significant tensions, which, in turn, undermined aspects of the "Darmstadt experiment" in the eyes of some artists, critics, and the public.

Between 1899 and 1914, an ever-changing roster of artists in residence mounted four major exhibitions at the colony. As one local promoter described it, the colony's assemblage of "major artists for the minor arts" would enable Darmstadt to transcend its provincial location and small-town identity. Economic sustainability proved elusive from the start, however, as an already reluctant state government withdrew its financial support following the colony's first exhibition. Only the continuing largesse of the grand duke enabled the colony to survive and, indeed, to continue growing. Grand Duke Ernst Ludwig, himself an amateur artist, provided sufficient support from his private coffers to ensure that professional artists could offer a major statement, if not a definitive model, for the reform of turn-of-the-century German attitudes toward architecture and the applied arts.

Grand Duke Ernst Ludwig's background played a central role in the genesis of the colony. Only twenty-three years old when he succeeded his deceased father in 1892, Ernst Ludwig was, like Kaiser Wilhelm II, a grandson of England's Queen Victoria. Not only was Ernst Ludwig raised and educated in England, but his mother, Alice, daughter to the Queen, was a friend of the legendary art critic and reformer John Ruskin. Aware of the British Arts and Crafts movement from an early age, Ernst Ludwig was drawn to the movement's general faith in the transformative power of the arts and applied arts, if not to its potentially revolutionary social message. His invitation to the English applied artist and architect M. H. Baillie Scott to design interiors for the Grand Ducal palace in Darmstadt in 1897–98 was only the beginning of Ernst Ludwig's engagement with the applied arts and dwelling reform in the name of large-scale Hessian economic and cultural reform.[30]

The grand duke found his strongest ally, adviser, and provocateur in Hessen's leading Art Education movement activist, Alexander Koch. Koch, a Darmstadt-based rug manufacturer and arts publisher who launched the influential journals *Innendekoration* in 1890 and *Deutsche Kunst und Dekoration* in 1896, was the local catalyst for the establishment of an artists' colony. His writings emphasized the cultural and economic significance of the new Applied Arts movement for modern Germany. Modeling *Deutsche Kunst und Dekoration* on Britain's *The Studio*, Koch underscored the national ambitions of his Darmstadt-based journal by adding the subtitle "Illustrated Monthly Journal for the Support of German Art and a Language of Form."

Koch's publishing activities amount to a kind of press campaign, particularly when seen in the light of the publisher's frequent meetings with Ernst Ludwig to discuss practical ways of developing Darmstadt into a center for the applied arts. His efforts culminated in the circulation of a memorandum to the grand duke, local and state officials, and influential Darmstadt personalities in April 1899. Echoing the tone of Theodor Fischer's campaign at the very same time for the Kohleninsel in Munich, he called for the immediate establishment of a "modern center for the applied arts" in the Hessian capital. The memorandum emphasized the necessity of acting quickly and seizing the initiative ahead of other German cities, which, Koch warned, were developing similar plans.[31]

Unlike the authorities in Bavaria, the grand duke embraced Koch's proposal from the first. By July 1, 1899, scarcely two months after receiving Koch's memorandum, Ernst Ludwig announced the appointment of four artists in residence to form the heart of a new artists' colony. Negotiating a series of three-year contracts, the grand ducal administration brought the Paris-based German painter and surface designer Hans Christiansen, the Brandenburg-born engraver and sculptor Rudolf Bosselt, the decorative painter Paul Bürck, and the applied artist Patriz Huber to the colony as founding members. Three additional appointments later that month brought the total number of artists to seven. Joseph Maria Olbrich, the young Viennese architect and talented understudy of the architect Otto Wagner, the Hamburg-born artist Peter Behrens, and the local sculptor Ludwig Habich filled out the ranks of initial appointees.[32]

Ernst Ludwig donated a private, walled-in hilltop park east of Darmstadt as a site for the colony.[33] Olbrich, the only trained architect among the seven invitees, received the commission for the colony's master plan as well as for the majority of its buildings (Fig. 13). This established him as the clear leader among the artists. His master plan proclaimed the aspirations of the privileged new colony atop the "Mathildenhöhe," as the park overlooking the town was now called. In

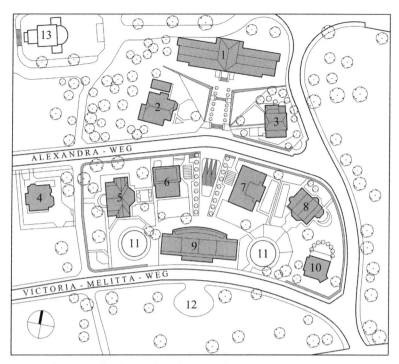

13. Joseph Maria Olbrich, site plan of Darmstadt Artists' Colony at the time of the exhibition "A Document of German Art," in 1901. 1. Ernst Ludwig House; 2. Christiansen house; 3. Olbrich house; 4. Behrens house; 5. First Glückert house; 6. Second Glückert house; 7. Habich house; 8. Keller house; 9. Pavilion for surface design (*Flächenkunst*); 10. Deiters house; 11. Basins; 12. Seating area; 13. Russian chapel (existing) (Drawing by Burak Erdim after site plan by J. M. Olbrich)

a special issue of *Deutsche Kunst und Dekoration* dedicated to the colony, Olbrich described in hyperbolic terms how the artists' collaboration would forge harmonious connections between art and life. The colony would fulfill, in short, the Art Education movement's general aspirations for fostering an exemplary German *Wohnkultur* – a contemporary culture of dwelling and living. These remarks built on Olbrich's earlier pronouncements regarding a commission for the *Hohe Warte* dwelling colony in Vienna, where the architect had called for a "city of beauty," a total work of art that encompassed plazas, streets, houses, and all manner of interior furnishings.[34]

Yet the actual circumstances surrounding the founding and operation of the Darmstadt colony were far more complex than Olbrich's vision of a hilltop "city of beauty." Presented by Koch and members of the press as an ideal, egalitarian artists' community, in reality the Darmstadt Mathildenhöhe set up rigid social and artistic hierarchies. Divisions between the artists were partly a function of varying recognition given to individual artists, along with sharply diverging salaries. For example, although colony members were encouraged to purchase land and build their own homes at generous terms offered by the grand duke, financial realities made such homes unaffordable to junior artists such as Bürck, Huber, and Bosselt.[35] Olbrich's dominance, too, was on clear display: He designed all the exhibition buildings and artists' residences in time for the first Darmstadt exhibition in 1901, with the sole exception of a house by Behrens, who retained complete control of the design of his dwelling.

For the government's part, the Hessian state legislature divided sharply over the matter of state subvention for the colony. In budget debates during the 1900 legislative session, some representatives objected to official backing for the applied arts as a form of interference in the "natural development" of the trades sector. Others added that the artists' reputed new stylistic experiments were insufficiently "of the people" (*volkstümlich*) to be valued by the general populace. The colony's legislative allies countered with the assertion that an artists' colony would benefit the totality of Darmstadt and Hessen's arts, crafts, and trades: Commissions attracted by well-known colony artists would not only introduce new ideas, techniques, and experiences to Hessian crafts enterprises and the buying public, but would also stimulate economic activity by spurring further commissions. This primarily economic argument eventually won the day. The legislature appropriated 20,000 Marks to the colony, an amount sufficient to cover approximately 20 percent of the construction costs for the colony's monumental atelier building, the Ernst Ludwig House (Fig. 14).[36] This state support disappeared after the colony's first exhibition in summer 1901, following cost overruns and accusations of egregious fiscal mismanagement associated with the exhibition. The grand duke's personal commitment and deep pockets, however, kept the colony afloat, and even enabled it to expand over the course of the next several years.[37]

Eighteen months of concentrated work enabled the artists of the colony to present themselves and their new buildings in a highly ritualized exhibition debut billed as "A Document of German Art." At the center of this exhibition, and at the highest point on the Mathildenhöhe, was Olbrich's Ernst Ludwig House – a communal art studio building housing the seven artists' ateliers, as well as apartments for Patriz Huber and Paul Bürck. Featuring a stark, symmetrical, monumental façade approached from below, the atelier building was the artistic and spiritual heart of the colony. Underscoring the building's monumentality, while Olbrich described his creation in cultlike terms as a "temple of work," were colossal stone sculptures of "Man and Woman," by Ludwig Habich, and smaller bronze "victory goddesses" by Rudolf Bosselt. Olbrich-designed homes for himself and Hans Christiansen flanked a "forum" immediately below and to either side of the Ernst Ludwig House. Further along were Olbrich-designed houses for Ludwig Habich and the Darmstadt furniture manufacturer Hans Glückert. Olbrich's site plan for this central portion of the arts and residential complex hinted at a kind of crystalline form nestled in the park's natural surroundings (Fig. 13). The crystal, inspired by the writings of the philosopher Friedrich Nietzsche, was a symbol of artistic rebirth and creativity that artists like Olbrich and Behrens enthusiastically embraced.

14. Darmstadt Artists' Colony opening ceremony, May 15, 1901, with Ernst Ludwig House in background (*Deutsche Kunst und Dekoration* 8, 1901)

Behrens, the second best-known artistic personality at the Darmstadt Artists' Colony after Olbrich, arranged for a crystal to be carried as a talisman during the solemn procession he organized with the poet George Fuchs for the opening ceremony of the 1901 exhibition (Fig. 14).[38] With much fanfare and religious-mystical ritual choreographed according to Nietzsche's notions of cultural rebirth, the entire Darmstadt architectural ensemble became the theatrical backdrop for ceremonies announcing the arrival of a new age for German art. No expense was spared as a Greek chorus dressed in elaborate costumes appeared on the steps of the atelier building and sang Fuchs's paean to the creative power of the human soul.

The colony provided Behrens with the opportunity to design his first house for himself and his wife Lilli, a textile designer, just west of Olbrich's symmetrical site composition (Figs. 13; 15–16). With this jewel-like, almost fairytale building Behrens launched what would become one of the Wilhelmine era's most prolific architectural design careers. As the architectural historian Tilmann Buddensieg has noted, Behrens incorporated into his "Zarathustrian" house numerous crystalline patterns, ancient Egyptian motifs, and forms such as the eagle and the diamond, symbolic of various aspects of Nietzsche's philosophy. According to Buddensieg, Behrens's house, which featured a fairly conventional single-family house plan with a music room, dining room, and drawing room off a main entrance hall (*Diele*), represented "a theater for the self-representation of the artist"

15. Peter Behrens, Behrens house, Darmstadt Artists' Colony, 1901, view from southwest (Fritz Hoeber, *Peter Behrens*, Munich, 1913)

and all his creations. The recurring diamond motif signified Nietzsche's *Edelstein*, intended to radiate "the virtues of a world that is not yet here."[39] This message was certainly consistent with the Darmstadt colony's overall reform effort. In fact, Darmstadt's artists struggled in their own ways to articulate personal visions for the fine and applied arts as vehicles for personal liberation, community rebirth, or artistic transcendence in a united Germany.

Yet Darmstadt was by no means the only location in which early-twentieth-century artists and architects competed to cast themselves as bearers of modern "Nietzschean" values. The philosopher's heroic depictions of artistic genius and creative independence struck a chord among German artists eager to facilitate a modern cultural renewal in their country. Behrens took the lead in designing projects that sought to create an orderly new synthesis out of all that was new, powerful, and unfamiliar in modern German society. In his German pavilion for the First International Exposition of Modern Decorative Art held in Turin in 1902, the architect organized displays of Germany's powerful new industries within a dramatically sky-lit interior; Zarathustra, cited explicitly in the

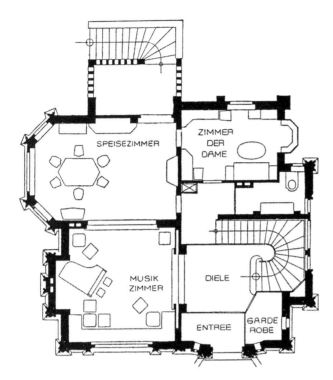

GRUNDRISS VOM ERDGESCHOSS

GRUNDRISS V. 1. OBERGESCHOSS

16. Peter Behrens, Behrens house, Darmstadt Artists' Colony, 1901, ground floor and first-floor plans (*Deutsche Kunst und Dekoration* 9, 1901–02)

exhibit, was said to be moving "towards the light," creating a link between the exhibit design and the notion that a new German culture was arising out of the country's national unity and economic organization.[40] Henry van de Velde, too, would design the interior of the Nietzsche archives in Weimar in 1903, using his own inimitable personal, fluid style to interpret the philosopher's message. Other architects such as Bruno Taut would eventually reinterpret the message of Zarathustra's mystical *Einsamkeitserlebnis*, or lonely mountain sojourns, in his post–World War I Expressionist "Alpine Architecture." Taut's fantastic architecture of color and light would reshape entire Alpine mountaintops with gleaming domes and crystalline palaces. These were to symbolize the birth of a new society that had escaped the destructive contradictions of modern physical, social, and political organization.[41]

Although Nietzsche constructed *Thus Spoke Zarathustra* as a tale of lonely mountain journeying and self-discovery, the book would nevertheless spark waves of mass tourism to the philosopher's favorite mountain region. This development could hardly go unnoticed by commentators at Darmstadt or by other contemporary Nietzsche scholars. The phenomenon confirmed, in a sense, the very philistinism of a mass age that the philosopher had been lamenting in the first place. Just as Behrens, Olbrich, and Taut used differing, highly personal interpretations of Nietzsche's philosophy in their search for new forms expressive of contemporary conditions, eminent German sociologists such as Ferdinand Tönnies, Georg Simmel, and others responded very differently to Nietzsche's prescriptions for German society. Tönnies, for example, after an initial phase of enthusiasm for Nietzsche's early books, reacted skeptically to the provocative aesthetic pronouncements and aphoristic tones of Nietzsche's late work. Publishing a sharp critique entitled "Nietzsche Nitwits," Tönnies warned that the cult following of Nietzsche's allegedly liberational philosophy endangered hopes for the reestablishment of German *Gemeinschaft*, or community, by furnishing young, disaffected members of society with half-baked justifications for a new brand of elitism. Simmel reacted differently, less interested in Tönnies's hopes for a re-created *Gemeinschaft* than in society's successful adjustment to a modern industrial and urban *Gesellschaft* (society). To Simmel, Nietzsche's final works symbolized the need for each individual to develop his or her ability to make personal distinctions about the complex modern world. These distinctions would enable each citizen to steer an ethical course through modern life's multiplying value systems and modes of existence.[42]

Critical reaction to the Darmstadt "Document of German Art" of 1901 were as varied as contemporary interpretations of Nietzsche's philosophy. On the whole, critics seemed to suggest, the colony balanced precariously between the poles of broad popular appeal and a pronounced elitism. The domestic exteriors presented visitors with a sincere attempt to update traditional German domestic forms in a festive atmosphere. Olbrich's houses followed central and south German regional building traditions while adding the architect's own, distinctive Viennese

17. Reconstruction model of Darmstadt Artists' Colony, view from the southeast; clockwise from bottom center of photo are the Habich house, the Second Glückert house, the Christiansen house, the Ernst Ludwig House, and the Olbrich house, with partial views of Helder House at bottom right, the pavilion for surface design at bottom left, and the First Glückert house at far left. All buildings designed by Joseph Maria Olbrich (Museum Künstlerkolonie, Darmstadt)

Secessionist flair to the stuccoed exteriors (Fig. 17). Bold folk murals and chimney details on the Christiansen house, for example, would give way to a more abstract pattern of colorful ceramic tiles on the Olbrich house. The hipped roofs, projecting bays, and balconies of a generalized, traditional German domestic architecture would be flattened or rendered orthogonally at the Habich house; by contrast, these would be rounded into provocatively shaped gables and adorned with abstracted reliefs of ornamental trees at the larger of two houses for furniture manufacturer Hans Glückert. Behrens's *Jugendstil* house, with its prominent gables and brick trim, recalled Northern German domestic building traditions.[43]

Some elements of Olbrich's buildings evoked Mediterranean or even ancient Near Eastern architecture. The wide expanses of clean, white stucco on the Habich house and Ernst Ludwig House, the two buildings' flat roofs, and the corner pylons and monumental sculpture of the Ernst Ludwig House all indicated the degree to which Viennese Secessionist forms derived vitality from the skillful incorporation of building traditions not necessarily native to Austria, but complementary to its architecture. As the architectural historian Barbara Miller Lane has pointed out, the Darmstadt examples fit within larger European currents of National Romanticism, the tradition in which late-nineteenth- and early-twentieth-century architects mined local and regional traditions to create personalized, evocative statements suggestive of an emergent national architecture, yet still appearing to be steeped in tradition.[44] By combining architectural elements from disparate, recently unified German-speaking regions with Mediterranean and monumental Near Eastern motifs, the colony's artists seemed to be groping toward the very architectural vocabulary embodied in Alexander Koch's phrase for a contemporary "German language of form" (*Deutsche Formensprache*).

Some critics, like Hermann Bahr – a friend of Olbrich's from Vienna – responded well to the display of individual artists' works, regarding them as both significant achievements in themselves and as the harbingers of increased social harmony to be promoted by artists. The most positive reactions saw in the exhibit's exquisitely coordinated architecture and furnishings the dawning of the very new age for German art and culture called for in the opening ceremony.[45] Others, however, saw not a document of German art, but an exaggerated tribute to the cult of individual artistic personality: expensive, fanciful houses saturated with luxury furnishings and detailing that the general public could ill afford. The exhibition's highly decorated domestic interiors provoked the harshest criticism. The journalist Richard Muther, for example, criticized the preciousness and fussiness of these interiors, the "prudishness" of endless roped off rooms in which, as he recalled, "on every table, on every stool, on every bed lies a note with the words '*Nichts anrühren*' (Don't touch anything)."[46] Far from offering an antidote to modern alienation, these displays of expensive commodities and plush surroundings suggested that for many exhibition visitors, the trappings of a new artistic age would remain, quite literally, inaccessible.

Other prominent visitors such as Harry Graf Kessler and Henry van de Velde, who made the journey from Weimar to view the Darmstadt exhibition, were also critical. They shared Muther's sentiment that the overprotective, curatorial obsessiveness of the Darmstadt displays, coupled with their enormous expense, undermined the very sense of artistic liveliness, freedom, and broad-based relevance that the colony ostensibly wished to promote. Kessler wrote that the "Darmstadt fiasco has proven that it takes time and patience in order to create something worthwhile, the gradual development of an entire industrial complex; that a sudden caprice cannot create something from nothing; and that success can only lie in the acceptance of modern life with its technology etc., and not in escapism and rubbishy nonsense with so-called beauty." Henry van de Velde was far less circumspect, and perhaps out of a sense of rivalry with Wilhelmine Germany's other best-known foreign artist, was alleged to have remarked: "Architecture for a bordello, and what's more, a bad bordello."[47]

Little is known concerning the exact reasons for the exodus of five of the Darmstadt colony's seven member artists shortly after the exhibition's close on October 15, 1901. It appears that the colony's numerous strong personalities, differing agendas, and enormous cost overruns combined to fuel the quarrels that prompted several of the departures. Patriz Huber, the talented

twenty-five-year-old interior designer who executed the abstract, geometric furnishings adorning several of Olbrich's interiors, tragically took his own life in
Berlin shortly after his contract at the colony went unrenewed. Behrens, feeling artistically suffocated, began negotiations in 1902 for a post as director of the
Dusseldorf Arts and Crafts School; Paul Bürck took a position teaching at another
of Prussia's applied arts schools, the Magdeburg School of Applied Arts.[48]

By 1903, only Olbrich and Habich remained as original members of the colony.
In December of that year, Ernst Ludwig invited the artists Paul Haustein, Johann
Vincenz Cissarz, and Daniel Greiner to join the colony. The new group prepared
a more modest exhibition for 1904, a statewide exhibition (*Landesausstellung*),
after which renewed quarrels led several members to depart again. With the
grand duke continually willing to underwrite operations, the colony overcame its
departures of personnel and added ceramics and glass workshops, an applied-arts
instructional institute, and a small applied-arts press in 1907. Olbrich produced
other important individual *Jugendstil* works such as the Marriage Tower of 1908,
but his death that year at the age of forty-one was a major blow to the colony
with which he had become so identified. His some-time rival and successor, the
Prussian architect Albin Müller, arrived from the Magdeburg School of Applied
Arts in 1906 and led the colony from the time of Olbrich's death until its final
exhibition in 1914.

The economic impact of the colony remained largely local, its hopes and ambitions hampered by Darmstadt's considerable remove from Europe's artistic centers. Critically, too, the colony continued to earn mixed reviews. Yet the Darmstadt Artists' Colony served as a beacon for the grand duke's wish to support
forward-thinking practitioners of architecture and the applied arts, attracting
numerous significant early-twentieth-century artists.

Whatever its financial woes and geographical disadvantages, the Darmstadt
experiment went anything but unnoticed. Indeed, the very fact of its existence
stimulated other German states to initiate their own decisive applied-arts reforms
in turn. Equally important, the colony lent credence to the notion that artists –
and especially architects and applied artists – could contribute in material terms to
a region's economic, artistic, and cultural renewal. This image of artists as leaders
of a modern German cultural milieu would endure well past the Wilhelmine era.

LEARNING FROM DARMSTADT: WÜRTTEMBERG AND THE "BUSINESS MODEL"

Of all German states, Hessen's nearby southern neighbor, the German kingdom of Württemberg, took the most immediate notice of Grand Duke Ernst
Ludwig's activities in Darmstadt. Its capital and royal residence, Stuttgart, lay
only 120 kilometers south of the Hessian capital, roughly between Darmstadt and
Munich. Like Darmstadt, Stuttgart did not enter the 1890s with a particularly

distinguished reputation as a center for art. In fact, the city's most ambitious art students tended to leave Stuttgart for Munich during the second half of the nineteenth century. The annals of the Württemberg Art Association record this as a time when a "permanent depression" afflicted the arts of Stuttgart and the Württemberg region.[49] As Richard Graul grimly observed in 1901, without the examples of Darmstadt, the Munich United Workshops, and van de Velde and Eckmann in Berlin, "no new spirit would have arisen in the high bastions of conservatism in Stuttgart."[50]

Within the first decade of the twentieth century, however, this situation would be reversed. Württemberg's King Wilhelm II, who ascended to the throne in October 1891 and was called by many the "learned king" (*gelernte König*), began to intervene personally in the kingdom's artistic milieu at the same time that Grand Duke Ernst Ludwig formed the Darmstadt colony.[51] Wilhelm II "very much understood himself as a bourgeois king (*Bürgerkönig*)," the noted German historian Thomas Nipperdey has written, and herein lies the key to understanding the significance of Württemberg's early-twentieth-century artistic reforms.[52] Specifically, between 1899 and 1910, royal initiatives put in place an entirely new physical and institutional infrastructure in support of the fine and applied arts. Rather than concentrating a privileged group of artists in a royal artists' colony, the "bourgeois king's" measures promoted commercial and intellectual life throughout Württemberg. To Max Diez, the art historian who served as the director of the State Art Museum in Stuttgart, Württemberg's King Wilhelm II acted out of the knowledge that the enhancement of art in individual German capital cities was "one of the ways by which royal authority can productively engage and preserve the desired many-sidedness of German intellectual life."[53] At a time when Prussian dominance and the undeniable centrality of Berlin as capital of the Reich was by no means a pleasant thought to all Germans, Diez's statement contained regional political undertones as well as a measure of particularist self-assertion.[54]

In the northern Württemberg city of Heilbronn, King Wilhelm II's new reform-minded arts associations found a political complement in the liberal circle around city councilman and silver manufacturer Peter Bruckmann and his colleague Ernst Jäckh, editor of Heilbronn's *Neckar Zeitung* newspaper. Together with the twenty-two-year-old journalist and political activist Theodor Heuss, and with the aid of Wolf Dohrn, a recent graduate from the economics seminar of Lujo Brentano at Munich University, these men made it possible for the politician, pastor, prolific writer, and liberal reformer Friedrich Naumann, a native of Saxony, to stand for election as an outsider in Heilbronn in 1907. This nexus of south German liberal activism and future Werkbund leadership grew in the fertile soil provided by a King Wilhelm II's reforms. The king's measures encouraged like-minded individuals from various fields to cooperate in the Württemberg setting, creating an environment in which future alliances could be forged and even institutionalized.

The first step was to attract leading personalities in the fine arts, applied arts, and architecture to Stuttgart. At the king's initiative, the royal administration tapped into the progressive energies of the Artists' Association (*Künstlerbund*) in the neighboring state of Baden. This group had seceded from the more traditional Karlsruhe Arts Society (*Kunstgenossenschaft*) in 1896. In 1899, the king hired the leading Artists' Association painter, Leopold Graf von Kalckreuth, along with – at Kalckreuth's insistence – the painters Carlos Grethe and Robert Poetzelberger, to relocate to Stuttgart. Paying Kalckreuth's and Grethe's salaries out of his own coffers, the king also agreed to finance a new atelier building for the artists. In administering these matters, the king overruled the objections of his own Minister of Culture and of some in the local arts community. As a Berlin newspaper observed at the time: "King Wilhelm II is clearly the only significant patron of art in Stuttgart. In spite of the many wealthy people who live there... the efforts they make on behalf of art are as good as nil."[55] The king's hiring of Kalckreuth, Grethe, and Poetzelberger signaled the beginning of changes that would have lasting effects on German art, architecture, and applied arts in the twentieth century.

Over the next few years Stuttgart's royal, state, and city administrations introduced ambitious measures that not only staunched the flow of turn-of-the-century artistic talent from Stuttgart to Munich, but in some instances reversed it. Württemberg responded directly to the example of the Darmstadt colony by placing special emphasis on improved practical training in the applied arts. Rejecting the model of a single privileged artists' colony, however, it promoted a multipronged approach to reform in architecture, the fine arts, and applied arts through new and existing institutions. Members of the Stuttgart city council, like the royal administration, would place great faith in economic justifications for artistic activity, holding that the "development of art in Stuttgart is unusually important and valuable, in part because many of the finer branches of industry (*feinere Industriezweige*) are directly or indirectly dependent upon art.... Thus, the economic prosperity (*Blüte*) of Stuttgart is to a certain degree conditioned by the flowering of art."[56]

To a greater extent than other states, and in recognition of these economic considerations, Württemberg's reformers reorganized training in the applied arts along modern entrepreneurial and business lines. Initially, and perhaps naively, the king and his advisers wanted simply to underwrite the cost of relocating the Munich United Workshops for Art in Handicraft to Stuttgart. In addition to paying for moving and operating costs, a portion of the subventions from this initial proposal would have paid for students to receive instruction from the United Workshops. Local applied-arts producers protested loudly, however, threatened by the potential competition the United Workshops represented. They insisted that the training of students for local applied-arts industries was a task solely for the schools and did not belong in practicing applied-arts firms.[57] Such protests from applied-arts practitioners would become an increasingly common refrain in the early years of the twentieth century, especially among members of the old *Mittelstand*. The complaints of the Württemberg craftsmen anticipated similar objections in Prussia by the Association for the Economic Interests of the Crafts (*Fachverband für die wirtschaftlichen Interessen des Kunstgewerbes*). The Association's protests led to the notorious "Muthesius Affair," the controversy that sparked the formation of the Werkbund; this controversy is examined in detail in Chapter 4.

Bowing to local pressures, the Württemberg administration abandoned its effort to relocate the Munich United Workshops and adopted a new tack. In 1901, and with the support of a new Württemberg Minister of Culture, von Weizsäcker, the king issued a decree for the founding of new Trials and Instructional Workshops at the Stuttgart School of Applied Arts. This new plan left in place the school's established curriculum, which focused on the reproduction of historical ornaments for application to interiors, furniture, and other products. However, there arose an alternative track that emphasized drawing from nature, not from plaster casts of the historic orders and ornaments. In addition, objects would be designed with greater attention to materials and constructional principles, and less to models of the past. These were the very methods popularized by educators in the British Arts and Crafts movement and adopted first in continental Europe by the Austrian School of Applied Arts in Vienna. The royal administration hired Otto Krüger and Bernhard Pankok of the United Workshops in Munich to head the new curriculum, while in 1903 they acquired the artist Bruno Paul as a teacher of surface design (*Flächenkunst*).[58] The administration's further hiring of Johann Cissarz and Paul Haustein away from the Darmstadt Artists' Colony after the colony's second exhibition in 1904 ignited new protests from the Württemberg applied-arts industries. Its members renewed complaints of unfair competition arising from the state-supported applied-arts workshops, which they accused of competing for profitable private commissions.[59]

These complaints appeared to have some basis: The Stuttgart instructional workshops were set up according to an unusually disciplined, entrepreneurial business model. Hermann von Seefeld, a visiting Prussian observer whom we will encounter later as Hermann Muthesius's first patron and the architect's close colleague in the reform of Prussian arts, crafts, and trade schools at the Ministry of Commerce in Prussia, reported after a lengthy study tour that Stuttgart's instructional workshops occupied a "special position" vis-à-vis the other applied-arts schools he surveyed in Württemberg, Baden, Elsass, Hessen, and Switzerland in 1903. This was particularly true in the fields of furniture, cabinet making, and metalworking. According to von Seefeld, Krüger and Pankok had outfitted the school and workshops for the express purpose of the "ennoblement of large-scale production" (*Veredelung des Grossbetriebes*), a term that would, in just four years, become one of the watchwords of the Deutscher Werkbund. For the time being, von Seefeld's use of this phrase referred to the relatively modest decorative arts process of "design[ing] simple, noble forms that can be manufactured through the means of modern techniques" and was not yet being applied to larger manu-facturing industries as such.[60]

Advanced students at the Stuttgart Applied Arts School, von Seefeld reported, benefited greatly from these "modern techniques." They worked as veritable employees in the school's instructional workshop for cabinet making, for example, where a large assortment of wood, marble, and metal material samples hanging from the ceiling inspired students to design their pieces from the outset with a particular material in mind. School personnel helped students calculate detailed budgets for each piece they developed and constructed, and the students kept track of their hours on weekly time cards. All projects were executed to the fullest extent possible, and in cases of private commissions that came from paying clients, students received compensation for their work.[61]

Pankok reinforced the Stuttgart School of Applied Arts' entrepreneurial spirit by leading student excursions to factories each summer to study the operations of applied-arts industries in greater detail. In winter, instructors supplemented lectures with class visits to historic local castles and museums, examining classic pieces in the history of furniture and the applied arts firsthand. Contrary to earlier pedagogical methods that would have emphasized the formal characteristics of these historical pieces, however, instructors accentuated the study of specific constructional and decorative techniques by which old masters in the applied arts had achieved high levels of technical and artistic quality in their works.[62]

These changes at Stuttgart's School of Applied Arts were only the beginning. In 1901, the Stuttgart Technical University gave a major boost to the reputation of its architecture school when it hired the architect and planner Theodor Fischer away from Munich. For the next seven years, Fischer's pedagogical, building, and planning activities would result in significant alterations to Stuttgart's physical as well as cultural landscape, launching a celebrated twentieth-century "Stuttgart school" of planners and architects renowned for mingling a focus on materials and local context with interventions at the urban scale.[63]

Building on his experience in Munich, Fischer developed a practice and an ar-chitecture curriculum that quickly made him one of the most highly respected and sought-after architects in Germany. Abandoning the curriculum of Skjold Neck-elmann, the predecessor whose careful academic historicism Fischer regarded as outdated, Fischer made the intense study of local Schwabian building traditions and characteristic urban forms into the basis of his Stuttgart teaching and prac-tice. Over the next several years in Stuttgart, and back in Munich beginning in 1908, Fischer's teaching and practice garnered him a national reputation as well as a huge following, with some of his students and apprentices going on to become luminaries of early-twentieth-century German architecture in their own right. Fischer's students are remarkable for their diversity of approach, itself a result of Fischer's particular pedagogy, and included such architects as Bruno Taut, Paul Bonatz, Erich Mendelsohn, Hugo Häring, Ernst May, and Dominikus Böhm.

During this time, Fischer worked on commissions for the Heilbronn City Theatre (1902–15), the expansion of the University of Jena (1903–08), the Garrison Church at Ulm (1906–10), and numerous other projects for museums, workers' housing settlements, and office buildings across Germany.

Fischer's towering pre–World War I reputation as an architect and teacher, and a career that has received no comprehensive treatment in English-speaking literature, call for a closer consideration of the degree to which Fischer's architecture and planning approaches helped establish south Germany's major capitals as modern architectural and cultural centers. The most obvious confirmation of Fischer's nationwide reputation was the Deutscher Werkbund's selection of him as the organization's first president at its founding meeting in Munich in October 1907. Later, back in Munich, Fischer's reputation drew young talents such as the Swiss-born architect Charles-Edouard Jeanneret, later Le Corbusier, and the young Dutch architect J. J. P Oud to visit in the years 1910 and 1911, respectively. After Jeanneret met with Fischer several times to see if he might be allowed to apprentice with him, an arrangement that did not come to pass, Jeanneret wrote a gushing letter to his Swiss mentor, Charles L'Eplattenier:

> I must tell you about Professor Theodor Fischer in Stuttgart. I saw a school of his, a church, an apartment house, and the new Garrison Church in Ulm – buildings which are of the greatest interest because of their architectonic construction: reinforced concrete materials, generous and full of power . . . they are characterized by a pleasing, lively vitality and are not at all morbid or dry . . . I wish to work for three or four months for an architect here, and when possible with one who builds in reinforced concrete . . . by Fischer I would be most happy.[64]

It is easy to understand why Jeanneret would have been drawn to advanced projects like the Garrison Church in the city of Ulm. This massive building, built between 1906 and 1910, could hold up to 2,000 Protestant worshippers from among the 10,000-man army garrison stationed along Württemberg's border with Bavaria (Figs. 18–20). The building illustrates the extent to which Fischer's sculptural approach and exploitation of concrete's unique spanning potential differed from the framing methods of Jeanneret's first mentor in concrete construction, the Parisian architect Auguste Perret. At the Garrison Church, Fischer allowed his roughcast, structural concrete buttresses and other framing elements to penetrate through the building's brick walls. This powerful assertion of the building's structural system ensured a lively contrast in color and material throughout the exterior. At the same time it referred visually back to such historic structural systems as the timber frame and the gothic buttress. Large, simple volumes like the circular apse enhanced the monumental language of the church, while the apse's cylindrical interior volume, flooded with daylight from above, betrayed an unexpected lightness and spatial continuity with the enormous nave (Fig. 20).

18. Theodor Fischer, Garrison Church, Ulm, 1908–10, general view (restored) (*Der Profanbau*, 1911)

At the Garrison Church the architect also undertook a radical reversal of the usual position of towers and apse, a move that helped the enormous building to retain its human scale. Instead of positioning the apse behind the altar, the architect designed it as a rounded entrance portico with open balcony above. Most adventurous, however, was the exposed twenty-eight-meter (ninety-two-foot) reinforced concrete ceiling span, among the largest concrete interior spans achieved in Europe before the First World War. With the nave ceiling, moreover, the architect took the step, uncommon for the time, of allowing the gentle curves of the concrete ceiling to express a new kind of tectonic reality for spaces of worship. Only a thin linear painted outline, whose curves recalled the gentle undulations of the side aisle column supports as well as the ceiling's primary supporting ribs, accented the concrete ceiling surface.

The architect oversaw the painting of interior wall murals by Adolf Hölzel, himself no traditionalist; among his best-known students at the Stuttgart Art Academy were Oskar Schlemmer and the Swiss artist Johannes Itten, both of

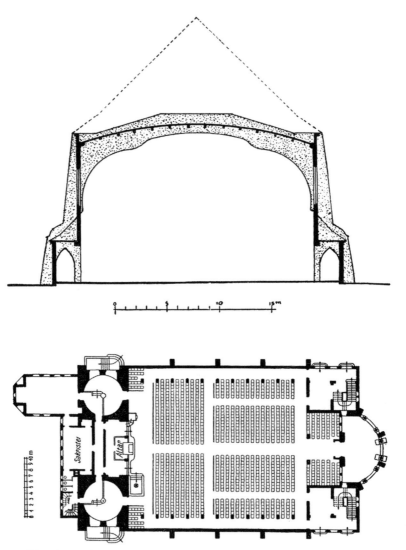

19. Theodor Fischer, Garrison Church, Ulm, 1908–10, transverse section and plan (Gustav A. Platz, *Die Baukunst der Neuesten Zeit*, Berlin, 1927)

later Bauhaus fame. Fischer's efforts to provide a familiar interior décor were not enough for some worshippers and critics. Many reacted with outrage at the untraditional nature of the building's numerous compositional and material innovations. Nonetheless, Fischer's Garrison Church marks an important contribution to a twentieth-century architectural tradition of exposed, reinforced concrete construction. Although Jeanneret never did get to work in Fischer's office, his exposure to buildings like this one made him one of the architect's many prewar converts.[65]

The young Stuttgart architecture school apprentices Paul Bonatz and Bruno Taut had better luck than Jeanneret at finding employment in Fischer's office. Bonatz in particular considered himself doubly fortunate, as Fischer also hired

20. Theodor Fischer, Garrison Church, Ulm, view of nave (*Jahrbuch des Deutschen Werkbundes*, Jena, 1912)

him to be his first teaching assistant at the Stuttgart Technical University. Echoing Jeanneret's enthusiasm, Bonatz offered strong, personal recollections of Fischer's methodical yet impassioned approach to architectural instruction.

As Bonatz recalled, Fischer engaged in pedagogical rituals his students found endearing. At desk-side critiques, the architect's remarks about a student's work would at first be painfully slow in coming. But when they finally emerged, Fischer's observations reflected what students regularly described as a seemingly effortless and thoughtful ability to interrelate the scales of an individual detail, a building, a large block, or an urban plan. Like his own teacher before him, Friedrich Thiersch, Fischer constantly dazzled students with his facility at working in an array of artistic and representational media. Eschewing normative architectural notions of his own, however, Fischer evinced a pedagogical self-assuredness that prompted him to nurture what he saw as the unique and worthwhile elements in students' often radically dissimilar formal designs. Bonatz's memoirs convey the characteristics, apart from Fischer's dedication and highly personalized approach, that gave the architect's work its path-breaking quality. The key to "Fischer's revival," as Bonatz called it,

> lay in his grasp of the crafts, of materials. He built with a sentiment that at last made things plastic again, filled them with blood and with life, conveying far more than the mere polish of an academic scheme. Naturally this

sort of creation had to build on tradition, and the precedents that lay closest to his heart were those of the bourgeoisie rather than the nobility. The
point of Fischer's teaching was not schematic imitation, but intuitive design
development (*intuitives Gestalten*). But he also implanted something in our
blood, above all in mine, his most eager adept: a sense of the romantic.[66]

With his flexibility of outlook, numerous commissions, and national reputation
as both an architect and teacher, it is little wonder that the Deutscher Werkbund's
diverse membership selected Fischer to serve as its first president in 1907. When
one contemplates the wide variety of approaches observable in devoted Fischer
students like Paul Bonatz, Erich Mendelsohn, Bruno Taut, and Hugo Häring,
one senses the ways in which Fischer's pedagogy and sense of the "romantic" –
which respected the originality of every student – lived on in a whole array of
influential twentieth-century German architects.

Württemberg and its capital, Stuttgart, likely would not have joined other
early-twentieth-century centers of architectural and applied-arts innovation had
the state and city not continued to support its newcomers after their arrival.
Accordingly, both Fischer and Bernhard Pankok received major commissions
for further arts buildings and cultural institutions. In 1907, for example, King
Wilhelm II supported Fischer's project for a new Stuttgart exhibition hall next
to the Baroque Royal Palace (Fig. 21). This so-called *Kunstgebäude* would host
exhibitions, concerts, and other cultural events. It also contained a large restau-
rant and club rooms for the Stuttgart Artists' Association. Completed between
1909 and 1913, the building featured a Renaissance arcade that simultaneously
evoked Brunelleschi's Foundling Hospital in Florence while employing, as Winfried Nerdinger has noted, an arcade "type" reminiscent of elements found in
the Pavilion of the late-sixteenth-century pleasure garden (*Lustgarten*) that had
earlier occupied the site. The new building was no mere historical quotation
or academic paraphrase, however. Rather, the project represented the conscious
reworking of a particular historical style that stood clearly apart from its royal
neighbor while maintaining a monumental, historically inflected link to it and, by
extension, to the royal grounds of which it was to become a part. The building's
largest feature, a sky-lit dome topping a multipurpose hall, established a dialogue
with three other domes close by in the surrounding city center. At the same time,
the dome enlarged the scale of the *Kunstgebäude* to allow the building to have an
independent presence alongside the comparative vastness of the Baroque Royal
Palace.[67]

Fischer's building was the subject of much debate. Critics complained about
the lack of stylistic unity, given the building's adjacency to the Royal Palace.
Those recognizing in Fischer a talent for anchoring innovative buildings flexibly
in their local context, while managing also to establish them within the larger flow
of historical tradition, favored it the most.[68] Like the tradition stretching back to
Karl Friedrich Schinkel's Altes Museum in Berlin of 1830, Fischer's *Kunstgebäude*

21. Theodor Fischer, Exhibition Hall for the Arts (*Kunstgebäude*), Stuttgart, 1909–1913, view circa 1930 (altered), with royal castle adjacent (Courtesy of Fiske Kimball Fine Arts Library Image Collection, University of Virginia)

represented the growing prominence of the bourgeoisie, the arts, and *Bildung* in city life. All of these were acknowledged by the royal patronage of Fischer's exhibition hall and embodied in the multipurpose building erected next to the king's palace.

Pankok, whose two projects for the *Kunstgebäude* were rejected in favor of Fischer's design, could derive consolation from a commission he received for King Wilhelm II's promised new studio building for the Association of Württemberg Friends of Art. This association enjoyed broad-based institutional support that extended well beyond the royal house. Built between 1905 and 1907 in the hills overlooking Stuttgart, Pankok's imposing edifice of concrete, stuccoed brick, and glass gave proud expression to Württemberg's alliance of royalty, state administration, industry, and businessmen (Fig. 4). With each group contributing funds to the new association, the alliance expressed the aim of "sweeping our state forward in further energetic efforts toward establishing ourselves as the born equals of the other peoples (*Stämmen*) of Germany."[69] From its ranks would emerge later the Deutscher Werkbund's longest-serving president, Peter Bruckmann, artistic director of the Württemberg Applied Arts Association and owner of the venerable firm P. Bruckmann and Sons, located in the northern Württemberg city of Heilbronn. Founded in 1805, P. Bruckmann and Sons had long been the *Hoflieferant* (Court Supplier) of high-quality silver goods to the Württemberg royal house.[70]

The Association of Württemberg Friends of Art differed greatly from the Darmstadt Artists' Colony in its organizational structure, approach to financing, and involvement of the public. Filling its coffers with required annual dues of 500 Marks per member, the association made clear that in return, members would receive the equivalent of one-fourth of this subscription rate in the form of fine- and applied-arts works of the member's choosing. Pankok's abstract, monumental design for the association's new atelier building seemed to celebrate the freshness of the art association's spirited and inclusive organizational approach: Giant pyramids of glass flooded the structure's eight studio spaces with controllable natural light, augmented by large window expanses along the north façade. Pankok's use of exposed concrete and plain, stuccoed surfaces and his rejection of handcrafted, applied historical ornament provoked outrage among more traditionally minded "friends of art" in the press, even though fans of the building were able to point to certain volumetric, material, and compositional resemblances to Josef Hoffmann's Purkersdorf Sanatorium of 1904 and Olbrich's Ernst Ludwig House in Darmstadt of 1901.[71] Given that his structure was completed between 1905 and 1907, the appearance of this stark building and its austere, unadorned volumes was bound to elicit shock among the many conservative members of Stuttgart's arts community. Yet Max Diez defended Stuttgart's maverick architect at the time with the remark, "it is a peculiar development that the people who most harshly criticize (Pankok) also display not a moment's doubt that they are dealing with a great talent."[72]

The Darmstadt colony artist Johann Vincenz Cissarz became one of the Art Association studio building's first occupants, joined by the painter Robert Weise. The studio positions came with teaching assignments in Pankok's Instructional Workshops at the School of Applied Arts, thus ensuring that artists would benefit from Württemberg's larger institutional framework. The Stuttgart Art Academy, meanwhile, also hired Ludwig Habich and Paul Haustein away from the Darmstadt colony to serve as new instructors. With new buildings, institutions, and artists, along with a network of supporting members from the capital city and throughout the kingdom, Württemberg provided a steady base of support for new directions in early-twentieth-century architecture, art, and the applied arts. It also furnished a point of orientation for such neighboring lands as Baden and Elsass-Lothringen, from which the Württemberg Association for the Friends of Art added subscribers. Moreover, the strength of Württemberg's broad-based institutional network would allow the kingdom's support for artistic and cultural endeavors to outlast the Wilhelmine period's catastrophic end in 1918. In the 1920s, Stuttgart's efforts to link cultural prestige, economic pragmatism, and progressive architecture and design would reach a climax with the city's sponsorship of "The New Dwelling," the exhibition that, under Ludwig Mies van der Rohe's oversight, produced the celebrated Weissenhofsiedlung in 1927, as well as Paul Schmitthenner's Kochenhofsiedlung, a rival demonstration housing estate located just a stone's throw from its more renowned avant-garde counterpart.

In the short term and prior to the First World War, however, individuals such as Theodor Fischer, Peter Bruckmann, the publicist and political manager Ernst Jäckh, and the politician Friedrich Naumann would all rise out of Württemberg's dynamic milieu to become prominent leaders of the pre-war Werkbund. Their important individual contributions to and battles within this association are discussed in Chapters 5 and 6.

APPLIED-ARTS REFORMS IN THE GRAND DUCHY OF SAXONY-WEIMAR-EISENACH

The Grand Duchy of Saxony-Weimar-Eisenach occupies a special place in the development of German architecture and the applied arts in the late nineteenth and early twentieth centuries. Like its neighbor directly to the west, Hessen, Saxony-Weimar-Eisenach was small enough to feel a major impact from the artistic initiatives of its grand duke, Wilhelm Ernst. His predecessor, the eighty-three year-old Grand Duke Carl Alexander, died in 1901 after a productive forty-eight-year reign. The twenty-five year-old Wilhelm Ernst began his rule at a young age, much like his counterpart in Darmstadt, Ernst Ludwig. But unlike the English-educated Ernst Ludwig, Wilhelm Ernst was not particularly interested in or informed about the arts. Nevertheless, eager to mark the beginning of his reign with a meaningful gesture, Wilhelm Ernst solicited suggestions from his advisers at court in response to the numerous reports of Ernst Ludwig's remarkable Darmstadt exhibition that summer.[73]

The long-standing minister of state Karl Rothe could recall two major arts initiatives from the reign of Carl Alexander, who had displayed a wide range of interests over the course of his reign.[74] The first was his founding of the Grand Ducal School of Art in Weimar in 1860, an institution inspired by the grand duke's completion of tours in Munich and Tirol in 1858.[75] Two decades later, in 1881, Carl Alexander authorized the creation of an Applied Arts Authority (*Zentralstelle fur Kunstgewerbe*). The authority offered practical advice to the duchy's decorative-arts industries and featured techniques that would only come into general use some two decades later. In fact, the activities of the authority's director, the architect Bruno Eelbo from Leipzig, give the lie to notions that the 1880s – too frequently dismissed as an unenlightened "age of historicism" – had nothing to offer by way of ideas for practical, functional design.

When the Weimar administration awarded Eelbo a three-year contract to advise the duchy's applied-arts producers on technical, aesthetic, and economic matters, he responded by warning local producers against the use of excessive ornament. For success in "the production of export goods," he wrote in his summary of activities for the ministry, the "highest quality of materials and work must go hand in hand with the most cautious application of artistic decoration, so that [these goods] can hold their own successfully against foreign competition. Every superfluous twist," he continued, "every inferior ornament makes the product more expensive and renders it uncompetitive."[76] From a long list of Thuringian applied-arts producers whom Eelbo either visited or advised in Weimar, several went on to build successful enterprises and even win medals in international exhibitions. During the authority's heyday in the early 1880s, Eelbo achieved considerable success in decorative-arts design reform by linking aesthetic and manufacturing issues to questions of economic viability and export potential. Eelbo's conclusions are surprisingly similar to those of other Wilhelmine figures who emphasized the commercial viability of redesigned applied-arts goods much later – men like the art historian Richard Streiter in Munich, the master cabinet maker and entrepreneur Karl Schmidt in Dresden, or Hermann Muthesius in Berlin, himself a native of Gross-Neuhausen, a tiny village in Saxony-Weimar-Eisenach. Eelbo's insistence that artist and manufacturer collaborate until "the typical form (*typische Form*) is developed" even anticipates by three decades the discussions of "type" and "typicality" (*Typisierung*) that would preoccupy the Werkbund between 1907 and 1914.[77] Financial difficulties whose origins – political or otherwise – are unclear seem to have ended the life of the Applied Arts Authority in 1890.[78]

In 1901, Karl Rothe recommended to Wilhelm Ernst that he revive a version of his grandfather's defunct Applied Arts Authority.[79] The two also discussed the possible appointment of two luminaries of the European art world, Harry Graf Kessler and Henry van de Velde, to prominent posts in Weimar.[80] This notion had the backing of Elizabeth Förster-Nietzsche, the sister of the recently deceased philosopher Friedrich Nietzsche.[81] As a result, Wilhelm Ernst appointed Kessler to replace Aimé von Palézieux as director of the permanent collection at the Weimar Museum of Art and Applied Art (*Museum für Kunst und Kunstgewerbe*) and van de Velde to head a new state arts and crafts "seminar" in Weimar. This seminar would take the form of a state-sponsored artistic consultancy to crafts enterprises across the grand duchy. The appointments took effect in 1902, only a few months after the two friends' joint visit to the Darmstadt Artists' Colony exhibition. Critical of the exhibition, as we have seen, Kessler and van de Velde shared an ambition to outperform Hessen artistically and to inaugurate a new golden age of art in Weimar.

Van de Velde began work in Weimar in mid-October 1902, concentrating on the agreed-upon task of "artistic improvement of the applied arts in the grand duchy" through the issuing of "expert advice" to trades practitioners, industries, and trades associations.[82] His Applied Arts Seminar (*Kunstgewerbliches Seminar*) was to be run as a private institute. Not only was van de Velde charged with the preparation of model drawings in various applied-arts fields, particularly in two-dimensional, ornamental surface design (*ornamentale Flächenkunst*), but he was also expected to counsel practitioners in such matters as "choice of materials and tools, the improvement of techniques, the acquisition of new trade opportunities, and the improvement of commercial relations."[83] Advised by a veteran factory inspector in Weimar, the Chamberlain (*Kammerherr*) von Nostitz, van de Velde not only breathed new life into Eelbo's Applied Arts Authority from the 1880s, but expanded on a recommendation made as far back as 1776 by Weimar's most famous resident, Johann Wolfgang von Goethe: that the grand duchy provide free classes for arts, crafts, and trades practitioners for "the general development of taste and support of industry."[84]

Van de Velde fought battles for recognition of his work in Weimar and gradually expanded his operations to a degree sufficient to warrant the founding of a new Weimar School of Arts and Crafts. What began as van de Velde's spurned application to the Ministry of State for an instructional workshop in applied arts for the modeling of porcelain, terra cotta, and ceramics in July 1903 broadened, by summer 1904, into a wider discussion about possible state funding for an applied-arts school. Seeing an opportunity, van de Velde stepped up his campaign with a memorandum to the grand duke on December 24, 1904. In it he enclosed a copy of a newly issued decree from the Prussian Ministry of Commerce and Trade, published just nine days earlier and crafted in the main by the architect and Commerce Ministry Privy Councillor Hermann Muthesius. The Prussian decree authorized the establishment of sixty-one new applied-arts workshops for leading arts, crafts, and trades schools (*Kunstgewerbe-und Handwerkerschulen*) in eighteen cities and towns across Prussia. Van de Velde was able to leverage his argument for new support from Wilhelm Ernst by underscoring "the extent to which the ideas concerning the form of training in this decree correspond to those that I have developed for your Highness."[85]

Van de Velde's gambit succeeded. By September 1906 he was moving his applied-arts operations into a building completed to his designs (Figs. 2–3) and situated directly across from the Weimar School of Art, the school founded by Carl Alexander in 1860. Van de Velde had been commissioned to renovate the School of Art in 1904, followed by a second renovation completed in 1911 (Fig. 1). To avoid obstructing the north-facing windows of the art school's painting studios, van de Velde gave his building a low, two-story profile and set it back from the street in two wings set at right angles. This layout created a forecourt as well as the sense of a shared precinct for the two schools. The Applied Arts School's most prominent feature was a distinctive horseshoe-shaped arch of cut stone that projected slightly outward from the south wall's plaster surfaces (Fig. 2). The arch wrapped around the windows of van de Velde's second-floor studio and office, a motif that, given the choice of materials and decorative flourish, can be seen as the application of a monumental accent to the school's all-important director's office. The school's main drafting room, located just below, received no such embellishment.[86] Now housed in a new building offering twenty-three new rooms for applied-arts instruction, van de Velde's Applied Arts Seminar continued as a state program within a school setting, taking the form of an advanced, fifth and final year of workshop-based instruction for especially talented applied-arts graduates.

Through fall 1907 van de Velde oversaw the outfitting of workshops for print-ing and bookbinding, goldsmithing, precious metal engraving, enameling, and textile and carpet weaving. He visited Muthesius in Berlin in December 1907 to discuss further the best means to manage workshop operations in the school context. The grand duchy's Ministry of State only agreed to finance two of the workshops, forcing van de Velde to find additional support from sources like the Weimar town council, local arts associations, and generous firms like Carl Zeiss of Jena. Later, the school also raised badly needed funds through proceeds from the sale of its own finished products. These were sold in annual Christmas exhi-bitions; during the school year products from the workshops were sold in a store fashioned out of a basement room in the school's forecourt. Although the school was up and running by late 1906, the school held its official opening on October 7, 1907 – just one day, as it happened, after the Werkbund held its founding meeting in Munich. Sixteen students enrolled in the first year, a number that would gradually increase to seventy-six in 1914.[87]

Van de Velde based the school's curriculum on his personal approach to deco-rative arts. Developed over the course of path-breaking experiences as an applied artist in Brussels, Paris, and Berlin, van de Velde's approach had captured the imaginations of Siegfried Bing, Julius Meier-Graefe, and other early patrons of Art Nouveau in the mid-1890s. Now van de Velde taught lessons in the evolution of linear and planar patterns, specifically suited to two-dimensional designs and decorative-arts products, and developed in a systematic way. An initial series of lines featuring simple curves and twists necessarily led, van de Velde taught, to further "dependent" linear formations elaborated from the initial lines. Simple, repetitive, reproducible linear sequences became rhythmic patterns whose care-ful application activated the surfaces and borders of objects to which they were applied. What began as simple lessons in line drawing developed into advanced methods of contrasting the positive and negative spaces between lines, or be-tween surfaces in volumes (Figs. 22–23). Van de Velde taught that lines possessed "the same logical and definite relations to one another as do numbers or musical notes," and in "their gliding and winding forward motion," they can "lift us up and raise our souls to that same exalted state, which only song and dance can awaken in us."[88]

Van de Velde's goal was to bring these dynamic graphic forms into harmony with the design and decoration of the broadest variety of applied-arts products; this was, he wrote, a "structural-linear and dynamic-graphic" (*strukto-lineare und dynamo-graphische*) approach to form-making.[89] It was a strongly personal ped-agogy and art, and one that van de Velde claimed was unique to him and his school. Wilhelm von Debschitz and Hermann Obrist, however, were teaching variations on these lessons concerning line, form, and abstraction in Munich, and, like instructors at Peter Behrens's Dusseldorf School of Applied Arts and teachers at the Cologne School of Applied Arts, were doing so in explicit rela-tion to forms studied in nature.[90] Van de Velde certainly had his own system in

22. Weimar School of Applied Arts, student drawings illustrating the development of linear and planar ornaments in Henry van de Velde's course for ornamental drawing, circa 1911 (drawing by author after Karl-Heinz Hüter, *Henry van de Velde*, Berlin, 1967)

approaching line, form, and decoration, yet his approach garnered criticism from some contemporaries who felt his methods placed too little emphasis on teaching students to be independently minded creative artists and not merely junior versions of their master. Walter Gropius, for example, would later go so far as to say that van de Velde trained assistants, but not independent creative personalities; Charles-Edouard Jeanneret's visit to the school left the Swiss observer impressed with the quality of the work – but less so with the school's emphasis on handmade articles.[91] The art historian Karl-Heinz Hüter, a van de Velde expert, has characterized the school as an "extension of van de Velde's own atelier."[92] Van de Velde defended himself against critics by pointing out that limited school resources,

23. Henry van de Velde, silver jewelry exhibited at the Third German Applied Arts Exhibition in Dresden, 1906 (Kuratorium der Ausstellung, *Das Deutsche Kunstgewerbe 1906: III. Deutsche Kunstgewerbeausstellung Dresden 1906*, Munich, 1906)

which were, in fact, quite real, prevented the funding of fully qualified artists to teach in the instructional workshops.

In any event, the Weimar School of Applied Arts was a major vehicle enabling van de Velde to pursue his stated mission of developing a new style for a new age. Like progressive thinkers and avant-garde artists all over Europe and the United States since the mid-nineteenth century, van de Velde insisted upon the creation of a style undeniably and recognizably different from past styles, and one arising out of the "intellectual, moral, and social currents of the times."[93] Van de Velde argued that only a radical break with the familiar styles of the past would permit a forging of a new whole out of the new conditions of modern life. Progress in this area needed guidance from the artist and his creative powers of synthesis, leading van de Velde to call upon all artists and applied artists to meet this challenge by standing together "as brothers in arms."[94]

Such polemics appeared throughout his books, *Lay Sermons on the Applied Arts* (*Kunstgewerblichen Laienpredigten*) in 1902 and *On the New Style* (*Vom Neuen Stil*) in 1907. They were rehearsed even earlier during an extensive tour of the grand duchy's decorative-arts enterprises in the company of the grand duke's mother, Pauline, in 1901.[95] Drawn in two magnificent grand ducal coaches complete with servants in livery, van de Velde's party made frequent stops at porcelain factories, furniture workshops, and other crafts enterprises throughout Saxony-Weimar-Eisenach. Here the artist would step down to make impromptu speeches to assembled workers, proclaiming the arrival of the new spirit in twentieth-century applied arts.[96]

There was nothing particularly German about this style, however, and influential Weimar residents, who saw themselves as defenders of a perceived "correct" German tradition, took notice. Signs of local difficulties emerged when Harry Graf Kessler's museum exhibition practices – which in 1906 included exhibits of nude female models drawn by the French sculptor Auguste Rodin – so provoked members of the court and community that they forced Kessler's resignation in 1906.[97] Wilhelm Ernst, for his part, favored the Weimar School of Art with full state recognition and support, obviously drawn to such loyal painters of "Heimat" landscapes as Paul Schultze-Naumburg, Fritz Mackensen, and Albin Egger-Lienz. In a clear raising of status for the Weimar School of Art, the state elevated this institution to the "College of Fine Art" (*Hochschule für bildende Kunst*) in 1910, while leaving van de Velde's school undersupported. Van de Velde's budget requests, along with the entreaty that his school at least be allowed to grant its graduates the title of "master craftsman" (*Meistertitel*), were rejected. By 1913, a time of great international tensions and mounting chauvinism, both the grand duke and Minister of State Rothe were taking active steps to remove van de Velde from his post. Fritz Mackensen of the College of Fine Art was asked to approach leading German artists as candidates for van de Velde's replacement, among them the architect Heinrich Tessenow. By July 25, 1914, van de Velde would tender his resignation, although his contract was extended to October 1, 1915, in order to allow students to complete their studies. His school was shut down, but in the event that it should ever be reopened, van de Velde recommended as possible successors Walter Gropius, August Endell, and Hermann Obrist – men he believed were sympathetic enough to his mission to carry it on. As Karl-Heinz Hüter has incisively observed in comparing van de Velde's Applied Arts School and Gropius's early Bauhaus:

> Both schools operated in the same location, but under completely different historical and cultural circumstances. Van de Velde had to assert himself against constant authoritarian control within the intellectual confines of a small, late feudal state (*Kleinstaat*). Gropius made his beginning in the wake of revolutionary social energies and expiring old orders; he saw, amid the chaos, an opening in which he might forge a new, more open form of education. Both schools met their end at the hand of reactionary political power: the Applied Arts School after eight years, the Weimar Bauhaus after six.[98]

THE SYNERGIES OF SAXONY

Residents of the kingdom of Saxony drew upon a broad spectrum of local, national, and international influences in their efforts to render their state a significant competitor in the new artistic developments of the late 1890s. Saxony and its capital, Dresden, seemed to possess all the ingredients for success as a noteworthy center of German culture: nationally significant journals and exhibitions; aggressive entrepreneurs who forged new linkages between applied-arts wares and modern markets; and city and state officials motivated by a search to link economic development with cultural prestige. These various ingredients came together at the Third German Applied Arts Exhibition of 1906, an event prominent in histories of twentieth-century German architecture and design, which dubbed it "the first Werkbund exhibition, in spirit." Justly famous for its new exhibition techniques and explicit efforts to feature leading artists more prominently than manufacturers or crafts producers, this exhibition is examined in detail in Chapters 3 and 4 in connection with the founding of the Werkbund. Yet the success of this exhibition has deep roots, depending on sustained cooperation between crafts entrepreneurs, patrons of art, local and state officials, architects, and educators that dated at least to the late 1880s.

The launching of the journal *Kunstwart* in 1887 gave the first major boost to Saxon discussions of a reform of Germany's applied arts and artistic taste. Its founder and editor, the Berlin-born, Dresden-based critic and journalist Ferdinand Avenarius, devoted the journal to a bi-weekly "overview of all fields of beauty," such as music, poetry, the fine arts, architecture, and the applied arts.[99] After modest beginnings in the late 1880s and early 1890s, subscriptions increased to approximately 1,000 in 1897, 8,000 by 1900, and 20,000 by 1903.[100] From very early in the life of his journal, Avenarius wished to educate the German public about the connections that could exist between German art, German civic life and morality, and a culture based on the marriage of German traditions with the realities of modern national life. By calling for a "party of realists" (*Partei der Sachlichen*) in 1888, Avenarius was the first to imbue the term *sachlich* with a combination of pragmatic and objective – yet still tradition-conscious – qualities.[101] Intellectually sophisticated but committed to an exclusively German aesthetic culture and way of life, Avenarius backed efforts to "monitor the national health" in ways that expanded beyond the limits of the journal alone.[102]

Avenarius gave the name "Kunstwart Enterprises" (*Kunstwart-Unternehmungen*) to a group of publications in arts and culture oriented toward the German family and released through his Munich-based publisher, Georg Callwey. The Saxon painter, architect, and principal of the Saaleck Workshops for Applied Arts Paul Schultze-Naumburg authored the best-known of these publications, the *Works of Culture* (*Kulturarbeiten*). This multivolume work, appearing as a serial in the *Kunstwart* beginning in 1901, polemically juxtaposed "good" and "bad" examples German buildings, villages, and landscapes.[103]

Schultze-Naumburg's books were emblematic of another pair of Saxony-based enterprises that quickly took on national significance. The first of these was Avenarius's "Dürerbund," founded in 1902. An enormously popular association of teachers, artists, and culturally active Germans, the Dürerbund sought to further national cultural development through newsletters, the organization of exhibitions, competitions, study fellowships, and petitions to governing authorities on a variety of cultural matters. The second organization, the German Association for Homeland Preservation (*Deutscher Bund Heimatschutz*), was likewise Dresden based and devoted to state, regional, and national preservation efforts. Schultze-Naumburg served as its chief executive, while Avenarius wrote proudly of the close cooperation between the two groups, observing: "The Heimatschutz [Bund] works with the Dürerbund in the manner of a cartel."[104] From applied arts to folk art, and from monument preservation to meditations by prominent German intellectuals on the proper responses to changes in German society and the landscape, Avenarius and his affiliated enterprises performed a vital function in expanding the network of art enthusiasts interested in anchoring a modern culture in perceived German national and ethnic traditions.[105] As the Applied Arts movement grew in both stature and sophistication, the Dürerbund, Werkbund, and several merchants' associations joined to publish the *Deutsches Warenbuch*, a catalog of exemplary products endorsed as examples of useful, high-quality housewares and as symbols of Germany's new domestic culture.[106]

SAXONY'S ENTREPRENEURIAL EXHIBITION CULTURE

By no means all Saxon reformers were as Teutonically focused as Avenarius or Schultze-Naumburg; nor, in spite of Avenarius's considerable success economically and nationally, were they in any way dependent upon him. Indeed, matching the energy of Saxony's Heimat-conscious reformers was the eagerness with which various individuals opened their gazes outward, building as well on cooperation between members of the governmental and private spheres. The Dresden professor of painting Gotthardt Kühl, appointed to the Dresden Academy of Art in 1895 following training in Munich and ten subsequent years in Paris, was especially significant for making international exposure an explicit focus of state art and applied-arts exhibitions. With the support of Dresden's mayor, Gustav Otto Beutler, Kühl planned the First International Art Exhibition in Dresden for 1897 – the same year, as we have seen, in which Munich artists and applied artists were allowed to exhibit in The International Art Exhibition at the Glaspalast. However, whereas Munich's applied-arts rooms featured works by Fischer, Riemerschmid, Paul, and other practitioners residing in or near the Bavarian capital, the Dresden International Exhibition displayed furniture by Henry van de Velde (acquired by Kühl in 1895 from Sigfried Bing in Paris) and glass works by Louis Comfort Tiffany imported from the United States, as well as works by applied artists from different regions of Germany.[107]

Although Saxony's broadening of artistic horizons resulted from such group efforts, one man, the master woodworker and home-furnishings entrepreneur Karl Schmidt, achieved results of inestimable importance to Germany's early-twentieth-century architectural and applied-arts reform efforts. Trained both in his native Saxon province of Zschopau and as a journeyman at firms in Denmark, Sweden, and England between 1892 and 1895, Schmidt displayed a particular interest in developing simple, affordable, well-designed furniture for Germany's *Mittelstand*. He founded the Dresden Workshops for Handcrafted Art (*Dresdener Werkstätten für Handwerkskunst*) with two assistant workers in 1898 and became sole owner in 1902. Winning prizes at numerous national and international exhibitions in recognition of its relatively simple, solid, homely (*volkstümlich*) furniture, Schmidt's firm produced works that contrasted greatly with the highly individualistic Art Nouveau and *Jugendstil* applied-arts ensembles that predominated at the World's Exhibition in Paris in 1900 and the Turin First International Exposition of Modern Decorative Arts in 1902. Following the firm's critical and commercial success closer to home at the officially sponsored "People's Exhibition for House and Home" in 1899, Schmidt was able to persuade Mayor Gustav Beutler to open a large portion of the Dresden Exhibition Palace for an exhibition dedicated exclusively to the Dresden Workshops' furniture and room displays in the winter of 1903–04.

As they had with the earlier sponsorship of international art exhibitions, the mayor, along with the Saxon administration, saw distinct economic, cultural, and political advantages to featuring the works of Schmidt's innovative firm. Whereas the applied-arts portion of Gotthard Kühl's national art exhibition in summer 1904 featured an assortment of applied-arts objects displayed in a gallery, Schmidt transformed the main space of the palace in his exhibition into thirty meticulously arranged, well-lit rooms simulating living accommodations as well as work environments. Never had the palace been devoted to the works of a single applied-arts entrepreneur, and never had the concept of the applied arts *Gesamtkunstwerk* been used to such effect in common domestic settings. Schmidt's interiors communicated the sense of livability, simplicity, and sturdy reliability in furniture produced to the designs of artists who had been asked explicitly to emphasize the *volkstümlich* in their efforts.

Schmidt featured the names of each artist first in the furniture and room displays, reversing older exhibition practices in which firms listed their own names above the names of artists, if the artist was mentioned at all. He paid the artists royalties on the number of pieces his firm sold; and, as an early member of the Deutscher Bund Heimatschutz, he connected his applied-arts products with local and national patriotic sentiments. In his introduction to the catalog of the Dresden International Art Exhibition of 1901, Schmidt wrote, "What brings [our firm] the highest satisfaction is the feeling that we are doing our part to transform our home city (*Vaterstadt*) Dresden, next to Munich, Darmstadt, and Stuttgart, once again into a powerful engine of applied-arts activities (*einem Kraftherd kunstgewerblicher Bewegung*), just as it was in earlier times."[108]

The payment of artists' royalties and the message of an especially German form of modern furniture production were only the first two ingredients driving Schmidt's rapid rise and success. Economically speaking, he benefited from the use of only local wood products; relied on no middle-men or merchants for distribution; trained apprentices through a supportive, in-house apprenticeship and mentorship program; and released numerous brochures and catalogs featuring language that connected the work of the firm to broader themes of social, ethical, and economic importance.[109] Schmidt's broad-ranging campaign also benefited from the entrepreneurial craftsman's determined efforts to keep educating himself through contact with leading German figures who worked at the intersection of economic, social, and applied-arts reform. He developed particularly close friendships with Friedrich Naumann and Hermann Muthesius and later with Theodor Heuss. These contacts aided Schmidt in the founding of the Garden City of Dresden-Hellerau in 1910, an epicenter of Germany's Garden City Society and of early Werkbund activity. Schmidt would begin relocating his operations to the Hellerau Garden City at about the same time as he was opening stores for furniture by the "German Workshops for Handcrafted Art" (*Deutsche Werkstätten für Handwerkskunst*) – so named after his firm merged with the Munich "Workshops for Home Furnishings" (*Werkstätten für Wohnungseinrichtung*) of Karl Bertsch – in cities like Munich, Hamburg, Berlin, Zurich, and Brussels.[110]

Schmidt features prominently in the subsequent developments discussed in Chapters 6 and 7 on the Garden City movement and the Werkbund. His early successes, too, proved extremely important in inspiring Dresden architects like the Bremen-born Fritz Schumacher, professor at the Dresden Technical University, and William Lossow, director of the Dresden School of Applied Arts, to adopt Schmidt's exhibition strategy of artist-designed, coordinated room ensembles as the formula for the Third German Applied Arts Exhibition in 1906. As one scholar from Saxony noted recently with a certain understandable pride, it was at the Third German Applied Arts Exhibition that "Dresden's way of thinking (*Gedankengut*) would become the national way of thinking."[111] In light of the cooperative yet competitive spirit with which artists in Dresden and Munich had been mounting exhibitions to demonstrate progress in the applied arts since the late 1890s, it is no surprise that authorities and artists alike would jump at the chance for Dresden to host the Third German Applied Arts Exhibition, once they learned in 1904 that a lack of interest had caused Munich to drop its plans to host another national applied-arts exhibition.

CONCLUSION

This brief analysis of the five states in central and southern Germany that saw the greatest proliferation of alternative approaches to the applied arts reveals some interesting tendencies in the cultural life of the Second Reich. First, applied artists found themselves making arrangements that very much reflected positive and negative local political conditions. Circumstances in the two small grand duchies, Hessen and Saxony-Weimar-Eisenach, favored more traditional, quasi-feudal arrangements in which highly individualistic artist-creators made their mark within local institutional settings. It is interesting to note as well that Hessen and Saxony-Weimar-Eisenach attracted the two most recognized foreign artistic personalities to contribute to design reforms in Germany prior to the First World War: the Viennese architect Joseph Maria Olbrich and the Belgian artist Henry van de Velde. Although these two artist-architects each created a sensation in their communities, their relative remove from larger cities and centers for art hampered their ambitions to effect broader changes. The Darmstadt Artists' Colony stimulated other states to take action in applied-arts reform, while in van de Velde's case, adversarial attitudes toward his art kept him from achieving broader results. He had to battle to protect the artistic mission and institutional direction he had come to shape and would carry this sense of mission with him into the Deutscher Werkbund later on. In both cases, the environment of a turn-of-the-century grand ducal court in a rural town setting placed great limitations on the leading artist's ability to affect seriously commerce or modern industrial production in Hessen or Saxony-Weimar-Eisenach.

Practical political realities in the capitals of the considerably larger kingdoms of Bavaria, Württemberg, and Saxony produced different and more varied results. Munich, relatively lacking in official programmatic sponsorship for experimental approaches to the applied arts, saw its most successful models for reform emerge in a private school, the Debschitzschule, and in a private workshop enterprise, the United Workshops for Art in Handcraft. The lack of government funding forced economic realities into the foreground of Munich-based artists' considerations of alternative applied-arts curricula and workshop-production schemes and led many leading practitioners to depart for greener pastures after the turn of the century.

Württemberg, the most industrialized of the four southern states, benefited immeasurably from having a sovereign who was intent on ensuring that cultural advance in his kingdom proceeded in line with possibilities for practical economic advantage. Württemberg's applied-arts reforms thus enjoyed royal patronage as well as private support. The result was a statewide network of different groups and institutional nodes that included the Stuttgart School of Applied Arts, the Technical University of Stuttgart (following the arrival of Theodor Fischer from Munich in 1901), the Württemberg Artists' Society, and the membership-driven Württemberg Society of the Friends of Art. Wide-ranging institutional support ensured as well that smaller towns such as Heilbronn could actually play a vital role in reform initiatives. This resulted from the involvement of such men as Peter Bruckmann, at once the town's largest employer, a city-council member, and an influential member of both the Württemberg Society of the Friends of Art and the election committee that helped the progressive outsider, Friedrich Naumann, achieve success.

Saxony, like Württemberg, was comparatively advanced industrially, and saw spirited involvement in the applied arts from official as well as private circles. Leaders of the Artistic Education movement like Ferdinand Avenarius, home-land preservation figures like Paul Schultze-Naumburg, entrepreneurs like Karl Schmidt, and leaders like Mayor Gustav Beutler of Dresden or the exhibition organizer Gotthardt Kühl cooperated to ensure Saxony a prominent role in affecting the future of the applied-arts industries in Germany.

The disparate experiences of leading applied-arts reformers in Germany's central and southern states also shaped individual expectations and new twentieth-century attitudes toward cooperation. Individual differences would emerge all the more sharply as regional alliances of artists, craftsman, and manufacturers undertook efforts to consolidate at the national level. This would occur, of course, with the founding of the Deutscher Werkbund, an association whose creation depended on the involvement of leading practitioners from all over Germany, including, of course, the state of Prussia, which is examined in the next chapter. The Werkbund would prove to be an alliance of disparate interests from all of the diverse states examined here. The development of this organization is in many respects a microcosm of the forces affecting Wilhelmine Germany before the First World War, from its disparate regional interests to the dominant forces of the Imperial government. The next chapters are devoted to placing the development of the Werkbund into a broader institutional context, demonstrating that design considerations were but one of a series of issues that both led to the founding of this organization and determined its fate.

CHAPTER TWO

THE PRUSSIAN COMMERCE MINISTRY
AND THE LESSONS OF THE BRITISH ARTS
AND CRAFTS MOVEMENT ◊◊

PRUSSIA'S DIVISION OF RESPONSIBILITY IN
APPLIED-ARTS TRAINING

"Prusso-Germany" is a name historians often use for the Second Reich of 1871–1918, and with good reason. Far and away the largest of the German states with some two-thirds of all German territory and 60 percent of its population, Prussia inevitably set the political and institutional tone for countless areas of German life (Fig. 9).[1] Constitutional prerogatives assured that Prussia's minister president (head of civil administration) was simultaneously the German Reich's chancellor; its proportion in the *Bundesrat* legislative branch would allow it to dominate the remaining German states; and its king was Germany's emperor and "All Highest," untouchable political authority.

From its vast landed estates of the east to the bastions of heavy industry in Silesia and the west, Prussia and its militantly conservative alliance of "iron and rye" assured that, in a very real sense, Prussia's politics became the Reich's politics. That is, Junker estate owners and heavy industrialists exercised enormous influence in their united determination to keep tariff barriers high for grains and industrial raw materials. This ensured profits for industry and economic survival for the Junker estates, all the while affecting areas of German policy as diverse as taxation, civil and military budgets, and social and economic measures. Finished-goods industries, including the applied-arts fields, suffered, as tariff structures forced German commercial manufacturers to pay higher relative prices for raw materials, making their wares less competitive. Although this is not a study of long-term structural changes in the German economy, it has to be noted that Prussian and German industrialization generally were altering conditions for Germany's traditional *Mittelstand* of arts, crafts, and trades producers in fundamental ways. The growth of commercial manufacturing put pressure on traditional small producers as well, even as the commercial, banking, and export sectors struggled to make political and financial headway against much more powerful conservative agrarians and heavy industrialists.[2]

Prussia's vast administrative bureaucracy mirrored the state's size, complexity, and diversity of interests in ways that had a direct impact on applied-arts training and reform efforts. Specifically, and since 1884, long-standing disputes between the Ministry of Culture and Ministry of Commerce had been resolved in such a way as to institutionalize divisions in the administration of applied-arts education. The Culture Ministry, which administered the state's universities as well as fine-arts academies, was left with only two schools of applied arts under its supervision. They were, however, two important schools: the Royal School of Applied Arts of the Applied Arts Museum in Berlin, and the School of Art and Applied Art in Breslau. High civil servants at the Culture Ministry such as Wilhelm von Bode, Ludwig Pallat, Peter Jessen, and Wilhelm Waetzold believed that growing divisions between the fine and applied arts, exacerbated by trends in nineteenth-century industrialization, had increasingly led to the education of an "artistic proletariat" (*Kunstproletariat*) – a class of applied-arts graduates unable to sustain themselves in the growing industrial and manufacturing economy.[3] Their solution was to appoint leading progressive artists as directors of the Breslau and Berlin schools and to have them run along the model of applied-arts "academies." Only the production of a smaller number of highly accomplished applied-arts "artists" would, in their mind, elevate the applied arts to a status that would maintain them as real contributors to German economic and cultural life.[4]

The Prussian Ministry of Commerce and Trade, by contrast, retained control over the vast system of arts, crafts, and trades education as a result of the administrative ruling of 1884. The vast majority of its schools, which numbered in the hundreds, had little to do with the arts or "high culture" generally. They trained students in basic trades skills ranging from machine operation and repair to textile weaving, drafting, or the building trades. However, a top tier of some three dozen applied-arts schools – extremely diverse in their makeup as a result of their individual histories and local contexts – were relevant to the state's economy and cultural affairs in ways that made them of interest to both the Ministry of Culture (from the artistic standpoint) and the Ministry of Commerce (from the economic standpoint) (Figs. 24–25; Appendix A). After the ruling of 1884 placed the schools back under the jurisdiction of the Ministry of Commerce, funding for arts, crafts, and trades education increased both course offerings and the number of schools. However, the curricula remained largely unchanged, and ministers of commerce preoccupied with much weightier issues of industrial and commercial growth delayed taking decisive action for well over a decade.

Significant signs of change began to emerge following the unusual appointment of a government architect, Hermann Muthesius, to a post as an official

24. Wilhelm Werdelmann, School of Applied Arts (*Kunstgewerbeschule*), Barmen, renovation, 1914–15, exterior view (altered) (S. Köhler, ed., *Deutschlands Städtebau: Barmen*, 2nd ed., Berlin, 1926)

Prussian government "technical reporter" at the German Embassy in London in 1896.[5] Muthesius had earned recognition as an award-winning examinee while passing his Prussian civil service exams in 1893 and had gone on to impress his superiors at the Ministry of Public Works with his engagement and output as the guest editor of its journal, the *Construction Administration Gazette* (*Centralblatt der Bauverwaltung*). Following a precedent the Prussian Commerce Ministry had set when it sent the legendary Prussian architect Karl Friedrich Schinkel on an official study tour of England in 1826, the ministry sought to derive similar lessons about engineering, architecture, technical education, and the applied arts when it sent Hermann Muthesius to report from the German Embassy in London exactly seventy years later. Because Muthesius played a central role in Commerce Ministry applied-arts reforms on his return to Berlin in 1903 and later in the founding and evolution of the Deutscher Werkbund beginning in 1907, it is important to examine both the motivation behind the government's assignment of Muthesius to England, as well as the substance of what he accomplished there. More than any other state, Prussia sought, in its Commerce Ministry–directed schools, to transform the applied arts into an effective arm of Prussian economic policy and *Mittelstandpolitik*, or policies affecting Prussia's endangered individual crafts entrepreneurs and small trades producers. Muthesius's critical evaluations of English arts, crafts, and architecture helped point the way for these reforms.

PRUSSIA'S ABSORPTION AND REWORKING OF BRITISH DEVELOPMENTS

During a six-year and nine-month assignment to the German Embassy in London between October 1, 1896, and June 30, 1903, Muthesius came to embody a Prussian institutional agenda that sought fulfillment through the study of economic, technical, and cultural practices abroad.[6] During his stay, the architect generated a bewildering array of technical reports, a flood of correspondence in both English and German, more than 100 articles in the architectural and popular press, and five books, the most significant of which were *Style-Architecture and Building Art* (*Stilarchitektur und Baukunst*) of 1902 and the landmark *The English House* (*Das englische Haus*), issued in three volumes in 1904–05.[7] These studies reflect Muthesius's direct confrontation with the variety of late-nineteenth-century architectural and artistic currents in England, centering around the British government's reforms of practical arts and technical education, on the one hand, and developments stemming from the Arts and Crafts movement, on the other.

Muthesius's assignment was to present coherent evaluations of English technical and cultural trends to the Prussian Ministry of Commerce and Trade and the Prussian Ministry of Public Works, especially where these could inform the development of Prussia's infrastructure and economic-development policies. Among duties that extended beyond his better-known publications on architecture and the applied arts, the architect also reported to the Prussian Railways Commission and the Ministry of State on technical aspects of the British railways and train design, infrastructure development, and breakthroughs in such technologies as wireless telegraph communications.[8]

Twentieth-century scholars of Muthesius placed comparatively little emphasis on the all-important flow of information from Muthesius to the different ministries to which he reported in Berlin. Instead, they emphasized the cultural impact that his studies of architecture and the applied arts had on German and

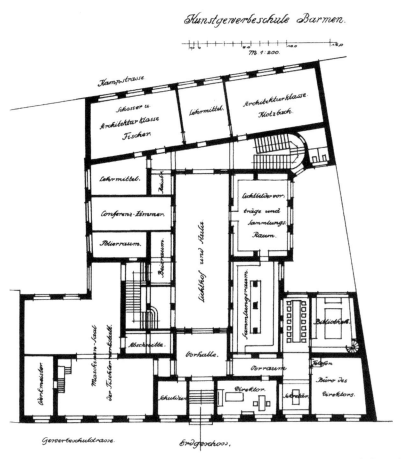

25. Wilhelm Werdelmann, School of Applied Arts, Barmen, 1914–15, ground-floor plan (Courtesy of Geheimes Staatsarchiv Preussischer Kulturbesitz, Berlin)

continental design developments. Whereas Muthesius typically has been characterized as the "German Embassy's Attaché for Architecture" or in some other similar capacity, his contributions ranged far more widely.[9] His books, articles, official reports, and correspondence provided building blocks for Prussian economic, social, and design reforms that were anchored in a reconfiguration of applied-arts education and production. The Prussian Ministry of Commerce and Trade, in particular, sought to learn all it could through Muthesius about British governmental and private efforts to improve product design and manufacture in the applied arts. The decorative arts, unlike architecture or the fine arts, were a particularly compelling area of study because the decorative arts involve not only questions of aesthetics but also functional considerations, production methods, and economic competition, as the art historian Nancy Troy has noted.[10]

The applied arts and artisanal trades in Prussia represented a neglected sector in what was Europe's most rapidly modernizing economy at the turn of the century. Employing the majority of Prussia's old and increasingly embattled trades

Mittelstand, the crafts and trades were also the area of production most affected by the rapid advance and consolidation of heavy industry.[11] Heavy industry had, in fact, replaced the artisanal trades in 1890 as the German economy's second-largest sector after agriculture, which continued to lead until industry surpassed it in 1910.[12] The surge of industry and concomitant decline of the crafts made the question of worker alienation and an upswing in support for the socialist movement into a pressing government concern.[13] Muthesius's study of crafts innovation, organization, and reform in Britain therefore had direct bearing on a much larger set of Prussian policy concerns at home.

Muthesius's professed interest in contributing to Germany's cultural renewal as a technical and cultural attaché was second only to his interest in fulfilling his Prussian government mission effectively. As an agent of his government and, later, as the embodiment of its institutional agenda, Muthesius conveyed modern English artistic and technical developments in terms that best fit his highly centralized government's outlook toward reform. For this reason, in seeking to derive pragmatic lessons for Prussian government-led reform efforts from the study of Britain's perceived strengths and weaknesses, Muthesius remained aloof from the study of collective citizen initiative in all its forms – whether manifested in socialism, the concern for workers' well-being shown by the Arts and Crafts guilds and trade associations, or the efforts of the Garden City movement.[14]

Responsible for reporting to the Prussian Ministries of Public Works as well as Commerce and Trade, Muthesius departed for England with only a general idea of his assignment to study and report on such technical and trade matters that his superiors in Berlin would find useful. In a short time, and at the senior Ministry of Public Works architect Otto March's urging to put aside "tedious engineering reports," Muthesius widened the scope of his inquiry to embrace cultural as well as technical considerations.[15] March, an Anglophile whose practice in Germany was based in part on the production of English-influenced suburban homes in Berlin and the Rhineland, agreed with Muthesius that British domestic architecture was especially worthy of study as an example of design from which German architects had much to learn.[16] March advised Muthesius in the production of such books as *The Newer Church Buildings of England* (*Die neuere kirchliche Baukunst in England*) and *The English Building Art of the Present* (*Die englische Baukunst der Gegenwart*).[17]

Muthesius's research agenda eventually expanded to include the study of infrastructure development, architecture, technical education, all manner of arts, crafts, and trades schools, exhibitions and museums, instructional workshops and master courses for craftsmen, trade associations, and administrative institutions that oversaw all of these activities.[18] The government reporter gradually formulated a recipe for comprehensive design reforms that would fit the Prussian state's eager quest for new approaches to pressing domestic problems of economic development, social reform, and modern government administration.[19] He developed concrete methods with which the Prussian state could apply the principle of *Bildung* – the idea of education and personal cultivation that had served the

Bürgertum so well – to a broad array of economic, social, and educational policy issues. Although this principle had long been in general circulation in matters of policy and nation-building, Muthesius was the first to promote its use in design reforms that were explicitly tied to the Wilhelmine state's economic development and social-policy goals.

MUTHESIUS'S STUDY OF BRITISH REFORMS

As an established empire and the world's first industrial power, Britain was a natural choice for closer study by Prussia, which had begun sending technical attachés abroad regularly in 1882.[20] The British government, for its part, took its first steps toward applying art to industry for the purpose of improving England's international competitiveness during the 1830s. In 1835, the House of Commons appointed a select committee to inquire into the "combination of beauty of design with machinery," eventually attracting the interest of the German-born Crown Prince Albert.[21] These early efforts culminated in the Great Exhibition in London in 1851, an exhibition that was later widely judged to have fallen short of success in the applied arts because of a lack of unity, beauty, and consistency in the design of ornamental objects. Henry Cole, an energetic British civil servant, was a major organizer of the exhibition under Prince Albert. He was subsequently appointed to the Board of Trade to organize the South Kensington Museum and School of Design to teach ornamental art, design, and, as Cole wrote, "the practical application of such knowledge to the improvement of Manufactures."[22]

Muthesius spent considerable time investigating this official British effort to improve the applied arts through its museum establishment. As he noted in "Drawing Instruction in London Grammar Schools" ("Der Zeichenunterricht in den Londoner Volksschulen"), Cole's reforms in the 1850s and 1860s developed a curriculum largely dependent on historicist, ornamental drawing instruction to address the forms and techniques of manufacture.[23] Nevertheless, by 1864 Cole's Department of Science and Art oversaw ninety schools and some 16,000 students in addition to overseeing the South Kensington Museum. By 1890, the museum had finally shifted its curriculum to reflect the innovative instructional techniques in numerous London grammar schools. The Council's schools had been influenced by the Arts and Crafts movement and took their inspiration not from historical ornaments but from nature.

In light of these changes in South Kensington, and perhaps weighing whether to open a similar institution to supplement the Berlin Applied Arts Museum (opened in 1867), the Prussian Commerce Ministry requested that Muthesius investigate the operations and budget of the South Kensington Museum in 1902. His report analyzed the institution's budget and the costs associated with the main arts and crafts school in South Kensington, the nonartistic and trades schools, and the teaching museum.[24] Although he judged the museum system to be complicated and bureaucratic, Muthesius also acknowledged the importance of its expanding array of programs, which taught drawing and related applied-arts skills to more than 2.4 million students per year.[25]

Muthesius spent a much greater proportion of his time reporting on the designers, creations, and organizations associated with the Arts and Crafts movement. A knowledgeable architect with an excellent command of English and the full backing of the German Embassy, Muthesius arranged to meet and correspond with leading British architects. His closest associations and written exchanges were with Richard Norman Shaw, Charles Rennie Mackintosh, Charles Voysey, and William Richard Lethaby, and to a lesser extent Charles Ashbee and M. H. Baillie Scott.[26] Through these architects and other official and unofficial contacts, Muthesius arranged to visit countless houses all over Britain, about which he wrote many critical reviews. Placing the buildings in historical context, he studied British houses with a thoroughness and acuity sufficient to earn such works as *Das englische Haus* a lasting place in the history of English domestic architecture.

Muthesius's work also diverged from the writing of history in the strictly scholarly sense: Intent on furnishing his government employer with a program for reforms in Prussia, the architect reinterpreted English architectural developments and the Arts and Crafts movement in a manner that would best reinforce Prussian policy priorities at home. In such works as *Style-Architecture and Building-Art (Stilarchitektur und Baukunst)* and *The English House (Das englische Haus)*, and as we will see in detail later, this reinterpretation was uniquely suited to strengthening the interests and the image of the Wilhelmine *Bürgertum*, or educated and professional middle class. Both books unabashedly viewed the *Bürgertum* as the natural heir to aristocratic power in a modern industrial age. In countless other articles on education, production, and exhibition policies in the applied arts, Muthesius outlined ideas that, although generated by his reflections on England, formed the basis of reforms that Muthesius would recommend and later implement when he returned to Berlin.[27] Just as *Das englische Haus* complemented a private architectural practice in Berlin, where Muthesius would design suburban homes for the successful Wilhelmine *Bürgertum* upon his return, his applied-arts studies provided the raw material for policies through which he would seek to reform Prussia's traditional applied-arts *Mittelstand* for service to a modernizing German economy. It is therefore important to relate Muthesius's analyses of British architects and their work to his studies of British institutional reform efforts and the Arts and Crafts movement, and to relate these back to his government's interests in making Germany more competitive.

Significantly, Muthesius's cultural and governmental biases prompted him to pay little specific attention to the principles of the Arts and Crafts movement's intellectual and spiritual father, the theorist and art critic John Ruskin. In such works as *The Seven Lamps of Architecture* of 1849 and *The Stones of Venice* of 1851–53, Ruskin had criticized what he saw as the moral and spiritual bankruptcy of the modern industrial age. Machinery, in Ruskin's opinion, did not just produce inferior goods but also debased the society that used them. So important was individual labor to Ruskin that, in his estimation, machine work and industrial influences needed to be banned from workplaces and building sites. This was the only way, he argued, to preserve the sacredness of architecture and the nobility of all work associated with building. Labor to Ruskin had to be a creative act that fostered curiosity and pleasure, for as he believed, "You must either make a tool of the creature, or a man of him. You cannot do both."[28]

Although he was a pragmatic government servant, Muthesius was also too careful a scholar to ignore the formative influence that Ruskin, like the architect Augustus Welby Pugin before him, had exercised on nineteenth-century art and architecture through the Gothic revival.[29] He devoted comparatively little attention, however, to Ruskin's doctrine of "honest" work – work performed by hand as a means to ensure the all-important integrity, health, and happiness of workers. Ruskin's vision, of course, had been the inspiration for the later collectivist and socialist impulses of Arts and Crafts practitioners, so it is of little surprise that these features of the movement also received short shrift from the Prussian government reporter.

Muthesius admired the way that the teachings of Pugin and Ruskin reestablished a valuable link to the craft values and working methods of the Middle Ages. These values and methods, in turn, had furnished the basis for a second generation of architects and decorative artists – men such as Philip Webb, Richard Norman Shaw, and William Morris – to work in what the German architect saw as a "modern" fashion not beholden to historical styles. As early as 1900, Muthesius had argued in one of his first book-length architectural studies, *The English Building Art of the Present* (*Die englische Baukunst der Gegenwart*), that the Gothic revival *qua* revival was doomed to "fall back into the stream of time." Its positive legacy, however, was a particular modern self-understanding that consisted of "the full freedom to form and shape the masses of a building without dependence on a particular style."[30] Webb's Red House of 1859 for William Morris and Shaw's New Zealand Chambers of 1873 exemplified, to Muthesius, rural and urban examples, respectively, of well-crafted structures that served modern functional needs while maintaining links to English building materials, forms, and constructional techniques (Figs. 26–31).[31] The architect Shaw, whom Muthesius proclaimed the "founder of the modern English art of building" (*Begründer der modernen englischen Baukunst*), demonstrated great facility at New Zealand Chambers in central London's dense, crowded City district. Here the architect had used thin cast-iron column supports and generously placed oriel windows to maximize floor space and natural light for one of London's most ingeniously designed speculative commercial buildings. The owners, James Temple and Walter Savill, were able to let well-ventilated and well-lit rooms from the basement to the top floor to a variety of merchants and businesses within an open, highly adaptable interior envelope.

26. Philip Webb, Red House, Bexley Heath, 1859, exterior view as photographed for Hermann Muthesius's *Das englische Haus* (Hermann Muthesius, *Das englische Haus*, Berlin, 1904–05)

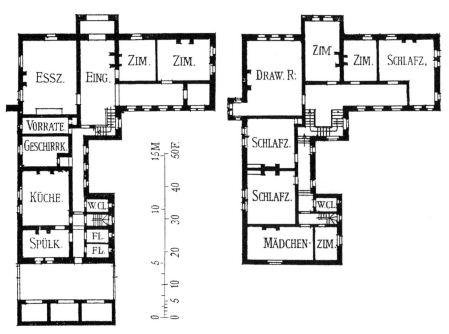

27. Philip Webb, Red House, Bexley Heath, 1859, ground-floor and first-floor plans (Hermann Muthesius, *Das englische Haus*, Berlin, 1904–05)

28. Richard Norman Shaw, New Zealand Chambers, London, 1873, exterior view (destroyed in World War II) (Hermann Muthesius, *Die englische Baukunst der Gegenwart*, Leipzig, 1900)

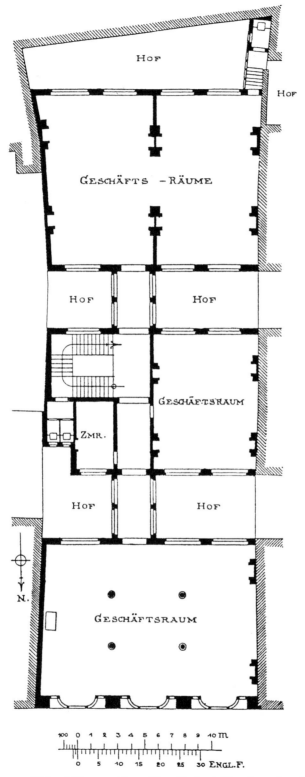

HOF

HOF

GESCHÄFTS – RÄUME

HOF

HOF

GESCHÄFTSRAUM

ZMR.

HOF

HOF

N.

GESCHÄFTSRAUM

100 0 1 2 3 4 5 6 7 8 9 10 m

0 5 10 15 20 25 30 ENGL.F.

29. Richard Norman Shaw, New Zealand Chambers, London, 1873, plan of upper floor (Hermann Muthesius, *Die englische Baukunst der Gegenwart*, Leipzig, 1900)

30. Richard Norman Shaw, Broadlands, Sunninghill, Berkshire, exterior view (demolished 1933) (Hermann Muthesius, *Das englische Haus*, vol. 2, Berlin, 1904–05)

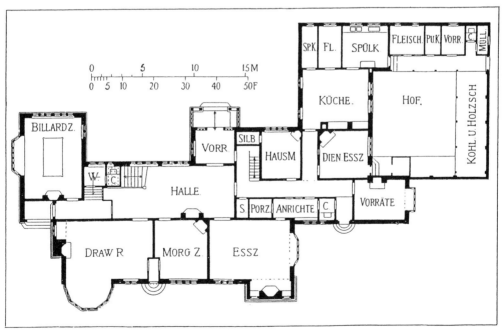

31. Richard Norman Shaw, Broadlands, ground-floor plan (demolished 1933) (Hermann Muthesius, *Das englische Haus*, vol. 2, Berlin, 1904–05)

Muthesius especially appreciated Shaw's artful adaptation of giant-order pilasters, painted oriels, and carved and chiseled brick decorations in the façade, which together represented a calculated swipe at nineteenth-century Gothicists and other academic revivalists. Compared to Shaw's modern creation, noted Muthesius, repeated attempts by Gothic revivalists to breathe new life into studied medieval forms were like "efforts to revive a corpse."[32] Shaw introduced an unprecedented urban massing of load-bearing girders fronted by brick pilasters, which alternated with vertically stacked oriels. Although some within the local building office objected, the brick pilasters technically satisfied metropolitan regulations that prohibited windows from projecting past the wall plane of the street façade. Having thrust the wall plane forward to match the plane of the oriel windows, Shaw produced a dynamic rhythm of solid and void that has been called both an expression of mercantile civic pride and, because of the furor with metropolitan regulators, the "*succès de scandale* of the Royal Academy Exhibition of 1873."[33] His fireproof window casings and designs for cut and chiseled brick in the old English tradition (originally brought by seventeenth-century Dutch craftsmen) completed the edifice. New Zealand Chambers demonstrated the ease with which Shaw could make modern building adaptations within an historical language that proved confounding to many critics and subsequent historians. Andrew Saint, the leading Shaw scholar, has identified this language as "neither Gothic, nor Queen Anne, nor middle-class domestic."[34] Instead, and quoting Muthesius's assessment from 1900 as the most accurate one, Saint argues that the style of New Zealand Chambers is best described as "'*bürgerlich*,' otherwise 'bourgeois.'"[35] This was the essence of Shaw's modernity in Muthesius's eyes: the innovative, practical adaptation of historical traditions to present realities and building needs, together with the avoidance of slavish imitation of particular stylistic precedents.

The historian Wendy Kaplan has correctly observed that the British Arts and Crafts movement was less a style than an approach to design; any definition based on style would exclude many of the movement's individualistic adherents.[36] As a pragmatic German reporter representing a highly centralized government studying a highly decentralized British artistic movement, Muthesius and the artists of the Arts and Crafts movement necessarily came from radically different organizational and cultural perspectives. Yet the movement held far greater interest for the German architect than the British government's reform efforts at South Kensington. Muthesius was particularly drawn to the movement's focus on the design of whole environments, from furniture and decorative arts to rooms and houses. He also expressed interest in the institutional side of the movement and in the effect that the Arts and Crafts had had on raising English standards of production, quality, and taste among the general public.

Each of the Arts and Crafts architects and designers, as the cultural historian Gillian Naylor has noted, defined for themselves in a very personal way what a socially conscious Arts and Crafts practice would look like.[37] Some, like William

Morris, founded a firm and became active in politics; others, like William R. Lethaby, became teachers; still others, like Arthur H. Mackmurdo and C. R. Ashbee, established guilds. All were concerned with responding after their own fashion to the effects of English industrialization and its accompanying degradation of working conditions, living standards, production quality, the beauties of the threatened English countryside, and even the simple, if idealized, values of village life.

No one had accomplished more in this regard than William Morris, a complex figure who left the single largest mark on the movement and who sought to realize Ruskin's ideals in virtually every area of decorative-arts practice. Commemorating Morris in an article of 1897 entitled "William Morris and the Fifth Exhibition of the Applied Arts Association and London," Muthesius noted that the Arts and Crafts movement was of the utmost artistic and economic significance for Germany and, under Morris's leadership, represented an important late-nineteenth-century sociological phenomenon that was no longer limited, as he put it, to the "upper ten thousand."[38] Morris died on October 3, 1896 – three days before the German architect arrived to begin his duties as technical and cultural attaché. Like many commentators on Morris, Muthesius focused on those aspects of his work that appealed to him most. As an immensely charismatic, strong, and energetic individual, Morris was remembered by one loyal friend, the artist Walter Crane, as having once wondered "which of six distinct personalities he himself really was"; Morris might have been referring, in other words, to any one of his recognized accomplishments as a poet, artist, craftsman, refined designer, knowledgeable businessman, or committed socialist.[39] Morris's dedication to socialism and art as means to create a better life for all was evident in his many lectures and articles, but came through in concentrated form in such observations as: "To the Socialist, a house, a knife, a cup, a steam engine, or what not, anything, I repeat, that is made by man and has form, must either be a work of art or destructive to art."[40]

Predictably, and in accordance with his mission, Muthesius focused on Morris's artistic ability, business success, and his tireless spread of the values of craftsmanship. Acknowledging the contradiction between Morris's avowed socialism and his sale of high-priced, hand-crafted luxury goods, Muthesius made no effort to inquire into the dilemmas faced by modern workers that had prompted Morris's political turn to the left.[41] Mentioning the founding role that Ruskin had played in drawing English attention to the linkage between art and morality, he avoided closer examination of the emphasis that Ruskin and his followers placed on remedying worker alienation in an industrial age. Instead, the Arts and Crafts mattered most to Muthesius as a movement that had simultaneously rediscovered English traditions and "values" while merging high art and low. To Muthesius, this was the most prominent sign of Britain's successful reaffirmation of its national character in the modern age, its achievement of a harmonious artistic culture through "a modern school based on the old."[42]

Among Muthesius's most important articles from his early years in England was a series that analyzed education and economic organization in the applied arts.[43] These detailed studies focused on the economic potential of educating crafts workers "artistically." Largely ignoring the intense individualism of Arts and Crafts practitioners, which existed in tension with the movement's enthusiasm for guilds, brotherhoods, and other forms of small-scale collective organization, Muthesius viewed the Arts and Crafts through the lenses of the German Art Education movement and the Prussian government's economic development priorities. This approach distorted the idealism not just of William Morris, but also of many leading Arts and Crafts associations, as the historian Alan Crawford has noted.[44] Muthesius, for example, characterized Ashbee's Guild and School of Handicraft in East London as

> a form which combines real commercial management with the best artistic standards, so eliminating the middle man in providing artistic goods and faultless craft work at reasonable prices. On these grounds more than on any other are these Guilds worthy before anything else of the most earnest consideration in Germany.[45]

To Muthesius, the success of such schools as Ashbee's Guild and School of Handicraft and the Birmingham Guild of Handicraft derived from teaching students to develop their projects while paying attention to the specific properties of materials. The goal of instruction was to lead students to discover how material properties could be turned to the best functional and aesthetic advantage. These small guild schools, Muthesius noted, were "nothing more than private commercial associations, but in them is a source of the healthiest and most important influence."[46] Further, to Muthesius, Ashbee was significant as just one of many English artists in the new decorative-arts movement who belonged to the Art Workers Guild. Muthesius praised the guild for the way in which nationally known artists "shared a common table" with coppersmiths, weavers, and other crafts workers. With its strict admission standards, the Art Workers Guild united artists and handworkers in a common mission: to "revive the crafts [*Handwerk*] once again and to reorganize life from the bottom up on artistic principles."[47]

Ashbee, a socialist who differed from Morris in his belief in gradual rather than revolutionary change, expressed his values through his insistence that "The Art problem must be worked out through the social problem."[48] His establishment of the Guild and School of Handicraft in the industrial, working-class neighborhoods of East London was an attempt by this self-confessed "Practical Idealist" to reform industrial conditions through the creation of a localized cell of enlightened crafts production. For this reason, in 1901 he would object strenuously to Muthesius's interpretation of his Guild in *An Endeavour Towards the Teaching of John Ruskin and William Morris*, in which he wrote,

There is something in the glamour that Herr Muthesius missed. There are
many of us in the field – I for one – who, if it was a mere business enterprise,
would have no further interest in it. Mere business we could pursue more
profitably elsewhere and unencumbered with altruism.... The Guild is a
protest against modern business methods, against the Trade point of view,
against the Commercial spirit.[49]

Ashbee captured the point precisely: It was this "Trade point of view" that Muthesius embodied as he distilled lessons for reformed crafts education and production. The Arts and Crafts movement was of interest to him only insofar as it could
aid Germans in improving their applied-arts production and so raise Germany's
economic as well as artistic status.

To this end Muthesius investigated the full range of British technical and
applied-arts education, from government-sponsored schools to guilds and associations. Besides the Department of Science and Art at the South Kensington
Museum, he analyzed the City and Guild of London Institute, the apprenticeship system of architectural training, the Central School of Arts and Crafts, and
the Home Arts and Industries Association.[50] Reporting on organizational structures, budgets, and training philosophies, he commented on the advantages each
element of the system offered. Unimpressed by the way apprenticeship-based
architectural training compared to the scientific education German architects
received at technical universities, Muthesius nevertheless saw some clear advantages in the English system. He praised the superior artistic component of British
architectural training and examinations, which focused on freehand drawing of
the human body, plants, and the natural world. "Here it is impossible to for-
get," he wrote, "that architecture belongs to the arts, not the sciences, and that
drawing is the language of the architect."[51] The naturalistic emphasis of Arts
and Crafts teachers and practitioners, who derived many lessons about structure,
form, and decoration from the study of flowers and plants, had, by the 1880s, also
clearly prevailed over the historicist, ornament-oriented instructional system of
the South Kensington Museum.

Of special importance to German reform efforts was the model provided by
the London County Council's Central School of Arts and Crafts. Founded in
1896, the school was an outgrowth of the Technical Education Act of 1889,
itself largely the product of reform efforts by Sidney Webb, a Fabian socialist
and London County Council Chairman of the Special Committee on Technical
Education.[52] Codirected by the architect and fellow socialist William Richard
Lethaby and the sculptor George Frampton, the radically experimental Central
School intentionally adopted an approach that was the opposite of the "academic"
model of the South Kensington Museum. Equally important, the Central School
furnished the model for reforms that the Prussian Commerce Ministry would
institute through Muthesius when the architect returned to Berlin in 1903. In
other words, British Fabian socialist-inspired reforms thus served as the direct

inspiration for the Prussian government's economic development program in the applied arts.

As might be expected of a Prussian civil servant, Muthesius made no mention of this left-wing inspiration in his glowing evaluation of the Central School. To Muthesius, the Central School combined the best of traditional arts-and-crafts apprentice education with the advantages offered by classroom training. For example, the school explicitly emphasized the teaching of drawing as a means to communicate design intentions. Lethaby expressed his educational philosophy clearly in *Leadwork*, a book of 1893, in which he wrote,

> It cannot be too strongly asserted that the *forms* of past art cannot be *copied*; that certain things have been done is evidence to show that we cannot do them over again... Commercially produced imitations of ornamental works are infinitely beneath the merely utilitarian object which serves its purpose and nothing more... New design must ever be founded on strict consideration of the exact purpose to be fulfilled by the proposed object, of how it will serve its purpose best, and show perfect suitability to the end in view, when made in this or that material by easy means. This, not the torturing of a material into forms which have not before been used, is the true ground of beauty, and this to a certain extent is enough without any ornamention.[53]

Muthesius praised Lethaby's practical design curriculum and the way it directly confronted questions of economic viability. He was particularly impressed with the way that a student was trained practically and "in the spirit of the techniques of his specific craft," and in a manner that, following one of Ruskin's edicts in "The Nature of Gothic" from *The Stones of Venice*, laid "special emphasis on the valuation of his own creative thoughts, as primitive as these might be in the beginning."[54]

Another influential part of the Central School curriculum was the introduction of instructional workshops in which students were taught to execute their designs. These derived from Lethaby's conviction that "[Technical Education Board] inspectors should be producing artists and have duties of a teaching kind," for "it cannot be too strongly emphasized that the artist must also be a producer."[55] Music to the ears of the pragmatically minded German attaché, Muthesius openly admired the way the school had students develop projects on the basis of "the study of nature in place of the copying of old examples" and emphasized the importance of instruction that led students to "consciousness of the limits of materials" as they "executed their works down to the last fine details."[56] Muthesius's evaluations of Lethaby's program must have caught the eye of his ministerial superiors, as he would be asked to re-create large portions of this system on German soil beginning in 1903.

Muthesius was sure that the education of applied-arts workers in "tasteful" design would simultaneously boost quality and raise the economic value of goods produced, while leading to a corresponding rise in cultural sophistication. Exactly who would be responsible for training the German population in matters of taste remained unclear, but Muthesius obtained some clues by studying Britain's class structure and the English approach to the problem.

The skillful management of the British Home Arts and Industries Association suggested one model. It was significant to Muthesius that the distance between the highest and the lowest social classes had grown so large in the past few years that it had become a commonly perceived duty in modern England for the upper classes to reach out a hand to help those of lesser means.[57] Momentarily putting aside purely economic arguments for reform, the German architect underscored artistic gains to be had from a study of English conditions. "If we want our contemporary arts and crafts to be spinning in the air less than is currently the case," he wrote, "then the raising of amateurs' abilities [*Diletantismus*] in the applied arts must be our next priority."[58] Just as the English had had to discourage actively the production of useless and purposeless objects in its cottage industries, so too would the Germans have to reeducate the public away from the creation of the "painted cowbells, sea mussels, and drums … that are preferred by certain classes."[59] Aggressively characterizing the English handling of the situation, Muthesius concluded that in England "this suppression has succeeded … and now the bed is more or less clear of weeds so that the plantings of culture [*Kulturpflanzen*] have begun to bloom."[60]

From observing the English, Muthesius declared that the first step toward the improvement of applied arts among German amateurs must be to improve the skills of those from the "better-off classes." Germany's applied-arts schools were the appropriate place for this to take place and were also the proper setting in which to train the teachers who would then engage in "the general education of the lower classes."[61] He advocated the introduction of an official body to organize annual exhibits that would be accompanied by prizes and professional criticism. School training alone, however, would not be sufficient. Muthesius argued that real progress could only be attained if amateur courses could be instituted along the same lines as professional instruction. In addition, he advocated the basic principles of simple, functional, and objective (*sachlich*) artistic creation as the central lesson that needed to be propagated at all levels of instruction. This important reform would simultaneously eliminate "naïve" crafts activity and replace forms of academic training that emphasized the copying of old masters.

From a pedagogical standpoint, Muthesius agreed with the prevailing English Arts and Crafts view that instructors in the visual arts should no longer use plaster models of historical ornaments for drawing instruction. Following Ruskin, Morris, and Lethaby, he wrote that teachers should initiate instruction by placing an ordinary plant before the students with an assignment to develop a simple but original design from its form. Paraphrasing the ideals of Ruskin and Morris, he wrote, "Better the simplest original project than the best copy; better ten misrepresentations in the rendering of one's own thoughts, than a masterpiece in the repetition of others!"[62]

Muthesius admitted that these new methods would appear objectionable to teachers for whom the old style of training was ingrained but insisted that the results of English student exhibits were compelling enough to justify changes in the German system. The superiority of the modern pedagogy became clear, he maintained, as soon as one observed the enthusiasm and quickness with which students learned to create independent projects from the very beginning of their instruction. The production of surrogates based on works that others had created in the past was always less satisfying and was bound to induce boredom on the part of students. The only thing left for students to enjoy from the act of copying was the satisfaction derived from representation, a satisfaction that paled in comparison to the feeling derived from displaying designs they had created themselves.

During his London stay officials in Berlin gradually came to recognize the policy potential of Muthesius's work. It was hardly a surprise, then, that Muthesius came to advocate the reproduction of an organization resembling the English Home Arts and Industries Association on German soil. Of critical interest to the Prussian Commerce Ministry, Muthesius's analysis of the association demonstrated the success with which the association had stimulated productive economic activity in the English provinces by teaching basic design skills and sound principles of production. His article provided the German government with the first in-depth look at how far advanced England was in comparison to Germany in linking concerns about economic development with improving the quality of production among crafts and trades practitioners and in propagating the principle of simple, functional design among the general population. At the same time, it offered insights into the ways that better-educated members of the German *Bürgertum* could lead the organization of schools and applied-arts practices so as to integrate Germany's faltering *Mittelstand* into a reforming economy and society. Muthesius's next goal was to relate his recommendations for design reforms to a broader concept of German cultural renewal and to give his arguments as wide an appeal as possible. He accomplished this task in *Style-Architecture and Building-Art*.

REFORM WITHIN THE EXISTING SOCIAL HIERARCHY: *STYLE-ARCHITECTURE AND BUILDING-ART*

In 1901, as Muthesius entered his fifth year in London, he synthesized the arguments that he had expressed in more than 100 articles and three books into a new, polemical formulation, entitled *Style-Architecture and Building-Art*.[63] Appearing as a sixty-seven-page essay in 1902 and then in an expanded, revised addition in 1903, the book combined an accessible popular tone with a program for German cultural reform. It was the first of Muthesius's books during his assignment in England to emphasize contemporary German issues rather than English cultural conditions.

Like the Viennese architect Otto Wagner and the German art historians Konrad Lange, Richard Streiter, and a host of other advocates of artistic education in German-speaking Europe, Muthesius highlighted the unique opportunities offered by the industrial present as a point of departure for the establishment of a more authentic German culture. In his important text of 1896, *Moderne Architektur*, Wagner had insisted that "modern life" provide the basis for a technologically sophisticated, urbane architectural culture.[64] Streiter, too, had sharpened Alfred Lichtwark's earlier arguments about the sober, realist, or objective design philosophy known as *Sachlichkeit* into a clarion call for architecture that objectively reflected local materials, atmosphere, and the character of its "milieu."[65]

Muthesius echoed these earlier arguments with his clear case for *Sachlichkeit* as a means to reintegrate the achievements of a scientific but "inartistic" nineteenth century. To Muthesius, a classical, "Latin" bias had dominated nineteenth-century architecture. This was plainly evident in the derivative classical styles of historicist "Architektur" – a German word arising from the Greek and redolent of Mediterranean, Latin associations. In place of what he termed a superficial "style-architecture" ("Stilarchitektur") Muthesius posited the German-rooted word "Baukunst," or "building-art," which he argued had its roots in the technical achievements of an Anglo-German, or "Nordic," Gothic revival.[66] Technical competence and the valuation of materials and constructional principles had been maintained in the nineteenth-century not by architects or applied artists, Muthesius argued, but primarily by pragmatic engineers.

Revealing the depth of his reading of Streiter's writings, as well as Robert Dohme's *Das englische Haus* of 1888 and Gottfried Semper's *Style in the Tectonic Arts* from the early 1860s, Muthesius pointed to the well-engineered steam ship, suspension bridge, bicycle, and iron-framed buildings such as exhibition halls as the quintessential examples of *sachlich* design and construction.[67] These utilitarian objects had not been absorbed into the fashion cycles of the consumer market, which were dependent on the seeming novelty of changing appearances. They differed fundamentally from the products of nineteenth-century applied-arts industries (*Kunstindustrie*), in which ornaments in various historical styles were frequently stamped, molded, or otherwise applied to create visual associations with other materials, objects, or historical styles.

A central ambition of *Style-Architecture and Building-Art* was to promote the arts as a means for further unifying the German people into a modern nation. From the outset Muthesius bemoaned the fallen and wholly "inartistic" state of German culture, pointing for evidence to the chaotic state of German architecture that, again borrowing from Ruskin, he insisted should be honored as "the mother of all the arts."[68] Like the Austrian architect Adolf Loos after him, Muthesius characterized architecture as a "conservative art," meaning that the utility associated with buildings led to slower innovation in architecture than in the other arts. The applied arts, he argued, must therefore develop and pull architecture in the direction of progress.[69]

Muthesius resolved the opposition between architecture as the "unifier of the arts" and the applied arts as the "basis for all other arts" by insisting that there was only one "great universal art."[70] Muthesius's depiction of an interdependent relationship between architecture and the applied arts was not unproblematic, for in his schema architecture and architects, in the end, retained a position of primacy that had deep implications for his later state design-school reforms. Though slowest to evolve, architecture was still the medium, in his view, to which the visual and plastic arts were answerable, rather than the other way around. As we will see in Chapter 7, Muthesius would not alter his position on the primacy of architecture among the arts until he helped organize the Deutscher Werkbund Exhibition of 1914 in Cologne, where he favored commerce and trade in a campaign to realize the government's economic development agenda.

Under "style-architecture" Muthesius referred to the neoclassical revival of the early nineteenth century and the neo-Gothic revival that came after it. The neoclassical revival was to blame, he felt, for architects' overemphasis on symmetry and formal expression, which prompted architects all too often to ignore issues of geography, climate, site, and local culture.[71] "One saw in the Greeks an artistic norm (*Normalkunst*) for the whole world and for all time," he wrote, "and thereby forgot that there can only exist one normal art (*eine normale Kunst*): namely, one that complies with the life and culture of the times."[72] He credited the English Romantic movement with rescuing the idea of individual creativity and Augustus Welby Pugin, in particular, with valuing authentic regional architectural expression through the neo-Gothic revival. Although neo-Gothic architects, too, became preoccupied with issues of stylistic representation, in Muthesius's eyes they nevertheless deserved credit for refocusing attention on indigenous building styles, quality workmanship, and buildings that addressed unique local conditions instead of conforming to principles of an ideal, abstract beauty.

Muthesius did, however, idealize ancient Greek architecture and the Gothic works of the Middle Ages to the extent that they represented collective achievements of integrated, fully developed, "perfect period[s] of art."[73] The nineteenth century, by contrast, had been overrun by the proliferation of historical styles, each competing for the attention of architects, theorists, and the public. In a "stylistic battle," Muthesius wrote, architects stampeded like a "hungry herd . . . in which the late Renaissance, Baroque, Rococo, Zopf (late Rococo), and Empire were slaughtered indifferently and, after a short period of blood sucking, were cast in the corner."[74]

As much as Pugin, Ruskin, and their followers had done to reawaken the English populace to the virtues of English Gothic architecture, Muthesius argued that there remained a self-deception inherent in trying to make a vital contemporary art out of the revival of the Gothic. To achieve the "true unfolding of the spirit" of the new art, it remained necessary to free architecture from the "dictatorial rule of outward Gothic appearances."[75] The only redeeming quality that Muthesius ascribed to historicism in *Style-Architecture and Building-Art* was that it nurtured late-nineteenth-century architects' abilities to generate a wide variety of historical styles; this schooling had at least sensitized contemporary architects to the nuances that different styles of building evoked. Although he ultimately dismissed the *Jugendstil* as a naturalistic "style-architecture" invented to succeed historicism, the architect also saw at least one positive point associated with *Jugendstil* art: In their search for originality of stylistic expression, *Jugendstil* artists took a necessary step toward thinking in terms of forms that broke with the academically reproduced patterns of the past.[76]

The individuality of spirit associated with the *Jugendstil* was a positive development that Muthesius linked to the Romantic ideal; and this individualist thinking, independent of historicist design, was crucial for the development of a truly modern art of building. Yet the *Jugendstil* suffered from the way that industry had learned to adapt it all too quickly for cheap reproduction in books, furniture, brass candlesticks, and other objects. Muthesius wished to see the development of a form of design that was less subject to the whims of artistic fashion and the market, and more suited to a pragmatic bourgeois class that he envisioned as an emerging leadership class in the early twentieth century. "In the case of any movement that wishes to effect reform today," Muthesius argued, "the task is not simply to develop a luxurious art (*Luxuskunst*); the purpose must be to bring forth an art suitable for bourgeois society (*bürgerliche Gesellschaft*), which in turn determines the overall character of our modern social relations."[77]

Muthesius was influenced to a degree by Gottfried Semper, a towering figure in nineteenth-century German architecture whose built works Muthesius admired, and whom the Prussian civil servant regarded as the second-greatest German architect of the nineteenth century after Schinkel. But Muthesius's regard for the Semper's Dresden Hoftheater and other buildings was tempered by the Saxon architect's preference for the classical. To Muthesius, Semper exemplified the late-nineteenth-century Classicists in an "age of strident party struggles between Romantics and Classicists."[78] Although the stylistic confusion seemed to deepen in the last quarter of the century, Muthesius saw great value in the reengagement with crafts and applied-arts education that occurred following national unification in 1871. Semper's analytical emphasis on production methods, materials, and technical processes did influence Muthesius to the extent that *Style-Architecture and Building-Art* identified "the style of our time" in "such new creations that serve truly new needs, as in our railway stations, exhibition halls, giant bridges, steamships, train cars, bicycles, etc." To Muthesius, the "scientific objectivity" evident in the design of these structures in no way contradicted the pleasing impression afforded by the "broad sweep of an iron bridge . . . the elegant landau, trim warship, or light bicycle," all of which had "a modern sensitivity inscribed within them."[79]

Muthesius's cultural arguments met with considerable approval among officials at home. This included even Kaiser Wilhelm II, whose competitive bent was prompted in part by his personal interest in and rivalry with England. As Queen Victoria's eldest grandchild, the Kaiser encouraged a policy of "global politics" (*Weltpolitik*) beginning in the late 1890s; a significant part of this national drive included an expansion of the German navy that was to influence deeply the dynamics of German party politics, industrial policy, and international diplomacy until the First World War.[80] When Muthesius returned to Germany to a post as the Commerce Ministry's leading arts, crafts, and trades school reformer, he personally arranged for the designer Richard Riemerschmid and the master craftsman and entrepreneur Karl Schmidt to design luxurious quarters for some of the German navy's newest ships. His reference in *Style-Architecture and Building-Art* to battleships as proper exemplars of modern design thinking, it seems, did not go unappreciated by Admiral von Tirpitz and his circle.[81] The artist Henry van de Velde, by contrast, was frustrated in his efforts to obtain prestigious commissions for Albert Ballin's Hamburg-America Shipping Line. Following a trip with Ballin to Italy, Greece, and the Near East, van de Velde saw his design plans blocked when the Kaiser intervened with Ballin to voice his objections to an artist known for his prominent position among international avant-garde artists.[82]

Semper's writings may have also played a role in prompting Muthesius to focus on the dwelling as the place where functional needs, material culture, and art intersected to produce "architecture." But where Semper worked historically and anthropologically to locate the roots of walls and spatial dividers in woven textile hangings, and where the Viennese architect Otto Wagner sought inspiration in modern technology and monumental urban forms, Muthesius focused exclusively on the recent experience of the English and the exemplary architects of the Domestic Revival. To Muthesius, as for many other adherents of the Art Education movement, art and the culture that accompanied it began in the home, and only from there could artistic sensibilities progress into the streets and the public environment. With the threads of the neo-Gothic tradition still present in the works of such architects as Norman Shaw, Philip Webb, and C. F. A. Voysey, the English were enjoying the fruits of an unpretentious, matter-of-fact bourgeois architecture, to which Muthesius specifically applied the word *sachlich*. This, he declared, was a national architecture, truly an expression of its time. Until Germans learned to value and create modern artistic homes, the new movement in the German applied arts would be limited to journals and exhibitions that featured objects fashionable only from one season to the next.

Muthesius admonished German architects to follow the English example of designing for local climate and health-oriented considerations of light and air, enjoining applied artists to make the house the focus of their activities as well. "The applied-arts movement in England," Muthesius assured, "knows exactly for whom it works: for the English house."[83] He concluded his polemic by calling for German architects to take the lead in rediscovering "local bourgeois and rural building motifs" that, when explored through each architect's "personal artistic views," would lead gradually to "not only a rational but also a national middle-class building-art."[84]

With this plea Muthesius promoted a full realization of what he saw as the "aesthetic-tectonic reform of peoples' outlooks that has steadily come to the fore and demanded a replacement of the earlier decorative arts with a sensible, objective art" (*sinngemässe sachliche Kunst*).[85] The English were Germanic folk, Muthesius reasoned, and it therefore made sense that Germans should be able to relate naturally to the developments of the Arts and Crafts movement and apply its lessons to present-day practices of engineering, building, and production. It remained, he said, only to heed the words of England's "artistic apostle," John Ruskin, and to reestablish architecture as the font of all artistic production. Muthesius's reading of Ruskin was again limited to this consideration, however, and largely ignored Ruskin's all-important emphasis on the well-being and happiness of workers.

Within *Style-Architecture and Building-Art* were the cultural messages that Muthesius would at once translate into Prussian state policy and articulate in his private architectural practice. In a second edition of the book released the following year (1903), Muthesius enlarged sections on the new artistic interior and stepped up his attack on the way that industries had quickly translated the *Jugendstil* into a source of cheap, mass-produced commercial wares. Arguing that Germany's achievement of success in architecture and the arts and crafts would be part of a multigenerational process, he stressed even more that modern aesthetic progress was inextricably linked to the self-realization of an enlightened twentieth-century bourgeoisie. Finally, he extended his polemic about the inferiority of mass-produced German goods and so-called machine surrogates, objects that had been made by machine to look as if they had been manufactured by hand. Improving the quality of German goods, Muthesius emphasized, would increase their value in the market and therefore would enhance the well-being of the entire nation.[86]

In the book's second edition, Muthesius revealed his escalating elitism as he wrote, "The masses appear incapable of grasping the fundamental nature of human problems."[87] This deficiency not only led the "masses" to be sucked into a cycle of buying inferior goods from competing industries rushing to make a profit; it also meant that solutions to large-scale economic and social problems would have to come from above. Macroeconomic solutions such as land reform, however, appeared to Muthesius to be out of the question. Although he objected to the unbridled land speculation that prevailed in Berlin's suburbs, he seemed to regard large-scale real-estate speculation as an unalterable fact.[88]

The second edition of *Style-Architecture and Building-Art* overlapped with Muthesius's appointment in Berlin to reform Prussia's arts, crafts, and trades school system for service to a modern economy. This is, in all likelihood, what prompted Muthesius to step up his focus on a socioeconomic project of "people's education" (*Volkserziehung*) – a pedagogical program, he explained, that would "fundamentally educate the people in the sense of the understanding of work of high-quality, a process that today has not yet even begun." The state, he wrote, must "immediately step in as an educator," in order to teach the German people by example to understand what solidity and quality, expressed by the word *Gediegenheit*, truly meant.[89]

Muthesius's prescriptive role for the state conformed exactly to the outlook of Prussia's new Commerce Minister Theodor Möller, who had been appointed on May 5, 1901. Apart from being a successful industrialist and recent member of the Reichstag representing the National Liberal Party, Möller took an especially active interest in the role that a modernized arts, crafts, and trades *Mittelstand* could play in contributing to Prussian commercial expansion.[90] As Möller grew familiar with Muthesius's many reports and well-reasoned, increasingly forceful views, he let the government architect know, through Otto March at the Public Works Ministry, that he foresaw a very active role for Muthesius at the Commerce Ministry in the near future – indeed, a role in which Muthesius could be expected to exercise "the greatest influence in the largest possible number of fields."[91] In *Style-Architecture and Building-Art* Minister Möller and other officials glimpsed both a program and a polemic, an achievement that was only outdone by Muthesius's monumental historical study *The English House*.

DAS ENGLISCHE HAUS: "OF BURNING INTEREST FOR GERMANY PRECISELY NOW"

The English House, containing a compendium and cultural history of exemplary English dwellings, was the magnum opus in Muthesius's crusade to transplant the values, if not the forms, of the English domestic revival onto German soil. The Berlin publishing house of Ernst Wasmuth released the book in three lavishly illustrated volumes in 1904 and 1905.[92] Although considered a classic work of architectural historical scholarship, the book was in equal measure, as Julius Posener has noted, the work "of a historian and a propagandist."[93] Muthesius conveyed the variety of English domestic architecture from pre-Norman times to the present in three carefully written volumes that covered development, layout and construction, gardens and landscape, and interiors. Reading extremely widely and documenting the richness of building traditions throughout Britain, Muthesius earned the praise of the British and Germans alike for his achievement. As William R. Lethaby recalled in reference to the work, "All the architects who at that time did any building were investigated, sorted, tabulated and, I must say, understood."[94]

Building on the arguments presented in *Style-Architecture and Building-Art*, *The English House* maintained that English domestic architecture reflected a level of

modern civilization yet to be attained in Germany. To Muthesius, newly unified Germany had been hampered by explosive urbanization, dangerous levels of
overcrowding in urban apartments, and rampant land and building speculation.
Berlin became the quintessential example of this growth as, during the "Founding Years" (*Gründerjahre*) after 1871, miles of speculative apartments were built
to house the lower classes in *Mietskasernen*, or "rental barracks" grouped around
multiple courtyards in deep, poorly lit city blocks. The middle and upper classes,
meanwhile, lived in decorous, generously proportioned apartment buildings carried out in various historical styles, including even the newer *Jugendstil*.[95] The
fact that the majority of the better-off classes in Germany continued to live in
urban apartments rather than relocating to the comfortable, green suburbs was
a confirmation, in Muthesius's eyes, that a modern German single-family house
culture had yet to develop.[96] Moreover, to Muthesius the impractical layout and
emphasis in many apartments on social presentation – rather than on comfort
and practicality – was further evidence of the bankruptcy of modern German domestic culture. Muthesius joined many contemporaries in condemning German
urban conditions; England was clearly the example for Germany to follow.[97]
Moving to houses in the suburbs and reestablishing peoples' connection to nature was essential for enhancing the well-being of the German people, he argued,
dutifully quoting Goethe, who wrote, "We must look upon our people as a store-
house from which the energies of failing humanity are continually replenished
and refreshed."[98]

The English house further represented a model with which Muthesius hoped
to revolutionize Germany's own thinking about building, manufacturing, and
artistic and cultural progress in general. "Our whole new movement," he wrote
in the first volume of the work, "is built on the results which England has achieved
from 1860 up to the mid 90s."[99] It was for this reason that Muthesius, when he
applied to Commerce Ministry officials in Berlin for a three-month extension of
his London stay to complete the manuscript of *The English House*, described English domestic architecture as "*the* field in which England has exhibited the most
valuable cultural progress." Occupying almost five of the years that Muthesius
spent in England, the book was "the actual general sum of that which I have been
working on here. The field is the most important that exists in England and is of
especially burning interest for Germany precisely now."[100] Because of its length
and significance, it was therefore essential to Muthesius to bring this study to
a conclusion before returning to Berlin to reform the Prussian schools for arts,
crafts, and trades in accordance with the tenets of the "new movement."

Muthesius's systematic study of English houses enabled him to synthesize his
accumulated knowledge about applied-arts reform and architectural development
during his years of government reporting in London. He obtained many of his
historical examples of Norman castles and Elizabethan houses from Robert Kerr's
inquiry of 1865, *The Gentleman's House*; from an earlier German study from 1888
by Robert Dohme that also bore the name *Das englische Haus*; and from articles

culled from such English journals as *The Builder, The Studio, The Architectural Record*, and *The Builder's Journal*.[101] He cataloged practical techniques of house planning that had evolved from older traditions of the English hall, the inglenook, and the Elizabethan garden, comparing them favorably with the less well-lit and less practical spaces in German apartment living such as the formal reception room (*Salon, gute Stube*). Interpreting cultural phenomena, as was common for the times, in ethnic terms, Muthesius categorized the resurgence of neovernacular English house design in the nineteenth century as a matter of "national instinct." He labored throughout the text to show how principles of English site planning enabled homes to take the best advantage of fresh air and sunlight so as to interact favorably with the outdoors and with their specific sites.[102]

By the 1860s, Muthesius argued, the ongoing decline of manorial power and rise of the middle classes had enabled a group of British architects to develop the "free plan" and to rediscover sensible, simple craftsmanship that bespoke an appropriate level of middle-class propriety and restraint. He discussed the ways in which architects such as Phillip Webb, Eden Nesfield, and Richard Norman Shaw rediscovered the craftsmanship of the master mason and the beauty of the village street, overcoming the overeducated academic architects' preoccupation with historical precedent as well as the pecuniary orientation of the speculative developer. He showed how leading British architects had translated the values of the Gothic revival into the Queen Anne and vernacular free forms that marked a rebirth of English domestic architecture in the late nineteenth century. Once again Shaw had been an important pioneer, evolving a picturesque vocabulary with homes like Broadlands (Sunninghill, Berkshire) to create irregular, rambling house plans that connected interiors to the outdoors while replacing the symmetry and discipline of classical representation with expressions of domestic comfort (Figs. 32–33). The insistence on the use of local materials and traditional building methods, together with picturesque massing and references to medieval construction, further reinforced the impression that the houses of a rising modern bourgeoisie were organically linked to the landscape and to English historical traditions. "In one to two centuries," wrote March to Muthesius, "we will also reach this point.[103]

Muthesius and March were captivated by the nonacademic, indigenous building forms and unfettered planning practices that seemed to go beyond mere expression of comfort to express steadfastness and cultural harmony amid the nineteenth century's rapidly changing social, economic, and political conditions. The countless exemplary English house designs that Muthesius paraded before an eager German readership accomplished two additional purposes: They introduced Germans to the notions of single-family dwelling and house ownership as phenomena characteristic of developed modern cultures; simultaneously, they inextricably linked ownership of a primary, suburban, architect-designed residence to a rapidly developing educated German bourgeoisie that hungered for its own distinguishing marks of cultural legitimacy.[104]

32. Richard Norman Shaw, houses in Bedford Park, near London, 1877–80, street view (altered) (Hermann Muthesius, *Das englische Haus*, vol. 1, Berlin, 1904–05)

As Muthesius reasoned in the first volume of the work, it mattered relatively little whether one or two dozen more large country mansions were erected in the early twentieth century: The real challenge for architects and for society in the modern world was the design and construction of the proper middle-class house ("*das Haus für den Mittelstand*"). "This class," he wrote, "has gained an undreamt of importance over the course of the nineteenth century and is

33. Richard Norman Shaw, houses in Bedford Park, sample plans (altered) (Hermann Muthesius, *Das englische Haus*, vol. 1, Berlin, 1904–05)

34. Charles Voysey, New Place, Haslemere, Surrey, exterior view (Hermann Muthesius, *Das englische Haus*, vol. 2, Berlin, 1904–05)

now of the utmost economic significance. It uncompromisingly demands its own art.... The challenge now is to solve the problem of the small house in a satisfying way, as Norman Shaw first did at Bedford Park" (Figs. 34–35).[105]

As Muthesius made clear in numerous subsequent publications, he would have liked very much to work along the lines followed in the 1870s at Bedford Park outside London, developed by the artistically minded British cloth merchant and developer Jonathan Carr. Eager for his development to achieve a successful mix of tasteful middle-class house design and commercial success, Carr had appointed Richard Norman Shaw to succeed E. W. Godwin as Bedford Park's estate architect in 1877. With Shaw's help Carr achieved an unprecedented balance of economy, functional convenience, and calculated artistic variety in the domestic architecture of England's first planned middle-class suburban community. Ridiculed by some as the playground of effete members of the Aesthetic movement, Bedford Park succeeded commercially and exercised a broad international influence, not least on the visiting Prussian state architect and government reporter.[106]

Beyond the inherent architectural interest of the single-family dwelling, house ownership conveyed to Muthesius the power of the private individual. No social class was a more fitting carrier of individuality than the educated middle class, which was made up of individuals who had gained their identity and distinction through education and personal cultivation in a particular field. The most important lesson that the Germans could learn from the English example, in

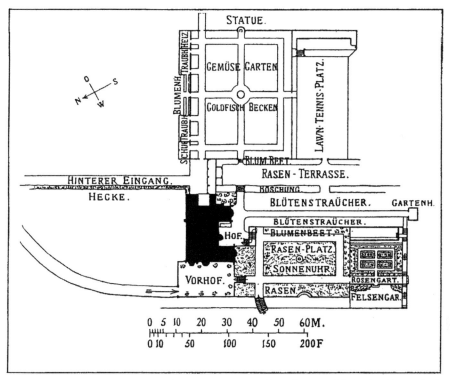

35. Charles Voysey, New Place, Haslemere, Surrey, site plan (Hermann Muthesius, *Das englische Haus*, vol. 2, Berlin, 1904–05)

Muthesius's eyes, was that the development of private house-dwelling was a crucial part of modern cultural advance. "For there can be no doubt," Muthesius asserted, "that to dwell in a private house is in every way a higher form of life."[107]

It was in the work of a younger generation of architects – men like C. H. Townsend, William Lethaby, Charles Voysey, M. H. Baillie Scott, and Charles Rennie Mackintosh – that Muthesius saw the creation of modern and "artistic" English houses in full flower. Each of these architects, and a host of others, were following Arts and Crafts principles to design houses that combined the valuation of local building traditions with a high level of technical execution and the use of fine materials.[108]

The individualism of these architects testified to their allegiance to Arts and Crafts ideals. Charles Voysey, a London-based architect at the height of his popularity at the turn of the century, impressed Muthesius and other critics with simple houses that blended vernacular and medieval elements in a manner so seamless, direct, and dignified that they were considered by many contemporaries, and by later historians, to be refreshingly modern. Houses like Greyfriars, Broadleys, and New Place, carried out for the most part for a growing bourgeois intellectual class with a taste for the arts – as Stuart Durant has shown – received Muthesius's praise in *Das englische Haus* and influenced him in his own house designs for a

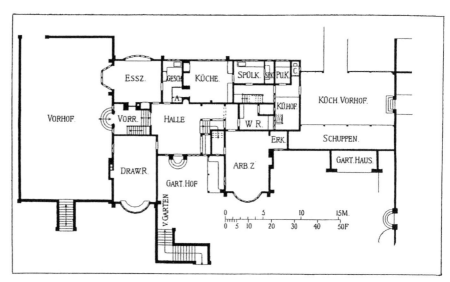

36. Charles Voysey, New Place, Haslemere, ground-floor plan (Hermann Muthesius, *Das englische Haus*, vol. 2, Berlin, 1904–05)

similar class of clients in Berlin (Figs. 36–38).[109] New Place by Haslemere in Surrey, in particular, seems to have inspired Muthesius to experiment with his own particular combinations of curved bays, projecting gables, balconies, terraces, and multilevel gardens at one of his best-known houses, the Freudenberg house in Berlin-Nicolassee (Fig. 37).[110]

Acknowledged by Muthesius as a "prophet of the new language of form," Voysey was outdone, in the German architect's estimation, only by Baillie Scott's more "poetic" design of houses with rooms that the architect had treated as individual creations linked by an overarching theme. As Muthesius put it, "It is the new thought of interior space as an independent work of art which Baillie Scott put into effect for the first time."[111] Shaw and the older, path-breaking architects of the Domestic Revival would gradually assume less importance to Muthesius during his ongoing campaign to promote a modern domestic architecture in Germany. By contrast, Muthesius would help Baillie Scott to obtain commissions in such German cities as Darmstadt and Dresden-Hellerau, while his houses and rich watercolor interior renderings would feature particularly prominently in the German architect's international compendium of contemporary (*neuzeitlich*) suburban houses of 1907, *Country House and Garden* (*Landhaus und Garten*) (Fig. 38).[112]

Muthesius admired the works of the Scottish architect Charles Rennie Mackintosh for their poetry and sophistication as well. To Muthesius, Mackintosh worked with his wife, the talented artist and designer Margaret Macdonald, imaginatively to combine interior decorations with inventive spatial treatments expressed outwardly through simplified, neovernacular forms. Muthesius publicized this young generation as the messengers of a new art of building in which architects, involved

37. Hermann Muthesius, Freudenberg house, Berlin-Nicolassee, 1907–08, view from northeast
(altered); the Muthesius house is in the background (*Die Kunst* 24, 1911)

38. M. H. Baillie Scott, design for a living room, watercolor perspective view, ca. 1897
(Hermann Muthesius, *Landhaus und Garten*, Munich, 1907)

in the design of houses as well as the furniture, wallpaper, and objects within them, brought the healthiest and most practical artistic sensibilities to bear on modern domestic culture.[113]

As March's comment to Muthesius indicated, however, the sustained nature of artistic and architectural progress among several generations of artists and architects had fostered developments in English house design for which the Germans could still only yearn. In his quest to provide an emerging middle-class sensibility of pragmatism, objectivity, or *Sachlichkeit* with an architectural and historical pedigree, Muthesius repeatedly claimed that the distinguishing features of modern British architects' houses were functionality, practicality, and sensible taste. Eschewing excessive ornament, ostentation, pretension, and "what one usually calls 'architecture,' i.e., the application of compositional and decorative elements," the modern English house found its "actual, decisive worth in its complete objectivity (*Sachlichkeit*)."[114]

CONCLUSION: BRINGING BRITISH LESSONS TO BERLIN

Before returning to Berlin for his new assignment with the Commerce Ministry, which began on July 1, 1903, Muthesius carried out one last major assignment in Britain for the Prussian government. He organized and led a tour that included a highly placed government adviser (*Ober-Geheimesregierungsrat*) from the Prussian Commerce Ministry, Fritz Dönhoff; another government adviser from the Prussian Ministry of Finance; as well as the artist Peter Behrens and the government adviser Eugen von Czihak. Muthesius led these men on a whirlwind study tour of twenty-seven British schools for arts, crafts, trades, and technical education during the month of June 1903. On their return, Dönhoff, Muthesius, and von Czihak filed a lengthy report with the Prussian lower legislative house, the Chamber of Deputies or *Abgeorgnetenhaus*, about their trip.[115]

Significantly, this final English tour in June dovetailed with Muthesius's first assignment at the Commerce Ministry once he arrived in Berlin in July. By mid-July, Muthesius set out to inspect ten of Prussia's own schools for arts, crafts, and trades education, the reform of which would be among Muthesius's main tasks over the next several years. Herein lay the full meaning of Muthesius's six years and nine months of study in England: Having produced an enormous oeuvre and accumulated a wealth of experience studying English applied-arts education, architecture, and cultural affairs, Muthesius was poised to exercise a decisive influence on Prussian and German design education and economic development policies from his new office at the Prussian Commerce Ministry. He was also given enough time in his post to establish himself in a private architectural practice that would concentrate on the reform of German domestic architecture.[116]

Joining Muthesius on the front line of Prussian school reform was a rising star of the German design world, Peter Behrens. The Commerce Ministry recruited the thirty-four-year-old Behrens to direct the Dusseldorf *Kunstgewerbeschule* in late 1902 – the same time that Muthesius had received his appointment. Writing to Muthesius in London in early 1903, Behrens voiced his hopes concerning the chaotic state of German artistic affairs. Elaborating on the upstart, industrializing German nation's "yearning for a culture" (*Sehnsucht nach einer Kultur*) that had seen such vivid expression at the Darmstadt Artists' Colony exhibition of 1901, Behrens wrote:

> What pleases me greatly in assuming this post is the opportunity it extends to be able, in a direct sense, to be subservient to the interests of the state. Where today from many sides the yearning for a culture is coming to expression – almost *ad nauseam* – I believe that little is helped through the seal of a slogan; . . . rather, the only possibility in this area lies in self-development or in the hands of the state. On this last point I regard your official appointment and the efforts of people like Professor Ludwig Pallat (an influential Culture Ministry art education reformer) as the best confirmation of my deeply held convictions.[117]

With this vote of confidence from the new Dusseldorf Applied Arts School director, and with the full support of his ministry, Muthesius was prepared to embark on the development of state policies that would address Prussia's arts, crafts, and trades schools, as well as the problem of what to do about the beleaguered *Mittelstand*. At the same time, these policies would help lay the foundations for the path-breaking German design organization, the Deutscher Werkbund.

⟪ CHAPTER THREE

PRUSSIAN APPLIED-ARTS REFORMS: CULTURE, CLASS, AND THE MODERN ECONOMY ⟫

THE TRANSFORMATION OF PRUSSIAN APPLIED-ARTS EDUCATION

The government post Muthesius assumed at the Prussian Ministry of Commerce and Trade in Berlin can be understood as a ministerial effort to bring the lessons of the British Arts and Crafts movement to bear on the modern Prussian economy. Even as turn-of-the-century considerations from modern economics and industry were altering earlier conceptions of the applied arts, Muthesius defined the lessons he learned in England in terms of their German applications rather than in relation to their British origins. As a consequence of Muthesius's efforts, and shortly after his return to Berlin in July 1903, the Prussian Ministry of Commerce and Trade became the sponsor of innovative applied-arts reform principles through its economic development policies. Operating at the point where economic development, design aesthetics, and educational reform converged, the Prussian Commerce Ministry institutionalized a veritable catalog of new design doctrines between 1903 and 1907 through the reform of its top three dozen schools for arts, crafts, and trades, or *Kunstgewerbe- und Handwerkerschulen*.

Recognized primarily as an architect and cofounder of the German Werkbund, Muthesius has received relatively little scholarly attention as a reformer of Prussian schools for arts, crafts, and trades.[1] Yet Muthesius's influential arts and crafts reforms represent one of the earliest, and certainly the largest, programmatic revisions of early-twentieth-century German approaches to applied-arts production, manufacture, and the act of "making" in general. The reforms he introduced between 1903 and 1907, designed to support the Commerce Ministry's agenda for improving Prusso-German production, export competitiveness, and domestic quality of life, were to have profound consequences for the arts, crafts, interior design, and architecture in Prussia and throughout Germany.

By far the most important consequence would be the formation, in 1907, of the Deutscher Werkbund, which is the subject of Chapter 4. The Werkbund, as Germany's seminal association of artists, architects, crafts practitioners, manufacturers, and politicians, enlarged the scope of activities begun in the Commerce Ministry and formalized many of Muthesius's applied-arts school-reform principles in this national design, manufacturing, and educational forum. This is not to say that other regions and important figures – the national politician Friedrich Naumann, Richard Riemerschmid of Munich, Peter Behrens of Dusseldorf, and Karl Schmidt of Dresden – were not working on similar ideas on their way to becoming co-initiators of the Werkbund. Rather, the way Muthesius worked from a position inside the government to connect industry, artists, and craftspeople on a level involving dozens of cities around Prussia, and the way he oriented people from different fields toward a common policy beginning in 1903, suggests that Muthesius and the Prussian government organizations for whom he worked provided, through their school reorganization and workshop-based design-reform policies, the blueprints for several of the Werkbund's most important principles in 1907.

Under Muthesius's guidance, the Commerce Ministry's reforms transmuted the values of the British Arts and Crafts movement into design techniques oriented toward materials, constructional principles, and local crafts industries in dozens of Prussian state schools. Among design principles that Muthesius placed at the core of a new ministerial economic-development package by 1904 were fitness of form to functional purpose (*Zweckmässigkeit*); the principle of objective, realist, or *sachlich* design; and tectonic, workshop-based instruction oriented to the relationship between materials and construction.[2] Muthesius advanced these principles as the core of a pedagogy oriented to present conditions in technology, materials, and production. At the same time, he invoked an idealized vision of traditions from Germany's preindustrial past – particularly the late eighteenth and early nineteenth centuries – when applied artists, fine artists, and architects allegedly worked in close harmony.[3]

Although Muthesius's reworking of Prussian schools and curricula drew on practices in Austria, the south German states of Bavaria, Baden and Württemberg,[4] his reforms benefited especially from his seven years of service as a government reporter in London. Muthesius drew on these experiences to demonstrate that modern aesthetic thinking, state economic development policies, and arts and crafts education could be made to converge. The Commerce Ministry's schools, located in more than thirty of Prussia's largest cities and towns from Aachen to Königsberg, and from Breslau to Flensburg, featured highly individualized curricula that Muthesius's reforms adapted for the Commerce Ministry's purposes (see Appendix A; also Figs. 22–23).

Prussia's applied-arts schools were more than simply a laboratory for furthering Prussian economic development, however: They fulfilled Commerce Minister Theodor Möller's mandate to train a new generation of artisans, building trades workers, and other members of Prussia's traditional "old" *Mittelstand* for service to a modern consumer economy.[5] Möller's position toward the *Mittelstand* was an outgrowth of his background and politics as a successful Westphalian industrialist. Although Möller has a mediocre reputation at best among historians of Wilhelmine politics, it was he who summoned Muthesius to the ministry as its most influential applied-arts reformer. Perhaps no less significant, Möller also recruited Peter Behrens to direct the Commerce Ministry's leading educational institution, the Dusseldorf School of Applied Arts.[6]

Möller's roots are important for understanding how he came to bring an architect like Muthesius into his ministry. Beginning in the 1880s, Möller had gained local popularity as an advocate of industrial interests in the Coal Producers' Association in Bielefeld and the Rhineland branch of the Central Association of German Industrialists (*Centralverband Deutscher Industrieller* – CDI). He ran successfully for a seat in the Reichstag in 1890 as a member of the National Liberal Party.[7] By the end of the 1890s, Möller became known as a supporter of a so-called "politics of rallying together," or *Sammlungspolitik*. *Sammlungspolitik* was essentially a revival of earlier efforts at coalition building during the Bismarck era that had brought together the famous alliance of "iron and rye," the agricultural Conservative Party of eastern Prussia and the industrial barons of western Prussia. Prussian Finance Minister Johannes von Miquel, from an industrial background himself, was responsible for the revival of *Sammlungspolitik* in 1897. This revival of an agrarian-industrial coalition (*Sammlung*) would meet with sporadic success as it was attempted during various periods of upheaval in the Wilhelmine Empire, as the historian Geoff Eley has shown.[8]

Möller managed to draw favorable attention from the regime when his support for the so-called "politics of the middle line" enabled him to achieve some degree of cooperation among dueling interests in Western heavy industry, Eastern agriculture, and commerce.[9] Although Kaiser Wilhelm II initially opposed Reich Chancellor Bernhard von Bülow's suggestion of Möller as Commerce Minister in 1901, it was precisely the Rhinelander's reputation for conciliatory tactics that won out in the end.[10] Many Prussian newspapers reacted favorably to the unusual appointment of an industrialist and party politician as Prussian Minister of Commerce; the Social Democratic Party's (SPD) main organ, *Vorwärts*, was an understandable exception. Fearing that the door had been opened to unacceptable levels of cooperation between government and capitalist interests, the SPD newspaper sarcastically recommended that the Prussian Ministry of Commerce and Trade change its name simply to "Ministry of the German Industrialists' Association."[11]

In his new role as Commerce Minister, Möller continued a long-standing practice of justifying political positions and policy decisions in terms of the general "good of all."[12] Möller saw the raising of exports as a primary goal. One month after his appointment he wrote to a family member: "without further development of exports we cannot feed the 800,000 people who are added to our population every year. From this standpoint the trade agreements are a question of national survival (*eine nationale Lebensfrage*)."[13] Möller further believed that Germany's political power was a function of its economic well-being.[14] He agreed with the policy of Bismarck's successor, Chancellor Leo von Caprivi, whose trade agreements sought an economically united *Mitteleuropa*, or German- and Austrian-led Central European trade bloc, as a guarantor of Germany's ability to compete effectively in the long run against the "powerful economic colossi" to the east and west, namely Russia, England, and the United States.[15]

Möller's interest in the trades *Mittelstand* – the primary group involved in arts, crafts, and trades as sole proprietors or, increasingly, in larger crafts enterprises – was therefore twofold. He believed that the duties of the Prussian state required the government to address the needs of this class in the face of burgeoning industrial concentration and production. Preventing the dissolution of the *Mittelstand* belonged to the state's primary responsibilities, not least to prevent increasing support for the growing Socialist Party. Second, and as an owner of factories for leather goods and textiles himself, Möller claimed that only by conferring on artisans "the advantages enjoyed by large enterprise" could German crafts workers compete effectively in a market increasingly dominated by mass-produced products.[16]

Although Möller was recognized by some of his peers for his interest in social policy, to the Social Democratic Party and the Left generally, Möller's social policy was far too weak. Hardly unusual for a German industrialist and National Liberal politician at the time, Möller believed unions should under no circumstances be associated with political parties or engage in politics in any way. In his view, the national interest and the preservation of the existing social order were top priorities. The best social reforms, therefore, were those that gave workers and artisans opportunities to work themselves out of unfavorable economic circumstances. In this context, Möller's steps to reform arts, crafts, and trades schools represented part of a modernization program and, as he wrote, should provide a series of "ladders upon which intelligent people of lesser means can climb up into the higher classes" (*höheren Stände*).[17]

Hermann Muthesius may or may not have been an active supporter of the National Liberal Party, but many of the views expressed by the architect in his writings and government reports closely matched those of the Commerce Minister and the party from which he came.[18] Among these were the belief in Germany's established social order, the rejection of socialism as a danger to state and nation, and the creation of state-sponsored opportunities for artisans to improve their lot and rise into the middle class. It is hardly a surprise, therefore, that Möller called on the government architect in November 1902 to return to a post in

Berlin to assist the Commerce Ministry government councillors Fritz Dönhoff, Hermann von Seefeld, and Heinrich Neuhaus in the reform of the entire system of applied-arts, crafts, and trades education.[19] One month later, the combined efforts of Theodor Möller, Mayor Wilhelm Marx of Dusseldorf, Ludwig Pallat from the Culture Ministry, and Fritz Dönhoff led to Peter Behrens's acceptance of an appointment to direct the Dusseldorf School of Applied Arts.[20] Behrens had come away from a series of lengthy interviews with Commerce Minister Möller and Privy Councillor Dönhoff in Berlin between November 17 and 20, 1902, feeling both honored and impressed. He indicated as much to a close friend, the poet Richard Dehmel, and added that "the people (at the ministry) are engaged in a drastic reorganization."[21]

The Commerce Ministry propagated its new tenets for applied-arts training through two major reform strategies. The first was the reorganization of school curricula around new instructional workshops in 1904; the second was the founding of a State Trades Board (*Landesgewerbeamt*) in early 1905.[22] These policies were a direct outgrowth of Muthesius's reform efforts and reflected the ministry's internalization of the recommendations he had made from London over the preceding seven years.

The State Trades Board, comprised of five permanent officials and various subcommittees, was created to render arts, crafts, and trades education compatible with the production systems of manufacturing and industry. The Board was also given the responsibility to promote exhibits of new tools, technology, and finished goods for the benefit of entrepreneurial master craftsmen, manufacturers, and consumers. Insisting that reformed schools and the new State Trades Board would improve the livelihood of crafts workers, the Commerce Ministry nonetheless refused the input of crafts associations in formulating the Trades Board's agenda; it limited artisanal representation in the Board's permanent membership to Muthesius as the ministry's own "arts and crafts architect."[23]

The Commerce Ministry shared the common view in the Prussian administration that improved working conditions for the arts, crafts, and trades *Mittelstand* would undercut support for an increasingly successful Social Democratic Party, which pioneered the practices of a mass political party in Germany after the lifting of antisocialist laws in 1890.[24] However, Minister Möller's efforts to ally disparate commercial, industrial, and *Mittelstand* interests alienated large numbers of craftsmen and tradesworkers in the applied arts. Many were dependent on established guild practices of historicist design reproduction and therefore resistant to change. Although some craftsmen benefited from the school-reform policies, larger numbers of master artisans expressed opposition in such conservative crafts associations as the Dusseldorf *Semperbund* as well as the national Association for the Economic Interests of the Crafts (*Fachverband für die wirtschaftlichen Interessen des Kunstgewerbes*). Independently employed artisans grew increasingly defensive about their established techniques of producing highly ornamental furniture and interior fittings in a variety of historical styles – an orientation that accompanied what the historian Shulamit Volkov has characterized as an "anti-modern" outlook.[25]

Under Muthesius's guidance, Prussian state applied-arts education would be redirected to engage an embryonic modern mass culture at the point of production and consumption, supply and demand. As the architect would later state at the first annual meeting of the Werkbund in 1908, where he was elected to the association's six-member leadership committee, the Arts and Crafts movement needed to be transformed in such a way as to effect the "new formulation of all forms of human expression."[26] The ministry's design reform and exhibition policies began this process by overlaying traditional notions of personal cultivation (*Bildung*) with the education of modern consumers, seeking simultaneously to refashion the artisans, workers, and small producers of Prussia's traditional *Mittelstand*, often with considerable resistance, into an arm of industrially based, export-oriented consumer economy.

Among several ways in which new state policies were realized, one of the most important was to ensure that Prussia's newly reformed, state-supported schools, curricula, and workshops were developed in accordance with the needs of local industries. Whether at the arts and crafts drawing academy in Kassel, the woodworking school in rural Warmbrunn, or the arts and crafts school in Dusseldorf, the Prussian Commerce Ministry encouraged schools to absorb the new teachings of *Sachlichkeit* and *Zweckmässigkeit*, apply them in classrooms and ateliers, and send them with their students into local-industry and crafts-workshop settings.

The Prussian school reforms sought to cultivate among the German people a sense of "modern" taste – a taste, that is, that no longer unquestioningly privileged copies of historical styles. To this end, Behrens and Riemerschmid worked for the Commerce Ministry at the behest of Muthesius and Möller. In their roles as designers and teachers they did much to propagate objective, practical, and purposeful design among students and teachers. Karl Schmidt, for his part, admired Muthesius and saw an opportunity to work with him and Riemerschmid for the advancement of his singularly successful applied-arts enterprise, the Dresden Workshops for Handicraft. As Saxony's best-known and most successful crafts entrepreneur, Schmidt supported Muthesius's efforts to reform applied-arts education. He brought the issue of German manufacturing quality to Muthesius's attention after reading *Style-Architecture and Building-Art* and served as a leading proponent of functional design from a craftsman's and manufacturer's perspective.[27] Schmidt also introduced Muthesius to the ideas of Friedrich Naumann, a prolific writer, Protestant minister, and politician of the Christian Left with firm ideas about how a modernized German economy could benefit workers while satisfying the expansionist aims of many leaders in German government and industry.

MUTHESIUS'S APPLIED-ARTS SCHOOL REFORMS: POLITICAL AND HISTORICAL BACKGROUND

Changes enacted by Möller, Muthesius, and other civil servants in the field of arts, crafts, and trades education cannot be separated from the broader political struggles taking place in Wilhelmine Prussia. To put Muthesius's reform contributions at the Commerce Ministry in perspective, it must be remembered that his period as a London-based reporter to the Prussian Public Works Ministry and the Commerce Ministry between 1896 and 1903 was part of a larger, two-decades-old effort at the Commerce Ministry to convert Prussian schools for arts and crafts into an effective arm of Prussian economic policy. Before this, the Prussian state had sought over two turbulent centuries to forge links between the fine arts, crafts, and trades, on the one hand, and programs to increase national economic prosperity on the other. The applied-arts reforms guided by Muthesius at the beginning of the twentieth century cannot be understood without some historical background on Prussia's earlier efforts in this area.

Prussia's arts, crafts, and trades schools had their roots in the state's eighteenth-century art and drawing academies. Training in the crafts and practical arts had been mentioned as early as 1696, when Crown Prince Frederick (later King Frederick I) founded Prussia's first Academy of Art (*Akademie der Künste*), modeled after the royal academy in Paris. However, it was not until Frederick the Great's reorganization and expansion of the schools in the late 1780s that the practical arts were explicitly connected to the fine-arts curriculum. Intent on broadening education in the practical arts to catch up with more established systems in France, Frederick the Great's administration expanded its educational infrastructure between 1790 and 1804 by founding provincial schools of art in the cities of Königsberg, Halle, Breslau, Magdeburg, Danzig, and Erfurt. The schools taught drafting, drawing techniques, and architectural delineation to craftsmen working in the decorative arts and building trades.[28]

The growth of the art academies and provincial schools of art was interrupted, like all areas of Prussian life, by the chaos brought by the Napoleonic Wars. Thereafter, support for the Prussian provincial schools fell sharply (all but the provincial art schools in Berlin, Breslau, and Königsberg were closed in the early nineteenth century), and even in peacetime most elements of the old system never recovered. The remaining schools gradually devolved and redirected their focus from a state system to local crafts instruction. German industrialization, at the same time, picked up as the nineteenth century progressed, particularly as machine manufacturing cut deeply into the share of products formerly produced in crafts and trades workshops.[29] A conflict was underway between a growing industrial manufacturing sector and more traditional methods of production in the crafts, between new and old methods of production and the modes of economic organization and social life that accompanied them. This struggle increased in intensity during the second half of the nineteenth century, and the closing of many Prussian provincial art schools was just one expression of the challenges that the applied arts faced.

The founding of the academy and other royal provincial schools, as the historian Norbert Eisold has shown, occurred at precisely the time when a greater split than ever before was emerging between design and execution, between creative artists and architects and those called to carry out designs in material form. Thus, rules governing the Berlin Academy in 1790 proclaimed the "fine arts" (*hohe Kunst*) the ruler of the applied arts; the praxis of the latter was to be made useful to the former. Similarly, an 1821 textbook of model projects for students edited by Peter Wilhelm Beuth and Karl Friedrich Schinkel took pains, Eisold writes, to caution manufacturers and crafts workers against making their own designs, imploring them to copy faithfully the designs given to them by trained artists.[30]

In his work as a Prussian school reformer, Muthesius downplayed the emerging power imbalances between artists and crafts practitioners that had been present during the early phases of state-led Prussian applied-arts education.[31] In Commerce Ministry publications, the architect made a point of noting that eighteenth-century crafts workers who had completed studies at the arts academy schools were given the title of "academic artist." In other words, the eighteenth century could be considered a time when crafts and trades practitioners executed their works with sufficient mastery to be regarded as artists themselves.[32] In general, Muthesius described the art academy's goal by 1790 as one of "raising taste in the crafts and improving production so as to raise the general welfare of the nation."[33]

These characterizations were crucial to Muthesius's thesis, put forth earlier in his popular polemic *Style-Architecture and Building-Art* of 1902, that the designation of whether a culture was "artistic" or "inartistic" depended on the extent to which the arts had been integrated and made accessible to the whole population. Interested in boosting the historical status of artisanal production, Muthesius linked the applied arts with the fine arts as a way to build support for school reforms in which artists and architects would play a leading role.[34] His historical characterization of the crafts as the foundation for all other artistic activity in such detailed Commerce Ministry publications as "The Historical Development of Arts and Crafts Teaching Institutions" ("Kunstgewerbliche und handwerkliche Unterrichtsanstalten: Geschichtliche Entwicklung") and "The Contemporary State of Arts and Crafts Instruction" ("Heutiger Stand des kunstgewerblichen Schulwesens in Preussen") mirrored precisely his discussion in *Style-Architecture and Building-Art*.[35] In *Style-Architecture* he ultimately leaned toward restoring the image of the architectural profession as – and here he used Ruskin's phrase – the "Mother of all the Arts." Giving primacy to different branches of the arts – in some cases to the applied arts, in others to architecture – Muthesius sought to balance different interests while betraying a degree of divided loyalty. As a government official in charge of crafts reform who received time off to manage a budding private architectural practice, Muthesius faced an early-twentieth-century conflict in which the applied arts and architecture struggled for primacy. The actual policies he recommended, and that the Commerce Ministry enacted, enforced a rigid hierarchy in which the crafts were the subject of thoroughgoing modernization at the hands of professionally trained artists and architects.

Muthesius's representation of the situation at eighteenth-century arts academies bolstered the claims he would make in support of his modern school reforms. These reforms placed more power than ever over arts, crafts, and trades education in the hands of artists and architects with academic training. Idealizing eighteenth-century Prussia's artistic scene for the state's twentieth-century reform purposes, Muthesius called for harmony where his reforms would, in fact, court division. Nevertheless, Muthesius's rhetoric was useful not only in the area of school reform: His program was also mindful of the Commerce Ministry's need for an economic program that would present an image of unity among classes where the political, economic, and social pressures of rapid industrialization and commercial development were driving Germans further apart.

TERMS OF DEVELOPMENT: *KUNSTGEWERK, KUNSTINDUSTRIE, KUNSTGEWERBE*

The chaotic state of the relationship between crafts and industry in the nineteenth and early twentieth centuries was mirrored in the language that developed to distinguish traditional methods of production from constantly developing new ones. A confusing array of terms evolved that, though it reflected changing attitudes across the decades, was never fully resolved even into the twentieth century. Complicating matters, of course, was the fact that the terminology cut across the artisanal trades, the fine arts, architecture, small-scale commercial enterprise, and industrial manufacture.[36]

Whereas eighteenth-century writers had described the crafts as "mechanical trades" (*mechanische Gewerbe*) or "mechanical arts" (*mechanische Künste*) in opposition to the fine arts (*Hohe Kunst*), by the early nineteenth century such terms as "art industry" (*Kunstindustrie*), "art work" (*Kunstgewerk*), and "technical arts" (*technische Künste*) had blurred somewhat the lines between the two.[37] Growing support for technical training was expressed in the emergence of new trades schools oriented to industry and more efficient mechanized production; these were opened and run by the Prussian Ministry of Commerce and Trade beginning in 1827 in Berlin. These schools devoted only a small part of their resources to crafts and drawing courses. As the state's support of new trades schools supplanted the state's funding of education in traditional crafts skills, the level of quality and performance in crafts production was perceived to have suffered. At the same time, innovations in mass production and the competition for ever cheaper means to manufacture finished goods were seen to have gradually eroded the quality of industrially produced goods as well.[38]

Official efforts to improve production and quality in the arts and crafts industry in order to boost economic success were first instigated by the English, following the disastrous reception of many industrial and crafts wares at the World's Exhibition in London in 1851. Gottfried Semper, the Dresden architect exiled after the 1848 revolution, advised the British government and aided Henry Cole to some extent in developing the path-breaking Department of Practical Art in 1852.[39] These official efforts to improve applied-arts production as an arm of economic policy were the target of criticism by such figures as the art critic John Ruskin, who insisted on moral grounds that the arts provided a basis for a full life and not simply for a narrowly construed economic program.[40] Nevertheless, authorities expanded the department in 1853 and renamed it the Department of Science and Art at the South Kensington Museum, home of a new National Art Training School. Just over a decade later, the Viennese followed the British example and founded the Austrian Museum of Art and Industry (*Österreichische Museum für Kunst und Industrie*) in 1864, which added an applied-arts school in 1868, while in Berlin the Prussian government founded the Berlin Museum for Art and Trade (*Kunst und Gewerbe*) in 1867. However, education efforts associated with Prussia's museum lagged behind those of the British as well as the Viennese.[41]

Also important during the 1860s was the elevation of the new term *Kunstgewerbe* from an array of related earlier terms, which signified the increased attention being devoted to the applied arts in German-speaking countries. The word's very construction as a "dual concept" (*Doppelbegriff*) reflected the conscious effort to reinject quality into overly mechanized crafts through the application of *Kunst*.[42] The term's popularity lasted well into the twentieth century, supplanting older eighteenth- and early-nineteenth-century terms. The word did not, however, displace other popular nineteenth-century terms such as applied arts (*angewandte Kunst*) or art industry (*Kunstindustrie*). The latter term gradually assumed a connotation for more machine-produced works.[43] Nor did the term *Kunstgewerbe* retain the same meaning from its appearance in the 1860s to its use at the time that Muthesius set about reforming the schools for arts, crafts, and trades.

One influential interpretation in the early twentieth century was produced by Heinrich Waentig in his history of the international Arts and Crafts movement, *Wirtschaft und Kunst* (Economy and Art), published in 1909. Stimulated by his pursuit of overlooked historical connections between art history and national economy, Waentig understood *Kunstgewerbe* to represent those methods of crafts production in which artistic treatment of everyday objects could simultaneously raise quality, performance, and aesthetic value. The question for Waentig was the degree to which artistic handling could be applied within these crafts, and this varied in accordance with the type of objects that were being considered.[44] Another contemporary, the political economist Werner Sombart, understood *Kunstgewerbe* differently. In his categorization of strictly practical, useful objects (the majority) versus objects that could be artistically treated, Sombart argued that an effort to treat objects artistically was errant from the beginning if they were meant solely for practical use. Sombart restricted the meaning of *Kunstgewerbe* to a degree that was unsatisfactory to ambitious turn-of-the-century artists and their wishes to reform culture in the broadest sense.[45]

These discussions of *Kunstgewerbe*, in focusing on types of objects that either could or could not be treated artistically, severely limited the application of *Kunstgewerbe* to broader fields of artistic reform. Muthesius, in linking *Kunstgewerbe* to the reform of all aspects of German culture along artistic lines, appears to have reached back for an embracing definition of *Kunstgewerbe* advanced by the Viennese Rudolf Eitelberger von Edelberg, founder of the Austrian Museum for Art and Industry. Art, von Edelberg had argued in 1876, figured into the total economic life of the peoples, for it had a role to play "wherever form or color are concerned"; even the name of his museum, in combining "art" and "industry," reflected the desire to spread this realization "from the house . . . to the state and to industry equally."[46]

Yet Prussian attitudes toward the applied arts, unlike those in Austria or England, did not see widespread revision after mid-century, nor after the founding of the Reich in 1871. One Prussian author, summarizing a popular conservative view in 1874 in the journal *Im neuen Reich*, insisted that the art industry should "remain focused on copying [historical styles], for the only real issue in the interest of the art industry consists in finding the right model and copying it in the right manner."[47] In the world's exhibitions in Paris in 1855 and 1867, in London in 1862, in Vienna in 1873, and in Philadelphia in 1876, German applied-arts goods were roundly criticized for their "technical backwardness, aesthetic inferiority, and economic worthlessness."[48] At the 1876 Philadelphia exhibition, in what some contemporaries as well as later historians of the applied arts regarded as the low point of Germany's nineteenth-century arts and crafts production, the German government exhibition commentator Franz Reuleaux penned a scathing review of his country's assortment of inferior mass-produced goods that imitated various historical styles without considering the relationship between materials, motifs, and constructional principles. In his *Letters from Philadelphia* of 1877, he did lasting damage to Germany's international reputation when he wrote, "the basic principle of German industry is cheap and bad."[49]

The government was slow to take action, hindered in part by complex divisions between the Culture Ministry and the Commerce Ministry in the oversight of arts, crafts, and trades education. The Commerce Ministry had outfitted the trades schools; yet the Culture Ministry, in addition to being responsible for state education generally, also erected and oversaw museums as part of the larger cultural and educational infrastructure. In 1879, the Prussian government opted to unify all educational responsibilities under the Culture Ministry (whose full name was the Ministry of Ecclesiastical, Educational, and Medical Affairs), and the trades schools were removed from the Commerce Ministry's oversight.[50]

Even more important, between the years 1880 and 1890, the Prussian Commerce Ministry was preoccupied with having to withstand the attacks, paradoxically, of its own Minister of Commerce, the Reich Chancellor Prince Otto von Bismarck. As the historian Hans Goldschmidt has shown in his book *The Empire and Prussia in the Battle for Supremacy*, Bismarck regarded commerce and trade as just two of the matters that he would fight to have administered on the level of the entire Reich.[51] In widespread anticipation that economic affairs would come to be administered at the Reich level soon after German unification, the kingdom of Bavaria had dissolved its Ministry of Commerce and Trade in 1871; the south German grand duchy of Baden did the same in 1881.[52] Taking for granted that a Reich Ministry of Commerce and Trade was in the offing, Bismarck sought to dissolve the state ministry into a new imperial authority that would be overseen by the Imperial Ministry of the Interior.[53]

Bismarck encountered stiff resistance from powerful leaders in the Prussian state administration. In conflicts that went to the heart of modern German self-definition and national identity, much energy was expended in the 1880s in struggles over state and imperial jurisdiction over commercial activities. In the end, and following Bismarck's direct onslaughts in 1881 and 1888, established Prussian interests in the Reichstag withstood Bismarck's attacks. Their successful resistance to Bismarck, and the survival of the Prussian Commerce Ministry, was a deciding factor in determining who ultimately would become responsible for design reforms affecting dozens of state crafts schools. The specially created Imperial Interior Ministry's Department for Economic Affairs, authorized by the Kaiser and intended by Bismarck to replace the Prussian Commerce Ministry, instead became preoccupied during the course of the 1880s with administering Bismarck's ever-expanding programs for workers' social insurance.[54]

Instead of shrinking or disappearing, the Prussian Commerce Ministry in fact grew. A Prussian special commission called to resolve the conflicts between the Commerce Ministry and the Ministry of Culture in 1884 placed the Commerce Ministry back in control over almost all of Prussia's arts, crafts, and trades schools. The ministry's chronicles recorded 1884 as a time of recognition that "the education of the youth needs to fit into the ever-stronger position of the German *Volk* in international competition;" education in the arts, crafts, and trades was henceforth to be considered "an inseparable part of the national economic policy."[55] Prussian schools for the arts, crafts, and trades for students at all levels increased from 715 in 1885 to 1,774 in 1900, while the ministry's education budget rose fivefold from 925,000 to 5,378,000 Marks.[56] Yet the thinking of the Ministry remained rigid, as progressive reform studies by such celebrated architects as Martin Gropius were ignored, and planners emphasized numerical increases over qualitative changes that would affect training or performance.[57]

When Theodor Möller became Commerce Minister in 1901, he took a very personal interest in reforming Prussia's burgeoning, outdated, and multilayered system of applied-arts and trades education. By then, the system had ballooned to encompass a top-tier of schools of applied art (*Kunstgewerbeschulen*, Figs. 24–25), mid-level schools of applied art and handcrafts (*Kunstgewerbe- und Handwerkerschulen*), which mingled advanced design training with the crafts and trades education, and purely artisan-oriented handcrafts schools (*Handwerkerschulen*), trades schools (*Gewerbeschulen*), and specialized trades schools (*Fachschulen*) (Appendix A).[58]

Commerce Minister Möller's first major act was to deliver a detailed statement concerning the arts, crafts, and trades schools to Prussia's provincial state authorities in Dusseldorf, Potsdam, Breslau, and six other cities.[59] At the heart of the statement was a six-part questionnaire asking such questions as: How should the applied-arts schools – the diverse, top tier of more than thirty-five schools for applied-arts production that Muthesius would soon come to oversee – be reorganized in each of the cities?[60] Opinions and recommendations in the local reports varied extremely widely as they came in from regional Prussian authorities (*Regierungspräsidenten*), school directors, and city mayors (sometimes one, sometimes all three) by the required date of March 1902. Immediate action for change appears to have been suspended in anticipation of other steps to reorganize a system that, in 1902, had grown more rather than less complicated during recent decades of unprecedented expansion.[61]

Significantly, it was at exactly this time that Muthesius was spelling out his formulas for the proper approach to applied-arts reform based on his reports from the German Embassy in London. These were based on his comparative study of English and German models in in-depth reports on architecture and design that he had filed in the previous several years, as well as in his more popular polemical tract, *Style-Architecture and Building-Art*. From the confusion that clearly reigned in the Commerce Ministry over the reform of a burgeoning system in dire need of reorganization, it is not unlikely that the Commerce Minister chose to wait for a time with the information he had gathered. He had appointed Muthesius to a post in Berlin in fall 1902 and likely chose to take no significant action to reform the vast array of Commerce Ministry design schools until Muthesius returned from England the following year.

ORGANIZATION OF THE PRUSSIAN COMMERCE MINISTRY'S APPLIED-ARTS SCHOOLS

At the top of an approximate, unofficial hierarchy of Commerce Ministry schools were the *Kunstgewerbeschulen* at Dusseldorf and Frankfurt-am-Main, which offered the highest degree of artistic training, mixed with a wide range of applied-arts and trades courses. The particular mission of this type of school was to develop the drawing, design, and execution abilities of students to a point where they were capable of designing independent projects in their chosen areas of the arts and crafts. These included areas such as furniture design, interior design, illustration and book design, ceramics, decorative painting, and fine metalworking and jewelry design.

School directors answering the Commerce Minister's questionnaire recounted many problems affecting the *Kunstgewerbeschulen*, and indeed the whole system.

Among them were the lack of skilled teachers, the shortage of instruction about techniques and materials, and the need for hands-on construction workshops in which designs could be carried out. The directors called especially for instructional workshops because many crafts workers' operations were smaller than they had ever been in view of recent industrial developments and could therefore no longer give apprentices broad-based instruction. Larger operations in the *Kunstindustrie* meanwhile, rarely took on apprentices for the type of training that used to be widely available.[62]

Among the schools in the top tier, the *Kunstgewerbeschule* at Dusseldorf would assert its preeminence after Peter Behrens assumed the directorship in 1903. Behrens's growing artistic celebrity status, as well as his close association with Muthesius while the latter was still in England in 1902 and early 1903, appeared to ensure that this school would enjoy a greater degree of independence to allow the thirty-four-year-old Behrens to direct the types of curriculum reforms about which he and Muthesius had already spoken in England and about which they had corresponded several times.[63]

Beneath the *Kunstgewerbeschulen* stood the rank of *Kunstgewerbe- und Handwerkerschulen*, nine of which existed with diverse programs in such cities as Krefeld, Magdeburg, Aachen, Cologne, Hannover, and Charlottenburg. These schools had an upper tier in which students were trained in the *Kunstgewerbe* (as at Dusseldorf), usually in a program lasting four years, to conceive and carry out their own independent designs. The *Handwerkerschule* section of these schools deemphasized the capabilities for independent design nurtured in the *Kunstgewerbler* and concentrated instead on teaching "accomplished craftsmen" how to execute previously prepared designs in a full range of crafts and applied-arts fields. The discouragement of design independence resembled that given by Schinkel and Beuth in the early nineteenth century, though the development of tectonic thinking – in which the nature of materials and constructional principles would have a direct influence on the form of objects – would become a goal for crafts training under Muthesius.[64]

Below this level of the hierarchy were three other main types of schools, the *Handwerkerschulen*, *Gewerbeschulen*, and the *Fortbildungsschulen*. The first two taught one or more of the various crafts and trades, featuring night or Sunday instruction for crafts workers already in employment (as did the guild schools, or *Innungsschulen*). They also offered courses to improve the skills, drawing abilities, and sense for quality workmanship among artisans – again discouraging them from working as independent designers. Some schools, like the *Keramische Fachschulen*, or ceramics schools, in cities like Bunzlau or Röhr, or the woodworking school at Warmbrunn (*Holzschnitzschule*), concentrated on a single specific craft. Their programs were almost always connected to a regional tradition dating back to Prussia's old provincial art schools or had emerged as a result of local economic or geographical conditions. Finally, dozens of *Fortbildungsschulen*, or general vocational schools for younger teenagers instructed students in various crafts and trades in larger numbers, serving as "feeder" schools for upper schools.

Depending on local initiative, schools could be reclassified and accorded a higher status based on the addition of new crafts fields, instructional workshops, and larger facilities. Thus, the administrative reports of the State Trades Board included annual summaries of local improvements to schools, accompanied by Commerce Ministry–approved name changes when the schools had attained the next highest level of qualification.

MUTHESIUS'S APPLIED-ARTS REFORMS AS A REFLECTION OF THEODOR MÖLLER'S POLITICS

The Prussian reform process began in earnest when Hermann Muthesius returned from London to assume his Commerce Ministry post in Berlin on July 1, 1903. There he joined a small team of civil servants in reforming Prussian applied-arts schools for service to a modern economy. Prominent among Muthesius's early colleagues were Fritz Dönhoff (to whom he had most often reported from London), Hermann von Seefeld, and Oskar Simon. All three men were experts on various aspects of German and international applied-arts and trades education.[65] The four men collaborated to propagate two major reform strategies for a series of new design tenets. Contained within the Commerce Ministry's changes to the applied-arts education system were the "ladders" Minister Möller had wished to offer less well-off classes of workers and tradespeople as a means of ascending to a higher social class.

Each step that Muthesius and the Commerce Ministry took in the school-reform process brought the schools more into line with the kind of economic thinking that was benefiting German industry at the turn of the twentieth century. Traditional crafts practitioners of the German *Mittelstand*, perceived to be stuck in their habits of producing historical copies and "surrogate" mass-produced goods, now faced direct competition from a state-mandated reform program that understood changes in applied-arts technique and economic change as mutually reinforcing impulses.

The earliest source of the Commerce Ministry's reform ideas is the report Muthesius filed with Commerce Minister Möller in August 1903, after his tour of Prussian applied-arts schools. In it the architect outlined a vision of reformed arts, crafts, and trades schools as the mainstays of a modern, tasteful middle-class production system guided by professionally trained artists and designers. He campaigned for a reorientation of design methods away from surface ornamentation and in the direction of tectonic, constructive thinking. This marked Prussia's shift from the "decorative" to the "tectonic" phase of applied-arts reform (see Chapter 1), undergone earlier in individual instances across Germany, but embraced now in a particularly consequential manner by the Prussian state school system. Raising the quality of education, Muthesius argued, would boost the quality of production for domestic and export markets. He repeatedly promoted the new middle-class and upper-middle-class standard of artistic taste in design that he had advocated in *Style-Architecture and Building-Art*, and emphasized the need to educate students about "tastefulness" so that they, in turn, could work to raise the standards of taste in the general public.

The methods that Muthesius recommended to curtail what he described as the prevailing "evil" in the Prussian school system sought to fulfill students' natural desires for originality by reorganizing courses in individual crafts and trades so that they focused on complete room interiors rather than on the production of individual objects. In this way, Prussian students of furniture, decorative painting, and other departments would realize that their pieces, rather than existing on their own, were conditioned by the spaces they were to occupy and therefore should be designed as parts of an artistic whole. Overdecoration as a source of ornamental distinction would be replaced by the design of practical, integrated works of furniture and decoration. These were to be drawn not simply in elevation or section, but in perspective, and designed according to a harmonious color scheme; they would further be fitted into a "bourgeois" (*bürgerlich*) interior that Muthesius argued need not be filled with cheap, machine-produced products mimicking historical styles, but should be distinguished by simplicity and elegance.[66]

A second tactic recommended in the report was to improve the quality of teachers, whose personal influence in raising students' taste was identified as one of the most important roles instructors could fulfill. Yet because most teachers taught students "to decorate rather than to design," they were in no position themselves to understand that "there can be just as much fineness, yes even genius, in the most simple object as in a highly decorated one."[67] Thus, older teachers who had mastered the reproduction of Rococo ornament, or teachers of sculpture who could model a head or a body, were still far from being capable of "designing tectonically ... which is a completely different field."[68] The aesthetic consideration of print and lettering, too, was absent from the schools. Thus, and even in cases where a successful tectonic drawing had been carried out, its bad lettering made it "just as un-stylish as a soldier with a ripped uniform."[69]

To remedy this situation Muthesius named such respected designers as Kolomann Moser in Vienna, Richard Riemerschmid in Munich, and Peter Behrens in Dusseldorf as potential instructors for badly needed *Lehrerkursen*, or courses for retraining Prussian teachers. He recommended Moser for surface design, Riemerschmid for interior space and furniture design, and Behrens for print and lettering. Aided by his immediate superior, Fritz Dönhoff, Muthesius arranged for Riemerschmid and Behrens (though not Moser) to teach courses in their respective cities of Munich and Dusseldorf in summers 1904, 1905, and 1906. The ministry also retained Alfred Mohrbutter, professor of decorative painting at the School of Applied Arts in Charlottenburg, to teach a four-week class in April 1906, a course that was similar to one taught by Bernhard Pankok in Württemberg. Also in the same year, Moritz Meurer was contacted to teach his drawing techniques to Prussian school instructors in a course at the Royal Museum of Applied Arts in Berlin, though he was unable to come.[70]

One of the Commerce Ministry's most significant reform strategies was to orient schools to their particular regional economies and local crafts industries. Muthesius's revised "Service Regulations for Directors and Instructors," completed on November 21, 1903, drew clear lines of authority from the teachers to school directors to boards of trustees, then to regional Prussian government authorities, and finally to the Commerce Minister. The new rules centralized control while allowing the schools to retain their individual characters. Rather than eliminating departments or replacing them with a standard, systemwide curriculum, the new rules introduced general, far-reaching principles into existing curricula, preparing the way for reforms that would match courses to the economic character of each school's surrounding region.[71]

Muthesius worked for six months on the most far-reaching reform policy to date, the ministry's Instructional Workshops Decree (*Lehrwerkstätten Erlass*) of December 4, 1904, which established trial and instruction workshops in the schools.[72] Instructional workshops were not a new concept: Many European schools had followed the example originally set by London's School of Practical Art where, beginning in 1853, Gottfried Semper led a combination of classroom and workshop training courses.[73] By the opening years of the twentieth century, individual schools in Vienna, Stuttgart, and Breslau had instituted instructional workshops, inspired in part by the example of the British Arts and Crafts movement and in part by the success of professional workshops operating in Dresden, Munich, and Vienna.

To emerge victorious in the "trades competition of the peoples," however, Prussia sought to effect reforms en masse.[74] To this end, Muthesius brought the attention of the Commerce Ministry to the successful efforts of a new wave of English Arts and Crafts–inspired schools, curricula, and instructional workshops led by William Richard Lethaby's Central School of Arts and Crafts and established in 1896 by the Technical Education Board.[75] Six years after reporting favorably on the Central School in the journal *Dekorative Kunst*, Muthesius virtually redefined the modus operandi of the Prussian arts, crafts, and trades schools when he incorporated much of Lethaby's philosophy into his final draft of the Commerce Ministry's Workshops Decree. Its language followed the Central School example closely, sweeping aside at a stroke decades of historicist pedagogical methods, concepts, and long-accepted definitions in the areas of drawing, design, and execution of student work. The following excerpt, which embodies the Central School philosophy while modifying it slightly, explains the new mission of the Prussian workshops as de facto centers of the schools:

> Teaching in instructional workshops will make it possible to bring the essential relationships between material and form to the express consciousness of

the student, and thereby teach him to develop his design more objectively, economically, and purposefully. This involvement with materials will further rid the student of the mistaken notion that producing outwardly pleasing drawings – which take no account of materials and their character – is a goal worth striving for. The workshops will also convey new worthwhile artistic impulses; instead of being based on outwardly transmitted forms, these will be grounded in the insights into the working possibilities of the material that have been gained through the student's own activities. . . . The essence of the *Kunstgewerbeschule* implies that artistic and technical instruction in the workshops go hand in hand.[76]

Under old methods from the 1870s, 1880s, and 1890s, students drew historical ornaments from plaster models, and then depicted them as objects applied to armoires, tables, or as part of interiors executed in various period styles (Figs. 39–40). Students typically produced designs for execution in workshops by craftspeople who had not participated in developing the drawings, but who had to figure out how to construct the object at hand to match the drawn forms. In this system the student remained at the drawing table to execute new designs, rather than studying, as Muthesius had noted in his 1903 schools report, how individual projects would look in space, relate to other objects in appearance, or respond to conditions of particular materials or methods of construction. The old methods, the decree explained, were a symptom of overspecialization that had led to "the one-sided training of arts and crafts draftsmen, who know nothing of materials and who are alienated from the activity of the craftsman."[77]

The Instructional Workshops Decree underscored the need for change with its immediate authorization of sixty-one new workshops for nineteen different schools (Figs. 5–6). Confronted in the workshops with the constructional limitations and possibilities of particular materials, students would learn about the tectonic relationship of form to assembly in hands-on fashion. At the same time, students of such subjects as decorative painting or cabinetry would no longer design works in isolation. Under the direction of a properly trained teaching artist or architect, they would develop individual designs for integration into an overall interior-design scheme. The emphasis was to be on "the bourgeois interior . . . of simple, solid appearance."[78] "Only in this way," Muthesius explained to the Commerce Minister, "can the student appreciate that a dresser or a mural is conditioned by the overall concept of the space, that these are not objects unto themselves, but parts of an artistic whole."[79]

Results from a Dusseldorf architecture class reflect the shift toward harmonious architectural interiors with complementary color schemes. Taught by the architect Max Benirschke, a member of the Vienna Secession who had studied under Josef Hoffmann, these classes brought together the teaching of drawing, applied-arts design, and architecture in the manner the decree prescribed. A perspective drawing for a living room from a Benirschke class in 1904, for example,

39. Wood ornaments from the advanced course for ornamental and figural woodworking, Dusseldorf School of Applied Arts, 1883 (*Bericht über die Kunstgewerbeschule zu Düsseldorf, 1883–1893, Düsseldorf, 1893*)

reflects an emphasis on functionality, reasonably integrated design of individual objects and spaces, and a decided lack of historical ornament (Fig. 41)

Both English and German school-reform documents referred to the workshops as "a supplement and not a replacement to instruction from master teachers." A further goal of both nations was for schools to "orient to industry."[80] Here, however, emerged the major difference between the 1895–96 mission statement

40. Student project for a staircase, wall, and niche from the advanced course for furniture, object, and architectural drawing, Dusseldorf School of Applied Arts, 1886, elevation (*Bericht über die Kunstgewerbeschule zu Düsseldorf, 1883–1893, Düsseldorf, 1893*)

41. Student project for a living room design from the advanced course for architectural design with instructor Max Benirschke, Dusseldorf School of Applied Arts, 1904, perspective (*Dekorative Kunst* 7, 1904)

and the 1904 Prussian decree: By its very nature, arts and crafts education in England remained on a path separate from that of industry. The London County Council expressed the wish to see the crafts made "useful to industry" and so promoted their study, but no specific policy materialized before the First World War. Until the British followed the example of the Deutscher Werkbund by establishing their own Design and Industries Association in 1915, the valuation of tradition, materials, and hand craftsmanship in the English Arts and Crafts remained marks of the search for honesty and ethics in the industrial age.[81]

Although he respected the accomplishments of the British Arts and Crafts movement, Muthesius also criticized the movement for its escapism, its refusal to recognize its own modern industrial potential. Even Lethaby's exploration of new building materials such as concrete in his project for a new Liverpool Cathedral in 1902–03, for instance, had met with little positive English response.[82] Certainly as inherited from John Ruskin, William Morris, and earlier Augustus Pugin, the Arts and Crafts movement's values of anticommercialism, anti-industrialism, and antiurbanism would remain incompatible with the modern industrial economy that the Prussian Commerce Ministry encouraged.

The Prussian decree articulated exactly where the instructional workshops were to stand with respect to industry. For example, schools establishing instructional workshops were advised "in the first place to consider local industries, following those working techniques in which artistic value will rest primarily on the work of the artist."[83] Feeding into local crafts industries while learning from them, workshops in Prussian schools were to execute commissions that sometimes drew on local crafts manufacturers' expertise. This would occur, for example, at the Third German Applied Arts Exhibition in Dresden. The decree supported having workshops led by master craftsmen (*Kunsthandwerker*) as long as these had demonstrated the "artistic capabilities" to teach equally the "artistic and the technical" sides of workshop courses. In cases where this was not so, then teaching was "to be divided between an artist and a technician (*Techniker*), in which the technician works under the direction of the artist."[84] Betraying the Prussian bureaucracy's confidence that traditional deference would support the reformed school hierarchy, Muthesius wrote,

> Doubts concerning any conflicts between artist and technician appear to me unfounded because, while the technician in such cases would be a common master craftsman, from the outset his social standing requires a recognition of the authority of the full teacher who is the institution's retained artist. The division between artist and technician in the described fashion is followed at the arts and crafts school in Vienna.[85]

That Muthesius's Commerce Ministry superiors responded well to his observations on the need for a strict hierarchy in the schools can be seen through marginalia in which Fritz Dönhoff wrote beneath Muthesius's observation: "Have the Chancellery Office record this in ink."[86] Although the Commerce Ministry gave the appearance that it wished to avoid conflict with existing arts, crafts, and trades producers, it could do little to hide the fact that academically trained artists were to remold the arts and crafts through their expertise. By reconfiguring the crafts workshops to place workers under their authority, these artists would exercise a fundamental influence on the artistic and economic value of their products.

The roots of a conflict that led to the formation of the Werkbund in 1907, well-known in design circles from its contemporary label as "The Muthesius Affair" (*Der Fall Muthesius*), can be traced directly to the controversies raised by the government's 1904 Workshops Decree. The decree came at a time when the question of arts and crafts instructional workshops was being hotly debated in Germany. Academics, crafts and trades unions, artists, and political economists all realized the potential for changes that went far beyond school workshops and into the realm of politics, crafts manufacturing, and the building of a "people's economy" (*Volkswirtschaft*), in which all classes and individuals were seen to be contributing to growth and stability on a national scale. For this reason, the workshops decree met with immediate responses from both sides of the debate, that is, from those who saw the decree as the proper fulfillment of a necessary new "applied-arts politics" (*Kunstgewerbepolitik*), on the one hand, to those who saw in it a betrayal of the crafts and the solid, ethical work traditions for which they stood, on the other.[87]

THE STATE TRADES BOARD: PRUSSIA'S
WERKBUND PREDECESSOR

The Prussian policy stood clearly on the side of the promotion of a new *Volkswirtschaft*, as its formation of the State Trades Board on the heels of the December 1904 workshops decree made clear. Given "All Highest" state sanction on January 16, 1905, the State Trades Board's function was to provide comprehensive educational and technical support to Prussia's many branches of the crafts, trades, and small enterprises.[88] The Commerce Minister appointed five experienced officials (four of whom, including Muthesius, were already employed in the Commerce Ministry) as full and permanent members of this new Commerce Ministry subdepartment, or *Nebenamt*. Appointed to oversee their respective areas of expertise – the building trades, the textile industry, the technical and machine-tool trades, lower schools and commercial training schools, and the arts, crafts, and trades schools – the five officials were led by a Commerce Ministry veteran, Heinrich Jakob Neuhaus, for whom Muthesius also designed one of the earliest houses in his private architectural practice.[89]

The State Trades Board quickly drew the attention of members of the Prussian Chamber of Deputies, or *Abgeordnetenhaus*. Representatives from the National Liberals, Conservatives, and Free Conservatives (*Freisinnige Volkspartei*), undoubtedly conscious of gains to be had from appearing to support trades and crafts workers, rushed to support and take credit for the founding of the State Trades Board in the sessions of February 1905. Expressing befuddlement at the chosen name of the agency, many referred colloquially to the new crafts-and-trades-support body as a "Crafts Ministry" (*Handwerksministerium*).[90] But the Free Conservatives vocalized fears that the artisanal class, as the nation's authentic "people's consciousness" (*Volksbewusstsein*), was not going to be represented in the Commerce Ministry's new subministry.[91] Minister Möller, who wrote about the lopsided support given to big industry in comparison to the government's support of crafts workers and other small tradespeople, defended the State Trades Board as an agency that would help equalize the balance of attention paid by the Commerce Ministry to large and small enterprises.[92] Backpedaling from the recommendations of trades associations that they be included in the State Trades Department's "Standing Committee for Education," he claimed the Ministry needed to "keep the organization small and expert" and that not everything that needed to be accomplished could be carried out at once.[93]

A network of twelve official but nonpermanent member experts linked the State Trades Board to other government agencies and regional educational institutions. In an organization whose structure and purpose anticipated the Werkbund, the State Trades Board cast an even wider net across the government and private sectors through its formation of a large, sixty-five-member commission designed to draw on the combined expertise of leaders in politics, business, trades, and education to improve production quality as well as training in all manner of arts, crafts, and trades schools. This part of the department, known as the "General Section of the Standing Committee for Trades' Educational Policy and the Support of Commerce," was composed of the Prussian Minister of Trade; trade association directors and other representatives of the trades (six in all); leaders of private industry; members of the Prussian legislature; directors of arts, crafts, and trades schools; the five permanent members of the State Trades Board; officials in the ministries for finance, education, and public works; and the mayors of such Prussian cities as Danzig, Magdeburg, and Hildesheim. Members of this section held their posts for five years and met on a biennial basis in Berlin.[94]

Muthesius interpreted the State Trades Board as a government tool to reeducate the public about taste and quality in design through exhibits of professional and student works that bore the stamp of the new design thinking. Revising his own school regulations from 1903, he persuaded State Trades Board Director Neuhaus and the Commerce Minister to allow school directors to exhibit student works outside their schools without having to seek the Commerce Minister's permission.[95] The State Trades Board also cooperated with the ministry in the founding of new commercial colleges such as the Berlin Commercial College (*Handelshochschule*), opened in 1906. Hermann Muthesius, the Board's own "arts and crafts architect," was appointed First Chair of Applied Arts.[96]

The State Trades Board represented the government's strongest commitment to date to top-down reforms aimed at integrating the artisanal and trades classes, as part of the fragmented *Mittelstand*, into an economy increasingly dominated by large industries and cartels. The Commerce Ministry would continue to pursue this policy toward the *Mittelstand*, even though by 1905, the politics surrounding big industry's mergers, cartels, and trusts had become sufficiently complicated as to bring about Theodor Möller's dismissal, or forced resignation, as a result of his role in a botched Commerce Ministry folly known as the "Hibernia Affair."[97]

To this day historians disagree about the exact details of the Hibernia Affair, named after the Hibernia Coal Company, but what seems sure is that Möller was the point man for the Prussian government's efforts to secure affordable, uninterrupted, and guaranteed coal supplies for its army and railroad system. These supplies were seen as endangered by the accelerating pace of cartellization in turn-of-the-century coal mining, distillation, and sales, dominated by a few enormous concerns in the Ruhr industrial coal belt. When word leaked out that it was the government's acquisition of Hibernia stocks through agents at the Dresdener Bank that was driving the company's stock values to unheard of levels, Ruhr industrialists August Thyssen, Hugo Stinnes, and others initiated a financial rearguard action that effectively prevented the government from acquiring a majority holding in the stock. Möller was forced to resign after the exposure of the government's covert and failed effort to break the growing concentration of the coal barons' power. On his way out of office, Möller was granted an aristocratic title by Kaiser Wilhelm II in recognition of his state service, making him known thereafter as Theodor von Möller. In the press and in industry circles, however, he was also marked as the man who betrayed fellow industrialists and used the state's power in a dishonorable fashion.[98]

Catastrophic for Möller's career and subsequent reputation, the incident did not appear to alter the Commerce Ministry's arts, crafts, and trades policies when Möller's successor, Clemens von Delbrück, took over as Commerce Minister.[99] However, the affair did reveal something of the unstable, or at least unpredictable nature of the Prussian bureaucracy's relationship to industry in an age of unprecedented vertical and horizontal integration. In the early years of the twentieth century, the government was showing an increased propensity to operate behind the scenes in an effort to shape economic processes that were quickly exceeding the government's capacity to control, let alone respond to, them effectively. The cartellized members of the Central Association of German Industrialists (Centralverband Deutscher Industrieller, or CDI), who had understood Möller as one of their own before he became Commerce Minister (he had, in fact, been a longstanding CDI member), felt stunned and angered by Möller's apparent behind-the-scenes dealings and turncoat behavior on behalf of his Prussian state masters. Commentators ranging from Walther Rathenau, heir to the AEG electricity cartel and company, to Maximilian Harden, insightful journalist and controversial editor of *Die Zukunft* (The Future), condemned Möller's actions, even though it is difficult to imagine that Möller would have gone forward with such a bold and ultimately reckless policy unless he had had the encouragement and support of more highly placed officials.

In any event, the newly disgraced (but ennobled) Möller was gone; but Clemens Delbrück, a powerful and rising bureaucratic insider who had been provincial governor of Prussia's Danzig district, saw to it that the Commerce Ministry's newly created State Trades Department worked toward its goals of "strengthening the tradeworker class" and "educating a workers' middle class" through an ambitious range of activities.[100] Apart from continued school and curriculum reorganization, the State Trades Department disseminated the latest technology and production techniques through regional information offices; organized exhibitions of new machines, tools, and motors suitable for improving the performance of small enterprises and traditional workshops; introduced courses to instruct interested crafts workers and tradesworkers in the uses, costs, and implications of upgrading their shops; and in general took measures to promote the Commerce Ministry's vision of "technical and commercial progress" for the trades classes.[101]

The State Trades Board also reworked Arts and Crafts principles with a further series of top-down, centralized government design reforms. This process began in earnest when Muthesius was asked to help in restructuring Prussian education in the building trades. He and other members of the department devised reforms that quickly brought the education of some 6,000 building-trades students in twenty-five schools into line with the Commerce Ministry's applied-arts curriculum.[102]

Beginning in 1907, the Board increased the duration of certification in the building trades from four semesters to six. It also restricted Prussian training in public and monumental building construction to technical university architecture programs. This freed building trades schools to focus on one priority: the housing sector, and particularly the design and construction of single-family dwellings.[103] New courses of gradually increasing complexity followed a model similar to the instructional workshops at the applied-arts schools. Building trades studies would henceforth unite the study of drawing, design, and construction in mutually reinforcing lessons. Teaching that "form-making depends less on art and ornament than on the fulfillment of function," the schools promoted "architectonic design as a consequence of function, construction, and material."[104] Likewise, the design of individual objects and interiors was to be coordinated from the outset so that students could appreciate the relationships among different scales and tasks in design. Such a reorientation of building-trades instruction spelled out clearly the role that masons, carpenters, and other types of interior finishing crafts- and tradesmen were to play in the state's vision of a modern, market-oriented system of housing production. Not just applied-arts goods, but now houses themselves were the subject of the state's efforts to enhance quality and increase competitiveness in a modern German building culture.

In a sign of growing political discontent with the Commerce Ministry's policies, the first conference of arts and crafts practitioners belonging to the Association for the Economic Interests of the Crafts degenerated into a virtual orgy of diatribes against many aspects of state-sponsored arts and crafts education. These emphasized the new pedagogical methods of the instructional workshops; the granting of "professor" titles to Prussian school instructors who had not necessarily earned them through study; and the privileges the state seemed to be assigning to new design experiments at the expense of historical practices and traditional styles. Alleging that teachers regularly violated the 1903 service regulations by using student labor to execute private commissions, master craftsmen complained that a "new class of arts and craftspeople was emerging, namely the school professors," while the "real" arts and crafts practitioners were in danger of "sinking to the level of common artisans."[105] On this end of the emerging applied-arts hierarchy, there was little willingness to embrace the subordination that Commerce Ministry officials had expected would accompany modern reforms: Where Muthesius and other Prussian civil servants expected deference from craftsmen as a function of their subordinate social standing, they encountered resistance from a group that no longer thought of itself as a deferential, preindustrial "estate," but as a modern, self-conscious class – and one that perceived its very existence as threatened.

Complaints at this March 1906 gathering in Berlin extended to preparations for the important Third German Crafts Exhibition. Scheduled to open two months later in Dresden, this exhibition united artists and architects with manufacturers in a conscious quest to improve the quality of German products by integrating product design with packaging design, artistic ability with commercial acumen. Advancing an era of maturing German mass production and consumerism in which designers would play a significant role, the Dresden exhibition has long been hailed by architectural and design historians as "the First Werkbund Exhibition, in spirit."[106]

Artisans from Dusseldorf's *Semperbund*, a group of conservative crafts practitioners who invoked Semper's name in an effort to fuse their outlook to a venerated national patrimony, complained that their efforts to secure exhibition space at the exhibit had been blocked by the Dusseldorf school director Peter Behrens and his close ally, Mayor Wilhelm Marx. Other members protested that the exhibition seemed as if it was meant "to show the world that the applied arts are at home only and in the main in the schools, so as to convince influential authorities of how important it is, that further resources be provided to them."[107] What was needed was to return the schools to their old form, these members insisted, or at least to rearrange school boards of trustees so that at least one-third of their members consisted of craftsmen recommended by the crafts and trades unions.[108]

When the director of the Altona School of Arts and Crafts tried to explain to the assembly the nature of instructional workshop-based reforms, the meeting hall erupted in a storm of protest. A member of the conference rose and motioned to ban all school directors from speaking, but the chairman of the meeting, a factory director, member of the Prussian Chamber of Deputies as well as the Berlin Chamber of Commerce, deflected this proposal and restored order.[109]

Resentment on the part of traditional crafts practitioners among Prussia's old *Mittelstand* had been building since the reform process began in earnest in 1903, but by 1906 the government and *Mittelstand* crafts and trades interest groups were clearly on a collision course. Both were determined and prepared for a fight, but this fight would not prove fair. On one side, the *Mittelstand*'s associations had only the past and traditional practices to hold onto amid the whirl of innovation taking place in industry, commercial manufacturing, and artist-directed applied-arts production. The progressive, industry-friendly crafts practitioners had the full backing, on the other side, of the Prussian state. It was clear that the Commerce Ministry was willing to sacrifice traditional elements opposed to its economic modernization plan, particularly since this plan was supported by arguments that firmly located the state on the side of "progress," as defined in relation to such modern social and cultural changes as large-scale economic concentration and the rise of a powerful commercial and industrial middle class. Those members of the *Mittelstand* who adopted the Commerce Ministry's reforms in practice, or joined in the work of the reformed schools, faced the prospect of joining a new kind of middle class of producers and consumers that was in the process of shaping a sophisticated commercial economy of copyrights, trademarks, and intellectual property. Those who resisted change saw themselves as guardians of venerated traditional crafts practices and protectors of the right to produce forms viewed as the common property of all.

Yet it was precisely these efforts by conservative crafts associations to cling to traditional practices of crafts production that were, in the eyes of Muthesius and the Commerce Ministry, the cause for Germany's poor performance in design and production, as well as the source of the nation's long-standing weakness in competitive international markets. The changes opposed by conservative practitioners were a necessary component of economic changes driven by technological innovations and competitive pressures. By backing Muthesius's reforms, the Commerce Ministry accepted that a new time was at hand for an altered relationship between the crafts, manufacturing, and economic development. There were still important battles to be fought, however, and it is to one of these – just on the horizon – that the Commerce Ministry gave its full support: to the Third German Crafts Exhibition in Dresden of 1906. The Prussian Culture Ministry would not send its schools to this exhibition, but the conservative crafts would find other reasons to take issue with the Prussian Culture Ministry's applied-arts polices. In control of only two schools of applied arts after the 1884 administrative reorganization, the Culture Ministry's alternative model for Prussian applied-arts reform is nevertheless an important one.

THE CULTURE MINISTRY AND THE APPLIED-ARTS "ARTIST"

Responsible for university education as well as for the academies of fine arts, the Prussian Ministry of Culture was left, after 1884, with jurisdiction over only two schools of applied arts: the Berlin School of Applied Arts (associated with the Royal Museum of Applied Arts) and the Breslau School of Art and Applied Arts in Silesia. Conscious of a widening gap between the arts academy and applied-arts education – the Academy of Fine Arts had dissolved its affiliation with the applied arts in the 1880s – the ministry steered its schools in Berlin and Breslau toward an "academy" model. The Culture Ministry nevertheless gave its applied-arts schools considerable latitude in the way they chose to promote the artistic aspects of applied-arts education. In the hopes of raising both the status of applied artists and the quality of their works, the Culture Ministry imposed stricter standards of admission and offered highly individualized training of "applied-arts artists." These measures were intended to bridge the gap between the fine arts and the applied arts.

As was the case at the Commerce Ministry, the Culture Ministry depended for its reforms on the appointment of teachers and school directors who were pursuing new directions in the applied arts. Culture Ministry officials Wilhelm von Bode, director of Berlin's museums, the pedagogue and reformer Ludwig Pallat, and Peter Jessen, director of the Arts Library in Berlin, collaborated in their search for new directors. Von Bode favored attracting leading artists from the progressive applied-arts movement that had been gaining in strength since the late 1890s. Pallat, meanwhile, was a strong supporter of the Art Education movement's effort to promote all forms of art among the German public; he helped organize national conferences on art education in Dresden in 1901, Weimar in 1903, and Hamburg in 1905.[110] The ministry appointed the architect Hans Poelzig to head the Breslau school in 1903 and the artist Bruno Paul to head the Berlin school in 1907. The new directors received considerable support in developing their individual "artists" of the applied arts.

At the Berlin School of Applied Arts, for example, a long tradition dating back to the teachings of Carl Boetticher and Moritz Meurer emphasized the decorative ornamentation of an object as an interpretive extension of its artistic essence, or "core form." Beginning in 1907, Bruno Paul changed this system with the introduction of crafts workshops in which applied-arts students – who were admitted only if they had already received a complete crafts education in the equivalent of one of the Commerce Ministry's schools – could see their designs executed for them by craftsmen. To Paul, ornament no longer furnished a decorative "vocabulary" of forms that communicated an underlying "essence" of the object it decorated. Rather, to Paul and his faculty, ornaments were to be a decorative illustration of the ways in which artists had mastered materials, forms, and the connection between a design and its execution.[111] The separation of the "artist" working in his studio from the "craftsman" in his workshop was a necessary one in Paul's philosophy. Differing from the outlook of the Commerce Ministry's reformed schools, where applied-arts students learned to execute their works in instructional workshops, Paul's school philosophy elevated applied-arts artists to a status above the crafts they had mastered on their way to being admitted to the Berlin School of Applied Arts.

Like Muthesius, Paul viewed the introduction of many more workshops into his school as a practical necessity. However, these workshops were not "instructional" in nature, as they were at Commerce Ministry schools. Rather, the artists-in-training were expected to design their works with careful attention from the outset to materials, constructional principles, and the implications of both of these for form. Craftsmen would execute these works in the workshops, or, if students wished, they could execute the projects themselves on their own time. It was important to Paul that his applied-arts students' execution of their designs not be a requisite part of individual applied-arts courses. Rather, his goal was to train his "artists" in such a way that their artistic conception included a sufficient degree of mastery of materials, constructional principles, and ornamentation that they did not need to work through design problems in the workshops, but could furnish fabrication-ready designs of high quality to the workshops.[112] Paul's methods, and indeed the traditions he promoted in his instruction and in professional works, resembled the Prussian classicism developed by Schinkel in the early nineteenth century. This fact was not lost on critics who admired the quality of Paul's designs for the Werkbund exhibition of 1914 in Cologne.[113]

Poelzig, too, thrived in an environment supported by the Culture Ministry's pro-academy stance. He had taught at the School of Art and Applied Arts in Breslau since 1900. For this reason, following his appointment to the directorship in 1903, he did not require the six-month preparation period that Behrens and Paul requested at their respective schools in Dusseldorf and Berlin. As Paul would do in Berlin, Poelzig raised admission requirements so that a crafts education became a prerequisite for entering his school. Although Poelzig eliminated introductory courses in the crafts, he placed each entering student in a workshop environment from his or her first term – a significant difference from Paul's approach. One-on-one conferences between students and faculty ensured highly individualized training in the development of each student's particular talents.[114]

Thanks to the support of Bode, Pallat, and Jessen, Poelzig was able to develop an early form of the "unified arts school" (*Einheitskunstschule*): a school model promoted by the Art Education movement activist Alfred Lichtwark of Hamburg. The unified arts school was any school that managed to bring together the study of fine arts and applied arts under the banner of architecture. Bruno Paul would achieve this goal at his Berlin school only in 1924; Walter Gropius would introduce a version at his Bauhaus in 1919.[115] Poelzig, on the other hand, launched his version of the "unified arts school" in 1903. Within a year he managed to design an exhibition house for the Breslau Applied Arts Association's summer exhibition of 1904 (Figs. 42–43; also Fig. 7). Where new applied-arts workshops served as the bridge between crafts theory and practice, commissions at the scale of an actual building united fine arts, applied arts, and architecture students in the completion of the model house and pavilion for Breslau applied-arts products.

The model Silesian house, designed by Poelzig in a modified Silesian farmhouse style, was Poelzig's first free-standing building and the first building in any German state to be completed through the collective efforts of an applied-arts school. Poelzig conceived the house "as a generous home for a fairly wealthy family on the outskirts of a large city."[116] Exhibition literature quoted Muthesius's writings at length, pointing out that the exhibition's goal was to teach the inhabitants of the Silesian Province about the possibilities for designing *sachlich*, affordable, contemporary houses for the bourgeoisie and *Mittelstand*.[117] The authors emphasized Poelzig's conscious effort to keep Silesia's rural traditions in mind while fulfilling the needs of the modern bourgeois family. To the Breslau director of the Museum of Applied Arts and Antiquities, Karl Masner, this meant shunning all ornamental inclinations that would make the house into "the degenerate offspring of the Italianate palace or the many-towered German town hall."[118] Poelzig's solution was to design a typical Northern European timber-framed structure with stuccoed exterior and soaring, peaked roof whose upswept forms resembled those found in Silesian farmhouses. Integrating living rooms and servant spaces around opposite sides of a two-story central square hall, the architect created a zone in which servants could circulate freely without passing through any of the main living areas of the house. Poelzig's model house effectively translated Muthesius's agenda for the development of contemporary yet tradition-conscious German houses into an architectural language appealing to residents of Breslau and the surrounding area. Masner called the house a "program for battle" (*Kampfprogramm*) on behalf of regional, *sachlich* design that turned its back on stylistic eclecticism and application of ornament for ornament's sake.[119] Poelzig's school would go on to complete other architectural projects throughout the Silesian province, most notably an addition to the town hall of Löwenburg, in 1905. Poelzig's students did not assist in their school director's many large commissions for industry, but these projects did reflect the same individualistic will that Poelzig taught in his courses – the will to design each building as a solution to a particular building problem.[120]

As a result of its reforms, the Culture Ministry, too, suffered its share of complaints from crafts associations and individual crafts practitioners. Once again, practitioners complained that state support for schools carrying out private commissions posed a threat to the livelihoods of those working in more traditional modes. In a few rare instances, cases of complaint were decided against the

42. Hans Poelzig, model single-family house at the Breslau Applied Arts Association Exhibition, 1904, general view (demolished) (Karl Masner, *Das Einfamilienhaus des Kunstgewerbevereins*, Berlin, 1905)

Breslau School of Art and Applied Arts. For example, the executive committee of the Breslau sculptors guild was able to demonstrate that Poelzig had hired three workers from outside his school to assist on a commission for an addition to the Löwenberg town hall. However, Poelzig's school had listed these workers as students and paid them a student per diem rather than the customary wage. Local Prussian state authorities treated the complaint as a minor problem at best; they asked Poelzig to correct this "misunderstanding" and in the end cited four proven complaints of unfair competition that occurred over several years as "small" and "solely in the interest of instruction."[121]

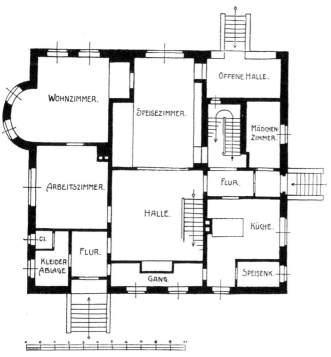

43. Hans Poelzig, model single-family house at the Breslau Applied Arts Association Exhibition, plan (Karl Masner, *Das Einfamilienhaus des Kunstgewerbevereins*, Berlin, 1905)

Lengthy reports and requests from the Association for the Economic Interests of the Crafts met with a series of dismissive responses from Bruno Paul, Peter Jessen, and Wilhelm von Bode. Paul reported that he was "too piled up with work" to answer the association's request for a detailed, publishable reply to a list of reforms being requested by the association for applied-arts school instruction.[122] Peter Jessen sarcastically cited verbatim portions of proceedings of the "so-called Congress of Applied-Arts Practitioners" as a way to illustrate the "intellectual heights" reached by speakers who complained loudly of the "slaughter" that the state was overseeing in the case of the traditional crafts.[123] Finally, Wilhelm von Bode wrote representing the view of the "general administration" when he observed that although the Berlin School of Applied Arts might "represent a thorn in the eye of the Association for the Economic Interests of the Crafts," this did not diminish the importance of the school's activities. For him, any "cooperation (*Entgegenkommen*) with the Association and its followers remained out of the question."[124] None of the authorities' rejections prevented the association from submitting detailed, often quite shrill complaints about the "illegitimacy" of both the ministerial school reforms and the instructional workshops, which they insisted were no substitute for proper apprenticeships in traditional techniques that emphasized the historical styles.[125]

Available evidence also suggests the existence of lingering competition between the Ministry of Culture and the Ministry of Commerce over applied-
arts education.[126] This manifested itself most clearly in the way that Commerce
Ministry schools took pains to advance themselves and obtain the next highest
state rank and title for their school. This they achieved through an increase in
offerings, size, budget, or number and variety of school workshops. Hermann
Muthesius himself journeyed to Breslau in 1911 to approve expansion plans
for the Commerce Ministry's Breslau School of Handcrafts (*Handwerkerschule*) –
and to negotiate with Hans Poelzig over curricular changes that this expansion and name change would necessitate. Once the city and state authorities had
agreed on the construction of a new building to bring the different branches
of the crafts from their scattered, rented quarters throughout the city under
one roof, the Commerce Ministry approved the city's application to change the
school's name to the Breslau Crafts and Applied Arts School (*Handwerker- und
Kunstgewerbeschule*). This, however, called for a more precise division of responsibilities with Poelzig's school, an arrangement involving both gains and losses.
Poelzig's school had to give up its woodworking workshop and dedicate itself to
providing more fine-arts training. For this his school received the elevated name
of "Academy of Art and Applied Arts."[127] Yet as the historian Hartmut Frank has
shown, certain expansionist tendencies on the part of Muthesius, the Commerce
Ministry, and its schools forced Poelzig to alter the configuration of his school
in ways he had not planned and certainly did not appreciate.[128] This, coupled
with the different philosophies of training that existed at Poelzig's school and the
Commerce Ministry's schools, may help explain why Poelzig was sympathetic
to the camp of so-called artistic "individualists" who battled Muthesius at the
Werkbund Congress of 1914; it may also account for Poelzig's characterization
of the Werkbund, from the time of its inception, as a kind of "monster."[129]

In any event, and by early 1906, the process of reform at the Prussian state
level – and in the Commerce Ministry's dozens of schools and in the State Trades
Board in particular – was provoking great tension with conservative applied-arts
associations. Saxony's energetic pursuit of a national forum at which to display the
breadth of changes taking place in Germany's applied-arts fields brought these
conflicts to a boil. Its Third German Applied Arts Exhibit in summer 1906 would
provide the national ingredients needed to unite reformers into a new, national
applied-arts association, the Deutscher Werkbund.

≈ CHAPTER FOUR

THE CONVERGENCE OF STATE AND PRIVATE REFORM IMPULSES IN THE DEUTSCHER WERKBUND ⟫

DRESDEN 1906: BEGINNINGS OF ARTISTIC CARTELLIZATION?

The Third German Applied-Arts Exhibition of 1906 assembled various constellations of reformers from Germany's different states for the first time. Held between May 12 and October 31, 1906, the exhibition offered a systematic overview of the German applied arts, which were divided into three distinct sections: *Kunst* (fine arts, which were exhibited in fully designed interiors, representing *Raumkunst*), *Kunsthandwerk* (handmade crafts), and *Kunstindustrie* (crafts industry). The cooperation of like-minded architects, artists, and craftsmen, coupled with the overtly economic agenda of applied-arts producers and the state, is precisely what made the Dresden exhibition of 1906 tantamount to the "First Werkbund Exhibition" for subsequent historians; all the basic ingredients, from personalities to exhibiting philosophy, were there for the organization that would form one year later.[1] As a national exhibition, it was meant as an expression of unity. But not atypically, the sense of competition among the states, and even among individual cities within the states, was palpable.[2] "A serious contest (*Wettstreit*) is to be expected among the German peoples (*Stämmen*)," wrote Prussian State Trades Board Director Heinrich Neuhaus to Commerce Minister Möller in his request for official support for Prussia's role in the undertaking. "Prussia's participation," he added, was "critical to the exhibition's effort to provide an unbiased overview of Germany's applied-arts achievements."[3]

Unlike the two prior national applied-arts exhibitions of 1876 and 1888 hosted by Munich, which had encouraged feelings of national unity and emphasized Renaissance, Baroque, and other examples of "Our Forefathers Works" (*Unsere Väter Werke*), the Dresden exhibition would feature highly exclusive exhibits aimed at stimulating a particular vision of an emerging "artists' economy" in the applied arts.[4] At the very least, the 1906 exhibition would prove the extent to which artist-oriented applied-arts enterprises, state applied-arts education policies and economic development priorities, and new arrangements emphasizing large-scale applied-arts production were acquiring national momentum.

Government authorities in Dresden and Saxony, as hosts to the exhibition, saw themselves as both beneficiaries and supporters of the promising developments in the growing applied-arts economy. No German city had pursued large-scale arts exhibitions with national and international dimensions with an intensity equal to that of Dresden in recent years: The city had devoted a total of six exhibitions to new developments in the arts between 1897 and 1904. Official Saxon support for progressive applied artists was undeniably on the upswing since the turn of the century – the opposite of the situation observed in Bavaria, where such support was flagging.[5] In fact, the special exhibition of artist-designed interiors by Karl Schmidt's Dresden Workshops for Handcrafted Art was still garnering favorable reviews in early 1904 when the Dresden Applied-Arts Association learned that its counterpart in Munich, after more than a year of deliberations, had shelved plans to organize a Third German Applied Arts Exhibition in the Bavarian capital. Acting swiftly, leaders of the applied-arts reform movement in Saxony scored what they saw as a significant victory for their capital city and region when they persuaded city and state authorities, along with the National Organization of German Applied-Arts Associations (*Verein Deutscher Kunstgewerbevereine*), to accept Dresden as the site of the exhibition.[6] The ready cooperation of the National Organization of German Applied-Arts Associations, with Muthesius as its president, ensured that a committee of like-minded organizers from across the nation would be assembled to plan the event.

The key commitments from local and state government as well as from applied-arts associations were in place by the end of March. By mid-1904, a program crafted by the Dresden committee made clear that the Third German Applied-Arts Exhibition sought to place design and production in the applied arts on a completely new footing, with great implications for this sector of the economy. Represented as a "Festive Procession of German Applied Arts" (*Festzug des deutschen Kunstgewerbes*), as the exhibition slogan proclaimed, the exhibition also displayed a serious polemical purpose that operated at a number of conceptual levels.

The exhibit organizers sought to secure for Germany's applied-arts practitioners a new system and standard of cooperation between independent artists, crafts and light industry manufacturers, and state applied-arts schools. All of these different elements, from sponsoring manufacturers to state applied-arts students, were given ample opportunity to display their products and wherewithal within ten carefully organized, conceptually elaborate exhibitions sections. At different times and in accordance with particular purposes, the directorate displayed wares by product type, region, or production method. The overarching concept for exhibitors, however, was the production of what the directorate called *Raumkunst*, the art of the room, or the art of interior space conceived and furnished as an architectonic whole. In this the directorate was indebted to the initiative Karl Schmidt's firm had shown at his 1903 exhibition in displaying not individual pieces designed by artists, but rather carefully arranged, fully outfitted rooms that integrated artist-designed furniture and other applied-arts works in an attractive, harmonious way. Schmidt was certainly not the only one conceiving of interiors as a complete whole around 1900: The *Gesamtkunstwerk* had been the approach of choice among individual *Jugendstil* designers, and orientation to complete, harmonious interiors was also at the heart of the Prussian Commerce Ministry's school reforms. However, Schmidt was the first German entrepreneur to direct his entire enterprise toward the employment of artists, craftsmen, and laborers for the purpose of creating and marketing such interiors. Instead of emphasizing the artist's individualistic vision, Schmidt's furniture and rooms strove to promote a simpler, *sachlich* Germanness, a furniture for the bourgeoisie and *Mittelstand* rather than for the connoisseur of art.

The initiative for the national exhibition came from leading figures within the Dresden *Kunstgewerbeverein*. A small group comprised of the architect Fritz Schumacher and the art historian Cornelius Gurlitt, both of the Dresden Technische Hochschule; William Lossow, an architect who directed the Dresden School of Applied Arts; the applied artist Karl Gross; and the Saxon government councillor Bernhard Stadler originated the concept for the exhibition. Dresden's mayor, a former Saxon state finance official named Gustav Otto Beutler, was also an important early supporter. Beutler had been impressed with the success of Karl Schmidt's Dresden Workshops for Applied Arts and particularly its 1903 exhibition of furniture designed by such luminaries as Charles Rennie Mackintosh, M. H. Baillie Scott, Joseph Maria Olbrich, Peter Behrens, and Richard Riemerschmid. Recognizing the cultural and economic significance of such exhibitions for the city, he immediately backed the Dresden Applied Arts Association's efforts to mount an applied-arts exhibition of national importance.[7]

Fritz Schumacher emerged from the group as one of the leaders of efforts to update exhibition practices to suit the aims of applied-arts reformers. As an influential Dresden architect and city planner who served as the celebrated city architect of Hamburg between 1909 and 1933, Schumacher exhibited a flair for creative organizational thinking.[8] He delivered a statement of organizing principles to the forty-five members of the Third German Applied Arts Exhibition's directorate at its first meeting in the Saxon capital on February 27, 1905. Unveiling the master plan of the exhibition palace and grounds, Schumacher explained that the exhibition was to be limited to commissioned works (Fig. 44). Further, a large architecture (*Raumkunst*) section of some 200 rooms and interiors, to be overseen by Schumacher himself, would admit only individual artists and architects as "authors" of exhibits, excluding the applied-arts manufacturers who had been listed as primary exhibitors in past exhibitions.[9] With these measures

Schumacher followed the local example set by the Dresden craftsman and entrepreneur Karl Schmidt, who since 1898 had begun a new practice of listing artists' names first and manufacturers second; Schmidt also paid artists a percentage of profits based on the number of their pieces sold by his firm, the Dresden Workshops for Applied Art.[10] Schumacher and the Dresden exhibition directorate also followed an international example, namely that of German applied artists exhibiting at the St. Louis International Exhibition of 1904. Rather than exhibiting highly personal, short-lived showpieces commissioned solely for exhibition purposes – as had still been largely the case during Turin's First Exhibition of Modern Decorative Arts of 1902 – German exhibitors showed commissioned projects that would be installed or delivered for their patrons' use after the close of the exhibition.[11]

The practical, integrated interior designs shown in St. Louis had prompted a group of German government reporters visiting the exhibition, among them Hermann Muthesius, to praise the St. Louis exhibition as an important breakthrough for German applied artists. At long last, Muthesius observed, German manufacturers and applied artists had overcome the clichéd reputation of exhibiting "cheap and bad" works and were now earning deserved international praise.[12] Such positive reviews, however, existed in abrupt contrast to the official government censorship of the fine-arts portion of the exhibition. Triggered by angry opposition from Emperor Wilhelm II – who had always disdained "foreign" influences in general and Secessionist painting in particular – government ministries blocked Secessionist painters from adding their works to those of more conventional artists in St. Louis's German pavilion.[13] For applied artists, however, the St. Louis exhibition marked the beginning of period of consolidation among adherents to the new movement.

The Dresden exhibition also coincided with a new wave of German government initiatives as well as consolidation in private industry. Cartellization, for example – the formation of cooperative vertical and horizontal arrangements of industries to control supply, production, and price – was particularly prevalent in the raw materials sectors of heavy industry. It extended as well to the electrical and chemical industries, where the formation of a cooperative association (*Interessengemeinschaft*) in 1906 by the three giants of the chemical industry – BASF, Bayer, and AGFA – was a typical development.[14] In November of the same year, dozens of companies combined to found a Standing Commission on Exhibitions for German Industry (*Ständige Ausstellungskommission für die Deutsche Industrie*), which aimed to coordinate exhibitions policies for greater efficiency and impact[15]; January 1907 saw both the opening of a new Commercial College (*Handelshochschule*) in Berlin[16] and the passing of new laws strengthening artistic copyrights.[17] Indeed, specialization and concentration were the watchwords of the Dresden exhibition as well. By defining its criteria for the 1906 exhibition in terms of the artist's relationship to producers and the manufacturing economy, exhibition organizers were able to limit participation sharply – a sign of their

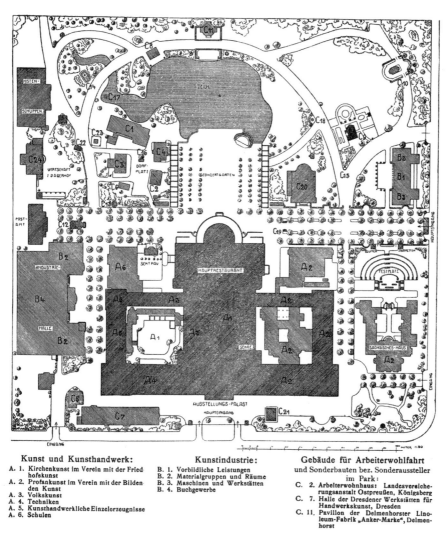

Kunst und Kunsthandwerk:
A. 1. Kirchenkunst im Verein mit der Friedhofskunst
A. 2. Profankunst im Verein mit der Bildenden Kunst
A. 3. Volkskunst
A. 4. Techniken
A. 5. Kunsthandwerkliche Einzelzeugnisse
A. 6. Schulen

Kunstindustrie:
B. 1. Vorbildliche Leistungen
B. 2. Materialgruppen und Räume
B. 3. Maschinen und Werkstätten
B. 4. Buchgewerbe

Gebäude für Arbeiterwohlfahrt
und Sonderbauten bez. Sonderaussteller
im Park:
C. 2. Arbeiterwohnhaus: Landesversicherungsanstalt Ostpreußen, Königsberg
C. 7. Halle der Dresdener Werkstätten für Handwerkskunst, Dresden
C. 11. Pavillon der Delmenhorster Linoleum-Fabrik „Anker-Marke", Delmenhorst

44. Fritz Schumacher, Third German Applied Arts Exhibition in Dresden, 1906, site plan (*Das Deutsche Kunstgewerbe 1906: III. Deutsche Kunstgewerbeausstellung Dresden 1906*, Munich, 1906)

increased awareness of the importance of new forms of organization for ensuring the success of the applied-arts sector. Exhibition planners, among them influential members of the state bureaucracy, excluded the *Fachverband* and *Semperbund* crafts traditionalists, dismissing them implicitly in their preliminary program by clearly separating their "uncomprehending imitation" from "what the creative men of our time really want."[18]

The Werkbund, too, as the most famous outgrowth of the Dresden exhibition, is best understood in the context of this wave of consolidation. Already there were many signs of coordination of the applied arts at the regional level and within individual states, which reflected in turn the character of private efforts at organization as well as governmental initiatives of various kinds. In Dresden, the practical work of Avenarius's Dürerbund had supported more coordinated activity on the part of applied artists, government authorities, citizens, and businesses since 1902.[19] In Munich one year later, an Alliance for Applied Art (*Vereinigung für angewandte Kunst*) – which also went by the name of the Munich Federation (*Münchener Bund*) – worked privately through publicity efforts and the organization of an exhibition in 1905 intended to place the applied and fine arts on an equal footing.[20] Württemberg's Society for the Friends of Art, too, had been creating a growing network of progressive artists, applied artists, producers, and other supporters in Baden and Württemberg since its founding in 1905. Although this group concentrated mainly on the fine arts, it was just one link in a chain of royal and private initiatives throughout the kingdom that brought Württemberg's applied artists and manufacturers closer together. And for similar purposes, though through decidedly less liberal means, Prussia's State Trades Board – Theodor Möller's "collegial authority" for the promotion of Prussia's arts, crafts, and trades – had initiated a standing committee of experts from local and state government, the crafts, industry, and applied-arts schools for the express purpose of promoting greater cooperation in pursuit of increasing the quality and competitiveness of German products.

Until 1906, members of these organizations were operating separately. Yet the circles of membership were expanding and overlapping with increasing frequency. It is hardly a coincidence that regional leaders from each of these organizations participated in the planning and execution of the Dresden exhibition of 1906: The seventeen exhibition "commissars," comprising a virtual "who's who" of applied-arts leaders from across Germany, coordinated their particular cities, regions, and organizations in Germany's first nationwide educational and propaganda effort in the applied arts to address explicitly the changing conditions of design and production in an industrial economy.[21] The exhibition's function as a catalyst was intentional, placing an explicitly bourgeois culture of artistic and economic organization onto a national stage.

THE EXHIBITION AS DIDACTIC PROGRAM

Virtually every planning and organizational decision taken in preparing the Third German Applied-Arts Exhibition supported a didactic purpose. The Dresden planners organized displays of hand-crafted works (*Kunsthandwerk*) separately from works produced with the assistance of machines (*Kunstindustrie*), where machines served at least partially as determinants of form. Freely acknowledging that there were considerable areas of overlap between these two areas of production, the exhibition's lead organizer, Fritz Schumacher, nonetheless considered the 1906 exhibition's educational mission in part to be the spelling out of potential advantages of machine production to producers and the public alike.[22] Deeming geographical classification as most appropriate for some areas of the

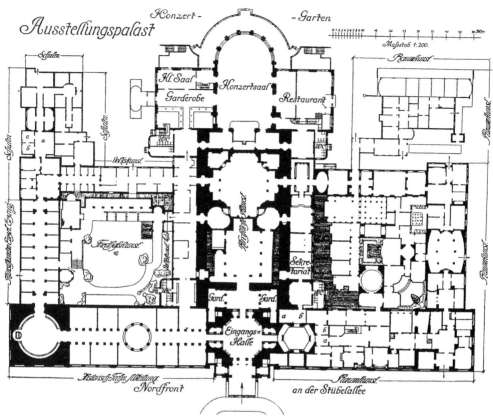

45. Exhibition palace, Third German Applied Arts Exhibition in Dresden, plan (*Das Deutsche Kunstgewerbe 1906: III. Deutsche Kunstgewerbeausstellung Dresden 1906*, Munich, 1906)

exhibition, elsewhere, as in the larger of two halls for *Kunstindustrie*, exhibition organizers arranged products according to production-oriented "material groups." The material groups targeted manufacturers so as to suit better "the world market interests of industry," as the official program of the exhibition noted.[23]

Social class provided an especially prominent organizational category for the exhibition. This was particularly true in the large section of more than 200 rooms in the exhibition palace devoted to architectonic arts (*Raumkunst*), the "natural focal point" of the exhibition, where unified displays of domestic interiors, entire houses, religious art, and landscape art were organized on the basis of class (Fig. 45). At the top of the hierarchy, Schumacher explained, the "individualistically formed space" of "luxury art" (*Luxuskunst*) appealed to the "art lover," typically a wealthy patron. Henry van de Velde's new entrance hall for the Weimar Museum of Applied Arts (Fig. 46) and Alfred Grenander's reception room were two such pieces. Beyond these rooms for privileged connoisseurs, other palace interiors – as well as a separate *Kunstindustrie* building dedicated entirely to Karl Schmidt's Dresden Workshops – explicitly targeted a bourgeois (*bürgerlich*)

46. Henry van de Velde, entrance hall for the Weimar Museum of Applied Arts, Third German Applied Arts Exhibition in Dresden, 1906, general view (*Das Deutsche Kunstgewerbe 1906: III. Deutsche Kunstgewerbeausstellung Dresden 1906*, Munich, 1906)

clientele. These "artistic spaces," Schumacher explained, "seek to be not at all individualistic, but quite the opposite, and are focused on fulfilling the average requirements of the *Bürger* in as typical a manner as possible."[24] Schumacher's own design for a living room in natural cherry wood typified this class of *Raumkunst* designs.

The prominent presence at the 1906 exhibition of Karl Schmidt's growing enterprise echoed his appearances at recent Dresden exhibitions in 1899, 1901, and 1903–04 and also exemplified an orientation toward the middle class. On one side of Schmidt's hall for *Kunstindustrie*, the entrepreneur recreated the assembly line of his furniture factory to illustrate plainly the unfamiliar processes of machine production; next door he displayed two completely furnished apartments as well as sixteen other examples of room interiors to present "tasteful" examples of middle-class furniture before the public. Highlighted in Schmidt's exhibits were the simple, rational designs of furniture that made efficient use of his machines. Each room featured ensembles designed by Richard Riemerschmid in close technical cooperation with Schmidt: The goal, as the official Dresden 1906 *Exhibition News* wrote, was to perfect a process for the manufacturing of "furniture that is technically as well as artistically completely superior

47. Richard Riemerschmid, view of dining room displaying "Machined Furniture," Third German Applied Arts Exhibition in Dresden, 1906 (*Das Deutsche Kunstgewerbe 1906: III. Deutsche Kunstgewerbeausstellung Dresden 1906*, Munich, 1906)

(*durchaus vorzüglich*), produced up to ninety percent by machine and therefore comparatively affordable, so that those of lesser means can afford to buy these items" (Fig. 47).[25] Schmidt and Riemerschmid had cooperated to develop "a furniture style out of the spirit of the machine," which quickly led to the name, "machined furniture" (*Maschinenmöbel*).[26]

Workers and, as Schumacher put it, those deemed to be "one economic step lower" than the middle classes were given an exhibit all their own, spatially segregated from exhibits for connoisseurs and the bourgeoisie in the palace's *Raumkunst* section.[27] A quaint village square of rural, petty-bourgeois houses provided the setting for a highly idealized vision of a Wilhelmine workers' environment. Architects like August Grothe and the young Max Taut produced simple workers' cottages set in functional gardens, and outfitted with lace curtains, patterned wainscoting, and copies of paintings by old masters on the walls (Figs. 48–49; also Item "C2" in Fig. 44).[28] The half-timbered dwellings with their hipped and half-hipped roofs depicted idyllic workers' homes that were the opposite of those lived in by the majority of German workers in overcrowded cities. In Berlin, for example, most workers lived in overcrowded, stifling apartments in "rental barracks," or *Mietskasernen*. The cottages, by contrast, could have been the creations of a paternalist large-scale industrialist such as the giant Krupp steelworks

48. Max Taut, workers' dwelling exhibited at the Third German Applied Arts Exhibition in Dresden, 1906, general view (*Das Deutsche Kunstgewerbe 1906: III. Deutsche Kunstgewerbeausstellung Dresden 1906*, Munich, 1906)

complex in Essen, or a prescription from Avenarius and the Dürerbund, or even a realization of the Prussian State Trades Board's stated aim at its inception in 1905 to "cultivate a middle class of crafts and trades workers."[29] Workers who successfully integrated themselves into Germany's modernizing production system, this portion of the exhibit seemed to say, could hope to rise on the "ladders" of Möller's National Liberal self-help program to live in a comfortable, if miniaturized bourgeois world.

Where planners of the Third German Applied-Arts Exhibition used conceptions of social class to organize the west wing of the exhibition palace and other portions of the exhibition devoted to *Raumkunst*, they organized the applied-arts sections in the palace's east wing along temporal lines. Implicit in this strategy was the notion of progress, suggested both in the language of the exhibition program and the spatial arrangements of the exhibition palace's east wing (Fig. 50). Located in the southeast wing of the palace, the schools were joined by exhibits of regional folk art on one side and individual objects from arts, crafts, and trades professionals on the other. An outdoor courtyard exhibit of gravestones for a churchyard cemetery was nearby, as was a "historical-technical" exhibit situated next to the palace's main entrance.

The directorate's placement of the schools in relation to the adjacent exhibits served two specific purposes: first, to demarcate the arts, crafts, and trades schools as the culmination of a historical development, and second, to represent them as the transmitters of modern design principles to a new generation of German applied-arts designers. Since the historical-technical section was next to the palace's main entrance, most visitors entering the palace encountered this part of the exhibit first. Its purpose was to illustrate works from different peoples and times in order to show the ways that "artistic methods developed from working with the essence of a given material." From this process, the program continued, "there arose inner laws that were not subject to the changes of historical styles."[30] In other words, the exhibit sought to convey the impression that artistic taste was consistently achievable through a correct understanding of the working of materials.

The folk-art exhibit, by contrast, presented visitors with the products of a "naive crafts activity" that deliberately stressed the "character of regionally accumulated traditions" over "the character of specific objects." Adjoining the schools exhibit from the other side were recent individual works of arts, crafts, and trades. These

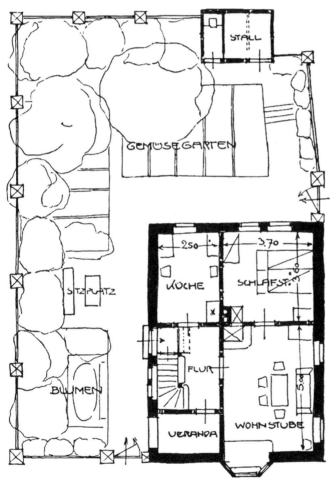

49. Max Taut, workers' dwelling exhibited at the Third German Applied Arts Exhibition in Dresden, 1906, plan and site plan (*Das Deutsche Kunstgewerbe 1906: III. Deutsche Kunstgewerbeausstellung Dresden 1906*, Munich, 1906)

products were displayed in a geographical survey of German regions in a manner that was supposed to depict "artistically arranged shops."[31]

These two exhibits provided the context in which visitors encountered the schools section, which was sandwiched between the "naive" folk arts on one side and the shoplike displays of modern products on the other. The plan layout, which juxtaposed old styles with new, emphasized the schools as carriers of the new movement. As the program put it, the schools exhibit was meant to "provide an overview of the extent to which the arts and crafts schools are propagating the products and traditions resulting from the *unmediated* working of materials" (emphasis original).[32] The folk-art display, although it honored German folk traditions, served simultaneously as a negative foil for the materials- and process-oriented modern product designs of the new movement. Besides showing the progress of the design schools, the schools exhibit was intended to awaken the public to the possibilities inherent in modern arts and crafts education.[33]

German state arts, crafts, and trades schools occupied approximately one-tenth of the palace's 10,382-square-meter exhibition area.[34] Seventeen Prussian *Kunstgewerbe- und Handwerkerschulen* were joined by smaller school delegations from Saxony, Württemberg, and Baden. Schools exhibiting from these three states shared a space that together roughly equalled that of the Prussian section (Fig. 50). After Prussia, the host state of Saxony had the largest section with some eleven rooms, though this state's exhibit surveyed the entire range of students and school types from the grammar schools to applied-arts schools and amateur applied-arts associations. Saxony was followed in size by Baden and Württemberg, which had one room each.[35] As Schumacher put it, the schools section would enable "everyone to see for himself the extent to which the life brought forth by the exhibition would be carried forward in seed form by the German state institutions."[36]

The State Trades Board's schools exhibit and catalog publicized what Prussian students were learning about modern materials and construction principles, even as it concretized the state's rejection of applied-arts education that had led to the training of traditional applied-arts draftsmen (*Kunstgewerbezeichner*). The Dresden exhibition's general emphasis on high-quality materials and tasteful orientation to commerce defined the Prussian schools exhibition as well. In a selection process of school projects that followed precisely Schumacher's criteria for professional work and unity of presentation, the exhibition directorate accepted only actual rooms, furniture, objects and finished projects; schools were explicitly prohibited, for example, from hanging student design drawings of unexecuted projects. By definition, and as the Dresden exhibition's "Schools Commissar" Muthesius pointed out, only Prussian schools with that epitome of school-reform thinking – instructional workshops (or other effective means to produce executed student works) – were fit to exhibit.

The relative prestige and capabilities of the individual Prussian schools determined the size and distribution of exhibition rooms in the schools' wing of the

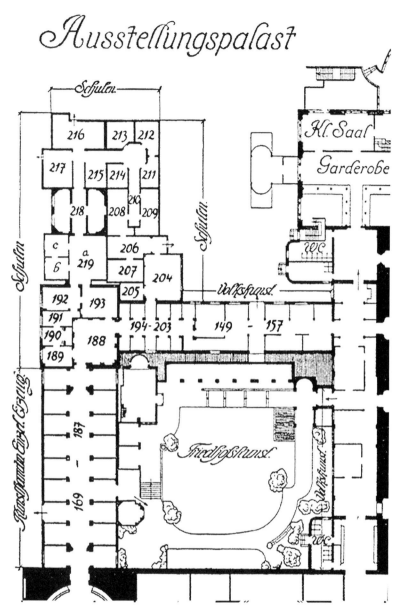

50. Third German Applied Arts Exhibition in Dresden, 1906, exhibition palace plan, detail of applied-arts firms' product exhibits (bays 169–187); applied-arts schools in Prussia (rooms 188–193; bays 194–203); Saxony (rooms 206–217, including Saxony's grammar schools); Baden (room 218); Württemberg (room 219); and folk-art exhibit (rooms 149–157) (*III. Deutsche Kunstgewerbeausstellung Dresden 1906*, Offizieller Katalog, Illustrierter Ausgabe, 1906)

exhibition palace. Of the seventeen Prussian schools exhibiting, Peter Behrens's Dusseldorf *Kunstgewerbeschule* received pride of place with a combined exhibit and reception room (Room 188), designed and filled with 277 student works (Fig. 51). It served as the main entrance to the palace's schools wing and terminated the

51. Dusseldorf School of Applied Arts, student exhibition and reception room at the Third German Applied Arts Exhibition in Dresden, 1906, general view (*Dekorative Kunst* 10, 1906/07)

corridor of professional applied artists' model shops. Its far doorway led down the passage in which Dusseldorf architecture students extended the pilaster and meander motif of their own room, helping to bind ten exhibition bays of smaller Prussian schools into a common exhibition framework. School bays such as that of the Royal Ceramic School of Bunzlau (*Königliche keramische Fachschule Bunzlau*) and the Crafts and Applied Arts School of Barmen (*Handwerker- und Kunstgewerbeschule Barmen*) were laid out like the shops, a further reminder of the close connection between the commercial and educational function of the design schools (Figs. 52–53).[37]

Every effort was made by the school's instructional workshops to bring to life at the level of exhibition interiors the prescribed principle of "tectonic thinking." Exhibition cabinets had been built to fit discreetly into their foreordained positions, where, as was particularly noticeable in the Dusseldorf room, they drew attention to the objects displayed inside them much more than to themselves. Smaller niches held sculptured podiums whose wooden forms and sculptured figures communicated the subtractive process of the tools that had shaped them. These podiums in turn held leather-bound, gold-lettered albums such as the *Golden Book of the Dusseldorf School of Applied Arts* from the school's own leather and book-binding workshops, featuring further information and projects from the school. With its wealth of objects and their promise of future student

52. View of Prussian applied-arts schools' exhibition bays at the Third German Applied Arts Exhibition in Dresden, 1906 (*Dekorative Kunst* 10, 1906/07)

53. Barmen School of Crafts and Applied Arts (*Handwerker und Kunstgewerbeschule*), detail of student product label designs from a course in lithography and surface design (*Fachklasse für Lithographie und Flächenkunst*), Third German Applied Arts Exhibition in Dresden, 1906 (*Das Deutsche Kunstgewerbe 1906: III. Deutsche Kunstgewerbeausstellung Dresden 1906*, Munich, 1906)

54. Students of the Magdeburg School of Crafts and Applied Arts (*Kunstgewerbe- und Handwerkerschule*), new director's office, Third German Applied Arts Exhibition in Dresden, 1906 (*Das Deutsche Kunstgewerbe 1906: III. Deutsche Kunstgewerbeausstellung Dresden 1906*, Munich, 1906)

performance, it was easy to see how this school earned so much national attention and praise in the arts press.[38]

No school had a larger number of contributions to the exhibition, but Dusseldorf was also not alone in designing entire rooms: The Magdeburg *Kunstgewerbe- und Handwerkerschule*, the Krefeld *Handwerker- und Kunstgewerbeschule*, and the *kunstgewerbliche Fachschule* from Flensburg also exhibited complete interiors (Fig. 54). The schools at Aachen, Elberfeld, Barmen, and Cologne contributed smaller interiors.[39] Magdeburg exhibited a new office for the school director Emil Thormählen, designed by students in the class of Albin Müller (one of the more successful exhibitors in St. Louis, where he helped put Magdeburg's applied arts on the map). This project, apart from involving the classes and instructional workshops for textiles, furniture, metalworking, and joincry, benefited from partnership with ten private Magdeburg firms that supplemented school work with specialized engraving, furniture assembly, and other tasks.[40] Krefeld furnished a complete exhibition room with its own furniture, display cabinets, and individual works from various studios, while

Flensburg, primarily a school for woodworking, exhibited furniture and equipment for a baptistry designed by its director, Anton Huber. The Barmen student workshops for surface design and lithography contributed designs for an assortment of products, true to both the Commerce Ministry's and the Dresden exhibition's spirit of infusing commerce with design (Fig. 53).[41]

The Prussian Commerce Minister gave as much support to Muthesius and "his schools," as Schumacher referred to them, as Minister Möller was able to support under difficult budgetary circumstances being faced by Prussia.[42] On one hand, Möller declined to give the Dresden exhibition's planning committee as much of a commitment of Muthesius's time as it had originally requested and proposed that several Prussian school directors join Muthesius in support of Prussia's effort.[43] On the other hand, when the state's desperate budget situation prompted the Finance Ministry to press Möller to reduce funding drastically for a Prussian schools exhibit, the Commerce Minister replied that he had taken measures to limit costs and that "Prussian interests" would be damaged if the schools' exhibit were reduced in size.[44] The Commerce Ministry was not free to spend lavishly and in the end arranged to provide matching funds for individual Prussian cities to cofinance construction of individual exhibition rooms for its top eight schools, headed by Dusseldorf, Magdeburg, and Krefeld.[45] As a further significant measure the ministry distributed 5,000 copies of a 150-page book about its arts, crafts, and trades schools at the Dresden exhibition, free of charge. When copies of this work at the exhibition ran out more quickly than anticipated, it printed and distributed 5,000 more. The work consisted of school programs, curriculum highlights, and addresses for more information, and opened with Muthesius's two articles about the history and new development of the arts, crafts, and trades schools that he had first published in 1905.[46] In all, the Commerce Ministry's contribution to exhibition costs was well above 50,000 Marks, an amount that excluded the costs of printing and distributing the 10,000 free books.[47]

Having devoted significant resources to arts, crafts, and trades schools since Commerce Minister Möller's arrival in 1901, the government might have been expected to trumpet the success of its school-reform program in the press as well as in its own publications. However, and mindful of the opposition of the *Fachverband*, *Semperbund*, and other conservative crafts practitioners virtually from the start of its reforms, the authorities kept their distance from linking government ministry officials too closely with the exhibition. Nowhere in the ministry's book on Prussia's arts, crafts, and trade schools were individuals from the State Trades Board or the Commerce Ministry credited by name in the whole process of either school reform or exhibition support. Muthesius's name as the author of the opening articles on Prussian arts and crafts education was omitted, as it was when his articles were reprinted in other exhibition literature.[48] The Commerce Ministry was, in fact, the only listed author of the book, but the institutional author's schools were not tied to any individuals' or reformers' efforts. In this way, the schools were made to fit seamlessly into the exhibition directorate's overall cultural program, without standing out as the product of years of specific state reforms.

Although successful by the school directors' and exhibition directorate's criteria, the schools' exhibit enraged many members of the German crafts and tradesworkers unions. Their resentment dated back earlier than the Dresden exhibition and stemmed largely from city and state government support for the applied-arts education system, which they saw as coming at the expense of traditional artisans' classes. Craftsmen at the 1907 conference of the Association for the Economic Interests of the Crafts spoke of the need to practice their skills flexibly and adaptably – essentially a euphemism for being able to work independently and in a wide variety of historical styles – which students were no longer learning. Had practicing artisans been favored "by Herr Regierungsrat Muthesius" with a secure place "in the state's nursery with, of course, life-long feeding," one *Semperbund* member declared, then, perhaps, working craftsmen too would be able to reject paying customers and concentrate instead on subsidized design experiments. In the meantime, craftspeople needed to make a living, and if the situation was not rectified, the speaker insisted, foreign competition stood to gain from unsatisfied customers who would look elsewhere while the German applied-arts producers invented untraditional, undesirable, confusing new forms.[49]

Exacerbating the frustration of the traditional crafts associations were the commissions for school directors and instructors in the different sections of the exhibition. The architects and school directors Wilhelm Werdelmann of Barmen, Anton Huber of Flensburg, Eberhard Abele of Aachen, and Peter Behrens of Dusseldorf all designed their respective exhibition rooms, while Behrens went on with commissions for the elegant, stylized Delmenhorst pavilion as well as a music room and "ceramics courtyard" in the *Raumkunst* section. Instructors like Johannes Lauweriks, Alfred Grenander, Rudolf Bosselt, Fritz Ehmcke, and Albin Müller were among the major designers of buildings, interiors, and objects in various sections of the exhibition, joining their counterparts from all over Germany and, in some cases, drawing manufacturers to exhibit with them.

Prussia's state applied-arts personnel were well represented in Dresden in part because Muthesius's revised regulations for school directors and teachers in 1903 had required school staff to maintain as much contact with the realm of design practice as possible, especially through commissions. This measure not only guaranteed that schools would be more closely linked to industry and manufacturers, but also alerted large numbers of Prussian and German businesses to the gains obtainable from working with trained designers oriented simultaneously to quality in production and to the competitive goals of business. What the Werkbund would later promote by way of *Industriekultur*, an industrial manufacturing culture ennobled (*veredelt*) through collaboration with artists, thus saw an early and important precedent in the policies of the Prussian state. This industrial culture would combine the rhetoric of improved manufacturing quality with national cultural advance, promoting Germany's long-sought-after competitive position in world markets. For their part, artist-designers linked the modern design and production process to the overall progress of a harmonious German "artistic culture."

Perhaps the single clearest manifestation of this nascent *Industriekultur* can be seen in the work carried out by Peter Behrens for the Delmenhorst Linoleum Company, a firm with which Behrens had a long-standing relationship. Behrens provided his first linoleum pattern designs to the Delmenhorst company while still at Darmstadt in 1900 and had designed an exhibition pavilion for the firm as part of an ensemble for the Oldenburg State, Industry, and Trade Exhibition in 1905.[50] Behrens's temple-like pavilion on the south side of the Dresden exhibition capitalized on his previous experiences of designing for the company, revealing Behrens's most distilled and integrated design for the company to date (Figs. 55–57; also Item "C11" at top of Fig. 44).

The building also completed an important shift in which the designer adapted monumental classical forms for buildings with modern commercial and industrial uses. With its symmetry, proportions, and formal clarity, the Delmenhorst pavilion presented an interlocking set of references to industry, commerce, culture, and, through its dramatic dome and central plan, even religion. Classical tradition effectively imbued this pavilion of a manufacturer of synthetic flooring material with an identity as a contemporary bearer of modern German culture. Its temple form helps recall the historian Fritz Stern's observation about

55. Peter Behrens, exhibition pavilion for the Delmenhorst Linoleum Company at the Third German Applied Arts Exhibition in Dresden, 1906, exterior (*Dekorative Kunst* 15, 1907)

56. Peter Behrens, exhibition pavilion of the Delmenhorst Linoleum Company at the Third German Applied Arts Exhibition in Dresden, 1906, interior (*Dekorative Kunst* 15, 1907)

Wilhelmine Germany as a place where, "perhaps even more than elsewhere, culture in the broadest sense became a secular equivalent of the sacred, and as such a revered possession of the educated middle classes."[51]

The pavilion's dramatic placement next to a reflecting pool in an open garden underscored the Delmenhorst Linoleum Company's role as a prominent participant and supporter of the exhibition. Everywhere the basic geometries of a circle and a square, which Behrens adapted from the sacral motif of the building's central plan, recurred in mutually reinforcing commercial and decorative forms. The company's "Ankermarke" (anchor brand) trademark, also inscribed in a circle and square and imprinted on the clear, white panels of the pavilion's exterior, created an iconic counterpoint to the company name and the stencil of the pavilion's plan located above the front entrance (Fig. 55).

Entering visitors found themselves immersed in a *Gesamtkunstwerk* of linoleum products (Fig. 56). Richly patterned floors, walls, and a frieze illustrated the possibilities this modern industrial material placed in the hands of artists and decorators. The pavilion's high dome and vertical windows lent a monumental cast to the linoleum rolls lining the room below. Abstract lines and circles further animated the space and demonstrated the Anchor Brand's decorative versatility, while beneath the circular dome an inset square of linoleum flooring featured an interweaving design of forest creatures.

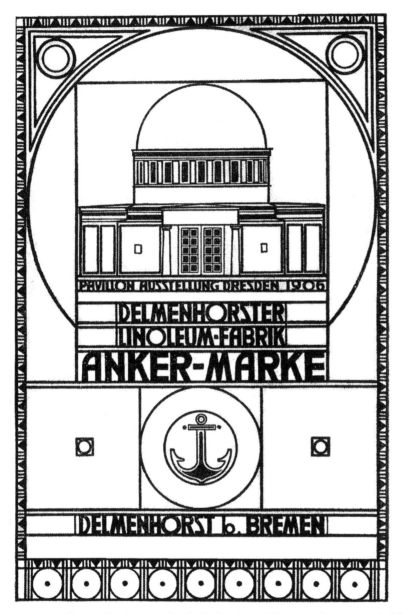

57. Peter Behrens, advertisement for the Delmenhorst Linoleum Company at the Third German Applied Arts Exhibition, 1906 (*Dritte Deutsche Kunstgewerbeausstellung Dresden 1906: Offizieller Katalog, Illustrierte Ausgabe*, Dresden, 1906)

Behrens's pavilion was the Dresden exhibition's best example of what in coming years would come to be known, in Werkbund circles, as the "spiritualization" (*Durchgeistigung*) of German work. This phrase would be adopted as the title theme of the first Werkbund Yearbook in 1912, expressing concisely early-twentieth-century German efforts to "spiritualize" industrial culture and commercial production as forms of a new secularized religion. Where the artist-designer transformed the Delmenhorst linoleum products into virtual cult objects, the clean lines of Behrens's temple of commerce lent themselves exceptionally well to further representational use.

For an advertising poster also featured on the back cover of the 1906 Dresden exhibition catalog, Behrens reproduced the front elevation of the manufacturer's pavilion above the trademark advertising the Anchor brand (Fig. 57). The familiar circle and square motifs reappeared as well, serving as frames for the trademark, Renaissance medallions, and further evocations of the pavilion-temple plan.[52] A major contributor to the exhibition, the Delmenhorst Linoleum Company succeeded in making the Anchor Brand the floor material of choice among artist-exhibitors in the *Raumkunst* section, and in many of the exhibits of arts, crafts, and trades schools. Apart from Behrens's other works at the exhibition, the integrated design of the exhibition pavilion, poster, and numerous linoleum patterns can only have helped convince Paul Jordan, director of the AEG's factories, to hire Behrens in 1907 as chief consultant to the AEG on all matters of design.[53]

THE POLITICAL ECONOMY OF THE THIRD GERMAN APPLIED ARTS EXHIBITION

The Dresden exhibition directorate highlighted artists as proprietors of their work. Debates over copyrights in artistic production had been raging in the Reichstag and in the pages of Germany's applied-arts journals since the early years of the twentieth century and continued to do so during summer 1906.[54] The Third German Applied Arts Exhibition played a part in this debate by projecting a vision of future design and production in which artists and applied-arts producers of the new movement asserted exclusive authorial rights to their designs. As Schumacher claimed, the exhibition was "not a reflection of that which we in Germany already have by way of an artistic culture, but rather only a reflection of the artistic culture that we could have."[55] The notion of "artistic culture," so popular among figures like Schumacher, Muthesius, the critic Karl Scheffler, and others, was a euphemism for a program extending well beyond the realm of aesthetics. The term often appeared interchangeably with "harmonious culture," and, for architects from Otto Wagner to critics like Richard Streiter, was related to the conviction that "modern life" provided the only legitimate basis for a new art.[56] In the case of the Dresden exhibition, the particularities of "modern life" that came especially to the fore were the conditions of modern production, the relationship between artists and producers, and the division of ownership rights over applied-arts product designs.

To Schumacher, an important step on the way to achieving an artistic culture for Germany involved balancing the rights of artists to own their designs as authors, on the one hand, and reigning in overly individualistic artistic production on the other. Like Muthesius, and perhaps influenced by him, Schumacher explicitly criticized what he perceived as the excessive willfulness of *Jugendstil* artists. Using language that closely paralleled that of the Prussian reformer's 1902 book, *Style-Architecture and Building-Art*, Schumacher called for a less personal approach to applied-arts production, quality, and form. Although the 1906 exhibition did not manifest fully the opposition between artistic individualism and "types" in design that would divide the Werkbund in 1914, the arguments advanced by different parties over the issues of form and style showed that backers of conformity in the name of cultural harmony were on a collision course with the advocates of individualistic, expressive designs.

Arguing for greater unity among exhibiting artists in Dresden, Schumacher took a swipe at the 1898, 1900, and 1901 exhibitions in Dresden, Paris, and Darmstadt respectively. These, he wrote, had been dominated by "individual courageous men seeking their own personal path." These artists had "made the new movement appear to be a movement of individual men who, with iconoclastic tastes that ignited mini-fashion movements with lightning speed, had their personal art misunderstood and caricatured by followers who only blurred the general reform thinking even further." Developments such as those in St. Louis, however, were revealing the movement "as something more general" and deserving of "a more systematic survey" – a survey that the Third National Applied-Arts Exhibition now claimed to deliver.[57] Emphasizing Germany's efforts to compete economically with other powers, the Dresden architect justified a national search for "a sure line amid the oscillating taste of our times." "The issue of taste," he wrote,

> is without question closely connected to matters of fundamental economic significance. In the competition of the world market each folk strives to become as independent as possible. The products of foreign industries are imitated and emulated, until one has equalled them; in the world market, then, the only products retaining enduring competitiveness and high value are those that one cannot imitate, and whose essence arises from the characteristic elements of its indigenous culture, which expresses itself in that which one calls taste.[58]

Responding to Schumacher's criticism of the *Jugendstil* and his elevation of economic concerns, Henry van de Velde protested vehemently against the overall impression communicated by Dresden exhibition and its organizers. He was no doubt defensive, in part, because his museum reception hall for the Weimar Museum of Art and Applied Arts, located immediately to the right of the exhibition palace main entrance, was the most forceful expression of the *Jugendstil* sensibility in the entire palace (Fig. 46). Van de Velde's assessment pulled no punches, declaring the Third German Applied Arts Exhibition so "backward looking" (*rückschrittlich*) that it threatened the very development of a modern style. The directorate's emphasis on unity of approach and artistic authorship of actual commissions was secondary, in van de Velde's mind, to the need for leading applied artists to develop a new style befitting the times. Among various rooms in which some artists had played "coquettishly" with a new style, van de Velde complained that a lifeless "skeleton" of columns, capitals, and other historical forms presented a reactionary display that was "simply disgusting."[59]

Where Schumacher praised the emphasis on workmanship and simplicity of design in the palace's *Raumkunst* displays, van de Velde accused the majority of exhibitors of producing uninspired, exhausted revivals of stuffy, Biedermeier sensibility. The "new style," van de Velde insisted, called for greater receptivity to the changed conditions of modern life than was evident in Dresden. A true cultural rebirth depended on artists banding together in recognition of the new qualities that made their time unique and deserving of new forms of expression. Van de Velde's artistic idealism and passionate rhetorical flourishes challenged his colleagues to reject the early-nineteenth-century *bürgerlich* and Biedermeier traditions that informed so many of their works.[60]

Schumacher, Muthesius, Lossow, and other members of the directorate certainly downplayed individual artistic differences in order to emphasize an underlying commonality of purpose among exhibition participants. Schumacher's assessment in the Dresden exhibition catalog, for example, optimistically claimed to see the beginning of an "inner unity" of creativity among artists whose individual works nonetheless still presented an "outwardly ununified image."[61] This diversity of styles and artistic personalities was undeniable: Behrens employed a decorative Neoclassicism for which he was becoming well-known; Heinrich Vogeler of the Worpswede artists' colony favored Rococo elements; Bernhard Pankok of Stuttgart preferred naturalistic motifs; and so on from the neo-Baroque of Wilhelm Kreis to the neo-Biedermeier of Bruno Paul, from the *Jugendstil* of Henry van de Velde to the *Heimatstil* of Paul Schultze-Naumburg.

Muthesius, for his part, played the diplomat, and like Schumacher, accentuated the exhibit's positive achievements to promote unity. He referred collectively to all the works produced for the exhibition as an affirmation of Germany's resurgent status as a rising "national cultural power" (*nationale Kulturmacht*). He wrote of a "respectable disposition" evident in the displays, of their "veracity" (*Wahrhaftigkeit*), and of their success at "in no way trying to appear more than they are" – all terms that referred to the applied-arts works and room interiors, but also, simultaneously, alluded to a model for bourgeois citizenship as well. For what was being achieved at the exhibition, Muthesius promised – and here he was very much in line with the campaigns of Ferdinand Avenarius in *Der Kunstwart* and in the Dürerbund – was both an elimination of the parvenu culture of imitation in the arts and a general rebirth of German artistic sensibilities.[62] "And with this strengthening of artistic character, with this turning away from the threadbare ideals of outdated German taste that had became completely lost in a culture of imitation and superficial appearance," he concluded,

> there will go hand in hand a further strengthening of the general character of the people (*Charakter des Volkes*), at least as far as this can be traced in expressions of outer culture. . . . The question of formal 'styles' retreats into the

background in the face of these principles. It is a matter of complete indifference (*Es ist völlig gleichgültig*) whether the works feature curved or straight lines, abstract or vegetative ornament, or closed or open compositions.[63]

Each in its own way, the arguments advanced by Schumacher and Muthesius papered over stylistic differences by emphasizing the commonality of purpose that inspired the exhibition: Whatever the preferences of individual artists, constituencies as diverse as the Prussian Commerce Ministry, the Dresden Workshops of Karl Schmidt, Dresden Mayor Gustav Beutler, and the various state applied-arts associations all strongly supported the notion of artist-designed products, furnishings, and rooms as a basis for improved quality in German production.

Conservative quarters of the applied-arts sector responded in kind. As Frederic Schwartz's study of the Werkbund has persuasively argued, members of the Association for the Economic Interests of the Crafts were not simply conservative crafts practitioners defending the production of historical styles. Rather, its members felt threatened by the way that state-supported schools and increased concentration in the crafts industries, along with new copyright and trademark laws, were distorting the playing field in ways unfavorable to traditional, undercapitalized applied-arts producers. As new laws threatened to extend copyrights to works of applied and visual art – a position the Dresden exhibition organizers clearly favored – the individual crafts producer and the common property of historicist design motifs looked to become obsolete.[64]

What at first glance might be perceived as an aesthetic conflict between traditional crafts practitioners and progressive designers was every bit as much a struggle over exactly who would benefit from the production and introduction of modern forms into the marketplace: the designer or the manufacturer. Historicism was the model favored by the association in large part because it enabled applied-arts practitioners to mine the forms of the past as a legally understood form of common property, whose sole "author" was the employer of the applied-arts workers who served him. The new movement, with the help of modern copyright laws that Kaiser Wilhelm II would sign into law in January 1907, elevated the artist to the status of a producer who received the backing of the courts.[65]

THE "MUTHESIUS AFFAIR" AND THE FOUNDING OF THE WERKBUND

Before, during, and after the Dresden exhibition of 1906, artisanal representatives and defenders of the traditional crafts approach continued to oppose reforms in states like Prussia, Saxony, and Württemberg, but to no avail.[66] In all states, funding for schools, exhibitions, and the Prussian State Trades Board's various programs and subcommittees only increased. At the same time, however, the

Prussian Ministry of Commerce consciously distanced itself from controversies with crafts associations that its own policies had done so much to provoke. For example, in January 1907 Muthesius, appointed first chair of the *Kunstgewerbe* at the newly opened, Commerce Ministry–supported Berlin Commercial College, publicly denounced traditional crafts practitioners in his inaugural lecture at the school, entitled "The Significance of the Applied Arts" (*Die Bedeutung des Kunstgewerbes*).[67] Holding old design techniques and shoddy material practices accountable for having made the words "'German' and 'tasteless' into practically identical concepts," he announced that the "future belongs to those producers who subscribe to the new movement."[68] At the heart of Muthesius's lecture was the linkage of new forms of economic organization in the applied arts to mass education and national progress. Specifically, Muthesius likened the education of consumers about the integrity of products and materials to the moral integrity of the masses and the nation. Practitioners of architecture and the applied arts, he insisted, had an ethical duty to pursue quality through modern means of machine manufacture.

Muthesius's moral argument certainly owed more to the philosophy of the Art Education movement (and to Avenarius in particular), the school reforms undertaken by the Prussian Commerce Ministry, and the tactics pursued by Theodor Möller as a leader of a moderate wing of Germany's National Liberal Party than to the arguments of Pugin, Ruskin, and Morris.[69] In spelling out the modern crafts' artistic and cultural significance, the new Chair of Applied Arts at the Berlin Commercial College challenged German light industrial manufacturers to embrace the modern crafts movement and imbue it with national economic significance. This economic breakthrough, as Muthesius explained, would walk hand in hand with a sweeping educational program to bring Germany's lower classes into the circle of a modern productive social order. "One thing is clear," Muthesius explained in his lecture:

> the arts and crafts are facing an educational task of the highest importance. And in this it already exceeds the boundaries popularly ascribed to it. More than mere applied art, it becomes a cultural means of education. The aim of the arts and crafts movement is to re-educate the social classes of today in solidity, truthfulness, and simple civic values. If it succeeds in this, then it will have the deepest effect on our cultural life and will produce far-reaching consequences. Not only will it change the German apartment and the German house, but it will directly influence the character of the generation, for a process of education which produces proper accommodations for us to live in can basically only be a character education, and one in which the pretentious and parvenu tendencies of today's interior design will be eliminated.[70]

Here Muthesius states most plainly his view that architecture and the applied arts are a "cultural means of education," agents of bourgeois *Bildung*. Manufacturers unwilling to subscribe to this outlook, he stated plainly, were standing in the way of Germany's national health and progress.

The controversy that erupted thereafter, widely publicized as the "Muthesius Affair" (*Der Fall Muthesius*), proved a focal point for contemporary debates about modern conditions of production as well as "traditional" versus "modern" crafts practices. The Association for the Economic Interests of the Crafts responded by petitioning Commerce Minister Delbrück and demanding angrily that he dismiss Muthesius from government service. In a reply to the Association, Minister Delbrück wrote that Muthesius had been acting "as an academic instructor . . . and independent from his activity as a member of the State Trades Board" and refused to dismiss him.[71] When the matter arose for debate in the Prussian Chamber of Deputies, Delbrück defended Muthesius as "an expert colleague" and "indispensable public servant." Referring indirectly to the Association for the Economic Interests of the Crafts, which had called for Muthesius's dismissal, he added that "the applied arts cannot be elevated by philistines."[72]

The Commerce Ministry, following Muthesius's recommendations, had put its full weight behind school reforms intended to renegotiate relationships between designers and manufacturers in the spirit of a new German culture – a culture in which traditional crafts practitioners were branded "philistines." Other interested parties, such as the Protestant minister, writer, social activist, and progressive politician Friedrich Naumann, saw an opportunity to recruit the applied arts for his worker-oriented policies of industrial and commercial expansion. His ideas about manufacturing quality and the modernization of German production had had a visible impact on Karl Schmidt of Dresden, as Schmidt himself informed Muthesius in March 1905, shortly after meeting Naumann for the first time.[73] Schmidt urged Muthesius to meet with Naumann and discuss their overlapping interests, an event that would take place at Muthesius's house in Berlin-Nicolassee in July of the same year.[74]

Naumann's broad-ranging interests and unique charisma certainly proved influential in prompting adherents of the new movement in the applied arts to organize a separate association of their own, in the same manner that his impassioned liberal vision had helped him to win an upset victory for a Reichstag seat representing the Württemberg town of Heilbronn.[75] Heilbronners Peter Bruckmann, Ernst Jäckh, and Theodor Heuss, along with Wolf Dohrn, all helped Naumann achieve his victory in Württemberg in the elections of 1907. Unlike Muthesius, however, Naumann sought specifically to aid workers through the progress of industry and manufacturing, whereas Muthesius believed workers would eventually benefit from changes that focused first and foremost on manufacturing and design quality.[76] The top-down reforms and patrician mentality of the Prussian bureaucrat, inflected by policies originating with a minister who was himself a National Liberal industrialist, clashed in the person of Muthesius with the south German, liberal, Württemberg-Saxon view of the social question, as embodied by Naumann.

Questions of national importance for applied artists and manufacturers in 1906–07 were thus being filtered through lenses of local culture, regional context, and individual political background. Of the greatest importance to Naumann was the formation of an association that coalesced around the interests of the new movement so that its collective talents could be mobilized for national economic growth and social progress. Though the two men would remain divided over the question of workers' welfare, Muthesius and Naumann shared common ground on the issue of improving German national competitiveness and promoting finished-goods exports of high quality in foreign markets. Lecturing at the 1906 Dresden exhibition, Naumann described the assembly of works as an expression of a new "national energy" and "national economy" and came to describe the Werkbund shortly after its creation as the institutional expression of these forces.[77]

Recollections of the precise history of the Werkbund's formation are marred by the fact that the archives of the early Werkbund were destroyed during the Second World War.[78] Fritz Schumacher, the chief organizer of the Dresden exhibition in 1906, recalled that "the principle of a brotherly association between artists and firms," seen in abundance at the exhibition, gave rise to "the suggestion from many sides to form a general German association on the basis of this idea."[79] Naumann was certainly one of those promoting the formation of a new applied-arts organization in summer 1906, as his protégé and biographer Theodor Heuss recorded.[80] The Werkbund journal *Die Form*, in its twenty-fifth anniversary issue commemorating the founding of the organization, also related that prior to the close of the exhibition, Muthesius, Karl Schmidt, Schmidt's business manager Wolf Dohrn, and Jacob Julius Scharvogel, the owner of a Munich ceramics factory, discussed the need for an association of artists and highly qualified members of the trades and industry to carry the message of the Dresden exhibition to a broader public.[81]

Recent as well as contemporary accounts of the Werkbund's formation agree that it was Muthesius's opening lecture at the Berlin Commercial College that provided the eventual spur to action for the new organization's founding. Karl Schmidt, too, played a decisive role, insofar as it was he who organized and submitted a "counterstatement" (*Gegeneingabe*) to the Prussian Commerce Minister against the petition of the Association for the Economic Interests of the Crafts, signed by himself and five Saxon applied-arts firms, six Munich applied-arts firms, and one Breslau applied-arts firm. Hefty written exchanges between Schmidt and the leadership of the Association for the Economic Interests of the Crafts followed.

Finally, at the June 1907, meeting of the Association for the Economic Interests of the Crafts in Dusseldorf, the Heilbronn silver manufacturer Peter Bruckmann, Wolf Dohrn (representing Schmidt's enterprises), and the Dresden-based Viennese art critic and *Hohe Warte* journal editor Joseph Lux (representing the Nymphenburg Royal Porcelain manufacturers and the applied arts firm of

Karl Bertsch in Munich) each gave short, approximately ten-minute speeches in defense of Muthesius and of the right of applied artists to design freely and independently from the association, and in concert with industry and manufacturers.[82] Although Bruckmann's firm of P. Bruckmann and Sons Silver Manufacturers was not a member of the Association, Bruckmann, as a specially invited guest, rose to thank the membership for its invitation to attend and speak at its congress. Bruckmann then warned the assembled group of some 180 firms that the new arrangements being reached between artists and producers represented "new ideas" of an unstoppable nature, the essence of which was "organized modern workshop production." Those members of the Association who resisted this new form of organization were, Bruckmann stated, "bound to find their strongest competition" coming from just these newly organized producers.[83]

Dohrn, speaking immediately after Bruckmann, announced that a movement for a new association representing the artistic and economic interests of the applied arts was gathering strength and planned to meet shortly in Munich.[84] Here Dohrn appeared to be alluding to discussions that had already taken place between his employer, Karl Schmidt, his mentor Naumann, and others. Lux, the last of the three to speak, drew a sharp distinction between the Association's craftsmen and the applied-arts *artists* whom the Association was trying to keep from working in their field. He reiterated the sentiment that the Association's behavior and protests against Muthesius had demonstrated the group's unworthiness to represent Germany's applied arts as they were taking shape in their forward-looking, modern form. On this basis he hoped that a future of honest and principled competition could be conducted between the Association and the backers of the new movement, more "through deeds than through words," as he put it. Dohrn then concluded sharply, "I am not putting my remarks up for discussion, and because we reject any notion of partnership with you, we will simply leave the hall right away."[85]

Less than two months later, by August 1907, 293 artists and firms deemed sympathetic to the new movement had received an "Invitation to the Inaugural Meeting of a German Applied-Arts Association (*Kunstgewerbebundes*)," held on October 5–6, 1907, in Munich. The invitations were signed by twelve artists and twelve applied-arts firms, a gesture of equality in the representation of artistic and economic interests.[86] Only at the Munich founding meeting, to which approximately one-third of the invitees came, did Karl Schmidt coin the name "Deutscher Werkbund," which was agreed to in recognition of the inability of the term "applied arts" (*Kunstgewerbe*) to any longer "express...the culture of trade and industry in its artistic, economic and social dimensions."[87] For its headquarters the Werkbund chose the administration building of Karl Schmidt's Dresden Workshops, moving shortly thereafter to Karl Schmidt's planned new "Hellerau Garden City" a few kilometers to the northeast of Dresden. On Naumann's suggestion, Schmidt's colleague, Wolf Dohrn, was appointed the Werkbund's business manager; he would retain this title until the Werkbund transferred its headquarters to Berlin on April 1, 1912, and replaced Dohrn with another Naumann colleague, the Württemberg journalist and Berlin political insider Ernst Jäckh.[88]

Although Muthesius prepared a speech and would go on to be one of the Werkbund's leading theorists of artist-designed industrial "types," he did not attend the organization's founding meeting in Munich. The Commerce Minister likely withheld Muthesius from the gathering because of the immediate furor surrounding the Association for the Economic Interests of the Crafts and the "Muthesius Case." Moreover, and as Commerce Minister Möller's actions (and those of his successor, Clemens von Delbrück) attest, the ministry wished to avoid publicizing its role as a strong supporter of the Third German Applied Arts Exhibition, the underlying positions of Muthesius's lecture at the Berlin Commercial College, and, now, the formation of a breakaway applied-arts association that openly opposed so many traditional German applied-arts producers.[89] Möller, after all, had recently forfeited his ministership by trying surreptitiously but forcefully to impose the state's will on the cartel of coal producers in the Rhineland during the disastrous "Hibernia Affair"; the press, banking, and industrial communities had all expressed outrage at the Prussian Commerce Ministry's overbearing behavior. In the case of the applied-arts and light-manufacturing sphere, even if industrial and banking muscle on the level of Stinnes, Thyssen, Rathenau, or Bleichröder would not act against the Commerce Ministry, the ministry had recently been handed a black eye in its failed takeover bid and stood to tarnish its image once again if its bureacracy continued to be branded by the press as too pro-active in the activities of the market economy.

Still, the long-standing supposition among historians of German architecture and design that Muthesius failed to attend the founding of the Werkbund because his speech ran counter to state policy is erroneous.[90] The aggressive provocation contained in Muthesius's opening address at the Berlin Commercial College did not violate the policies of state. Instead, it was an extension, and in many ways a culmination of policies he had helped to develop first in the Commerce Ministry and later brought into the Werkbund. By broadening his focus on the applied arts and exhorting German manufacturers explicitly to embrace the rational principles of *Sachlichkeit*, purposefulness (*Zweckmässigkeit*), and tectonically consistent use of materials and constructional principles, he was following several years of ministerial economic development policies and *Mittelstandpolitik* to their logical conclusion. The concept of the Werkbund as a national association of artists and manufacturers, aided as it was by the political vision of Naumann and the practical, open-minded entrepreneur Karl Schmidt, enjoyed mixed paternity from the governmental and private spheres. Although the ministry in all likelihood withheld Muthesius from the public spotlight momentarily, the speech that earned him the epithet "Father of the Werkbund" fulfilled the development policies of the Prussian Commerce Ministry all too well.[91] Karl Schmidt for his part, and within the space of a decade, would go from founding a three-man firm to developing an entire "garden city" at Dresden-Hellerau as the base for an ever-expanding enterprise with overlapping economic, social, and cultural ambitions. Although exceptional, Schmidt's phenomenal success had national implications, which are examined more closely in Chapter 6.

THE WERKBUND: DESIGN FORUM AND AGENT
OF ECONOMIC EXPANSION

Shortly after the inaugural meeting of the Werkbund in Munich in October 1907, Muthesius assumed a position of leadership in the organization. His work in the Werkbund, scant evidence of which exists in surviving files of the Commerce Ministry, the State Trades Board, or the Standing Committee on German Industrial Exhibitions, allowed him to articulate in an extragovernmental setting the Prussian Commerce Ministry's long-standing goals of strengthening manufacturing quality in Germany's applied arts and stimulating German exports. In 1908 Werkbund members elected Muthesius to the six-member Werkbund leadership council, and he served as the organization's vocal vice president between 1912 and 1916.

Where Naumann would not serve as an officer in the organization or participate in its day-to-day managerial activities, his regular keynote speeches at Werkbund annual meetings met with thunderous approval, and the politician did serve, as Walter Gropius later noted, in a moral leadership role. Likewise, Naumann's contacts furnished the organization with many of its most able members, including Bruckmann, Jäckh, Dohrn, and Heuss. Muthesius, on the other hand, was very active in the Werkbund's day-to-day affairs. In fact, and as we will see in Chapters 6 and 7, the more time that passed, the more some Werkbund members grew to resent the intensity and increasingly domineering nature of Muthesius's involvement in the association.

At the time of the Werkbund's founding, Muthesius found much to say that linked his ideas for the organization to statements he had been making in recent years. His unused speech for the Werkbund inaugural meeting, for example, contains many of the same points as his Berlin College of Commerce inaugural lecture – which in turn built on arguments the architect had developed in *Stilarchitektur und Baukunst* in 1902 and *Kultur und Kunst* in 1904. Several points establish direct links between the architect's work produced while in government service and his efforts in the Werkbund. These include the emphasis on the applied arts as an "architectonic movement" that contributed to the production of orderly, comfortable surroundings, and not just isolated objects; the discussion of the leading role that the state should play by educating applied artists and the public to appreciate *sachlich*, well-constructed applied-arts products and domestic furnishings; and the stress on quality as the key to German economic success.[92]

Muthesius maintained this continuity with his remarks at the first annual meeting of the Werkbund in Munich in 1908. Here, too, he stressed the reform of applied-arts design, production, and consumption as matters of national importance, adding a call for "a total reform of our human forms of expression" consonant with the approaches of objectivity and functionality.[93] He argued that Germany's relative paucity of foreign colonies and shortage of indigenous raw materials demanded an emphasis on higher quality in design and production to enable the nation to compete effectively. The architect had raised this point many years earlier in one of his first articles for a government publication, his review of Konrad Lange's *The Artistic Education of German Youth* of 1893 in the Public Works Ministry journal, *Centralblatt der Bauverwaltung*. Yet this formulation was also common enough in the argumentation of his former National Liberal minister, Theodor Möller.[94] Expanding on principles he had already put in place in the Prussian schools, he spoke explicitly of the need for Werkbund artists and member industries to search for an "assured method of cooperation" that would provide a model for a national production program.[95]

In light of the successes being enjoyed by big industry, Muthesius also asserted – to the loud cheers of his audience – that "mass production cannot be ignored, and must be improved. And therein," he added, "lies the actual contemporary, the modern in the idea of the Deutscher Werkbund." The organization would strive for the broadest possible effect, as he made clear when he defined the young association as "an organization of experts that seeks to enlighten, teach, and educate the greater public about the concept of quality. [It] seeks through its activities to have an effect like yeast among the whole folk."[96]

A strong German export economy, he noted at the close of his 1908 address, could not be based on the customary cheap exports for which Germany had hitherto been known. The improved national economy being promoted by the Werkbund would contribute to the solution of social problems by lifting working-class living standards up on a rising tide of German production, exports, and wages. This, of course, was the same strategy that the Commerce Ministry had advocated in its rationale for reforming the schools and modernizing the trades *Mittelstand* beginning in 1903.[97] The Werkbund's efforts to improve the economy, Muthesius stated confidently, would also solve problems of aesthetic disharmony and inconsistency through the creation of an harmonious national mode of design expression.[98]

The Werkbund closed its 1908 meeting with the general resolution that "The goal of the organization is the ennoblement of work in the trades in a cooperative effort of art, industry, and handwork through education, propaganda, and decisive positions on associated issues."[99] Of all the speakers, Muthesius's remarks gave the greatest amount of scope and detail to the Werkbund program. Although its members would disagree in the coming years about many aspects of the Werkbund's program and purpose, its basic goals were agreed upon in 1907 and left considerable latitude for different firms and artists, once they were accepted to the association, to generate their own forms and products.

In the absence of complete archival records, the precise relationship between the Commerce Ministry's pre-war policy efforts and the Werkbund's activities remains blurred. Nonetheless, government files and the Werkbund's illustrious series of yearbooks establish some important links. The Werkbund's Schools Commission, for example, focused on the area of "commerce" (*Handel*), a word that, as the historian Angelika Thiekötter has observed, the Werkbund's official program never mentioned.[100] Among the Schools Commission's accomplishments was the development of a lecture series planned by Muthesius and other Werkbund members during the 1908 meeting. This series bore the title "Lectures to Educate the Taste of German Merchants." By 1910, more than 5,000 salespeople had attended lectures, seminars, and courses on the education of consumer taste as important components of the national economy. Muthesius delivered many talks on this subject himself, while two of his superiors at the Commerce Ministry, Privy Councillor Hermann von Seefeld and State Trades Board Director Heinrich Neuhaus, imposed strict standards on private business training schools throughout Prussia in an effort to make them better serve the modernizing industrial and commercial economy.[101]

The Commerce Ministry funded an additional Werkbund initiative that grew out of the schools program in 1910. This was the creation of the so-called Higher Specialty School for Decorative Art (*Höhere Fachschule für Dekorationskunst*) in Berlin. The Specialty School was responsible for educating merchants and applied artists in the making of tasteful product displays, advertising, and shop-window decorations for the purpose of improving product sales.[102] Muthesius rose to become chairman of the school's board of trustees by 1912; the work of the school's graduates featured prominently in stores and shops throughout Berlin, as well as in the Werkbund yearbook of 1913. Among its better known faculty were the painters and advertising poster designers Lucian Bernhard and Julius Klinger, as well as the designers Else Oppler-Legband and Lilly Reich.[103]

Although a systematic linkage of applied-arts education, modern means of manufacture, and the development of a modern German consumer consciousness was encouraged first in the Commerce Ministry's reform of its schools through Prussia's well-developed bureaucratic apparatus, it was the Deutscher Werkbund that brought this set of issues to a national audience. Having withstood Bismarck's onslaughts in the 1880s, the Prussian Commerce Ministry, now acting as Germany's de facto Imperial Commerce Ministry, likely saw in the Werkbund a private organization that could help it disseminate Prussian policies throughout the nation without interfering with the governments of any other states or, for that matter, other departments in the German Imperial bureaucracy.

Other states, of course, had developed their own approaches to the applied arts, embracing and supporting reform measures in different ways and to different degrees, as we saw in Chapter 1. The approaches of Naumann, Schmidt, Bruckmann, and others played important roles in establishing the Werkbund and helping it to define its identity in the pre–World War I years. Their input brought crucial, non-Prussian attitudes to the table that made an organization like the Werkbund possible in the first place. With respect to Muthesius, we have seen how he helped the Commerce Ministry to reorganize two-thirds of Germany's state system of applied-arts education and production in a manner that had far-reaching consequences. This work also represented an opportunity for architects like himself to advance to the top of an emerging Wilhelmine social, political, and economic order. The "modern German artistic culture" to which Muthesius and many of his Werkbund contemporaries referred was, in fact, a euphemism for a Wilhelmine governmental and private effort to strengthen the nation's applied arts, light manufacturing, and export sectors; advance the image of the design professions as carriers of an affirmative Wilhelmine bourgeois identity; and integrate different classes of workers into the modernizing German economy.

For this reason, Muthesius's service as a reformer of government applied-arts schools and schools for the building trades cannot be understood apart from his work as an architect in Berlin. After all, his school reforms subordinated the crafts to the organizing wishes of the architect, mirroring many of the structural and legal changes taking place in this sector of the economy around the turn of the century.[104] In his capacity as a private architect, too, Muthesius played the role of chief arbiter in all matters of design for his own buildings and interiors. His policies for the government therefore found their counterparts in the principles he realized in his private house designs. Similarly, his privately published criticisms of Germany's architectural, social, and economic circumstances found legitimation in the substance of Commerce Ministry decrees.

Neither the Werkbund nor government service occupied all of Muthesius's time as a cultural reformer. His private architectural practice, which focused on modern suburban "country house" (*Landhaus*) architecture for a new elite, provided yet another venue in which he articulated a vision of Wilhelmine social and cultural reform. Like the other spheres of his activity, his architecture evinced a particular Wilhelmine blend of social conservatism and progressive design thinking, held in a tension characteristic of German culture in the years before the First World War. It is in Muthesius's architectural practice, launched initially by private commissions from his Commerce Ministry superiors, that the social, political, and economic dimensions of Muthesius's governmental and Werkbund-based reforms are manifested in architectural form.

CHAPTER FIVE

HERMANN MUTHESIUS: ARCHITECTURAL PRACTICE BETWEEN GOVERNMENT SERVICE AND WERKBUND ACTIVISM

THE *LANDHAUS* MOVEMENT AND BERLIN'S RISING BOURGEOIS LEADERSHIP CLASS

In order to give the reform movement in the applied arts and light manufacturing national expression in the Deutscher Werkbund, men like Friedrich Naumann, Karl Schmidt, and Hermann Muthesius drew from ever-widening circles of German business and society.[1] Between 1907 and 1914, corporate membership in the Werkbund's "cartel for quality" would grow from 143 to more than 300 companies. Oriented at its inception to artists and applied-arts manufacturers, the Werkbund within a few years would welcome newer, technically oriented industrial firms with names like Bosch, Bayer, BASF, Daimler, Benz, and Mannesmann. These firms joined the AEG, an early Werkbund giant, in representing Germany's increasingly influential mechanical, chemical, and electrical industries.[2]

Even as the Werkbund's national base expanded, however, regional power centers and local political outlooks continued to play an important role in determining the organization's growth and identity. From their respective bases in Dresden, Heilbronn, and Berlin, leaders like Schmidt, Naumann, and Muthesius attracted new members and firms, published their evolving views about the association's mission, and shaped the organization's agenda through contributions at national annual meetings. Additional centers of Werkbund activity also arose in the first few years, most notably at Karl Ernst Osthaus's German Museum of Art in Commerce and Industry in Hagen (Deutsches Museum für Kunst im Handel und Industrie), a town in the industrial Ruhr district. Osthaus, a wealthy art patron who had operated the Folkwang Museum for avant-garde European art since 1902 using funds inherited from a family banking fortune, founded the

Museum for Art in Commerce and Industry in mid-1909 in cooperation with the Werkbund and as an outgrowth of his Folkwang museum activities.[3] Tensions grew within the Werkbund as membership expanded and figures like Muthesius, Naumann, Osthaus, Schmidt, and van de Velde struggled to impose divergent views concerning the organization's overall strategy and tactics.

Each of these important Werkbund figures gained influence from the particular institutions and local contexts in which they worked. Hermann Muthesius was no exception, and in some ways was a special case. For while the architect introduced ground-breaking, mutually reinforcing reforms into state applied-arts institutions and the Werkbund, he simultaneously cultivated an architectural practice in suburban Berlin that catered to leading members of his governmental and Werkbund client base. Muthesius's architectural commissions, when analyzed in the context of fast-paced changes taking place in Wilhelmine Berlin, illuminate important relationships between the architect's reform efforts in the government, the Werkbund, and in private practice. Perhaps more than any other single Werkbund member, Muthesius employed what one of his colleagues termed the architect's "concentric talents" in writing, policy making, the applied arts, and architectural design to advance the interests of the bourgeois class (*Bürgertum*) both within and outside government circles.[4]

The high-level civil servants, industrialists, entrepreneurs, artists, and educators who commissioned houses by Muthesius joined the architect in projecting a vision of Germany's capital as home to a new, modern, artistically sophisticated bourgeois leadership class. Not simply an outgrowth of his theoretical writings on architecture, as they often have been portrayed, Muthesius's buildings were the architectural embodiments of reforms the architect was enacting in the Prussian Commerce Ministry's arts, crafts, and trades education system, and, later, in the Werkbund's programs for producer, merchant, and consumer education. In fact, many of Muthesius's Berlin-based clients, highly accomplished and generally operating at the top of their respective professions, made quite conscious efforts in their own fields to further the very initiatives that Muthesius was advancing in both his government and Werkbund guises.

THE *LANDHAUS*: ARCHITECTURAL EMBODIMENT OF MUTHESIUS'S REFORM AMBITIONS

In his private practice Muthesius propagated a suburban version of the "country house" known as the *Landhaus* (Figs. 58–60). A term in popular use since the early nineteenth century, the *Landhaus* was typically a primary suburban residence that emphasized domestic comfort, cultured bourgeois living, and close contact with its natural surroundings. Architecturally speaking, the *Landhaus* differed from its grand residential counterpart, the villa, in one essential respect: The villa typically stood above a garden with its main floor, or *piano nobile*, atop a

58. Hermann Muthesius, Hermann von Seefeld house, Zehlendorf by Berlin, 1904–05, view from Knesebeckstrasse (altered) (Courtesy of Zehlendorf Heimatverein und Archiv, Berlin)

59. Hermann Muthesius, Hermann von Seefeld house, Zehlendorf by Berlin, 1904–05, view of garden façade (*Berliner Architekturwelt* 10, 1907)

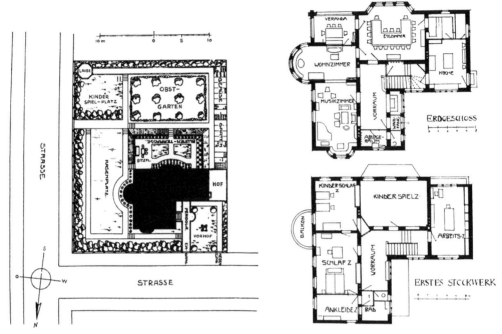

60. Hermann Muthesius, Hermann von Seefeld house, Zehlendorf by Berlin, 1904–05, site plan, ground- and first-floor plans (Hermann Muthesius, *Landhaus und Garten*, Munich, 1907)

submerged half-basement (Fig. 61). This half-basement, while lifting the main rooms of the house above the garden and contributing to the overall verticality of the building volume, provided space for servants' quarters, storage rooms, and other service spaces such as the kitchen and scullery. Garden access in the villa was usually obtained by passing through a winter garden or terrace and then down a staircase. The *Landhaus*, by contrast, tended to feature a main floor placed as close to ground level as possible, affording immediate access to the outdoors (Fig. 59).[5] As designed by architects like Muthesius, Erich Blunck, Otto Spalding, and others, individual rooms in the *Landhaus* opened directly onto terraces, lawns, kitchen gardens, and other rationally planned outdoor spaces. Large windows and projecting bays further maximized daylighting for the interior.[6]

Landhaus architects explicitly designed their houses to be in close contact with nature. Connoting healthy living while bringing residents closer symbolically to "German soil," the typical *Landhaus* offered comfort, privacy, maximum contact with sunlight, fresh air and the outdoors, and a measure of cultural significa-tion. Often more spread out horizontally on their sites than their villa coun-terparts, these edifices also tended to feature elements borrowed from German and northern European vernacular architecture: steep, soaring roofs and a vari-ety of windows, gables, and bays. The high, sloping roof symbolized a particular German and Nordic domesticity as it sheltered the house from the wet, icy climate of northern Europe.[7] Although architects like Alfred Messel, Alfred Grenander,

Erdmann u. Spindler, Arch.   Holzstich v. O. Ebel, Berlin.
Villa Ebeling.

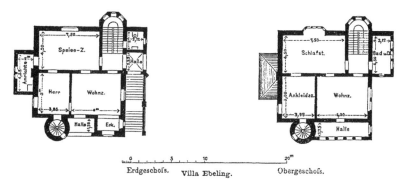

Erdgeschofs.   Villa Ebeling.   Obergeschofs.

61. Gustav Erdmann and Ernst Spindler, Villa Ebeling, Wannsee, 1893, perspective rendering from southwest with plans of ground floor and first floor (altered) (*Centralblatt der Bauverwaltung* 13, 1893)

and Otto March began importing some features of English country house design into Germany toward the end of the nineteenth century, it was Muthesius who, in the opening years of the twentieth century, first formalized the lessons of the British Arts and Crafts movement into a reform program for German architectural and cultural renewal.[8]

To Muthesius, this *Landhaus* design philosophy carried an important social message. Imparting a socially conservative slant to the position of such mid-nineteenth-century German single-family-house advocates as Victor Aimé Huber, a supporter of housing for workers, Muthesius explained that the modern *Landhaus* movement embodied the ascent of the *Bildungsbürgertum* as modern Germany's true leadership class.[9] In *Style-Architecture and Building-Art* and *The English House*, he had argued that the German house must replace the urban apartment as the center of a revitalized domestic culture.

Muthesius designed his suburban country houses to accommodate diverse social functions, family requirements, servants, and work spaces. The buildings would exhibit a particular Wilhelmine form of *Sachlichkeit* through their floor plans, massing, and careful calibration of indoor and outdoor spaces. *Sachlichkeit* in this context meant planning and design that paid particular attention to the orientation, lighting, and furnishing requirements of every room and garden space so as to fulfill specific domestic functions and the rituals of modern bourgeois family life. Taking cues from the British Arts and Crafts movement, Muthesius strove to provide the rising new German bourgeoisie with an appealing, dignified, historically rooted architecture – a German variant of the suburban British houses that he had observed by architects like Richard Norman Shaw, Charles Voysey, and M. H. Baillie Scott. At the same time, Muthesius used carefully chosen materials, construction techniques, and artful, restrained decorations to set his bourgeois houses well apart from those that, in parvenu fashion, merely mimicked historical styles and ornaments associated with periods of aristocratic hegemony.[10] A hall he designed for the Bernhard house in Berlin-Grunewald, his second commission, was typical: It featured oak-paneled sliding doors, an elevated podium containing a well-lit seating area, double-layered casement "flower windows" (*Blumenfenster*) affording passive solar warmth for plants in winter conditions, an inglenook, custom lighting, and colorful rugs and upholstery featuring fabrics from the firm of William Morris (Fig. 62).

Muthesius designed more than two dozen houses in Berlin's wealthy suburbs between 1904 and the outbreak of the First World War. He also had commissions for large country estates outside of Berlin for German industrialists, bankers, and aristocrats, just as he had commissions for *Landhäuser* in cities such as Frankfurt and Lübeck, as well as in the Hapsburg regions of Bohemia and Silesia. At one socioeconomic extreme Muthesius designed large stone houses and aristocratic country estates (*Herrenhäuser*) such as the Wendgraben Estate near Loburg (outside Magdeburg) and the Villa Dryander for a country estate in the province of Zabitz in Saxony.[11] These were extensive commissions with enormous budgets and square footage requirements, but as Muthesius himself had written in *The English House*, the cultural challenge of designing proper houses for modern *Bürgers* in the early twentieth century by far outweighed the production of a few more country estates.[12] At the other extreme were Muthesius's designs for workers' housing in garden-suburb housing schemes, the only place where the architect could realize his wish to design houses that were unified at the level of the street block rather than merely within an individual site.[13] Muthesius built

62. Hermann Muthesius, Bernhard house, Berlin-Grunewald, 1904–05, view of hall (altered)
(Hermann Muthesius, *Landhäuser von Hermann Muthesius*, Munich, 1912)

some two dozen additional *Landhäuser* after the war and until his death in 1927, but these no longer carried the same forceful message for bourgeois reform in the radically altered architectural culture of the Weimar Republic.[14]

The bulk of Muthesius's *Landhaus* commissions, however, came from Berlin, and most of his early-twentieth-century houses appeared in the new belt of suburbs and villa colonies that had been springing up among the woodlands and lakes of the Grunewald forest since the late 1880s and early 1890s (Fig. 63). These suburbs were located from two to eight miles to the west and southwest of Berlin and included the villa colonies of Schlachtensee (founded 1894), Zehlendorf-Grunewald (founded 1898), Nicolassee (founded 1900), and Zehlendorf-West (founded 1903), and extended as well to such suburbs as Dahlem and Wannsee.[15]

To succeed in the private architectural practice that he operated alongside his employment with the Prussian Ministry of Commerce and Trade, Muthesius declared war on traditional, academically trained architects and on that class of traditional master masons, architects, and speculative builders whom Muthesius blamed for creating the burgeoning "style-architecture" of Berlin's suburbs and villa colonies. A veritable flood of articles, books, and lectures about the modern German home aided him in this campaign. Besides promoting *The English House* as a chronicle of English architectural and cultural evolution from which Germany could benefit, Muthesius released lavish new catalogs in 1904, 1905, 1907, and 1912 bearing the titles *The Modern Country House* (*Das moderne Landhaus*), *Country House and Garden* (*Landhaus und Garten*), and, for a catalog of his own buildings, simply *Country Houses* (*Landhäuser*).[16] The first two works comprised international folios of recently produced, architect-designed houses for upper-middle-class clients in such countries as Germany, Austria, England, the United States, and Finland. Their timely release enabled Muthesius to propagate the image that an enlightened, international upper-middle class was participating in a *Landhaus* movement that stretched from Oak Park, Illinois, to the suburbs of Helsinki and Stockholm. Those Germans who wished to participate as modern arbiters of culture and taste, the books implied, would commission an architect like Muthesius to design a *Landhaus* for them as well.

In other writings Muthesius reiterated the many causes to which he attributed the decline of German taste in the nineteenth century: the demise of the crafts tradition, misguided new forms of fabrication, social changes that had catapulted a new class lacking in taste to the top of the social order, and Germany's sharply limited economic success during the first half of the century. "But nothing," he admonished, "has had so shocking and disastrous an effect [on German taste] as the parvenu class of the last thirty years."[17] The architect also attacked speculative building companies (*Terraingesellschaften*) for employing poorly trained draftsmen to design villas that were cheap and poorly thought through and then selling them to the public. In the 1907 edition of *Landhaus und Garten* he wrote,

> Villa-building real-estate companies (*Terraingesellschaften*) show how little intelligence and artistic ability is regarded as necessary for house building … [They] mostly employ the cheapest drafting labor in their projects to produce dozens of villas which are inferior even to those of the building contractors in their tastelessness and impracticality. That this occurs is the most telling sign of Germany's artistic backwardness.[18]

Invoking the example of Norman Shaw's work on the series of small but tasteful houses for Bedford Park in the 1880s (Figs. 32–33), Muthesius called the failure

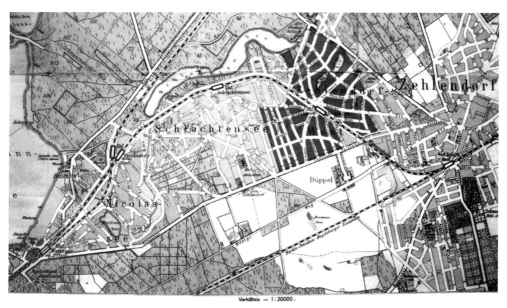

63. Map of villa colonies southwest of Berlin, 1905, detail depicting old village core of Zehlendorf and the villa colonies Zehlendorf-West (shaded), Schlachtensee, and Nicolassee (Landesarchiv Berlin, Kartenabteilung, Acc. 2561 Nr. 26, 1905, detail)

of the German building companies to employ architects of the first rank to design their suburban villa colony houses a "sin of omission" in both the cultural and economic senses. The building companies' villas were, in short, "signs of an anti-culture."[19]

The builders' and development companies' collective success at selling their houses to the public was only further proof, to Muthesius, that Berlin's citizens of means were completely out of touch with the spirit of the times – times that were becoming ever more resolutely defined by middle-class economic, social, and political relations. Failing to understand that such items as their plain business suits, functionally designed bicycles, and other well-engineered contemporary modes of transport were the real symbols of modern times, Berlin's new rich had rushed to re-create the trappings and illusions of aristocratic culture. Even worse, he felt, the example set by the rich was being followed by those of lesser means. Late-nineteenth-century German industry, too, had all too quickly learned to produce cheap surrogates of historical ornaments formerly popular among the aristocracy. In Muthesius's view, the trajectory of the *Jugendstil* – from artistic invention in 1898 to signature style of mass-produced commercial product lines by 1902 – was indicative of the speed with which modern industry had learned to play on the general population's desire to imitate the tastes of more privileged classes.[20]

Against such trends Muthesius reminded readers that architecture was a conservative art, accountable to economic forces as well as human patterns of use in

64. View of houses along Burgrafenstrasse, Zehlendorf by Berlin, 1904 (Courtesy of Zehlendorf Heimatverein und Archiv, Berlin)

ways not true of painting, sculpture, or many of the applied arts.[21] He sought to make his very first house commission, built in Zehlendorf for Privy Councillor Hermann von Seefeld from the Prussian Commerce Ministry, an embodiment of this maxim (Figs. 58–60). Differing greatly from the typical houses being erected in Zehlendorf at this time (Fig. 64), the von Seefeld house illustrated particularly well the closeness of the connection between Muthesius's approach to architecture and his work for the government.[22]

At the von Seefeld house Muthesius demonstrated the degree to which siting and the disposition of individual rooms were a function of the architect's analysis of specific site conditions, solar orientation, views, and the home's particular relationship to the outdoors. At his houses for von Seefeld and a second early patron from the Prussian Commerce Ministry, the State Trades Board director Heinrich Neuhaus, for example, site plans and house plans reveal the extent to which the placement of the dwelling and disposition of individual rooms were a function of each building's orientation to the sun, the garden, and the street (Figs. 58–60; 65–66). For both projects, locating the building in the northernmost portion of the site offered distinct advantages. First, primary living rooms as well as upstairs bedrooms could be located along south-facing façades overlooking terraces and the garden. Second, such service and circulation spaces as the kitchen, pantry, wash rooms, and entrance hall could be placed along less advantageously lit north façades, either facing the street as at the von Seefeld house or facing a service court in the case of the Neuhaus house.

Health, privacy, and enjoyment of the outdoors took precedence over the presentation of a noble façade or the orientation of main living rooms of a *piano nobile*

65. Hermann Muthesius, *Landhaus* for Heinrich Neuhaus, Dahlem (Berlin), 1906–07, view of entrance façade and garden façade (altered) (*Dekorative Kunst* 19, 1910)

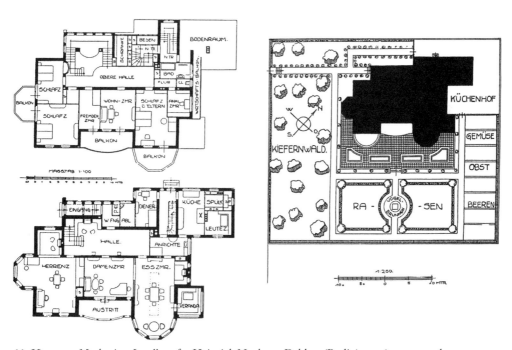

66. Hermann Muthesius, *Landhaus* for Heinrich Neuhaus, Dahlem (Berlin), 1906–07, ground-floor and first-floor plans, site plan (*Dekorative Kunst* 19, 1910)

toward the street. Muthesius's rational approach further used shifts in plan and section to divide the house into distinct rooms and zones for family use, for work, and for entry and circulation; for example, the architect located von Seefeld's ample study (*Arbeitszimmer*) on its own half storey off the middle stair landing (Fig. 60). Although no contemporary interior views of the von Seefeld house survive, Muthesius's plans further illustrate the degree to which each room was conceived with particular uses, furniture, and options for rearrangement in mind. Retractable doors, for instance, enabled the music rooms and living room to be united into a continuous space for large gatherings, while removable window panels on three sides of the veranda made it possible to extend this space even further into the outdoors. Built-in seating and oak, cherry, and maple furniture by highly reputable firms such as Karl Schmidt's Dresden Workshops contributed to the richness of these domestic surroundings.[23]

To adherents of the Applied Arts movement, such a reformed interior represented more than a statement about artistic taste: It was part of a program for the comprehensive bourgeois reform of life (*Lebensreform*), a way of reconnecting with a proud, family oriented, and preindustrial – if idealized – early-nineteenth-century Biedermeier sensibility. As Karl Scheffler wrote in *The Architect* (1907), a volume in a series on "social psychology" edited by Martin Buber:

> The renovation (*Erneuerung*) of the interior presupposes a complete renewal of the conditions and objects of life (*Lebensformen*) of the residents, or, at the very least, a re-organization of their consciousness. It must be called a victory of an all-encompassing conception of life when an artist finally finds in architecture his true field of activity. Alongside artistic self-education comes an education in sociability (*Erziehung zur sozialen Kultur*).[24]

This passage resembles Muthesius's comments about the applied arts involving an all-encompassing "character education," and, indeed, has much in common with the statements of Alfred Lichtwark, Ferdinand Avenarius, and other members of the Art Education movement.

Von Seefeld appreciated Muthesius's design approach and its results on several levels. Active in Zehlendorf's local government and a member of its town council beginning in 1907, von Seefeld was a close personal friend of Muthesius's and was known for hosting frequent large gatherings at which artists, writers, journalists, government officials, and members of the Reichstag mixed with other Berlin notables.[25] Moreover, in his work von Seefeld was part of the Muthesius-led team that drafted the Commerce Ministry's Instructional Workshops Decree. As we saw in Chapter 3, this decree transformed Prussian applied-arts education and, when it was published in December 1904, served as a model for Henry van de Velde in his efforts to enlarge the scope of his Weimar Applied Arts Seminar by adding instructional workshops to his teaching. The decree placed applied-arts training under the guiding hand of an architect, so that all furniture, decorative elements, and color schemes would contribute to unified, harmonious interiors. Muthesius modeled just this type of approach in designing the house for von Seefeld, who was willing to launch Muthesius's private practice with a personal, extragovernmental validation of the measures the two men were helping to advance at Commerce Ministry applied-arts schools throughout Prussia. With von Seefeld's prominent position in local government and in the state bureacracy, Muthesius's first *Landhaus* functioned admirably as both symbol and vehicle for state-sponsored applied-arts reforms.[26]

It is important to note that although an approach oriented to function and use resulted in asymmetrical, Arts and Crafts–influenced house plans, Muthesius's garden plans owed much to Elizabethan formal garden traditions. These, too, had been revived by such Arts and Crafts architects as Phillip Webb, Norman Shaw, and Eden Nesfield in the early 1860s. The formal solution was the rational one for the garden, practical in comparison to the nineteenth-century Romantic landscape tradition's curving pathways and picturesque grottoes. The von Seefeld kitchen thus opened onto a small courtyard and vegetable garden, the dining room and veranda onto a terraced rose garden, and the living room and music room overlooked a lawn (Fig. 60). As Muthesius was fond of explaining to readers and prospective clients:

> One sees in the garden a continuation of the spaces of the house, to a certain degree an array of individual exterior spaces in which each fulfills a specific purpose. In this manner, the garden extends the house into nature and frames it in nature without making it stand in its environment as an alien body. An ordered garden is, aesthetically speaking, like a base on which the house stands, like a statue on its pedestal.[27]

Comparing this with the popular nineteenth-century picturesque approach, which aspired to create artworks in imitation of nature, Muthesius likened Romantic gardens to lifeless figures in a "wax-figure museum."[28]

A brief comparison of a suburban house by Muthesius and those being produced by master masons like Wilhelm Schuffenhauer, the academically trained architects Gustav Erdmann and Ernst Spindler, and the Homestead Joint Stock Company – all active at the same time and in the same suburbs as Muthesius – further illustrates the difference the *Landhaus* architect sought to make in the Berlin domestic environment. At the 1906 house Muthesius designed in Berlin-Dahlem for his Commerce Ministry superior, Heinrich Neuhaus, the architect placed the building on its site so as to maximize forest and garden views, outdoor access, and natural light for major domestic spaces lining the home's southern, western, and eastern fronts (Figs. 65–66). By 1907, Muthesius systemized his rational approach to site planning and building placement even further: He published a schematic diagram illustrating the "ideal" siting of a typical suburban house, given certain conditions (Fig. 67). This diagram maximized advantages of

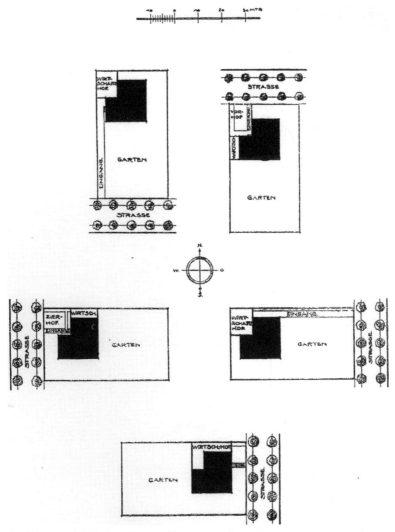

67. Hermann Muthesius, diagram illustrating relationship between house and site as a function of site and solar orientation (Hermann Muthesius, *Landhaus und Garten*, Munich, 1907)

aspect, prospect, and privacy for the house and its most important rooms in cases that assumed a fixed compass direction and particular relationship of each land parcel to the street. The Neuhaus and von Seefeld Houses corresponded to the top two examples in the architect's diagram.[29]

The less advantageously lit north side of the Neuhaus residence contained the entrance foyer and a separate wing for servants and dependent spaces including the kitchen, pantry, and other service rooms. The architect laid out the grand entrance hall, service room, and veranda walls in such a way as to minimize visual and personal contact with domestic personnel (Fig. 66). Taking a page from his own Instructional Workshops Decree and from the Arts and Crafts architects who inspired it, he designed each room's furnishings using high-quality materials, simple, coordinated decorative motifs and harmonized color schemes – all of which conferred a dignity and utility that he called bourgeois (*bürgerlich*) in the best sense of the word (Fig. 68). At the same time, rooms like the slightly sequestered study (*Herrenzimmer*), ladies' drawing room (*Damenzimmer*), and adjoining dining room (*Esszimmer*) all opened outward to a terrace overlooking a rose garden. Other outdoor spaces such as the work yard and kitchen garden aligned with the service wing (Fig. 66).

68. Hermann Muthesius, Neuhaus house, Dahlem (Berlin), 1906–07, view of hall (*Dekorative Kunst* 19, 1910)

By contrast, many houses by Muthesius's competitors aspired to present a noble, dignified appearance by employing elements of the "style-architecture" so decried by the government architect. At one end of the spectrum of suburban housing production were houses by Schuffenhauer, a master mason and small-scale entrepreneur of the *Mittelstand*, who had done a brisk business at his Atelier for Architecture and Building Construction in Zehlendorf since the 1870s. Schuffenhauer became known for his naïve application of Renaissance and Baroque decorations to Italianate villas that, underneath their flattened roofs, retained the scale and proportions of early-nineteenth-century houses found around Berlin and Brandenburg (Fig. 69).[30]

By the turn of the twentieth century, however, new legal and economic factors militated against the success of master masons like Schuffenhauer. As early as 1914, the sociologist Else Meissner's study, *The Relationship of the Artist to the Contractor in Construction and the Applied Arts* (*Das Verhältnis des Künstlers zum Unternehmer im Bau- und Kunstgewerbe*) confirmed that modern architects were gradually replacing traditional master masons and other accomplished crafts workers as leaders of a comprehensive design, construction, and interior finishing process.[31] Rising levels of specialization and the hierarchical organization of labor processes were clear signs, in Meissner's view, of the superimposition of modern market forces onto the housing production process at the expense of more traditional arrangements between master masons and other craftsmen.[32]

In 1897, new German laws had made it far more difficult for craftsmen to obtain the title of *Baumeister*, or "master builder"; these laws resembled new copyright laws that began to protect the works of individual applied artists in 1907, as the art historian Frederic Schwartz has shown.[33] Professional architects benefited as well from maturing market conditions that made turn-of-the-century German house building part of a complex system of supply, distribution, and increasingly specialized production. This further restricted crafts workers from participating as individual leaders of the design and building process and ensured that masons like Schuffenhauer would become part of an endangered breed of artisanal home builder.[34] Meissner's work corroborates for German developments what researchers such as Gwendolyn Wright have identified in the suburban architecture of turn-of-the-century America – namely that middle-class domestic architecture "relied absolutely upon the industrial production and commercialism (that) the home supposedly transcended."[35]

Changes in the law and the use of modern, industrially manufactured materials and construction processes – which Muthesius took as an inspiration for his philosophy of *Sachlichkeit* – subordinated craftsmen in the building trades as surely as other professional organizations, such as the Deutscher Werkbund, were beginning to overshadow artisanal practices in traditional, individualized *Mittelstand* occupations. To the extent that Muthesius advocated *Sachlichkeit* as the proper approach to single-family home design, it might equally have been read by Meissner as the contemporary expression of the rationalization of production processes in

69. Wilhelm Schuffenhauer, Schuffenhauer house, Zehlendorf by Berlin, 1875, street façade (demolished) (Courtesy of Zehlendorf Heimatverein und Archiv, Berlin)

architecture, construction, and the applied arts. Muthesius's arguments in *Style-Architecture and Building-Art* (1902) and *The English House* (1904–05) – in which he expressed the need to rework artistic and socioeconomic processes to reflect the modern Zeitgeist – were not merely a prelude to the economic and sociological analyses of his contemporaries: They were an aesthetic interpretation of these very same processes.

At the other end of the commercial scale, and by the 1890s, large real-estate development firms like the Homestead Joint Stock Company competed against Schuffenhauer and similar small-scale enterprises by featuring a broad array of historicist suburban villa designs in company catalogs. The company's houses could be built to order or bought "key ready" for immediate occupancy in one of several districts being developed by the company. A catalog from 1901, for example, offered a medieval castle replete with crenelated walls, a turret, and towers; more rustic, half-timbered, gabled variants with quite similar, nonsite-specific floor plans were also available (Figs. 70–71).[36]

Like the ornamented, historicist furniture that Muthesius had criticized in traditional applied-arts industries, "style-architecture" emphasized the application of surface ornament for picturesque effects. Even academically trained architects like Gustav Erdmann and Ernst Spindler seemed to ignore issues of solar orientation, practical room placement, and functional garden design. Their Villa Ebeling, commissioned as "a stately *Landhaus* for a young bachelor," was the type of house that epitomized all that was wrong with the prevailing "style-architecture" in Muthesius's eyes: Like so many Wilhelmine architects, the

Projekt No. 100.

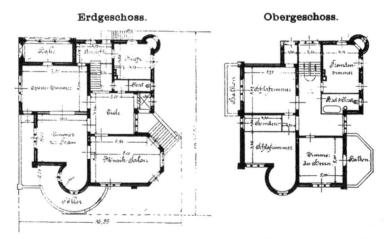

70. Homestead Joint Stock Company, project for a villa in suburban Berlin, early 1900s, elevation, ground- and first-floor plans (Heimstätten-Aktien-Gesellschaft, *Die Villenkolonien an den Bahnhöfen Schlachtensee, Nicolassee, Wannsee, Carlshorst, Mahlow*, Berlin, 1901, courtesy of Zehlendorf Heimatverein und Archiv, Berlin)

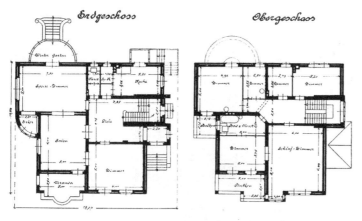

71. Homestead Joint Stock Company, project for a villa in suburban Berlin, early 1900s, elevation, ground- and first-floor plans (Heimstätten-Aktien-Gesellschaft, *Die Villenkolonien an den Bahnhöfen Schlachtensee, Nicolassee, Wannsee, Carlshorst, Mahlow*, Berlin, 1901, courtesy of Zehlendorf Heimatverein und Archiv, Berlin)

designers sought to create an architecture of image at the expense of comfort, adequate ventilation, natural lighting, and functional planning. In their long, narrow site Erdmann and Spindler placed the villa behind a picturesque medieval wall and tower (Figs. 72; 61). Its gatehouse was designed, as one complementary review noted at the time, so that "from the dwelling house one could enjoy no less a charming architectural picture (*Architekturbild*) than one enjoyed from the street."[37] The main house, too, was a picturesque arrangement of a tower, a Renaissance arcade, and a mansard roof executed in a mixture of red brick, yellow

Villa Ebeling.
Abb. 3. Thorgebäude.

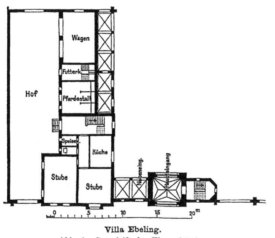

Villa Ebeling.
Abb. 4. Grundriſs des Thorgebäudes.

72. Gustav Erdmann and Ernst Spindler, Villa Ebeling in Wannsee, 1893 gatehouse elevation
and plan (altered) (*Centralblatt der Bauverwaltung* 13, 1893)

sandstone, white plaster, and half-timbered construction. Service spaces such as
bathrooms, the main stair tower, and the hall occupied the well-lit southeast
corner of the building, while the architects placed the sole window for their
patron's office and smoking room on the building's unlit north side (Fig. 61). None
of the main living rooms enjoyed any direct access to the garden or to a terrace, and
the only mention of the garden in a review of the Villa Ebeling in the architectural
press was a "great architectonically designed ornamental fountain."[38]

The project's emphasis on external appearance over Vitruvian fitness and comfort was, in Muthesius's view, living proof of late-nineteenth-century Germany's
parvenu philosophy. It was precisely the absence of a "culture of the German

house" that had led, he thought, to the chaos he saw reigning in German house design and that he called "the cause of the cancer that afflicts all of German art."[39] By the time Muthesius published his second edition of *Style-Architecture and Building-Art* in 1903, he had spelled out his position on the type of client he wished to serve in his private architectural practice. At the close of the book he wrote,

> As the bearer of new ideas, the new spiritual aristocracy arises, which this time stems from the best of the middle class rather than the hereditary aristocratic elements, and this especially clearly signals the new and enlarged goal of the movement: the creation of a contemporary middle-class art.... The goal remains sincerity, straightforwardness (*Sachlichkeit*), and a purity of artistic sensibility, qualities that avoid all secondary considerations and superficialities, so that one can be fully dedicated to the great problem of the time.... If from the labyrinth of the arts of the last hundred years we are ever again to succeed to artistic conditions that bear even a remote similarity to the great epochs of the history of art, then architecture must assume leadership in the community of the arts.[40]

Enunciating this position further in the book *Landhaus und Garten* in 1907, Muthesius described how he sought in his practice to provide homes for the "small community that had recognized the unbearable state of recent artistic affairs and has rebelled against the providers of shoddy art (*Afterkunst*)." This community recognized that Germany's growing Arts and Crafts movement had still to "spread to neighboring fields, above all to domestic architecture, before it can have a thorough and decisive effect."[41]

Muthesius's own house and the adjacent Freudenberg house illustrate the architect's varied approach to house plans, materials, and external appearance (Figs. 73–77). At a bend in Nicolassee's stream and riparian corridor, known as the "Rehwiese," Muthesius found the perfect site on which to showcase a German version of houses he had studied in England. As Voysey had done with large adjoining sites at such projects as Hollybank and the Orchard, Muthesius designed the neighboring Muthesius and Freudenberg houses to create the impression that his projects were completely at home in their natural surroundings and had long stood on their sites.[42]

Muthesius organized his own house beneath a half-hipped roof structure that intersected with an even higher gambrel roof, forms that invoked the traditional German farmhouse (Fig. 74). He arranged simple, quadratic, well-proportioned rooms to take advantage first and foremost of grand views from the edge of the plateau to the northwest, and second to receive abundant light from the south and east. The most prominent room in the house was a long and well-lit music room with a simple white barrel vault and an intricate parquet floor (Fig. 78). Designed with a minimum of rugs, upholstery, and other sound deadening accoutrements, the room formed a center for entertainment and for private music making for the

73. Hermann Muthesius, Freudenberg house and Muthesius house, Nicolassee, ca. 1910, view from the east looking down the Rehwiese meadow (Hermann Muthesius, *Landhäuser von Hermann Muthesius*, Munich, 1912)

74. Hermann Muthesius, Muthesius house, Nicolassee, 1906–07, with atelier wing added 1909, view from northeast (altered) (*Blätter für Architektur und Kunsthandwerk* 24, 1911)

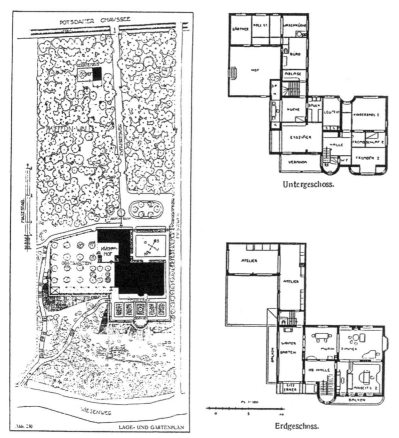

Untergeschoss.

Erdgeschoss.

75. Hermann Muthesius, Muthesius house, Nicolassee, site plan, ground- and first-floor plans, 1909 (Hermann Muthesius, *Landhäuser*, Munich, 1912; *Blätter für Architektur und Kunsthandwerk* 24, 1911)

76. Hermann Muthesius, Freudenberg house, Nicolassee, 1907–08, view of garden façade as seen from the Rehwiese meadow (altered) (*Blätter für Architektur und Kunsthandwerk* 24, 1911)

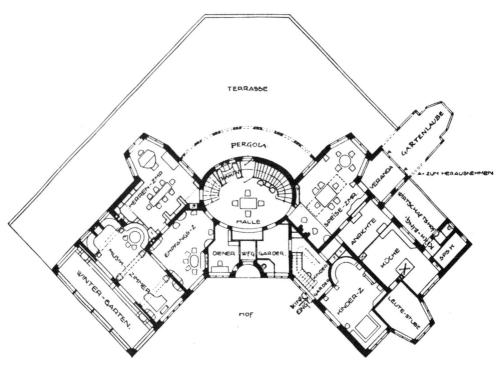

77. Hermann Muthesius, Freudenberg house, Nicolassee, 1907–08, ground-floor plan
(Hermann Muthesius, *Landhäuser von Hermann Muthesius*, Munich, 1912)

78. Hermann Muthesius, Muthesius house, Nicolassee, 1906–07; 1909, music room (*Deutsche Kunst und Dekoration* 12, 1908)

79. Hermann Muthesius, Muthesius house, Nicolassee, winter garden, 1906–07; 1909, (*Deutsche Kunst und Dekoration* 12, 1908)

architect, an accomplished pianist, and his wife, Anna, a professional singer prior to their marriage. The winter garden bore the influence of the architect Charles Rennie Mackintosh, who was godfather to Muthesius's son Eckart (Fig. 79). Two gifts of the Scottish architect's own design occupied prominent positions in the house: a stained-glass window hung in the second floor of the stair tower, and a round chandelier with spherical bulbs hung in Muthesius's office (Fig. 80).[43] The office, reduced in size from the two-story scheme the architect had devised in 1906, was efficiently planned to offer maximum built-in seating and storage space in bookcases and cupboards that surrounded the room's elevated podium and primary work area.[44] As was customary in his office designs, the architect positioned the main desk to assure that it was well lit from the left side by a row of windows. The architect completed his *Landhaus* with the addition of an atelier in 1909 (Figs. 74–75). In its final form, the L-shaped atelier wing enclosed a new service courtyard with the help of an additional wall. As if to suggest that no age was too early to expose his children to the world of commerce and trade, the architect built a kiosk outfitted as a miniature "department store" (*Kaufhaus Eckchen*) into the corner of the children's playroom.[45]

The Freudenberg house, by contrast, was a much more formal, stately edifice that attended to domestic comforts within the extended wings of a butterfly plan (Figs. 76–77; 81; 37). In England Muthesius had studied the possibilities afforded by this plan in the works of Norman Shaw, Edward Prior, M. H. Baillie Scott,

80. Hermann Muthesius, Muthesius house, Nicolassee, 1906–07; 1909, office (*Deutsche Kunst und Dekoration* 12, 1908)

81. Hermann Muthesius, Freudenberg house, Nicolassee, 1907–08, view of entrance façade (Hermann Muthesius, *Landhäuser von Hermann Muthesius*, Munich, 1912)

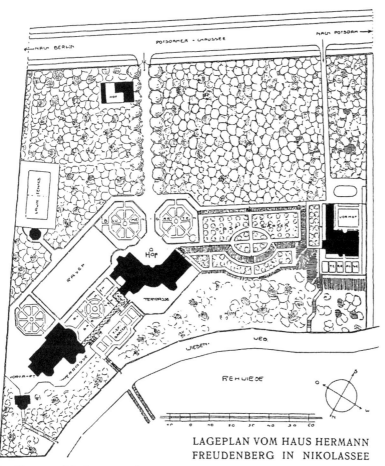

LAGEPLAN VOM HAUS HERMANN
FREUDENBERG IN NIKOLASSEE

82. Hermann Muthesius, preliminary site plan of the houses Freudenberg and Muthesius, Nicolassee, ca. 1907 (*Dekorative Kunst* 14, 1910)

and others, and appropriated it as an example of Northern European domestic architecture suitable for Germany.[46] The German architect used this plan to full advantage in an auspicious site atop the plateau, nestling the house in a bend of the winding Rehwiese meadow (Figs. 73; 76; 82). The extended wings maximized views in the two directions up and down the meadow at the rear of the house, while in front the building's geometry worked to create an imposing, formal entry and forecourt at the end of an allée of trees (Fig. 81).

The architect transformed a half-timbered gable above the entranceway into a monumental element that jutted out over the entrance courtyard and was on axis with the entrance approach. Muthesius enlisted local master bricklayers to clad the gable in a seemingly endless variety of panels featuring clover-leaf, diagonal, and hexagonal patterns in between the gable's half timbers (Fig. 81). Further details like the stenciled meander pattern in the window frames, dormers, and gables added to the impression that the client, the owner of the fashionable

Hermann Gerson home-furnishings and department store, must indeed have been one of the leading members of Berlin's modern artistic culture.[47] Decorative accents and details were a recurring theme in *Landhaus* façades that otherwise differed widely from one another, but few of Muthesius's projects received as much attention to structural and applied detail as the Freudenberg residence.

Another distinguishing design feature of the Freudenberg house was what the architectural historian Julius Posener has classified as Muthesius's "jigsaw puzzle plan," a series of irregularly shaped rooms fitted into a whole (Fig. 77).[48] As in the exterior of the house, an eclectic mix of regular and irregular geometries in the plan maintained a balance between formality and informality. Along the entrance axis, visitors were shown through a foyer into one of Muthesius's grandest entrance and stair halls – a Baroque-influenced, double-height oval room panelled with lustrous inlaid mahogany (Fig. 83). Muthesius maintained the plan's symmetry only along the entrance axis of the building, continuing it through the hall and out the back door, leading under a pergola and onto the terrace over the Rehwiese.

The garden façade of the Freudenberg house expressed the oval shape of the hall in a manner that reworked such structural motifs as those Muthesius had observed in Voysey's New Place at Haslemere in Surrey (Figs. 34–36). Where Voysey had favored a projecting triangular gable supported by recessed round bays, Muthesius applied brick pilasters between the hall's double-height windows to give the Freudenberg structure a Baroque expression. The swooping curve of the window bay above the windows and pilasters only added to the effect of eclectic, crafted aristocratic grandeur.

That Muthesius thought of, or at least depicted, the Freudenberg and Muthesius houses as related units is clear from his comprehensive garden and site plan (Fig. 82). This plan employed elliptical and octagonal flower beds and numerous pathways to link the Muthesius house, the Freudenberg house, and a projected house for Freudenberg's brother into a harmonious ensemble. Muthesius apparently was able to acquire the land for these sites – approximately three-and-a-half hectares – from the villa colony's Homestead Stock Company even before the land was officially advertised as parcels in the villa colony's market.[49]

The site plan presented a unified image of sizable, carefully landscaped country estates in a suburban context, thereby heightening the impression of updated aristocratic grandeur.[50] Unlike the house for Hermann Freudenberg, however, the house for Julius Freudenberg never materialized; nor did an agreement to bridge the Muthesius and Freudenberg sites by means of the large formal garden. Instead, the land appears to have been divided by the owners along the axis bisecting the garden in a line perpendicular to the nearby main boulevard, the Potsdamer Chaussee (Fig. 75). Muthesius nevertheless published his grand and unified initial design even after the completion of the houses, perhaps to maximize the impression that he was indeed building at a scale befitting a new "spiritual aristocracy."

83. Hermann Muthesius, Freudenberg house, Nicolassee, 1907–08, view of hall (Hermann Muthesius, *Landhäuser von Hermann Muthesius*, Munich, 1912)

Both *Landhäuser*, as embodiments of Muthesius's architectural reform efforts, were used for frequent entertainment, the staging of outdoor summer plays, and receptions for Commerce Ministry and Werkbund events. Significantly, the Muthesius and Freudenberg houses served jointly as the venue for the closing reception of the June 1910 Werkbund annual congress in Berlin. Among those who enjoyed mingling with Muthesius, Freudenberg, von Seefeld, and prominent members of the Werkbund was the visiting Charles-Edouard Jeanneret (the future Le Corbusier), who was in Berlin as part of his study tour of German architecture and applied arts commissioned by his home town of La Chaux-de-Fonds.[51]

BERLIN: BATTLEGROUND OF SUBURBAN DEVELOPMENT

Despite his lofty ambitions, Muthesius's far-reaching vision for architectural reform was complicated and to a significant degree confounded by the competitive environment of Germany's expanding imperial capital. For all of Germany's progress in pioneering such aspects of city planning and differential zoning in the nineteenth century, turn-of-the-century Berlin ranked last among German cities in enacting zoning and building regulations.[52] Land speculation thus abounded as new suburban municipalities arose outside the city's jurisdiction. Berlin's local government exercised little control over these suburbs before the First World War, for its boundaries remained unchanged in the explosive period of growth spanning the adoption of James Hobrecht's Plan in 1862 and the Greater Berlin expansion of 1920. Consequently, German planning in Berlin showed fewer signs

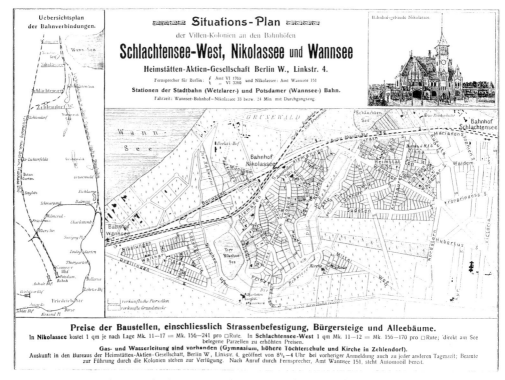

84. Joseph Brix and Felix Genzmer, for Homestead Joint Stock Company, plan of the Nicolassee villa colony, 1905 (Landesarchiv Berlin, Kartenabteilung Acc. 2561 Nr. 26, 1905)

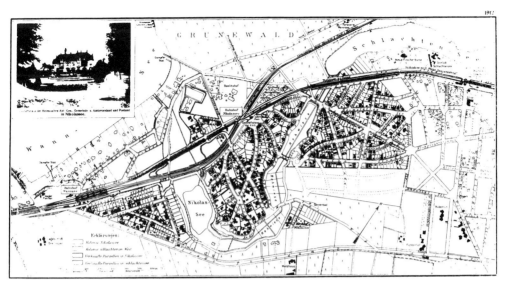

85. Joseph Brix and Felix Genzmer, for Homestead Joint Stock Company, plan of the Nicolassee villa colony, 1912 (Landesarchiv Berlin, Kartenabteilung B 246/1912)

of dramatic gains around the turn of the century than Britain, with its Garden City and Town Planning movement, or the United States, with its City Beautiful movement and vigorous program of public park construction.[53]

As a result of these local conditions in Berlin, Muthesius was unable to convince suburban real-estate developers to retain him as an estate architect for one of the many "villa colonies" that had been springing up in the forests outside the city. As discussed in Chapter 2, and as Muthesius spelled out in his publications, the architect would have preferred to adopt the precedent set in the 1870s at Bedford Park outside London, developed by the artistically minded cloth merchant and developer Jonathan Carr. Working with the architects E. W. Godwin and Richard Norman Shaw, Carr had successfully balanced economic, functional, and artistic considerations in England's first planned middle-class suburban community (Figs. 32–33).

More typical of the Berlin suburban development boom around 1900 was the villa colony of Nicolassee, where Muthesius located his own house and architectural practice. Founded in 1900 by the Homestead Joint Stock Company, the colony featured a scenic forested lake, a stream, and the bucolic Rehwiese, the 100-meter-wide riparian corridor that snaked its way through the area's sloping hills and wooded bluffs (Figs. 73; 84–85). The mixture of natural beauty, attractive houses built along gently winding streets, and a diverse population of artists, writers, and professionals prompted some residents to observe in hindsight that the "remarkable colony Nicolassee lay outside of the usual Berlin and actually quite outside the Prussia of those times."[54] However, the peacefulness of this suburban setting belied the conflicting forces that shaped it. The evolution of the

Nicolassee villa colony pitted a hugely profitable, large-scale capitalist economic development against the elitist artistic and social-reform agenda of the colony's best-known resident architect.

Though far more accustomed to achieving results with the centralized authority of the state behind him, Muthesius was forced to operate within the confines of the modern marketplace with its intense profit-based constraints. For its part, the company studied the fashionable techniques of English garden city planners less to fulfill a social-reform agenda than to facilitate the organization of its business enterprise and to accelerate the sale of housing units to Berlin's growing suburban professional middle and upper-middle classes. The company emphasized the colony's conveniently planned transportation that offered access to a broad array of affordable, contractor-built model homes and building lots within a wide price range. This strategy enabled the Homestead Company to sell its homes quickly and cheaply, thereby thwarting the self-fashioned expert architect's ambition for suburbwide success.

The Homestead Company hired the architects Joseph Brix and Felix Genzmer to design the Nicolassee general plan. Their picturesque solution produced gently undulating streets with views over the lake, stream, and surrounding Rehwiese meadow. The focal point of the Nicolassee plan was a single large public square, the "Hohenzollern Platz," in which the company erected a picturesque ensemble consisting of a new neo-Gothic Nicolassee railway station and, directly across from it, a palatial edifice that housed its main business and sales offices as well as the Nicolassee post office. The prominent location of the company's headquarters at the far side of the plaza meant that the commercial structure, also in the neo-Gothic style, provided a monumental gateway to the winding, forested suburban streets beyond. The radiating principal streets of the development offered salesmen, residents, and customers who had just arrived at Hohenzollern Platz quick and easy access to the suburb's model homes and vacant building sites. As if to underscore physically the company's centrality to the Nicolassee scheme, a town hall constructed on the Hohenzollern Platz in subsequent years was forced to occupy a position off the main axis to one side of the plaza. Mindful of the marketing potential of the plaza's Gothic structures, the company proudly reproduced images of the railway station and company headquarters in its successive promotional sales maps for Nicolassee (Figs. 84–85).

In its quest to take maximum advantage of the latest trends in modern suburban planning, the Homestead Company also adopted as a model for its Nicolassee marketing materials the advertising and publicity format followed by the English Garden City Association at its first Garden City of Letchworth (Fig. 86). Founded in 1902, Letchworth was the practical result of efforts by Ebenezer Howard and the Garden City Association to shift development from overcrowded English cities to the countryside.

The German developer produced its first marketing brochure for the Nicolassee villa colony in 1903, following as closely as possible the techniques

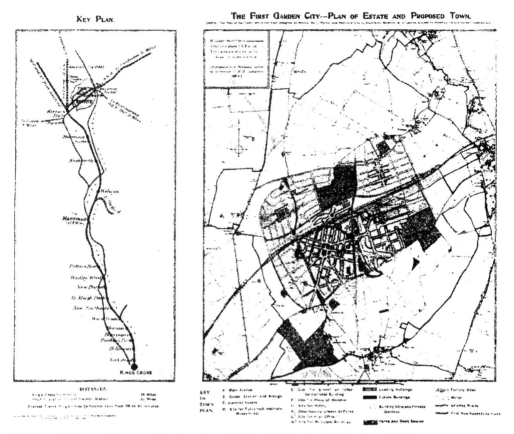

86. Barry Parker and Raymond Unwin, plan of the English Garden City Letchworth, circa 1901 (Deutsche Gartenstadt-Gesellschaft, *Die Gartenstadt im Wort und Bild*, Flugschrift 7, Berlin, 1906)

that Barry Parker and Raymond Unwin used to produce the Letchworth estate plan of 1902. In a move that may have intentionally given the Nicolassee prospectus a scale and layout similar to those in contemporary plans for Letchworth, the Homestead Company represented the villa colony of Nicolassee together with the adjacent suburb of Schlachtensee, laid out in 1894 (Fig. 84). At Schlachtensee, the company's planners had followed a precedent used at Charlottenburg castle to the west of Berlin, but projected the layout of a palatial, thirty-room rural retreat constructed in the 1880s into the suburban fabric. Making the most of Schlachtensee's formal planning elements and Nicolassee's picturesque features, the Homestead Company brochure of 1903 employed a system of cross-hatching to draw attention to the variety of planning elements.

The plans produced by Parker and Unwin for Letchworth in 1903–04 also served as a model for the Nicolassee prospectus in another way: The Homestead Company reproduced a schematic railway map showing the location of the colony relative to the main stations in downtown Berlin. Located to the left of the development plan, the railway map occupied exactly the same position

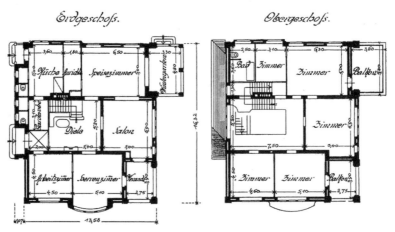

87. Homestead Joint Stock Company, "key ready" single-family house in Schlachtensee villa colony, ca. 1910 (Heimstätten-Aktien-Gesellschaft, *Die Villenkolonien Nikolassee, Schlachtensee-West, und Karlshorst*, Leipzig, 1913, courtesy of Zehlendorf Heimatverein und Archiv, Berlin)

as a similar map in the prospectus for Letchworth (Figs. 84; 86).[55] This similarity prompted the German *Gartenstadtgesellschaft*, or Garden City Society, to feature the plans for Nicolassee and Letchworth as part of a discussion in one of its "propaganda pamphlets," entitled *The Garden City in Word and Image*.[56] Two prominent members of the German Garden City Society, the brothers Julius and Heinrich Hart, actually rented the sprawling Schlachtensee retreat house and used it as the communal home and headquarters for their bohemian literary and artistic society, the *Neue Gemeinschaft* (New Community).[57] From the contemporary literature it is clear that the developer's profit-motive intersected with the German garden city reformers' utopian agenda in the early years of the twentieth century, a phenomenon that is explored in greater detail in the next chapter. The Homestead Stock Company went on to capitalize further on English Garden City ideas in its private developments by employing the same architects, Brix and Genzmer, to design Frohnau Garden City in the suburbs northwest of Berlin in 1909.[58]

Following the strategy it had employed in neighboring Schlachtensee, the Homestead Stock Company advertised Nicolassee as the location of a variety of model homes set in "pure air and in God's free nature" and intended for academics, civil servants, business people, and other members of an "educated *Mittelstand*."[59] In its brochures, the company described an array of affordable homes that could be ordered or purchased as already built. Seeking directly to capture segments of the market that were interested in the lifestyle or the image connoted by the *Landhaus*, the Homestead Company also advertised "key ready" homes in a *Landhaus* style bearing the distinct "influences of the . . . Nikolassee architect Hermann Muthesius" (Fig. 87).[60]

More rectilinear in plan than Muthesius's houses, these homes nevertheless projected the solidity and scale of a *Landhaus* on the exterior. By 1912, such houses as Muthesius's *Landhaus* Hirschowitz and his "*Landhaus* with two apartments" showed that the architect and the company were pitching scaled-down *Landhaus* models to the same clientele (Figs. 88–90).[61] The Hirschowitz house and duplex residence may well reflect Muthesius's growing interest in "types" at this time, which are discussed in greater detail in Chapters 6 and 7.

88. Hermann Muthesius, Hirschowitz house, Nicolassee, street view (Hermann Muthesius, *Landhäuser*, Munich, 1922)

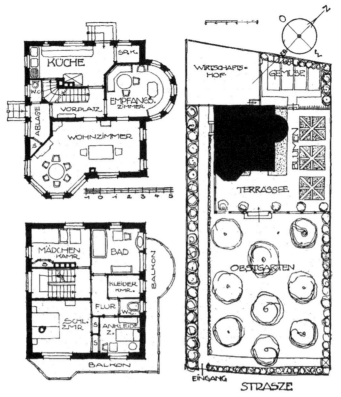

89. Hermann Muthesius, Hirschowitz house, Nicolassee, site plan, ground- and first-floor plans (Hermann Muthesius, *Landhäuser*, Munich, 1922)

90. Hermann Muthesius, *Landhaus* with two apartments, Berlin, 1908 (Hermann Muthesius, *Kann ich auch jetzt noch mein Haus bauen?*, Munich, 1920)

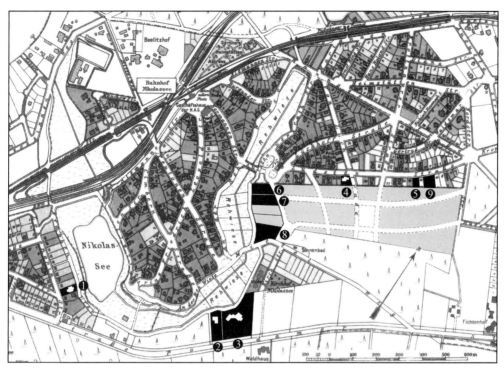

91. Map of Nicolassee depicting Muthesius's *Landhaus* projects and sites: 1. Soetbeer house (completed 1907); 2. Muthesius house (1906; 1909); 3. Freudenberg house (1908); 4. Bloch house (1907); 5. Hirschowitz house (1912); 6. Wild house (1914); 7. Stern house (1913); 8. Mertens house ("Mittelhof," 1915); 9. Vowinckel house (1921). (Landesarchiv Berlin, Kartenabteilung, Kartenabteilung B 246/1912, additions by author, drawing by Joe Corridore)

At favorable prices and financing rates, prospective Nicolassee clients could opt to purchase from among several cottage designs or, alternatively, "hipped-roof villas in the round-arch style." An upscale *Landhaus* with a half-timbered upper story, a wooden veranda, pointed gables and towers, and generously proportioned rooms was another typical example (Fig. 71). The company brochure informed clients that in most cases, they could choose the exact composition of timber framing, gables, and arches in the house façades.[62] The company also encouraged potential buyers to consider purchasing a parcel and arranging to build the house with the building company of their choice. However, given the additional cost of retaining an architect to design a custom dwelling, many clients simply chose one of the company's models that were available on site.

Muthesius, by contrast, completed an ensemble of custom *Landhäuser* that would confront the contractor-built homes of the Homestead Joint Stock Company from across the Rehwiese meadow (Fig. 91). Emphasizing the same qualities of sobriety, fitness, and material quality that he promoted in Prussia's applied-arts schools, Muthesius consciously set his houses for a new Wilhelmine elite against those built by contractors and developers. This architectural confrontation, recorded in the spatial disposition of suburbs like Nicolassee, was a direct parallel to the conflict that pitted Muthesius and the applied artists of the new movement against the crafts practitioners of the traditional *Mittelstand.* Eventually ringing the development company's model homes, houses such as the Freudenberg house, the Soetbeer house, and his own house became part of a suburban architectural "standoff" in which, on either side of the Nicolassee escarpment and stream bed, architect-designed individual houses described a vision of advanced German taste, while opposite them, larger numbers of speculative, contractor-built dwellings satisfied the burgeoning demand for attractive and affordable middle-class suburban homes.

The Muthesius and Freudenberg houses came to form the nucleus of a collection of *Landhaus* projects that Muthesius realized in Nicolassee (Fig. 91). He completed the Soetbeer house, which overlooked the Rehwiese and the Nicolassee lake, in 1907 (Figs. 92–93). In the same year he also designed a *Landhaus* for the engineer Albert Bloch in the nearby Sudeten Strasse (now Shopenhauer Strasse). By 1915 a total of six Muthesius houses would line the southern side of the Rehwiese as Muthesius completed the Stern house (Kirchweg 27, completed 1913), the adjacent Wild house (Kirchweg 25, completed 1914), and a very large house for Wilhelm Mertens, known as "Mittelhof" (Kirchweg

92. Hermann Muthesius, Heinrich Soetbeer house, Nicolassee, 1907, view of garden façade (Hermann Muthesius, *Landhäuser von Hermann Muthesius*, Munich, 1912)

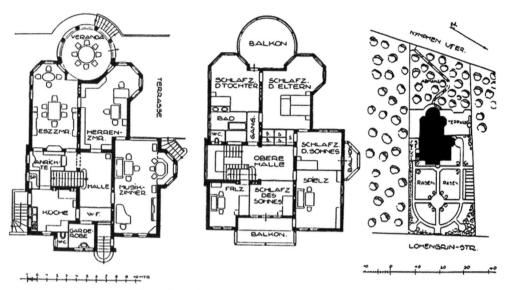

93. Hermann Muthesius, Heinrich Soetbeer house, Nicolassee, 1907, site plan, ground- and first-floor plans (Hermann Muthesius, *Landhäuser von Hermann Muthesius*, Munich, 1912)

33, completed 1915). With between ten and twelve assistants preparing finished drawings and models in his Nicolassee atelier, Muthesius also added the Hirschowitz house to Sudeten Strasse in 1912 (Figs. 88–89), along with two more houses after the war: the Vowinckel house (Sudeten Strasse 12 and 14, completed 1921), and a second "guest" house for Erich Wild at Kirchweg 24 (completed 1925), situated across from the 1914 house.[63]

THE OVERLAPPING REFORM GOALS OF MUTHESIUS'S *LANDHAUS* CLIENTS

Although commentators on Muthesius's architecture have discussed the ways that the Freudenberg house exterior recalls the butterfly house plans and forms of such Arts and Crafts houses as "The Barn" by Edward S. Prior, the exact identity of Hermann Freudenberg, Muthesius's nextdoor neighbor, turns out to have enormous significance for both the Deutscher Werkbund and the German Applied Arts movement generally. Freudenberg, a leading figure in Berlin's applied-arts manufacturing and sales spheres, was an important ally in Muthesius's and the Werkbund's efforts to advance the quality of German applied-arts production. A close friend of Muthesius's who, like Hermann von Seefeld, was fêted in verse in one of Anna Muthesius's published poems, Freudenberg became a member of the Werkbund in 1910.[64] Much like one of the Prussian Commerce Ministry's own reformed applied-arts schools, the Hermann Gerson department store trained cabinet makers and interior finishing craftsmen of all types in its own in-house instructional workshops (Fig. 94).[65] From Freudenberg's highly respected Gerson store and workshops – situated across the street from Karl Schinkel's Neogothic Werder church in central Berlin – came interiors for his own Muthesius-designed house and many other Berlin *Landhäuser*; for sumptuous new officers' quarters onboard German merchant marine and navy ships in Admiral Tirpitz's accelerated ship-building plan; and for exhibition pavilion interiors designed by Muthesius, Walter Gropius, and Bruno Paul at the Werkbund exhibition in Cologne in 1914.[66]

With the Werkbund's increased interest in luxury fashion design beginning in 1914, Freudenberg became chairman of the Association for the German Fashion Industry (*Verband Deutsche Modeindustrie*), an offshoot of the Werkbund's Commission for the Fashion Industry (*Ausschuss für Mode-Industrie*). The close support of the government in these efforts can be seen through its sponsorship of the Deutscher Werkbund Fashion Show of March 1915, held in the Prussian Chamber of Deputies' banquet hall, across the street from the Berlin Applied Arts Museum and Bruno Paul's school.[67]

At the time of Freudenberg's death in 1924, Peter Jessen of the Berlin Applied Arts Museum declared Freudenberg's worth to Germany's Applied Arts movement to have equalled "the value of many men." Statements he quoted of Freudenberg's from various speeches, in fact, displayed a tone virtually indistinguishable from that of Muthesius in his capacities as Commerce Ministry privy councilor and Werkbund vice president. "In the global market of the future," Freudenberg said for example, "only independent, unique German products of the highest and most tasteful quality will play a role; otherwise no German product will retain its worth for export in the long run."[68] Freudenberg was a powerful Muthesius ally, whether collaborating on house interiors and Werkbund pavilions or supporting the Werkbund's commercial and cultural policies.

Two additional patrons of Muthesius-designed houses in Nicolassee had traceable connections to Muthesius's overlapping efforts at reform in the Werkbund and in government applied-arts reform. Erich Wild, a sculptor for whom Muthesius designed a *Landhaus* overlooking the Nicolassee Rehwiese in 1914, executed the sculptures adorning Walter Gropius's and Adolf Meyer's Model Factory at the Werkbund Exhibition in Cologne in 1914.[69] Heinrich Soetbeer, Muthesius's neighbor a few houses to the west along the Rehwiese (Figs. 92–93), was a manufacturer of rubber products who also served as the general secretary of the Association of German Chambers of Commerce (*Deutscher Handelstag*) and as a member of the Standing Committee on Industrial Exhibitions (*Ständige Ausstellungskommission für die Deutsche Industrie*).[70] The latter shared the goals of the Werkbund: The committee worked closely with the Prussian Ministry of Commerce, the Imperial Ministry of the Interior, and the Foreign Office to improve heavy and light industry's efforts to improve competitiveness and raise the status of German industry at home and abroad. The committee also analyzed the viability of firms and markets in all sectors for participation in industrial exhibitions, including the applied arts.[71] These functions complemented the efforts

HERRMANN GERSON

BERLIN W.

Ausstellungsräume: Möbel-Fabrik:
Werderstr. 9—12   Kadinerstr. 20

Aus dem englischen Speisezimmer des Herrn Bankdirektor Hermann W., Lützow-Ufer.
Entwurf: Dipl.-Ing. Mor. Ernst Lesser—Ausführung aller Holzarbeiten in eigener Tischlerei.

Künstlerische Entwürfe
für Einrichtungen von Villen, Etagenwohnungen, Hôtels usw.

Grosses Lager interessanter antiker und moderner Möbel, Stoffe und Teppiche.

Augenblicklich: Ausstellung alter Tapisserien des XVIII. und XIX. Jahrhunderts.

94. Advertisement for the Herrmann Gerson Home Furnishings Store and Workshops, Berlin, 1913 (*Kunst und Künstler* 12, 1913)

of the Werkbund in the applied-arts industries, a fact that Muthesius and other Werkbund leaders certainly appreciated.

Soetbeer was well positioned to advise German businesses and chambers of commerce nationwide on the impact that state- and Werkbund-sponsored design reforms stood to have on German competitiveness and productivity. The Commerce Ministry, in fact, was active in centralizing the authority of the very chambers of commerce for which Soetbeer was responsible.[72] Soetbeer, who was a Werkbund member, backed government measures that would enhance the Werkbund's influence by strengthening the representation of industry in German government and society. Soetbeer argued that the interests of industrialists, who in 1910 made up some two-thirds of the members of Germany's 167 chambers of commerce, were underserved by the chambers of commerce and required separate

95. Hermann Muthesius, factory for the Michels & Cie. Silk Manufacturers, Nowawes by Potsdam, exterior view (*Dekorative Kunst* 19, 1916)

chambers of industry (*Industriekammern*) to represent their interests more effectively in the German economy and in relation to the state. Changes at this level proved to be unforthcoming from the leadership of the Commerce Ministry and Imperial Interior Ministry, however, for these ministries both feared losing influence over industry if these new authorities were created.[73] The central role of industrial interest groups and the government in influencing Werkbund policy in the years before the First World War is examined more closely in Chapter 7.

Although not all of Muthesius's *Landhaus* projects were commissioned by government officials, Werkbund members, or other supporters of progressive developments in architecture and the applied arts, it is surprising how many of them were. For example, Hans Bredow, a high official at the Imperial Post Ministry, commissioned a house from Muthesius in Berlin-Dahlem in 1916.[74] From his position inside the ministry, Bredow was the most likely figure to help arrange for Muthesius to receive another very large commission outside Potsdam: the wireless telegraph station in Nauen. Completed between 1916 and 1920, the station was Europe's largest and most powerful broadcaster of wireless telegraph signals.[75]

Gustav von Velsen, the Prussian Commerce Ministry's chief overseer of the mining industry, also commissioned a Muthesius house in Zehlendorf-West in 1907. As the historian Gerald Feldman has noted, von Velsen was the "driving force" behind Prussian efforts to engineer the state takeover of the Hibernia Coal Company in 1905 – even though it was Commerce Minister Theodor Möller who ultimately paid the price for this failed takeover bid by forfeiting his post.[76] Yet another patron, the industrialist and government commercial adviser (*Kommerzienrat*) Fritz Gugenheim, commissioned Muthesius to design the palatial Michels & Cie. Silk Factory in Nowawes, outside Potsdam (Fig. 95), in

96. Charles de Burlet house, Schlachtensee, view of garden façade (Hermann Muthesius, *Landhäuser von Hermann Muthesius*, Munich, 1922)

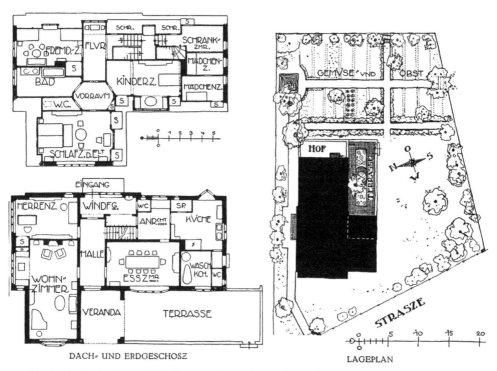

97. Charles de Burlet house, Schlachtensee, floor plans and site plan (Hermann Muthesius, *Landhäuser von Hermann Muthesius*, Munich, 1922)

1912, as well as a house in Berlin-Tiergarten in 1914.[77] In addition to owning the Michels & Cie. Silk Factory, Gugenheim was a member of the board of the Commerce Ministry- and Werkbund-supported Higher Specialty School for Decorative Arts and a founding member of the Werkbund's Commission for the Fashion Industry. Gugenheim, like Muthesius and Heinrich Soetbeer, epitomized that brand of prominent Wilhelmine citizens who saw their influence multiplied through professional positions that placed them at the crossroads of state service, private enterprise, and reform-minded associations like the Werkbund.[78] Wilhelmine applied-arts reformers, economic development officials, industrialists, and other prominent members of the upper-middle class (*Bürgertum*) strengthened their ties through such interconnecting webs of association. The possibility for numerous reforms that favored the expansion of Wilhelmine bourgeois power and influence rested in their hands.

Even some of the smaller houses that Muthesius began designing amid tightening market conditions after 1907 were commissioned by promoters of Berlin's modern "artistic culture." Charles de Burlet, for example, commissioned a small, elegant brick residence in 1911 (Figs. 96–97). De Burlet served the high end of Berlin's market for fine art by operating a gallery space (also designed by Muthesius) out of the prestigious Hotel Adlon, located across from the Brandenburg gate on the Pariser Platz.[79] A neighbor of de Burlet's in Zehlendorf-West, the decorative painter Alfred Mohrbutter, also commissioned a house and studio from Muthesius in 1913. A well-recognized painter and innovator, Mohrbutter received an appointment from the Commerce Ministry to work as an instructor in decorative painting at the Charlottenburg School of Applied Arts (*Kunstgewerbeschule*) in 1904. He collaborated with numerous Berlin fashion designers and carried out commissions as a decorative painter with Hermann Freudenberg's Gerson store.[80] These three houses were close enough together in the nearby colony of Zehlendorf-West to form another cluster of Muthesius-designed *Landhäuser*. They were located midway between his largest concentration of houses in Nicolassee and the homes he completed for Neuhaus, Bredow, and others in Dahlem. Where the houses embodied Muthesius's proclamations of a new kind of German domestic architecture and bourgeois culture, some of their occupants led the growth of commerce and industry, while others advanced an array of state- and Werkbund-sponsored reforms.

No prosopographical study has ever established the careers and identities of all of Muthesius's patrons; even a full count of his houses is difficult, and some attributions continue to be in dispute.[81] It is reasonable, however, to estimate that up to one-third of Muthesius's private commissions came from clients occupying leading positions either in commerce and industry, government posts related to economic development, or in positions in direct support of Werkbund aims. In the foregoing preliminary analysis of a number of *Landhaus* projects and their clients, we can see that Muthesius's architectural practice, government work, and Werkbund work overlapped to a considerable degree. The "ennoblement of German work" – a classic Werkbund tenet – belonged every bit as much to Muthesius's efforts to design houses for Berlin's new "spiritual aristocracy" as it did to the Commerce Ministry's and Werkbund's bid to boost German exports. The architect's designs and careful direction of a variety of applied-arts workers in the completion of custom interiors further reflected the practices Muthesius wished to propagate throughout northern Germany through the reform of Prussia's applied-arts schools and schools for the building trades.

Exercising his authority as chief designer and integrator of the applied-arts and constructional processes, Muthesius expressed a conception of modern Wilhelmine domestic architecture in which the architect not only had to be the master of artistic, planning, and domestic design traditions, but also had to organize and deploy an array of master craftsmen beneath him to complete the transformation of what was essentially a contractor-built edifice into "a work of art."[82] Firmly embedded in the state institutional structures that had enabled him to rise from *Mittelstand* roots to relative prominence, Muthesius practiced a form of residential design that expressed a very particular conception of Wilhelmine socioeconomic organization. This approach borrowed from the traditions of the hierarchically organized Prussian bureaucracy in the same manner that nineteenth-century German industrial enterprises – Siemens or the AEG, Germany's General Electric Company, for example – had been nurtured in the shadow of an advanced, educated, and centralized bureaucratic culture. Muthesius, in other words, shunned the competitive efficiencies and leveling tendencies of modern real-estate markets in favor of a system that depended on centralization, hierarchy, and strict accountability.[83]

Fundamentally different from the British Arts and Crafts movement's decentralized and individualistic guild approach, the architect's embrace of a professionalized applied-arts philosophy valued high-quality work for its economic value and cultural signification, but at the expense of the worker independence and integrity preached by John Ruskin, William Morris, or Charles Ashbee. This high-quality work manifested itself nevertheless in the exterior and interior of the Freudenberg and Muthesius houses and was carried through to the interiors as well by such crafts entrepreneurs as Karl Schmidt's Dresden Workshops for the Applied Arts. Schmidt, one of the leading craftsmen involved in initiating the Werkbund, worked on furniture and interior finishing for Muthesius's *Landhäuser* beginning with the architect's very first house for Hermann von Seefeld.[84]

By no means the only architect designing important new houses in Berlin – one thinks of Peter Behrens, Alfred Messel, and the young Ludwig Mies van der Rohe – Muthesius's houses nevertheless embodied new ways of thinking, building, and living in the Berlin suburban environment.[85] Moreover, his approach to designing and building the *Landhaus* revealed the same top-down reform philosophy that he brought to his school reforms. As he expanded his practice, the architect was forced to face the limitations imposed by an extremely competitive market economy dominated by developers and enterprising contractors.

Meanwhile, and as conditions in the Garden City movement and the Werkbund grew more tense, Muthesius gradually turned to a search for greater consistency and regularity of form as a guarantor of economic success and fulfilment of his claims of achieving the broad-based artistic culture he sought to promote. His work with the Prussian state would help him, and to a certain extent prompt him in his effort to promote "types" as evidence of a maturing German design culture, but not, as we will see, without a struggle from other Werkbund quarters.

◀◖ CHAPTER SIX

CULTURAL FAULT LINES IN THE WILHELMINE GARDEN CITY MOVEMENT ◠◡

A GROWING RIFT: PRAGMATISM VERSUS INDIVIDUALISM IN WILHELMINE REFORM

Karl Schmidt's Garden City of Dresden-Hellerau was the acknowledged flagship of the German Garden City movement. Germany's first garden city to be built along lines inspired by British examples, Hellerau also quickly became the locus of hotly contested debates between different factions of the Werkbund and German Garden City Society (*Gartenstadtgesellschaft*; hereafter GCS), two organizations whose memberships overlapped significantly. Even as men like Karl Schmidt, Hermann Muthesius, Richard Riemerschmid, and Theodor Fischer joined the GCS in order to broaden the reach of the Werkbund's architectural, applied-arts, and social-reform ideas to applied-arts workers in the German *Mittelstand*, they clashed with younger men whose ideas about modern architecture and art were at cross purposes with the pragmatic, business-oriented approach of the senior Wilhelmine figures. Led by the architect Heinrich Tessenow and the idealistic business manager of the Werkbund Wolf Dohrn, the men who introduced classicized monumental architecture to Hellerau at the artist and choreographer Jacques Dalcroze's Institute for Rhythmic Movement elaborated utopian ideas for the protection and glorification of art. Hellerau, however, was founded by Schmidt to serve as a progressive factory suburb for his expanding and phenomenally successful German Workshops for Handcrafted Art, arguably the Werkbund's leading applied-arts industry.[1] Schmidt was by no means alone in feeling that there scarcely was room at Hellerau for the strongly individualistic expressions of art espoused by Tessenow, Dohrn, and other younger members of the Garden City movement.

This chapter examines the efforts of Schmidt, Muthesius, Fischer, and Riemerschmid – as members of a hardening Wilhelmine old guard – to steer an agenda for architectural and socioeconomic reform through the cross currents of Wilhelmine cultural development in the years leading up to World War I. Concentrating on the cultural politics of the German Garden City movement, it shows how philosophical and generational differences introduced serious tensions into the movement's leadership and into the built environment of Hellerau. These tensions naturally carried over into the Deutscher Werkbund, to which many Garden City movement adherents also belonged. The conflicts in the Werkbund, expressed particularly strongly in the years leading up to the first Deutscher Werkbund Exhibition in Cologne in 1914, are the subject of the next chapter, while the conclusion examines the effect that these conflicts had on the early incarnation and promotion of the Bauhaus.

CONFLICTING EARLY IMPULSES OF THE GERMAN GARDEN CITY MOVEMENT

Like the Werkbund, the German Garden City movement – and particularly its Garden City Society (GCS) – became an institutional focal point for a variety of social, political, and design agendas. When the Garden City movement first attained formal status in Germany with the founding of the German GCS in 1902, it was little more than a literary mouthpiece for an array of utopian social-reform groups. Chief among these was the New Community (*Neue Gemeinschaft*), a literary circle led by the brothers Heinrich and Julius Hart, which attracted such future GCS leaders as the brothers Paul and Bernhard Kampffmeyer along with their cousin, Hans Kampffmeyer.[2] The GCS also absorbed members from such nature-loving groups as the Wandering Bird Group (*Wandervogelgruppe*) as well as from other adherents to Germany's burgeoning youth movement (*Jugendbewegung*) from the 1890s.[3] These optimistic groups, comprised mainly of middle- and upper-class intellectuals, gravitated to the English example of the garden city as a way to express their progressive reform impulses in concrete terms. More engaged with literary production and experiments in alternative living, however, the early GCS lacked resources to realize even minor plans for communal housing to have been designed by the young architect Bruno Taut.[4] For this reason, the building association promoter Franz Oppenheimer was prompted to observe that whereas the blooms of the Garden City movement were springing up in the English countryside, in Germany the movement was "still a weak hothouse plant." He added that the GCS resembled some early-nineteenth-century utopian communities that had failed because there were "plenty of philosophers but very few who were willing to dig potatoes."[5]

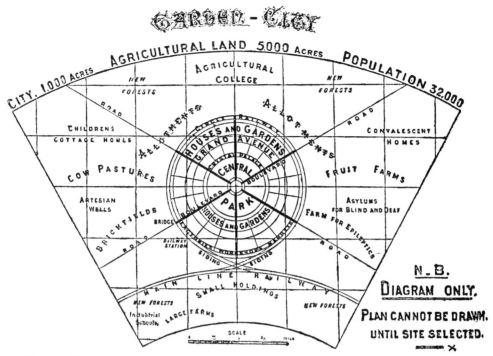

98. Ebenezer Howard, Garden City diagram, 1898 (reprinted from Deutsche Gartenstadt-Gesellschaft, *Die Gartenstadt im Wort und Bild*, Flugschrift 7, Berlin, 1906)

Successful or not, the German GCS modeled itself after the English Garden City Association that had formed in 1899. Like its English counterpart, the German society had been directly inspired by Ebenezer Howard's book from 1898, *To-Morrow: A Peaceful Path to Real Reform*. Howard argued that industrialization, the flight from the countryside to the cities, and urban overcrowding all could be ameliorated through the foundation of new, communally owned towns. With approximately 30,000 residents each, these "garden cities" would help to repopulate the countryside, decentralize cities, and alleviate overcrowding and associated social ills (Fig. 98). Quoted frequently and at length by German reformers, Howard's original book was reprinted as *Garden Cities of Tomorrow* in 1902 and translated into German in an edition published by Eugen Diederichs in 1907.[6]

The English were by no means alone in exploring the idea of planning new towns to relieve urban overcrowding and industrial blight. In 1896, two years before Howard's work appeared, a German sociologist by the name of Theodor Fritsch investigated precisely this theme in a work entitled *The City of the Future* (*Die Stadt der Zukunft*). However, this largely theoretical work offered a vision of ideal cities in which radial boulevards and streets were arranged according to a strict physical and social hierarchy.[7] Moreover, and as the architectural historian

Wolfgang Voigt has noted, Fritsch "wanted the garden city to be understood as a stroke against Jewry," for in the sociologist's opinion, "it was they who controlled the cities" and threatened the German race.[8] *Die Stadt der Zukunft* complemented a series of other sociological works in which Fritsch outlined his nationalist, racist, and anti-Semitic program, and as a result his work received scant attention in GCS circles.

Howard's proposal, by contrast, engaged practical questions of economic organization and land reform in a communal spirit; his work, consequently, held much broader appeal. In schematic diagrams, Howard surrounded a typical, 1,000-acre city with 5,000 acres of a green "girdle" of farmland, factories removed from residential city cores, and various social institutions. His garden city projects for up to 32,000 inhabitants inspired the founding of the English Garden City Association in 1899 and led, after four years of campaigning and planning, to the founding of the first garden city at Letchworth in 1903.[9]

While Adolf Otto, the brothers Paul and Bernhard Kampffmeyer, and other idealist reformers propagated the ideas of the English Garden City movement in the publications of the GCS, men like Karl Schmidt and Hermann Muthesius embarked on an effort to convert the movement into a tool to advance the economic development and social-reform programs on which they collaborated from their respective positions in private enterprise and in the Prussian bureaucracy. Virtually from the moment when, in September 1906, Schmidt received unanimous support in a meeting with his workers for his idea of an expanded factory settlement with communally owned houses and rental units, he had begun planning the ambitious project in earnest with his brother-in-law, Richard Riemerschmid.[10] Moreover, men like Schmidt, Riemerschmid, and Muthesius had shown an interest in improved housing for workers and the trades *Mittelstand* in the form of the village square exhibited at the Third German Crafts Exhibition in summer 1906.[11]

Friedrich Naumann was every bit as enthusiastic as Schmidt to see a rapidly expanding industry relocate to larger facilities with housing for workers set in a model landscape. He helped Schmidt raised the one million Marks in necessary capital to embark on the project.[12] Both Naumann and Schmidt saw tremendous economic and social potential in an expanded workshop enterprise in which workers actively helped plan housing that would rise not in the form of the infamous rental "barracks" in proletarianized cities but as picturesque villages. Moreover, to Naumann the workers belonged to the "rising classes" who had to be respected and empowered, as he stated in his programmatic *New German Economic Policy* (*Neudeutsche Wirtschaftspolitik*) of 1906. This book, completed at exactly the same time that Schmidt was beginning to plan Hellerau, represented Naumann's latest recipe for attempting to reconcile liberals and socialists, as well as the bourgeoisie and working-classes, in the service of Germany's expansion.[13]

Muthesius, a great supporter of Schmidt and of Hellerau, had very different reasons for backing the Garden City movement and Schmidt's project in particular.

First, its centralized planning authority enabled him to exert control over the built environment at a scale that had eluded him in the villa colonies and suburbs of Berlin, as we saw in Chapter 5. Second, it offered the hope that architects could indeed play a central role in designing communities that supported a modernizing industrial and urban economy while expressing a holistic, if conservative, architectural and social vision. As he modernized the Commerce Ministry's applied-arts schools, enlarged his private architectural practice, and cultivated fresh ties for the newly formed Deutscher Werkbund, Muthesius also embraced the Garden City movement as a vehicle for fashioning applied-arts workers of the lower *Mittelstand* into a cohesive trades middle class. By re-creating the conditions of hierarchical authority and centralized control that had allowed him to achieve success in his reforms for the arts, crafts, and trades schools, Muthesius hoped to overcome the vagaries of the modern real-estate market and execute comprehensive, paternalistic design at the garden city of Hellerau. At all times, in fact, Muthesius had fought to maximize the power that architects would exert over design processes in Germany's growing industrial and commercial economy. The models he sought in England, like the garden city developments he supported beginning with Hellerau in 1907, stood out for the ways in which their architects set standards of taste in order to cultivate workers' artistic instincts while integrating the working classes into a stable social hierarchy and modern capitalist production system. The Garden City movement proved useful in the ongoing Wilhelmine campaign to prevent the proletarianization of German workers from reaching the levels that it had in English cities like Manchester, Liverpool, and Birmingham. Like his measures on behalf of the state to integrate crafts workers into a modernized system of design and production, Muthesius's garden city efforts encouraged the design of a new kind of residential environment friendly to workers, thereby helping to allay the deep-seated fear of socialism among Germany's upper and middle classes. This perceived threat to national progress and stability became more real as the percentage of Germany's working-class population increased and as the Social Democratic Party met with increasing pre-war electoral success after 1909.[14]

To Muthesius, then, garden city projects were working- and middle-class counterparts of that architectural embodiment of Muthesius's vision for a modern, enlightened German upper class, the *Landhaus*. The consolidation of the new upper class – as Muthesius's hierarchical reorganization of the schools and editorial collaboration with elite journals such as *Hohe Warte* (High View) made clear – was based in part on a molding of the trades *Mittelstand* into dutiful adherents to a modern, hierarchical Wilhelmine social order.[15] Two years after the Viennese art critic Joseph August Lux launched *Hohe Warte* in 1904, in fact, the journal introduced a supplement entitled "Garden City," which reported on developments in the movement. By 1908, this supplement had expanded sufficiently to become a journal in its own right under the editorship of Hans Kampffmeyer. Together, the two journals reflect the ways in which the educated upper-middle classes extended the impulses of the Art Education movement of the 1890s to refashion the physical environments, modes of production, and consumption habits of less-privileged classes.

In this context, the cultural role of the *Landhaus*, too, became more than simply symbolic: It represented both the pinnacle and the container of a new domestic culture that was at once sophisticated, aesthetically self-conscious, and increasingly consumer oriented. Here, the German family unit – so important to social conservatives such as Muthesius – would thrive in artistically planned surroundings that had been integrated with the outdoors and outfitted with tasteful furniture and domestic accoutrements.[16] As he had argued in *Style-Architecture and Building-Art* in 1902, "The Significance of the Applied Arts" in 1907, and elsewhere, the stability of Wilhelmine Germany depended on propagating a new set of domestic values among the middle and lower classes through a combined cultural and artistic pedagogy. Educating Germans of all classes about taste, domesticity, and suburban house ownership would integrate society into a culture that architects had helped to define and would additionally create a domestic market for the improved export goods that the Commerce Ministry wished to have produced in its restructured system of applied-arts industries and their associated arts, crafts, and trades schools.

The Commerce Ministry's reform of its arts and crafts schools would thus provide a governmental linchpin to Muthesius's larger cultural reform agenda, an agenda that the Werkbund, of course, would propagate at a national level. As much as possible, Muthesius fused Prussia's economic development program for the applied-arts industries with prescriptions for a new German domestic architecture that featured the *Landhaus* for the upper classes and, via the Garden City movement, smaller houses in decentralized garden city developments for the middle and working classes of the German *Mittelstand*. Houses and apartments would flourish in orderly, planned settlements and provide an antidote to the "barracks-city" (*Mietkasernenstadt*) that many critics feared Berlin had become.[17] Muthesius's domestic design philosophy did not reach the extremes of Paul Schultze-Naumburg, the prominent conservative architect who was also a leader in the German movement for national "homeland" preservation, or *Heimatschutzbewegung*. Nevertheless, his philosophy did translate into physical terms Schultze-Naumburg's conviction that domestic architecture should provide a clear mirror of an ideal social hierarchy – what Schultze-Naumburg referred to as an "aesthetic order of estates."[18]

Just as Muthesius and his Commerce Ministry colleagues expected members of the working classes and trades classes to adapt to the new productive conditions being imposed on them by the government's reforms, he similarly believed they would embrace the new domestic and urban order prescribed by garden city architects. Muthesius's overlapping campaigns for a new German *Landhaus* architecture, the improvement of German production through artistic intervention in the Werkbund, and the spread of middle-class (*bürgerlich*) values in garden city-inspired workers' settlements became linked as overlapping features of a comprehensive Wilhelmine architectural, socioeconomic, and cultural program.

Muthesius's goals dovetailed perfectly with those of Karl Schmidt and his company, and the two men collaborated frequently as well. Virtually from the inception of the Dresden Workshops for the Applied Arts, Karl Schmidt had demonstrated a fine-tuned ability to pitch his furniture and design services to a wide range of customers in different social classes. Whether asking Muthesius to lobby Admiral von Tirpitz for the commission for a potential workers' settlement in Wilhelmshaven, or requesting one-page marketing statements to explain the economic and political significance of his applied-arts business to public officials, businesspeople, and the general public, Schmidt appreciated the value of working closely with the Prussian government architect.[19] He likewise had the government architect to thank for commissions received by Riemerschmid and himself to design and execute luxury cabins for the German shipping company Norddeutsche Lloyd. Schmidt in turn ensured that the Prussian architect would meet influential Saxon officials who were smoothing the way for the construction of Schmidt's garden city and would commission him to design some sixty-eight buildings there.[20]

Although the utopian ideas of Robert Owen and Charles Fourier influenced the Garden City movement, Muthesius and Schmidt – each for their own reasons – favored workers' settlements and factory towns as another form of garden city precedent. Schmidt may well have been inspired by Muthesius in his thinking on this front, as he had written of being inspired by *Style-Architecture and Building-Art* in the past. Muthesius particularly favored the paternalistic workers' colonies of such progressive British industrialists as George Cadbury, who built the Bournville estate for the Cadbury chocolate concern, and W. H. Lever, who constructed a colony for his giant soap factory at Port Sunlight. Lever, in fact, became a leading supporter of the Garden City movement in his home country. In 1902 he received an enthusiastic letter from the German Embassy in London in which Muthesius claimed he was "very anxious to report on your movement to the German government."[21] Significantly, however, the scope of Muthesius's reporting in this area was limited to a two-part article on "The Factory Village Port Sunlight by Liverpool."[22] Having left the issue virtually untouched in his seven-year term as a London-based government reporter, it was left to Muthesius's successor at the German Embassy to report on the larger movement.[23]

The garden city theme, too, offers a view into Muthesius's search for balance in industrial development while the government and ruling classes maintained order. His article "England as World Power and Culture-State" of 1899, a review of an eponymous work by the Swedish commentator Gustav Steffens, had argued that English workers' misery and "hell on earth," born of "the relations toward which big industrialism tends," might soon develop in nations such as Germany, where industrialization was accelerating.[24] Ignoring the early stirrings of the Garden City movement, Muthesius identified the workers' colony model as a promising source of rational organization, idealism, and intensive education of the working population – a process known in German as *Volksbildung*. Even in 1903, Muthesius shied from trying to identify the causes of "difficult social scientific questions to which I have until now been able to devote little attention."[25] Rather, he held to a position he had outlined late in 1899 – shortly after completing his study of Port Sunlight – when he wrote: "It must also be possible to become great in industry without stamping a class of people into the ground, maintaining intact a harmonious care for the inner qualities of the nation."[26]

It was undoubtedly the role reserved for architects at Port Sunlight and other English workers' colonies that also fired the German architect's enthusiasm. At the 140-acre factory "village" of Port Sunlight, begun by W. H. Lever in the late 1880s, settlement planners had taken their cues from the picturesque traditions of what Muthesius referred to as contemporary English "*Landhaus* building" (*Landhausbau*).[27] This had occurred with such success and to such an extent, the architect gushed, that "whoever . . . . comes to the village Port Sunlight experiences the greatest surprise."[28] Second, a group of well-known professional architects – including Ernest Newton, William Owen, Ernest George, T. N. Lockwood, and others – had produced "a model menu of the best of English *Landhaus* building," using "not far-fetched ingredients, not overextended concepts of abstract beauty, but [relying] instead solely on a revival of specific local traditions" (Fig. 99).[29] The paternalism that Muthesius clearly valued as a Prussian state functionary had also received fitting architectural expression in ample school buildings, social centers, and above all in dwellings. As his review underscored, the multiunit apartment houses for workers – constructed using the architectural *Landhaus* vocabulary of the class whose mores and habits the factory owners and the observing German architect most wanted workers to absorb – expressed properly the reigning social hierarchy "in artistic terms of outstanding significance."[30]

The colony, in short, exemplified to Muthesius what forward-thinking industrialists could accomplish when paternalistic housing schemes were designed by skilled architects. With their attractive buildings and prospects for workers' home ownership, colonies such as Port Sunlight represented a marked improvement over such German industrial workers' colonies as those of the industrialist Krupp outside of Essen.[31] Paternalist schemes also appealed to Muthesius because they resisted the communitarian social organization of earlier utopian socialists and preserved the family as the basic unit of social organization – a value that the German *New Community* and GCS adherents did not share. The focus on the family linked Muthesius to an older tradition of abortive Prussian state housing reforms initiated in the Rhineland during the 1840s by the architect C. W. Hoffmann and the anti-Owenite reformer Victor Aimé Huber.[32]

Muthesius argued that Lever's use of different architects at Port Sunlight had enabled his colony to outdo Norman Shaw's suburban bourgeois community of thirty years earlier, Bedford Park, in variety and charm.[33] Muthesius devoted little attention to the workers' house per se as he evaluated these colonies; he concentrated instead on the role that architects could play in improving the living

99. Port Sunlight worker's housing, 1892, street view (Hermann Muthesius, *Die englische Baukunst der Gegenwart*, Leipzig, 1900)

conditions of workers through practical and artistic design. Doubtful that these efforts would solve the decades-old problem of overcrowding in English cities, he argued that workers' colonies, garden cities, or government-sponsored urban housing could at least help to alleviate the problem.[34] Linking the improvement of living conditions and workers' taste to the architects' potential role in addressing the "social question," he concluded that Port Sunlight and Bournville "fulfilled in an ideal way . . . . the transfer of art into the life of the working classes."[35]

In both England and Germany, the factory colonies at Port Sunlight and Bournville evolved into symbols of the Garden City movement and were cited indiscriminately as "garden cities" as the movement searched for promising models. Consequently, the chocolate-making colony and the soap-making colony – which generated 3,000 tons of Sunlight soap weekly – gained considerable attention from the press.[36] They also served even more directly as models for the flagship of German garden cities, the garden city of Dresden-Hellerau.

HELLERAU GARDEN CITY: REFORM IN A GERMAN FACTORY COLONY

Hellerau Garden City became a crucible for ideas about town planning, architecture, design, artistic education, and social reform. It was organized around Karl Schmidt's greatly expanded and newly minted "German Workshops for

Handcrafted Art" (*Deutsche Werkstätten für Handwerkskunst*) – a joint stock company formed through the merger of his Dresden Workshops for the Applied Arts and Karl Bertsch's Workshops for Home Furnishings of Munich in 1907.[37] By 1909, Schmidt was using small, private exhibitions of interiors as a springboard to establish new stores in many large German cities; he also pursued prospects for outlets in Vienna, Zurich, Brussels, and as far away as Cairo and Alexandria.[38]

Schmidt enthusiastically kept Muthesius abreast of the company's leading position in Germany's emerging "artists' economy."[39] The steady expansion of his enterprise, coupled with the mergers with the Bavarian firms, enabled him to initiate the Hellerau Garden City as a planned factory community designed completely in the spirit of the architectural and applied-arts reform movement. His constant correspondence with Muthesius, Riemerschmid, and other influential figures since early 1903 reveals common attitudes toward the improvement of production and elevation of German taste through design.

Schmidt also introduced Muthesius to the writings of his friend Friedrich Naumann, the minister, writer, social activist, and politician who published voluminously on all manner of social, religious, and artistic questions in his journal, *Assistance* (*Die Hilfe*). As a pastor, founder of the National Social Union in 1896, and eventual member of the Reichstag's *Fortschrittliche Volkspartei* (Progressive People's Party) ten years later, Naumann advocated aggressively expansionist economic policies as part of a broader socialist domestic program. Although Naumann and Muthesius met in 1905 and collaborated with Schmidt and others in the genesis of the Werkbund, Naumann's commitment to industrial capital, machine production, and the applied-arts economy as means to solve the "social question" clashed with Muthesius's more conservative views on how best to aid workers.[40] Naumann published his opinions in his manifesto for the Werkbund, "Deutsche Gewerbekunst," written in 1908.[41] Accepted by some historians as the definitive statement of the Werkbund's program, the article is better understood as an elaboration of Naumann's political orientation to the connection between workers' welfare and the national welfare.[42] These views were shared by Naumann's prominent allies from the Württemberg city of Heilbronn, most notably by Theodor Heuss, but also to some extent by Peter Bruckmann and Ernst Jäckh. Naumann's manifesto should be seen as a valuable contribution to debates that ranged beyond the issues customarily raised by politicians, including questions of aesthetics, creative authorship of applied-arts products, and the issue of individually designed forms versus the "types" advocated by Muthesius as evidence of economic and cultural progress. As the historian Kevin Repp has noted, Naumann contributed much to discussions among bourgeois reformers who founded their own programs, institutions, and associations as a form of Wilhelmine "anti-politics" – that is, direct action taken outside of legislation and governing bodies.

The Third German Applied Arts Exhibition in Dresden, so critical for the formation of the Werkbund, had also been critical to Schmidt's campaign to relocate his expanding firm in a new garden city. Two months prior to the exhibition's opening, Schmidt wrote to Muthesius of his wish to use the exhibition in Dresden to deliver a "powerful, energetic blow against the old society" that clung to the fashions of "Empire" and "Louis XVI" styles. Seeking the most effective strategy to wage his campaign, Schmidt turned to another increasingly sophisticated modern institution: the media. He wrote to Muthesius: "Most effective, I believe, would be to release a large polemic in the newspapers, large enough so that even the dailies would take it up and express opinions on the matter as well."[43] Schmidt regretted that Muthesius's government position most likely disqualified him from orchestrating such a campaign and immediately mentioned as an alternative the conservative art critic Karl Scheffler, another supporter of Muthesius. The press campaign was the best method that Schmidt could imagine for dealing "strongly and directly" with the increasingly vocal opposition from such groups as the Association for the Economic Interests of the Crafts.[44]

Muthesius did not go on to organize Schmidt's campaign, but he served as a strong advocate for Schmidt in other ways. At Schmidt's request, and following similar support he had given the crafts entrepreneur in 1903, Muthesius generated propaganda texts that highlighted Richard Riemerschmid's innovative designs for Germany's first machine-produced furniture (*Maschinenmöbel*), produced by Schmidt's firm.[45] Tables, chairs, and cabinets were all assembled from prefabricated and mass-produced parts that had been designed through a collaboration between the artist and manufacturer (Fig. 47). To Muthesius, the low-cost furniture deserved the epithet "RESPECTABLE FURNITURE FOR THE COMMON MAN," a phrase he capitalized to highlight its importance in his catalog description, "Machine Furniture" (*Das Maschinenmöbel*). "This is what is still totally lacking in Germany," he continued, "a furniture that is not based on pretty appearance, a furniture that will be a loyal servant to its master."[46] It is worth noting the close parallel between the architect's choice of a social metaphor in the context of his larger vision of a justly stratified, hierarchical Wilhelmine society. At Hellerau Garden City, workers would be responsible for the manufacture of this new type of furniture that combined quality with a price that a trades middle class could afford.

One must also understand Muthesius's influential speech of 1907, "The Significance of the Applied Arts," which led directly to the formation of the Werkbund, as part of the propaganda campaign advocated so forcefully by Schmidt. This broad-ranging speech forged direct connections to the Garden City movement and GCS by linking the integrity of products and materials to the moral integrity of the masses and the nation.[47] And as Muthesius asserted scarcely three months later in a speech about "Economic Forms in the Applied Arts," garden cities such as Hellerau offered the advantage of simultaneously educating worker-producers as well as consumers in an integrated living and working environment designed by architects.[48]

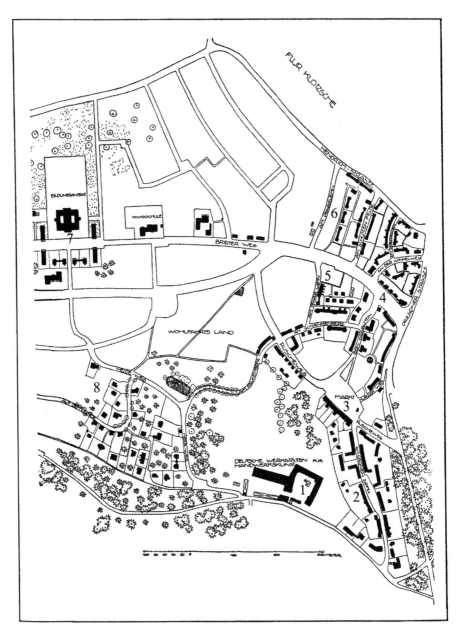

100. Richard Riemerschmid, master plan for Hellerau Garden City, 1907. 1. Factory complex; 2. Housing "Am Grünen Zipfel" by Riemerschmid; 3. Market square; 4. Housing "Beim
Gräbchen" and "An der Winkelwiese" by Muthesius; 5. Housing "Ruscheweg" by Tessenow;
6. Housing "Am Schützen Felde" by Frick; 7. Dalcroze Institute by Tessenow; 8. Villa quarter (Hermann Muthesius, *Kleinhaus und Kleinsiedlung*, 2nd ed., Munich, 1920, with numbered
additions by author)

101. Richard Riemerschmid, German Workshops for Handcrafted Art (*Deutsche Werkstätten für Handwerkskunst*), factory complex, Hellerau Garden City, 1910, street view (Walter Müller-Wulckow, *Deutsche Baukunst der Gegenwart: Bauten der Arbeit und des Verkehrs*, Königstein im Taunus & Leipzig, 1929)

Whereas Muthesius's Prussian applied-arts schools registered their presence at the Dresden exhibition of 1906 as carriers of a future generation of applied-arts producers informed by industry, Schmidt's workshops were the only crafts industry at the exhibition to exhibit in its own hall.[49] Shortly after the exhibition closed, Schmidt wrote to Riemerschmid on the topic of the large factory community he was planning to found for his enlarged workshops on open farmland just outside Dresden.[50] Consulting initial sketches provided by Schmidt, Riemerschmid accepted the job of chief designer for the Hellerau Garden City, designing the general plan, the factory complex, the first rowhouse developments, and the commercial buildings on the market square (Figs. 100–104). Where Muthesius had retained Riemerschmid to instruct teachers in the Commerce Ministry's arts, crafts, and trades schools in 1904 and 1905, now Schmidt and the Garden City Society gave Riemerschmid the opportunity to exercise his talents at an unprecedented scale.

As plans for Hellerau Garden City developed through fall 1906 and winter 1907, the German Garden City Society itself underwent a significant transformation with the influx of influential new members. Not only Schmidt, Riemerschmid, and Muthesius, but also Ferdinand Avenarius, Theodor Fischer, Joseph Lux, and Eugen Diederichs – all of whom became influential members of the Werkbund in 1907 as well – brought their collective expertise and varied reform agendas into the circle of an expanded GCS.[51]

102. Richard Riemerschmid, workers' housing "Am Grünen Zipfel," designed according to types (*Typenhäuser*) and using serialized parts, Hellerau Garden City, after 1908, general view (SLUB/Deutsche Fotothek, Dresden)

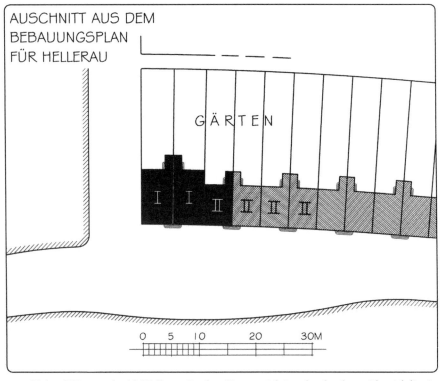

AUSCHNITT AUS DEM
BEBAUUNGSPLAN
FÜR HELLERAU

GÄRTEN

0 5 10   20   30M

103. Richard Riemerschmid, Hellerau Garden City, partial site plan for the residential district "Am Grünen Zipfel," circa 1910 (after Riemerschmid in Hartmann, redrawn by Burak Erdim)

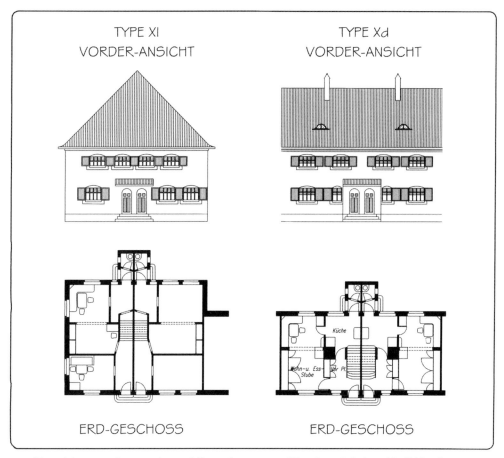

104. Two of the more than two dozen different house types (*Typenhäuser*) designed by Richard Riemerschmid for Hellerau Garden City, elevations and plans for Types XI and Xd (after Riemerschmid in Hartmann, redrawn by Burak Erdim)

The leaders of the GCS – new as well as old – expressed their visions for Hellerau in the first "Garden City Supplement" to the journal *Hohe Warte*. In it, Hellerau became a vehicle for authors' views on the themes of art, crafts, architecture, and economic and social reform. Hans Kampffmeyer opened *Hohe Warte*'s "Garden City Number" by rehearsing a theme with which readers of Muthesius's works were already familiar: The single-family house, Kampffmeyer wrote, was the dominant housing form in England, the nation with the greatest level of industrialization. In Germany, however, speculation inhibited the propagation in wider circles of living conditions prevalent in German villa colonies, thereby necessitating the foundation of garden city settlements.[52] Joseph Lux, *Hohe Warte*'s senior editor, introduced the topic of Hellerau with an article that focused on the intimate linkage between Hellerau Garden City and the unification of Germany's two leading professional crafts workshops into the combined German Workshops for Art in Handicrafts, Ltd. The specific challenge at Hellerau, Lux wrote, was "to solve the artistic-social problem of [building] the smallest house for the smallest income [group]." This would be accomplished by joining "hygiene and beauty in objectively artistic forms to become a new type, which the Hellerau Garden City will exemplify."[53]

Although Schmidt had been the primary force behind the founding of Hellerau Garden City, he shared control over design decisions from the very beginning with committees from the Garden City Society's leadership. At the suggestion of Riemerschmid, a workers' "Commission of Seven" arranged for each of more than one hundred workers in the factory to fill out detailed questionnaires examining their existing and desired living conditions. The questionnaire also asked workers to sketch, to the best of their ability, their existing and desired apartment plans.[54]

As he had in previous publications, Muthesius, too, reacted extremely favorably to Schmidt's plans in his contribution to the *Hohe Warte* issue. He boosted the project in terms that matched the goals of his ministerial work as well as his private practice. For example, he pointed to the contributions Hellerau would make to raising the quality of German crafts production, thereby helping to ensure the stability and well-being of the working class. Urging Schmidt to "realize the plan as soon and as fully as possible," Muthesius compared the entrepreneur's announced plans for training workshops with courses that the Prussian architect had observed in New York while touring the United States on his way to the St. Louis World's Exposition of 1904. Based on the successes achieved by Americans in five-month courses for mechanics, woodworkers, masons, and building-trades workers, Muthesius expressed confidence that "a rationalized method of training crafts workers" in Dresden would be most suitable for "the very people who are best situated to raise the level of the trades working class."[55] He further agreed to advise Schmidt on the introduction of an instructional workshop curriculum for workers at Hellerau, reviewing drafts of the program and offering encouragement and advice.[56] In one notable objection to passages in the curriculum discussions written by Theodor Fischer, Muthesius argued that Fischer seemed to be proceeding from

> the unjustified assumption that the schools should rescue the failing crafts [*Handwerk*] and will bring them back to a golden existence. The time is clearly at hand in which one cannot expect this from even the best school, for the decline of the crafts has economic and social bases upon which a school cannot have even the most distant influence.[57]

This revealing passage is a frank admission that Prussia's leading reformer of arts, crafts, and trades schools could not foresee any of the schools surviving intact with the identities they had had at their inception: They had to conform to modern commercial and industrial developments. It was precisely such changes that the Commerce Ministry was doing its best to anticipate and guide, with full awareness of the consequences for the small-scale crafts practitioners of the traditional *Mittelstand*.

COMPETING VISIONS OF PLANNING AND
ARCHITECTURE AT HELLERAU

Following the examples of Port Sunlight and Bournville, Karl Schmidt selected a design team for Hellerau that represented a cross-section of the best-known designers that Germany's new movement had to offer. Learning from his friend and Munich associate Theodor Fischer, Richard Riemerschmid would carry out the general plan as well as designs for houses and commercial buildings, while Muthesius, Heinrich Tessenow, and Kurt Frick would each design blocks of workers' houses according to their own respective tastes. All designs would have to be approved by a Building and Arts Commission consisting of Muthesius, Fischer, Riemerschmid, Fritz Schumacher, Otto Gussmann of Dresden, the artist Adolf von Hildebrand of Munich, and Hans Poelzig of Breslau.[58] This commission, in turn, received input about the living conditions and desires of the workers gathered by the Commission of Seven from Schmidt's factory.[59]

The Commission of Seven represented the agenda of the progressive wing of the German Garden City movement, as did a Hellerau Building Cooperative. The latter organization constructed workers' housing that bore no legal connection to the German Workshops for Art in Handicrafts. By allowing residents to settle in, rent, and eventually own houses independent of the factory enterprise, the Hellerau Building Cooperative was the feature that enabled Hellerau to most resemble an English garden city such as Letchworth. Although Hellerau remained, in the end, a factory suburb with a significant cultural component, it did offer a measure of independent ownership for workers that did not exist in such workers' colonies as *Alfredshof* and *Margaretenhöhe* of the Krupp industrial empire in Essen, the latter being executed to the designs of the architect Georg Metzendorf. Nor did such ownership options exist at the Staaken Garden City, a workers' settlement designed by the architect Paul Schmitthenner for western Berlin's Staaken munitions factory.[60] As a factory suburb, however, Hellerau also promoted house ownership to a lesser degree than such cooperative association housing developments as Falkenberg-bei-Berlin, by Fischer's former assistant Bruno Taut, or Berlin's Freie Scholle, planned before the First World War but built only after fighting had ended.[61]

Progressive features such as workers' surveys and ownership options, designed to assure overall aesthetic quality as well as improved living conditions for workers, were nevertheless organized into a layout that was plainly hierarchical. The design of Hellerau expressed physically the overall social structure of the company town while enabling individual architects to provide their own particular inflections in the districts to which they were assigned. Hellerau's residential quarters became a crossroads for varying building philosophies and geographical influences, as various architects imported the traditions from different parts of Germany that inspired them most. Once again Karl Schmidt – the initiator of Hellerau but also a major innovator during the events leading up to the path-breaking Third German Applied Arts Exhibition of 1906 – was playing a leading role in bringing together architects and applied artists from disparate regions of Germany to work on Saxon soil.

After he executed the general plan in 1908, Richard Riemerschmid, for example, carried out commissions for the first groups of terraced workers' housing, the factory complex, and the main commercial building on the market square, all of which were completed between 1909 and 1911 (Figs. 101–104).[62] It was Riemerschmid who had suggested that workers' surveys be carried out as an instrument to aid in design, and it was he who worked out his designs for more than two dozen standardized house "types" (*Typenhäuser*) in the greatest detail. His housing was to be the first example of a workers' residential district developed in consultation with the workers and following the principles of the modern crafts movement.

As he had been doing for nearly a decade in his furniture designs and independent architectural commissions, Riemerschmid employed a stylistic vocabulary anchored firmly in the German vernacular tradition. However, his numerous variations on a variety of house types, when mixed together in his irregular plan, disguised the architect's use of a standardized kit of parts for doors, windows, and most fixtures (Figs. 102–104). Like the Machined Furniture produced in 1906, Riemerschmid's houses mingled a crafts philosophy with machine production for efficiency and economy. Their appearance belied the use of modern technology to project an image of quaintness, peacefulness, and rootedness in tradition.[63] This atmosphere was to prevail in all of Riemerschmid's contributions to Hellerau, including the factory and market square buildings.

Riemerschmid learned much from Theodor Fischer, teacher of students such as Bruno Taut, Erich Mendelsohn, Hugo Häring, Ernst May, and Fred Forbat, as we saw in Chapter 1. Riemerschmid appears to have followed closely the picturesque planning principles, conscious mixing of a fixed number of house types, and southern German vernacular architecture employed by Fischer at projects like the Gmindersdorf Workers' Colony in Reutlingen, completed between 1903 and 1908 (Fig. 105). In limiting the variety of his Hellerau house types to a set of variations within seven distinct groups, Riemerschmid may have taken another cue from Fischer, who lamented the "unsatisfying appearance of the all-too-great variety" found in the nineteen distinct house types he developed for the Gmindersdorf colony.[64]

Riemerschmid employed many of the same techniques used by Fischer to achieve a studied vernacular perfection at Hellerau. He designed the main residential street in his district, the Green Point (*Grüner Zipfel*), to meander along the sloping contour of the landscape. After numerous sketches and studies, he

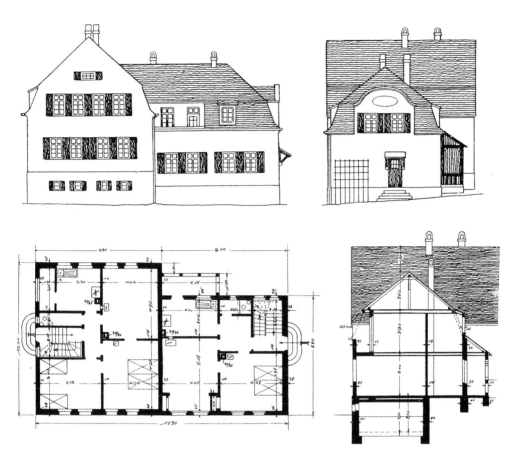

105. Theodor Fischer, housing at workers' colony of Gmindersdorf, Reutlingen, 1903–08, elevations, plans, and section of house type 10 (Casimir H. Baer, *Kleinbauten und Siedelungen*, Stuttgart, 1919)

arranged the blocks of houses to form courtyards, residential alleys, and pathways to create the overall impression of an old German village. Irregular street widths and a combination of building projections and setbacks all contributed to the planned informality of the picturesque residences (Figs. 102–104). Gently curving building façades and streets molded space into informal gathering places and quaint plazas. Riemerschmid's planning principles, absorbed from Fischer who in turn had been inspired by Camillo Sitte, enabled the architect to create the appearance of a traditional village that would serve as a model for Germany's homeland preservation movement, or *Heimatschutzbewegung*, for years to come.

Riemerschmid's carefully researched workers' surveys and typology of standardized fittings combined the germ for an idea of fulfilling a worker's basic needs (*Existenzminimum*), which would become popular in the 1920s, with a studiously arranged *Gesamtkunstwerk*, or total work of art, of imagined traditional German village life. Completed on the eve of the modern German city-planning debates that would form the heart of the greater Berlin planning exhibition of

1910 – which would erupt in the pages of Camillo Sitte's and Theodor Goecke's journal *Der Städtebau* in the same year – Riemerschmid's *Am Grünen Zipfel* elaborated the type of program that had been on exhibit in the *Heimatstil* village square at the Third Dresden Crafts Exhibition of 1906 (Figs. 48–49).[65] In the exhibition context and now in the paternalist environment of the factory suburb, the traditional village projected a nostalgic, static image of *Heimat* community onto a modern working class.

Riemerschmid's village design, a consummately antiurban statement, borrowed from the dreams of organic community, as expressed by Ferdinand Tönnies, to resist the fractured life of German urban and industrial society.[66] A scene seemingly frozen in an idealized past, the houses along the Grüner Zipfel fit in comfortably with the planned segregation and hierarchical social and economic visions of the new owning class. Riemerschmid's artistic image of community was the antithesis of workers' uprooted proletarian existence in contemporary industrial *Mietskasernen* cities such as Berlin. Riemerschmid wrote that when one had designed a village and its houses as thoroughly as he had, then

> the result must be that inside and out, the homes reflect the same charac-
> teristics that we would like to see in their residents: honest and upstanding,
> unpretentious, modest, and also proud and calm, self aware, cheerful and
> loyal. When one meets a group of worker-residents standing together on
> one of these lanes, not in a row or in ranks, not dressed up, not in some way
> displaying themselves, but rather in no strict order but also without any
> one pushing themselves burdensomely forward, in shirt sleeves perhaps,
> and with a pipe between their teeth, in comfortable conversation, then one
> should have to think to oneself: "yes, they suit one another, these houses
> and these people."[67]

Some reviewers claimed that the settlement had raised the conditions of the work-ing class to the point of creating a "workers' aristocracy" (*Arbeiteraristokratie*). Yet Hellerau improved living conditions while leaving intact fundamental differences in social class and economic power in Wilhelmine Germany's foremost garden city development.[68] This was most evident in the creation of the workers' hous-ing districts apart from the individual *Landhäuser* in the hills. The latter homes were built for managers, artists, and more privileged residents such as Jacques Dalcroze, the celebrated dance and movement instructor from Geneva who was brought to Hellerau by that faction of the garden city, led by the Werkbund ex-ecutive secretary Wolf Dohrn, who wished the settlement to be a center for new forms of artistic expression and aesthetic experimentation.[69]

Riemerschmid's factory complex for the German Workshops for Art in Hand-icraft was similarly romantic, yet pleasantly situated, well lit, and attentive to modern hygienic and functional needs (Fig. 101). With the appearance of over-sized farmhouse buildings at a manorial estate arranged to resemble, in plan, a woodworker's vise (Fig. 100), the factory complex did little to express its highly rationalized organization of a modern industrial production process. Long, relatively narrow workshop spaces assured individual woodworkers, furniture assemblers, and apprentice craftsmen adequate natural light from generously proportioned windows located along one wall. Machines, too, were accommodated to smooth the flow of work processes and dispose of waste through centralized exhaust ducts, features that experienced workers noted as a significant advance.[70]

The Hellerau factory's modern functionality, if not its appearance, prompted some contemporaries to liken Riemerschmid's building to the celebrated AEG Turbine factory in Berlin by Peter Behrens, even though the latter building's scale and updated classical temple front contrasted markedly with the rural, domestic forms of Riemerschmid's Hellerau factory. Designers of a younger generation working in Behrens's office at the time, such as Walter Gropius, complained that Riemerschmid's structure was an architectural anachronism that employed a "subjective farmhouse romanticism" (*unsachliche Bauernhausromantik*) to disguise a modern factory.[71] Gropius and his partner, Adolf Meyer, were much more interested in exploring an urban, industrial, and often heroic vocabulary that developed out of the classical tradition being reinterpreted by Behrens in his buildings for the AEG, as well as in his project for a new German Embassy in St. Petersburg.[72] Riemerschmid, Muthesius, and Schmidt opposed the use of classicism at Schmidt's garden city, which was meant, in their eyes, to epitomize a new German community anchored in a landscape through the deployment of Germanic and Nordic architectural traditions.

Muthesius, too, used his residential district to design workers' housing as a model of lower-middle-class prosperity and the antithesis of the urban *Mietskaserne*. He took a very different approach from that of Riemerschmid, however. His terraced houses and courtyard groupings owed much to the practices that Barry Parker and Raymond Unwin employed at such developments as the Birds' Hill Estate at Letchworth Garden City, begun in 1905.[73] Muthesius did not repeat the English designers' pioneering use of the cul-de-sac, but he did divorce the building groups from the roadway line – an English planning innovation regarded by some historians as the Garden City movement's "main invention" (Figs. 106–107).[74] Muthesius employed the same English repetitive rhythm of plain white gables that he had seen in the almshouses of Bournville and that were updated in the low-rent housing of Letchworth's Rushby Mead in 1908. He also adopted the simple cornice lines separating the first and second floors evident at Asmuns Hill and, in general, seemed to think it appropriate that the planning and building traditions of Europe's leading garden city builders appear on German soil as well. Parker and Unwin, after all, did not hesitate to import traditional German house and town forms in their search for picturesque motifs to blend with their updated synthesis of Baroque planning principles with elements of planned irregularity.[75]

Hellerau enabled Muthesius to build one of the largest districts of houses in his career, which was part of his stated mission "to re-educate the social classes

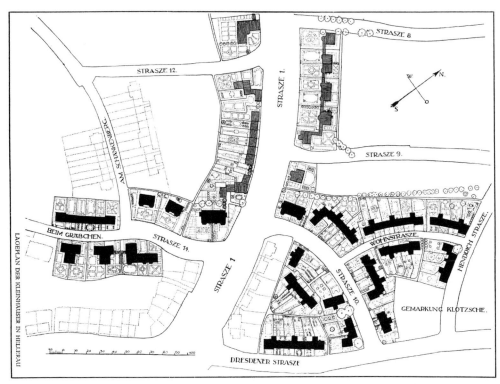

106. Hermann Muthesius, residential district at Hellerau, site plan, 1910 (Hermann Muthesius, *Landhäuser von Hermann Muthesius*, Munich, 1922)

of today in solidity, truthfulness, and simple civic values."[76] His efforts in city planning, however, were minor in comparison with those of Parker and Unwin. Their works on *The Art of Building of Home* (1901) and Unwin's *Town Planning in Practice* (1911) demonstrated a commitment on the part of the British architects to integrate comfortable working-class housing with community and town planning in a way that Muthesius, with his early emphasis on the *Landhaus* and upper-class domestic architecture, never attained.[77] Instead, his terraced houses and *Landhaus* projects for Hellerau exemplified socioeconomic and cultural views – expressed in the lecture "The Significance of the Applied Arts" in 1907 – that united the Werkbund and the German Garden City movement in a common mission of national education and prosperity.

While reinforcing his hierarchical social vision, Muthesius's workers' houses and projects for a *Landhaus* quarter at Hellerau employed the planning philosophy that he had advocated in *Landhaus und Garten*. In the workers' district, three-bedroom row houses in groups of four and six were clustered in a picturesque manner along five different streets (Figs. 106–107). Larger duplex homes designed for master craftsmen punctuated the workers' housing. Muthesius's plan laid a particular emphasis on the orderly gardens outside each of the houses and in the arrangement of house groups into courtyards, where setbacks and breaks in rowhouse plans differentiated individual units and added to the privacy of individual garden plots. The largest courtyard was a trapezoid formed by three large groups of rowhouses and two duplex houses. This arrangement offered the advantage of southern exposure for the majority of houses while providing an informal courtyard off the main traffic street. Critics responded well to Muthesius's deployment of steep gables above individual house entryways. The further choice of white plaster facades, terra-cotta tile roofs, green window frames and shutters, and white fences – while uniform – communicated both comfort and a sense of individual ownership, even pride, to the individual structures.

Whereas Muthesius's workers' houses were divided into blocks for six, four, and two families, his *Landhaus* designs at Hellerau were for one or occasionally two families and were predictably more spacious and elaborate. Like Riemerschmid, Muthesius designed his houses according to "types" (*Typen*).[78] For his single-family houses, he appears to have adapted typical floor plans for such individual rooms as the living room (*Wohnzimmer*), reception room (*Empfangszimmer*), and entrance hall (*Flur*) to suit local site conditions. Exterior massing, room plans, and window, bay, and balcony features all prove quite similar when one compares his

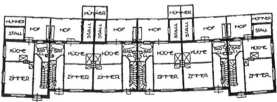

107. Hermann Muthesius, workers' houses designed according to types (*Typenhäuser*), Hellerau Garden City, 1910, street view and plan (Hermann Muthesius, *Landhäuser von Hermann Muthesius*, Munich, 1912; Hermann Muthesius, *Kleinhaus und Kleinsiedlung*, 2nd ed., Munich, 1920)

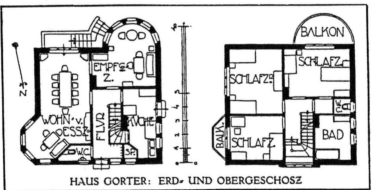

108. Hermann Muthesius, Gorter House, Hellerau, 1910, view and plans (*Landhäuser von Hermann Muthesius*, Munich, 1912)

Gorter house at Hellerau of 1911 (Fig. 108), the Hirschowitz house in Berlin-Nicolassee of 1912 (Figs. 88–89), and some of the houses he designed for an entire Muthesius "villa quarter" at Hellerau (Fig. 109). Although Muthesius's villa quarter design remained unexecuted, it offers by far the clearest insight into his conception of economic efficiency of construction, artistic unity of appearance, and a comprehensive planning approach that was so absent, in his mind, from such developments as the Homestead Company's villa colony at Nicolassee.

Grouped around streets with private gardens and common living courtyards in the style of Unwin, the houses of Muthesius's proposed Hellerau "villa quarter" all shared such common features as steep mansard roofs, simple rectangular dormers,

109. Hermann Muthesius, projected houses (*Typenhäuser*) for a "villa quarter" (*Villenviertel*) in Hellerau Garden City, 1911, bird's-eye view (*Die Kunst*, 24, 1911)

projecting bays and balconies, and shuttered windows. This building typology can be interpreted as a rare architectural expression of arguments Muthesius was to promote shortly thereafter in the Werkbund for the evolution of "types" in modern manufacturing and architectural production. In place of Muthesius's unified design, however, there arose a broad mix of more than two dozen houses designed on spacious plots by Riemerschmid, Fischer, Muthesius, Tessenow, and even the British architect Baillie Scott. These architects' individually designed houses occupied the garden city's highest hill overlooking the rest of the new town.

In the same year that Muthesius produced the drawing of a unified *Landhaus* quarter, he delivered the address "Where Do We Stand?" (*Wo Stehen Wir?*) at the 1911 Werkbund Annual Meeting. This lecture marked a shift for Muthesius in the direction of a renewed interest in form, which in his newly revised view needed to be considered "above purpose, material, and technique" if architecture and production were not to "remain raw" or incomplete.[79] Arguing that supporters of the historic preservation movement "suffer from the deception that the ailing body of architecture can be cured with the prescription 'healing serum 1830,'" the architect insisted to his colleagues that the most important tasks for Werkbund members were the "reawakening of the understanding of form and the rejuvenation of architectonic perception."[80] His vision for what this meant was spelled out in the project for the *Landhaus* quarter: windows, doors, and fittings of high quality would contribute to a uniformity that architects would render both practical and aesthetically pleasing.

Muthesius contributed other garden city–influenced housing designs for settlements at Duisburg near the Rhine and Stettin on the Baltic coast. In his description of these projects, he argued for the Garden City movement as a partial solution to urban overpopulation and unhealthy living conditions in large German cities.[81] The garden city was not the impractical utopia that building speculators accused it of being, Muthesius would insist in "The Meaning of the Garden City movement," a slide lecture delivered before a royal audience in the *Herrenhaus*, the upper house of the Prussian legislature, in early 1914. The matter was one of utmost complexity, he maintained, for speculative real-estate companies "have appropriated the catchy name 'garden city' [for their developments] in order to attract the interest of the public" (Fig. 110).[82] Garden cities that offered real socioeconomic benefits and elements of land reform, he argued, were a necessity for Germany as well as for the health and productivity of its population. They would assure healthy living conditions for workers, boost entrepreneurship and creative thinking, and increase German productivity as the nation struggled to succeed in extremely competitive world markets.[83]

THREATENING THE OLD WORLD ORDER: TESSENOW'S ALTERNATIVE DESIGNS

Heinrich Tessenow, fifteen years Muthesius's junior, had ideas about Hellerau Garden City architecture that differed from those of both Riemerschmid and the Prussian government architect. The young architect from north Germany saw no need to subordinate modern constructional possibilities to the projection of Riemerschmid's rural idyll or Muthesius's Anglo-Saxon suburban landscape. Erecting only five groups of workers' houses in comparison with Muthesius's fourteen and Riemerschmid's fifteen, Tessenow reduced his houses to "*sachlich* and puritanical" gabled roof structures of the utmost simplicity (Figs. 111–112).[84] Moving beyond the use of mass production merely in fixtures or windows and doors, he drove down building costs even further by developing a "Tessenow patented wall," a prefabricated party wall between houses.[85]

The Dresden professor of architecture Erich Haenel, author of *The Modern Single-Family House* (*Das Einzelwohnhaus der Neuzeit*) of 1910, viewed Tessenow's houses as a reflection of a northern German sensibility that tended to be off-putting and even cold, especially when compared to the comfortable and richly detailed south German ensemble by Riemerschmid.[86] The young architect Martin Wagner, an apprentice in Muthesius's home-based architectural practice who later served as Berlin's chief city planner during the final years of the Weimar Republic, strongly disagreed.[87] Tessenow's architecture, Wagner wrote in 1910 in his article "Garden City Houses," was that of an urbanist fully aware of the divide separating urban workplaces from suburban domiciles. Neither of these

Broich-Speldorfer
Wald-und Gartenstadt
Akt. Ges.

Mülheim / Ruhr
Fernsprecher Nr. 1640

Billige und ideale Waldansiedlung
ersten Ranges im Stadtkreis
Mülheim-Ruhr.

Bebauungsplan und Charakter als Wald-
und Gartenstadt garantiert ❧ Wege mit
Gas, Wasser und Elektrizität ❧ Elek-
trische Straßenbahn nach dem Mittel-
punkt von Mülheim-Ruhr, Essen, Duisburg, Oberhausen ❧ 50 km Reitwege.

Prospekt, Lageplan, Auskunft, Beratung und Führung kostenlos.

110. Broich-Speldorfer Forest- and Garden City Joint Stock Company (*Wald- und Gartenstadt Aktien Gesellschaft*), advertisement for "cheap and ideal forested living colony of the first class in the Mülheim-Ruhr metropolitan area," 1914 (F. Biel, *Wirtschaftliche und technische Gesichtspunkte zur Gartenstadtbewegung*, Leipzig, 1914)

contexts, in any case, necessitated the creation of villagelike escapes that denied the essential modernity of Hellerau as a center for modern living and production just outside of Saxony's metropolitan capital. To Wagner, Tessenow had built for workers who had modern urban characters as well as needs – a situation that the architect's designs frankly acknowledged.[88] This was the very type of argument that

111. Heinrich Tessenow, workers' housing for Hellerau Garden City, 1911, street façade
(Heinrich Tessenow, *Hausbau und dergleichen*, Berlin, 1916)

Walter Curt Behrendt, editor of the progressive journal *Neudeutsche Bauzeitung*
in which the article appeared, must have looked upon favorably as a justification
for Tessenow's work.

The leadership committees could live with this difference of opinion over
Hellerau's residential architecture. This proved to be no longer the case, however,
when it came to Tessenow's design for the Hellerau Institute of Rhythmic Movement and Dance (Fig. 113). The institute was to be run by the internationally
known artist and choreographer Jacques Dalcroze and was strongly supported
by Wolf Dohrn, the fellow founder of Hellerau Garden City, vice director of

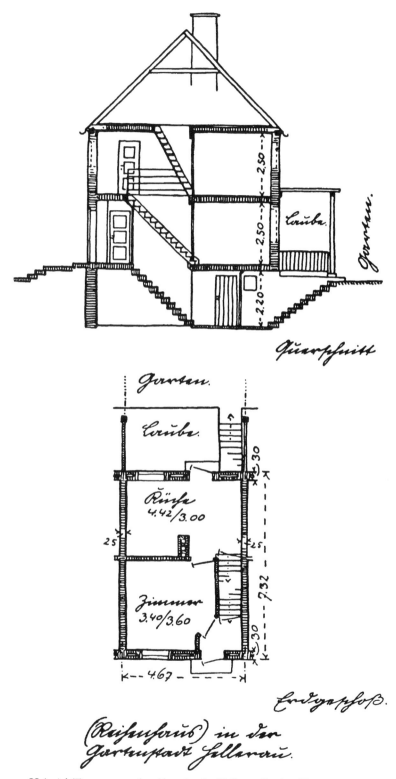

112. Heinrich Tessenow, workers' housing for Hellerau Garden City, 1911, section and ground-floor plan (Heinrich Tessenow, *Hausbau und dergleichen*, Berlin, 1916)

the Dresden Workshops for the Applied Arts, and secretary of the Werkbund.[89] Among the architects whom Dohrn had suggested for this project were Hans Poelzig of Breslau and Josef Hoffman of Vienna, but Tessenow's youthful energy, consummate graphic skills, and compelling design led Dohrn to back him in this, the architect's first major commission. The decision to favor Tessenow placed Dohrn's position in jeopardy.[90]

The classical monumentality of Tessenow's design, its abstracted columns, its lofty pediment stamped with a prominent Taoist symbol denoting the eternal rhythm, swirling movement, and equilibrium of universal "yin" and "yang" – all were like a slap in the face to Schmidt and Riemerschmid. The design, strongly supported by Dalcroze and Dohrn as a monumental, purpose-built, and artistic expression of the flexible spaces needed for movement and glorious dance performances, was contested by Schmidt, Riemerschmid, Muthesius, and Fischer. Where each of the architects' housing projects could arguably be connected to one or another aspect of German or Nordic building traditions, the Dalcroze school clearly updated classical models. Although Tessenow could argue that his building established links to the German classical tradition as advanced by Leo von Klenze, Karl Schinkel, and others, it was nevertheless deemed unacceptable in a landscape of Heimat-inflected buildings. Lengthy negotiations produced a compromise: The site of the institute was moved from Hellerau's center to the colony's periphery, while Tessenow's project was allowed to break ground in April 1911.

The split over the design expressed a greater rift between early and later GCS reformers. Men like Bernhard and Hans Kampffmeyer, the brothers Hart, and later Wolf Dohrn identified with the Garden City movement's liberative, educational, and artistic potential, as indeed they had since the formation of the GCS in 1902. Relative latecomers to the Garden City movement such as Karl Schmidt, Hermann Muthesius, and Richard Riemerschmid, joining the GCS only in 1907, regarded the garden city as a place for the fusion of modern business, a conservative and *bürgerlich* Wilhelmine social hierarchy, and healthy suburban living through neotraditional design. Concerning conflicts within the GCS leadership, Schmidt complained to his friend Simon Israel, owner of a textile factory and workshops in the Berlin fashion district's Hausvogteiplatz and, later, a member of the Werkbund's Fashion Industry Committee:

> It is essential that the nice, idealistic people from the leadership of the Garden City Society, who have truly unclear heads, not prevail. These men, for example, have no architectonic judgment whatsoever. In this matter it is quite critical that the leadership committee consist of the best and most capable people, particularly [when considered] from a purely business standpoint.[91]

Idealist impulses were a threat to Schmidt and his business; the entrepreneur recommended that for a sensible conversation about this matter, his friend should

113. Heinrich Tessenow, Institute of Rhythmic Movement and Dance at Hellerau Garden City, view of entrance façade, 1911–12 (Walter Müller-Wulckow, *Deutsche Baukunst der Gegenwart: Bauten der Gemeinschaft*, Königstein im Taunus & Leipzig, 1928)

seek out Hermann Muthesius of the State Trades Board, across the street from Messel's Wertheim store on the Leipzigerplatz, top floor.[92]

The compromise that allowed Tessenow's dance institute to move forward proved fatal to the Hellerau Building Commission. Riemerschmid, Muthesius, and Fischer all resigned in protest over the project in early 1913, and no new leadership for the commission could be agreed on before the First World War. The situation was proving much the same in the Werkbund, where increasingly tense debates and struggles for control of the organization made it increasingly difficult for cool heads to prevail. Wolf Dohrn, the idealistic secretary of the Werkbund since 1910, was replaced by Naumann's influential colleague Ernst Jäckh early in 1912 (after brief interim service by Alfons Paquet), in spite of Dohrn's friendship with Karl Schmidt. This friendship had undergone significant strain in the conflict over the dance institute, with Dohrn and Schmidt finding themselves at opposite ends of the spectrum of the pragmatic and the artistic. Pragmatism and good business sense were Schmidt's watchwords; Dohrn remained, as Friedrich Naumann characterized him, an idealist, a seeker, and "a fisherman of new ideas."[93] With the transfer of the Werkbund's administrative headquarters to Berlin from Dresden-Hellerau in April 1912, the stage was set for a new phase in the expansion of the organization. Whether the Werkbund could survive the pains associated with its own growth, however, was not at all clear – particularly as personalities, tempers, and political agendas collided with the approach of the First Werkbund Exhibition in Cologne in 1914.

CHAPTER SEVEN

WERKBUNDPOLITIK AND *WELTPOLITIK*: THE GERMAN STATE'S INTEREST IN GLOBAL COMMERCE AND "GOOD DESIGN," 1912–1914 ♒

GERMAN POLITICS AND WERKBUND POLICY, 1912–1914

The Deutscher Werkbund Congress of 1914 produced a showdown of fundamental importance to the subsequent history of twentieth-century German architecture and design. The weekend conference, held between July 3–4 in a festival hall designed by Peter Behrens on the grounds of the First Werkbund Exhibition in Cologne, featured familiar keynote speakers: Hermann Muthesius gave the conference's first major address, and, as was also customary, Friedrich Naumann closed the conference with a rousing speech on the final night (Figs. 114–115).[1]

There is a long-standing consensus among historians of architecture, art, and design about what took place: At the conclusion of Muthesius's speech on July 3, entitled "The Future Work of the Werkbund" ("Die Werkbundarbeit der Zukunft"), the artist Henry van de Velde rose to read a statement prepared the night before opposing virtually every recommendation Muthesius's speech had just made. The ensuing storm of controversy dominated the remainder of the conference. Various speakers rose to attack or defend the apparent heart of Muthesius's speech – his advocacy of "types" in design and industry – while others supported van de Velde's impassioned defense of artists' individual creative freedom. When it finally came time for Friedrich Naumann's closing address, entitled "The Werkbund and the World Economy" ("Werkbund und Weltwirtschaft"), the charismatic politician did his best to rally his audience around a common goal by assuring them that the Werkbund, despite its differences, was destined to raise the status of German exports and cultural production to unprecedented heights. Increased exports were a national necessity, Naumann reminded his audience, for

114. Peter Behrens, Festival Hall at Cologne Werkbund Exhibition, general view (*Jahrbuch des Deutschen Werkbundes 1914: Deutsche Form im Kriegsjahr*, Munich, 1915)

115. Peter Behrens, Festival Hall at Cologne Werkbund Exhibition, interior view (*Moderne Bauformen* 13, 1914)

Germany's great good fortune – its ever-growing population – required a steady expansion of exports to sustain the health and wealth of the nation.

As soon as the conference closed, Werkbund members who had been in attendance began writing articles and letters in a contentious, drawn-out effort not only to determine what, exactly, had just transpired, but also to try to influence subsequent developments. It was clear to all that Henry van de Velde had countered Muthesius's presentation of ten "guiding principles" (*Leitsätze*) justifying "types" (*Typisierung*) in design with ten "counter-principles" (*Gegenleitsätze*) defending artistic individuality against the encroachment of industrial and economic imperatives (Appendix B). Ten days before delivering his lecture, Muthesius had circulated his ten principles among the fourteen speakers scheduled to address the conference. Where Muthesius's keynote address traced the development of types as an historical process, his ten theses distilled the speech into a set of principles that the Werkbund – in concert with industry and the state, and virtually by decree – would use to set new standards for exports and for industry.

Muthesius appears intentionally to have kept his theses general, sweeping, and maddeningly unspecific with regard to execution or to specific, practical implications for artists, industry, retailers, and the state. He avoided using the word "standardization" (*Standardisierung*), although his coinage of the term *Typisierung* ("making of types") left room for listeners to infer this; he also never outlined the new structures of authority that would be needed to put such a comprehensive scheme into place. Muthesius's first priority, it seemed, was to steer the organization toward acceptance of the new direction, and one thing appeared certain: If the Werkbund followed the new course, the nature of its activities would be altered forever, enlarged to an extent that the Werkbund would henceforth work closely with industry and the state to establish readily identifiable, artist-designed "types" for seemingly every scale of product manufactured by Werkbund industries.[2] If Muthesius had his way, typical, "tasteful" products of high quality would be made available in unprecedented quantities for coordinated, worldwide distribution as German national exports in an expanding *Weltwirtschaft*, or global economy. Architecture would continue to lead the way in coordinating the applied arts and ensuring Germany's continued development toward a contemporary "harmonious culture."[3]

What the Werkbund membership would gradually come to know in the weeks between the Congress of July 3–4 and the outbreak of the First World War in early August is that Muthesius and Naumann – with Werkbund members like Gustav Stresemann and Ernst Jäckh, the Werkbund managing director, in key supporting roles – represented forces at work in German politics and in the Werkbund that far exceeded the ability of individual artists or small, private institutions like Osthaus's German Museum for Art in Commerce and Industry (*Deutsches Museum für Kunst in Handel und Gewerbe*) to mount effective, meaningful resistance. Muthesius and Naumann, as two of the Werkbund's most influential

founders and leaders, had also come more than ever to represent two even more
formidable factions joined in alliance in the radically charged political environment that was Wilhelmine Germany between 1911 and 1914. Muthesius, as we
have seen, represented the interests of the Prussian Commerce Ministry, now
joined in a constellation of ministerial and governmental actors that reflected
the unique political circumstances of these increasingly tension-filled, jingoistic
years. Chancellor Bethmann-Hollweg and three powerful ministries – Minister
Clemens von Delbrück's Imperial Interior Ministry, Reinhold Sydow's Prussian
Commerce Ministry, and Arthur Kiderlen-Wächter and Gottlieb von Jagow's
Imperial Foreign Office – gradually aligned themselves with increasingly risky,
aggressive bids to expand German foreign trade and territorial influence. They
lent greater support to commerce, exports, and the finished-goods industries, in
spite of the continued political dominance of coal, iron, and steel producers in
concert with agrarian Conservatives. In the nomenclature of the powerful but
fractious industrial interest groups, the Chancellor and these three ministries
grew more receptive to light industry's Association of Industrialists (*Bund der
Industriellen*, or BDI) and the Hansa League for Commerce, Trade, and Industry
(*Hansabund für Handel, Gewerbe, und Industrie*), relative to their traditional backing
of heavy industry's Central Association of German Industrialists (*Centralverband
Deutscher Industrieller*, or CDI).[4]

Naumann, for his part, was no creature of the ministerial bureaucracy, but the
left-leaning progressive mouthpiece of an expansionist program for a German-
led trade zone in Central Europe and the Balkans – a region he called "Mitteleuropa." But Naumann was anything but alone in promoting plans that reflected
Germany's bid to rise into the ranks of such global powers as Britain, France,
Russia, and the United States. Werkbund managing director Ernst Jäckh, a long-
time Naumann disciple, emerged as the forceful advocate of a German-led alliance stretching "from Berlin to Baghdad" via the Austro-Hungarian Empire,
the Balkans, and Turkey. Naumann, Jäckh, and Gustav Stresemann – a National
Liberal Reichstag member and the galvanizing head of the Association of Saxon
Industrialists (the BDI's single largest corporate member) – were all aggressive
promoters of imperialism at a time in Germany when, as the historian Klaus
Wernecke has noted, "the word imperialism had no negative associations for its
proponents."[5]

In domestic policy, Naumann was a hopeful advocate of ever-elusive representative democracy as a safeguard against socialist revolution and, simultaneously,
as a weapon against heavy industrialists and feudal landowning Junkers allied in
their stubborn maintenance of tariff rates favorable to Germany's purveyors of
"iron and rye." Although Muthesius and Naumann had never been able to agree
on a proper *Sozialpolitik* for the treatment of Germany's workers, trade expan-
sionism and imperialism provided a common ground for the Prussian Commerce
Ministry privy councillor and Württemberg's leading progressive politician.

To men like Muthesius, Naumann, and Jäckh, then, the Werkbund operated at the intersection of art's claims to represent a civilizing German *Kultur* and industry's claims to political influence commensurate with its growing preeminence in German economic life. Like other organizations top-heavy with a membership drawn primarily from the Wilhelmine bourgeoisie, the Werkbund embodied what the historian Geoff Eley has discussed as a growing Wilhelmine bourgeois push for "equality of status" (*Gleichberechtigung*) in a political system singularly ill-prepared to brook compromise, or to embrace new and increasingly powerful bourgeois and working-class interests.[6]

Given the imperial Wilhelmine political system's unwillingness to broaden the franchise or alter the fundamental structure of government, leading Werkbund figures such as Naumann and Muthesius adjusted their views in ways that remained loyal, in the end, to the conservative power structures they served. Their advocacy of "types" in 1914, occurring as it did in the context of larger political efforts to accelerate trade, concentrate production, and increase Germany's colonial and global influence, can hardly be considered apart from the political programs that began working their way through ministries as diverse as the Imperial Interior Ministry, the Foreign Office, the Colonial Office, the Prussian Commerce Ministry, and the Reich Chancellor's Office after 1912.

The first storm clouds began to gather over the Werkbund Congress when, ten days before Muthesius's scheduled address, he distributed his ten guiding principles to the fourteen scheduled Congress speakers. Back in 1907, Muthesius's controversial lecture on "The Significance of the Applied Arts" at the opening of the Berlin College of Commerce had culminated four years of intensive, state-supported design reforms by challenging traditional applied-arts producers to join a national, modern applied-arts production system; the result, a split between conservative and self-proclaimed progressive applied-arts forces, had effectively called the Werkbund into being in October of that year. This time, in 1914, Muthesius threw down the gauntlet to the organization's own membership. From the state's point of view – and with the help of Muthesius's interpolation of trends in economics, art, culture, and politics – national priorities dictated that only a concentration of Werkbund efforts on the development of "types" in architecture, the applied arts, and finished-goods industries could ensure German economic competitiveness and the emergence of a coherent, readily identifiable German "style" worthy of representing German culture both at home and abroad. In essence, and dating at least as far back as spring 1912, Muthesius supported increased government efforts to involve its huge bureaucratic and imperial apparatus in organizing export industries and promoting Germany's bid to assert itself as the world's newest international power. Treating the Werkbund less like a voluntary association and more like a semiofficial guardian of quality in production, Muthesius approached the 1914 exhibition as a place to display German productive capacity as a collective achievement in need of further disciplined organization.

Cooperating with Henry van de Velde in the resistance to Muthesius's proposed "new course" were such figures as Karl Ernst Osthaus, Walter Gropius, and August Endell. Osthaus, the most influential member of the anti-Muthesius faction, was an independently minded reformist missionary with consummate "individualist" credentials. He had used a private family fortune in his hometown of Hagen to open the Folkwang Museum to promote avant-garde art in 1900. As the applied-arts section of the Folkwang Museum expanded, he converted it in 1909 into a separate institution, the German Museum for Art in Commerce and Industry. Muthesius, for a time, had supported the efforts of the latter museum, and the Werkbund made a modest contribution to its budget.[7] As Frederick Schwartz has persuasively argued in his account of the Werkbund's evolving attitudes toward form in the increasingly complex German economy, "For Osthaus the artist always preceded the organization" – whether it was the German Museum or the Werkbund.[8]

Specializing in advertising and staking a claim for the modern artist's place in the commercial economy's domain of circulation and exchange, Osthaus assumed an important role as a patron, promoter, and organizer, and is therefore sometimes referred to by historians of the Werkbund as the artist-individualists' "mentor." Osthaus received the support of the Werkbund for his museum and its traveling exhibitions of modern German products; their success prompted him to appeal for further support to the German Foreign Ministry to continue sending exhibitions of German products abroad.[9] Not averse to the idea of government support for his personal projects, Osthaus only objected when it became apparent that government priorities concerning industry and export production were beginning to dictate the agenda of the Werkbund's 1914 exhibition. This process, which culminated in the confrontation between Muthesius, van de Velde, and their respective supporters, began just over two years before the opening of the exhibition.

When looked at chronologically and in some detail, the exhibition planning process confirms the overlapping nature of Muthesius's program for the Werkbund and broader political and economic goals being pursued by men like Delbrück, Sydow, Naumann, Jäckh, and Stresemann. As we will see, the radical new course projected by Muthesius for the Werkbund coincided with efforts by German light industry interest groups and advocates of expansionist economic policies to gain unprecedented new influence in the months leading up to the Werkbund Exhibition of 1914.

REDIRECTING THE WERKBUND: THE ORGANIZATION EXPANDS

The first day of April 1912 marked two related, major changes that would place the Werkbund on a new course: Its headquarters were moved from Dresden-Hellerau to Berlin, and a new managing director, Ernst Jäckh, was appointed to run the office. Leaving his close friend and fellow "Naumannite" Theodor Heuss to assume his post as editor of the liberal Heilbronn newspaper the *Neckar Zeitung*, Jäckh appeared to rejoice at the prospect of relocating to the center of Prussian and imperial power. Quite unlike the first, idealistic, long-time Werkbund managing director, Wolf Dohrn, Jäckh took virtually no interest in artistic matters. His passion was politics, at which he excelled, even though his memoirs and other writings display an occasional tendency to inflate his importance and closeness to the Kaiser and other top government officials.[10] Known as an able manager and a well-connected political insider in Berlin, Jäckh was thrilled to exercise his influence as "an adept of the Foreign Office" to build on international connections at the German mission in Turkey, to which he had been assigned, and to organize a powerful network on behalf of Werkbund-related causes.[11] A more effective organizer, recruiter, and propagandist than politician, Jäckh enthused to associates at the Foreign Office about the long list of German and Austrian journals and newspapers "with whom I am employed ... with which I have influence, [and which] I favor depending on the theme and the situation."[12] In its new, expansionist phase, the Werkbund would rely more than it ever had on aggressive press propaganda to advance its domestic and foreign goals.

Yet the appointment of Jäckh and the relocation of the Werkbund's headquarters to the imperial capital were only the beginning of fundamental organizational changes. At the fifth annual congress of the Werkbund in Vienna in June 1912 – the first ever to be convened on foreign soil – several other important measures heralded what Jäckh, in the organization's official report, called "a high point in the development of the Werkbund," as well as "a promising point of departure" for its future growth.[13] To begin with, Prussian and German government officials attended the meeting in greater numbers than ever before and were joined by their counterparts in the Habsburg Imperial administration. Among German ministries represented were the Prussian Commerce Ministry, the Imperial Foreign Ministry – with whom Jäckh enjoyed particularly strong ties – and the Ministry of the Interior. Clemens Delbrück, who as Prussian Minister of Commerce had defended Muthesius in the Prussian Chamber of Deputies during the "Muthesius Affair" in 1907, had been promoted to Imperial Interior Minister in 1909. From this position he became Chancellor Theobald von Bethmann-Hollweg's second in command and "most trusted" ministerial colleague, as well as a strong Werkbund advocate.[14] Fritz Dönhoff, Muthesius's closest official correspondent from Muthesius's days stationed at the German Embassy in London beginning in 1896, came to Vienna representing the Prussian Commerce Ministry.[15] Werkbund President Peter Bruckmann, in his address "On the Next Tasks of the Deutscher Werkbund," repeatedly emphasized that while "the Werkbund is the leader of the new movement in the applied arts," it must "in the next few years be recognized and respected by the imperial and state authorities as the official representative of the German applied arts."[16]

DEUTSCHE WERKBUND-AUSSTELLUNG CÖLN 1914
GESAMTPLAN DER AUSSTELLUNG

1. Eingangsgebäude	13. Atelierhaus	20. Weinrestaurant
2. Glashaus	14. Bierrestaurant	21. Haus der Frau
3. Verwaltungsgebäude	15. Österreichisches Haus	22. Theater
4. Cölner Haus	16. Sächsisches Haus	23. Krankenhaus
5. Stadlerhaus	17. Kolonialanlage	24. Gewächshaus
6. Ladenstraße	18. Haupthalle	25. Fabrik und Büro
7. Farbenschau	19. Festhaus	26. Bremen-Oldenburger
8. Hapag		Haus
9. Verkehrshalle		27. Etagenhaus
10. Haus Heinersdorf		
11. Teehaus mit Mario-		
netten-Theater		
12. Café		

116. Carl Rehorst, general plan of Deutscher Werkbund Exhibition in Cologne, 1914 (*Die Woche,* June 6, 1914)

Internal changes to the Werkbund affecting the organization far more directly included a resolution adopted in Vienna to enlarge the executive committee from six members to twelve. Harmless enough at first glance, this enlargement in fact put executive committee members Osthaus and van de Velde – later of "individualist" faction fame – at a considerable numerical disadvantage for important committee votes. The executive committee was henceforth dominated by such pro-government and pro-industry figures – and future *Typisierung* advocates – as executive committee chairman Bruckmann, vice chairman Muthesius, Friedrich Naumann, Bruno Paul, Richard Riemerschmid, Karl Schmidt, Ernst Jäckh, and Carl Rehorst, an architect and member of the Cologne City Council.[17] A second resolution altered the Werkbund's by-laws to permit supporters or "patrons" (*Förderer*) to join the Werkbund as either individual or corporate members. This step was taken explicitly to boost Werkbund revenues, membership, and prestige.[18]

A final resolution adopted at the Vienna congress enabled Rehorst to join the executive committee in the first place: The new resolution permitted the committee to appoint new members solely on the basis of their association with a particular cause. Thus, Rehorst joined the executive committee in his capacity as manager of the newly formed Cologne Association for the Planning of the Deutscher Werkbund Exhibition. Active in the urban planning and shaping of twentieth-century Cologne, Rehorst worked to publicize Cologne as a fast-growing German commercial and financial center. He was also responsible for the master plan of the Cologne Exhibition (Fig. 116). Cologne's rapid development, it was widely felt, made the city a most appropriate host for the Werkbund exhibition. Fittingly, Rehorst helped arrange for posters that would jointly advertise the Werkbund Exhibition and an exhibition featuring Cologne's "development from a Roman city to a modern metropolis" (Fig. 117).[19]

In addition to welcoming Rehorst to the Werkbund, Bruckmann's address in Vienna took pains to emphasize the reputation and respected abilities of the newly appointed Ernst Jäckh. To Bruckmann, Jäckh was to be the key figure in helping the Werkbund obtain official government recognition, along with dramatic increases in funding and membership. Muthesius seconded Bruckmann's high opinion of Jäckh, to whom Muthesius wrote:

> We in the Werkbund... agree completely with the Foreign Minister that you should continue the promising Middle East policy and foreign policy work you began in Heilbronn and Constantinople, and that, alongside your management of the Werkbund, you should carry on with this work in Berlin. I have understanding for this type of honorary position and the extension of one's professional duties, and am convinced that your energy and initiative will do complete justice to both of these tasks. I will speak quite openly: we know of no one whom we can trust more than you to rescue the Werkbund and restore it from its ash-heap existence in Hellerau and to develop it into a German center of culture.[20]

Muthesius naturally saw greater state involvement in Werkbund affairs as a blessing for the organization. Others, of course, would shortly see it as a curse. But from the government architect's perspective, the Werkbund stood positioned to become the linchpin of an overarching plan according to which powerful German industries, influenced if not controlled directly by government, would deliver German products of high quality in a commercial economy defined by an unprecedented degree of organization.

THE WERKBUND BETWEEN MINISTERIAL POLICIES AND INTEREST GROUP POLITICS, 1912–1914

The radical alteration of course Muthesius sought to impose on the Werkbund cannot be understood apart from changes taking place in German politics between 1912–1914 – years that the historian Thomas Nipperdey has described as a time of "stable crisis."[21] Perhaps the defining event for these years was the Reichstag election of January 1912, which yielded results that shook the German Empire to its foundations: The Social Democratic Party captured an unprecedented 34.8 percent of the vote. With its 110 delegates, the party formed the Reichstag's largest bloc, a feat all the more considerable in view of the party's illegality between 1878 and 1890 and the discriminatory three-class German voting system that allotted votes on the basis of property ownership.[22]

The resulting intensification and radicalization of German politics affected virtually every party, interest group, and political association. Changes in the

117. Poster advertising the "Deutscher Werkbund Exhibition: Art in Craft, Industry, and Commerce, Architecture," and the "Exhibition of Old and New Cologne: The Development of the City of Cologne from Roman Town to Modern Metropolis," Cologne, May through October 1914, and featuring the front view of Theodor Fischer's Main Exhibition Hall for the Werkbund Exhibition (*Die Woche* June 6, 1914)

organization of the Werkbund fit into this matrix of larger shifts, in which government ministries and interest groups struggled to make progress on constructive domestic and foreign policies amid antisocialist agitation that ranged from mild to hysterical. For the next two years, Chancellor Bethmann-Hollweg swung between two equally problematic poles in domestic policy. Appeasement of the socialists' loud calls for a just social policy (*Sozialpolitik*) was impossible, since this was anathema to Prussia's controlling Junker and heavy industrial interests, to say nothing of the Kaiser. On the political Right, heavy industry's Central Association of German Industrialists (*Centralverband Deutscher Industrieller* – CDI) maintained repeated hard-line calls for the dissolution of the Reichstag, the banning of public demonstrations, and resurrection of Bismarck's antisocialist laws. Heavy industry and agrarian leaders alike attacked Bethmann-Hollweg and Delbrück for refusing to disband the Reichstag and crush the socialists. The Chancellor and his Interior Minister, for their part, would disappoint moderates and especially the Left as well, paying only lip service to the idea of greater recognition and support for workers in 1912 before backing off entirely from the development of a social policy by early 1914.[23]

If the government of Bethmann-Hollweg was not experiencing complete paralysis in these areas of domestic policy, then it certainly had very little maneuvering room. For groups that represented commercial, trade, and finished-goods manufacturing interests, however, the dilemmas being faced by Bethmann-Hollweg and Delbrück actually opened an unprecedented – if by no means assured – window of opportunity. The BDI, for one thing, emerged as a natural partner to Werkbund interests. It had formed initially in 1895 to unite small and middle-sized finished-goods industries, which typically did not belong to cartels, in an effort to break the overwhelming influence and domination of well-organized, cartellized heavy industry.[24]

For another, the BDI enjoyed gradually increasing ties to the Hansa League for Commerce, Trade, and Industry, a second, even younger interest group dominated by light manufacturing industries. The Hansa League had formed in 1909 during battles over the reform of Imperial finances and represented a further important step in the organization of Wilhelmine commercial, banking, and white-collar employee (*Privatangestellten*) interests. Active members and leaders of these groups like Emil Rathenau, Gustav Stresemann, and Friedrich Naumann railed against the government's unfavorable treatment of finished-goods industries as compared to its sustained support for tariff agreements favorable to the old alliance (*Sammlung*) of heavy industry and agriculture.[25] In fact, the BDI and its closest political ally, the National Liberals of the "broad middle" of Basserman and Stresemann, had been agitating for years to gain fair representation for commercial, banking, and light manufacturing interests in the Imperial Interior Ministry's Economic Commission for Industry (*Wirtschaftliche Ausschuss beim Reichsamt des Innern*).[26] Complaining about the stubborn and ongoing refusals of Conservatives to accept inheritance taxes and to roll back finished-goods tax hikes that were damaging to German commerce and consumers, Naumann had protested, "Liberals pay the most taxes, but get little say [in government]. Social Democrats provide the most soldiers of all the parties and get even less."[27]

Bethmann-Hollweg and Delbrück did not expand light industry representation on the Economic Commission, just as they refused either to ban the socialist party outright or appease it with a meaningful social policy. They did, however, step up calls for imperialist expansion and initiatives promoting Germany's commercial success. A "gunboat diplomacy" dimension of this policy shift fell short, as the brinksmanship of Chancellor Bethmann-Hollweg and Foreign Minister Alfred von Kiderlen-Wächter during the Morocco Crisis of 1911 raised the ire of the French and British and failed to produce the hoped-for wave of nationalist fervor that would carry Conservatives to victory in the elections of 1912. Kiderlen-Wächter, a close friend of Ernst Jäckh from their Constantinople days, worked closely with Bethmann-Hollweg on foreign policy until his unexpected death on December 30, 1912.[28]

A second dimension of this policy, a bid for expanding Germany's trade territories in order to compete effectively with such global powers as Britain and the United States, seemed to offer greater prospects. For example, the Foreign Office responded well to calls from the BDI and Stresemann, its most influential member, to mobilize Germany's worldwide network of diplomatic consulates as energetic facilitators of German commerce and foreign trade. German diplomatic outposts in Rio de Janeiro, Beirut, Calcutta, Genoa, and other cities received official notice of the Werkbund and its bid to improve the quality of German products and support German culture through the cooperation of artists, manufacturers, and merchants. The Chancellor's Office also requested that consulates furnish it with addresses of all German businesses and professionals operating in foreign territory who could serve as appropriate conduits for Werkbund propaganda, which the ministry wished to have businesses disseminate as widely as possible in these countries.[29]

In a related effort, the Chancellor and Foreign Office arranged free passage on a luxury steamer from South America to Germany for Major Joâo Simplicio de Carvalho, Brazil's incoming Minister of Transport and one-time War Ministry attaché, so that he could tour the planned Werkbund Exhibition of 1914. He was to be shown German industry's finest examples of locomotives, passenger train cars, automobiles, and planes and was to be treated as an honored minister of state throughout his visit. As the Chancellor noted in a letter to the German consul in Brazil, the Krupp Company, one of Germany's only heavy industries to join the Werkbund, would also take Major Carvalho on one of its tours through the legendary Krupp steel works, which encompassed eighty factories in nearby Essen alone.[30] Here family patriarch Gustav Krupp von Bohlen und Halbach would usher the Brazilian dignitary through detailed explanations of the Krupp steel-production process, followed by a visit to sales displays of Germany's finest steel-plated armor, naval guns, artillery field pieces, and railway wheels and rails.[31] Between the Werkbund Exhibition and the Krupp tour, Foreign Office officials were confident that Major de Carvalho's "far-reaching influence would soon be of benefit to German commerce, German industry, and shipping."[32]

As the Foreign Office was given to understand through documentation submitted by Ernst Jäckh and Carl Rehorst, the Werkbund Exhibition Planning Committee was working to assure that official foreign visitors would encounter the best selection of German industrial products in Cologne as well. For strategic reasons, the planning committee had chosen to abandon the Werkbund's traditional emphasis on the "*quality of the exhibitor*" and instead decided to focus attention on the "quality of the *exhibited products*" (emphasis original). "This broadening of the exhibition's base," explained Rehorst's and Jäckh's annotated report to the Standing Committee for German Industrial Exhibitions, "will especially help to realize the goal of the exhibition in its national-economic dimension, far better than if one were to limit oneself only to people and firms that are in the Werkbund and have already been won over to its ideas."[33] In other words, the Cologne Exhibition committee was opening its doors to all German industries and products deemed to be of sufficient quality. This move cast the Werkbund as a kind of umbrella organization whose principles stood to become those of the invited, non-Werkbund German industries as well. The Foreign Ministry further used the Werkbund Exhibition for training and education of its diplomatic and consular staff. Its trainees attended the exhibition and heard lectures on various national efforts to promote quality in Germany's export industries.[34]

None of the Foreign Office's measures, of course, proceeded in a vacuum. Interior Minister Delbrück, for example, assured Foreign Minister Gottlieb von Jagow that the Werkbund Exhibition had his full support.[35] The Imperial Colonial Office (*Reichs-Kolonialamt*), too, signed on to display Germany's colonial products in its own Werkbund Exhibition pavilion. Colonial Office officials laid particular emphasis on exhibiting examples of Germany's colonial architecture, which they felt were in dire need of improvement given the sophisticated colonial buildings of the rival British Empire.[36]

As it had in 1906, the Prussian Commerce Ministry arranged for its applied-arts schools to exhibit in Cologne, although at a much smaller scale in view of even tighter budgetary constraints.[37] In general, the Commerce Ministry engaged in unprecedented levels of government involvement in domestic economic organization between 1910 and 1914. Commerce Minister Reinhold Sydow, appointed in July 1909 following Clemens Delbrück's accession to Imperial Minister of the Interior, enlarged the influence of the Commerce Ministry to a far greater degree than either Delbrück or Möller before him.[38] Continuing the control of private commercial and accounting schools begun by Heinrich Neuhaus and Hermann von Seefeld, the Commerce Ministry also moved to consolidate the activities of decentralized chambers of commerce with growing commercial associations to improve cooperation in trade.[39]

Significantly for the Werkbund, the Commerce Ministry also asserted its authority over aspects of the electric power industry and the coal industry after 1910. For example, a ministerial decree of July 1912 ordered state-led, public-private associations to assume control of the generation and distribution of electric power in the name of serving the public and preventing "private exploitation."[40] Likewise, Commerce Minister Sydow reenergized ministerial efforts begun under Theodor von Möller to purchase a controlling interest in the Hibernia Coal Co., one of the largest firms in the Rhineland Coal Syndicate. The Commerce Minister was not interested in an outright state take-over of the coal industry; rather, and as the historian Hans-Heinrich Borchard has shown, Sydow "wanted to enlarge the state's financial possessions only to an extent that would allow the state to exercise influence over price, production, and supply."[41] The ministry's actions with respect to the electrical and coal industries suggest that what may have been planned for the Werkbund – had not the outbreak of war superceded all other plans – was a way to convert it, as well, into a form of state-led, public-private association. In this guise the Werkbund could oversee design and production quality in an array of finished-goods industries that would be subjected to increasing discipline and concentration, much as the Commerce Ministry was already doing with the electrical and coal industries.

Light industry interest groups, too, mobilized to urge greater recognition of their importance to the German economy on the part of government. Naumann and Stresemann strengthened ties between the BDI and Hansa League to the point where the two associations formed a special "industry council" (*Industrierat*) for noncartellized German export industries in late 1912. Hartmann Oswald Freiherr von Richthofen, a banker and National Liberal who assumed the post of business manager for the Hansa League in May 1912, proclaimed to a Hansa League audience in Dresden on November 17, 1912, that a new "mercantile imperialism," a "healthy – not chauvinistic – imperialism," was henceforth to serve as the inspiration for Hansa League activities.[42] Here, and as the historian Dirk Stegmann has noted, von Richthofen was following a course set by BDI spokesman Stresemann just one week earlier. In a speech at the second "Hansa Week" in Berlin on November 11, where Naumann and Professor Hans Delbrück, a "socialist of the lectern" and editor of the *Prussian Yearbooks* (*Preussische Jahrbücher*) had also spoken, Stresemann asserted: "The success of a people's global economic policies (*Weltwirtschaft*) is dependent on the global politics (*Weltpolitik*) of that people. The times have changed... and if the world outside is being divided up [among established colonial powers], then Germany must also participate."[43]

Such remarks went hand in hand with the Hansa League's domestic-policy efforts. As commentator Emil Lederer observed in 1912: The Hansa League sought for the first time ever, and "in a consequential manner," to bring the "small tradespeople and small merchants into a state of economic and political solidarity with the entire urban upper-middle class (*städtischen Bürgertum*)."[44] This was congruent with Stresemann's own campaign to encourage group identity among private industrial and commercial white-collar employees, known as *Privatbeamten*. Stresemann specifically targeted the *Privatbeamten* so as to stimulate a middle-class political awareness disinclined to support trade unions.[45]

The closer ties between the BDI and Hansa League underscored the suspicion of these two associations toward the so-called cartel of productive estates (*Kartell der schaffenden Stände*), an alliance viewed with distrust given its support for the anticommerce tariff positions favored by the agrarians and heavy industry.[46] The BDI also approached selected leaders of heavy industry in an effort to establish a German Society for World Commerce (*Deutscher Gesellschaft fur Weltwirtschaft*), but negotiating efforts fell apart. Regional associations such as the Foreign Society Ltd. (*Auslands GmbH*), however, formed smaller coalitions of heavy and light industry in parts of Germany. This effort succeeded particularly well among industries in the Rhineland and Westphalia, where Cologne, significantly, was a major industrial and financial center.[47] As Rehorst had proclaimed in 1911: "The Rhineland is economically on the rise – it is with Westphalia the site of our largest and most important industries. Together they yield 38 percent of Prussia's taxes, and in relation to the size of the rest of the state and its provinces, the West nourishes the East."[48]

In concert with official policies and with measures being taken by interest groups and associations, Friedrich Naumann and especially Ernst Jäckh stepped up measures to sketch a pre-war road map for German imperialism. Friedrich Naumann's *Assistance* (*Die Hilfe*) generally "took a strongly imperialist line," while Jäckh, a regular contributor, launched a series of additional publishing projects to spell out the terms for a bold, expansive, German-led alliance.[49] The foundation of the German-Austro-Hungarian Economic Association in September 1913, only a year after the Werkbund's Congress in Vienna, lent fuel to Jäckh's vision of a gigantic trading bloc dominated politically and economically by Germany.[50] Such programs for customs unions and various degrees of unification of East Central Europe under German hegemony were certainly part of a long tradition of discussions among pan-Germanists and colonialists like Albert Ritter, Heinrich Class, Paul Rohrbach, and others; it seems significant in this context that Jäckh, as the Werkbund managing director, propagandist, and close liaison to the Foreign Office, pushed so strongly for such a program at a time when the Foreign Office and other ministries were acting especially favorably toward the Werkbund as an official representative of German export ideals and cultural values.[51]

Jäckh optimistically and perhaps naively assumed that a German challenge to the British Empire at two of its "sorest spots," namely Egypt and India, could succeed without provoking war.[52] He was certainly not alone among factions of German industry in advocating a "Berlin to Baghdad line" – a rail line and axis of trade projected to stretch well beyond Germany, Austria–Hungary, through the Balkans and Turkey, and ultimately to the Persian Gulf (Fig. 118).[53] Cultivating Germany's alliance with the Ottoman Empire had been one of Jäckh's and

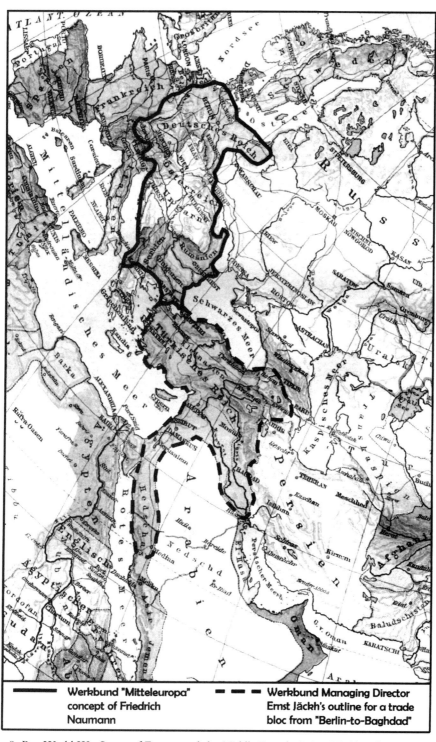

118. Pre–World War I map of Europe and the Middle East depicting Werkbund strategists' plans for *Mitteleuropa* (Friedrich Naumann) and the projected German-led trade bloc from "Berlin to Baghdad" (Ernst Jäckh) (*Diercke Schulatlas für Höhere Lehranstalten*, Braunschweig, 1917, with additions by author, drawing by Burak Erdim)

Kiderlen-Wächter's specialties, and although skeptics regarded Turkey derisively as the "sick man of Europe," Ottoman territory represented to many Germans the Wilhelmine Empire's last and best hope of coming to dominate a portion of the globe that had not yet been claimed by any other colonial power. Jäckh would continue efforts to draw the Ottomans and Germans closer together as head of the German-Turkish Union, which, with funding from Werkbund firm owner Robert Bosch, would hold a competition for a "House of Friendship" to symbolize the coming together of the two empires (Fig. 119).[54]

In the plans of Jäckh, Naumann, and Stresemann, as well as Pan-Germanists like Paul Liman and Heinrich Class, Germany would be able to purchase badly needed raw material supplies from new markets in the Balkans, Turkey, and beyond. In exchange, these allies and trade partners would receive products from Germany's burgeoning finished-goods industries. Commercial, banking, and industrial interests in the BDI, Hansa Bund, and Association for Trade Agreement Negotiations generally backed these types of measures, while Jäckh's patriotic and boosterist propaganda publications detailed ambitions for challenging England's "Pax Britannica" with an alternative "Pax Germanica." To promote this cause Jäckh produced such publications as *Germany in the Near East Following the Balkan War* of 1913, *Greater Germany* of 1914, *The Rising Crescent: On the Path to German and Turkish Union* of 1915, and *Werkbund and Mitteleuropa* of 1916.[55] Jäckh's program was notably more expansive than Naumann's calls for a pan-German and East Central European *Mitteleuropa*, although Naumann's book of the same name, published in 1915, espoused similar economic ambitions. Naumann's *Mitteleuropa* was to become the politician's best-selling, most-translated, and most-discussed publication.[56]

Jäckh's pre-war publications are just the furthest projection of a pan-German global economic and political power scenario that squared with the evolving policies of government and the lobbying efforts of Germany's largest industrial associations between 1911 in 1914. They are also of a piece with Muthesius's July 1914 lecture "The Future Work of the Werkbund," and with Naumann's address a few days later, "The Werkbund and the World Economy." But only the internal Werkbund politics surrounding the planning of the Cologne Exhibition of 1914, the Werkbund Congress of July 3–4, and its bruising aftermath can demonstrate the tactics being pursued to change the course of an organization that, only seven years earlier, had consisted primarily of artists, craftsmen, architects, and applied-arts manufacturers.

THE WERKBUND'S INTERNAL CONFLICTS AND THE STRUGGLE FOR CONTROL AT COLOGNE

Events leading to the 1914 "Werkbund debate" strongly suggest that the role of government and industry in planning the Cologne exhibition was indeed the

119. Hans Poelzig, project for House of German-Turkish Friendship, Istanbul, 1916, perspective view (Theodor Heuss, *Das Haus der Freundschaft in Konstantinopel*, Munich, 1918)

major, probably even the decisive cause for a faction comprised of Osthaus, Gropius, van de Velde, and August Endell to seek to topple Muthesius from the Werkbund leadership at the Congress of July 1914. Osthaus, in particular, suffered the greatest frustration as a delegate to the Werkbund's official exhibition planning committee, which began meeting in fall 1912. His correspondence – which, unlike Muthesius's Werkbund-related correspondence, survived wartime destruction[57] – recounts a none-too-subtle "stacking" of the Werkbund exhibition planning committee with members distinctly ill-disposed toward Osthaus's artistic views.

When it first met, the exhibition planning committee had consisted of eight Cologne representatives, plus Osthaus and Bruckmann as the Werkbund's designated delegates. At the committee's second meeting, however, there appeared two additional Werkbund representatives: Muthesius and Jäckh. As Osthaus recalled, "a position of 'second chairman' was expressly created for Muthesius." Claiming to have had no prior knowledge of the planning committee's enlargement, Osthaus insisted that "through Muthesius's selection my influence was meant to be paralyzed."[58] Osthaus's complaints are consistent with letters exchanged among Osthaus, Walter Gropius, and Peter Bruckmann, which recount with some bitterness Muthesius's efforts to replace Osthaus with a Prussian civil servant as author of an article on railway-station architecture for the 1914 Werkbund Yearbook.[59]

Ernst Jäckh, by contrast, held Muthesius in very high regard, particularly where the Werkbund's political affairs were concerned. In his memoirs he characterized the government architect as the most decisive personality in the Werkbund, for "he alone had the accurate conception of politics . . . as a synthesis of all human relations, ranging from physical matters to the metaphysics of psychology, from 'material' to 'form.'"[60] Such unqualified praise for Muthesius would become a rarity as 1914 approached. Evidently influenced by developments and policy shifts at the Commerce Ministry and Interior Ministry over the past few years, Muthesius took on a role – a personality, even – that pointed to a significant shift in attitude, a subordination of his previous valuation of architecture and artistic culture to a particularly strong emphasis on commerce.

Since its beginnings in 1907, the Werkbund had taken a cue from Muthesius's speech on the "The Meaning of the Applied Arts" and emphasized the leading role that government should play in educating consumers and acting as promoters of good taste. The organization had even included this point in the guiding principles it formulated in its inaugural meeting.[61] With Muthesius's influential presence as second chairman of the Cologne Exhibition planning committee, the government's involvement reached new levels. The "great interest [in the exhibition] shown by decisive officials in the German Empire," the building trade journal *Deutsche Bauhütte* reported, could be explained in part by the prospect that Germany's best-known architects would be contributing buildings to the exhibition.[62] Muthesius and Jäckh, meanwhile, cooperated to ensure that the exhibition's appearance and content would place the Werkbund's economic and artistic ideas in what they saw as the most favorable light in order to appeal expressly to potential new Werkbund industries in the rich Rhineland region.[63]

The commercial emphasis of the exhibition quickly became apparent, as the committee concentrated on finished goods products and, led by Muthesius, made efforts to deliver commissions to architects who were likely to design understated, conservative exhibition halls rather than radical, experimental buildings. In his efforts to keep the exhibition unified and subdued, Muthesius even opposed Peter Behrens, who had presented a preliminary plan for the exhibition at the Vienna meeting of 1912.[64] Behrens complained to Carl Rehorst that Muthesius's rejection of his plan seemed to stem from the government architect's "absurd" impression that Behrens "wished to consider the exhibition as an individual exhibit of his works and would therefore prevent the Werkbund from expressing itself."[65] Osthaus assuaged Behrens's anger and his wish to conduct an immediate "counter-agitation" against Muthesius, assuring him that there was surely "much room for improvement in the current Werkbund operations" and that action would be taken "at the next opportunity."[66]

The Osthaus correspondence is rife with evidence of various other artists' efforts to avoid entirely or circumvent Muthesius's domineering tendencies in the

120. Henry van de Velde, Theater, Cologne Werkbund Exhibition, 1914, general view
(*Jahrbuch des Deutschen Werkbundes 1914: Deutsche Form im Kriegsjahr*, Munich, 1915)

planning of the exhibition. Victims of the planning committee second chairman's intransigence included such older individualists from the *Jugendstil* tradition as August Endell and Henry van de Velde, whom Muthesius resisted as potential exhibition architects.[67] Even after the committee commissioned van de Velde to design the exhibition's theater (Fig. 120), the Belgian architect continued to face difficulties. To begin with, Muthesius arranged to take over the original site for van de Velde's theater, a location close to the entrance gate, so he could design a pavilion for the Hamburg-America Shipping Line as an annex to his pavilion for a display of color in design.[68] Commerce appeared to be displacing culture in the competition for the exhibition's most favorable sites: Instead of entering the Werkbund Exhibition to find van de Velde's signature Art Nouveau theater grouped among the initial ensemble of buildings visitors would encounter, guests would instead find themselves immersed in a sober, unified exhibition environment of domed buildings and classical arcades. Conventional classical edifices that would greet visitors included Muthesius's domed pavilion for Color Display (*Farbenschau*, Fig. 121) for BASF, Bayer, and other top manufacturers of colors and dyes, and the pavilion of the Hamburg-America Line.[69] Van de Velde's theater, along with other "radical" buildings like Walter Gropius's model factory and administration building (Fig. 122), would be relegated to the far end of the main grounds, while Bruno Taut's glass pavilion would be excluded from the main exhibition area altogether (Fig. 123).

The exhibition planning committee, and especially the triumvirate of Bruckmann, Jäckh, and Muthesius, compounded van de Velde's frustrations by requiring him to submit seven laboriously revised proposals and designs. They only

121. Hermann Muthesius Pavilion for Color Display (*Farbenschau*), Cologne Werkbund Exhibition, 1914, general view (*Jahrbuch des Deutschen Werkbundes 1914: Deutsche Form im Kriegsjahr*, Munich, 1915)

122. Walter Gropius, Model Factory and Administration Building, Cologne Werkbund Exhibition, 1914, general view (Gustav A. Platz, *Die Baukunst der Neuesten Zeit*, Berlin, 1927)

123. Bruno Taut, Glass Pavilion at Cologne Werkbund Exhibition, 1914, general view (Gustav A. Platz, *Die Baukunst der Neuesten Zeit*, Berlin, 1927)

granted van de Velde eleventh-hour approval in early March 1914. This serious delay to the start of construction meant the theater could only begin operating in mid-June, one month after the exhibition had opened, and left only six weeks of the exhibition in which the theater could actually operate.[70]

Another recipient of Muthesius's censorial behavior, the Munich architect August Endell, also had origins in the *Jugendstil* tradition, and most likely for this reason represented a threat to the unity and integrity of the exhibition in the judgment of the government architect. Endell had first achieved renown as the designer of the singularly un-*sachlich Jugendstil* façade and interior of the Munich Photography Atelier "Elvira" in 1897, a building that could not possibly have attracted Muthesius as a fan (Fig. 10). In spite of Endell's pronounced hopes to obtain a large and meaningful commission for the Cologne exhibition, he faced a series of disappointments. When awarded a commission for a glass exhibition hall in December 1913 – at a planning meeting that Muthesius was unable to attend – Endell prepared a design, only to discover later that his commission had been revoked in a subsequent and unexplained reversal of the planning committee's position. Endell settled for a smaller exhibition interior that Osthaus arranged for him, but in his frustration threatened to bring the matter of Muthesius's opposition "to every larger work" for the Cologne exhibition out into the open, so that it could be "reckoned with before the public."[71]

Muthesius also hindered the exhibition ambitions of the young Walter Gropius. In 1914, at the age of fifty-three, Muthesius was Gropius's senior by twenty-three years. Separated by a generation and divided in their orientation and outlook, the two men clashed. First, Muthesius displaced Gropius as the designer of a pavilion for the Hamburg-America Shipping Line, a project in which Muthesius worked closely with Hermann Freudenberg's Hermann Gerson Store.[72] Second, when Gropius obtained the opportunity to design the model factory and administration building in place of Hans Poelzig, who gave up the commission in mid-1913, he found himself once again facing Muthesius's opposition. Significantly, Poelzig appears to have stayed away from the Werkbund Exhibition out of a rising disgust for the organization. He threatened to resign from the organization altogether – especially if Gropius followed through with his germinating proposal to found a *Sonderbund*, or alternative association to the Werkbund. If this occurred, "a miracle would have to follow," wrote Poelzig to Gropius, "and all those would have to resign who have made the Werkbund into a monster, which it actually was right from its inception."[73] Festering differences that had long divided the outlooks of the Commerce Ministry and the Culture Ministry came into high relief with the clear commercial emphasis of the Cologne preparations, and Poelzig was clearly bitter.[74] Yet the architect would feel differently toward the Werkbund after Muthesius's departure from the organization in 1916; he would succeed Muthesius as vice president in 1916 and rise to become Werkbund president in 1919.

Gropius, who had made a name for himself with the design of the Fagus Shoe-Last Factory in Alfeld in 1911, rallied numerous Werkbund allies to support him in his design of the exhibition's model factory and machine hall (Fig. 122). First, he successfully fought off a proposal by the firm of Breuer, Schumacher & Co., a Cologne industrial manufacturer, to display a gargantuan armor-plate press in the courtyard of the model factory. Gropius argued that the presence of this fourteen-meter-high hydraulic press, which produced armor plating for Admiral Tirpitz's sixty-ship battle fleet, would completely disrupt the scale and proportions of his carefully planned building. Thereafter, the commission vetoed the architect's efforts to place a reflecting pool alongside the machine hall, even after Gropius offered to finance the building of the pool himself. The exhibition planning commission preferred to line the machine hall exterior with a series of memorial pavilions. Angry at being unable to convince the commission to withdraw this measure, Gropius submitted a petition signed by other exhibition artists and architects, at which point the committee backed down.[75] Gropius continued his agitation for a secession of artists from the Werkbund in protest of Muthesius's domineering tactics, but was told by Werkbund president Peter Bruckmann that, for reasons of pre-exhibition publicity, a large confrontation or secession before the opening of the exhibition needed to be avoided at all costs. Bruckmann did submit, however, that the Cologne Werkbund conference would offer a much-needed opportunity for "clear declarations, in which differing opinions must be allowed to collide with one another."[76]

Significantly, the buildings most opposed by the exhibition's organizing committee are the ones that received the most critical acclaim. Gropius's model factory and van de Velde's theater were, from the beginning, the most popular buildings of the 1914 exhibition (Figs. 122, 120). Gropius, who had expressed concern for the artistic potential of new materials like steel, glass, and concrete in industrial architecture, nevertheless saw his building interpreted by subsequent critics such as Nikolaus Pevsner and Reyner Banham as an example of anonymous, mechanized architecture that some suggested Muthesius was promoting in his Werkbund Congress speech of 1914. In other words, where Gropius saw himself as promoting individual artistic excellence and monumentality in the production of modern architecture, subsequent interpreters would see an expression of the rationality and standardization associated with a "machine aesthetic."[77]

Bruno Taut's glass pavilion, built for the German Luxfer-Prism-Syndicate of glass manufacturers, also proved extremely popular (Fig. 123). Taut's project, however, received a site close to the main entrance gate and amusement park and far away from the main exhibition buildings. Nor did the multicolored pavilion, dedicated to the utopian writer Paul Scheerbart, appear on many site plans or published maps depicting locations of the exhibition's attractions. Instead, it stood in a line of small police, fire, and service pavilions. Taut, who had initiated the project and provided most of the financial backing himself, convinced the glass industry to support his pavilion design.[78] The fantasy and charm of Taut's crystalline form, glass construction, and shifting kaleidoscopic projections suggested the possibility of a Werkbund Exhibition that celebrated artistic creativity even as it introduced the public to new building materials and their potential applications. However, the planning committee's predominant concern with economic, political, and export-oriented goals produced far different results.

The buildings by architects of the older generation – Behrens's Neoclassical convention hall (Figs. 114–115), Fischer's main exhibition hall (Fig. 117), and Muthesius's hall for color design (Fig. 121) – were largely panned by contemporary critics. They displayed what Julius Posener has called a "listless classicism."[79] Yet these buildings were the calculated result of the planning committee's efforts to enforce restraint and respectability in order to avoid challenging the sensibilities of potential new Werkbund industrial partners, who were central to the success of the exhibition. Moreover, and to the extent that state ministries, industrial interests, and commercial imperatives exerted unprecedented influence over the Werkbund in the years 1912–1914, this collection of Neoclassical pavilions can be seen as the clear stylistic expression of that influence.

The pre-war period of cartellization, concentration, and intense military build-up were all components of Germany's unprecedented, albeit increasingly worrying, national power. The commercially oriented design savvy of Emil Rathenau's

124. Hugo Röttcher, Cologne-Deutz railroad station, 1914, general view (*Moderne Bauformen* 13, 1914)

AEG company and the progressivism of such Werkbund firms as Bosch-Stuttgart and Bahlsen-Hannover notwithstanding, a deep cultural and economic conservativism was characteristic of Germany's industrial interests. In their Wilhelmine form, and in their growing prominence as forces to be reckoned with by both state authorities and Werkbund leaders, industrial interests were far less likely to

125. Walter Gropius, salon at Cologne Werkbund Exhibition, 1914 (*Moderne Bauformen* 13, 1914)

126. Bruno Paul, music hall, Cologne Werkbund Exhibition, 1914 (*Moderne Bauformen* 13, 1914)

promote architectural exuberance and experimentation of a sort one might otherwise deem appropriate for exhibition buildings that were, after all, temporary. A glance at the contemporary architecture of Cologne's large banks, insurance companies, and industrial headquarters, or even at Hugo Röttcher's new railway station of Cologne-Deutz outside the Werkbund Exhibition's entry gate (Fig. 124), confirms that the exhibition planning committee's adoption of updated classical forms mirrored precisely the architectural preferences displayed in Cologne's newest commercial, industrial, and administrative structures.[80] This display of conventional forms, while far from adventurous, may well have been one expression of Muthesius's concept of evolving "types" in Wilhelmine architecture, grounded as they were in a familiar common language. Cologne's display of neoclassical architecture for financial and commercial headquarters in the city and its self-presentation as a "modern metropolis" at the Werkbund Exhibition fit very well with the vast majority of exhibition interiors, too, which catered to conservative, neo-Biedermeier tastes. Most of these attained a high quality of workmanship and materials without threatening to challenge exhibition visitors' aesthetic sensibilities (Figs. 125–126). Walter Gropius included progressive art from the Expressionist movement in some of his exhibition rooms and model factory building, and Osthaus backed progressive artists as well. But on the whole, commerce was king at the 1914 Cologne exhibition and threatened to reduce many artists' battles for expression to a kind of rearguard action.

ECONOMIC DESTINY, CULTURAL HARMONY, AND THE "TYPE" IN DESIGN

It is in this context, and amid the economic and political consequences of greatly increased industrial concentration, that Muthesius's development of ten theses for the development of "types" can best be understood. What began as a meditation on the essence and importance of form in his 1911 speech "Where Do We Stand?" evolved over the course of the exhibition planning phase into a firm commitment to the identification and reproduction of "types" in design. In his contribution to the 1913 Werkbund Yearbook, entitled "The Problem of Form in Engineering Construction," Muthesius urged all Werkbund members to recognize that aspects of beauty and function interacted dynamically from the beginning of any design process, whether concerned with a household object or a building. The vital work for generations of artists in any period, he argued, was to evolve fitting aesthetic forms for each newly invented object. This could be shown historically through an examination of the design efforts that had surrounded the first steamships (in which a steam engine was mounted on a sailing ship), the first railway wagons (which resembled mail coaches), or early gas lights (whose forms resembled candles). Over time, designers learned to relate the forms of these objects to the expression of their capabilities and functional requirements.[81]

Muthesius's development of this new and more forcible position regarding the "typical" coincided with the transfer of the Werkbund's headquarters to Berlin, and even more closely with the planning phase of the First Werkbund Exhibition between 1912 and 1914. His philosophical shift and his contemporaneous actions in the exhibition planning committee seemed calculated to favor a stronger push toward exports and toward new forms of production in industry. Yet his introduction of the term *Typisierung* (making of types) was nothing if not imprecise and confusing. Muthesius apparently did not mean standardization (*Standardisierung*), although some, with good reason, did read this meaning into his use of the term. Some of his theses seemed to imply mass production, yet the architect specifically avoided using this term as well in the ten "theses" he distributed prior to the Werkbund's seventh annual meeting at the exhibition in early July (Appendix B).[82] In stopping short of an outright call for standardization, Muthesius advocated a contemporary recognition of tendencies toward the "typical," which he claimed could be identified through the analysis of any era known for the greatness of its architectural, artistic, or applied-arts production. The identification and collective recognition of "types" of products and designs was the best way, he reasoned, for Werkbund artists and designers to aid German industry. Artists executing individual commissions, by contrast, could hardly hope to have a measurable effect on the export market that the Werkbund, the Commerce Ministry, and the finished-goods industries so wished to increase. One thing, at least, was clear to Muthesius: Collective and sustained efforts by Werkbund artists and industries in the direction of developing standard "types" would lead to a vastly increased output of products of high quality. These, in turn, would prove more attractive to foreign consumers, leading to increased exports, while the same improved products would also raise the tastes of average Germans at home. "Productively capable and dependably tasteful large enterprises," Muthesius wrote in his ninth thesis, "are the precondition for such an export. [By contrast], the individually produced, artist-designed object cannot even begin to fulfill domestic demand."[83] Muthesius contended further in his other "theses" that Germany's progress in arts and crafts design and production needed to be publicized widely through a propaganda campaign and through publicly subsidized exhibitions, and was a national matter of life and death. The world, he explained, would ask for German products once these goods possessed a "convincing expression of style," for which the German movement recently had provided the basis. "Architecture, and with it the whole area of the Werkbund's activites, is pressing toward the making of types," the very first thesis proclaimed, and herein lay the key to Germany's reestablishment of a "harmonious culture" (Appendix B).[84] During the course of his long government service, Muthesius had become accustomed to producing the insightful textual syntheses that had been incorporated or effectively translated into Commerce Ministry policy. This process can be seen in the influence that such articles as "Artistic Education for Craftsmen in England" (1898), "The Home Arts and Industries Association and Amateurism in the Applied Arts in England" (1900), and books like *Style-Architecture and Building-Art* (1902) and *The English House* (1904–05) had on Commerce Ministry officials in the early twentieth century.[85] In his reform of the ministry's applied-arts schools, moreover, Muthesius exhibited a seemingly typical Wilhelmine Prussian bureaucratic willingness to exert the authority of the state to reproduce hierarchical social and institutional relations in the name of German growth and cultural progress.

At a later point the Commerce Minister himself had defended Muthesius as an exemplary public servant in the Prussian Chamber of Deputies and had provided ministerial funding for one of the Werkbund's pioneering commercial schools in Berlin, the Higher Specialty School for Decorative Art. Now at the Cologne exhibition of 1914, it appeared, Muthesius was again relying on the cachet of his privileged government position in an effort to impose the will of the Commerce Ministry on a newly inaugurated phase of Werkbund policy. Just as his writings and lectures analyzed the conditions underlying cultural developments across generations or even centuries, his policy recommendations most often attempted to produce similar results by decree. At the Werkbund conference in 1914, this autocratic approach was once again evident: His speech to the assembly spoke of the tendency of advanced cultures to evolve types in design over time, whereas his theses suggested the immediate redirection of design and production with some measure of guidance from the state.

This arrogant expectation of obedience, coupled with the authoritarian behavior displayed by Muthesius as second chairman of the exhibition planning committee, is most likely what made the Werkbund into a "monster" in Poelzig's estimation and turned Muthesius into a "black sheep" in Gropius's eyes – or into a conduit, as Osthaus wrote, for "underground" and "subaltern" forces.[86] All of these men battled for levels of artistic integrity, independence, and individuality that they saw evaporating from the Werkbund in the years prior to the exhibition and in the months immediately preceding the outbreak of war. These artistic "individualists," as they would come to be known, were rebelling against a state-guided structure described by an outside observer, the French critic Paul Valéry, as one in which "fortress, factory, and school are linked with one another and are only different aspects of the same, soundly constructed Germany.... One must grant that the one and the other victory (military and commercial victories – author's note) are achieved by one and the same system."[87]

Seven years earlier, in 1907, it had been the traditional crafts practitioners of the Association for the Economic Interests of the Crafts who had opposed Muthesius's advancement of the Commerce Ministry's will. At the Werkbund Exhibition of 1914, it was the elite cadre of artists, architects, and supporters of artistic independence whose ire was aroused. The Weimar-based Belgian architect and applied artist van de Velde, with the support of Walter Gropius and Karl Ernst Osthaus, drafted ten "countertheses" in defence of absolute creative independence for the Werkbund's artists. Van de Velde read the countertheses immediately following Muthesius's address on July 3. These theses protested against the introduction of types as well as against "every suggestion of a canon" that Muthesius's types seemed to imply.[88] Not only had many designers' talents been suppressed in the preparations for the exhibition, but there was also a palpable sense that the artists, who so valued their independence and creative freedom, were simply being drafted as part of an economic program in applied-arts manufacturing over which they would have little or no control.

Yet this counterprotest, supported by many of the architects and artists aggrieved during the exhibition planning process, can hardly be regarded as having been against the principle of types per se, but against the wanton, undiplomatic, and autocratic way in which Muthesius had imposed his (and the government's) will on the Werkbund membership. Werkbund discussions about the development of "types" took place well before 1914, but had not been anywhere near as heated. Osthaus, for example, had reacted favorably to Muthesius's introduction of the "type" in Werkbund discussions following the government architect's address, "Where Do We Stand?" delivered during the 1911 annual meeting.[89] Van de Velde, too, was not a foe of industry or the concept of serial production in itself, as he had made plain in the journal *Pan* as early as 1897. There he had proclaimed a desire "to avoid systematically everything in furniture that could not be realized by big industry. My ideal," he wrote at the time, "would be a thousand-fold multiplication of my creations."[90] Similarly, Gropius had written a proposal for the industrial production of prefabricated houses for workers as early as 1910, and as such had clearly anticipated an aspect of Muthesius's modern "types" in architectural terms.[91] By opposing Muthesius in 1914, Osthaus, van de Velde, and Gropius were rebelling against statist efforts to commandeer their skills for a greater institutional and national agenda, for in principle Muthesius's ideas concerning the type did not run contrary to artistic views they had expressed earlier in their careers under less aggravated circumstances.

Knowing that van de Velde had prepared his countertheses, Muthesius toned down the address he gave before the entire assembly. Entitled "The Future Work of the Werkbund," the speech sought diplomatically to appraise the exhibition and to promote the new Werkbund orientation as a positive step for all. Admitting that the exhibition suffered from "a certain stillness...not to say listlessness," Muthesius agreed that the fractious Werkbund, by staying together in spite of having been called "an association of the most intimate enemies," offered "the best proof of the greatness of the idea that moves us beyond all differences of opinion."[92]

It was true that artistry had suffered at the hands of efforts to give the exhibition the broadest possible appeal, the architect admitted. But on the positive side, businesses had begun taking the Werkbund seriously – to the point that "today the whole merchant class and the great majority of industrial producers seek to work with us." Underlining this as the purpose of the whole exhibition, he continued, "It is of the greatest importance to establish this here. And this confirmation calls forth a certain reproach, that actual new [Werkbund] products are only to be seen in such small numbers. It raises the question, what does the Deutscher Werkbund want?"[93] The Werkbund, Muthesius argued, must in the end choose the direction of developing the "typical," for that was the direction of development during all great eras of art. By shunning the unusual and seeking the orderly, the typical nevertheless also managed to bear within it the paradoxical quality of retaining "the worthwhile particular, the personal, and the unique."

Muthesius assured his audience that the call for the typical was not a demand for the artist to concentrate only on a single form: "The artist follows only his own inner drive. He enjoys complete freedom, because he can only work in this way."[94] Nevertheless, the character of the present day called for acknowledgment of unprecedented levels of international exchange, as well as technological developments that "practically overcome the boundaries of time and space." With this international quality of contemporary life arose the tendency toward "a certain similarity to the architectonic forms over the entire globe."[95]

Muthesius did not explicitly advocate standardization or mass production by machines as the basis for a new style; nor did he discuss either of these industrial processes in his speech. He did, however, speak clearly of a wish to put the Werkbund at the forefront of discovering what the style representative of contemporary life would be. The faction that coalesced around van de Velde, however, took even the intimation of "types" as a sure sign that artists were being recruited to serve the assembly line.

Naumann's closing address of the next day, "The Werkbund and the World Economy," reinforced Muthesius's arguments from an economic, rather than artistic or cultural point of view. In his customary fashion, Naumann blended economic and demographic statistics with anecdotal evidence and persuasive examples in an effort to bring Werkbund artists into line with the new economic thinking. Artists need not take the economic arguments so hard, Naumann suggested, for those not interested in focusing on the design of export wares would not be affected. Nevertheless, he proclaimed,

> Let us be expansionists . . . and when artists say that their freedom suffers as a result, then let us be honest with ourselves and say, that he who wishes to participate, must sacrifice. . . . It is not the highest art to converse only with oneself; rather the artist should know for whom and for what place he creates (*für wen und wohin er schafft*). We need German artists who have so much of a sense of America, that they work for America in a German manner! That is our expanded mission, i.e., in the last analysis: the Werkbund and the world economy.[96]

The assembly took no collective decisions at the end of the July Congress, for the proceedings following Muthesius's address were drowned in a sea of debate. The arguments reflected the pent-up emotions of the individuals who had been slighted or thwarted in their various ambitions for the exhibition. It was evident that the power struggle over the leadership of the Werkbund was every bit as important, indeed if not more important, than the confused arguments over artistry, aesthetics, and quality. Hermann Obrist mockingly posed the question whether, following two decades of innovation in Germany's applied-arts movement, the exhibition's "pseudo-Romanesque, pseudo-Baroque, pseudo-classical, and pseudo-Biedermeier buildings" represented "the 'types' with which we are supposed to conquer the world?"[97] The young Bruno Taut, one of eighteen speakers who responded on July 4 to the "theses" and "anti-theses" read to the assembly the previous day, even suggested that a great artist, someone like Henry van de Velde, should be appointed to a rotating three-year position as "art-dictator" to assume control over all aesthetic issues affecting the Werkbund.[98]

At the end of this stormy session, Muthesius rose to respond with a final comment to the assembly. He withdrew his ten theses by way of seeking conciliation with the artistic faction. He claimed that he would rather "make a sacrifice of himself" and withdraw from the Werkbund than see its larger purposes damaged.[99] This intimation of offering to resign, however, was identical to tactics he was accustomed to employing in the Prussian Commerce Ministry during the embattled days of the 1907 "Muthesius Affair." As he had written to Richard

Riemerschmid, in times of difficulty he typically "reduced to nothing" objections made against him by "offering [my] resignation" to then Commerce Minister Delbrück, whom Muthesius knew preferred to keep the government architect in his ministry.[100] Similarly, he employed another tactic familiar from Delbrück's defence of him during the "Muthesius Affair," in which the Commerce Minister had characterized Muthesius's opening speech to the Berlin Commercial College as purely academic and private in nature, and not, in fact, the logical extension of four years of Commerce Ministry work. Similarly, in 1914 Muthesius claimed before the Werkbund assembly to have been giving a lecture "as a private individual, as Hermann Muthesius," as if to suggest that he was just another Werkbund member and not the organization's vice president, not an influential government councillor, and not the domineering vice chair of the exhibition planning committee. He stood by his lecture and assured his audience that his withdrawal of the theses represented no true act of renunciation, for "that which is written here in the theses is also contained line for line in my lecture."[101] Although Muthesius would close the July Congress with these lines, it was far from being the last rhetorical sleight of hand to which the Werkbund membership would be subjected in summer 1914.

MANAGING DISSENT: THE WERKBUND, THE STATE, AND THE *BERLINER TAGEBLATT*

The split that occurred between defenders and critics of Muthesius at the July Congress led to renewed controversy and power struggles of particular intensity in the month between the Werkbund Congress and the outbreak of the First World War. Letters and telegrams raced back and forth among members of the various factions and the Werkbund leadership, seeking to make sense of recent events and their implications. Conflicts only escalated as Osthaus, van de Velde, and Gropius reacted to the most blatant of efforts by the Werkbund leadership (*Leitung*) to use the press to cast events of the preceding days in such a way as to proclaim a clear, nearly unanimous victory for the Werkbund's new industrial and commercial orientation as outlined in Muthesius's speech.

The first volley in these exchanges came from a Dr. Mahlberg, a friend of August Endell and Henry van de Velde, who published a review of the Werkbund Congress on July 7 that strongly favored van de Velde's interpretation of the events that had transpired. His review appeared in Rudolf Mosse's *Berliner Tageblatt* and prompted an immediate reply from the Werkbund leadership in the evening edition the very next day. The *Berliner Tageblatt* – pro-commerce, liberal on free trade, and regarded by historians as the "protector" of light industry's BDI – quickly became the venue for the resolution of private disagreements, grievances, and negotiated statements that rendered the Werkbund's internal differences innocuous before the public.[102]

With the *Berliner Tageblatt* under the distinct influence of commercial and Werkbund-related interests, Osthaus, van de Velde, and Gropius faced a marked disadvantage in attempting to clarify their points of view before the Werkbund membership and the broader public. For example, the *Berliner Tageblatt* was one of the newspapers with which Ernst Jäckh enjoyed sufficiently close ties to allow him to boast to the Imperial Foreign Office that he both "worked with" and "had influence" at this paper.[103] Moreover, as Dr. Mahlberg reported to Osthaus, the newspaper's editors had informed him that "influential personages [had been] intervening on Muthesius's behalf," thereby prompting them to deny Mahlberg the opportunity to publish a defense of his views following the Werkbund leadership's own article on the matter. Instead, the newspaper prepared to publish an article by Muthesius.[104]

These developments represented a critical blow to those ill-disposed toward Muthesius, and above all to Osthaus, Gropius, and van de Velde, for it enabled the Werkbund management to shape public opinion in ways that have echoed in Werkbund historiography to this day. Specifically, the Werkbund office, and presumably its politically engaged newspaper editor and managing director Ernst Jäckh, crafted a reply to Mahlberg in the *Berliner Tageblatt*'s evening addition of July 8, maintaining that Muthesius's retraction of his theses at the Werkbund Congress had been a mere "formality" and that the new direction of the Werkbund discussed in Muthesius's lecture had received approval from an optimistic and vocal majority. It further suggested that a "van de Velde group" had received printed copies of Muthesius's theses prior to the conference. In actual fact – and as numerous correspondents repeatedly pointed out over the course of the July exchanges – no such clearly formed "van de Velde group" had ever existed prior to the conference; all fourteen scheduled conference speakers, who represented a great diversity of opinion, had been given printed copies of the theses.[105]

Shortly thereafter, a Muthesius article in the *Berliner Tageblatt* of July 12 took further steps to downplay the seriousness of the thunderous debates at the Congress, dismissing them merely as "expressions of nervousness" on the part of a "small group" of Werkbund artists concerned about the Werkbund's new direction.[106] Incensed by such a blatant "rearrangement of the facts" (*Verschiebung der Tatsachen*), Osthaus and Gropius fired off indignant letters to Jäckh and the *Berliner Tageblatt* demanding clarifications and a retraction. They even suggested that Muthesius's misrepresentation of events discredited him to such a degree that he should resign his position on the Werkbund executive committee – a result that Gropius appeared especially eager to achieve.[107]

But once more the figures at the helm – Jäckh, Bruckmann, and Muthesius – were one step ahead in the use of publicity both to manage dissent within the Werkbund and to control the image of the organization in the public sphere. The Werkbund leadership called an emergency executive committee meeting in Berlin on Friday, July 17, at which Jäckh, Bruckmann, Muthesius, and Osthaus negotiated a short, line-by-line "clarification" of events to be published in the

Berliner Tageblatt. This was to help clear the air following the Werkbund's skirmishes and allow the association to present a unified front following the Congress and its troubling aftermath. At their emergency meeting, the executive committee members all seemed to agree on the need to avoid compromising the "power position" the Werkbund directors believed the organization had achieved as a result of its exhibition in Cologne, which was still underway. In composing the clarification, Osthaus wrote to Gropius that he "had to fight for the sentence" in which the Werkbund executive committee claimed it had not known about Muthesius's retraction of his theses at the time that it wrote to claim victory for the Muthesius position in the *Berliner Tageblatt* article of July 8.[108] The brief, paragraph-long clarification ultimately agreed on by the Werkbund's executive committee concluded, "Through the discussions today the tensions that temporarily affected the Werkbund as a result of this miscommunication have been brought to a peaceful solution."[109] With this, the executive committee adjourned its tense meeting in the hope that matters had been brought to rest.

Yet once again Osthaus, Gropius, and van de Velde were in for a shock: after unanimous agreement in the committee that the negotiated one-paragraph clarification would be published without any additions whatsoever, a second long passage mysteriously appeared as a rider to the published piece. This extra material once again greatly favored the position of Muthesius, Jäckh, and Bruckmann, and is in all likelihood the result of Jäckh's customary influence – or interference – with the press. The additional sentences effectively minimized the entire Werkbund Congress controversy by arguing that the Werkbund leadership, "like so many others, did not understand the practical meaning of the conflict and above all the passionate excitement" aroused by it. "In the end the only thing that happened," it continued, "was that Muthesius warned against an overemphasis on the personal, and others have already made such statements more sharply in the past. Only the rather unfortunate word *Typisierung* could have caused misunderstanding. For now, the unity of all Werkbund artists is more important than the assertion of individual opinions."[110]

Osthaus, understandably livid, immediately communicated his outrage to Muthesius concerning the mysterious appearance of the article's additional lines. Muthesius replied that the original agreed-on passage "had been given to Herr Jäckh for delivery" and that after that point he, Muthesius, "stood far removed from whatever happened."[111] Gropius was even more beside himself when he heard the news, persisting in efforts to promote a secession of artists from the Werkbund to such a degree that it remained for Osthaus to intervene and convince him that such actions could no longer lead to anything constructive.[112]

Just days later, the beginning of the First World War and Germany's general mobilization in early August eclipsed the Werkbund's bitter internal struggles. The Cologne Exhibition shut down immediately and before its scheduled end, while the proximity of the city to the Western front assured that within days, several of the exhibition halls would be in use as spaces for receiving wounded

German soldiers.[113] Gropius and Osthaus, instead of achieving their desired result of driving Muthesius to resign from the Werkbund leadership, instead saw Henry van de Velde forced out of his directorship in Weimar; because of his Belgian citizenship and the outbreak of hostilities, van de Velde was now labeled a hostile foreign alien.[114] Jäckh, Naumann, and Muthesius would continue a variety of Werkbund propaganda efforts during the war, including the blatantly anti-French "Werkbund Fashion Show" in the Prussian Chamber of Deputies in 1915, the "House of German-Turkish Friendship" architectural competition in 1916, and various additional publications.[115] However, the painful events and privations of a devastating, four-year mechanized war gradually made it apparent that the expansive plans of the Werkbund, the government, and light industry associations would suffer the same disastrous fate as the government's military campaign. The Werkbund would survive as an organization, but never again in the particular Wilhelmine configuration it had achieved as part of a nexus involving government ministries, industry, and exporters of German goods. The interaction of these various forces had done the most to shape the Cologne Werkbund Exhibition of 1914, and it was these forces that young architects like Walter Gropius would seek to escape after completing army service as a sergeant in a Hussar Reserve Regiment in 1918, and moving on to found the "State Bauhaus in Weimar" (*Staatliches Bauhaus in Weimar*) in spring 1919.[116]

CONCLUSION ❧

WORLD WAR I, WERKBUND PROPAGANDA, AND APPLIED-ARTS REFORM

In the first months of World War I, the euphoric "spirit of 1914" bolstered German national unity and prompted many Germans to anticipate a quick victory. Hermann Muthesius, Ernst Jäckh, Gustav Stresemann, and Friedrich Naumann – all protagonists in the government-backed policies of Werkbund-led commercial expansion – produced numerous writings that seamlessly blended the Werkbund's message with wartime propaganda. In more than fifty pamphlets edited by Ernst Jäckh and published under the series title "The German War" (Der Deutsche Krieg), Stresemann, Naumann, Muthesius, and Jäckh addressed a variety of war-related economic and political themes.[1]

In a typical piece from Jäckh's series, *The Future of German Form* (*Die Zukunft der Deutschen Form*) of 1915, Muthesius interpreted progress in German architecture and design as a sign of the Wilhelmine Empire's elevation to the status of a world power.[2] Extreme in its nationalism, Muthesius's essay proclaimed the triumph of "German form" as the coming new "global form" (*Weltform*). If Muthesius avoided specific descriptions of "German form," he took pains to differentiate between tasteful, artistically designed German products and the flood of mass-produced "Hurrah-kitsch" (*Hurrakitsch*) that arose in the wake of mass patriotism and war-time profiteering.[3]

Muthesius's piece was notable for the way it enlarged on claims advanced by the Werkbund leadership in Rudolf Mosse's *Berliner Tageblatt* in the immediate aftermath of the Werkbund's fractious debates in Cologne in July 1914.[4] Muthesius specifically argued that German form was prepared to conquer competitors in international markets as surely as the German military would achieve victory in the battlefield. "We are not only in a position to create a German form," he wrote,

> but we have one already in most fields of activity. In the fields of design and production we are just as well armed as in our military, financial, and economic spheres . . . [T]he entire younger artists' community is unified on this point. As they are led forward in further activity, we will achieve the eagerly desired German form in the whole nation, in every field, and in the farthest corners of our national production.[5]

Downplaying strong differences of opinion that continued to divide the Werkbund membership, Muthesius's declarations in *The Future of German Form* projected the government's and Werkbund leadership's strategy for global commercial expansion well into the first year of the war. The triumphalist conclusion of Muthesius's 1915 piece goes so far as to equate the Werkbund's objectives with those of the Second Reich. The nation's goal, he wrote, involves

> more than simply ruling the world, financing it, teaching it, or flooding it with wares and goods. It has to do with giving the world a new face (*Es gilt, ihr das Gesicht zu geben*). The people that accomplishes this feat will truly stand at the top of the world. And Germany must become this people.[6]

Such wartime rhetoric in the early days of conflict could easily support the conclusion that long-standing promoters of German architecture and design reform had succumbed entirely to the kind of "war mania" that the British, among others, ascribed to the Germans.[7] The reality, however, was more complex and grew all the more so as the war lengthened in duration from months to years. Critics like Eugen Kalkschmidt, for example, were less wedded to the expansionist program so avidly pursued by the Wilhelmine government and the Werkbund. Kalkschmidt directly questioned the legitimacy of a Werkbund that had formed initially to express a new, freer spirit of German design and production, yet had settled, by 1914, for the largely historicist, decorous classical forms exhibited at the First Werkbund Exhibition in Cologne.[8]

Another applied-arts critic, Paul Westheim, noted optimistically that applied-arts enterprises were successfully converting from the production of furniture to the fabrication of such military equipment as ammunition cartridge cases; from decorative coverings for radiators to swords and bayonet blades; and from electric lamps to spiked metal tops for German army helmets. Perhaps, both Kalkschmidt and Westheim suggested, a temporary end to the cyclical, seasonal introduction of new luxury goods and fashionable product lines would have a salutary long-term effect on the quality of German production.[9]

Yet the widespread misery and privation that set in during the campaigns of 1916 and 1917 provoked new responses to the predicament facing architects, applied artists, and fine artists during the war. At first, Hermann Muthesius did not participate in this press-based discussion: He was forced to withdraw from the

Werkbund in June 1916 due to apparent illness, likely exacerbated by wartime shortages and ongoing stresses in the Werkbund organization.[10] Hans Poelzig – who, as we saw in the previous chapter, had denounced the Werkbund as a "monster" shortly before the war – replaced Muthesius as the Werkbund's new vice president; he would rise to become president in 1919.[11] Other Werkbund members, directors of art academies and applied-arts schools, and civil servants engaged in a sustained debate about proper ways for German institutions to address a growing number of problems affecting artistic training and practice. Among these was the question of appropriate measures for education in the arts, crafts, and trades at a time when, many felt, fine-arts academies in many cities had succeeded all too well at producing legions of unemployed painters and sculptors. It was from this national debate – with its many regional inflections – that the groundwork for post-war architecture and design education was laid.

Some, like Wilhelm von Bode, the venerable director of Berlin's museums at the Ministry of Culture, argued that the times called for the absorption of applied-arts school curricula into the fine-arts academies. The laws of supply and demand, von Bode felt, dictated that the majority of artists should receive practical applied-arts training, while the fine arts should be reserved for a select, talented few. If a noble and truly "German" art were to be cultivated after the cessation of hostilities, von Bode argued, then measures such as these would strengthen the academies' offerings while stemming the tide of graduates in the fine arts. The improvement of academy curricula would, moreover, help ensure that radical new movements such as Cubism and Expressionism met the same well-deserved fate as the *Jugendstil* a decade before: These movements would, von Bode predicted, face decline as soon as the novelty of new stylistic expressions had ceased to captivate the attention of younger artists and critics.[12]

Von Bode promoted the "unified arts school" (*Einheitskunstschule*) as the basis for a reformed artistic education. The combination of educational programs for the applied and fine arts offered by these schools was similar, von Bode noted, to programs in place since 1903 at Hans Poelzig's Breslau School of Art and Applied Arts in Silesia, and since 1907 at Bruno Paul's Royal School of Applied Arts in Berlin.[13] Significantly, both examples cited by von Bode were schools administered by von Bode's employer, the Prussian Ministry of Culture, and not by its rival schools administered by the Prussian Ministry of Commerce. Endorsing prototypes developed in Culture Ministry schools, von Bode emphasized the manner in which unified arts schools would impart solid basic skills in the applied arts while assuring that only the most talented students would achieve the designation of fine artist.

Hermann Muthesius, who regained his health by 1918 but remained active in the Werkbund in name only, took exception to von Bode's Culture Ministry–inspired approach to educating the "applied-arts artist." Muthesius wrote an article in the Berlin journal *The Week* (*Die Woche*), in part to answer von Bode's earlier article of 1916 and in part to protest the dissolution of the Dusseldorf

School of Applied Arts and the reassignment of its applied-arts classes to the Dusseldorf Academy of Art.[14] Reflecting his long-time allegiance to the Prussian Commerce Ministry, Muthesius defended applied-arts schools' traditional independence from academic institutions and their emphasis on providing useful, practical applied-arts skills.

In keeping with their divergent philosophies and ministerial allegiances, Muthesius and von Bode disagreed on the fundamental nature of Germany's early-twentieth-century Applied Arts movement. Von Bode and Arthur Kampf, director of the Berlin Academy of Art (another Culture Ministry institution), claimed that fine artists had been the true leaders of the Applied Arts movement of the previous two decades. Muthesius, by contrast, insisted that reformed, workshop-based applied-arts schools had guaranteed the early-twentieth-century Applied Arts movement its broad base and assured its sustained success.

Applied-arts schools, Muthesius further insisted, taught underlying lessons about materials, constructional principles, form, and color, and equipped students with a variety of practical craft techniques. The applied-arts schools, in short, were ideal for the basic training of large numbers of applied-arts students. Fine-arts practitioners and architects, he added, should rightly emerge as the most gifted graduates of applied-arts schools – after they had proven their talent and potential. They should not, as von Bode seemed to argue, receive applied-arts training retroactively as part of academy programs to revitalize problem-ridden fine-arts curricula. Muthesius offered one final reason for continuing the independent support of applied-arts schools: Architects and fine artists regularly depended on competent applied artists for the practical execution of their artistic designs in material form; the training of competent workers in these less-creative, manual skills belonged in separate schools for applied arts.[15]

Debates concerning the proper way to reform artistic education continued throughout World War I and well into the Weimar era. As they had during the Wilhelmine period, these debates brought results that varied by region and were strongly influenced by local political conditions. In Berlin, for example, Bruno Paul's vision of "applied-arts artists" proved entirely compatible with von Bode's ideas for a closer relationship between art academies and applied-arts schools. Yet Paul did not envision a radical transformation of society or a curriculum that exalted architecture, as Gropius would at the Bauhaus. Instead, Paul's goal was to impart training that placed the applied arts and fine arts on an equal footing.[16]

After much negotiation among local Berlin authorities and within the Prussian Culture Ministry, Paul succeeded in joining the Academy of Art with the Royal School of Applied Arts into the "United State Schools for Free and Applied Art" (*Vereinigten Staatsschulen für freie und angewandte Kunst*) in 1924. The continued division of administrative responsibilities between the Prussian Ministries of Culture and Commerce, however, meant that Paul's school would remain the only one of its kind in Prussia after the war. Muthesius and his colleagues at the Commerce Ministry, meanwhile, continued to administer the Prussian system of arts, crafts, and trades schools at a level commensurate with the scarce resources of the post-war Weimar Republic.[17]

At the same time, school reform efforts throughout Germany brought a variety of results. In the western Prussian city of Frankfurt am Main, local authorities created a far less advanced version of the "unified arts school" with the formation of its "Frankfurt Art School for Free and Applied Art" (*Frankfurter Kunstschule für freie und angewandte Kunst*) in 1924. In the Bavarian capital, Richard Riemerschmid's efforts to found a unified arts school in Munich foundered on opposition led by the architect German Bestelmeyer. As we saw in Chapter 1, Munich had suffered a significant artistic "brain drain" at the turn of the century as a result, in part, of the lack of official support for progressive developments in the applied arts. Nearly two decades later, similar tendencies thwarted Riemerschmid's efforts to convert the Munich School of Applied Arts into a unified arts school.[18]

Elsewhere in southern Germany, Stuttgart, too, proved unable to resolve opposition between its applied- and fine-arts institutions. Neighboring Karlsruhe, the proud grand ducal seat of Baden, was more successful. In 1921, Karlsruhe recovered some of the prestige it had forfeited at the turn of the century when Baden's Academy of Art lost the important artists Leopold Graf von Kalckreuth, Carlos Grethe, and Robert Poetzelberger to the Stuttgart Academy of Art. In keeping with post-war national progressive trends, Baden authorities successfully combined Karlsruhe's Academy of Art and School of Applied Arts into a unified "State School of Art" (*Landeskunstschule*) in 1921.[19]

THE "UNIFIED ARTS SCHOOLS" AND POST–WORLD WAR I APPLIED-ARTS REFORM

Post-war changes wrought by Walter Gropius at the Weimar Academy of Art and Weimar School of Applied Arts must be understood against the broader background of nationwide reforms and debates over the "unified arts school" concept. Although certainly not unique among German schools in pursuing a combined applied-arts and fine-arts curriculum, Gropius's Bauhaus was, in spring 1919, the first unified arts school to become operational after the war. Likewise, the Bauhaus was the earliest school to combine a curriculum that regarded architecture as the highest of the arts with radical rhetoric that called for German societal renewal. As Marcel Franciscono, Gillian Naylor, Barbara Miller Lane, and other scholars of the Bauhaus have noted, Gropius's declaration of artistic radicalism coincided with his membership, with Bruno Taut, Otto Bartning, and Adolf Meyer, in the radical Workers' Council for Art, or *Arbeitsrat für Kunst*, formed in the wake of Germany's abortive revolution in November 1918.[20] Prior to this, in January 1916, Gropius had submitted a far more conventional, unprovocative eight-page memorandum to the Grand Ducal Ministry of State in Weimar outlining ways to revive Thuringian crafts industries.[21]

The beginnings of Gropius's radical turn can be traced to the harsh winter of 1916–17, with its battlefront stalemates and desperate food shortages on the home front. The gloomy state of affairs by 1917 suggested to many – even to the loyal, long-time civil servant Hermann Muthesius – that Prusso-German political and military leaders were needlessly prolonging the war and deepening the nation's suffering. In dramatic contrast to his jingoistic Werkbund literature of 1915, Muthesius wrote privately to a close family friend, Max Pfarrer, in 1917: "And so the saying has some merit, that Germany today needs only two institutions – the prison for those who break the war laws, and the asylum for those who obey them. We find ourselves in a terrible, lopsided state in every respect, including the ethical." The ill will that the rest of the world bore toward Germany Muthesius ascribed "above all to our backward inner political relations, the unjustified Prussian superior tone (*Schnauzton*), and our arrogant behavior."[22]

Walter Gropius exhibited an even harsher view of Germany's plight. The younger architect angrily blamed the entire structure of a Wilhelmine society that had seemed well on the way to subordinating architecture and design to imperialist and commercial imperatives on the eve of war. Writing shortly after the revolutionary events of November 7–9, 1918 – which included the abdication of Kaiser Wilhelm II and his replacement by the Social Democratic Party leader Friedrich Ebert – Gropius reflected the prevailing left-wing turn of criticism when he condemned a pervasive Wilhelmine culture of "bourgeois philistinism." His article "Art and the Free People's State," published in 1919 in the *German Revolutionary Almanac*, stated:

> Capitalism and power politics have made our generation creatively sluggish, and our vital art is mired in a broad bourgeois philistinism (*ein breites bürgerliches Philisterium*). The intellectual bourgeois of the old Empire – tepid and unimaginative, mentally slow, arrogant and incorrectly trained – has proven his incapacity to be the bearer of German culture. His benumbed world is now toppled, its spirit is overthrown, and is in the midst of being recast in a new mold.[23]

Gropius shared similar sentiments with Bauhaus faculty and students at his speech honoring the first exhibition of students works in June 1919:

> We find ourselves in a colossal catastrophe of world history, in a transformation of the whole of life.... Before the war we put the cart before the horse and wanted to drag art backward into the public sphere by means of organization. We designed artistic ashtrays and beer mugs, and in that way hoped to work up to the great building.... That was an incredible presumption upon which we were shipwrecked, and now things will be reversed. No large spiritual organizations, but small, secret, self-contained societies, lodges.[24]

To Gropius and many other young architects it seemed that real opportunities for post-war progress in the applied arts and architecture lay in fostering crafts-based renewal, individual creativity, and the exploration of such new movements as Expressionism and Cubism – the very movements condemned by von Bode and other members of the Wilhelmine old guard.[25] As Karl-Heinz Hüter has noted, Social Democrat August Bebel's proclamation in the Reichstag in 1911 of the "twilight of the bourgeois world" (*Götterdämmerung der bürgerlichen Welt*) seemed, in the wake of the November 1918 revolution, on the verge of becoming reality.[26]

Gropius had begun developing his new views on artistic education during noncombat periods at the Western front. Besides his proposal for the post-war revival of crafts industries in Weimar, he corresponded with Karl Ernst Osthaus and the artist Fritz Mackensen, who directed the Weimar Academy of Art until October 1918. His letters to Osthaus reveal that the Werkbund's discussions of the development of "types" seemed to agitate him more than the bullets whistling around his ears, as the historian Angelika Thiekötter has observed.[27] Named by Henry van de Velde as a possible successor to the directorship of the Weimar School of Applied Arts in 1915, Gropius corresponded with Mackensen and the Ministry of State in Weimar in an effort to strengthen his candidacy.[28]

By late 1918, Gropius had ample opportunities to enrich his thinking about possibilities for the Weimar school through close contact with fellow artists and architects in the newly formed Workers' Council for Art in Berlin. The organization modeled itself on revolutionary workers' councils, or soviets, in Russia, and overlapped closely in its membership with the November Group (*November-gruppe*), a second radical association of artists and architects formed in the wake of the November Revolution. Among the members of the Workers' Council for Art the architect Otto Bartning, in particular, had written in a 1919 issue of the *Deutscher Werkbund Bulletin* of the need to expose students to a unified artistic education. Such an education would begin with crafts training and fine-arts train-ing, and would culminate with architecture as a "total work of art." This broad spectrum of artistic education would take place within the confines of a single, integrated school whose focus was to be the free artistic development of each individual.[29]

Bartning's conception resembled contemporaneous proposals by Bruno Paul, Richard Riemerschmid, Wilhelm von Debschitz, and others who retained the crafts and workshop-based education of the pre-war years as the basis for design education.[30] In the same manner that the German word "Werk" in "Werkbund" drew on associations with centuries-old guild terminology for "work" or "ware," Bartning's text – and later Gropius's Bauhaus program – placed terms from the Middle Ages like "apprentice," "journeyman," and "master" at the center of edu-cational proposals intended to rid schools of their professorial titles and academic connotations. By emphasizing the placement of the applied and fine arts on an equal footing, Gropius's Bauhaus program projected a new, post-war egalitarian vision for German society. Although this imagery offered a salutary counterpoint to the large-scale organization of the pre-war period, actual equality among master craftsmen (*Werkmeister*) and artists (*Formmeister*) at the Bauhaus proved every bit as elusive in practice as it had during Muthesius's introduction of workshop-based design education at numerous Prussian applied-arts schools beginning in 1903.[31]

Gropius's thinking benefited greatly from contact with Workers' Council members Bartning and Bruno Taut.[32] After Gropius became chairman of the Workers' Council for Art in February 1919, he adopted much of the language from Taut's pamphlet for "An Architecture Program" ("Ein Architektur-Programm") of December 1918 for the utopian Bauhaus program of April 1919. Gropius wrote to Osthaus, his friend and old Werkbund ally, in February 1919 to explain that he had found Bartning's and Taut's language "deeply appealing and in my own spirit" (*tief sympatisch und aus meinem Geiste*), as the architectural historian Winfried Nerdinger has noted.[33]

Gropius's Bauhaus program maintained the applied arts and fine arts as independent entities within a larger unified whole. As director of the new school, he took pains to retain separate designations for the fine and applied arts in the Bauhaus's lengthy official title, which read "The State Bauhaus in Weimar (Combined former Grand Ducal Academy of Art and former Grand Ducal School of Applied Arts)" (*Staatliches Bauhaus in Weimar, Vereinigte ehemalige Grossherzogliche Hochschule für bildende Kunst und ehemalige Grossherzogliche Kunstgewerbeschule*).[34] Although the school opened with modest beginnings and no official fanfare, the Thuringian government approved the school's new name on April 12, 1919.[35]

With Bartning's and Taut's help, Gropius created a curriculum that invoked a distant, ideal German past in which small artisans' guilds collaborated with artists, sculptors, and architects on such symbols of community and faith as the Gothic cathedral. Craft was the "ancient source" of all artistic activity, Gropius maintained, and so the post-war Bauhaus would promote egalitarian unity in the collaborative process of forging a "crystal symbol of the coming faith" (*kristallenes Sinnbild eines kommenden Glaubens*).[36] The American-born German painter Lyonel Feininger lent visual impact to Gropius's utopian Bauhaus program when he designed an Expressionist woodcut for its cover (Fig. 127). Feininger's design depicted a cathedral topped by three stars, apparently symbolizing the trinity of the fine arts, applied arts, and architecture. With the crafts as their unifying base, the arts would experience a revival in a process that paralleled the revival of German society from below. As Gropius put it in his *German Revolutionary Almanac* article, "New, intellectually undeveloped levels of our people are rising from the depths. They are our chief hope."[37]

The ideas of Gropius, Bartning, and Taut – and indeed the entire German artistic and intellectual atmosphere immediately following World War I – owed much to Oswald Spengler's immensely popular, epoch-making study of 1918, *The*

127. Lyonel Feininger, cover of Bauhaus Program of 1919, woodcut (Busch-Reisinger Museum, Harvard University)

Decline of the West (*Der Untergang des Abendlandes*).[38] Spengler cast the Middle Ages as the "springtime" of German cultural achievements, a time of antimaterialism, cultural synthesis, and social harmony that existed in dramatic contrast to Germany's failed imperialist ambitions, expansionist policies, and grim post–World War I realities. By modeling the Bauhaus as a small community or "lodge" of masters and apprentices, Gropius, too, could tap into this idealized past as a way of escaping the horrors of prolonged, mechanized mass warfare and the social, political, and economic chaos that followed national defeat. The Gothic period furnished Gropius with a parable of a harmonious German society in which practitioners of the crafts, fine arts, and architecture cooperated in a purer, less mediated, and realizable form of artistic production. Even the name "Bauhaus" evoked the ancient German word *Bauhütte*, a medieval guild of craftsmen and building-trades workers, and strengthened the modern school's mythical ties to medieval lodges.

BAUHAUS DEBTS TO THE WILHELMINE ERA

With revolutionary, optimistic language that sought to inspire a nation struggling to recover from devastating human, material, and spiritual loss, the Bauhaus program also appeared to model itself on everything that Muthesius's version of the Werkbund in 1914 was not. More was at stake, however, than the continuing divide that separated artists from industrialists within the Werkbund.[39] As Gropius's statements in the *Revolutionary Almanac* and elsewhere indicated, generational differences played a significant role as well in determining the direction that individuals like Gropius took after the war. Born in 1883 and only thirty-five years of age when he began directing the Bauhaus in 1919, Gropius – like Otto Bartning, Bruno Taut, Erich Mendelsohn, and Ludwig Mies van der Rohe – came of age professionally just as the war got underway.[40] All of these men, part of a veritable "generation of the 1880s," were also young enough to ride out changes wrought by the war. As Gropius, Taut, Mendelsohn, and others demonstrated, this generation was young enough as well to adapt sufficiently to post-war realities to have a significant hand in shaping the direction of Weimar-era design. These architects would do the most to further such movements as Expressionism, the New Objectivity (*Neue Sachlichkeit*), and the New Building (*Neues Bauen*) during the Weimar Republic's short life span from 1919 to 1933.

An older cohort born in the 1860s – including architects such as Hermann Muthesius, Peter Behrens, Theodor Fischer, and Richard Riemerschmid – had been embedded far more deeply in the political, economic, and social structures of the Wilhelmine era.[41] As this study has argued, each of these men participated at the top levels of various institutions in a fast-growing industrial and commercial society; their theories and practices in no small measure helped to set the parameters for early-twentieth-century Wilhelmine architecture and design culture. While practicing architecture and the applied arts, this group also occupied prominent roles in such fields as government policy making and education, and in the new fields of urban planning administration and corporate image design. As a result, their efforts helped determine what German architecture and design could be at the very time when the *Kaiserreich* surpassed traditional European powers as a center of modern production and innovation. Consequently, after the war shattered the German Empire this "generation of the 1860s" was in a far less auspicious position to shape the new directions of post-war design in the Weimar Republic, though they continued to obtain commissions and work productively in their fields as respected practitioners and teachers.

Assembled from the broken pieces of Wilhelmine architectural and design culture, the Bauhaus, as the most prominent of the post-war unified arts schools, recast the lessons of an expansionist, imperial age in a mold that combined nostalgia for the Middle Ages with visions of post-war communitarian rebirth. Within Gropius's Bauhaus were the remnants of van de Velde's defunct Weimar School of Applied Arts, along with those of its neighbor, Fritz Mackensen's Academy of Fine Arts (Figs. 1–3). Amid the reformist ferment that emerged during the prolonged First World War, the Bauhaus and the unified arts school movement in general capitalized on the best of the Wilhelmine era's progressive ideas. As noted earlier, Gropius's fusion of two schools resembled a model established by Hans Poelzig at the Breslau School of Art and Applied Arts in 1903 – the year in which Poelzig oversaw a particular synthesis of fine-arts and applied-arts curricula under the banner of architecture. Gropius's Bauhaus curriculum also bore some resemblance to that of Wilhelm von Debschitz at the Instructional and Trials Workshops for Applied and Fine Arts in Munich, founded in 1902, as well as to the program begun in 1903 by Peter Behrens at the Dusseldorf School of Applied Arts. Like these schools, Gropius's Bauhaus developed a curriculum that emphasized Arts and Crafts–inspired workshop instruction, which facilitated mastery of materials, constructional principles, and craftsmanship.

When Gropius reopened several of Henry van de Velde's original workshops after the war (Fig. 128), he was reviving facilities that had been modeled after Hermann Muthesius's Instructional Workshops Decree, issued by the Prussian Commerce Ministry in 1904. When Johannes Itten introduced his acclaimed Bauhaus introductory course in 1919, he advanced significantly exercises introduced in Debschitz's Munich school, Poelzig's Breslau school, and others – practices that maximized individual creative development in the context of inventive approaches to form, line, color, and pattern recognition in everyday objects. Lastly, Gropius's efforts to lead the Bauhaus benefited directly from the advice of such experienced Prussian applied-arts school directors as Richard Riemerschmid of Munich and Rudolf Bosselt of Magdeburg on curriculum and organizational matters.[42] Both men had been important players in the Prussian state's pre-war reform efforts and directed schools after the war as well.

The Bauhaus thus popularized and recast what numerous Wilhelmine schools, absorbing the lessons of the British Arts and Crafts movement, had pioneered on German soil: the introduction of hands-on instructional workshops; the orientation of all branches of the fine and applied arts toward the design of architectonically integrated, harmonious interiors (Fig. 129); the embrace of a spirit

128. Bauhaus instructional workshop for metalworking, general view (Bauhaus-Archiv, Berlin)

of individual experimentation selectively informed by tradition; and the belief that applied-arts education needed to evolve in order to address changing socio-economic conditions.[43] Although Wilhelmine applied-arts schools took various, regionally inflected forms, many of their most progressive features informed Walter Gropius's development of the Bauhaus curriculum after the First World War. These new approaches, in turn, were part of a larger recognition that changes in Germany's growing industrial and commercial sectors had to be met by applied artists head-on if they were to avoid the fate of the traditional *Mittelstand*. Even during the Weimar era, crafts practitioners of this threatened "middle estate" continued to be squeezed by rapid changes in systems of production, exchange, and consumption – consequences of Germany's renewed industrial and commercial growth in the 1920s.[44]

Yet Gropius emphasized uniqueness at his school, not continuity. Or rather, and perhaps understandably, he sought continuities with a safer, more politically distant German past than that of the discredited Germany of Kaiser Wilhelm II. Nowhere did Gropius's Bauhaus program or literature acknowledge debts to the Prussian school directors, the principles disseminated by the Deutscher Werkbund, the writings of Wilhelm von Bode, or the reforms of the influential former Werkbund vice president Hermann Muthesius. As we have seen, Gropius and his associates Henry van de Velde and Karl Ernst Osthaus had suffered much at the hands of Muthesius – a man whom, between 1912 and 1914, they had come to view not only as an imperious government functionary, but as a shameless panderer to industrial, commercial, and governmental interests. Accurate or not, Gropius's characterization of the "intellectual bourgeois of the old Empire" as "tepid and unimaginative, mentally slow, arrogant and incorrectly trained" may well have been aimed at Muthesius, his old antagonist; Gropius's statements at least, seemed to carry echoes of the anger Gropius had experienced in his confrontations with Muthesius during the Werkbund debacle at Cologne in summer 1914. This anger appears to have been shared by architects like Bruno Taut and Gustav Adolph Platz, each of whom would omit Muthesius entirely from their celebrated accounts of twentieth-century German architecture's rise.[45]

Much to the chagrin of men like von Bode, who initially approved of Gropius's more modest proposals for the revival of the crafts in Weimar in 1916, Gropius staffed the Bauhaus with an internationally recognized avant-garde faculty. This faculty would help Gropius to fashion his new school as both a standard-bearer for

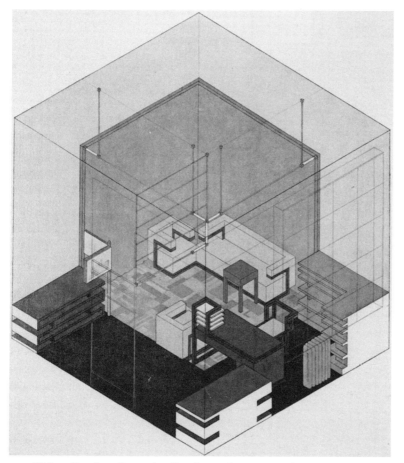

129. Walter Gropius, director's office for at the State Bauhaus in Weimar, isometric view executed by Herbert Bayer (Bauhaus-Archiv Berlin; © 2004 Artists Rights Society (ARS), New York/VG Bild-Kunst, Bonn)

progressive art and as an agent for the reform of post-war German society. The appointment in 1919 of the painters Lyonel Feininger and Johannes Itten and the sculptor Gerhard Marcks as Bauhaus instructors sent a clear signal to incumbent Weimar Art Academy faculty that Gropius in no way favored their preferred pedagogical traditions of naturalism and historical genre painting. By 1922 Gropius strengthened the school and solidified its reputation as a bastion of the German and international avant-garde by adding to the faculty Paul Klee, Wassily Kandinsky, George Muche, Oskar Schlemmer, and other important twentieth-century innovators.

With renewed idealism and a strong distaste for everything the pre-war Werkbund had come to represent, Gropius employed his organizational talents to distance himself and his new school from pre-war precedents. Muthesius, who reformed so many Prussian applied-arts schools for service to a modern Wilhelmine economy, had pursued a politics of export and economic expansion that gradually subordinated applied-arts schools and the Werkbund alike to a highly organized, quasi-planned Wilhelmine economy. The early Bauhaus, by contrast, emphasized the renewal of the crafts, artistic experimentation in Johannes Itten's introductory course, and individualistic instruction from a variety of Bauhaus masters.

Yet by the early 1920s Gropius altered course. He dismissed the highly charismatic and idiosyncratic Itten in 1923 and increased contact with Germany's reviving industries. Gropius also expanded the Bauhaus's workshop-based education to begin contemplating anew the concept of the "type," which assumed greater relevance as industrial production in Germany began to recover.[46] Gropius also announced the school's quest to forge a "new unity" between art and technology. In contact with such movements as De Stijl in Holland and Constructivism in Russia, the Weimar Bauhaus set out to generate new forms representative of the new era.

Evincing qualities of a new formal language for the twentieth century, many Bauhaus designs nevertheless drew strength from reformist impulses that had energized progressive applied-arts education during the Wilhelmine era. Except for occasional explanations of the way his early triumphs at the Fagus Factory of 1911 and the Model Factory and Administration Building of 1914 had helped pave the way for the development of a broad-based "modern movement" in the 1920s and 1930s, Gropius would largely avoid discussing the Wilhelmine era's particular mix of design reform, industrial and commercial expansion, and government policy. This would remain true as Gropius's long career unfolded in Weimar, Dessau, Berlin, London, and by 1937, at Harvard University's Graduate School of Design in Cambridge, Massachusetts, where he would remain an influential department chair, teacher, and formidable presence until his death in 1969.[47]

Developing alongside Gropius's influential career as an internationally celebrated leader of twentieth-century architecture, the historiography of the Werkbund, too, was similarly "formalized, depoliticized, and de-culturalized (*entkulturalisiert*)," as the architectural historian Werner Oechslin has persuasively argued.[48] The reason for German scholars' neglect of the pre-war Werkbund's political and cultural context is plain: After Germany's disastrous defeat in 1918 completely discredited the policies and structure of the Wilhelmine Imperial government, historians in a new Weimar Republic were loath to identify the government of the *Kaiserreich* as in any way associated with leading originators or supporters of avant-garde design. Later historians continued the tradition of divorcing considerations of German government policy from the cultural sphere, a sphere in which avant-garde tendencies most often have been singled out for their redemptive potential. Recent historical studies such as Jeffrey Herf's *Reactionary Modernism*, however, have shown that post–World War I Germans and their institutions were capable of reconciling conservatism with technological progress, formulating that oddest of German mass social phenomena, a populist, Volkish modernism of the right-wing.[49] In an analogous development before the First World War, Wilhelmine government officials such as Commerce Minister Theodor Möller proved perfectly capable of recognizing the advantages to be derived from fostering progressive design principles in a regime pilloried by at least one generation of post-1945 historians as a bastion of conservatism, militarism, and reactionary art policies.

Governmental involvement in Wilhelmine design reform was every bit as important – and improvised – as the Werkbund membership's own approach to defining such contested terms as "culture," the "economy," "style," "fashion," and the "type."[50] As we saw in Prussian Commerce Minister Theodor Möller's failed hostile takeover bid to acquire the Hibernia Coal Company in 1905, Germany's captains of banking and finance capital rallied to block the government's efforts to lessen the power of heavy industry cartels and their dominance of the supply chain. This setback only highlighted the early-twentieth-century central government's difficulties in negotiating the increasingly complex terrain of commerce, industry, and finance.

Struggling to overcome burdensome gaps between constitutionally weak legislative power, bureaucratic initiative at the ministerial level, imperial authoritarian rule, and pronounced German regional differences, authorities like the Prussian Commerce Ministry backed such voluntary associations as the Deutscher Werkbund from their inception. Significant for architectural and design history on its own terms, the Werkbund must also be understood, from the government's point of view, as an attractive option for the mobilization of highly educated, national middle-class and upper-middle-class interests that could aid particular ministries in their struggle to advance new policy goals.

In the most recent and influential literature on the Deutscher Werkbund, Frederic Schwartz has provided what is undoubtedly the most original analysis of the variety of outlooks toward cultural reform in pre–World War I Germany. Accompanying the emergence of a Wilhelmine "industrial culture" that was, in Schwartz's account, inverted to form the Weimar-era "culture industry," however, lay many unstable relations and tensions characteristic of broader Wilhelmine life: disparity between the number of left-wing voters and their constitutionally limited franchise; the inability of heavy and light industry to overcome their differences and assert collective influence; lack of confidence in an unpredictable emperor eager for German national self-assertion; and, of great significance to Schwartz, the emergence of a sophisticated German mass culture driven by new mechanisms of demand, supply, advertising, and distribution.

The language of signs, reification, and advertising manipulation so crisply and admirably illuminated by Schwartz's account of Wilhelmine design culture offer a more complex and valuable tale of Wilhelmine modernity. The German capitalist economy certainly developed more rapidly and had greater influence on debates over form and design than researchers prior to Schwartz have ever detailed. But these developments, along with their fascinating cultural consequences, in no way took place apart from the mediating government authorities that remain largely absent from Schwartz's account – authorities that were themselves struggling to develop effective responses to Germany's phenomenal growth and transformation.[51] Beyond the changing legal environment that had profound implications for ownership of applied-arts designs in the increasingly sophisticated cultural sphere, royal and grand ducal houses, national and state party legislators, urban administrations, and bureaucrats at various levels exercised considerable influence in establishing the conditions of possibility for capitalist development and its cultural corollaries.

Thus for Walter Gropius, as for many other young German architects, the formative years of training and early practice in the *Kaiserreich* could hardly have provided a more stimulating – if also contentious – twentieth-century training ground. The Wilhelmine era produced innovations in architecture and the applied arts that went hand in hand with the accelerating pace of developments in industry, commercial design, government policy, and economic globalization. Twentieth-century architects simply could not succeed without a sophisticated understanding of broader economic, social, and political changes that had a fundamental impact on the design professions. For this reason, and with the further intensification of global networks and international competition, pre–World War I German approaches to architecture and design were virtually guaranteed to reappear in some form in progressive design curricula of the Weimar era. However transformed, enlarged, or disguised, the debts of "Bauhaus thinking" to German architecture and design culture before the First World War remained greater than Gropius – along with other members of the "generation of the 1880s" – ever cared to admit. Recovered here and placed in the context of Wilhelmine political, economic, and social history, this generation's omissions reveal as much about the evolution of twentieth-century German architecture and design culture as the writings, buildings, and spoken accounts they chose to leave behind.

APPENDIX A

Summary Report on Prussian Schools of Arts, Crafts, and Trades (*Kunstgewerbe- und Handwerkerschulen*)

Source: Prussian State Trades Board, Ministry of Commerce (*VB* 1905)

N	Location of School	Type of School	Year Open'd	Annual Local Expenditures 1897	1900	1903	1905	The State 1897	1900	1903	1905	Other Sources 1897	1900	1903	1905	Winter 1902/03 Full-Time	Total	Summer 1903 Full-Time	Total	Winter 1903/04 Full-Time	Total	Summer 1904 Full-Time	Total	Winter 1904/05 Full-Time	Total
A. State-Supported Schools																									
1	BUNZLAU	Kgl. Keramische Fachschule	1897	12 717	24 900	31 048	33 166	9 390	21 170	27 158	29 276	2 572	3 000	3 000	3 000	28	69	28	72	25	72	29	69	27	62
2	BROMBERG	Kgl. Handwerker-u. Kunstgewerbeschule		not yet open																					
3	CASSEL	Kgl. Kunstgew. u. gewerbl. Zeichenschule (1903 Staatsanstalt)	1869	42 420	50 890	73 532	70 882	21 610	21 040	38 472	36 262	20 810	20 040	23 000	22 500	141	565	95	302	126	355	79	241	118	215
4	HANNAU	Kgl. Zeichenakademie	1772	69 793	86 850	93 635	97 090	69 740	74 400	81 225	84 930	53	148	108	108	76	318	97	343	91	320	97	341	97	322
5	HOHR	Kgl. Keramische Fachschule	1880	8 350	19 290	23 286	28 456	16 038	17 900	22 156	27 074	400	500	500	500	16	49	30	70	23	67	20	63	25	84
6	ISERLOHN	Kgl. Fachschule für die Metallindustrie	1879	belongs to machine building training																					
7	KONIGSBERG	Kgl. Provinzial-Kunrst-u. Gewerkschule	1790	20 770	31 104	35 910	40 645	20 770	29 364	33 350	38 685	–	–	–	–	19	192	6	110	18	178	6	126	21	188
B. State- and Locally Supported Schools																									
8	AACHEN	Gewerbliche Tagesschule	1886	20 230	48 810	66 746	62 915	10 115	18 450	24 423	26 317	10 115	18 450	24 423	26 317	236	236	188	188	185	185	200	200	218	218
9	AACHEN	Zeichen- u. Kunstgewerbeschule	1886	26 360	50 090	64 612	80 102	18 200	20 220	26 496	34 971	17 720	17 720	23 496	31 971	36	1 154	–	839	15	992	–	885	9	893
10	BARMEN	Handwerker- u. Kunstgewerbeschule	1896	32 300	61 400	85 212	100 398	17 900	28 630	41 034	47 524	14 400	25 130	37 774	44 004	71	724	35	455	64	700	41	511	69	767
11	CHARLOTTENBURG	Kunstgewerbe- u. Handgewerkschule	1896	23 566	26 410	82 270	95 754	13 280	13 280	38 789	43 957	10 280	10 280	37 231	44 257	39	806	25	590	40	815	33	665	60	1 016
12	COLN	Kunstgewerbe- u. Handgewerkschule	1879	38 880	39 220	48 960	55 570	19 440	15 700	20 127	22 075	19 440	15 700	20 127	22 075	76	514	37	435	71	539	34	505	50	490
13	ELBERFELD	Handwerker- u. Kunstgewerbeschule	1897	46 300	52 695	100 260	91 967	21 150	25 590	43 181	44 030	21 150	21 590	49 681	40 030	117	827	81	576	112	741	106	574	92	642
14	ERFURT	Handwerker- u. Kunstgewerbeschule	1898	–	50 100	47 610	57 910	–	24 600	23 685	28 305	–	20 600	19 685	24 305	54	476	25	446	37	410	23	360	71	432
15	HALLE A/S.	Handwerkerschule	1870	–	28 300	69 525	68 475	10 190	12 850	30 578	31 045	9 190	11 845	28 578	28 005	88	1 052	21	867	81	942	22	780	119	847
16	HANNOVER	Handwerker- u. Kunstgewerbeschule	1890	92 230	122 784	147 902	158 682	44 615	49 477	53 477	65 356	49 477	50 225	65 356	70 644	251	2 528	105	2 476	207	2 478	109	2 544	227	2 589
17	MAGDEBURG	Kunstgewerbe- u. Handwerkerschule	1887	76 990	92 660	130 790	145 016	35 145	38 235	54 209	61 909	35 145	38 235	60 255	69 758	141	1 194	86	1 084	141	1 078	92	1 048	116	1 004
C. Locally Supported Schools to Which the State Contributes Support																									
18	ALTONA	Handwerker- u. Kunstgewerbeschule	1900	–	69 410	74 330	77 600	–	28 150	28 000	28 000	–	28 150	34 896	34 696	31	507	19	464	56	515	42	529	61	583
19	BERLIN	I. Handwerkerschule	1880	119 248	165 266	192 670	195 690	99 248	108 742	134 391	137 409	99 248	108 742	134 391	137 409	210	2 480	83	1 830	184	2 396	83	1 773	138	2 354
20	BRESLAU	Handwerkerschule	1903	–	–	88 096	111 530	–	–	30 000	30 000	–	–	26 000	26 000	–	–	–	–	76	698	67	506	138	624
21	CREFELD	Handwerker- u. Kunstgewerbeschule	1904	–	–	50 546	69 550	–	–	–	25 000	–	–	–	31 750	–	–	–	–	–	–	35	410	74	415
22	DANZIG	Handels- u. Gewerbeschule	1892	–	–	97 000	126 803	80 000	80 000	80 000	80 000	–	–	–	–	–	3 008	–	3 008	–	3 108	–	3 250	–	3 607
23	DORTMUND	Handwerkerschule	1904	–	–	–	62 860	–	–	–	15 000	–	–	–	42 238	–	–	–	–	–	–	–	–	3 667	3 667
24	DUSSELDORF	Kunstgewerbeschule	1883	43 630	75 000	83 330	101 500	23 690	30 000	34 500	42 000	23 690	35 187	38 830	49 500	147	304	75	158	128	252	79	162	157	286
25	ELBING	Gewerbeschule	1901	–	50 000	45 000	45 000	–	45 000	45 000	45 000	–	–	–	–	–	–	–	–	–	–	–	–	39	289
26	ESSEN	Gewerbeschule	1900	–	50 000	51 450	53 860	–	23 000	23 000	23 000	–	22 550	21 200	24 190	67	415	27	274	60	353	40	202	118	301
27	FLENSBURG	Kunstgewerbliche Fachschule	1890	–	12 750	–	25 439	–	–	5 500	12 500	–	–	6 250	10 800	–	–	–	–	20	24	18	20	13	13
28	FRANKFURT A/M.	Kunstgewerbeschule	1879	93 780	111 550	81 095	85 595	69 780	65 850	48 695	51 905	–	–	–	–	33	274	31	272	37	262	34	264	35	270
29	GNESEN	Handels- u. Gewerbeschule	1901	–	–	79 242	78 970	–	46 300	21 982	48 800	–	–	16 123	15 593	41	508	38	487	34	515	40	483	42	565
30	HILDESHEIM	Handwerkerschule	1903	–	–	37 202	36 165	–	–	15 000	16 382	–	–	16 123	15 593	75	276	8	191	71	278	11	200	79	335
31	KIEL	Handwerkerschule	1905	–	–	–	–	–	–	–	–	–	–	–	–	–	–	–	–	–	–	–	–	–	–
32	SOLINGEN	Fachschule für die Stahlwarenindustrie	1904	–	–	–	17 707	–	–	–	8 500	–	–	–	8 847	–	–	–	–	–	–	–	–	–	–
33	TRIER	Gewerbeschule	1904	–	–	–	27 183	–	–	–	12 268	–	–	–	12 667	–	–	–	–	–	–	–	–	–	–
34	WARMBRUNN	Holzschnitzschule	1902	–	–	18 000	23 900	–	–	12 000	14 500	–	–	5 500	5 500	19	52	19	52	20	58	21	70	22	74

The following theses and "anti"-theses are reproduced from the publication *The Future Work of the Werkbund and Discussion Thereof* (*Die Werkbundarbeit der Zukunft und Aussprache darüber*), edited by Hermann Muthesius and published in 1914. The original German text appears as it did in 1914, following a translation that has been adjusted by the author to reflect more closely the meanings, arguments, and evidence presented in the latter chapters of this book.

The most obvious adjustment in translation occurs in the rendering of the awkward, difficult, and even tendentious German word *Typisierung*. Hitherto translated without comment or criticism as "standardization," the word *Typisierung* might perhaps be better understood as the "making of types," or the even slightly more grating "typification." Even specialists present at Muthesius's speech and subsequent debates at the Werkbund Congress of 1914 readily admitted that they were unclear what the vague term *Typisierung* actually meant. One thing is certain, however: Not once in his ten theses did Muthesius use the word *Standardisierung*, German for "standardization." Moreover, Hermann Muthesius and Richard Riemerschmid wrote of and designed housing explicitly in terms of "types," or *Typen*, at Karl Schmidt's Hellerau Garden City (Figs. 102, 104). In fact, Theodor Fischer – Riemerschmid's acknowledged mentor in matters architectural – had been designing workers' housing in terms of regularized yet adaptable "types" since at least as far back as 1903 (Fig. 105), while Muthesius had begun discussing the "type" in detail as early as 1911 in his speech to the Werkbund congress of that year.

Certainly many parts for doors, window frames, and metal fittings in these houses reflected a level of standardization. But it is misleading to think that the primary interest of these senior Wilhelmine architects was in industrial form, industrial processes of making, or "standardization" as such. To the contrary: Each of these architects demonstrated a career-long interest in striking a balance between German domestic building traditions and the new advantages of production and cost to be derived from the radically transformed German industrial and commercial economy. Since the formation of the Deutscher Werkbund in 1907, Werkbund artists, craftsmen, and architects had been demonstrating the variety of ways that industry could benefit from the rethinking of product designs.

To Muthesius in 1914, the vagaries of the word "type" and "typification" allowed him to begin seeking a change in the Werkbund's orientation in a manner he hoped would satisfy the variety of constituencies involved: political, economic, as well as artistic. When Muthesius met opposition from van de Velde and others during the debates that ensued at the July congress in Cologne, he pursued firmer measures to ensure that the Werkbund would adopt the new commercial and expansionist course. These we saw in the maneuvering of Muthesius, Ernst Jäckh, and others in Rudolf Mosse's newspaper the *Berliner Tageblatt*. By early August 1914, however, the outbreak of World War I replaced Germany's Werkbund-aided bid for increased economic competitiveness abroad with the more immediate demands of military conflict. Rather than paving the way for new national forms of expression anchored in German traditions, the "type" would give way after the war to discussions of functional, industrially produced housing and standardization as symbols of a new, more forward-looking era. Investigations of the "type" as a possible mediator between traditional and progressive, new forms in the pre–World War I era have by no means been exhausted.

PRINCIPLES FROM THE LECTURE BY HERMANN MUTHESIUS

1. Architecture, and with it the whole area of the Werkbund's activities, is pressing toward the making of types (typification, or *Typisierung*), and only through typification can it recover that universal significance that was characteristic of it in times of harmonious culture.

2. Only the making of types – to be understood as the result of a beneficial concentration – will make possible the development of a universally valid, unfailing good taste.

3. As long as a universal high level of taste has not been achieved, we cannot count on the German applied arts to make their influence effectively felt abroad.

4. The world will demand our products only when they are the vehicles of a convincing stylistic expression. The foundations for this have now been laid by the German movement.

5. The creative development of what has already been achieved is the most urgent task of the time. Upon it the movement's ultimate success will depend.

Any relapse and deterioration into imitation would today mean the squandering of a valuable possession.

6. Starting from the conviction that it is a matter of life and death for Germany constantly to ennoble its production, the Deutscher Werkbund, as an association of artists, industrialists, and merchants, must concentrate its attention upon creating the preconditions for the export of its industrial arts.

7. Germany's advances in applied arts and architecture must be brought to the attention of foreign countries through effective propaganda. Next to exhibitions the most obvious means of doing this is by periodic illustrated publications.

8. Exhibitions by the Deutscher Werkbund are only meaningful when they are expressly restricted to the best and most exemplary. Applied-arts exhibitions abroad must be looked upon as a national matter and hence require public subsidy.

9. Productively capable and dependably tasteful large enterprises are the precondition for such an export. With the individually produced, artist-designed object, not even domestic demand could begin to be fulfilled.

10. For national reasons large distribution and transport enterprises whose activities are directed abroad ought to link up with the new movement, now that it has borne fruit, in order consciously to represent German art in the world.

HENRY VAN DE VELDE: COUNTER-THESES

1. So long as there are still artists in the Werkbund and so long as they exercise some influence on its destiny, they will protest against every suggestion for the establishment of a canon and for typification. By his innermost essence the artist is a burning idealist, a free spontaneous creator. Of his own free will he will never subordinate himself to a discipline that imposes upon him a type, a canon. Instinctively he distrusts everything that might sterilize his actions, and everyone who preaches a rule that might prevent him from thinking his thoughts through to their own free end, or that attempts to drive him into a universally valid form, in which he sees only a mask that seeks to make a virtue out of incapacity.

2. Certainly the artist who practices a "beneficial concentration" has always recognized that ¨currents that are stronger than his own will and thought demand of him that he should acknowledge what is in essential correspondence to the spirit of his age. These currents may be very manifold; he absorbs them unconsciously and consciously as general influences; there is something materially and morally compelling about them for him. He willingly subordinates himself to them and is full of enthusiasm for the idea

of a new style per se. And for twenty years many of us have been seeking forms and decorations entirely in keeping with our epoch.

3. Nevertheless it has not occurred to any of us that henceforth we ought to try to impose these forms and decorations, which we have sought or found, upon others as types. We know that several generations will have to work upon what we have started before the physiognomy of the new style is established, and that we can talk of types and typification only after the passage of a whole period of endeavours.

4. But we also know that as long as this goal has not been reached our endeavours will still have the charm of creative impetus. Gradually the energies, the gifts of all, begin to combine together, antitheses become neutralized, and at precisely that moment when individual strivings begin to slacken, the physiognomy will be esablished. The era of imitation will begin and forms and decorations will be used, the production of which no longer calls for any creative impulse: the age of infertility will then have commenced.

5. The desire to see a type come into being before the establishment of a style is exactly like wanting to see the effect before the cause. It would be to destroy the embryo in the egg. Is anyone really going to let themselves be dazzled by the apparent possibility of thereby achieving quick results? These premature effects have all the less prospect of enabling German arts and crafts to exercise an effective influence abroad, because foreign countries are a jump ahead of us in the old tradition and the old culture of good taste.

6. Germany, on the other hand, has the great advantage of still possessing gifts that other, older, wearier peoples are losing: the gifts of invention, of brilliant personal creative inspirations. And it would mean nothing short of castration to regulate this rich, many-sided, creative upswing so soon.

7. The efforts of the Werkbund should be directed toward cultivating precisely these gifts, as well as the gifts of individual manual skill, joy, and belief in the beauty of highly differentiated execution, not toward inhibiting them through typification at the very moment when foreign countries are beginning to take an interest in German work. As far as fostering these gifts is concerned, almost everything still remains to be done.

8. We do not deny anyone's good will and we are very well aware of the difficulties that have to be overcome in carrying this out. We know that the workers' organization has done a very great deal for the workers' material welfare, but it can hardly find an excuse for having done so little toward arousing enthusiasm for consummately fine workmanship in those who ought to be our most joyful collaborators. On the other hand, we are well aware of the need to export that lies like a curse upon our industry.

9. And yet nothing, nothing good and splendid, was ever created out of mere consideration for exports. Quality will not be created out of the spirit of export. Quality is always first created exclusively for a quite limited

circle of connoisseurs and those who commission the work. These gradually gain confidence in their artists; slowly there develops first a narrower, then a national notice of this quality. It is a complete misunderstanding of the situation to make the industrialists believe that they would increase their chances in the world market if they produced a priori types for this world market before these types had become well tried common property at home. The wonderful works being exported to us now were none of them originally created for export: think of Tiffany glasses, Copenhagen porcelain, jewelery by Jensen, the books of Cobden-Sanderson, and so on.

10. Every exhibition must have as its purpose to show the world this native quality, and it is quite true that the Werkbund's exhibitions will have meaning only when, as Herr Muthesius so rightly says, they restrict themselves radically to the best and most exemplary.

ORIGINAL GERMAN TEXT FROM *DIE WERKBUNDARBEIT DER ZUKUNFT UND AUSSPRACHE DARÜBER*, JENA: 1914

Hermann Muthesius

Leitsätze

1. Die Architektur und mit ihr das ganze Werkbundschaffensgebiet drängt nach Typisierung und kann nur durch sie diejenige allgemeine Bedeutung wiedererlangen, die ihr in Zeiten harmonischer Kultur eigen war.

2. Nur mit der Typisierung, die als das Ergebnis einer heilsamen Konzentration aufzufassen ist, kann wieder ein allgemein geltender, sicherer Geschmack Eingang finden.

3. Solange eine geschmackvolle Allgemeinhöhe nicht erreicht ist, kann auf eine wirksame Ausstrahlung des deutschen Kunstgewerbes auf das Ausland nicht gerechnet werden.

4. Die Welt wird erst dann nach unseren Erzeugnissen fragen, wenn aus ihnen ein überzeugender Stilausdruck spricht. Für diesen hat die bisherige deutsche Bewegung die Grundlagen geschaffen.

5. Der schöpferische Weiterausbau des Errungenen ist die dringendste Aufgabe der Zeit. Von ihr wird der endgültige Erfolg der Bewegung abhängen. Jedes Zurück- und Abfallen in die Nachahmung würde heute die Verschleuderung eines wertvollen Besitzes bedeuten.

6. Von der Überzeugung ausgehend, dass es für Deutschland eine Lebensfrage ist, seine Produktion mehr und mehr zu veredeln, hat der Deutsche Werkbund als eine Vereinigung von Künstlern, Industriellen und Kaufleuten sein Augenmerk darauf zu richten, die Vorbedingungen fuer einen kunstindustriellen Export zu schaffen.

7. Die Fortschritte Deutschlands in Kunstgewerbe und Architektur sollten dem Ausland durch eine wirksame Propaganda bekanntgemacht werden. Als nächstliegendes Mittel hierfür empfehlen sich neben Ausstellungen periodische illustrierte Veröffentlichungen.

8. Ausstellungen des Deutschen Werkbundes haben nur dann Sinn, wenn sie sich grundsätzlich auf Bestes und Vorbildliches beschränken. Kunstgewerbliche Ausstellungen im Ausland sind als eine nationale Angelegenheit zu betrachten und bedürfen daher öffentlicher Unterstützung.

9. Für einen etwaigen Export ist das Vorhandensein leistungsfähiger und geschmacklich sicherer Grossgeschäfte die Vorbedingung. Mit dem vom Künstler für den Einzelfall entworfenen Gegenstand würde nicht einmal der einheimische Bedarf gedeckt werden können.

10. Aus nationalen Gründen sollten sich grosse, nach dem Ausland arbeitende Vertriebs- und Verkehrsgesellschaften jetzt, nachdem die Bewegung ihre Früchte gezeitigt hat, der neuen Bewegung anschliessen und die deutsche Kunst mit Bewusstsein in der Welt vertreten.

Henry van de Velde (Gegenthesen)

Ich bin von mehreren Herren, die eine grosse Gefahr darin sehen, dass die Leitsätze zum Vortrag des Herrn Muthesius nur einen Augenblick hauptsächlich in Bezug auf die Typisierung als die allgemeine Meinung des Vorstandes und des Vorsitzenden des Werkbundes aufgefasst werden können, in der gestrigen Vorstandssitzung beauftragt worden, nicht bis morgen zu warten, sondern gleich jetzt die Erklärung abzugeben, dass die Leitsätze des Herrn Muthesius den ganzen Werkbund nicht engagieren. Ich wurde dann beauftragt, heute noch zu reden, auch ein Vertreter des österreichischen Werkbundes. Ich werde mich darauf beschränken, 10 Gegenleitsätze vorzulegen, ohne irgend welchen Kommentar daran zu knüpfen. Dies bleibt meinen Freunden vorbehalten, welche morgen Stellung dazu nehmen werden. (Der Redner verliest die Leitsätze, die mit starken Beifallskundgebungen aufgenommen werden.)

Die Leitsätze lauten

1. Solange es noch Künstler im Werkbund geben wird und solange diese noch einen Einfluss auf dessen Geschicke haben werden, werden sie gegen jeden Vorschlag eines Kanons oder einer Typisierung protestieren. Der Künstler ist seiner innersten Essenz nach glühender Individualist, freier spontaner Schöpfer; aus freien Stücken wird er niemals einer Disziplin sich unterordnen, die ihm einen Typ, einen Kanon aufzwingt. Instinktiv misstraut er allem, was seine Handlungen sterilisieren könnte und jedem, der eine Regel predigt, die ihn verhindern könnte, seine Gedanken bis zu

ihrem eigenen freien Ende durchzudenken oder die ihn in eine allgemeingültige Form hineintreiben will, in der er doch nur eine Maske sieht, die aus einer Unfähigkeit eine Tugend machen möchte.

2. Gewiss hat der Künstler, der eine heilsame "Konzentration" treibt, immer erkannt, dass Strömungen, die stärker sind als sein einzelnes Wollen und Denken, von ihm verlangen, dass er erkenne, was wesentlich seinem Zeitgeist entspricht. Diese Strömungen können sehr vielfältige sein, er nimmt sie unbewusst und bewusst als allgemeine Einflüsse auf, sie haben materiell und moralisch etwas für ihn Zwingendes; er ordnet sich ihnen willig unter und ist für die Idee eines neuen Stiles an sich begeistert. Und seit 20 Jahren suchen manche unter uns die Formen und die Verzierungen, die restlos unserer Epoche entsprechen.

3. Keinem von uns ist es jedoch eingefallen, diese von uns gesuchten oder gefundenen Formen oder Verzierungen anderen nunmehr als Typen aufzwingen zu wollen. Wir wissen, dass mehrere Generationen an dem noch arbeiten müssen, was wir angefangen haben, ehe die Physiognomie des neuen Stiles fixiert sein wird, und dass erst nach Verlauf einer ganzen Periode von Anstrengungen die Rede von Typen und Typisierung sein kann.

4. Wir wissen aber auch, dass nur solange dieses Ziel nicht erreicht ist, unsere Anstrengungen noch den Reiz des schöpferischen Schwunges haben werden. Langsam fangen die Kräfte, die Gaben aller an, ineinander überzugehen, die Gegensätze werden neutralisiert, und in eben dem Augenblick, wo die individuellen Anstrengungen anfangen zu erlahmen, wird die Physiognomie fixiert; die Ära der Nachahmung fängt an, und es setzt der Gebrauch von Formen und von Verzierungen ein, bei deren Herstellung niemand mehr den schöpferischen Impuls aufbringt: die Zeit der Unfruchtbarkeit ist dann eingetreten.

5. Das Verlangen, einen Typ noch vor dem Werden eines Stiles erstehen zu sehen, ist geradezu dem Verlangen gleichzusetzen, die Wirkung vor der Ursache sehen zu wollen. Es heisst, den Keim im Ei zerstören. Sollte wirklich jemand sich durch den Schein, damit rasche Resultate erzielen zu können, blenden lassen? Diese vorzeitigen Wirkungen haben um so weniger Aussicht, eine wirksame Ausstrahlung des deutschen Kunstgewerbes auf das Ausland zu erreichen, als eben dieses Ausland einen Vorsprung vor uns voraus hat in der alten Tradition und der alten Kultur des Geschmacks.

6. Deutschland hingegen hat den grossen Vorzug, noch Gaben zu haben, die anderen älteren, müderen Völkern abgehen, die Gaben der Erfindung, der persönlichen geistreichen Einfälle. Und es heisst geradezu, eine Kastration vornehmen, wenn man diesen reichen, vielseitigen schöpferischen Aufschwung jetzt schon festlegen will.

7. Die Anstrengungen des Werkbundes sollten dahin abzielen, gerade diese Gaben sowie die Gaben der individuellen Handfertigkeit, die Freude und

die Glauben an die Schönheit einer möglichst differenzierten Ausführung zu pflegen und nicht sie durch eine Typisierung zu hemmen, gerade in dem Moment, wo das Ausland anfängt, an deutscher Arbeit Interesse zu empfinden. Auf dem Gebiet dieser Förderung bleibt fast noch alles zu tun übrig.

8. Wir verkennen niemandes guten Willen und erkennen sehr wohl die Schwierigkeiten, die dabei zu überwinden sind. Wir wissen, dass die Arbeiterorganisation viel für das materielle Wohl des Arbeiters getan hat, aber kaum eine Entschuldigung dafür vorbringen kann, so wenig dafür getan zu haben, die Begeisterung für vollendet schöne Arbeit bei denen zu wecken, die unsere freudigsten Mitarbeiter sein müssten. Andererseits ist uns der Fluch wohl bekannt, der auf unserer Industrie lastet, exportieren zu müssen.

9. Und dennoch ist nie etwas Gutes und Herrliches geschaffen worden aus blosser Rücksicht auf den Export. Qualität wird nicht aus dem Geist des Exports geschaffen. Qualität wird immer nur zuerst fuer einen ganz beschränkten Kreis von Auftraggebern und Kennern geschaffen. Diese bekommen allmählich Zutrauen zu ihren Künstlern, langsam entwickelt sich erst eine engere, dann eine rein nationale Kundschaft, und dann erst nimmt das Ausland und die Welt langsam Notiz von dieser Qualität. Es ist ein vollkommenes Verkennen des Tatbestandes, wenn man die Industriellen glauben macht, sie vermehrten ihre Chancen auf dem Weltmarkt, wenn sie a priori Typen produzierten für diesen Weltmarkt, ehe diese ein zu Hause ausprobiertes Gemeingut geworden seien. Die wundervollen Werke, die jetzt zu uns exportiert werden, sind niemals ursprünglich für den Export erschaffen worden, man denke an Tiffany-Gläser, Kopenhagener Porzellan, Schmuck von Jensen, die Bücher von Cobden-Sanderson usw.

10. Jede Ausstellung muss das Ziel verfolgen, der Welt diese heimische Qualität zu zeigen, und die Ausstellungen des Werkbundes haben in der Tat nur dann einen Sinn, wenn sie sich, wie Herr Muthesius so trefflich sagt, grundsätzlich auf Bestes und Vorbildliches beschränken.

Leitsätze zum Vortrag von Hermann Muthesius

1. Die Architektur und mit ihr das ganze Werkbundschaffensgebiet drängt nach Typisierung, und kann nur durch sie diejenige allgemeine Bedeutung wieder erlangen, die ihr in Zeiten harmonischer Kultur eigen war.

2. Nur mit der Typisierung die als das Ergebnis einer heilsamen Konzentration aufzufassen ist, kann wieder ein allgemein geltender, sicherer Geschmack Eingang finden.

3. Solange eine geschmackvolle Allgemeinhöhe nicht erreicht ist, kann auf eine wirksame Ausstrahlung des deutschen Kunstgewerbes auf das Ausland nicht gerechnet werden.

4. Die Welt wird erst dann nach unseren Erzeugnissen fragen, wenn aus ihnen ein überzeugender Stilausdruck spricht. Für diesen hat die bisherige deutsche Bewegung die Grundlagen geschaffen.

5. Der schöpferische Weiterausbau des Errungenen ist die dringenste Aufgabe der Zeit. Von ihr wird der endgültige Erfolg der Bewegung abhängen. Jedes Zurück- und Abfallen in die Nachahmung würde heute die Verschleuderung eines wertvollen Besitzes bedeuten.

6. Von der Überzeugung ausgehend, daß es für Deutschland eine Lebensfrage ist, seine Produktion mehr und mehr zu veredeln, hat der Deutsche Werkbund als eine Vereinigung von Künstlern, Industriellen und Kaufleuten sein Augenmerk darauf zu richten, die Vorbedingungen für einen kunstindustriellen Export zu schaffen.

7. Die Fortschritte Deutschlands in Kunstgewerbe und Architektur sollten dem Auslande durch eine wirksame Propaganda bekannt gemacht werden. Als nächstliegendes Mittel hierfür empfehlen sich neben Ausstellungen periodische illustrierte Veröffentlichungen.

8. Ausstellungen des Deutschen Werkbundes haben nur dann Sinn, wenn sie sich grundsätzlich auf Bestes und Vorbildliches beschränken. Kunstgewerbliche Ausstellungen im Auslande sind als eine nationale Angelegenheit zu betrachten und bedürfen daher öffentlicher Unterstützung.

9. Für einen etwaigen Export ist das Vorhandensein leistungsfähiger und geschmacklich sicherer Großgeschäfte die Vorbedingung. Mit dem vom Künstler für den Einzelfall entworfenen Gegenstand würde nicht einmal der einheimische Bedarf gedeckt werden können.

10. Aus nationalen Gründen sollten sich große nach dem Ausland arbeitende Vertriebs- und Verkehrsgesellschaften jetzt, nach dem die Bewegung ihre Früchte gezeitigt hat, der neuen Bewegung anschließen und die deutsche Kunst mit Bewußtsein in der Welt vertreten.

Van de Velde

Ich bin von mehreren Herren, die eine große Gefahr darin sehen, daß die Leitsätze zum Vortrag des Herrn Muthesius nur einen Augenblick hauptsächlich in Bezug auf die Typisierung als die allgemeine Meinung des Vorstandes und des Vorsitzenden des Werkbundes aufgefaßt werden können, in der gestrigen Vorstandssitzung beauftragt worden, nicht bis morgen zu warten, sondern gleich jetzt die Erklärung abzugeben, daß die Leitsätze des Herrn Muthesius den ganzen Werkbund nicht engagieren. Ich wurde dann beauftragt, heute noch zu reden, auch ein Vertreter des österreichischen Werkbundes. Ich werde mich darauf beschränken, 10 Gegenleitsätze vorzulegen, ohne irgend welchen Kommentar daran zu knüpfen. Dies bleibt meinen Freunden vorbehalten, welche morgen Stellung dazu nehmen werden. (Der Redner verliest die Leitsätze, die mit starken Beifallskundgebungen aufgenommen werden.)

Die Leitsätze lauten:

1. Solange es noch Künstler im Werkbunde geben wird und solange diese noch einen Einfluß auf dessen Geschicke haben werden, werden sie gegen jeden Vorschlag eines Kanons oder einer Typisierung protestieren. Der Künstler ist seiner innersten Essenz nach glühender Individualist, freier spontaner Schöpfer; aus freien Stücken wird er niemals einer Disziplin sich unterordnen, die ihm einen Typ, einen Kanon aufzwingt. Instinktiv mißtraut er allem, was seine Handlungen sterilisieren könnte und jedem, der eine Regel predigt, die ihn verhindern könnte, seine Gedanken bis zu ihrem eigenen freien Ende durchzudenken oder die ihn in eine allgemein gültige Form hineintreiben will, in der er doch nur eine Maske sieht, die aus einer Unfähigkeit eine Tugend machen möchte.

2. Gewiß hat der Künstler, der eine „heilsame Konzentration" treibt, immer erkannt, daß Strömungen, die stärker sind, als sein einzelnes Wollen und Denken von ihm verlangen, daß er erkenne, was wesentlich seinem Zeitgeist entspricht. Diese Strömungen können sehr vielfältige sein, er nimmt sie unbewußt und bewußt als allgemeine Einflüsse auf, sie haben materiell und moralisch etwas für ihn Zwingendes; er ordnet sich ihnen willig unter und ist für die Idee eines neuen Stiles an sich begeistert. Und seit 20 Jahren suchen manche unter uns die Formen und die Verzierungen, die restlos unserer Epoche entsprechen.

3. Keinem unter uns ist es jedoch eingefallen, diese von uns gesuchte oder gefundenen Formen oder Verzierungen anderen nunmehr als Typen aufzwingen zu wollen. Wir wissen, daß mehrere Generationen an dem noch arbeiten müssen, was wir angefangen haben, bis die Physiognomie des neuen Stiles fixiert sein wird, und daß erst nach Verlauf einer ganzen Periode von Anstrengungen die Rede von Typen und Typisierung sein kann.

4. Wir wissen aber auch, daß nur so lange dieses Ziel nicht erreicht ist, unsere Anstrengungen noch den Reiz des schöpferischen Schwunges haben werden. Langsam fangen die Kräfte, die Gaben aller an, ineinander überzugehen, die Gegensätze werden neutralisiert, und in eben dem Augenblicke, wo die individuellen Anstrengungen anfangen, zu erlahmen, wird die Physiognomie fixiert; Die Aera der Nachahmung fängt an, und es setzt der Gebrauch von Formen und von Verzierungen ein, deren niemand mehr den schöpferischen Impuls aufbringt: die Zeit der Unfruchtbarkeit ist dann eingetreten.

5. Das Verlangen, einen Typ noch vor dem Werden eines Stiles erstehen zu sehen, ist gerade dem Verlangen gleichzusetzen, die Wirkung vor der Ursache sehen zu wollen. Es heißt, den Keim im Ei zerstören. Sollte wirklich jemand sich durch den Schein, damit rasche Resultate erzielen zu können, blenden lassen? Diese vorzeitigen Wirkungen haben umsoweniger Aussicht, eine wirksame Ausstrahlung des deutschen Kunstgewerbes auf das Ausland zu erreichen, als eben dieses Ausland einen Vorsprung vor uns voraus hat in der alten Tradition und der alten Kultur des Geschmackes.

6. Deutschland hingegen hat den großen Vorzug, noch Gaben zu haben, die anderen älteren, müderen Völkern abgehen, die Gaben der Erfindung nämlich, der persönlichen geistreichen Einfälle. Und es heißt geradezu, eine Kastration vornehmen, wenn man diesen reichen, vielseitigen schöpferischen Aufschwung jetzt schon festlegen will.

7. Die Anstrengungen des Werkbundes sollten dahin abzielen, gerade diese Gaben, sowie die Gaben der individuellen Handfertigkeit, die Freude und den Glauben an die Schönheit einer möglichst differenzierten Ausführung zu pflegen und nicht sie durch eine Typisierung zu hemmen, gerade in dem Momente, wo das Ausland anfängt, an deutscher Arbeit Interesse zu finden. Auf dem Gebiete dieser Förderung bleibt fast noch alles zu tun übrig.

8. Wir verkennen Niemandes guten Willen und erkennen sehr wohl die Schwierigkeiten, die dabei zu überwinden sind. Wir wissen, daß die Arbeiterorganisation viel für das materielle Wohl des Arbeiters getan hat, aber kaum eine Entschuldigung dafür vorbringen kann, so wenig dafür getan zu haben, die Begeisterung für vollendet schöne Arbeit bei deren Herstellung niemand mehr den schöpferischen Impuls aufbringt: die Zeit der Unfruchtbarkeit ist dann eingetreten. Andererseits ist uns der Fluch wohl bekannt, der auf unserer Industrie lastet, exportieren zu müssen.

9. Und dennoch ist nie etwas Gutes und Herrliches geschaffen worden aus bloßer Rücksicht auf den Export. Qualität wird nicht aus dem Geiste des Exports geschaffen. Qualität wird immer nur zuerst für einen ganz beschränkten Kreis von Auftraggebern und Kennern geschaffen. Diese bekommen allmäh-

lich Zutrauen zu ihren Künstlern, langsam entwickelt sich erst eine engere, dann eine reinnationale Kundschaft, und dann erst nimmt das Ausland und die Welt langsam Notiz von dieser Qualität. Es ist ein vollkommenes Verkennen des Tatbestandes, wenn man die Industriellen glauben macht, sie vermehrten ihre Chancen auf dem Weltmarkt, wenn sie a priori Typen produzierten für diesen Weltmarkt, ehe diese ein zu Hause ausprobiertes Gemeingut geworden seien.

Die wundervollen Werke, die jetzt zu uns exportiert werden, sind niemals ursprünglich für den Export erschaffen worden, man denke an Tiffany-Gläser, Kopenhagener Porzellan, Schmuck von Jensen, die Bücher von Cobben-Sanderson etc.

10. Jede Ausstellung muß das Ziel verfolgen, der Welt diese heimische Qualität zu zeigen, und die Ausstellungen des Werkbundes haben in der Tat nur dann einen Sinn, wenn sie sich, wie Herr Muthesius so trefflich sagt, grundsätzlich auf Bestes und Vorbildliches beschränken.

NOTES ∾

INTRODUCTION

1. The literature on the Bauhaus is vast. A recent, brief account of the school's origins and development can be found in Ute Ackermann, "Einleitung: Zur Funktion und Geschichte des Meisterrates am Staatlichen Bauhaus Weimar," in Volker Wahl and Ute Ackermann, eds., *Die Meisterratsprotokolle des Staatlichen Bauhauses Weimar, 1919 bis 1925*, Veröffentlichungen aus thüringischen Staatsarchiven Band 6 (Weimar: Verlag Hermann Böhlaus Nachfolger, 2001), 18–40. Classic accounts in English of the school and its origins include Marcel Franciscono, *Walter Gropius and the Creation of the Bauhaus in Weimar: The Ideals and Artistic Theories of its Founding Years* (Urbana: University of Illinois Press, 1971); Gillian Naylor, *The Bauhaus Reassessed: Sources and Design Theory* (New York: E. P. Dutton, 1985); Hans Maria Wingler, *The Bauhaus: Weimar, Dessau, Berlin, Chicago*, translated by W. Jabs and Basil Gilbert (Cambridge, Mass.: MIT Press, 1978). For a recent reassessment see Jeannine Fiedler and Peter Feierabend, eds., *Bauhaus* (Cologne: Könemann Verlagsgessellschaft, 1999); on the pedagogical contributions of Gropius, Klee, Kandinsky, Itten, and others see Rainer K. Wick, *Teaching at the Bauhaus* (Ostfildern-Ruit, Germany: Hatje Cantz Verlag, 2000).

2. See the discussion of the term "crafts" below, and in note 10.

3. Walter Gropius, "Proposed Budget for the Art Academy and School of Fine Arts in Weimar, 1919–1920," in Hans Wingler, *The Bauhaus, 1919–1933: Weimar, Dessau, Berlin, Chicago* (Cambridge, Mass.: MIT Press, 1969), 26.

4. Among recent reassessments see Paul Betts, "The Bauhaus as Cold-War Legend: West German Modernism Revisited," *German Politics and Society* 14 (Summer 1996): 75–100; Paul Betts, *The Authority of Everyday Objects: A Cultural History of West German Industrial Design* (Berkeley: University of California Press, 2004); Margaret Kentgens-Craig,

The Bauhaus and America: First Contacts, 1919–1936 (Cambridge, Mass.: MIT Press, 1999); Ute Ackermann, "Einleitung: Zur Funktion und Geschichte des Meisterrats am Staatlichen Bauhaus Weimar" (note 1); and Juliet Koss, "Bauhaus Theater of Human Dolls," *Art Bulletin* 85 (December 2003): 724–45. On the Bauhaus in the context of Weimar politics and culture, see John Willett, *Art and Politics in the Weimar Period: The New Sobriety, 1917–1933* (New York: Pantheon, 1978); Barbara Miller Lane, *Architecture and Politics in Germany, 1918–1945* (Cambridge, Mass.: Harvard University Press, 1968).

5. Characterizing Walter Gropius in the 1920s as a virtual "wandering preacher of the modern" (*Wanderprediger der Moderne*), the architectural historian Winfried Nerdinger has observed that "one could practically assemble a weekly itinerary of [Gropius's] lecture tours throughout Germany and Europe, from which emerged hundreds of essays and articles." Quoted in Winfried Nerdinger, "Walter Gropius' Beitrag zur Architektur des 20. Jahrhunderts," in Peter Hahn and Hans M. Wingler, eds., *100 Jahre Walter Gropius: Schliessung des Bauhauses 1933* (Berlin: Bauhaus-Archiv, 1983), 17–36, quotation from p. 18. Unless otherwise noted, all translations are by the author. Bibliographies on Walter Gropius and the Bauhaus include William Bainter O'Neal, ed., *Walter Gropius*, The American Association of Architectural Bibliographers papers, vol. 9 (Charlottesville: University Press of Virginia, 1972); Ruth Cook, *A Bibliography of Walter Gropius, 1919–1950* (Chicago: American Institute of Architects, Chicago Chapter, 1951); Robert P. Harmon, *The Bauhaus: Art and Architecture in Harmony, A Selected Bibliography* (Monticello, Ill.: Vance, 1980).

6. See the discussion, "Learning from Darmstadt: Württemberg and the 'Business Model,'" in Chapter 1, this volume.

7. On the German Applied Arts movement see John Heskett, *German Design: 1870–1918* (New York: Taplinger, 1986); Angelika Thiekötter and Eckhard Siepmann, *Packeis und Pressglas: Von der*

Kunstgewerbebewegung zum Deutschen Werkbund (Giessen: Anabas Verlag, 1987); Gisela Moeller, *Peter Behrens in Düsseldorf: Die Jahre von 1903 bis 1907* (Weinheim: VCH Verlag, 1991).

8. Hartmut Frank, "Ein Bauhaus vor dem Bauhaus," *Bauwelt* 41 (1983): 1640–58. For a recent reassessment, see Jerzy Ilkosz and Beate Störtkuhl, eds., *Hans Poelzig in Breslau: Architektur und Kunst 1900–1916* (Delmenhorst: Aschenbeck und Holstein Verlag, 2000). Poelzig and his school are discussed in greater detail in Chapter 4, this volume.

9. The historian Karl Erich Born notes that no separate statistics were kept to distinguish the crafts and industry in German economic output between 1871 and 1914. This began to change in a qualified manner with the founding of Crafts Chambers (*Handwerkskammern*) in 1897. As Born notes, the net share of the domestic national product (*Nettoinlandsprodukt*) deriving from industry and the crafts was 29.7 percent in 1874, 35.6 percent in 1899, and 40.9 percent in 1913. See Karl Erich Born, *Wirtschafts- und Sozialgeschichte des Deutschen Kaiserreichs (1867/71–1914)* (Wiesbaden: Verlag Franz Steiner, 1985), 45–52, figures from p. 45; see also Wolfram Fischer, "Vom Agrastaat zur Industriegesellschaft," in Dieter Langewiesche, ed., *Ploetz. Das deutsche Kaiserreich 1867/71 bis 1918: Bilanz einer Epoche* (Freiburg, Würzburg: Verlag Ploetz, 1984), 64–72.

10. The "crafts" can be taken to encompass many areas of activity; for the purpose of this book, the crafts denote all those fields in which skilled labor is employed in a variety of specialized fields for the production of objects. Usually these are objects of use, although they can be also objects of decoration (e.g., a decorative frieze or other ornamental work). Thus the crafts include activities such as weaving, pottery, metalwork and jewelry work, carpentry and the interior finishing trades, leatherwork and bookbinding, and the like. Although the building trades often are taken to belong to a separate field of activity (i.e., the "trades"), during the Wilhelmine era these were often characterized as part of the general field of "Handwerk," or "crafts and trades." In this study the word "crafts" will appear interchangably with terms like the "applied arts," "decorative arts," or "practical arts," although these latter terms will usually be employed when there is a distinction being made between forms of skilled labor and the "fine arts" of painting and sculpture, on the one hand, and products made by industry, on the other. I am grateful to Alan Crawford for a discussion of this point; for a discussion of the galaxy of craft-related terms and their nuances in the German language, see Stefan Muthesius, "Handwerk/Kunsthandwerk," *Journal of Design History* 11 (1998): 85–95.

11. The title of the Deutscher Werkbund's Yearbook for 1912 is *The Spiritualization of German Production* (*Die Durchgeistigung der Deutschen Arbeit*), while the explicit goal of the organization, as asserted by the architect Fritz Schumacher in his keynote address at the Werkbund's founding meeting, was the "reconquest of a harmonious culture" (*Wiedereroberung einer harmonischen Kultur*). See DWB 1912, *Die Durchgeistigung der Deutschen Arbeit: Wege und Ziele in Zusammenhang von Industrie/Handwerk und Kunst* (Jena: Eugen Diederichs, 1912), and Fritz Schumacher, "Gründungsrede des Deutschen Werkbundes 1907 in München," *Die Form* 7 (1932): 331, as reprinted in Kurt Junghanns, *Der Deutsche Werkbund: Sein erstes Jahrzehnt* (Berlin: Henschelverlag, 1982), 141. Standard works on the Werkbund include Joan Campbell, *The German Werkbund: The Politics of Reform in the Applied Arts* (Princeton: Princeton University Press, 1978), and Frederic J. Schwartz, *The Werkbund Design Theory and Mass Culture before the First World War* (New Haven: Yale, 1996). See also Frederic J. Schwartz's "Afterword" to the recently reissued *Jahrbuch des Deutschen Werkbundes 1913: Die Kunst in Industrie und Handel* (Berlin: Gebr. Mann Verlag, 2000), 18–32.

12. Fritz Schumacher, "Gründungsrede des Deutschen Werkbundes 1907 in München," in Junghanns, *Der Deutsche Werkbund*, p. 141.

13. On aspects of the Art Education movement, see Gerhard Kratzsch, *Kunstwart und Dürerbund: Ein Beitrag zur Geschichte der Gebildeten im Zeitalter des Imperialismus* (Göttingen: Van den Hoeck & Ruprecht, 1969); Wolfgang J. Mommsen, *Bürgerliche Kultur und Künstlerische Avantgarde: Kultur und Politik im deutschen Kaiserreich, 1870 bis 1918* (Frankfurt a. M.: Propyläen Verlag, 1994); also Jennifer Jenkins, "The Kitsch Collections and *The Spirit in the Furniture*: Cultural Reform and National Culture in Germany," *Social History* 21 (May 1996): 123–41; Laurie A. Stein and Irmela Franzke, "German Design and National Identity 1890–1914," in Wendy Kaplan, ed., *Designing Modernity: The Arts of Reform and Persuasion, 1885–1945* (New York: Thames and Hudson, 1995), 49–78.

14. On developments in Hamburg, see Jennifer Jenkins, *Provincial Modernity: Local Culture and Liberal Politics in Fin-de-Siècle Hamburg* (Ithaca, N.Y.: Cornell University Press, 2003); on Osthaus and the Folkwang Museum, see Herta Hesse-Frielinghaus, gen. ed., *Karl Ernst Osthaus: Leben und Werk* (Recklinghausen: Verlag Aurel Bongers, 1971).

15. Konrad Lange, *Die künstlerische Erziehung der deutschen Jugend* (Darmstadt: Verlag Arnold Bergstraesser, 1893); Julius Langbehn, *Rembrandt als Erzieher: Von Einem Deutschen* (Leipzig: Verlag E. L. Hirschfeld, 1893). On Langbehn, see Fritz Stern, *The Politics of Cultural Despair* (Berkeley: University of California Press, 1961), 97–182.

16. See George Mosse, *The Crisis of German Ideology: Intellectual Origins of the Third Reich* (New York: Grosset and Dunlap, 1964).

17. The various groups that converged in the German Garden City movement are discussed in detail in Chapter 6, this volume.

18. Charles-Edouard Jeanneret, *Étude sur le mouvement d'art décoratif en Allemagne* (New York: De Capo Press, 1968 [1912 edition reprint]), 15. On Jeanneret's extensive study tour of Germany in 1910–11, see H. Allen Brooks, *Le Corbusier's Formative Years: Charles-Edouard Jeanneret at La Chaux-de-Fonds* (Chicago: University of Chicago Press, 1997).

19. Ibid.

20. In the extensive literature on Second Empire Germany, brief accounts of the structure of the Empire can be found in Gerhard Loewenberg, *Parliament in the German Political System* (Ithaca, NY: Cornell University Press, 1967), 1–18; James Retallack, *Germany in the Age of Kaiser Wilhelm II* (New York: St. Martin's Press, 1996), 34–52; see also the contributions by Roger Chickering, Dan S. White, Michael John, and Andrew Lees in Roger Chickering, ed., *Imperial Germany: A Historiographical Companion* (Westport, Conn.: Greenwood Press, 1996).

21. Over time, the term *Heimat* took on new meanings that blurred the distinctions between the local "hometown," "homeland," and the nation. This made it possible for local *Heimat* traditions as well as new local initiatives to take on significance as contributions to national culture. See Celia Applegate, *A Nation of Provincials: The German Idea of Heimat* (Berkeley: University of California Press, 1990); Alon Confino, *The Nation as Local Metaphor: Württemberg, Imperial Germany, and National Memory, 1871–1918* (Chapel Hill: University of North Carolina Press, 1997); also classic is Mack Walker, *German Home Towns: Community, Estate, General Estate, 1648–1871* (Ithaca, N.Y.: Cornell University Press, 1971).

22. See Michael John, "Constitution, Administration, and the Law," and Dan S. White, "Regionalism and Particularism," both in Chickering, ed., *Imperial Germany: A Historiographical Companion*, pp. 185–214; 131–55; also see Gerhard Loewenberg, *Parliament in The German Political System*, pp. 1–19.

23. Jeanneret worked for Behrens, whom he referred to as "the bear" (*le ours*), between November 1, 1910, and April 1, 1911. See H. Allen Brooks, *Le Corbusier's Formative Years*, 235–46.

24. The following works have been part of the lively and extensive historical debates on Wilhelmine Germany: Fritz Fischer, *Griff nach der Weltmacht: Die Kriegszielpolitik Kaiserlichen Deutschland 1914–1918* (Dusseldorf: Droste, 1961); Fritz Fischer, *War of Illusions: German Policies from 1911 to 1914*, trans. by Marian Jackson (Dusseldorf:

Droste, 1975); Dirk Stegmann, *Die Erben Bismarcks, Parteien und Verbände in der Spätphase Wilhelminischen Deutschlands: Sammlungspolitik 1897–1918* (Köln: Kiepenheuer & Witsch, 1970); V. R. Berghahn, *Germany and the Approach of War in 1914*, 2nd ed. (London: Macmillan, 1993); Richard J. Evans, ed., *Society and Politics in Wilhelmine Germany* (London: Croom Helm, 1978); John C. G. Röhl and Nicolaus Sombart, *Kaiser Wilhelm II: New Interpretations* (Cambridge, UK: Cambridge University Press, 1982); Hans-Ulrich Wehler, *The German Empire 1871–1918*, trans. by Kim Traynor (Dover, N.H.: Berg Publishers, 1985); Hans-Ulrich Wehler, *Deutsche Gesellschaftsgeschichte. Band 3: Von der "Deutschen Doppelrevolution" bis zum Beginn des Ersten Weltkrieges, 1849–1914* (München: C.H. Beck, 1995); David Blackbourn and Geoff Eley, *The Peculiarities of German History: Bourgeois Society and Politics in Nineteenth-Century Germany* (Oxford: Oxford University Press, 1984); Geoff Eley, *Reshaping the German Right: Radical Nationalism and Political Change after Bismarck* (New Haven, Conn.: Yale University Press, 1980); Geoff Eley, ed., *Society, Culture and the State in Germany, 1870–1930* (Ann Arbor: University of Michigan Press, 1996); Thomas Nipperdey, *Deutsche Geschichte, 1866–1918, Zweiter Band: Machtstaat vor der Demokratie* (Munich: C.H. Beck, 1992); Roger Chickering, ed., *Imperial Germany: A Historiographical Companion*. See also the important recent contributions by Margaret Lavinia Anderson, *Practicing Democracy: Elections and Political Culture in Imperial Germany* (Princeton: Princeton University Press, 2000); and Kevin Repp, *Reformers, Critics, and the Paths of German Modernity: Anti-Politics and of the Search for Alternatives, 1890–1914* (Cambridge, Mass.: Harvard University Press, 2000). For a useful reconsideration of Kaiser Wilhelm II, himself the subject of a string of recent reappraisals, see Christopher Clark, *Kaiser Wilhelm II, Profiles in Power* (Essex: Pearson Education Limited, 2000). Finally, see Geoff Eley and James Retallack eds., *Wilhelminism and Its Legacies: German Modernities, Imperialism, and the Meanings of Reform, 1890–1930* (New York: Berghahn Books, 2003).

25. Three recent studies that shed new light on Wilhelmine architectural and design developments include Barbara Miller Lane, *National Romanticism and Modern Architecture in Germany and The Scandinavian Countries* (Cambridge, UK: Cambridge University Press, 2000); Frederic J. Schwartz, *The Werkbund: Design Theory and Mass Culture* (New Haven, Conn.: Yale University Press, 1996); and Matthew Jeffries, *Politics and Culture in Wilhelmine Germany: The Case of Industrial Architecture* (Oxford: Berg Publishers, 1995).

26. Posener's studies remain foundational in their importance; see Julius Posener, *Berlin auf dem Wege*

zu einer neuen Architektur: Das Zeitalter Wilhelms II (München: Prestel, 1979); Julius Posener, "Vorlesungen zur Geschichte der Neuen Architektur: Das Zeitalter Wilhelms des Zweiten," *Arch+* 39 (October 1981): 4–75; Julius Posener, *Anfänge des Funktionalismus: Von Arts and Crafts zum Deutschen Werkbund*, Bauwelt Fundamente Nr.11 (Frankfurt: Ullstein, 1964); see also Joan Campbell, *The German Werkbund*; Heskett, *German Design: 1870–1918*. Also useful for understanding the political and economic contexts of the fine and applied arts are Ekkehard Mai et al. eds., *Kunstpolitik und Kunstförderung im Kaiserreich: Kunst im Wandel der Sozial- und Wirtschaftsgeschichte*, Band 2 (Berlin: Gebr. Mann Verlag, 1982); Peter Paret, *The Berlin Secession: Modernism and its Enemies in Imperial Germany* (Cambridge, Mass.: Harvard University Press, 1980); Maria Makela, *The Munich Secession: Art and Artists in Turn-of-the-Century Munich* (Princeton: Princeton University Press, 1990).

27. Lane, *National Romanticism*; Schwartz, *The Werkbund*; and Jeffries, *Politics and Culture in Wilhelmine Germany*.

28. See Gary Bonham, *Ideology and Interests in the German State* (New York: Garland, 1991); also Friedrich Facius, *Wirtschaft und Staat: Die Entwicklung der staatlichen Wirtschaftsverwaltung in Deutschland vom 17. Jahrhundert bis 1945*, Schriften des Bundesarchivs 6 (Boppard am Rhein: Harald Boldt Verlag, 1959); and Goldschmidt, *Das Reich und Preussen im Kampf um die Führung*.

29. Thomas Nipperdey, who helped edit the fourth volume (political writings) of Friedrich Naumann's *Werke*, has judged Naumann's influence and legacy to have been somewhat overrated, and that especially through his disciple Theodor Heuss, Naumann emerged later in the twentieth century as a "kind of myth" (*[eine] Art Mythos*). See Nipperdey, *Deutsche Geschichte 1866–1918*, vol. 2, p. 531, as quoted and discussed in Ursula Krey, "Der Naumann-Kreis: Charisma und politische Emanzipation," in Rüdiger vom Bruch, ed., *Friedrich Naumann in seiner Zeit* (Berlin: Walter de Gruyter, 2000), 115–47, here especially pp. 118–19.

30. Jeffries' findings are significant enough to quote in their entirety: "Although most authors mention [Naumann's] membership in the Reichstag, many fail to place him in the right party. Stanford Anderson, in his thesis on Peter Behrens, refers to 'the nationalist and social democratic politician Friedrich Naumann'; Kenneth Frampton's *Modern Architecture* mentions Naumann as a 'Christian-Social Democrat'; the Werkbund Archive's own publication *Packeis und Pressglas* states that 'the Freisinnige Volkspartei was the party which was particularly close to the Deutscher Werkbund'; whilst the same Werkbund Archive speaks in another pamphlet of 'Friedrich Naumann's national-liberal circle.' If these errors highlight the tendency of art historians to underestimate the importance of historical accuracy," Jeffries continues, "then the silent response of political historians, such as Naumann's most recent biographer Peter Theiner, to Naumann's 'artistic' activities is even more alarming. Far from being an irrelevant self-indulgence, the Werkbund and its preoccupations were central to the new vision of Germany propagated by Naumann and his followers." As Jeffries notes, Naumann had founded the short-lived National Social Union (*Nationalsoziale Verein*) in 1896. It disbanded in 1903, at which time Naumann associated himself with the left-liberal *Freisinnige Vereinigung*. In 1910 he helped form the Progressive People's Party (*Fortschrittliche Volkspartei*), a single left-liberal party comprised of the *Freisinnige Vereinigung*, the *Freisinnige Volkspartei*, and the south German Democrats. See Matthew Jeffries, *Politics and Culture in Wilhelmine Germany: The Case of Industrial Architecture* (Oxford: Berg Publishers, 1995), 149–50, and footnotes 7–11.

31. Three important recent sources on Muthesius that continue the nearly century-old tradition of downplaying or ignoring entirely the architect's thirty-three-year government career are Fedor Roth, *Hermann Muthesius und die Idee der harmonischen Kultur* (Berlin: Gebr. Mann, 2001); Uwe Schneider, *Hermann Muthesius und die Reformdiskussion in der Gartenarchitektur des frühen 20. Jahrhunderts* (Worms: Wernersche Verlagsgesellschaft, 2000); and Laurent Stalder, *Wie man ein Haus baut: Hermann Muthesius (1861–1927) – Das Landhaus als Kulturgeschichtlicher Entwurf* (Ph.D. dissertation, ETH-Zürich, 2002).

32. See Repp, *Reformers, Critics, and the Paths of German Modernity*.

33. Heinrich A. Winkler, *Mittelstand, Demokratie, und Nationalsozialismus* (Cologne: Verlag Kiepenhauer & Witsch, 1972); Herman Lebovics, *Social Conservatism and the Middle Classes in Germany, 1914–1933*; Jürgen Kocka, "Vorindustrielle Faktoren in der deutschen Industrialisierung: Industriebürokratie und 'neuer Mittelstand,'" in Michael Stürmer, ed., *Das kaiserliche Deutschland: Politik und Gesellschaft, 1870–1918* (Dusseldorf: Droste Verlag, 1970), 255–86; and David Blackbourn, "The *Mittelstand* in German Society and Politics, 1871–1914," *Social History* 4 (1977): 409–33.

34. See the helpful discussion of the German upper-middle class in Jonathan Sperber, "Bürger, Bürgertum, Bürgerlichkeit, Bürgerliche Gesellschaft: Studies of the German (Upper) Middle Class and Its Sociocultural World," *Journal of Modern History* 69 (June 1997): 271–97; also David Blackbourn and Richard J. Evans, eds., *The German Bourgeoisie: Essays on the Social History of the German Middle Class from the Late Eighteenth to the Early Twentieth*

Century (New York: Routledge, 1991), and Werner Conze und Jürgen Kocka, eds., *Bildungsbürgertum im 19. Jahrhundert, Teil I: Bildungssystem und Professionalisierung in internationalen Vergleichen*, in Werner Conze, ed., Industrielle Welt, Band 38 (Stuttgart: Klett-Cotta, 1985).

35. See the discussion of the relationship between Prussian social policies and police control over the working classes in Volker R. Berghahn, *Imperial Germany, 1871–1914: Economy, Society, Culture and Politics* (Providence: Berghahn Books, 1994), 247–61.

36. Otto von Bismarck, speech to the Prussian Landtag on October 18, 1849, as quoted in Karl Scheffler, *Lesebuch aus dem Handwerk* (Berlin: P. List Verlag, 1942), 324, and reproduced in Sonja Günther, *Interieurs um 1900: Bernhard Pankok, Bruno Paul und Richard Riemerschmid als Mitarbeiter der Vereinigten Werkstätten für Kunst im Handwerk* (München: W. Fink Verlag, 1971), 17, n. 14.

37. The importance of the *Mittelstand* as nineteenth-century German society's broad base was also emphasized by German-speaking Europe's leading prophet of socialism, Karl Marx. Where Bismarck and other conservatives regarded German social divisions as firm, if in need of defense, Marx increasingly read the advance of industrial capitalism as a menace to the boundary between workers and members of the *Mittelstand*, threatening to fuse these groups into a single exploited mass. See Winkler, *Mittelstand, Demokratie, und Nationalsozialismus*, pp. 21–22; Lebovics, *Social Conservatism and the Middle Classes in Germany*, pp. 6–11.

38. Shulamit Volkov, *The Rise of Popular Anti-Modernism in Germany: The Urban Master Artisans, 1873–1896* (Princeton: Princeton University Press, 1978).

39. Kocka, "Vorindustrielle Faktoren," pp. 276–77.

40. Quoted in Heidrun Walther, *Theodor Adolf von Möller, 1840–1925: Lebensbild eines westfälischen Industriellen* (Neustadt an der Aisch: Verlag Degener & Co., 1958), 157. Theodor von Möller was ennobled by Kaiser Wilhelm II on the occasion of his forced resignation in 1905 following the Hibernia Affair; he is therefore referred to here, in events that predate his dismissal and ennoblement, without the aristocratic "von" before his name. Möller is discussed in detail in Chapter 3.

41. Blackbourn, "The *Mittelstand* in German Society and Politics, 1871–1914"; Wehler, *Deutsche Gesellschaftsgeschichte*, pp. 683–85.

42. See Theodor Möller on *Sammlungspolitik*, or the "politics of rallying-together," in the National Liberal Party's discussions of 1898 at the *Allgemeiner Delegiertentag der Nationalliberalen Partei* (Berlin, 1898), as excerpted in Eley, *Reshaping the*

German Right, pp. 37–38. See also the excellent and detailed analysis of Stegmann, *Die Erben Bismarcks*.

43. See the helpful discussion of this term in Sperber, "Bürger, Bürgertum, Bürgerlichkeit, Bürgerliche Gesellschaft" (note 34).

44. Biographical information is available in Hermann Muthesius, "Mein Lebens- und Bildungsgang " (25 September 1900), NMWA; see also Eckhard Siepmann and Angelika Thiekötter, eds., *Hermann Muthesius im Werkbund-Archiv*, Ausstellung des Werkbund-Archivs im Martin-Gropius-Bau vom 11. Oktober bis 11. November 1990, (Berlin: Werkbund-Archiv, 1990), 105–28. Facts in these sources as well as the government files at the Prussian State Archives, which are used to account for Muthesius's activities in later chapters, contradict some of the published biographical details on Muthesius in, for example, Wiltrud Petsch-Bahr, "Hermann Muthesius," in Wolfgang Ribbe and Wolfgang Schäche, eds. *Baumeister, Architekten, Stadtplaner: Biographien zur baulichen Entwicklung Berlins* (Berlin: Historische Kommission zu Berlin, 1987), 321–40; also Dennis Sharp, "Introduction" to Hermann Muthesius, *The English House*, trans. by Janet Seligman (New York: Rizzoli Press, 1979), xiii–xvii.

45. Fritz K. Ringer, *The Decline of the German Mandarins: The German Academic Community, 1890–1933* (Cambridge, Mass.: Harvard University Press, 1969).

46. Emil Klein, "Die sociale Bedeutung des evangelischen Pfarrhauses," in Emil Zettel, hrsg., *Studien der evangelisch-protestantischen Geistlichen des Grossherzogtums Baden*, 2 (1876): 20–34, as discussed in Ulrich Engelhardt, *Bildungsbürgertum: Begriffs- und Dogmengeschichte eines Etiketts* (Stuttgart: Klett-Cotta, 1986), 160–62.

47. Eckart Muthesius, "Muthesius," in *Hermann Muthesius, 1861–1927*, Exhibition Catalog (London: Architectural Association, 1979), 3; on Hermann Muthesius's years in Japan, see John V. Maciuika, *Hermann Muthesius and the Reform of German Architecture, Arts, and Crafts* (Ph.D. dissertation, University of California Berkeley, 1998).

48. Jürgen Pasche, "Der Nachlass von Hermann Muthesius im Werkbund-Archiv," in Eckhard Siepmann and Angelika Thiekötter, eds., *Hermann Muthesius im Werkbund-Archiv*, p. 108; Muthesius, "Mein Lebens- und Bildungsgang." On the sociology of the architectural profession and the context of nineteenth-century professionalization, see Jürgen Kocka, ed., *Angestellte im europäischen Vergleich: Die Herausbildung angestellter Mittelschichten seit dem späten 19. Jahrhundert* (Göttingen: Vandenhoeck & Ruprecht, 1981); Conze and Kocka, eds., *Bildungsbürgertum im 19. Jahrhundert*; Vincent Clark, "A Struggle for Existence: The Professionalization of German Architects," in Geoffrey Cocks and Konrad

H. Jarausch, eds., *German Professions, 1800–1950* (New York: Oxford University Press, 1990), 143–60.

49. Kocka, "Vorindustrielle Faktoren in der deutschen Industrialisierung: Industriebürokratie und 'neuer Mittelstand,'" 255–86; see also Jürgen Kocka, "Capitalism and Bureaucracy in German Industrialization before 1914," *Economic History Review* 34 (1981): 453–68.

50. The architectural historian Gavin Stamp notes that "revivalism is the most potent force in English culture"; quoted in *The English House 1860–1914: The Flowering of English Domestic Architecture* (London: Faber & Faber, 1986), 19; also Mark Girouard, *Sweetness and Light: The 'Queen Anne' Movement, 1860–1900* (Oxford: Oxford University Press, 1977).

51. See David Bindman and Gottfried Riemann, eds., *Karl Friedrich Schinkel: "The English Journey," Journal of a Visit to France and Britain in 1826*, trans. by F. Gayna Walls (New Haven, Conn.: Yale University Press, 1993); also Barry Bergdoll, *Karl Friedrich Schinkel: An Architecture for Prussia* (New York: Rizzoli, 1994), 177–84.

52. Fritz K. Ringer, *The Decline of the German Mandarins*, p. 29.

53. Hermann Muthesius, *Stilarchitektur und Baukunst: Wandlungen der Architektur im XIX. Jahrhundert und ihr heutiger Standpunkt*, (Mülheim-Ruhr: Verlag von K. Schimmelpfeng, 1902), 49–51. See also Stanford Anderson's translation and introductory essay to Hermann Muthesius, *Style-Architecture and Building-Art: Transformations of Architecture in the Nineteenth Century and its Present Condition*, trans. by Stanford Anderson (Santa Monica, Calif.: Getty Center for the Arts and Humanities, 1994). Quotations are from the original 1902 edition unless otherwise noted. A good recent account of Muthesius's intellectual heritage appears in Roth, *Hermann Muthesius und die Idee einer harmonischen Kultur*, pp. 42–50; 97–107.

54. Muthesius, *Stilarchitektur und Baukunst*, pp. 25–56.

55. Facius, *Wirtschaft und Staat*, p. 68.

56. Ibid., p. 67.

57. Hans Goldschmidt, *Das Reich und Preussen im Kampf um die Führung* (Berlin: Carl Heymanns Verlag, 1931); see especially pp. 15–16, 280–83.

58. Wilhelm Waetzoldt, "Die Entwicklung des kunstgewerblichen Unterrichtswesens in Preussen," *Deutsche Rundschau* 176 (1918): 228–45; 365–80.

59. This point is also made by Nancy J. Troy in her study *Modernism and the Decorative Arts in France: Art Nouveau to Le Corbusier* (New Haven, Conn.: Yale University Press, 1991), 3.

60. Waetzoldt, "Die Entwicklung des kunstgewerblichen Unterrichtswesens in Preussen," p. 366.

61. "Rückblick auf die Entwickelung des gewerblichen Schulwesens in Preussen von 1884–1909," *Ministerial-Blatt der Handels-und Gewerbe-Verwaltung* 11 (6. Mai 1910) (Beilage): 155–64, quotation from p. 155.

62. Bismarck, in addition to being Reich Chancellor, Minister President, and Prussian Minister of Foreign Affairs, was also made Prussian Commerce Minister on September 13, 1880 (a post he held until January 31, 1890). October 1880 marked the first use of the term "economy" (*Wirtschaft*) in official imperial decrees, part of Bismarck's effort to redirect the Prussian government's control over "commerce and trade" (*Handel und Gewerbe*) toward an imperially administered "economy" (*Wirtschaft*) through a new branch of the Interior Ministry, the "Department of Economic Affairs" (*Abteilung für wirtschaftliche Angelegenheiten*). See Facius, *Wirtschaft und Staat*, pp. 65–77 and p. 70 n. 138; also Goldschmidt, *Das Reich und Preussen im Kampf um die Führung*, pp. 15–16; 280–83; and Hans-Heinrich Borchard, *50 Jahre Preussisches Ministerium für Handel und Gewerbe, 1879–1929* (Berlin: Reichsverlag H. Kalkoff, 1929), 30–38. See also Chapter 3, this volume.

63. Heinrich Waentig pointed out in *Wirtschaft und Kunst*, his study of 1909, that the percentage of manufactured goods in German exports rose from 40.1 percent in 1873 to 70.2 percent in 1907, and correctly believed this to be part of a long-term upward trend; quoted in Jeffries, *Politics and Culture in Wilhelmine Germany*, p. 168.

64. Theodor Möller and the Prussian Commerce Ministry's state effort to take over the Hibernia Coal Mining Company is discussed in Chapter 4, this volume.

65. Thomas Nipperdey, *Deutsche Geschichte, 1866–1918*, p. 173.

66. Much of the pedigree of such twentieth-century architectural movements as "modernism" and the "International Style" counted on the simplistic translation of *Typisierung* to mean simply "standardization"; from here it was a relatively small step to argue that the Werkbund debate paved the way for an industrial "factory aesthetic" and a universal, acontextual "functionalism," both of which were key components of the twentieth-century "modern movement." The nuances of the term *Typisierung* are addressed in Chapter 7, this volume.

67. Stephen Jay Greenblatt, *Renaissance Self-Fashioning: From More to Shakespeare* (Chicago: University of Chicago Press, 1980); Nikolaus Pevsner, *Pioneers of Modern Design from William Morris to Walter Gropius* (New York: Penguin Books, 1960). [Originally *Pioneers of the Modern Movement* (New York: Faber & Faber, 1936).] Interestingly, Pevsner, a German émigré to England in the 1930s and originally a scholar of the Baroque period, seems to have learned and borrowed much from his readings of

books by Muthesius about England and the British Arts and Crafts movement. These were written in German and untranslated at the time, leading to the interesting historiographical twist that much of what we know about key nineteenth-century developments leading to the "modern movement" came from Muthesius as filtered through Pevsner for English-speaking readers. This is by no means to argue that Muthesius was the only one writing meaningfully on this period, but that his works, which are discussed in some detail in Chapter 2, this volume, provided much analysis and condensation of material about the Domestic Revival, the Arts and Crafts movement, and changes in design culture generally. Sigfried Giedion, *Space, Time, and Architecture: The Growth of a New Tradition*, 3rd ed. (Cambridge, Mass.: Harvard University Press, 1954).

ONE. DESIGN REFORM IN GERMANY'S CENTRAL AND SOUTHERN STATES, 1890–1914

1. The list of important figures and individual institutions that promoted new attitudes toward design in turn-of-the-century Germany is, in fact, far more extensive than can be covered in any study concentrating on "architecture, politics, and the German state."

2. For background on the fine arts and applied arts in Munich, see Maria Makela, *The Munich Secession*; Kathryn Bloom Hiesinger, ed., *Art Nouveau in Munich* (Philadelphia: Philadelphia Museum of Art, 1988); Gillian Naylor, "Munich: Secession and Jugendstil," in Paul Greenhalgh, ed., *Art Nouveau:1890–1914* (London: V&A Publications, 2000) 286–297; Winfried Nerdinger, "Riemerschmids Weg vom Jugendstil zum Werkbund," in Winfried Nerdinger, ed., *Richard Riemerschmid: vom Jugendstil zum Werkbund* (München: Prestel Verlag, 1982), 13–38; Robin Lenman, "Politics and Culture: The State and the Avant-Garde in Munich, 1864–1914," in Richard Evans, ed., *Society and Politics in Wilhelmine Germany* (New York: Harper and Row, 1978), 90–111; for a more recent comparative discussion of Munich and Dresden as centers for applied-arts experimentation, see Alfred Ziffer, "Impulse – München und Dresden," in Gisela Haase, ed., *Jugendstil in Dresden: Aufbruch in die Moderne* (Wolfratshausen: Edition Minerva, 1999), 179–87.

3. Makela, *The Munich Secession*, pp. 16, 32–33.

4. See the discussion in John Heskett, *German Design, 1870–1918* (New York: Taplinger, 1986), 57–62.

5. Among the earliest appraisals of these developments are Richard Streiter, "Das deutsche Kunstgewerbe und die englisch-amerikanische Bewegung" (1896), in Richard Streiter, *Ausgewählte Schriften zur Aesthetik und Kunst-Geschichte*, ed. Franz von Reber and Emil Sulger-Ebbing (Munich: Delphin, 1913), 1–29; Richard Graul, "Deutschland," in Richard Graul, ed., *Die Krisis im Kunstgewerbe: Studien über Wege und Ziele der modernen Richtung* (Leipzig: S. Hirzel, 1901), 39–51. Both articles place great emphasis on the economic consequences for Germany of English and French success in the applied arts.

6. Hermann Muthesius, "Englische und kontinentale Nutzkunst," *KuH* (1899): 326, as quoted in Winfried Nerdinger, "Riemerschmids Weg," p. 14. On the nineteenth-century German reception of English architectural culture, see Stefan Muthesius, *Das englische Vorbild: Eine Studie zu den deutschen Reformbewegungen in Architektur, Wohnbau und Kunstgewerbe im späteren 19. Jahrhundert* (Munich: Prestel, 1974).

7. Hermann Obrist draws attention to this fact in "Die Zukunft unserer Architektur," *DK* 8 (1901): 329–49, esp. p. 338. Although Peter Behrens moved to Munich in 1890 and was active in founding the Munich Secession and participating in the Münchener Werkstätten, he was also very active in the Bavarian city of Nürnberg. See Peter-Klaus Schuster, ed., *Peter Behrens und Nürnberg, Geschmackswandel in Deutschland: Historismus, Jugendstil und die Anfänge der Industriereform* (Munich: Prestel, 1980).

8. Ekkehard Mai, "Problemgeschichte der Münchener Kunstakademie bis in die zwanziger Jahre," in Thomas Zacharias, ed., *Tradition und Widerspruch: 175 Jahre Kunstakademie München* (München: Prestel, 1985), 103–43.

9. See "Hof-Atelier Elvira," *DK* 6 (1900): 298–305; Naylor, "Munich: Secession and Jugendstil," pp. 292–93; R. Herz and B. Bruns, eds., *Hof-Atelier Elvira: 1887–1928* (Munich: Münchener Stadtmuseum, 1986).

10. Bavarian Applied Arts Association circular of January 1897, as quoted in Winfried Nerdinger, "Riemerschmids Weg," p. 14. The text of the Bavarian Applied Arts Association circular can be found in the Architecture Collection of the Munich Technical University. The urge to "reflect the character, ideals, and needs of their time" places the exhibition planners very much in the current of progressive artists throughout Europe who sought to express the "spirit of the age." See the discussion in Richard A. Etlin, *Frank Lloyd Wright and Le Corbusier: The Romantic Legacy* (Manchester: Manchester University Press, 1994), chapter 4.

11. See Hans Eduard van Berlepsch-Valendas, "Endlich ein Umschwung!" *Deutsche Kunst und Dekoration* 1 (1897): 1–12; Richard Graul, "Deutschland," in Graul, ed., *Die Krisis im Kunstgewerbe*; Ekkehard Mai, "Akademie, Sezession und Avantgarde – München um 1900," in Zacharias, ed., *Tradition und Widerspruch*, pp. 145–78.

12. Mai, "Akademie, Sezession und Avantgarde – München um 1900," pp. 160–65; Ziffer, "Impulse – München und Dresden," pp. 181–82. See also Stefan

Muthesius, "The *'altdeutsche' zimmer*, or Cosiness in Plain Pine: An 1870s Contribution to the Definition of Interior Design," *Journal of Design History* 16 (2003): 269–90.

13. Other artists who sent designs to the United Workshops for production of furniture and applied-arts wares included Karl Bertsch, Heinrich Vogeler, Wilhelm Kreis, and Emanuel Seidl. All were later to become members of the Werkbund. Morris's *News from Nowhere* first appeared in German translation in the socialist journal *Die neue Zeit* in 1892–93; see Winfried Nerdinger, "Riemerschmids Weg," p. 16. "Vereinigte Werkstätten für Kunst im Handwerk, München," DK 1 (1898): 137–38; Günther, *Interieurs um 1900*, p. 10 n. 3; 24.

14. Ziffer, "Impulse – München und Dresden," p. 187.

15. Wilhelm von Debschitz, "Eine Methode des Kunstunterrichts," *DK* (1904): 209–26; Helga Schmoll-Eisenwerth, "Die Münchener Debschitz-Schule," in Hans M. Wingler, ed., *Kunstschulreform 1900–1933* (Berlin: Gebr. Mann, 1977), 68–85.

16. On Obrist see "Hermann Obrist," *DK* 1 (1898): 138–39; Hermann Obrist, "Die Zukunft unserer Architektur," *DK* 8 (1901): 329–49; Silvie Lampe von Bennigsen, *Hermann Obrist: Erinnerungen* (Munich: Verlag Herbert Post, 1970), and Siegfried Wichmann, *Hermann Obrist: Wegbereiter der Moderne* (Munich: Villa Stück/Karl M. Lipp, 1968).

17. Debschitz quoted in Schmoll-Eisenwerth, "Die Münchener Debschitz-Schule," p. 71.

18. Wilhelm Waetzoldt, "Die Entwicklung des kunstgewerblichen Unterrichtswesens in Preussen"; Streiter registered complaint about the decorative excesses of the 1890s when he observed more than twenty years earlier, "Es wird zu viel dekoriert, zu wenig tektonisch gestaltet" (There is too much decoration, not enough tectonic expression); Streiter, "Das deutsche Kunstgewerbe...", p. 16; Kirchner and Klee are mentioned in Schmoll-Eisenwerth, "Die Münchener Debschitz-Schule," pp. 69, 77.

19. Unlike the Bauhaus, of course, the Debschitzschule did not culminate its curriculum sequence with architecture; nor is it the purpose here to confuse these very different institutions, which emerged during very different times. Significantly, however, Walter Gropius stayed in touch with Wilhelm von Debschitz and is known to have paid more than one visit to the school. Obrist quoted in Schmoll-Eisenwerth, "Die Münchener Debschitz-Schule," p. 71.

20. Winfried Nerdinger, *Theodor Fischer: Architekt und Städtebauer, 1862–1938* (Berlin: Ernst & Sohn, 1988), 26–46. A brief account of Fischer's career in English is Winfried Nerdinger, "Theodor Fischer," *Architectural Review* 180 (1986): 61–65. See also

Rudolf Pfister, *Theodor Fischer: Leben und Wirken eines deutschen Baumeisters* (Munich: Verlag Georg D.W. Callwey, 1968).

21. Quotation from *Architektonische Rundschau* (1902): 47, as quoted in Nerdinger, *Theodor Fischer*, p. 189.

22. Letter from Fischer to Riemerschmid, June 10, 1912, GNM-ABK, Nachlass Riemerschmid; the discussion by Nerdinger provides the context of this conflict; see Nerdinger, *Theodor Fischer*, pp. 13, 49–50, 189; also Ziffer, "Impulse – München und Dresden," pp. 182–84.

23. Hans-Joachim Hubrich points out that many anti-academy, progressive trends around the turn of the twentieth century, including the Applied Arts movement (*Kunstgewerbebewegung*), the *Jugendstil*, and promoters of a new *Sachlichkeit* or Functionalism, were commonly grouped under the umbrella term *neue Bewegung*, or "new movement," and were not necessarily perceived as being in tension or conflict with one another. See Hans-Joachim Hubrich, *Hermann Muthesius: Die Schriften zu Architektur, Kunstgewerbe, Industrie in der "Neuen Bewegung"* (Berlin: Gebr. Mann Verlag, 1981), 9.

24. Quoted in Ekkehard Mai, "Problemgeschichte der Münchener Kunstakademie," in Zacharias, ed., *Tradition und Widerspruch*, pp. 130–31; 142 n. 83; see also the documentation on "Unternehmungen am Rande" in Winfried Nerdinger, ed., *Richard Riemerschmid: vom Jugendstil zum Werkbund* (München: Prestel Verlag, 1982), pp. 485–87; also Peter-Klaus Schuster, "Behrens in Nürnberg und ein Nürnberger Auftrag an Behrens," in Schuster, ed., *Peter Behrens und Nürnberg*, pp. 95–165.

25. See the discussion in John Heskett, *German Design, 1870–1918*, pp. 57–62; also Günther, *Interieurs um 1900*, pp. 37–74.

26. Nerdinger, "Riemerschmids Weg," p. 16.

27. See "Darmstadt, Stuttgart und München als Heim-Stätten moderner Gewerbe Kunst" *DkuD* 9 (1902): 247–50; note especially the detailed "Tafel der künstlerischen Migration aus München 1897–1902."

28. One commentator, Ernst von Wolzogen, observed in 1917 that turn-of-the-century Darmstadt "competed for the prize for petty bourgeois sleepiness with many other smaller noble residence towns." Quoted in Gerhard Bott, "Darmstadt und die Mathildenhöhe," in Gerd Wietek, ed., *Deutsche Künstlerkolonien und Künstlerorte* (München: Verlag K. Thiemig, 1976), 154–61; quotation from p. 154.

29. See the discussion in Bott, "Darmstadt und die Mathildenhöhe." Thorough analysis from numerous perspectives appears in the exhibition catalogs *Darmstadt, Ein Dokument Deutscher Kunst 1901–1976,*

5 vols. (Darmstadt: Eduard Roether Verlag, 1976). For documentation of the Darmstadt colony's restoration and treatment as a cumulative, century-long achievement, see Christiane Geelhaar, ed., *Mathildenhöhe Darmstadt, 100 Jahre Planen und Bauen für die Stadtkrone, 1899–1999*, 2 vols. (Darmstadt: J. Häusser, 2000).

30. See Bott, "Darmstadt und die Mathildenhöhe," pp. 154–55.

31. Ibid., p. 154.

32. Ibid., pp. 154–55; also *Ein Dokument Deutscher Kunst 1901–1976*, vol. 4, pp. 2–4. Another useful discussion is contained in Fritz Schmalenbach, *Jugendstil: Ein Beitrag zu Theorie und Geschichte der Flächenkunst* (Würzburg: Verlag Konrad Triltsch, 1935), 110–117.

33. The park was known to the public as the "Thursday Park," since this had hitherto been the only day of the week that the park was made accessible to visitors. Henceforth it was known as the "Mathildenhöhe."

34. Eva Huber, "Die Darmstädter Künstlerkolonie: Anspruch und Verwirklichung ihrer künsterischer Zielsetzungen," in *Ein Dokument Deutscher Kunst 1901–1976*, vol. 5, p. 60.

35. Annette Wolde, "Der ökonomische Hintergrund der Künstlerkolonie," in *Ein Dokument Deutscher Kunst 1901–1976*, vol. 5, pp. 49–51.

36. The Ernst Ludwig House cost 92,000 Marks for construction and interior furnishings – as compared to 200,000 Marks and 75,000 Marks paid respectively by Behrens and Olbrich for their houses. See the excellent discussion by Annette Wolde, "Der ökonomische Hintergrund der Künstlerkolonie," in *Ein Dokument Deutscher Kunst 1901–1976*, vol. 5, pp. 49–50.

37. A financial scandal resulting from mismanagement of the 1901 exhibition forced the liquidation of 96 percent of a 260,000 Mark insurance guarantee fund in order to cover the exhibition's deficits. Wolde, "Der ökonomische Hintergrund der Künstlerkolonie," p. 50.

38. "Eröffnungs-Feier der Darmstädter Kunst-Ausstellung," *DKuD* 8 (1901): 446–48.

39. See Tilmann Buddensieg, "Das Wohnhaus als Kultbau: Zum Darmstädter Haus von Behrens," in Schuster, ed., *Peter Behrens in Nürnberg*, pp. 37–48, quotations from pp. 39, 46.

40. On the themes of the "national" and "international" at the 1902 exposition see Richard A. Etlin, "Turin 1902: The Search for a Modern Italian Architecture," *Journal of Decorative and Propaganda Arts* 13 (Summer 1989): 94–109.

41. See Bruno Taut, *Alpine Architektur* (Vienna: Hagen, 1919) and the translation by James Palmer and Shirley Palmer in Dennis Sharp, ed., *Glass Architecture by Paul Scheerbart and Alpine Architecture by*

Bruno Taut (New York: Praeger, 1972); also the excellent introductory essay in John A. Stuart, *The Gray Cloth: Paul Scheerbart's Novel on Glass Architecture*, trans. by John A. Stuart (Cambridge, Mass.: MIT Press, 2001), and Stephen R. Ascheim, *The Nietzsche Legacy in Germany, 1890–1990* (Berkeley: University of California Press, 1992), 30–41. On Expressionist architecture generally, see Wolfgang Pehnt, *Expressionist Architecture*, trans. by J. A. Underwood and Edith Küstner (London: Thames and Hudson, 1973).

42. Ascheim, *The Nietzsche Legacy in Germany*, pp. 30–41; also Werner Oechslin, "Politisches, allzu Politisches...: 'Nietzschelinge', der 'Wille zur Kunst' und der Deutsche Werkbund vor 1914," in Werner Oechslin, *Moderne entwerfen: Architektur und Kulturgeschichte* (Köln: Dumont, 1999), 116–71.

43. See the documentation in Huber, "Die Darmstädter Künstlerkolonie," in *Ein Dokument Deutscher Kunst 1901–1976*, vol. 5, pp. 107–65.

44. Barbara Miller Lane, *National Romanticism and Modern Architecture in Germany and the Scandinavian Countries*, pp. 126–44.

45. Huber's article, "Die Darmstädter Künstlerkolonie," gives the best critical overview of the reception of the first Darmstadt exhibition. Richard Hamann and Jost Hermand see the 1901 exhibition as a "transitional" phase from artistic individualism to a more general concern with characteristics of realist, functional design in *Stilkunst um 1900*, Epochen deutscher Kultur von 1870 bis zur Gegenwart, vol. 4, 2nd ed. (Frankfurt a. M.: Fischer Taschenbuch Verlag, 1977), 256–57.

46. Muther remarks: "Es wird durch die zimperliche Hausfrauenbesorgnis gerade das zunichte gemacht, was dem Unternehmen seine Eigenart, seinen stimmungsvollsten Reiz gegeben hätte." Richard Muther, *Studien und Kritiken II* (Wien, 1901), 88, as quoted in Eva Huber, "Die Darmstädter Künstlerkolonie," p. 61.

47. Letter from Kessler to Eberhard von Bodenhausen, September 6, 1901; both this letter and van de Velde are quoted in Laird McLeod Easton, *The Red Count: The Life and Times of Harry Kessler* (Berkeley: University of California Press, 2002), 94–95.

48. Wolde, "Der ökonomische Hintergrund der Künstlerkolonie," pp. 51–52.

49. See the discussion in Matthias Freytag, *Theodor Fischers Stuttgarter Kunstgebäude am Schlossplatz: Entstehung und architektonische Form* (Stuttgart: Silberburg Verlag, 1989), esp. the section "Aufstrebendes Kunstleben," 9–21; Fritz Schneider, *Lebendige Funken. 125 Jahre Württembergischer Kunstverein, 1827–1952* (Stuttgart: Württembergischer Kunstverein, 1953), 31–32; quotation from p. 32.

50. Graul, "Deutschland," p. 50.

51. On Württemberg's King Wilhelm II and the background of arts reform, see Anni Willman, *Der gelernte König, Wilhelm II Von Württemberg: Ein Porträt in Geschichten* (Stuttgart: DRW-Verlag, 1993), 98–135; Otto Borst, *Württemberg und seine Herren: Landesgeschichte in Lebensbildern* (Esslingen-München: Bechtle Verlag, 1988), 307–36; Julius Baum, ed., *Stuttgarter Kunst der Gegenwart* (Stuttgart: Deutsche Verlags-Anstalt, 1913); Victor Bruns, ed., *Württemberg unter der Regierung König Wilhelms II* (Stuttgart: Deutsche Verlags-Anstalt, 1916), 601–80.

52. Thomas Nipperdey, *Deutsche Geschichte 1866–1918*, p. 615.

53. Max Diez, "Neuzeitliche Kunst-Bestrebungen in Württemberg," *DKuD* 20 (1907): 117–65, quotation from p. 121.

54. As Laird McLeod Easton notes aptly in a recent biography of Harry Graf Kessler, "The legacy of Germany's centuries of political fragmentation weighed heavily even after the founding of the Reich: cities with proud pasts as independent city-states or commercial centers such as Hamburg, Frankfurt am Main, and Cologne could not be relegated so easily to the status of provincial centers of mere regional importance. Indeed, much smaller towns had shaped German culture to a degree unimaginable in France, England, Spain, or Russia." Quoted in Easton, *The Red Count*, p. 59. On the general phenomenon of Württemberg's relationship to the Reich, see Alon Confino, *The Nation as Local Metaphor*.

55. *Der Tag* (Berlin), Nr. 135 (21 March 1902), as quoted in Freytag, *Theodor Fischers Stuttgarter Kunstgebäude am Schlossplatz*, p. 13.

56. Protocols of the Stuttgart City Council, July 20, 1909, as quoted in Freytag, *Theodor Fischers Stuttgarter Kunstgebäude am Schlossplatz*, p. 20.

57. Diez, "Neuzeitliche Kunst-Bestrebungen in Württemberg," pp. 119–28; "Kleine Mitteilungen: Stuttgart," *KgB*, N.F. 13 (1902): 121; Schmalenbach, *Jugendstil*, p. 108.

58. "Die künstlerische Leitung des Münchener Unternehmens geht nach Stuttgart über." "Kleine Mitteilungen: München," *KgB*, N.F. 13 (1902): 120–21, quotation from p. 121. Krüger would return to Munich only one year after his arrival in Stuttgart, leaving Pankok in charge.

59. Diez, "Neuzeitliche Kunst-Bestrebungen," pp. 127–28.

60. Hermann von Seefeld, "Die Förderung des Kleingewerbes in Hessen, Baden, Württemberg, Elsass-Lothringen und der Schweiz, Auf Grund einer Studienreise im Jahre 1903," in *Sammlung der Drucksachen des preussischen Hauses der Abgeordneten*, 20. Legislatur-periode, I. Session 1904/05, Bd.4, Drucksache 142 (Berlin: W. Moeser, 1904), 2159–214, quotation from p. 2194.

61. Ibid.

62. Ibid.

63. For sources on Fischer generally, see note 20, this chapter; on Fischer's Stuttgart context, see Jürgen Joedicke, "Die unterschiedlichen Wege der Architekturlehre in Stuttgart: Von der Real- und Gewerbeschule zur Universität, in Lothar Fehn et al., *Stuttgarter Architekturschule: Vielfalt als Konzept* (Stuttgart: Karl Krämer Verlag, 1992), 16–35.

64. Jeanneret to L'Eplattenier, April 16, 1910, as quoted in Winfried Nerdinger, "Le Corbusier und Deutschland: Genesis und Wirkungsgeschichte eines Konflikts, 1910–1933," *Arch+* 20 (August 1987): 80–86, quotation from p. 80.

65. In Munich Jeanneret busied himself, in between social invitations to Fischer's home, by studying the writings of Camillo Sitte and other works on city planning in the Bavarian State Library. Nerdinger, "Le Corbusier und Deutschland," p. 80; also Winfried Nerdinger, *Theodor Fischer*, pp. 103–09; 235–38.

66. Paul Bonatz, *Leben und Bauen* (Stuttgart: 1950), as quoted in Werner Durth, *Deutsche Architekten: Biographische Verflechtungen, 1900–1970* (München: DTV, 1992), 62. On Bonatz's legacy, see Gerhard Graubner, ed., *Paul Bonatz und seine Schüler* (Stuttgart: Verlag Deutsche Bauten (1932?)).

67. Winfried Nerdinger, *Theodor Fischer*, pp. 71–73; 255–58; Freytag, *Theodor Fischers Stuttgarter Kunstgebäude am Schlossplatz*, pp. 42–62.

68. Winfried Nerdinger, *Theodor Fischer*, pp. 255–58; Freytag, *Theodor Fischers Stuttgarter Kunstgebäude am Schlossplatz*, pp. 86–95.

69. Max Diez, "Neuzeitliche Kunstbestrebungen in Württemberg," *Deutsche Kunst und Dekoration* 20 (1907): 117–63; quotation from p. 163.

70. The special status and achievements of the firm P. Bruckmann & Söhne is described and placed in context in Gustav E. Pazaurek, "Das Kunstgewerbe in Württemberg," V. Bruns, ed., *Württemberg unter der Regierung König Wilhelms II*, pp. 661–68; a recent excellent treatment of the Württemberg milieu and the case study of Peter Bruckmann, Friedrich Naumann, and Ernst Jäckh in Heilbronn is in Matthew Jeffries, *Politics and Culture in Wilhelmine Germany*, pp. 146–79.

71. See Eduard Sekler's analysis of the Purkersdorf Sanatorium in Eduard F. Sekler, *Josef Hoffmann: The Architectural Work* (Princeton: Princeton University Press, 1985), 67–72; more recently see Leslie Topp, "An Architecture for Modern Nerves: Josef Hoffmann's Purkersdorf Sanatorium," *JSAH* 56 Nr. 4 (December 1997): 414–37.

72. Diez, "Neuzeitliche Kunstbestrebungen in Württemberg," p. 144.

73. Harry Graf Kessler, a court insider in more countries than just Germany, characterized Grand Duke Wilhelm Ernst's motivations for considering

the appointment of the artist Henry van de Velde in a diary entry of November 4, 1901, as "the wish to do something to inaugurate his reign in a grand way." Kessler is quoted in Easton, *The Red Count*, p. 101.

74. Between 1896 and 1900, for example, Carl Alexander solicited an array of infrastructure-related information from the government's technical and cultural attaché in London, the Thurinigian-born architect Hermann Muthesius. Muthesius owed Carl Alexander a great deal, as the grand duke had arranged for Muthesius's first independent building commission, the German evangelical church in Tokyo, when the architect made his start working on government buildings in Japan between 1888 and 1890. Muthesius in turn served the Grand Duke in the late 1890s when he supplied a steady stream of information about state-of-the-art British railway engineering, canal construction, the control of factory emissions in the duchy's fisheries and waterways, and other industry-related data. The Muthesius–Carl Alexander correspondence can be found in NMWA, Berlin; the detailed and enthusiastic letters about all the lessons England has to offer the grand duchy strongly suggest an alternative to Laird Easton's portrayal of the last decades of Carl Alexander's reign as "a long, undistinguished twilight" in which Weimar "became a truly provincial *Museumstadt*, vegetating peacefully with its memories, undisturbed by any contact with living culture." This does not appear to have been true, at least, on the administrative level. Quotation from Easton, *The Red Count*, p. 100. Among Carl Alexander's noble titles was that of Protector of the German evangelical community in Japan. See Hermann Muthesius, "Deutsche evangelische Kirche in Tokyo," *CdB* 11 (1891): 339; Muthesius's years in Japan and debts to Carl Alexander are discussed in John V. Maciuika, *Hermann Muthesius and the Reform of German Architecture, Arts, and Crafts* (Ph.D. dissertation, University of California Berkeley, 1998), 36–57.

75. See Carl Alexander, Grossherzog von Sachsen-Weimar-Eisenach, "Mein Kunst-Glaubensbekenntnis nach der Münchener Reise 1858," reprinted in Achim Preiss and Klaus-Jürgen Winkler, eds., *Weimarer Konzepte: Die Kunst- und Bauhochschule 1860–1995* (Weimar: VDG, 1996), 59.

76. Bruno Eelbo, "Bericht uber die dreijährige Tätigkeit der Großherzoglich-Sächsische Zentralstelle für Kunstgewerbe 1881–1884," reprinted in Preiss and Winkler, eds., *Weimarer Konzepte*, pp. 91–95, quotation from p. 92.

77. Eelbo, "Bericht," as quoted in Karl-Heinz Hüter, "Hoffnung, Illusion und Enttäuschung: Henry van de Veldes Kunstgewerbeschule und das frühe Bauhaus," in Klaus-Jürgen Sembach and Birgit Schulte, eds., *Henry van de Velde: Ein europäischer*

Künstler seiner Zeit (Hagen: Karl-Ernst-Osthaus Museum, 1992), 285–337, quotation from p. 287.

78. Ibid., p. 286.

79. As Harry Graf Kessler recalled, "(Minister of State) Rothe suggested the Grand Duke appoint van de Velde with the open-ended assignment of advising and improving the crafts and trades in the grand duchy." Kessler diary entry of December 21, 1901, as quoted in Hüter, "Hoffnung, Illusion und Entäuschung," p. 285.

80. On Henry van de Velde's early development, see Amy F. Ogata, *Art Nouveau and the Social Vision for Modern Living: Belgian Artists in a European Context* (Cambridge, UK: Cambridge University Press, 2001), 27–31; 46–48; 89–103; on van de Velde in Germany, see Sembach and Schulte, eds., *Henry van de Velde*; Karl-Heinz Hüter, *Henry van de Velde: Sein Werk bis zum Ende seinen Tätigkeit in Deutschland* (Berlin: Akademie Verlag, 1967).

81. Easton, *The Red Count*, p. 94.

82. *Staatshandbuch für das Großherzogtum Sachsen* (1904), p. 57, as quoted in Karl-Heinz Hüter, "Henry van de Veldes Kunstgewerbeschule in Weimar," *Wissenschaftliche Zeitschrift der Hochschule für Architektur und Bauwesen Weimar* 9 (1962): 12.

83. Hüter, "Henry van de Veldes Kunstgewerbeschule in Weimar," p. 12.

84. Quoted in ibid., p. 10. For a detailed chronology of van de Velde's work in Weimar, see "Annalen der Wiemarer Zeit," in Hochschule für Architektur und Bauwesen Weimar, ed., *Henry van de Velde, Weimar 1902–1915: Gedächtnisausstellung zu Seinem 100. Geburtstag am 3. April 1963* (Weimar: Hochschule für Architektur und Bauwesen Weimar, 1963), 11–16.

85. Letter from Henry van de Velde to Grand Duke Wilhelm Ernst, December 24, 1904, reprinted in Preiss and Winkler, eds., *Weimarer Konzepte*, Document 22, p. 96. See also document 23, pp. 96–99, the reprint of van de Velde's report of October 8, 1907, describing to the grand duke the organization and operation of the school workshops. See also the discussion in Hüter, "Henry van de Veldes Kunstgewerbeschule in Weimar," p. 14.

86. See Dieter Dolgner, *Henry van de Velde in Weimar, 1902–1917* (Weimar: VDG, 1996), 56–57.

87. Hüter, "Hoffnung, Illusion und Enttäuschung," p. 319.

88. Henry van de Velde, "Die Linie," essay of 1910 in van de Velde, *Essays* (1910), cited here in reprinted form in Henry van de Velde, *Zum Neuen Stil* (Munich: R. Piper, 1955), 186; see also Hüter, "Hoffnung, Illusion und Enttäuschung," pp. 326–27.

89. Hüter, "Hoffnung, Illusion und Enttäuschung," p. 287.

90. Ibid., p. 329; Moeller, *Peter Behrens in Düsseldorf*, pp. 35–72.

91. Hüter, "Hoffnung, Illusion und Enttäuschung," p. 331; Jeanneret, *Étude*, pp. 68–69.

92. Hüter, "Hoffnung, Illusion und Enttäuschung," p. 331.

93. Ibid. See also the discussion in Etlin, "The Spirit of the Age," in *Frank Lloyd Wright and Le Corbusier*, Chapter 4.

94. Henry van de Velde, *Vom Neuen Stil* (Leipzig: Insel, 1907), 41, 48.

95. Henry van de Velde, *Kunstgewerbliche Laienpredigten*, 2 vols. (Leipzig: Hermann Seemann Nachfolger, 1902) and *Vom Neuen Stil* (Leipzig: Insel, 1907).

96. Easton, *The Red Count*, pp. 104–05.

97. Easton gives a nuanced account of the many circumstances surrounding this incident and Kessler's particular difficulties in the *The Red Count*, pp. 148–56.

98. Hüter, "Hoffnung, Illusion und Enttäuschung," p. 336.

99. *Kunstwart* changed the journal's subtitle from an "overview of all fields of beauty" (*Rundschau über alle Gebiete des Schönen*) to, in 1907, the broader "bi-weekly overview of the culture of [artistic] expression in all areas of life" (*Halbmonatsrundschau für Ausdruckskultur auf allen Lebensgebieten*). See the discussion in Gerald Heres, "Kunstwart – Dürerbund – Heimatschutz," in Gisela Haase, ed., *Jugendstil in Dresden*, p. 172.

100. Gerhard Kratzsch, *Kunstwart und Dürerbund*, p. 133.

101. Ferdinand Avenarius, "Pro domo," *KW* 2 (1888): 81; see the discussion in Kratzsch, *Kunstwart und Dürerbund*, p. 180.

102. Kratzsch, *Kunstwart und Dürerbund*, p. 180.

103. Paul Schultze-Naumburg, *Kulturarbeiten*, 9 vols. (Munich: G. D. W. Callwey, 1902–17). See also Christian Otto, "Modern Environment and Historical Continuity: The Heimatschutz Discourse in Germany," *Art Journal* 43, Nr. 2 (Summer 1983): 148–57.

104. Ferdinand Avenarius in *Kunstwartarbeit* (Munich: 1908), as quoted in Heres, p. 176.

105. Among those frequently publishing in *Kunstwart* were Ernst Troeltsch, Ferdinand Tönnies, and Wilhelm Dilthey; see Kratzsch, *Kunstwart und Dürerbund* p. 196.

106. *Deutsches Warenbuch* (Hellerau: Dürerbund-Werkbund Genossenschaft, 1915); also Ferdinand Avenarius, "Das Deutsche Warenbuch," *Der Kunstwart* 29 (1915): 19–22, and Kratzsch, *Kunstwart und Dürerbund*, pp. 266–67.

107. Alfred Ziffer, "Impulse – München und Dresden," in Gisela Haase, ed., *Jugendstil in Dresden: Aufbruch in die Moderne* (Dresden: Minerva, 1999), 179–87.

108. Karl Schmidt in Johannes Kleinpaul, "Das Kunstgewerbe auf der internationalen Kunstausstel-

lung Dresden 1901, *KgBl* N.F. 13 (1902): 13–35, quote on p. 14, as quoted in Petra Hölscher, "Dekorative Kunst auf Ausstellungen in Dresden – nur Dekoration?" in Gisela Haase, ed., *Jugendstil in Dresden*, p. 63.

109. Ziffer, "Mobelbau in Dresden," in Haase, *Jugendstil in Dresden*, p. 84.

110. Schmidt's expansion abroad led him to place his furniture at stores in Zurich and Brussels, rather than opening his own branch stores there. See Schmidt to Muthesius, May 7, 1909, NMWA; also Ziffer, "Möbelbau in Dresden," in Haase, *Jugendstil in Dresden*, p. 87.

111. Hölscher, "Dekorative Kunst auf Ausstellungen," in Haase, *Jugendstil in Dresden*, p. 63.

TWO. THE PRUSSIAN COMMERCE MINISTRY AND THE LESSONS OF THE BRITISH ARTS AND CRAFTS MOVEMENT

1. Nipperdey, *Deutsche Geschichte*, Band 2, p. 173.

2. Although certainly not the focus of the present study, it is important to note that as for so many topics in the Wihelmine era, there is debate over the exact ways in which economic development and interest-group politics played out between 1871 and 1914. See, for example, Kenneth D. Barkin, *The Controversy over German Industrialization, 1890–1902* (Chicago: University of Chicago Press, 1970); Hartmut Kaelble, *Industrielle Interessenpolitik in der Wilhelminische Gesellschaft*, Veröffentlichungen der Historischen Kommission zu Berlin, Band 27 (Berlin: Walter de Gruyter & Co., 1967); W. O. Henderson, *The Rise of German Industrial Power, 1834–1914* (Berkeley: University of California Press, 1975); Karl Erich Born, *Wirtschafts- und Sozialgeschichte des Deutschen Kaiserreichs (1867/71–1914)* (Wiesbaden/Stuttgart: Franz Steiner Verlag, 1985); Geoff Eley, ed., *Society, Culture, and the State in Germany, 1870–1930*; the topic also receives some consideration from the perspective of applied-arts developments in Heinrich Waentig, *Wirtschaft und Kunst: Eine Untersuchung über Geschichte und Theorie der Modernen Kunstgewerbebewegung* (Jena: Gustav Fischer, 1909).

3. Wilhelm Waetzoldt, "Die Entwicklung des kunstgewerblichen Unterrichtswesens in Preussen," *Deutsche Rundschau* 176 (1918): 228–45; 368–80.

4. The reforms led by the artist Bruno Paul at the Berlin School of Applied Arts and the architect Hans Poelzig at the Breslau School of Art and Applied Art will be examined in Chapter 3, where Prussia's arts, crafts, and trades reforms are considered in greater depth.

5. There was no such post at the German embassy prior to 1896; it appears to have been created for Muthesius.

6. Muthesius began serving as a civil servant in the Prussian Ministry of Public Works in 1893 and began working for the Commerce Ministry in 1897. See Hermann Muthesius, "Mein Lebens- und Bildungsgang" (September 25, 1900); see also Eckhard Siepmann and Angelika Thiekötter, eds., *Hermann Muthesius im Werkbund-Archiv*, Ausstellung des Werkbund-Archivs im Martin-Gropius-Bau vom 11. Oktober bis 11. November 1990 (Berlin: Werkbund-Archiv, 1990), 105–28. Two important new sources on Muthesius are Fedor Roth, *Hermann Muthesius und die Idee der harmonischen Kultur*, and Uwe Schneider, *Hermann Muthesius und die Reformdiskussion in der Gartenarchitektur des frühen 20. Jahrhunderts*.

7. Hermann Muthesius, *Stilarchitektur und Baukunst: Wandlungen der Architektur im XIX. Jahrhundert und ihr heutiger Standpunkt* (Mülheim-Ruhr: Verlag von K. Schimmelpfeng, 1902). I borrow the terms "style-architecture" and "building-art" from the recent translation by Stanford Anderson of Hermann Muthesius, *Style-Architecture and Building-Art: Transformations of Architecture in the Nineteenth Century and its Present Condition*, trans. by Stanford Anderson (Santa Monica, Calif.: Getty Center for the Arts and Humanities, 1994); hereafter cited as *Style-Architecture and Building-Art*. Quotations are from the 1902 edition unless otherwise noted; *Das englische Haus: Entwicklung, Bedingungen, Anlage, Aufbau, Einrichtung und Innenraum*, 3 vols. (Berlin: Ernst Wasmuth, 1904–05).

8. See Hermann Muthesius, Letter Book II, NMWA; also Hermann Muthesius, "Bericht über den Vortrag von Guglielmo Marconi am 2. März im 'Institution of Civil Engineers' in London," Bundesarchiv, Abteilungen Potsdam, Reichspostakten RPA, Nr. 15137, Bl. 3f, as reproduced in Michael Bollé, *Die Grossfunkstation Nauen und ihre Bauten von Hermann Muthesius* (Berlin: Verlag Willmuth Arenhövel, 1996), 62. The Ministry of Commerce and Trade and Ministry of Public Works had been joined in a single ministry until 1878, but continued to work closely together as separate ministries on such matters as railways, canal development, and other infrastructure vital for commercial growth. Muthesius reported most frequently to the architect Otto March at Public Works and Fritz Dönhoff at Commerce; the architect's earliest reports from London concern the English railway system and are at NMWA.

9. Julius Posener, *Anfänge des Funktionalismus*, p. 109; Jürgen Pasche, "Der Nachlass von Hermann Muthesius im Werkbund-Archiv," p. 108; Wiltrud Petsch-Bahr, "Hermann Muthesius," p. 324. The recent wave of literature on Muthesius does little to offset this view; see Roth, *Hermann Muthesius und die Idee der harmonischen Kultur*; Schneider, *Hermann Muthesius und die Reformdiskussion in der*

Gartenarchitektur des frühen 20. Jahrhunderts; and Laurent Stalder, *Wie man ein Haus baut: Hermann Muthesius (1861–1927) – Das Landhaus als Kulturgeschichtlicher Entwurf*.

10. Nancy J. Troy, *Modernism and the Decorative Arts in France: Art Nouveau to Le Corbusier* (New Haven, Conn.: Yale University Press, 1991), 3. In studies of turn-of-the-century Germany, only Hans-Joachim Hubrich and Reyner Banham have discussed Muthesius's role as an instrument of German economic policy in this area. Their treatments, however, do not do justice to many important features of the government servant's work. See Reyner Banham, *Theory and Design in the First Machine Age*, 2nd ed. (Cambridge, Mass.: MIT Press, 1980), 68–87; Hans-Joachim Hubrich is better in his summary of Muthesius's activities, but does not relate them back to his other important spheres of activity, notably as the catalyst in the founding of the Werkbund or as an architectural reformer; see Hubrich, *Hermann Muthesius: Die Schriften zu Architektur, Kunstgewerbe, Industrie in der "Neuen Bewegung"* (Berlin: Gebr. Mann Verlag, 1981), 191–218.

11. For an explanation of the term "Mittelstand," roughly translatable as "middle estate," see the Introduction, pp. 13+. The term "decorative arts" is insufficient in this context to describe Muthesius's areas of inquiry, since he was also interested in questions affecting infrastructure and such "practical" or "applied" arts as metal work and the various building trades. For a recent discussion of the complexity associated with terms for the applied arts and trades in a multilingual context, see Stefan Muthesius, "Handwerk/Kunst-handwerk," *Journal of Design History* 11 (1998): 85–95.

12. Karl Heinrich Kaufhold, "Fragen der Gewerbepolitik und der Gewerbeförderung," in Ekkehard Mai et al., eds., *Kunstpolitik und Kunstförderung im Kaiserreich*, pp. 95–96; Minister für Handel und Gewerbe Theodor von Möller, "Denkschrift über den Stand der Gewerbeförderung im Königreiche Preussen," *Sammlung der Drucksachen des Preussischen Hauses der Abgeordneten* [Anlagen zu den Stenographischen Berichten], 19. Legislaturperiode, V. Session, 1903, Drucksache 92, 1999–2016.

13. Carl Schorske, *German Social Democracy, 1905–1917: The Development of the Great Schism* (Cambridge, Mass.: Harvard University Press, 1955), 9–32.

14. In 1907 Muthesius would assume a prominent role in the German Garden City movement, seeking again to bend the German Garden City Society (*Deutsche Gartenstadtgesellschaft*), founded in 1902, in the direction of centralized, government-influenced reforms. This is discussed in detail in Chapter 6, this volume.

15. Otto March to Hermann Muthesius, July 1, 1897, NMWA. March encourages Muthesius to

develop his study of the English house and other projects in letters from June 16, 1897, and August 27, 1897. On the March–Muthesius correspondence, see the comments of Wiltrud Petsch-Bahr, "Anmerkungen zu dem Briefwechsel von Herman Muthesius aus dem Jahren 1896 bis 1909," in Sonja Günther and Julius Posener, eds., *Hermann Muthesius, 1861–1927*, Ausstellung in der Akademie der Künste von 11. Dezember bis 22, Januar, 1978 (Berlin: Akademie der Künste, 1978), 23–28, esp. 24–26 (hereafter cited as *Muthesius Ausstellungskatalog*).

16. See Werner March, ed., *Otto March 1845–1912: Ein schöpferischer Berliner Architekt der Jahrhundertwende* (Tübingen: Verlag Ernst Wasmuth, 1972); also Stefan Muthesius, *Das englische Vorbild: Eine Studie zu den deutschen Reformbewegungen in Architektur, Wohnbau und Kunstgewerbe im späteren 19. Jahrhundert* (Munich: Prestel Verlag, 1974), 107–10.

17. *Die englische Baukunst der Gegenwart: Beispiele neuer englischer Profanbauten* (Leipzig und Berlin: Cosmos, 1900); *Die neuere kirchliche Baukunst in England: Entwicklung, Bedingungen und Grundzüge des Kirchenbaues der englischen Staatskirche und der Secten* (Berlin: Wilhelm Ernst und Sohn, 1901). See also Laurent Stalder, "'In Wort und Bild': Bemerkungen zum Mappenwerk *Die englische Baukunst der Gegenwart* von Hermann Muthesius," *Scholion* 1 (2002): 123–32.

18. See Muthesius, Letter Book II, NMWA, as well as the discussion in Pasche, "Der Nachlass von Hermann Muthesius im Werkbund-Archiv," pp. 112–13.

19. Prussian goals are discussed in Nipperdey, *Deutsche Geschichte 1866–1918*, Band 2, pp. 621–757; Wehler, *The German Empire, 1871–1918*; Gordon A. Craig, *Germany 1866–1945* (New York: Oxford University Press, 1978), 224–338.

20. Otto Sarazin, "Attachirung von Bautechnikern an einzelne diplomatische Vertretungen im Auslande," *CdB* 2 (1882): 22–23; "Berichte im Ausland," *CdB* 7 (1887): 379–81.

21. Gillian Naylor, *The Arts and Crafts Movement: A Study of Its Sources, Deals, and Influence on Design Theory* (London: Studio Vista, 1971), 15–17, 147, quotation from select committee on p. 147.

22. Letter from Henry Cole to J. W. Henley, March 10, 1852, as quoted in Harry Francis Mallgrave, *Gottfried Semper: Architect of the Nineteenth Century* (New Haven, Conn.: Yale University Press, 1996), 209. See also John Physick, *The Victoria and Albert Museum: The History of Its Building* (Oxford: Phaidon, 1982), 13–32.

23. Hermann Muthesius, "Der Zeichenunterricht in den Londoner Volksschulen," in Karl Muthesius, hrsg., *Beiträge zur Lehrerbildung und Lehrerfortbildung*, Heft 16 (1900), 4–12.

24. GSPK, File I.HA Rep. 120 EX Fach 1. Nr.1 Bd.13 file IIIb.5696 (Oktober 1902).

25. Hermann Muthesius, "Künstlerische Unterricht für Handwerker in England," *Dekorative Kunst* 1 (1898): 15–20, figures from p. 17.

26. More than 100 letters between Muthesius and these architects are part of the Muthesius papers at the Berlin Werkbund Archive (NMWA).

27. A few exemplary articles include: Hermann Muthesius, "Die 'Guild and School of Handicraft' in London," *DK* 2 (1898): 41–48; "Künstlerischer Unterricht für Handwerker in England," *DK* 1 (1898): 15–20; "Der Verein für häusliche Kunstindustrie (Home Arts and Industries Association) und der Diletantismus in den Kleinkünsten in England," *CdB* 20 (1900): 165–67, 173–74, 197–99, 209–12; "Der Zeichenunterricht in den Londoner Volksschulen," in Karl Muthesius, ed., *Beiträge zur Lehrerbildung und Lehrerfortbildung*, Heft 16 (1900). The most complete bibliography of Muthesius's writings is in Hubrich, *Hermann Muthesius*, pp. 317–32.

28. Ruskin, *The Stones of Venice*, 3 vols. (London: Smith, Elder & Co., 1851–53); quotation from vol. 2 of the 1913 edition (Boston: Dana Estes & Co.), 162.

29. Muthesius, *Die englische Baukunst der Gegenwart: Beispiele neuer englischer Profanbauten*, pp. 5–12; Hermann Muthesius, "William Morris und die Fünfte Ausstellung des Kunstgewerbe-Vereins in London," *CdB* 17 (1897): 3–5; 29–30; 39–41, especially p. 4. See also Laurent Stalder, "John Ruskin als Erzieher: Muthesius, England, und die neue nationale Tradition," in Werner Oechslin, ed., *Studien und Texte zur Geschichte der Architekturtheorie: Akten des Colloquiums "John Ruskin: Werk und Wirkung"* (Zürich: GTA Verlag, 2002), 158–69.

30. Muthesius, *Die englische Baukunst der Gegenwart*, p. 20. Muthesius also discusses Shaw at length in *Das englische Haus*, but outlines Shaw's importance most forcefully in this earlier oversized folio work of 1900.

31. Ibid., pp. 18–21.

32. Ibid., p. 20.

33. Andrew Saint, *Richard Norman Shaw* (New Haven, Conn.: Yale University Press, 1976), 133.

34. Ibid., p. 137.

35. Ibid.

36. Wendy Kaplan, "The Lamp of British Precedent: An Introduction to the Arts and Crafts Movement," in Wendy Kaplan, ed., *"The Art That Is Life": The Arts and Crafts Movement in America, 1875–1920* (New York: Little, Brown and Co., 1987), 52.

37. Gillian Naylor, *The Arts and Crafts Movement*, pp. 7–8.

38. Hermann Muthesius, "William Morris und die Fünfte Ausstellung des Kunstgewerbe-Vereins in

London," *CdB* 17 (1897): 3–5; 29–30; 39–41; quotation from p. 4.

39. Peter Stansky, *Redesigning the World: William Morris, the 1880s, and the Arts and Crafts* (Princeton: Princeton University Press, 1985), 262–64; quotation from p. 262.

40. William Morris, "The Socialist Ideal of Art," *New Review* (January 1891), as quoted in Stansky, *Redesigning the World*, p. 66.

41. Muthesius, "William Morris und die Fünfte Ausstellung des Kunstgewerbe-Vereins in London," p. 5; Morris's socialist allegiance is explored in detail in E. P. Thompson, *William Morris: Romantic to Revolutionary* (New York: Pantheon Books, 1955), while a review of English misreadings of Morris's politics can be found in Martin J. Wiener, "The Myth of William Morris," *Albion* 8 (Spring 1976): 67–82.

42. Muthesius, "William Morris und die Fünfte Ausstellung des Kunstgewerbe-Vereins in London," pp. 4–5; 40–41; quotation from p. 5.

43. Hermann Muthesius, "Die 'Guild and School of Handicraft' in London," *DK* 2 (1898): 41–48; "Künstlerischer Unterricht für Handwerker in England," *DK* 1 (1898): 15–20; "Der Verein für häusliche Kunstindustrie (Home Arts and Industries Association) und der Diletantismus in den Kleinkünsten in England," *CdB* 20 (1900): 165–67, 173–74, 197–99, 209–12; "Der Zeichenunterricht in den Londoner Volksschulen," in Karl Muthesius, hrsg., *Beiträge zur Lehrerbildung und Lehrerfortbildung*, Heft 16 (1900).

44. Alan Crawford, *C.R. Ashbee: Architect, Designer, and Romantic Socialist* (New Haven, Conn.: Yale University Press, 1985), 410.

45. Hermann Muthesius, "Die 'Guild and School of Handicraft' in London." I am using the translation as it appears in Crawford, *C.R. Ashbee: Architect, Designer, and Romantic Socialist*, p. 410.

46. Muthesius, "Künstlerischer Unterricht für Handwerker in England," p. 16.

47. Ibid., p. 20.

48. Ashbee as quoted in Crawford, *C.R. Ashbee*, p. 54.

49. C. R. Ashbee, *An Endeavour towards the Teaching of John Ruskin and William Morris* (London: Essex House Press, 1901), 20, as quoted in Crawford, *C.R. Ashbee*, p. 410.

50. Hermann Muthesius, "Die 'Guild and School of Handicraft' in London," *DK* 2 (1898): 41–48; "Künstlerischer Unterricht für Handwerker in England," *DK* 1 (1898): 15–20; "Der Verein für häusliche Kunstindustrie (Home Arts and Industries Association) und der Diletantismus in den Kleinkünsten in England," *CdB* 20 (1900): 165–67, 173–74, 197–99, 209–12; "Der Zeichenunterricht in den Londoner Volksschulen," in Karl Muthesius, hrsg., *Beiträge zur Lehrerbildung und Lehrerfortbildung*, Heft 16 (1900);

Hermann Muthesius "Die Ausbildung des englischen Architekten," *CdB* 17 (1897): 446–48; 459–61.

51. Muthesius "Die Ausbildung des englischen Architekten," p. 447.

52. Godfrey Rubens, *William Richard Lethaby: His Life and Work 1857–1931* (London: The Architectural Press, 1986), 177.

53. Lethaby quoted in ibid., p. 181.

54. Muthesius, "Künstlerischer Unterricht für Handwerker in England," p. 19.

55. Rubens, *William Richard Lethaby: His Life and Work 1857–1931*, p. 183.

56. Muthesius "Künstlerischer Unterricht für Handwerker in England," p. 19. The "study of nature" in the Arts and Crafts movement, of course, is also a major component in the rise of the Art Nouveau at the end of the nineteenth century; see Meredith L. Clausen, *Frantz Jourdain and the Samaritaine: Art Nouveau Theory and Criticism* (Leiden: E.J. Brill, 1987); Amy Ogata, *Art Nouveau and the Social Vision of Modern Living*; Debora L. Silverman, *Art Nouveau in Fin-de-Siècle France: Politics, Psychology, and Style* (Berkeley: University of California Press, 1989).

57. Muthesius's observations about the social structure of arts and crafts education and the role of women of different classes is corroborated in Anthea Callen's study, *Women Artists of the Arts and Crafts Movement, 1870–1914* (New York: Pantheon, 1979), especially pp. 2–15.

58. Muthesius, "Der Verein fuer häusliches Kunstindustrie," p. 211.

59. Ibid.

60. Ibid.

61. Ibid.

62. Ibid.

63. Muthesius, *Stilarchitektur und Baukunst* (see Introduction, this volume, n. 53).

64. Otto Wagner, *Modern Architecture: A Guidebook for his Students to This Field of Art*, trans. by Harry Francis Mallgrave (Santa Monica, Calif.: Getty Center for the History of Art and the Humanities, 1988). See also Harry Francis Mallgrave, ed., *Otto Wagner: Reflections on the Raiment of Modernity* (Santa Monica, Calif.: Getty Center for the History of Art and the Humanities, 1993).

65. Richard Streiter, "Aus München," (1896), in Richard Streiter, *Ausgewählte Schriften zur Aesthetik und Kunstgeschichte* (Munich: Delphin, 1913), 32, as quoted and discussed in Stanford Anderson, "Style-Architecture and Building-Art: Realist Architecture as the Vehicle for a Renewal of Culture," introduction to Hermann Muthesius, *Style-Architecture and Building-Art: Transformations of Architecture in the Nineteenth Century and Its Present Condition* (Santa Monica, Calif.: Getty Center for the History of Art and the Humanities, 1994), 16.

66. Muthesius, *Stilarchitektur und Baukunst*, 25–30; 49–66; for a broader discussion of architects' debates about the relevance of classical and Gothic tradition for nineteenth- and twentieth-century architecture, see Richard A. Etlin, *Frank Lloyd Wright and Le Corbusier: The Romantic Legacy* (Manchester: Manchester University Press, 1994), 150–99.

67. See Dohme's discussion of the "grace of line that derives from the purposefulness" of such objects as "modern wagons and ships" in Dohme, *Das englische Haus*, p. 42. Also Streiter, *Ausgewählte Schriften*, pp. 11, 83.

68. Ibid., pp. 7, 9.

69. Ibid., pp. 53, 56; see Adolf Loos, "Architektur" (1910), *Sämtliche Schriften* (Wien: Verlag Herold, 1962), 302–18.

70. Muthesius, *Stilarchitektur und Baukunst*, p. 66.

71. In this view Muthesius was influenced by Heinrich Hübsch, *In What Style Shall We Build?* (1828) (Santa Monica, Calif.: Getty Center for the History of Art and the Humanities, 1993).

72. Muthesius, *Stilarchitektur und Baukunst*, pp. 24–25.

73. Ibid., p. 10.

74. Ibid., p. 36. For this quotation I have used the translation by Stanford Anderson as he has rendered it in Hermann Muthesius, *Style-Architecture and Building-Art*, p. 69.

75. *Stilarchitektur und Baukunst*, p. 34.

76. Ibid., pp. 57–58. This positive regard for one element of *Jugendstil* design helps to explain Muthesius's decision to design a *Jugendstil* cover for the book's first edition. The architect's sketch for this cover is at the Berlin Werkbund Archives and is also reproduced in Siepmann and Thiekötter, eds., *Hermann Muthesius im Werkbund-Archiv*, p. 22. By the time Muthesius published the second edition in 1903 – in which he was much more critical of the *Jugendstil* – the cover had been replaced with more straightforward block lettering.

77. Muthesius, *Stilarchitektur und Baukunst*, p. 59. A recent discussion of the relationship of style to fashion in the development of modern German design can be found in Frederic J. Schwartz, *The Werkbund*.

78. Muthesius, *Stilarchitektur und Baukunst*, pp. 34–35.

79. Ibid., pp. 50–51; I am here using the translation in Anderson, *Style-Architecture and Building-Art*, p. 79. On Semper, see Wolfgang Hermann, *Gottfried Semper: In Search of Architecture* (Cambridge, Mass.: MIT Press, 1984); Harry Francis Mallgrave foregrounds Muthesius's respect for Semper's built works and for Semper's book *Der Stil* in his book *Gottfried Semper: Architect of the Nineteenth Century* (New Haven, Conn.: Yale University Press, 1996), 370–71.

80. On Kaiser Wilhelm II and the German Naval policies, see V. R. Berghahn, *Germany and the Approach of War in 1914*, 2nd ed. (London: Macmillan Press, 1993); John C. G. Röhl, *The Kaiser and his Court: Wilhelm II and the Government of Germany*, trans. by Terence F. Cole (Cambridge: Cambridge University Press, 1994), 3–69; Eckart Kehr, *Battleship Building and Party Politics in Germany* (Chicago: University of Chicago Press, 1975); Christopher Clark, *Kaiser Wilhelm II: Profiles in Power* (Essex: Pearson Education Ltd., 2000).

81. See Schmidt's letter of thanks to Muthesius, June 3, 1906, NMWA, as well as the illustrations of the officers' dining quarters and officers' lounge on His Majesty's Battle Cruiser "Danzig" in Direktorium der Ausstellung, *Das Deutsche Kunstgewerbe 1906: III. Deutsche Kunstgewerbe-Ausstellung Dresden 1906* (Munich: F. Bruckmann, 1906), 156 (hereafter the book title is abbreviated as *Das Deutsche Kunstgewerbe 1906*). Muthesius would also design the Kaiser's personal quarters, or "Kaiser-Kabinen," on the steamer *Bismarck* for the Deutscher Werkbund Exhibition in Cologne in 1914.

82. "Annalen der Weimarer Zeit," in *Henry van de Velde: Weimar, 1902–1915* Exhibition Catalog from March 31 to April 28, 1963, (Weimar: Kunsthalle Weimar, 1963), 12.

83. Muthesius, *Stilarchitektur und Baukunst*, p. 62.

84. Ibid.

85. Ibid., p. 64.

86. *Stilarchitektur und Baukunst*, 2nd ed. (Mühlheim-Ruhr: Verlag K. Schimmelpfeng, 1903), 60–81.

87. Ibid., p. 60; here I am using the translation by Stanford Anderson, *Style-Architecture and Building-Art*, p. 87.

88. Ibid., p. 75.

89. Ibid., pp. 69–70.

90. See, for example, GStA PK, File I.H.A. Rep.120 E X Fach 1 Nr. 6, *Die Organisation der Handwerker- und Kunstgewerbeschulen* [Dez. 1901–Nov. 1904]. The basis for this file is the directive and questionnaire by Minister für Handel und Gewerbe Theodor von Möller, "An die Herren Regierungs-Präsidenten zu Düsseldorf," pp. 1–6. The complete list of cities included Dusseldorf, Potsdam, Breslau, Posen, Cologne, Cassel, Magdeburg, Erfurt, and Hannover.

91. March to Muthesius, October 26, 1904, NMWA.

92. Wasmuth would become famous for publishing the large-format "Wasmuth Portfolio" of the American architect Frank Lloyd Wright's works in 1910.

93. Ibid., p. 11.

94. William R. Lethaby, *Form in Civilization* (London: Oxford University Press, 1922), as quoted

in Posener, "Muthesius in England," in Architectural Association, ed., *Hermann Muthesius 1861–1927*, Exhibition of the Architectural Association in London in September 1979 (London: Architectural Association, 1979), 6.

95. Julius Posener and Burkhard Bergius, "Individuell geplante Einfamilienhäuser 1896–1918," in Architekten- und Ingenieur-Verein zu Berlin, ed., *Berlin und seine Bauten*, Teil 4, Bd. C: Wohnungsbau (Berlin: Ernst & Sohn, 1975), 11. The classic work on Berlin's Mietskaserne phenomenon remains Werner Hegemann, *Das steinerne Berlin*, Bauwelt Fundamente 3 (Frankfurt a. M.: Ullstein Verlag, 1963).

96. *Stilarchitektur und Baukunst*, 2nd ed., p. 75.

97. Posener and Bergius, "Individuell geplante Einfamilienhäuser 1896–1918," especially the section "Stadtfeindschaft und ihr Einfluss auf die Entstehung der Villenvororte," in *Berlin und seine Bauten*, pp. 4–5.

98. Muthesius, *Das englische Haus*, 3 vols. (Berlin: Ernst Wasmuth, 1904), vol. 1: Entwicklung, 6.

99. Muthesius, *Das englische Haus*, vol. 1, p. 178.

100. Muthesius to the Commerce Ministry's Geheimrat Dönhoff, January 9, 1903, NMWA, Letter Book II (emphasis original); Muthesius to Public Works Ministry, January 10, 1903, NMWA, Letter Book II.

101. Robert Kerr, *The Gentleman's House or How to Plan English Residences, from the Parsonage to the Palace* (London: John Murray, 1865); Robert Dohme *Das englische Haus: eine Kultur-und baugeschichtliche Skizze* (Braunschweig: George Westermann, 1888). Articles clipped by Muthesius from English journals are contained in a large binder entitled *Material englisches Haus*, which Muthesius brought back with him from London, NMWA.

102. Muthesius, *Das englische Haus*, vol. 1, pp. 13–87; quotation from p. 150.

103. March to Muthesius, July 1, 1897, and June 16, 1897; quotation from July 1, 1897, NMWA.

104. Andrew Jackson Downing, *Cottage Residences; or, A Series of Designs for the Rural Cottages and Cottage Villas, and Their Gardens and Grounds, Adapted to North America*, 2nd ed. (New York and London: Wiley and Putnam, 1844); A. J. Downing, *The Architecture of Country Houses, Including Designs for Cottages, Farm-Houses, and Villas, with Remarks on Interiors, Furniture, and the Best Modes of Warming and Insulating* (New York: D. Appleton & Co., 1853); Robert Kerr, *The Gentleman's House*; Robert Dohme, *Das englische Haus*. Muthesius's three-volume work follows in the tradition of these writings, of which his studies and extensive research in British libraries had made him aware. Although Muthesius makes no mention of Downing's work in the United States in *Das englische Haus*, he was likely aware of it, just

as he was aware of American domestic architectural developments; Muthesius began featuring the works of American architects in books like *Landhaus und Garten* in 1907 (Munich: F. Bruckmann, 1907).

105. Muthesius, *Das englische* Haus, vol. 1, p. 139.

106. Andrew Saint, *Richard Norman Shaw*, pp. 201–10; Mark Girouard, *Sweetness and Light: The 'Queen Anne' Movement, 1860–1900* (Oxford: Oxford University Press, 1977), 160–76; Elizabeth Aslin, *The Aesthetic Movement: Prelude to Art Nouveau* (New York: Frederick A. Praeger, 1969), 14–16; 49–66. Muthesius's polemics concerning home design, real-estate development, and Bedford Park – written in conjunction with the growth of his Berlin-based architectural practice beginning in 1904 – are examined in Chapter 5, this volume.

107. Ibid., p. 5.

108. As James Kornwulf has pointed out, the younger generation appeared to Muthesius to have moved beyond the lingering *Stilarchitektur* of the generation of Shaw. This generation, which had mingled elements from past styles in the Queen Anne, had given way to an energetic young group of practitioners of a modern *Baukunst*. James D. Kornwulf, *M. H. Baillie Scott and the Arts and Crafts Movement* (Baltimore, Md.: Johns Hopkins Press, 1972), 324.

109. Stuart Durant, *CFA Voysey, 1857–1941*, Architectural Monographs No. 19 (London: St. Martin's Press, 1992), 15; see also Wendy Hitchmough, *C. F. A. Voysey* (London: Phaidon, 1995).

110. The Freudenberg house and other Muthesius projects are examined in their particular architectural and cultural context in Chapter 5, this volume.

111. Muthesius, *Das englische Haus*, vol. 1, p. 177, as quoted in Kornwulf, *M.H. Baillie Scott and the Arts and Crafts Movement*, p. 324. Hermann Muthesius, *Das moderne Landhaus und seine innere Ausstattung* (Munich: F. Bruckmann, 1904); *Das moderne Landhaus und seine innere Ausstattung*, 2. verbesserte und vermehrte Auflage (Munich: F. Bruckmann, 1905); *Landhaus und Garten: Beispiele neuzeitlicher Landhäuser nebst Grundrissen, Innenräumen und Gärten* (Munich: F. Bruckmann, 1907).

112. Hermann Muthesius, *Landhaus und Garten*.

113. Muthesius and his wife, Anna, developed a close relationship with Mackintosh and Margaret Macdonald-Mackintosh; Charles Rennie Mackintosh, for example, was godfather to Muthesius's youngest son, Eckart (1904–89; also an architect), and two gifts from the Mackintoshes, a hanging lamp and a stained-glass window, hung in the Muthesius home in Berlin-Nikolassee. On Eckart Muthesius, see Reto Niggl, *Eckart Muthesius: Der Palast des Maharadschas in Indore, Architektur und Interieur* (Stuttgart: Arnoldsche, 1996).

114. Muthesius, *Das englische Haus*, vol. 2, p. 237; vol. 3, p. 240.

115. On the English study tour, see Geheimes Ober-Regierungsrat Dönhoff, Regierungs und Gewerbeschulrat von Czihak, und Landbauinspektor Doctor Muthesius, "Das Gewerbliche Unterrichtswesen in Grossbritannien, auf Grund einer Studienreise im Jahre 1903," in Preussischen Haus der Abgeordneten, 20. Legislatur-Periode, I. Session 1904–05, Drucksache Nr. 70, pp. 1347–80.

116. The significance of Muthesius's architectural practice for his Berlin context is examined in Chapter 5, this volume.

117. Behrens to Muthesius, January 21, 1903, NMWA.

THREE. PRUSSIAN APPLIED-ARTS REFORMS: CULTURE, CLASS, AND THE MODERN ECONOMY

1. No published research to date is based on either the Commerce Ministry or the *Landesgewerbeamt* files at the Prussian State Archives. Until 1989 the relevant materials were in the difficult-to-access city of Merseberg in the former GDR, as several scholars of this subject have noted. See Jan S. Kunstreich, "Hermann Muthesius (1861–1927) und die Reform der preussischen Kunstgewerbeschulen," *Nordelbingen: Beitraege zur Kunst- und Kulturgeschichte* 47 (1978): 128–40. Gisela Moeller, "Die preussischen Kunstgewerbeschulen," in Ekkehard Mai et al., eds., *Kunstpolitik und Kunstforderung im Kaiserreich: Kunst im Wandel der Sozial- und Wirtschaftsgeschichte*, vol. 2 (Berlin: Gebr. Mann Verlag, 1982), 113–29. The best coverage of Muthesius's published writings in connection to Prussian school reform efforts is in Hans-Joachim Hubrich, *Hermann Muthesius: Die Schriften zu Architektur, Kunstgewerbe, Industrie in der "Neuen Bewegung,"* pp. 191–218. Gisela Moeller draws connections between Muthesius's school reforms and Peter Behrens's activities as director of the Prussian Arts and Crafts school (or *Kunstgewerbeschule*) in Dusseldorf in her model study, *Peter Behrens in Düsseldorf: Die Jahre von 1903 bis 1907* (Weinheim: VCH Verlagsgesellschaft, 1991).

2. The words *sachlich*, *wirtschaftlich*, and *zweckmässig* appear in the Commerce Minister's "Instructional Workshops Decree" (*Lehrwerkstätten Erlass*) of December 15, 1904. See the development of Muthesius's increasingly forcible drafts in GStA PK, I.HA Rep. 120 EX Fach 1 Nr. 1 Bd. 14, file III b.8731.

3. The historical circumstances behind Muthesius's representation of the early nineteenth century in this way are examined later in this chapter.

4. Prussia's Commerce Ministry studied other regions intently during the early years of the twentieth century to glean precise knowledge of what other states and nations were doing to overhaul their arts, crafts, and trades education systems for greater effectiveness in a modern economy. See the Commerce Ministry reports to the Prussian legislature (*Abgeordnetenhaus*): F. Doenhoff, Eugen von Czihak, and Hermann Muthesius, "Das gewerbliche Unterrichtswesen in Grossbritannien, Auf Grund einer Studienreise im Jahre 1903," in *Sammlung der Drucksachen des preussischen Hauses der Abgeordneten*, 20. Legislatur-periode, I. Session 1904/05, Bd.2, Drucksache 70 (Berlin: W. Moeser, 1904), 1347–80; "Bericht des Geheimen Ober-Regierungsrats Simon ueber die im Mai 1903 nach Oesterreich unternommene Studienreise," in ibid., pp. 1312–46; Hermann von Seefeld, "Die Förderung des Kleingewerbes in Hessen, Baden, Württemberg, Elsass-Lothringen und der Schweiz, Auf Grund einer Studienreise im Jahre 1903," 20. Legislaturperiode, I. Session 1904/05, Bd.4, Drucksache 142 (Berlin: W. Moeser, 1904), 2159–214.

5. Heinrich A. Winkler, *Mittelstand, Demokratie, und Nationalsozialismus* (Cologne: Kiepenheuer & Witsch, 1972); Herman Lebovics, *Social Conservatism and the Middle Classes in Germany, 1914–1933* (Princeton: Princeton University Press, 1969), 6–11. After Theodor Möller's dismissal in 1905, Kaiser Wilhelm II granted him the customary aristocratic title in recognition of his state service. In the years that he served as Commerce Minister, however (1901–05), he was not yet Theodor *von* Möller, and will be referred to as Theodor Möller.

6. Both Muthesius and Behrens agreed to work for the ministry in late 1902, although they would not begin service until early 1903 in Behrens's case, and summer 1903 in Muthesius's case.

7. Heidrun Walther, *Theodor Adolf von Möller, 1840–1925: Lebensbild eines westfälischen Industriellen* (Neustadt an der Aisch: Verlag Degener & Co., 1958), 54–55. On Möller, see also Hans-Heinrich Borchard, *50 Jahre Preussisches Ministerium für Handel und Gewerbe, 1879–1929* (Berlin: Reichsverlag H. Kalkoff, 1929), 52–55; 149–50; Stefan Hartmann, "Theodor Adolf von Möller," in Historische Kommission bei der Bayerischen Akademie der Wissenschaften, ed., *Neue Deutsche Biographie* 18 (Berlin: Duncker & Humblot, 1994), 634–35.

8. Geoff Eley, *Reshaping the German Right: Radical Nationalism and Political Change after Bismarck* (New Haven, Conn.: Yale University Press, 1980).

9. Walther, *Möller*, pp. 30–49; 62–64.

10. Ibid., p. 62.

11. Quoted in Walther, *Möller*, p. 64.

12. Ibid. p. 93.

13. Letter from Theodor Möller to his daughter, Irmgard Möller, May 5, 1901, as quoted in Walther, *Möller*, pp. 67–68.

14. Ibid., p. 152.

15. Ibid. On Caprivi, see J. Alden Nichols, *Germany after Bismarck: The Caprivi Era, 1890–1914* (Cambridge, Mass.: Harvard University Press, 1958).

16. Ministerium für Handel und Gewerbe, "Denkschrift über die Begründung eines Landesgewerbeamts und eines ständigen Beirats," in *Anlagen zum Staatshaushalts-Etat für das Etatsjahr 1905*, II. Band (Nr.16, Beilage G, Handels- u. Gewerbeverwaltung), 92.

17. Möller, as quoted in Walther, *Möller*, p. 157.

18. See Chapter 2, this volume.

19. Hermann von Seefeld and Heinrich Neuhaus commissioned among the earliest private homes from Muthesius, helping him launch his architectural practice in 1904; this is discussed in Chapter 5, this volume.

20. For details of the process by which Behrens was hired, see Gisela Moeller, *Peter Behrens in Düsseldorf: Die Jahre von 1903 bis 1907* (Weinheim: VCH Verlagsgesellschaft, 1991), pp. 17–22.

21. Letter from Behrens to Dehmel, November 27, 1902, as quoted in Moeller, *Peter Behrens in Düsseldorf*, p. 22.

22. The State Trades Board (*Landesgewerbeamt*) differs from a "State Board of Trade" (with which Muthesius is often errantly associated). A Board of Trade implies commerce, whereas the purpose of the Commerce Ministry's State Trades Board was to regulate and improve conditions in the trades – fields such as textile weaving, machine assembly, the building trades, and the applied arts.

23. "Denkschrift über die Begründung eines Landesgewerbeamts und eines ständigen Beirats," p. 93.

24. Wehler, *Deutsche Gesellschaftsgeschichte*, Bd. 3 pp. 683–85.

25. Shulamit Volkov, *The Rise of Popular Anti-Modernism in Germany*.

26. Hermann Muthesius, "Diskussion auf der 1. Jahresversammlung des Deutschen Werkbundes München 1908," in Siepmann und Thiekötter, eds., *Hermann Muthesius im Werkbund-Archiv*, p. 58.

27. Letter from Karl Schmidt to Muthesius, March 16, 1903, NMWA.

28. See Wilhelm Waetzoldt, "Die Entwicklung des kunstgewerblichen Unterrichtswesens in Preussen," *Deutsche Rundschau* 176 (1918): 228–45; 368–80; Miron Mislin, "Zum Verhältnis von Architektur, Kunstgewerbe und Industrie 1790–1850," in Eckhard Siepmann und Angelika Thiekoetter, eds., *Packeis und Pressglas: Von der Kunstgewerbebewegung zum Deutschen Werkbund*, Werkbund Archiv Band 16 (Giessen: Anabas-Verlag, 1987), 41–48.

29. Waetzold, pp. 371–80; Moeller "Die preußischen Kunstgewerbeschulen," pp. 114, 127. Both Waetzold and Moeller cite another work, by Oskar Simon, as an invaluable source on crafts and trades education: Oskar Simon, *Die Fachausbildung des preussischen Gewerbe- und Handelsstandes im 18.*

und 19. Jahrhundert (Berlin: Wasmuth, 1902), especially pp. 669–77 and 709–20. Contrary to popular historical opinion, the crafts and small trades did not all suffer uniformly throughout Germany during nineteenth-century industrialization: In some regions, crafts and other *kleingewerbliche* economic activities, as well as the relative incomes of their producers, actually increased. See Karl Heinrich Kaufhold, "Fragen der Gewerbepolitik und der Gewerbeförderung," in Mai et al., eds., *Kunstpolitik und Kunstforderung im Kaiserreich*, vol. 2, pp. 95–110; also see Frank B. Tipton Jr., *Regional Variations in the Economic Development of Germany during the Nineteenth Century* (Middletown: Weslyan University Press, 1976).

30. Norbert Eisold, *Die Kunstgewerbe- und Handwerkerschule Magdeburg 1793–1963* (Magdeburg: Kloster, 1993), 14–17.

31. Hermann Muthesius wrote two major articles on the historical background and contemporary circumstances of Prussia's schools, subdivided into sections on origins, pedagogical methods, administrative reforms, and levels of state support. See "Kunstgewerbliche und handwerkliche Unterrichtsanstalten: Geschichtliche Entwicklung," *I. Verwaltungsbericht des Koeniglich Preussischen Landesgewerbeamts 1905* (Berlin: Carl Heymanns Verlag, 1906), 88–106, and, in the same volume, "Heutiger Stand des kunstgewerblichen und handwerklichen Schulwesens," pp. 107–29 (hereafter abbreviated *VB* (1905); subsequent years of this report follow the "*VB*" in brackets). *Verwaltungsbericht* articles, like other articles by government officials, were more often than not published without any author's name. Nevertheless reviewed, excerpted, and republished in various publications that supported the new direction that the arts and crafts were taking in Germany in the opening years of the twentieth century, these two Muthesius articles in particular enjoyed an enduring publishing history that lasted through the 1920s. See "Geschichtliche Entwicklung des Kunstunterrichts im XVIII. Jahrhundert. Für Preussen Bearbeitet von Dr. Hermann Muthesius," *Hohe Warte* 2 (1905): 159. Also see "Auszug aus dem Verwaltungsbericht des Königl. Preussischen Landesgewerbeamts 1905: Die neuere Entwicklung der Kunstgewerbeschulen" and "Heutiger Stand des kunstgewerblichen Schulwesens in Preussen," in Königliches Preussisches Ministerium für Handel und Gewerbe, *Nachrichten über die Preussischen Kunstgewerbeschulen: Zusammengestellt gelegentlich der mit der 3. Deutschen Kunstgewerbeausstellung in Dresden 1906 Verbundenen Ausstellung Preussische Kunstgewerbeschulen* (Berlin: Julius Sittenfeld, o. J. (1906)): 9–17; 18–47. Also in Direktorium der Austellung, hrsg., *3. Deutsche Kunstgewerbe Ausstellung Dresden 1906, Ausstellungszeitung* (Dresden: Wilh. Baensch, 1906), 225–28; 244–45. The articles' succinct yet

detailed review of historical developments in the German and Prussian arts and crafts industries and in education undoubtedly contributed to their popularity in the 1920s, when they were reproduced in abridged form with slightly altered titles. See, for example, Hermann Muthesius, "Die neuere Entwicklung des kunstgewerblichen Gedankens und ihr Einfluss auf die Schulen," *Zeitschrift für Berufs- und Fachschulwesen*, 43 (1928): 1–3.

32. Muthesius, *VB* (1905), pp. 89, 101. Muthesius's characterization of eighteenth-century relations across the spectrum of artistic fields as harmonious also recalled the descriptions of his popular 1902 tract, *Stilarchitektur und Baukunst*; see esp. pp. 7–12.

33. Muthesius, *VB* (1905), pp. 88–89.

34. See Muthesius, *Stilarchitektur und Baukunst* (1902), pp. 7–9; 56.

35. See note 31, this chapter.

36. Our language still bears the traces of the imprecision and slippages that occur when a term like "design" is used to refer to industrial design, decorative arts, or even architecture itself, as when architecture practitioners can still be heard to refer to themselves as "designers."

37. Goethe had classified the crafts and trades as "strict arts" (*strenge Kuenste*), as opposed to the "free arts" (*freie Kuenste*). Barbara Mundt, *Die deutsche Kunstgewerbemuseen im 19. Jahrhundert* (Munich: Prestel, 1974), 14–15. See also Monika Franke, "Schoenheit und Bruttosozialprodukt: Motive der Kunstgewerbebewegung," in Siepmann und Thiekoetter (1987), pp. 167–73.

38. Muthesius, *VB* (1905), p. 92; Moeller (1982), p. 114.

39. Heinrich Waentig identified the interruption of Semper's career in Dresden, and particularly the way he took care in such works as the Dresden opera house to design down to the last crafts detail, as the first half of the nineteenth century's failed "last attempt to save art for the crafts," after which the undermining of the crafts by machine production was unstoppable. Heinrich Waentig, *Wirtschaft und Kunst: Eine Untersuchung über Geschichte und Theorie der Modernen Kunstgewerbebewegung* (Jena: Gustav Fischer, 1909), 233–38.

40. Ruskin's critique is discussed in Chapter 2, this volume, and for this reason is left out of the analysis of government reform efforts here.

41. The establishment of nineteenth-century museums as centers of crafts education and revival is discussed in Mundt, *Die deutsche Kunstgewerbemuseen*, pp. 152–64. Muthesius railed against these institutions in his own *Stilarchitektur und Baukunst* polemic, calling them useless warehouses of art that missed valuable opportunities to educate the public when they could well have taken on this role; see

Stilarchitektur und Baukunst, pp. 22–23. Mundt, the current director of the Berlin Kunstgewerbemuseum, defends nineteenth-century museums against accusations that they were bastions of historicism and bad taste (cf. Mundt, *Die deutsche Kunstgewerbemuseen*, p. 17).

42. Mundt, *Die deutsche Kunstgewerbemuseen*, p. 15. Used in isolated instances earlier in the nineteenth century, the word *Kunstgewerbe* had even appeared in the title of Nürnberg's *Kunstgewerbeschule*, but this usage was one of the rare exceptions until after the mid-1860s. The word still had not appeared in the second edition of Meyer's *Neuem Konversations-Lexikon* in 1865, while in Grimm's dictionary in 1873 the words *Kunstgewerbe* and *Kunstindustrie* appeared as synonyms. See also Monika Fraenke, "Schoenheit und Bruttosozialprodukt: Motive der Kunstgewerbebewegung," in Siepmann and Thiekötter, eds., *Packeis und Pressglas*, p. 47.

43. Mundt, *Die deutsche Kunstgewerbemuseen*, pp. 14–15; Fraenke, in Siepmann und Thiekötter, pp. 41–48.

44. Waentig, *Wirtschaft und Kunst*, especially his concluding chapters "Kunst und Arbeit," and "Kunst und Beduerfnis," pp. 298–410. I am also indebted to the discussion in Günther von Pechmann's *Die Qualitätsarbeit: Ein Handbuch für Industrielle, Kaufleute, Gewerbepolitiker* (Frankfurt: Frankfurter Societäts-Druckerei, 1924), 54–56.

45. Von Pechmann, *Die Qualitätsarbeit*, pp. 54–56.

46. Von Eitelberg's address to the Munich *Kunstgewerbeausstellung* of 1876 is quoted in von Pechmann, *Die Qualitätsarbeit*, p. 58. Von Eitelberg's statements hearkened back to those made in the 1820s by Henri de Saint-Simon, inventor of the term "avant-garde," who in his time was a strong advocate of artists as leaders in a cooperative union of scientists and industrial producers. See Frank Trommler, "The Creation of a Culture of *Sachlichkeit*," in Geoff Eley, ed., *Society, Culture and the State in Germany, 1870–1930* (Ann Arbor: University of Michigan Press, 1996), 481–82.

47. Anton Springer, "Reform des Kunstgewerbes," *Im neuen Reich* (1874), cited in Kunstreich, p. 132.

48. See Wilhelm Waetzoldt, "Die Entwicklung des kunstgewerblichen Unterrichtswesens in Preussen," p. 366.

49. "Deutschlands Industrie hat das Grundprinzip billig und schlecht." Franz Reuleaux, *Briefe aus Philadelphia* (Braunschweig: 1877), p. 5, quoted in Moeller, "Die preussischen Kunstgewerbeschulen," p. 115.

50. The ministry's name is even more imposing in the original: *Das Ministerium der geistlichen, Unterrichts- und Medizinalangelegenheiten*. "Rückblick auf die Entwickelung des

gewerblichen Schulwesens in Preussen von 1884–1909." *Ministerial-Blatt der Handels- und Gewerbe-Verwaltung* 11 (6. Mai 1910) (Beilage): 155–64.

51. Hans Goldschmidt, *Das Reich und Preussen im Kampf um die Führung* (Berlin: Carl Heymanns Verlag, 1931), 15–16; 280–83.

52. Friedrich Facius, *Wirtschaft und Staat: Die Entwicklung der staatlichen Wirtschaftsverwaltung in Deutschland vom 17. Jahrhundert bis 1945*, Schriften des Bundesarchivs 6 (Boppard am Rhein: Harald Boldt Verlag, 1959), 68.

53. As already noted in the Introduction to this volume, Bismarck would argue that "The Prussian Commerce Ministry is in the long run a political impossibility, just as is one from Mecklenburg or Saxony." Ibid., p. 67.

54. Friedrich Facius, *Wirtschaft und Staat*, pp. 59–60; also Rudolf Morsey, *Die Oberste Reichsverwaltung Unter Bismarck, 1867–1890* (Münster: Verlag Aschendorf, 1957), 210–13.

55. "Rückblick auf die Entwickelung des gewerblichen Schulwesens in Preussen von 1884–1909," pp. 155–64; quote from p. 155.

56. "Denkschrift über die Begründung eines Landesgewerbeamts und eines ständigen Beirats," p. 91.

57. Muthesius cites an 1868 report from Martin Gropius, Walter Gropius's great uncle and the architect of the Berlin *Kunstgewerbemuseum*, as a model for progressive thinking that was lost in the midst of the reshuffling of ministerial responsibilities, as well as an 1891 memorandum that blindly recommended a new school for every city above 33,000 residents, regardless of the type of school or the economic background of the region. Muthesius, *VB* (1906), pp. 93, 98.

58. Minister für Handel und Gewerbe Theodor von Möller, "An die Herren Regierungs-Präsidenten zu Düsseldorf," GStA PK, I.H.A. Rep.120 E X Fach 1 Nr. 6, *Die Organisation der Handwerker- und Kunstgewerbeschulen* (Dez. 1901–Nov. 1904), especially pp. 1–6, which contain von Möller's detailed questionnaire about individual schools throughout Prussia.

59. GStA PK, File I.H.A. Rep.120 E X Fach 1 Nr. 6, *Die Organisation der Handwerker- und Kunstgewerbeschulen* (Dez. 1901–Nov. 1904). The basis for this file is the directive and questionnaire by Minister Theodor Möller, "An die Herren Regierungs-Praesidenten zu Duesseldorf" (2 December 1901), pp. 1–6. The complete list of cities included Dusseldorf, Potsdam, Breslau, Posen, Cologne, Cassel, Magdeburg, Erfurt, and Hannover.

60. The memorandum also asked local officials whether a particular school in each region should be singled out and improved by the state to educate especially talented students; how preparatory school education could be fitted better to the needs of the arts and crafts schools; how specialized schools should teach in relation to the general schools and the lower schools; and how the strengths of particular arts, crafts, and trades schools could best be oriented to serve the needs of local economies. Other important questions involved the need for and organization of instructional workshops, the consideration of fixed curricula across schools and subject areas, requirements for the acceptance of students, and the question of whether and how to institute school fees. Ibid., pp. 2–3.

61. See Minister für Handel und Gewerbe Möller, "Denkschrift über den Stand der Gewerbeförderung im Königreiche Preussen," *Sammlung der Drucksachen des Preussischen Hauses der Abgeordneten* (Anlagen zu den Stenographischen Berichten), 19. Legislaturperiode, V. Session, 1903, Drucksache 92, 1999–2016. The first page of this report to the legislature by the Commerce Minister gives the official view explaining why the "sharp delimitation of the *Handwerkerschulen* relative to the *Fortbildungsschulen* below them and the *Kunstgewerbeschulen* above them has not yet succeeded."

62. Report of *Kunstgewerbe- und Handwerkerschuldirektor* Emil Thormählen in Magdeburg (February 1902), in GStA PK, *Die Organisation der Handwerker- und Kunstgewerbeschulen*, p. 20. Report of the Breslau *Regierungs-Präsident*, March 10, 1902, in ibid., pp. 57, 60, 75. Interestingly, the latter report also warns against the danger that the Austrians represented to the quality of teaching in the German schools in light of increasing international competition. The Austrian journals, it appears, after twenty years of advertising for teachers of Austrian *Kunstgewerbeschulen* only in their domestic press, had recently begun advertising these positions in the German arts journals as well.

63. The England school study tour, for which Behrens joined Muthesius for sixteen of the twenty-seven schools visited, was certainly one occasion in which school reform must have been the topic of extended discussion; other occasions are clear from correspondence between Muthesius and Behrens concentrated in fall 1902 and winter 1903 (see Behrens to Muthesius, 1/23/1903, 4/14/03, and 8/1/03 in Werkbund-Archiv, Nachlass Muthesius). Peter Behrens's years in Dusseldorf are recounted in detail in Gisela Moeller, *Peter Behrens in Düsseldorf*.

64. Christian P. W. Beuth und Karl Friedrich Schinkel, "Vorbilder für Fabrikanten und Handwerker (Berlin: 1821), as discussed in Norbert Eisold, *Die Kunstgewerbe- und Handwerkerschule Magdeburg 1793–1963* (Magdeburg: Kloster, 1993), 14–17.

65. Dönhoff, Muthesius, von Seefeld, and Simon undertook a series of applied-arts school study tours to glean precise knowledge of what neighboring states and nations were doing to overhaul their arts, crafts, and trades education systems for greater effectiveness in a modern economy. See the Commerce Ministry reports to the Prussian Chamber of Deputies (*Abgeordnetenhaus*): F. Dönhoff, Eugen von Czihak, and Hermann Muthesius, "Das gewerbliche Unterrichtswesen in Grossbritannien, Auf Grund einer Studienreise im Jahre 1903," in *Sammlung der Drucksachen des preussischen Hauses der Abgeordneten*, 20. Legislatur-periode, I. Session 1904/05, Bd.2, Drucksache 70 (Berlin: W. Moeser, 1904), 1347–80 (Peter Behrens went to Britain especially to join this tour); Oskar Simon, "Bericht des Geheimen Ober-Regierungsrats Simon über die im Mai 1903 nach Oesterreich unternommene Studienreise," in ibid., pp. 1312–46; Hermann Von Seefeld, "Die Förderung des Kleingewerbes in Hessen, Baden, Württemberg, Elsass-Lothringen und der Schweiz, Auf Grund einer Studienreise im Jahre 1903," *Sammlung der Drucksachen des preussischen Hauses der Abgeordneten*, 20. Legislatur-periode, I. Session 1904/05, Bd.4, Drucksache 142 (Berlin: W. Moeser, 1904), 2159–2214.

66. GStA PK, I.HA 120 EX Fach1 Nr.1 Bd.13 File IIIb.8130, "Ergebnisse der Besichtigung der Kunstgewerbe- und Handwerkerschulen in Düsseldorf, Crefeld, Elberfeld, Barmen, Coeln, Iserlohn, Halle, Erfurt, Kassel und Hannover im Juli und August 1903" (signed and dated Hermann Muthesius, Oktober 15, 1903), 8; the forty-two-page report is hereafter cited as "Ergebnisse."

67. Ibid., p. 10.

68. "Es handelt sich um die Fähigkeit, tektonisch zu bilden, eine Fähigkeit, die auf einem völlig andern Gebiete liegt." Ibid., p. 11.

69. "[E]ine tektonische Zeichnung mit schlechter Schrift ist genau so stillos wie ein Soldat mit zerrissenem Rock." Ibid., p. 8.

70. Ibid., cover note attachment from Dönhoff to Muthesius, dated February 17, 1904. Also GStA PK, File I.HA Rep. 120 EX Fach 1 Nr.14, *Kurse zur Ausbildung von Lehrern an Kunstgewerbe und Handwerkerschulen*, file IV.9858. Mohrbutter, a friend of Muthesius's and later a client for one of the architect's suburban houses in Berlin, is discussed further in Chapter 5, this volume.

71. GStA PK, I.HA. Rep. 120 EX Fach 1 Nr.7 Bd.1, 104–118; also published in the *Ministerialblatt der Handels- und Gewerbe-Verwaltung*, 3.Jg. Nr.23 (Dez. 7. 1903), pp. 381–88; and in *VB* (1905), pp. 165–74.

72. "Der Minister für Handel und Gewerbe an sämtliche Herren Regierungs-präsidenten" ("Lehrwerkstätten Erlass," Dez. 15. 1904), GStA PK, I.HA Rep. 120 EX Fach 1. Nr. 1 Bd.14,

file IIIb.8731. Muthesius produced revised drafts between June and December; he justified instructional workshops and supplied budget figures to the Finance Ministry in GStA PK, I.HA Rep. 120 EX Fach 1. Nr. 1 Bd.14, files IIIb.8731 and IIIb.5613.

73. H. E. von Berlepsch-Valendas, "Kunstgewerbeschulen und Lehrwerkstätten," *DK* 12 (1904), 326–28. For a recent dicussion, see Harry Francis Mallgrave, *Gottfried Semper: Architect of the Nineteenth Century* (New Haven, Conn.: Yale University Press, 1996), 210–14.

74. See "Denkschrift über die Begründung eines Landesgewerbeamts und eines ständigen Beirats," p. 92.

75. Muthesius's evaluation of this school is discussed in Chapter 2, this volume.

76. Because this passage signifies a sea change in Prussian applied-arts education policy, it is reproduced here in the original: "Der Unterricht in Lehrwerkstätten wird das Mittel an die Hand geben, dem Schüler die notwendigen Beziehungen zwischen Werkstoff und Form nachdrücklich zum Bewusstsein zu bringen und ihn dazu erziehen, seinen Entwurf sachlicher, wirtschaftlicher und zweckmässiger zu entwickeln. Durch die Beschäftigung mit dem Material wird ferner im Schüler die auf Abwege führende Vorstellung beseitigt werden, als ob die Herstellung äusserlich gefälliger Zeichnungen ein erstrebenswertes Ziel wäre, ohne Rücksicht darauf, ob sie dem Material und seiner Eigenart gehörig Rechnung tragen. Auch rein künstlerisch wird die Werkstätte neue wertvolle Anregungen vermitteln können, die sich statt auf äusserlich übermittelte Formen auf die durch eigene Tätigkeit gewonnene Einsicht in die Gestaltungsmöglichkeiten des Materials gründen. . . . Das Wesen der Kunstgewerbeschule bedingt es, dass in der Werkstätte die künstlerische Unterweisung mit der technischen Hand in Hand geht." GStA PK, I.HA Rep. 120 EX Fach 1. Nr. 1 Bd.14, file IIIb.8731. The decree was first published in the *Ministerial-Blatt der Handels- und Gewerbe Verwaltung*, 4 Nr.24 (Dez. 28. 1904): 494–95, and then again in the *Landesgewerbeamt*'s first administrative report, *VB* (1905), pp. 159–61. Subsequent quotations refer to page numbers from the *VB* (1905) edition.

77. "Ergebnisse," pp. 22–30; *VB* (1905), p. 159.

78. "Zu pflegen wäre der *bürgerliche* Innenraum und das Hauptaugenmark wäre auf eine einfache, gediegene Erscheinung zu legen, bei voller Verfeinerung in der *Farbe*" (emphasis original). "Ergebnisse," pp. 6–7.

79. "Ergebnisse," pp. 10–11; *VB* (1905), pp. 159–60.

80. A London County Council report from 1895–96 on the founding of the Central School of Arts and

Crafts is quoted in Posener, *Anfänge des Funktional-ismus*, p. 27.

81. See Deutscher Werkbund, ed., *Design and Industries Association, London: Englands Kunst-industrie und der Deutsche Werkbund, Übersetzungen von Begründungs- und Werbeschriften der englischen Gesellschaft "Design and Industries Association,"* 2nd ed. (Munich: F. Bruckmann, 1916).

82. Posener, *Anfänge des Funktionalismus*, pp. 10–17; also Peter Davey, *Arts and Crafts Architecture*, pp. 70–77.

83. *VB* (1905), p. 159.

84. *VB* (1905), pp. 159–60.

85. "Bedenken wegen etwaiger Conflikte zwischen Künstler und Techniker erscheinen mir deshalb unbegründet, weil der Techniker in solchem Falle ein gewöhnlicher Werkmeister sein wird, dessen sociale Stellung schon zu einer Anerkennung der Autorität des als voller Lehrer von der Anstalt beschäftigten Künstlers nötigt. – Muthesius." "Lehrwerkstätten Erlass," comment on p. 5 of decree draft.

86. Ibid.

87. Contemporary sources in this debate include Peter Stubmann, "Kunstgewerbepolitik," *DK* 6 (1903): 214–26; "Kunstgewerbeschulen und Lehrwerkstätten," *DK* 12 (1904): 326–28; "Neue Lehrwerkstätten," *Hohe Warte* 2 Nr.7 (1905): 175; "Unterricht an Kunstgewerbeschulen," *DK* 13 (1905): 379–80; Friedrich Carstanjen, "Kunstgewerbliche Erziehung," *DKuD* 16 (1905): 478–80; 486–87.

88. Kaiser Wilhelm II to Ministry of State (*Staatsministerium*), GStA PK, I. HA Rep. 89 Nr.27688, p. 5. The department began functioning on April 1 of the same year.

89. "Akten betreffend das Landesgewerbeamt," GStA PK, I. HA Rep. 89 Nr.27688, pp. 6–15; *Ministerial-Blatt der Handels- und Gewerbe-Verwaltung* 5 (April 6, 1905): 75. "Organisation des Landesgewerbeamtes und des Beirates," *VB* (1907), pp. 1–9. See also "Denkschrift über die Begründung eines Landesgewerbeamts und eines ständigen Beirats," pp. 91–95.

90. *Verhandlungen des Preussischen Hauses der Abgeordneten*, 20. Legislaturperiode, I. Session 1904/05, 136. Sitzung am 9. Februar 1905, pp. 9723–66.

91. Ibid., pp. 9723–24.

92. Minister von Möller, "Denkschrift über den Stand der Gewerbeförderung im Königreiche Preussen," pp. 2011–14.

93. *Verhandlungen des Preussischen Hauses der Abgeordneten*, 20. Legislaturperiode, I.Session 1904/05, 136. Sitzung am Februar 9. 1905, pp. 9724–26.

94. See the description of the Landesgewerbeamt in *VB* (1906).

95. Landesgewerbeamt Ministerialdirektor Neuhaus to Minister für Handel und Gewerbe Delbrück, Mai 19. 1906, in GStA PK, I.HA Rep.120 EX Fach 1 Nr.7, p. 228; Minister für Handel und Gewerbe Delbrück (Neuhaus, im Auftrage) to *Regierungspräsidenten und Oberpräsidenten* in Potsdam, "Betr. Ausstellungen von Schuelerarbeiten," Juni 1. 1906, *Ministerial-Blatt der Handels- und Gewerbe-Verwaltung*, 6 Nr.12 (June 16, 1906), p. 230.

96. Quotation from "Denkschrift über die Begründung eines Landesgewerbeamts," p. 92.

97. Minister Möller, it was announced in the Prussian Chamber of Deputies, had "been informed that he was tired of office" (*Amtsmüde*); see *Verhandlungen des Preussischen Hauses der Abgeordneten*, 9. Sitzung, January 15, 1906, p. 504.

98. On the Hibernia Affair, see the correspondence between Maximilian Harden and Walther Rathenau in Hans Dieter Hellige, ed., *Walther Rathenau – Maximilian Harden: Briefwechsel, 1897–1920* (Munich: Gotthold Müller Verlag, 1983), 375–81; Gerald D. Feldman, *Hugo Stinnes: Biographie eines Industriellen, 1870–1924* (Munich: C. H. Beck), 92–99; Hans Fürstenberg, *Carl Fürstenberg: Die Lebensgeschichte eines deutschen Bankiers, 1870–1914* (Berlin: Ullstein, 1931), 400–15; Charles Medalen, "State Monopoly Capitalism in Germany: The Hibernia Affair," *Past and Present* 78 (February 1978): 82–112; Heidrun Walther, *Theodor Adolf von Möller*, pp. 86–100.

99. On Clemens von Delbrück see Richard Bahr, *Clemens von Delbrück: Staatssekretär des Innern von 1909 bis 1916* (Berlin: Reichsverlag Hermann Kalkoff (1916)); Clemens von Delbrück, *Reden: 1906–1916* (Berlin: Verlag Reimar Hobbing, 1917); Borchard, *50 Jahre Preussische Ministerium für Handel und Gewerbe*, pp. 58–63.

100. "Denkschrift über die Begründung eines Landesgewerbeamts und eines ständigen Beirats," p. 92.

101. "Denkschrift über die Begründung eines Landesgewerbeamts und eines ständigen Beirats," pp. 92–95, quotation from p. 92; see also "Das neue Landesgewerbeamt," *Kölnische Zeitung*, 12 January 1905, p. 26; "Das neue Landesgewerbeamt," *Berliner Tageblatt*, Jan. 11, 1905, p. 27; "Liberale Grundsätze bei der Handwerkerförderung," *Königsberger Hartungsche Zeitung*, 6 April 1905, p. 1; "Bericht über die Sitzung des Ausschusses des Deutschen Handwerks- und Gewerbekammertages," *Handwerker-Zeitung für die Provinzen Hannover und Schleswig-Holstein und die Fürstentümer Pyrmont und Schaumburg-Lippe: Amtliches Organ der Handwerkskammern zu Altona, Flensburg, Hannover, Harburg, Hildesheim, und Stadthagen*, vol. 10, Nr.14 (8 April 1905), p. 59; all of these newspaper clippings are in GStA PK, I.HA 120 EI Gen. Nr. 27 Bd.1.

102. Muthesius's drafts for principles guiding the reform of the building trades schools are at NMWA.

103. *VB* (1909), pp. 66–67; 292–99; "Denkschrift des Landesgewerbeamts über die Notwendigkeit

einiger Änderungen im Betriebe der Baugewerkschulen," in *Ministerial-Blatt der Handels- und
Gewerbe-Verwaltung* 18 (1906, Beilage), 322–33.

104. "Es wird leichter als bisher dazu zu erziehen
sein, daß es für ihn (den Schüler) bei der Formgebung
weniger auf Kunst und Schmuck als auf Erfüllung
des Zweckes ankommt, und dass die architektonische
Gestaltung das Resultat aus Zweck, Konstruktion
und Material sein muss." Quoted in "Denkschrift des
Landesgewerbeamts über die Notwendigkeit einiger
Änderungen im Betriebe der Baugewerkschulen,"
p. 327.

105. Fachverband für die wirtschaftlichen
Interessen des Kunstgewerbes, *Bericht über die
Versammlung deutscher Kunstgewerbetreibender,*
Berlin Jägerstr. 22, März 9. 1906 (Berlin: H.
Bergmann, 1906), pp. 38–48; quotation from
p. 48.

106. Posener, *Anfänge des Funktionalismus*, p. 21;
Hubrich, *Hermann Muthesius: Die Schriften zu Architektur, Kunstgewerbe, Industrie in der "Neuen Bewegung,"* p. 167.

107. Fachverband für die wirtschaftlichen Interessen des Kunstgewerbes, *Bericht . . . März* 9. 1906,
p. 12.

108. Ibid., pp. 12–13.

109. Ibid., pp. 12–18.

110. See Gisela Moeller, *Peter Behrens in
Düsseldorf*, p. 19, n. 67.

111. Johann D. A. Ferdinand Graf Rothkirch-
Trach, *Die Unterrichtsanstalt des Kunstgewerbemuse-
ums in Berlin zwischen 1866 und 1933: Eine Studie zur
Kunstentwicklung in Deutschland* (Ph.D. dissertation,
Friedrich-Wilhelm University, Bonn, 1984), 145–63.
See also Andreas Bode, "Bruno Paul als Direktor der
Unterrichtsanstalt des Kunstgewerbemuseums und
ihrer Nachfolgeinstitutionen," *Stadt: Monatshefte für
Wohnungs- und Städtebau* 29 (October 1982): 8–14,
71–72.

112. Rothkirch-Trach, *Die Unterrichtsanstalt des
Kunstgewerbemuseums in Berlin*, pp. 140–43.

113. Eugen Kalkschmidt, "Die Möbel- und
Raumkunst auf der Werkbund-Ausstellung zu Köln
a. Rh.," *Moderne Bauformen* 15 (1914): 401–76, especially pp. 462–67.

114. *Lehrplan der Königliche Kunst- und Kunstgewerbeschule zu Breslau* (Breslau: A. Stenzel, 1897);
n.a., "Von der Königlichen Kunst und Kunstgewerbeschule," *Schlesische Zeitung* (30 April 1903),
clipping from GStA PK 120 EX Fach 2 Nr. 26 Bd.
2, pp. 24–25; also Rothkirch-Trach, *Die Unterrichtsanstalt des Kunstgewerbemuseums in Berlin*, pp. 140–
43. On Poelzig's life and work, see Jerzy Ilkosz and
Beate Störtkuhl, eds., *Hans Poelzig in Breslau: Architektur und Kunst, 1900–1916* (Delmenhorst: Aschenbeck und Holstein, 2000); Julius Posener, *Hans
Poelzig: Reflections On His Life and Work* (Cambridge, Mass.: MIT Press, 1992); Julius Posener,

Hans Poelzig: Gesammelte Schriften und Werke (Berlin:
Gebr. Mann, 1970).

115. See the excellent introductory essay in
Katja Schneider, *Burg Giebichenstein: Die Kunstgewerbeschule unter Leitung von Paul Thiersch und Gerhard Marcks 1915 bis 1933* (Weinheim: VCH Verlag,
1992), 19–20. The "unified arts school" is discussed
further in the Conclusion, this volume.

116. Hans Poelzig, "Das Einfamilienhaus auf der
Ausstellung fur Handwerk und Kunstgewerbe in
Breslau, *CdB* 24 (1904): 547–48; quotation from
p. 547.

117. Conrad Buchwald, *Sonderausstellung des Kunstgewerbevereins für Breslau und die Provinz Schlesien
Ausstellung für Handwerk und Kunstgewerbe Breslau
1904* (Breslau, 1904), as excerpted in Jerzy Ilkosz
and Beate Störtkuhl, eds., *Hans Poelzig in Breslau:
Architektur und Kunst, 1900–1916* (Delmenhorst: Aschenbeck und Holstein, 2000), 480–81.

118. Karl Masner, *Das Einfamilienhaus des Kunstgewerbevereins für Breslau und die Provinz Schlesien auf
der Ausstellung für Handwerk und Kunstgewerbe in Breslau 1904* (Berlin: Ernst Wasmuth, 1905), 7.

119. Ibid.

120. See Hans Poelzig, "Der neuzeitliche Fab-
rikbau," *Der Industriebau* 2 (1911): 100–06; Joanna
Janas-Fürnwein, "Monumente für die Industrie:
Hans Poelzigs Industrie und Ingenieurbauten der
Breslauer Zeit," in Ilkosz and Störtkuhl, Hans *Poelzig
in Breslau*, pp. 245–80.

121. Obermeister Andrés (Vorstand der Bild-
hauerzwangsinnung zu Breslau) to Staatsminister
für Kultus und Medizinalangelegenheiten, 27 April
1908, in GStA PK, I. Rep. 120 EX2 Nr. 26 Bd.2,
85–8; "Regierungspräsident Breslau an die Handw-
erkskammer zu Breslau," 31 October 1907, same file,
pp. 92–94; "Regierungspräsident an Herrn Direktor Poelzig in Breslau," October 31, 1907, same file,
p. 95.

122. Letter from A. Matthias, business manager of
the journal *Der Maler*, to Bruno Paul, July 21, 1908,
in UdK 7, 132, file U08/1728.

123. Report of Peter Jessen from January 23,
1912, on the letter of complaint from the Association for Economic Interests to Minister of Culture,
November 30, 1911, in UdK 7, 132, file U2010/11.

124. Wilhelm von Bode to Minister of Culture,
March 8, 1912, in UdK 7, 132, files U241/12 and
U898/10.

125. See UdK 7, 132.

126. Bode remarked that the Association's agitation against the Berlin Museum of Applied Arts and
its school was "doubtless" an effort to enable the
Commerce Ministry to gain influence over the two
institutions, "a development with which the Herr
Minister would not be displeased." Wilhelm von
Bode to von Falke and Paul, April 26, 1910, in UdK
7, 132, file U898/10, 1.

127. See Muthesius's summary of his meeting with Poelzig in his letter to Breslau Crafts School director Heyer, February 23, 1911, in GStA PK, I. Rep. 120 EX2 Nr. 26 Bd.2, 146–47. Also *VB* 1912, 257–58.

128. Hartmut Frank, "Ein Bauhaus vor dem Bauhaus," *Bauwelt* 41 (1983): 1640–58, here especially pp. 1646–47.

129. Poelzig to Gropius, June 30, 1914, as reprinted in Marcel Franiscono, *Walter Gropius and the Creation of the Bauhaus in Weimar*, p. 263. The circumstances surrounding these remarks are dealt with in greater detail in Chapter 7, this volume.

FOUR. THE CONVERGENCE OF STATE AND PRIVATE REFORM IMPULSES IN THE DEUTSCHER WERKBUND

1. See Julius Posener, *Anfänge des Funktionalismus*, p. 21; also Hans Joachim Hubrich, *Hermann Muthesius: Die Schriften zu Architektur, Kunstgewerbe, Industrie in der "Neuen Bewegung,"* p. 167.

2. This was particularly true of cities like Magdeburg, "the city of the sugar beet and sauerkraut," whose name in arts journals had until recently "at most been a geographical concept." So wrote the Magdeburg School of Applied Arts instructor Paul Dobert, insisting that beginning with its performance in St. Louis and now in Dresden two years later, the work of Magdeburg applied artists "did not qualitatively rank below the achievements of the 'cities of art' (*Kunststädte*) Dusseldorf, Munich, and Darmstadt." Paul Dobert, "Das Magdeburger Kunstgewerbe auf der Ausstellung in Dresden," in Direktorium der Ausstellung, ed., *Dritte Deutsche Kunstgewerbeausstellung Dresden 1906, Ausstellungszeitung* (Dresden: Wilhelm Baensch, 1906), 136–37.

3. Neuhaus to Möller, October 5, 1904, GStA PK I 120 EXVI.3 Nr.1G Bd.1, 20.

4. Quoted in letter from Schmidt to Muthesius, March 28, 1906, in NMWA.

5. Initiatives in the applied arts taken by municipal and state authorities in Dresden and Munich are discussed in Chapter 1, this volume.

6. Schumacher, Gurlitt, Lossow, Gross, and Stadler were the initiators of the exhibition. See Petzold-Hermann, "Die Dritte Deutsche Kunstgewerbeausstellung Dresden 1906," in Haase, ed., *Jugendstil in Dresden*, p. 65.

7. Hans Wichmann, *Aufbruch zum neuen Wohnen: Deutsche Werkstätten und WK-Verband, Ihr Beitrag zur Kultur unseres Jahrhunderts* (Basel: Birkhäuser, 1978), 19; on Beutler, who served as Finance Chairman for the 1906 exhibition, see Petzold-Hermann, "Die Dritte Deutsche Kunstgewerbeausstellung Dresden 1906," p. 67.

8. Schumacher attributed his ability to think creatively and "outside the box," as it were, to the decade he and his brother spent growing up in New York City, where his father served as German Consul General between 1875 and 1883. Catapulted at the age of thirteen from ten years of a "free and independent" childhood in New York to the strict, regimented society of his family's native Bremen, Schumacher realized that among his German peers he simply "thought differently." Attending university in Munich and Berlin, Schumacher enjoyed access to the most privileged circles of high society by virtue of his upbringing in one of Bremen's oldest and most distinguished families. In the Bavarian and Prussian capitals Schumacher studied architecture under Friedrich von Thiersch and Carl Schäfer respectively, finding employment afterward in the architectural office of Gabriel von Seidl. Fritz Schumacher, from *Stufen des Lebens: Erinnerungen eines Baumeisters* (Stuttgart und Berlin: Deutsche Verlags-Anstalt, 1935), as quoted in Dagmar Löbert, *Fritz Schumacher, 1869–1947: Reformarchitekt zwischen Tradition und Moderne* (Bremen: Donat, 1999), 16; 18–21.

9. Petzold-Hermann, "Die Dritte Deutsche Kunstgewerbeausstellung Dresden 1906," pp. 65–66; for further literature by and about Schumacher see Fritz Schumacher, *Streifzüge eines Architekten: Gesammelte Aufsätze* (Jena: Eugen Diederichs, 1907); Fritz Schumacher, *Stufen des Lebens: Erinnerungen eines Baumeisters*; also Hartmut Frank, ed., *Fritz Schumacher: Reformkultur und Moderne* (Stuttgart: Hatje, 1994); Jennifer Jenkins, *Provincial Modernity*, Chapter 8.

10. Wichmann, *Aufbruch zum neuen Wohnen*, p. 15.

11. Fritz Schumacher, "Zur Geschichte der Ausstellung," in Direktorium der Ausstellung, *Das Deutsche Kunstgewerbe 1906: III. Deutsche Kunstgewerbe-Ausstellung Dresden 1906* (Munich: F. Bruckmann, 1906), 11 (hereafter the book title is abbreviated as *Das Deutsche Kunstgewerbe 1906*).

12. Hermann Muthesius visited the United States with the German government delegation to report on the exhibition in spring 1904. See Hermann Muthesius, "Das Kunstgewerbe, insbesondere die Wohnungskunst [auf der Weltausstellung in St. Louis]," in *Amtlicher Bericht ueber die Weltaustellung in St. Louis 1904*, Teil 2 (Berlin: Reichsdruckerei, 1905), 263–96. This government report is filled with the paeans and informative appraisals of the delegation. Different from the official report, a reworked and more widely circulated article by Muthesius appeared as "Die Wohnungskunst auf der Welt-Ausstellung in St. Louis," *DKuD* 15 (October 1904–March 1905): 209–27.

13. Peter Paret describes the St. Louis experience as "paradigmatic" for conflicts over modern fine arts in the Wilhelmine era: Anxious imperialist impulses initially drove up a meager world's exhibition budget, the government bureaucracy sought to administer the exhibition organization fairly, and the decrees

of the emperor superceded all previous measures by imposing a narrow, dictatorial order over the fine arts. Progressive applied artists, who for several years had been arguing that their art and the fine arts enjoyed the same status, nevertheless had an experience that must be differentiated from that of the painters. See Paret, *The Berlin Secession*, pp. 112–55.

14. See the essay, "Together and Apart: Fritz Haber and Albert Einstein," in Fritz Stern, *Einstein's German World* (Princeton: Princeton University Press, 1999), 82.

15. Reichsminister of the Interior Graf Posadowsky to Prussian Commerce Minister Clemens Delbrück, December 27, 1906, in GStA PK, I. H.A. 120 EXVI.1 Nr.3 Bd.1.

16. Not the first modern Commercial College in Germany or in Prussia (Leipzig and Aachen each opened a *Handelshochschule* in 1898, in each case as part of their local universities), Berlin's school, featuring faculty like Werner Sombart, Else Meissner, and Hermann Muthesius, was nevertheless arguably the most significant. See GStA PK, I. H.A. 120 EXIII. Fach 3 Nr.5 Bd.1, and Korporation der Kaufmannschaft von Berlin, *Die Eröffnung der Handelshochschule Berlin am 27. Oktober 1906* (Berlin: Verlag von G. Reimer, 1906).

17. See Schwartz, *The Werkbund*, pp. 151–63.

18. Das Direktorium, *3. Deutsche Kunstgewerbe-Ausstellung Dresden 1906*, printed preliminary exhibition program (no publisher, no date) attached to memorandum from William Lossow to Theodor Möller, October 5, 1904, in GStA PK, I. H.A. EXVI.3 Nr. 1G Bd.1, pp. 10–19; quotation from pp. 13–14.

19. Haase, *Jugendstil in Dresden*, p. 173.

20. Ibid., p. 187.

21. The commissars, listed alphabetically, included: Peter Behrens (Düsseldorf), Wilhelm Bertsch (Munich), Justus Brinckmann (Hamburg), Ludwig Dettmann (Königsberg), Richard Graul (Leipzig), Alfred Grenander (Berlin), M. Haug (Stassburg/Elsass), Emil Högg (Bremen), Harry Graf Kessler (Weimar), Otto Krüger (Munich), Otto Lehmann (Altona), Albin Müller (Magdeburg), Hermann Muthesius (Prussia's schools), Joseph Maria Olbrich (Darmstadt), Bernhard Pankok (Stuttgart), Max Seliger (Leipzig), Bernhard Stadler (Saxony), and L. Volkmann (Leipzig). Fritz Schumacher, "Zur Geschichte der Ausstellung," p. 12; also Petzold-Hermann, "Die Dritte Deutsche Kunstgewerbeausstellung Dresden 1906," p. 65.

22. Schumacher, "Die Ziele der III. Deutschen Kunstgewerbeausstellung," in Schumacher, *Streifzüge eines Architekten*, pp. 208–15.

23. "Das Programm der Ausstellung," *Das Deutsche Kunstgewerbe 1906*, p. 16. Such material groups, it should be noted, were hardly new, and had

been used in the Dresden Applied Arts Exhibition of 1896, which had gone under the name, "Die alte Stadt."

24. Schumacher, "Ziele," p. 219.

25. M. Buhle, "Kunstindustrielle Maschinen und Werkstaetten," in *Dritte Deutsche Kunstgewerbeausstellung Dresden 1906, Ausstellungszeitung*, Nr. 7 (April 1906), as quoted in Klaus-Peter Arnold, *Vom Sofakissen zum Städtebau*, p. 80.

26. Dresdner Werkstätten für Handwerkskunst, *Preisbuch Dresdner Hausgerät* (Dresden: 1906), as quoted in Arnold, *Vom Sofakissen zum Städtebau*, p. 80.

27. Schumacher, "Ziele," p. 219.

28. Gebäude für Arbeiter- und Volkswohlfahrt, *Das Deutsche Kunstgewerbe 1906*, pp. 268–78.

29. "Denkschrift über die Begründung eines Landesgewerbeamts und eines ständigen Beirats," p. 92.

30. "Das Programm der Ausstellung," *Das Deutsche Kunstgewerbe 1906*, p. 15. The original language is significant here for its untranslatable nuances concerning the exhibition planners' agenda: "Es soll ohne Unterschied der Zeiten und Völker an bezeichnenden Beispielen zur Anschauung gebracht werden, wie aus dem Wesen des Stoffes die künstlerische Bearbeitung sich entwickelt hat und hieraus innere Gesetze entstehen, die ebenfalls dem Wechsel geschichtlicher Stile nicht unterworfen sind. Dabei soll möglichst deutlich der Stand unserer heutigen kunsthandwerklichen Techniken gegenueber denjenigen früherer Zeiten zum Ausdruck kommen."

31. Ibid. "Eine der Volkskunst gewidmete Abteilung soll zeigen, wie die naive kunstgewerbliche Betätigung, die nicht die Eigenart des einzelnen, sondern die Eigenart einer örtlichen Überlieferung pflegt, im Wechsel der geschichtlichen Stile frisch bleibt"; and for *Kunsthandwerkliche Einzelerzeugnisse*: "Es wird beabsichtigt, diese Gruppen in Form von künstlerisch angeordeneten Läden zu zeigen."

32. Ibid. "Es soll ein Überblick zu geben versucht werden, inwieweit unsere der Ausbildung des Kunsthandwerks gewidmeten Schulen durch Arbeit u n m i t t e l b a r im Material diese aus der technik sich ergebenden Ueberlieferungen und Fertigkeiten weiter fortpflanzen (emphasis original)."

33. *VB* (1904), p. 151.

34. Schumacher, "Ziele," p. 217.

35. *Dritte Deutsche Kunst-Gewerbe-Ausstellung Dresden 1906, Offizieller Katalog*, Illustrierte Ausgabe, pp. 115–38.

36. Schumacher, "Ziele," p. 217.

37. Specific background about the Dusseldorf exhibit contributions and its various student and teacher contributions can be found in Gisela Moeller, *Peter Behrens in Dusseldorf*, pp. 119–24.

38. *Dekorative Kunst* was especially thorough in documenting the rise and success of Behrens – even

before Dusseldorf. Reforms in drawing techniques, their effects on student projects, and the bringing together of artistic specialties under the organizing unit of the architectonically treated interior were, for example, the subject of a feature article by H. Board, "Die Kunstgewerbeschule zu Düsseldorf," *DK* 12 (1904): 409–32. Julius Meier-Graefe produced his own feature the following year, "Peter Behrens-Duesseldorf," *DK* 13 (1905): 381–90; 391–413. On the exhibition see Wilhelm Niemeyer, "Die Arbeiten der Kunstgewerbeschule Duesseldorf," *DK* 14 (1906): 167–76.

39. *VB* (1907), p. 153.

40. The local firms were mostly small, carrying such names as Möbelfabrik Wilhelm Grimpe, Gravieranstalt Herman Held, and eight others. *Dritte Deutsche Kunst-Gewerbe-Ausstellung Dresden 1906, Offizieller Katalog*, 12.Mai–Ende Oktober 1906, Illustrierte Ausgabe (Dresden: Wilhelm Baensch, 1906), 122.

41. The Barmen product-design efforts echoed Fritz Schumacher's design for the professional exhibit of shops in the exhibition's "shopping street." Ibid., p. 119.

42. On financial pressures facing Prussia and the Reich in 1905, see Gordon Craig, *Germany 1866–1945* (Oxford: Oxford University Press, 1978), 278–79; V. R. Berghahn, *Germany and the Approach of War in 1914*, 2nd ed., pp. 85–87. The quotation concerning Muthesius and "his schools" is from Schumacher, "Zur Geschichte der Ausstellung," p. 12; information about schools' invitations and preparations corroborated on p. 13; see also Moeller, *Peter Behrens in Düsseldorf*, p. 119, n. 443.

43. Möller to Ministry of Culture, December 8, 1904, which includes Möller's objections to overparticipation by Muthesius due to time constraints, as well as a draft joint reply from the two ministries to the Dresden 1906 exhibition directorate; in GStA PK, I 120 E XVI.3 Nr.1G Bd.1, 24.

44. Ministry of Finance to Commerce Minister, June 21, 1905, for objections to exhibition funding proposal; Möller to Finance Ministry August 22, 1905, with defense of spending plan and refusal to damage "Prussian interests" by cutting costs further, in GStA PK, I 120 E XVI.3 Nr.1G Bd.1, 143–45. Möller explained further measures taken to decrease Prussia's involvement and expense at the 1906 exhibition: He limited the Royal Porcelain Manufacturers' exhibit and excluded Silesia from the exhibition.

45. The ministry paid entirely the construction costs of the corridor of bays for the nine additional, smaller Prussian schools that had their own instructional workshop-produced wares. Muthesius to Herrn Minister für Handel und Gewerbe, "Einrichtung und Kosten der Fachausstellung in Dresden 1906," in GStA PK, I. H. A. EXVI.3 Nr. 1G Bd.1, pp. 238–43. Also Muthesius, "Die Beteiligung der preussischen Kunstgewerbeschulen an der III. Deutschen Kunstgewerbeausstellung in Dresden 1906," *VB* (1907), p. 151.

46. Hermann Muthesius, "Kunstgewerbliche und handwerkliche Unterrichtsanstalten: Geschichtliche Entwicklung," *VB* (1905), pp. 88–106, and, in the same volume, "Heutiger Stand des kunstgewerblichen und handwerklichen Schulwesens," pp. 107–29. See also the discussion of these articles in Chapter 3, this volume, n. 35.

47. Königliches Preussisches Ministerium für Handel und Gewerbe, Berlin. *Nachrichten über die Preussischen Kunstgewerbeschulen: Zusammengestellt gelegentlich der mit der 3. Deutschen Kunstgewerbeausstellung in Dresden 1906 Verbundenen Ausstellung Preussische Kunstgewerbeschulen* (Berlin: Julius Sittenfeld, o.J., 1906) (abbreviated hereafter as *Nachrichten*). This book is also discussed in *VB* (1907), pp. 151–52.

48. See, for example, "Die neuere Entwicklung der Kunstgewerbeschulen" and "Heutiger Stand des kunstgewerblichen Schulwesens in Preussen," in *Nachrichten*, pp. 9–17; 18–47. These articles are both listed as excerpts from the *Landesgewerbeamt* administrative report [*Verwaltungsbericht*] of 1905. The remainder of the *Nachrichten* book consists of excerpts from annual reports (1903–04, 1904–05, and 1905–06) from the seventeen schools that took part in the exhibit; see, for example, "Mitteilungen aus den Jahresprogrammen der an der Schulausstellung in Dresden 1906 beteiligten kunstgewerblichen Anstalten," *Nachrichten*, pp. 49–150. This section leads off with the Dusseldorf Kunstgewerbeschule, "Aus dem Jahresbericht der Kunstgewerbeschule zu Duesseldorf fuer das Schuljahr 1904/05," pp. 49–52, and lists the following information: Director P. Behrens; Gründung April 3, 1883; participating in Dresden in 1906 were thirty-six architecture students, fifty-one decorative painters, and thirty-three applied-arts draftsmen (*Kunstgewerbliche Zeichner*).

49. Craftsman Paul Beumers, quoted in Fachverband für die wirtschaftlichen Interessen des Kunstgewerbes, *Stenographischer Bericht über den 2. Kongress deutscher Kunstgewerbetreibender*, Dusseldorf, 14. Juni 1907 (Berlin: H. Bergmann, 1907), 114–15.

50. For a detailed discussion of Behrens's buildings for the Oldenburg State, Industry, and Trade Exhibition see Gisela Moeller, *Peter Behrens in Düsseldorf*, pp. 192–241; on Behrens's relationship to the Delmenhorst Linoleum Company and its owner, Gustav Gericke, see Matthew Jeffries, *Politics and Culture in Wilhelmine Germany*, pp. 244–83.

51. Fritz Stern, *Einstein's German World*, p. 38.

52. The works of the Dusseldorf *Kunstgewerbeschule* at the Dresden 1906 exhibition as

well as Behrens's company poster are discussed in Gisela Moeller, *Peter Behrens in Düsseldorf*. I am also grateful to Professor Tilmann Buddensieg for a discussion of this subject.

53. Buddensieg, "Industriekultur: Peter Behrens and the AEG, 1907–1914," pp. 9–12; Moeller (1991), pp. 43–45.

54. See Schwartz, *The Werkbund*, pp. 151–63.

55. Schumacher, "Ziele," quotation from pp. 226–27.

56. See the discussion in Fedor Roth, *Hermann Muthesius*, pp. 52–53.

57. Schumacher, "Zur Geschichte der Ausstellung," p. 11.

58. Schumacher, "Ziele," p. 223.

59. Henry van de Velde, *Vom Neuen Stil, Der Laienpredigten II* (Leipzig: Insel Verlag, 1907), 40.

60. Ibid., pp. 41–49, quotation from p. 48.

61. Schumacher, "Die Geschichte der Ausstellung," p. 13.

62. Avenarius, too, wrote of the need for "veracity" (*Wahrhaftigkeit*) in the applied arts, and the double need for the applied arts to serve as a medium of expression and a means for education at once. See Kratzsch, *Kunstwart und Dürerbund*, pp. 134–38; 201–03.

63. Hermann Muthesius, "Die Bedeutung der 3. Deutschen Kunstgewerbe-Ausstellung," *Leipziger Bauzeitung* (19 April 1906), pp. 155–56, quotations from p. 155, clipping in NMWA.

64. Schwartz, *The Werkbund*, pp. 155–57.

65. Ibid., pp. 151–63.

66. The Free Union of Dresden Furniture and Decorator Stores sent detailed complaints about the selection conditions and plans for the Dresden exhibition, and about the instructional workshops at the Dresden School of Applied Arts, to the Saxon Ministry of Economics (*Wirtschaftsministerium*), as detailed in Klaus-Peter Arnold, *Vom Sofakissen zum Städtebau*, pp. 86–90. Complaints of the *Fachverband* to Prussian authorities are discussed in Chapter 3, this volume, and similar agitation against state-supported applied-arts reforms in Württemberg in Chapter 1, this volume.

67. The Berlin *Handelshochschule*, which opened in 1906, is discussed in Max Osborn, *Berlin 1870–1929: Der Aufstieg zur Weltstadt* (Berlin: Gebr. Mann Verlag, 1994), 188–89. Support for new *Handelshochschulen* was part of the Commerce Ministry's expanding educational policy by the 1890s as well. See Facius, *Wirtschaft und Staat*, p. 60. Ministerial documentation concerning the school is in GStA PK, I. H.A. 120 EXIII. Fach 3 Nr.5 Bd.1.

68. Hermann Muthesius, "Die Bedeutung des Kunstgewerbes," *DK* 15 (1907): 184, 190.

69. Muthesius, "Die Bedeutung des Kunstgewerbes," p. 183. See also "Werkbundaktivitäten zur Konsumentenerziehung," in Siepmann und Thiekötter, eds., *Herman Muthesius im Werkbund-Archiv*, pp. 61–66.

70. Again, the original language is indispensable here for an appreciation of the multiple meanings in the speaker's layered rhetoric:

> Aber eins ist klar: das Kunstgewerbe hat hier eine erzieherische Aufgabe von eminenter Bedeutung vor sich. Und es überschreitet hier bereits die Grenzen, die ihm nach populärer Auffassung zugeschrieben werden, es wird mehr als Kunstgewerbe, es wird ein kulturelles Erziehungsmittel. Das Kunstgewerbe hat das Ziel, die heutigen Gesellschaftsklassen zur Gediegenheit, Wahrhaftigkeit und bürgerlichen Einfachheit zurückzuerziehen. Gelingt ihm das, so wird es aufs tiefste in unser Kulturleben eingreifen und die weitesten Folgen ziehen. Es wird nicht nur die deutsche Wohnung und das deutsche Haus verändern, sondern es wird direkt auf den Charakter der Generation einwirken, denn auch die Erziehung zur anständigen Gestaltung der Räume, in denen wir wohnen, kann im Grunde nur eine Charaktererziehung sein, die die prätentiösen und parvenuhaften Neigungen, die zu der heutigen Zimmerausstattung geführt haben, unterdrückt.

Muthesius, "Die Bedeutung des Kunstgewerbes," p. 183.

71. Minister Delbrück to Fachverband für die wirtschaftlichen Interessen des Kunstgewerbes, May 15, 1907, reprinted in "Der Fall Muthesius: Ein Vortrag mit Akten und Briefen," *Hohe Warte* 3 (1907): 238.

72. *Verhandlungen des Preussischen Hauses der Abgeordneten*, 23. Sitzung am February 3, 1908, p. 1527, as cited in Hubrich, *Hermann Muthesius*, p. 277.

73. Schmidt to Muthesius, March 11, 1905, NMWA.

74. Schmidt to Muthesius, July 24, 1905, NMWA; see also the discussion in Angelika Thiekötter, "Erste Kontakte," in Siepmann und Thiekötter, eds., *Hermann Muthesius im Werkbund-Archiv*, p. 25.

75. Riemerschmid designed the cover of Naumann's journal *Die Hilfe*; Behrens adopted many of Naumann's economic ideas and repeated them in articles like his "Kunst und Technik" of 1910; and Theodor Fischer realized three buildings known as "Volkshäuser" on the secular-communal model outlined by Naumann. Avenarius and Eugen Diederichs were also Naumann supporters. See Kurt Junghanns, *Der Deutsche Werkbund: sein erstes Jahrzehnt* (Berlin: Henschel Verlag, 1982), 13.

76. The best discussions of Naumann in relation to the applied-arts movement are in Jeffries, *Politics and Culture in Wilhelmine Germany*, pp. 146–79;

Julius Posener, "Das Prinzip Wachstum: Friedrich Naumann," in *Berlin auf dem Wege zu einer neuen Architektur*, pp. 49–54, with Naumann excerpts from pp. 55–80; and Junghanns, *Der Deutsche Werkbund*, pp. 10–13. Jeffries makes an extremely important point about the one-sided nature of knowledge of Naumann among historians and art historians alike: As he points out, eminent architectural historians as well as two of the Werkbund Archive's own publications all misidentify Naumann's all-important political party affiliation, while political historians like Peter Theiner, a biographer of Naumann and author of the book *Sozialer Liberalismus und deutsche Weltpolitik* (Baden-Baden, 1983), "fail to mention the Deutscher Werkbund once in three hundred pages." See Jeffries, p. 150.

77. See "Kunst und Industrie: Ein Vortrag in der Dresdener Kunstgewerbe-Ausstellung," in Friedrich Naumann, *Werke*, Band 6: Ästhetische Schriften, ed. Heinz Ladendorf (Köln: Westdeutscher Verlag, 1964), 433–47, and "Deutsche Gewerbekunst: Eine Arbeit über die Organisation des Deutschen Werkbundes" (Berlin, 1908), in ibid., pp. 254–89.

78. Siepmann and Thiekötter, eds., *Hermann Muthesius im Werkbund-Archiv*, p. 61.

79. Fritz Schumacher, *Stufen meines Lebens: Erinnerungen eines Baumeisters*, pp. 330–31, as excerpted in Siepmann and Thiekötter, eds., *Hermann Muthesius im Werkbund-Archiv*, p. 52.

80. Theodor Heuss, *Friedrich Naumann: der Mann, das Werk, die Zeit*, 2nd ed. (Stuttgart and Tübingen: Deutsche Verlags-Anstalt, 1949), pp. 223–24.

81. "Zur Gründungsgeschichte des Deutschen Werkbundes," *Die Form* 7 (1932): 229, as excerpted in Siepmann and Thiekötter, eds., *Hermann Muthesius im Werkbund-Archiv*, p. 50.

82. These speeches are reproduced with commentary in *Hohe Warte* 3 (1907): 245–48; with Joseph A. Lux as its editor, this journal was very much on the side of the new movement and against the Association.

83. Peter Bruckmann in ibid., p. 245.

84. Dohrn in ibid., pp. 246–47.

85. Dohrn in ibid., pp. 247–48.

86. The twelve artists were Peter Behrens, Theodor Fischer, Josef Hoffmann, Wilhelm Kreis, Max Laeuger, Adelbert Niemeyer, Joseph Maria Olbrich, Bruno Paul, Richard Riemerschmid, Julius Scharvogel, Paul Schultze-Naumburg, and Fritz Schumacher; the twelve firms were Peter Bruckmann und Söhne, Deutsche Werkstätten für Handwerkskunst Dresden, Eugen Diederichs (Verlag), Gebrüder Klingspor Kunstdruckerei, Künstlerbund Karlsruhe, Pöschel und Trepte-Leipzig, Saalecker Werkstätten, Vereinigte Werkstätten für Kunst im Handwerk-München, Werkstätten für Deutschen Hausrat Theophil Müller Dresden, Wiener Werkstätte, Wilhelm und Co., Gottlob Wunderlich-Zschopau. Cited in Posener, *Anfänge des Funktionalismus*, p. 22, n. 1.

87. Quoted in Joseph August Lux, "Der Deutsche Werkbund," *Fachblatt für Holzarbeiter* 7 (1907): 217–18.

88. Siepmann and Thiekötter, eds., *Hermann Muthesius im Werkbund-Archiv*, p. 42; Klaus-Peter Arnold, *Vom Sofakissen zum Städtebau*, p. 93.

89. The ministry's increasingly cautious approach to publicity in matters affecting the crafts sector supports this conclusion, but there are, unfortunately, no documents discovered to date that convey the ministry's particular reasoning on this point.

90. See, for example, the discussion in Frederic J. Schwartz, *The Werkbund*, pp. 9, 15.

91. The designation of Muthesius as "Father of the Werkbund" is from Karl Scheffler, *Die fetten und die mageren Jahre*, p. 42.

92. Hermann Muthesius, "Unbenutzter Werkbundaufruf," in Siepmann and Thiekötter, eds., *Hermann Muthesius im Werkbund-Archiv*, pp. 52–57.

93. Hermann Muthesius, "Programrede auf der 1. Jahresversammlung des DWB München 1908," in Siepmann and Thiekötter, eds., *Hermann Muthesius im Werkbund-Archiv*, p. 58. Fritz Stahl noted in his report on the 1908 Werkbund meeting that government representatives in attendance included Fritz Dönhoff of the Prussian Commerce Ministry, Privy Councillor Albert from the Imperial Ministry of the Interior, and "other officials"; quoted in Fritz Stahl, "Chronik," *Berliner Architekturwelt* 10 (1908): 199.

94. Hermann Muthesius, "Die künstlerische Erziehung der deutschen Jugend" (A review of Konrad Lange, *Die künstlerische Erziehung der deutschen Jugend*) (Darmstadt: Verlag Arnold Bergstrasser, 1893), *CdB* 13 (1893): 527–28; Heidrun Walther, *Theodor Adolf von Möller*, pp. 152–54.

95. Muthesius, "Programrede 1908," in Siepmann and Thiekötter, eds., p. 58.

96. Ibid.

97. See, for example, the discussion in "Denkschrift über die Begründung eines Landesgewerbeamts."

98. Muthesius, "Programrede auf der 1. Jahresversammlung des DWB München 1908," in Siepmann and Thiekötter, eds., *Hermann Muthesius im Werkbund-Archiv*, p. 59.

99. "Die Veredelung der gewerblichen Arbeit im Zusammenwirken von Kunst, Industrie und Handwerk." Verhandlung des Deutschen Werkbundes zu München 11. und 12. Juli 1908, Leipzig (1908), as quoted in ibid., p. 60.

100. "Werkbund Aktivitäten zur Konsumerziehung," in Siepmann and Thiekötter, eds., *Hermann Muthesius im Werkbund-Archiv*, p. 61.

101. Ibid., p. 62. See Neuhaus's and von Seefeld's reviews of private business schools and selected school closures in GStA PK, I. HA 120 EX IIIa Fach 3 Nr. 8 Bd. 5 (Die privaten Handelslehranstalten), files IV 3150, IV 8282, IV 9789; while local government authorities (*Regierungspräsidenten*) closed schools, directors appealed to the State Trades Board, who mostly supported local authorities, but sometimes rejected their judgments as well.

102. See Else Oppler-Legband's contribution to the *Jahrbuch des Deutschen Werkbundes 1912: Die Durchgeistigung der Deutschen Arbeit* (Jena: Eugen Diederichs, 1912), 105–10. Files on the Prussian Commerce Ministry's relationship to the school, with copious Werkbund material, are in GStA PK, I. HA 120 E XIIIa Fach3 Nr. 2 adh.1 Bd.1.

103. See the examples of the school's window displays in *Jahrbuch des Deutschen Werkbundes 1913: Die Kunst in Industrie und Handel* (Jena: Eugen Diederichs, 1913), 100–08; see also August Endell, "Ladeneinrichtungen," in ibid., pp. 55–58; Karl Ernst Osthaus, "Das Schaufenster," pp. 59–69; Hans Weidenmüller, "Die Durchgeistigung der Geschäftlichen Werbearbeit," pp. 70–74. On the merger with the Reimannschule see Albert Reimann to Senior Privy Councillor Fritz Dönhoff, December 20, 1911, in GStA PK, I.HA 120 E XIIIa Fach3 Nr. 2 adh.1 Bd.1, 32. The story of this school has not been told in full, but would make an excellent and fascinating institutional study, especially as it merged with the highly regarded Reimann School, the respected Berlin private applied-arts school operated by Albert Reimann beginning in 1911.

104. On Muthesius's reform of the schools for the building trades see his edited manuscript of the Union of German Architects and Engineers, "Leitsätze zur Frage der Umgestaltung der Baugewerkschulen," aufgestellt von Verbande deutscher Architekten-und Ingenieur-Vereine, typed manuscript dated 1906, NMWA.

FIVE. HERMANN MUTHESIUS: ARCHITECTURAL PRACTICE BETWEEN GOVERNMENT SERVICE AND WERKBUND ACTIVISM

1. Significant research has been devoted to understanding the local contexts of most, but not all, of the Werkbund's leading figures. Matthew Jeffries has done much to fill in gaps concerning Friedrich Naumann's "Heilbronn connection," his mobilization of a network of supporters for the purpose of harnessing the Werkbund to expansionist, worker-oriented liberal policies; see Jeffries, *Politics and Culture in Wilhelmine Germany*, pp. 146–79. Kristiana Hartmann, Winfried Nerdinger, and others have demonstrated that Karl Schmidt's Hellerau Garden City, home to the Werkbund for its first four years, was an exceptional case of entrepreneurial expansion that simultaneously carried out architectural, social, and cultural experiments in the spirit of Naumann, Schmidt, and Wolf Dohrn; see Kristiana Hartmann, *Deutsche Gartenstadtbewegung: Kultur, Politik, und Gesellschaftsreform* (Munich: Heinz Moos Verlag, 1976); Klaus-Peter Arnold, *Vom Sofakissen zum Städtebau: Die Geschichte der Deutschen Werkstätten und der Gartenstadt Hellerau* (Dresden, Basel: Verlag der Kunst, 1993); Hans Wichmann, *Deutsche Werkstätten und WK-Verband, 1898–1990: Aufbruch zum neuen Wohnen* (Munich: Prestel, 1992), 14–127; Winfried Nerdinger, ed., *Richard Riemerschmid*, pp. 13–26; 400–06. Books that concentrate on Muthesius's written and built works, but not his Berlin-based practice or his government work in relation to his work for the Werkbund, include Fedor Roth, *Hermann Muthesius und die Idee der harmonischen Kultur*; Uwe Schneider, *Hermann Muthesius und die Reformdiskussion in der Gartenarchitektur des frühen 20. Jahrhunderts*.

2. Jeffries, *Politics and Culture in Wilhelmine Germany*, p. 202.

3. Osthaus's Museum for Art in Commerce and Industry has been analyzed as a center for artistic patronage in the commercial sphere, a place where artists and firms came together in a dawning age of twentieth-century commercial and visual culture. On Osthaus and his museum work, see Herta Hesse-Frielinghaus, ed., *Karl Ernst Osthaus: Leben und Werk* (Recklinghausen: Verlag Aurel Bongers, 1971); Bettina Heil and Andrea Sinzel, eds., *Briefe an Karl Ernst Osthaus* (Hagen: Karl Ernst Osthaus Museum, 2000); for a recent assessment of Osthaus's Museum of Art in Commerce and Industry, see Schwartz, *The Werkbund*, pp. 164–91.

4. Fritz Hellwag took the occasion of Muthesius's fiftieth birthday to praise the architect's "concentric talents, which developed early," in "Kunstgewerbliche Rundschau," *Kgbl*, N.F. (1911): 138.

5. The distinction between "villa" and *Landhaus* was not always strictly observed by Wilhelmine architects and critics – or, perhaps, not always understood as a hard and fast difference. At the journal *Berliner Architekturwelt*, for example, the critic Ernst Schur wrote, on the one hand, "The concept 'villa' is disappearing; the *Landhaus* dominates. And so the ground for the regeneration of our domestic architecture is secured." On the other hand, in the very same issue, there appeared photographs Muthesius's own *Landhaus* with the caption, "The Villa Muthesius" – a designation to which Berlin's leading *Landhaus* architect could only have objected. Quote from Ernst Schur, "Malerei, Plastik, Architektur auf den Grossen Berliner Kunstausstellung 1907," *Berliner*

Architekturwelt 10 (1907): 126; the "Villa Muthesius in Nikolassee bei Berlin" is illustrated on p. 56 of the same issue.

6. This discussion of the *Landhaus* is based on the analyses of Julius Posener in *Berlin auf dem Wege zu einer neuen Architektur*, pp. 127–74, and especially pp. 160–61; also Julius Posener and Burkhard Bergius, "Individuell geplante Einfamilienhäuser 1896–1918," in Architekten- und Ingenieur-Verein zu Berlin, ed., *Berlin und seine Bauten*, Teil 4, Bd. C: Wohnungsbau (Berlin: Ernst & Sohn, 1975); and Goerd Peschken, "Zur deutschen Bürgervilla 1800–1914: Grundzüge einer Baugeschichte der Berliner Villa," in Goerd Peschken, ed., *Baugeschichte politisch: Schinkel, Stadt Berlin, preussische Schlösser*, Bauwelt Fundamente 96 (Braunschweig: Vieweg, 1993), 94–115. The divisions between the *Landhaus* and the villa were not always cut and dry: turn-of-the-century architecture journals and the press sometimes used the terms loosely, almost interchangeably at times, while architects also were known to combine elements from these two types in the same building.

7. Laurent Stalder provides a detailed discussion of the significance of the sloping, high roof as well as other "Nordic" building features in late-nineteenth-century German scholarship on German domestic architecture in his dissertation *Wie man ein Haus baut: Hermann Muthesius (1861–1927) – Das Landhaus als kulturgeschichtlicher Entwurf* (Ph.D. dissertation, ETH-Zürich, 2002), 72–77.

8. Noted in Posener, *Berlin auf dem Wege zu einer neuen Architektur*, pp. 160–61.

9. On Victor Aimé Huber and other mid-nineteenth-century German housing reformers, see Hartmann, *Deutsche Gartenstadtbewegung*, pp. 22–6; Anthony Sutcliffe, *Towards the Planned City: Germany, Britain, the United States and France 1780–1914* (Oxford: Basil Blackwell: 1981), 30–32.

10. Interestingly, and in contrast to architects like Adolf Loos, ornament had a place in Muthesius's Wilhelmine philosophy of *Sachlichkeit* in domestic architecture, much as he deemed the use of exposed iron trusswork appropriately *sachlich* in a modern engineered bridge. For example, his featuring of cherubs above the windows of the Gugenheim house of 1914 in the Tiergarten – Berlin's elegant diplomatic quarter – recalls the architect's statements in the book *Landhaus und Garten*, from 1907: "Modern man has become extremely uncomfortable with ornament precisely due to the mass ornamentation produced over the last several decades. One has surely become aware once again that ornament is an art. Art can never be a mass-produced object, but rather only the individual creation of an artist." To the extent that Muthesius's façade decorations partook of the decorative language common to the urban villas of the area, bespeaking the wealth and status of the

building's owner, they helped make the Gugenheim house "*sachlich*," or objectively suited to its upscale residential context. The quotation is from Muthesius, *Landhaus und Garten*, p. xxxx (sic).

11. See Muthesius, *Landhäuser* (1912), pp. 19–28; 101–10.

12. Muthesius, *Das englische Haus*, vol. 1, p. 139; see also the discussion in Chapter 2, this volume.

13. Examples of Muthesius's working class housing are discussed in Chapter 6, this volume.

14. See Hermann Muthesius, *Landhäuser* (Munich: F. Bruckmann, 1922); *Landhaus und Garten*, 4th ed. (Munich: F. Bruckmann, 1925).

15. On the growth of Berlin's suburbs see Clemens Zimmermann, "Suburbanisierung – Die wachsende Peripherie," in Tilman Harlander, ed., *Villa und Eigenheim: Suburbaner Städtebau in Deutschland* (Stuttgart, Munich: Deutsche Verlags-Anstalt, 2001), 50–63; Landesdenkmalamt Berlin, ed., *Baudenkmale in Berlin: Bezirk Zehlendorf, Ortsteil Zehlendorf* (Berlin: Landesdenkmalamt Berlin, 1995), 23–37 (hereafter cited as *Baudenkmale in Berlin*); Julius Posener, "Vorortgründungen," *Arch+* 7 (1975): 1–10.

16. Hermann Muthesius, *Das moderne Landhaus und seine innere Ausstattung* (Munich: F. Bruckmann, 1904); *Das moderne Landhaus und seine innere Ausstattung*, 2. verbesserte und vermehrte Auflage (Munich: F. Bruckmann, 1905); *Landhaus und Garten: Beispiele neuzeitlicher Landhäuser nebst Grundrissen, Innenräumen und Gärten* (Munich: F. Bruckmann, 1907); *Landhäuser von Hermann Muthesius: Abbildungen und Pläne ausgeführter Bauten mit Erläuterungen des Architekten* (Munich: F. Bruckmann, 1912) (hereafter cited as *Das moderne Landhaus, Landhaus und Garten*, and *Landhäuser*, respectively).

17. Hermann Muthesius, "Kultur und Kunst," in *Kultur und Kunst: Gesammelte Aufsätze über Künstlerische Fragen der Gegenwart* (Jena: Eugen Diederichs, 1904), 36. This essay first appeared in *Die Kunst für Alle* 15 (1900): 487–508, and as such represents a significant precedent to many of the arguments that reappeared in *Stilarchitektur und Baukunst* of 1902.

18. Muthesius, *Landhaus und Garten*, p. xv.

19. Ibid.

20. Muthesius discusses the relationship between stylistic fashions and "anti-culture" in "Kultur und Kunst," pp. 17–25. See also the analysis in Schwartz, *The Werkbund*, pp. 26–43.

21. *Stilarchitektur und Baukunst* (1902), p. 53.

22. Joining the Commerce Ministry in 1897 with a background in law and economics, von Seefeld rose gradually to become a Commerce Ministry undersecretary in the Weimar Republic. Von Seefeld published some two dozen articles and gave lectures on state support for the traditional *Mittelstand*,

pedagogical methods in primary schools and trades schools, and the trades education system. A bibliography of his writings can be found in Alfred Von Seefeld, "Anlass des 100. Geburtstages von Hermann von Seefeld am 21. December 1963," Archiv-Heimatmuseum Zehlendorf, typescript, 9. I am grateful to Benno Carus of the Archiv-Heimatmuseum for his generous insights on von Seefeld's family and estate materials. See also the helpful discussion in Kurt Trumpa, *Zehlendorf in der Kaiserzeit: vom Dorf zum Vorort* (Berlin: Grundkreditbank EG, 1985), 96–97. Further information about Zehlendorf and its evolution is in Jürgen Wetzel, *Zehlendorf*, Geschichte der Berliner Verwaltungsbezirke, Band 12, ed. by Wolfgang Ribbe (Berlin: Colloquium Verlag, 1988); Heimatverein Zehlendorf, ed., *Zehlendorf: Handel und Wandel eines Berliner Bezirks* (Berlin: Heimatverein Zehlendorf, 1996); n.a., "Die neue Vorortbahn Berlin-Potsdam (Wannseebahn), *CdB* 11 (1891): 378–79.

23. Muthesius corresponded with Schmidt about furniture being produced for the von Seefeld house in March and April 1905; see Schmidt to Muthesius March 16 and 25 and April 22, 1905, NMWA.

24. Karl Scheffler, *Der Architekt* (Frankfurt a. M.: 1907), vol. 10 in the series, Die Gesellschaft: Sammlung sozialpsychologischer Monographien, ed. Martin Buber, as quoted in Hartmut Frank, "Ein Bauhaus vor dem Bauhaus," p. 1645.

25. Anna Muthesius's self-published verse contains a poem entitled "Herrn von Seefeld," a birthday poem that is a testimony to the close friendship that existed between the Muthesius and von Seefeld families. See Anna Muthesius, *Gereimtes und Ungereimtes* (Privatdruck, Charlottenburg: Kunstgewerbe- und Handwerkerschule Charlottenburg, 1926), 35; I am grateful to Laurent Stalder for bringing Anna Muthesius's publication to my attention; see also Kurt Trumpa, *Zehlendorf in der Kaiserzeit*, pp. 47, 96–97, 176. On von Seefeld's work as a Zehlendorf town councilman see LAB A Rep 040 Nr. 232.

26. Von Seefeld appears to have also been in a position to help Muthesius in ways extending beyond his role as a sympathetic Commerce Ministry official. Just as he had commissioned Muthesius's first house, it is likely that von Seefeld, in his capacity as a Zehlendorf town councilman, also supported Muthesius's appointment to Zehlendorf's newly created design-review board. Bearing the official title of "Town Commission Against Disfigurement" (*Gemeindekommission gegen Verunstaltung*), the board was comprised of Muthesius and other local architects, among them Paul Mebes, the author of the architectural folio of buildings from *Around 1800* (*Um 1800*). The Commission Against Disfigurement boosted member architects' influence by allowing them to pass judgment on the works of their peers in order to prevent

"botches" and to enforce a relatively consistent, if conservative, aesthetic standard. At the commission's direction, the *Landhaus* form became the "required binding element" for the building ensemble by Otto Kuhlmann that came to surround the plaza of the new S-bahn station at Zehlendorf-West. Trumpa, *Zehlendorf in der Kaiserzeit*, p. 61; Landesdenkmalamt Berlin, *Baudenkmale in Berlin*, pp. 142–44.

27. The original language gives the clearest sense of Muthesius's intentions:

> Man erblickt im Garten eine Fortsetzung der Räume des Hauses, gewissermaßen eine Reihe einzelner Außenräume, von denen jeder in sich geschlossen eine gesonderte Bestimmung erfüllt. So erweitert der Garten das Haus in die Natur hinein, zugleich gibt er ihm den Rahmen in der Natur, ohne den es in seiner Umgebung als Fremdkörper stehen würde. Der geordnete Garten ist für das Haus, ästhetisch genommen, die Basis, auf der es sich aufbaut, wie das Standbild auf dem Sockel.

Muthesius, *Das englische Haus*, vol. 2: Bedingungen, 85.

28. Quoted in Schneider, *Hermann Muthesius*, p. 51.

29. Muthesius, *Landhaus und Garten*, p. 23. Following the von Seefeld House Muthesius completed a *Landhaus* for the Swiss engineer Eduard Bernhard in Berlin-Grunewald (1904–05) (no relation to Karl Bernhard, Behrens's engineer for the AEG Turbine factory). The 1978 Akademie der Künste exhibition catalog of Muthesius's built work, *Hermann Muthesius 1861–1927*, incorrectly lists the dates of the von Schuckmann house as 1905 and the Neuhaus house as 1906; Julius Posener publishes the correct date of 1907 for both houses in his updated history, *Berlin auf dem Wege zu einer neuen Architektur: Das Zeitalter Wilhelms II*. pp. 137–38. Permission to break ground on the Neuhaus house was granted by local building authorities on June 30, 1906, and the house was ready the following year. See Bau- und Wohnungsaufsichtsamt Zehlendorf, Grundstücksakte Bernadottestr. 56/58 (Haus Neuhaus), Dahlem, vol. 1, 30. I am grateful to Dr. Peter Heynert, who renovated the Neuhaus house and is its current owner, for his generous assistance in my study of this residence.

30. Trumpa, *Zehlendorf in der Kaiserzeit*, p. 50.

31. Else Meissner, *Das Verhältnis des Künstlers zum Unternehmer im Bau- und Kunstgewerbe* (Munich: Verlag von Duncker und Humbolt, 1915), in Gustav Schmoller und Max Sering, eds., *Staats- und sozialwissenschaftliche Forschungen*, Heft 185, pp. 36–37 (hereafter *Das Verhältnis*); see also Trumpa, *Zehlendorf in der Kaiserzeit*, p. 50.

32. Meissner, *Das Verhältnis*, pp. 81–3.

33. See Schwartz, *The Werkbund*, pp. 147–63.

34. Meissner, *Das Verhältnis*, pp. 36–37.

35. Gwendolyn Wright, *Moralism and the Model Home: Domestic Architecture and Cultural Conflict in Chicago, 1873–1913* (Chicago: University of Chicago Press, 1980), 98.

36. Villen- und Landhaus-Baugesellschaft "Heimstaedten-Aktien-Gesellschaft," *Werbeschrift* (Berlin: 1897); Landesdenkmalamt Berlin, ed., *Baudenkmale in Berlin*, p. 33; Trumpa, *Zehlendorf in der Kaiserzeit*, p. 194.

37. Quoted in "Villa Ebeling in Wannsee," *CdB* 13 (1893): 69; see also Landesdenkmalamt Berlin, ed., *Baudenkmale in Berlin*, 74–77; 185–86.

38. "Villa Ebeling in Wannsee," p. 70.

39. Muthesius, *Stilarchitektur und Baukunst* (1902), pp. 59–60.

40. Muthesius, *Stilarchitektur und Baukunst*, 2nd ed. (1903), pp. 80–81; I am here using the translation by Stanford Anderson, *Style-Architecture and Building-Art*, p. 100.

41. Muthesius, *Landhaus und Garten*, p. xiv.

42. See, for example, Stuart Durant, *CFA Voysey*, Architectural Monographs No. 19 (London: Academy Editions), 21.

43. The latter piece still hangs in its original position in the house, while the former is at the Hamburg Museum of Applied Arts.

44. Initial design drawings, BWAZ, Grundstücksakte Potsdamer Chausee 49a, Nikolassee, Bd. I, 16.

45. See *DKuD* 12 (October 1908): 21.

46. Muthesius, *Das englische Haus*, vol. 2, p. 131; Jill Franklin, "Edwardian Butterfly Houses," *Architectural Review* 157 (April 1975): 220–25; Hermann Muthesius, "Vorwort," *Baillie Scott, London: Haus eines Kunstfreundes*, in Meister der Innenkunst, Bd. I (Darmstadt: Alexander Koch, 1902).

47. Letter from Eckart Muthesius to Julius Posener, January 15, 1977, NMWA.

48. Akademie der Künste, *Hermann Muthesius 1861–1927*, p. 92; Posener, *Berlin auf dem Wege zu einer neuen Architektur*, pp. 137–46.

49. As a result of frequent and close contact among members of the Commerce Ministry and the Finance Ministry, Muthesius may even have been able to purchase this land directly from the government, though there is no conclusive proof of this. See LAB, Acc.2561 Nr.26 (1905); also Acc.373 Nr.13 (1913).

50. See Hermann Muthesius "Mein Haus in Nikolassee," *DKuD* 12 (Oktober 1908): 4; Muthesius, "Landhäuser," *DK* 14 (Oktober 1910): 2.

51. Deutscher Werkbund, "Programm der III. Jahresversammlung, Berlin 10–12 Juni 1910," UdK 7, 135. Jeanneret might well have met Muthesius's friend and colleague Hermann von Seefeld at Muthesius's Werkbund reception, which would have enabled the visiting Swiss architect and the Prussian privy councillor to establish that von Seefeld, in turn, had been visiting Jeanneret's applied-arts school on a government-commissioned study tour of his own exactly eight years earlier, while Jeanneret was studying there under L'Eplattenier. Jeanneret spent two additional days in Nicolassee sketching and painting houses, calling the suburb one of the best laid out and pleasant parts of Berlin he had seen. See H. Allen Brooks, *Le Corbusier's Formative Years*, pp. 220–21.

52. Anthony Sutcliffe, *Towards the Planned City*, p. 43; Brian Ladd, *Urban Planning and Civic Order in Germany, 1860–1914* (Cambridge: Harvard University Press, 1990); Posener, "Vorortgründungen," pp. 1–10; Landesdenkmalamt Berlin, ed., *Baudenkmale in Berlin*, pp. 14–48.

53. Sutcliffe, *Towards the Planned City*, pp. 43–45; George R. Collins and Christiane Crasemann Collins, *Camillo Sitte: The Birth of Modern City Planning* (New York: Rizzoli, 1986), 35–43; 91–94.

54. "Erinnerungen an Nikolassee: Aus einem Gespräch, dass Eckart Muthesius im Herbst 1977 mit Richard Friedenthal in London führte," in Akademie der Künste, *Hermann Muthesius 1861–1927*, p. 29. See also the paeans to life in Nicolassee in Anna Muthesius, *Gereimtes und Ungereimtes*.

55. Plans for Letchworth Garden City had been under discussion since 1901, though it is not clear when the German architects first viewed Parker and Unwin's plan. See Walter L. Creese, *The Search for Environment, The Garden City: Before and After*, expanded ed. (Baltimore, Md.: Johns Hopkins University Press, 1992), 108–43; Stanley Buder, *Visionaries and Planners: The Garden City Movement and the Modern Community* (New York: Oxford University Press, 1990), 81–87.

56. Deutsche Gartenstadt-Gesellschaft, *Die Gartenstadt im Wort und Bild*, Flugschrift 7, Prospekt für Lichtbilder-Vorträge (Berlin: Deutsche Gartenstadt-Gesellschaft, 1906), 8, 13.

57. See Eva Bartsch, Benno Carus, and Kurt Trumpa, "Weltgeist, wo bist du? Lebensreformer ziehen an den Schlachtensee: Die Neue Gemeinschaft, 1902–1904," *Zehlendorfer Heimatbrief: Mitteilungen und Regionalgeschichtliche Beiträge* 41 (March 1998): 3–7. This article takes its title from Stanislaw Przybyszewski's memoirs of literary Berlin, who remembered his friend, the Expressionist writer and visionary Paul Scheerbarth, this way: "After his third glass he would fall under the table, slam the floor with his fist, begin to cry, and moan, 'World Spirit, where are you?'"; quoted from p. 3; see also Ulrich Wyrwa, "Das Haus der 'Neuen Gemeinschaft' am Schlachtensee," in Helmut Engel et al., eds., *Zehlendorf*, Geschichtslandschaft Berlin, Band 4 (Berlin: Nicolai Verlag, 1992), 347–61.

58. "Gartendstadt Frohnau bei Berlin," LAB, Kartenabteilung Acc. 2561 Nr. 28 (1909); Posener,

Berlin auf dem Wege zu einer neuen Architektur, pp. 300–04.

59. Villen- und Landhaus-Baugesellschaft, "Heimstaedten-Aktien-Gesellschaft" Werbeschrift (Berlin: 1897), 1, as quoted in Landesdenkmalamt Berlin, hrsg. *Baudenkmale in Berlin,* p. 33.

60. Trumpa, *Zehlendorf in der Kaiserzeit,* p. 194.

61. See Günther and Posener, eds., *Hermann Muthesius 1861–1927,* p. 83.

62. The Office for the Protection of Monuments in Berlin notes that the houses were not typical or serial houses in the strict standardized sense, but were "model in character." Landesdenkmalamt Berlin, hrsg. *Baudenkmale in Berlin,* p. 33.

63. See Akademie der Künste, *Hermann Muthesius 1861–1927,* pp. 64–66; 94–98; also the individual discussions of these houses in Muthesius, *Landhäuser* (1912 and 1922).

64. See "Dem Nachbarn Freudenberg," in Anna Muthesius, *Gereimtes und Ungereimtes,* p. 36.

65. These were located in the Hermann Gerson block of buildings across from Karl Friedrich Schinkel's Werder Church at the center of town, one block north of the wealthy clothing and fashion district surrounding the Hausvogteiplatz and Jerusalemerstrasse. The store, with its workshops and warehouse complex built over the course of several additions and alterations between 1880 and 1910, was torn down after receiving heavy bomb and fire damage in the Second World War. See the file "Grundstücksblock Gerson," in LAB, Sign. A Pr. Br. Rep. 042.

66. The Hamburg-Amerika Shipping Line was a major Gerson client; the Gerson workshops also carried out Hermann Muthesius's designs for Kaiser Wilhelm II's personal quarters aboard the steamer, "Bismarck." At the First Werkbund Exhibition in Cologne in 1914, Freudenberg's Gerson workshops executed numerous other works: Hermann Muthesius's pavilion interior for the Hamburg-Amerika Line; Gropius's suite of rooms for the Gerson firm's own exhibit; and the interior of Bruno Paul's "Yellow House." See Peter Jessen, "Nachruf für Hermann Freudenberg," in *Mitteilungen des Verbandes der Deutschen Moden-Industrie,* N.F., Heft 1 (1924): 3–8; Eugen Kalkschmidt, "Die Möbel- und Raumkunst auf der Werkbund-Ausstellung zu Köln a. Rh.," *MB* 15 (1914): 401–76, especially pp. 426–31 and 462–67.

67. This was the first noncommercial fashion show to be held in Germany. See the detailed account in Adelheid Rasche, "Peter Jessen, der Berliner Verein Moden-Museum und der Verband der deutschen Mode-Industrie, 1916 bis 1925," in *Waffen- und Kostümkunde* 37 (1995): 65–92, here pp. 80–81.

68. See Jessen, "Nachruf für Hermann Freudenberg," quotations from pp. 7–8.

69. Karin Wilhelm, *Walter Gropius: Industriearchitekt* (Braunschweig: Fr. Vieweg & Sohn,

1983), 77. On the Wild house see Muthesius, *Landhäuser* (1922), pp. 5–10. Anna Muthesius wrote a poem to Ruth Wild as well, "An Ruth Wild," in *Gereimtes und Ungereimtes,* p. 37.

70. "Dr. Phil. Heinrich Soetbeer," *Reichshandbuch der Deutschen Gesellschaft,* Bd. 2 (Berlin: Deutscher Wirtschaftsverlag, 1930): 1798. See also Hans Peter Ullmann, *Der Bund der Industriellen,* pp. 202–10.

71. See, for example, Muthesius's address to the committee's special congress held with the three aforementioned ministries and the full committee membership. Muthesius spoke to the assembly of the intimate connection between applied-arts manufacturing and the continual need to educate the public and improve their sense of taste as both consumers and citizens, a goal that could be furthered through exhibitions. He also reminded the assembled industrialists of the value that artists could bring to all industries through participation in various aspects of their business. See *Ausstellungskonferenz Düsseldorf 11 Januar 1908, Einberufen im Einvernehmen mit dem Auswärtigen Amt, dem Reichsamt des Innern und dem Preussischen Ministerium für Handel und Gewerbe von der Ständigen Ausstellungskommission für die Deutsche Industrie* (Vertraulich!), Stenographischer Bericht, GStA PK I 120 EXVI.1 Nr.3 Bd.1 (1907–11), 241–45; also pp. 8–10.

72. Borchard, *50 Jahre Preussisches Ministerium für Handel und Gewerbe,* p. 69.

73. Soetbeer's views are quoted in W. Wendlandt, "Die Einführung eines 'Deutschen Industrietages,'" in *Jahresbericht des Bundes der Industriellen für das Geschäftsjahr 1905/06* (Berlin: Klokow, 1907), 94–104.

74. See Akademie der Künste, *Hermann Muthesius 1861–1927,* pp. 100–01.

75. Information obtained from the special exhibition, "Funkstadt Nauen: 90 Jahre Funkgeschichte," Sonderausstellung des Museums der Stadt Nauen, August 1996. See also Jürgen Graaf, ed., *Telefunken: 90 Jahre Fortschritt in der Sendetechnik* (Berlin: Berlin Telefunken Sendertechnik Gmbh, 1993); Michael Bollé, *Die Grossfunkstation Nauen und ihre Bauten von Hermann Muthesius* (Berlin: Verlag Willmuth Arenhövel, 1996); also Akademie der Künste, *Hermann Muthesius 1861–1927,* p. 124.

76. On the Hibernia Affair, see Charles Medalen, "State Monopoly Capitalism in Germany: The Hibernia Affair, *Past and Present* 78 (February 1978): 82–112; Borchard, *50 Jahre Preussisches Ministerium für Handel und Gewerbe,* pp. 67–68; Walther, *Aus dem Leben von Theodor Adolf von Möller,* pp. 84–99; Lerman, *The Chancellor as Courtier,* pp. 134–35; Hans Fürstenberg, ed., *Carl Fürstenberg,* pp. 400–16; Feldman, *Hugo Stinnes,* pp. 92–98; Hellige und Schulin, eds., *Walther Rathenau-Maximilian Harden: Briefwechsel 1897–1920,* pp. 375–79; see also the discussion in Chapter 4, this volume; the von

Velsen house is mentioned in Akademie der Künste, *Hermann Muthesius 1861–1927*, pp. 64–65; see also "Haus von Velsen," *BAK* 13 (Juli 1910): 25; Muthesius, *Landhäuser* (1922), pp. 43–46.

77. See Akademie der Künste, *Hermann Muthesius 1861–1927*, pp. 47; 122–24. On the Gugenheim house see LAB, Rep. 202 Acc. 1806 Nr. 3750; also Muthesius, *Landhäuser* (1922), pp. 123–24.

78. Hermann Muthesius, "Die mechanische Seidenweberei Michels & Cie. in Nowawes bei Potsdam," *DK* 19 (1916): 190–95. Julius Posener has noted that Muthesius's Michels & Cie. factory was an anticipation of Le Corbusier's *usine verte*; see Akademie der Künste, *Hermann Muthesius 1861–1927*, p. 123.

79. De Burlet proved an important client for Muthesius. Not only did Muthesius design de Burlet's gallery space at the hotel, but it was through de Burlet that an avid hunter and art collector, a Herr Dryander, met the architect and subsequently hired him to build the aforementioned Dryander estate in Saxony. I am grateful to Hubertus Adam for this information, which he provided in the lecture "Zwischen Individualität und Representation: Hermann Muthesius, Haus Dryander, und der Landhaus Gedanke," Hermann-Muthesius-Symposion, symposium at the Muthesius-designed Dryander house in Zabitz, September 21, 1996.

80. See Anna Muthesius, *Das Eigenkleid der Frau* (Krefeld: Verlag von Kramer und Baum, 1903); also *Dekorative Kunst* (1904), clipping in GStA PK, I.HA 120 EX Fach 2 Nr.21 Bd. 7, file IIIb.2135.

81. The most knowledgeable source on the range and extent of Muthesius's projects is undoubtedly Uwe Schneider; his accumulation of extensive information on the architect's *Landhäuser* exceeds that of the Akademie der Künste catalog, *Hermann Muthesius, 1861–1927*, but it has, however, unfortunately never been published.

82. The Freudenberg house shell, for example, was constructed by the construction firm Joseph Frankel, while the majority of the interior work was done by craftsmen employed by the firm of Hermann Gerson; both were Berlin-based companies. See "Landhaus Hermann Freudenberg in Nikolassee," *BAK* 23 (Februar 1910): 5–6.

83. Jürgen Kocka, "Vorindustrielle Faktoren in der deutschen Industrialisierung: Industriebürokratie und 'neuer Mittelstand,'" pp. 269–71.

84. See the letters from Schmidt to Muthesius, March 16, 1905, and August 9, 1905, NMWA.

85. See Moeller, *Peter Behrens in Düsseldorf*, pp. 407–30; Anderson, *Peter Behrens*; Fritz Stahl, "Alfred Messel!," *Berliner Architekturwelt* 9 (Sonderheft, 1911); Walter Curt Behrendt, *Alfred Messel* (Berlin: Bruno Cassirer, 1911); Posener, *Berlin auf dem Wege zu einer neuen Architektur*, pp. 160–74; Barry Bergdoll, "The Nature of Mies's Space," and

Wolf Tegethoff, "Catching the Spirit: Mies's Early Work and the Impact of the 'Prussian Style,'" in Barry Bergdoll and Terence Riley, eds., *Mies in Berlin* (New York: Museum of Modern Art, 2001), 66–105; 134–52.

SIX. CULTURAL FAULT LINES IN THE WILHELMINE GARDEN CITY MOVEMENT

1. No less an authority than Julius Posener describes Hellerau as a "factory settlement with communitarian ideas." See Posener, *Berlin auf dem Wege zu einer neuen Architektur*, p. 275. Recent reassessments of Hellerau have placed particular emphasis on the garden city's active arts scene; see, for example, Dresdener Geschichtsverein, gen. ed., *Gartenstadt Hellerau: Der Alltag einer Utopie* (Dresden: Dresdener Geschichtsverein, 1997); Michael Fasshauer, *Das Phänomen Hellerau: Die Geschichte der Gartenstadt* (Dresden: Hellerau-Verlag, 1997); Karl Lorenz, *Wege nach Hellerau: Auf den Spuren der Rhythmik* (Dresden: Hellerau-Verlag, 1994). I am grateful to Kevin Repp for helpful discussions of this dimension of the Hellerau Garden City.

2. See Eva Bartsch, Benno Carus, and Kurt Trumpa, "Weltgeist, wo bist du? Lebensreformer ziehen an den Schlachtensee: Die Neue Gemeinschaft, 1902–1904," *Zehlendorfer Heimatbrief: Mitteilungen und Regionalgeschichtliche Beiträge* 41 (March 1998): 3–7. Further useful background can be found in Jost Hermann, "Meister Fidus: Vom Jugendstil-Hippie zum Germanenschwärmer," in Jost Hermann, *Avantgarde und Regression: 200 Jahre deutsche Kunst* (Leipzig: Edition Leipzig, 1995), 72–89.

3. The society and the early development of the German Garden City movement are discussed in Axel Schollmeier, *Gartenstädte in Deutschland: Ihre Geschichte, städtebauliche Entwicklung und Architektur zu Beginn des 20. Jahrhunderts* (Münster: Lit Verlag 1990), 57–61; Kristiana Hartmann, *Deutsche Gartenstadtbewegung: Kultur, Politik, und Gesellschaftsreform*, pp. 27–32; Julius Posener, *Berlin auf dem Wege zu einer neuen Architektur*, pp. 264–79; and Franziska Bollerey and Kristina Hartmann, "A Patriarchal Utopia: The Garden City and Housing Reform in Germany at the Turn of the Century," in Anthony Sutcliffe, ed., *The Rise of Modern Urban Planning* (New York: St. Martin's Press, 1980), 135–64; on the *Jugendbewegung*, see Fritz Stern, *The Politics of Cultural Despair*, pp. 176–80.

4. See Bartsch, Carus, and Trumpa, "Weltgeist, wo bist du?" p. 6.

5. Franz Oppenheimer, "Die Gartenstadt," *Neue Deutsche Rundschau* 14 (1903): 897, as quoted in Hartmann, *Deutsche Gartenstadtbewegung*, p. 28.

6. Ebenezer Howard, *To-Morrow: A Peaceful Path to Real Reform* (London: 1898); a second edition of Howard's book appeared as *Garden Cities of Tomorrow* in 1902, and was translated into German with the title *Gartenstädte in Sicht* (Jena: Eugen Diederichs, 1907). Extended discussions and quotations of Howard's argument appear, for example, in Deutsche Gartenstadt-Gesellschaft, *Gartenstädte*, Flugschrift 1 (Berlin: Verlag der Gartenstadt-Gesellschaft, 1903); Bernhard Kampffmeyer, *Die englische Gartenstadtbewegung*, Flugschrift 2 (Berlin: VGG, 1903); *Der Zug der Industrie aufs Land: eine Innenkolonisation*, Flugschrift 5 (Berlin: VGG, 1905); and *Die Gartenstadt im Wort und Bild*, Flugschrift 7 (Berlin: VGG, 1906).

7. Theodor Fritsch, *Die Stadt der Zukunft* (Leipzig: Hammer Verlag, 1896); Schollmeier, *Gartenstädte in Deutschland*, pp. 55–56.

8. Wolfgang Voigt, "The Garden City as Eugenic Utopia," *Planning Perspectives* 4 (1989): 295–312, quotation from p. 300.

9. Simon Pepper, "The Garden City Legacy," *The Architectural Review* 43 (June 1978): 321–24; Mervin Miller, *Letchworth: The First Garden City* (Chichester: Phillimore, 1989); Walter L. Creese, *The Search for Environment, The Garden City: Before and After*; also Stanley Buder, *Visionaries and Planners: The Garden City Movement and the Modern Community*.

10. Letter from Schmidt to Riemerschmid, September 26, 1906, quoted in Kristiana Hartmann, *Deutsche Gartenstadtbewegung*, p. 49. The complete correspondence is in GNM-ABK (Nachlass Riemerschmid).

11. Gebäude für Arbeiter- und Volkswohlfahrt, *Das Deutsche Kunstgewerbe 1906*, pp. 268–78; see also the description of this village in Chapter 4, this volume.

12. Ibid., p. 48.

13. Friedrich Naumann, *Neudeutsche Wirtschaftspolitik*, 3rd ed. (Berlin: Fortschritt, 1911). I am grateful to Kevin Repp for his discussion of this work and its connection to Naumann's larger thinking, in Repp, *Reformers, Critics, and the Paths of German Modernity*, pp. 58–63.

14. Carl Schorske, *Germany Social Democracy, 1905–1917: The Development of the Great Schism* (Cambridge: Harvard, 1955), 224–56; Hartmann, *Deutsche Gartenstadtbewegung*, p. 130, n. 5.

15. *Hohe Warte: Illustrierte Halbmonatsschrift für die künstlerischen, geistigen und wirtschaftlichen Interessen der städtischen Kultur*. The full title of this journal is significant for an understanding of its elite outlook: *High View: Illustrated biweekly Journal for the Artistic, Intellectual and Economic Interests of Urban Culture. Hohe Warte* was founded by Joseph Lux in 1904, and was supported by an editorial board of leading international architects and cultural figures including Muthesius, Otto Wagner and Kolomann

Moser of Vienna, Paul Schultze-Naumburg, Cornelius Gurlitt, and Alfred Lichtwark.

16. On social conservatism, see Lebovics, *Social Conservatism and the Middle Classes in Germany*, pp. vii–viii, 4–10.

17. The foremost critic was Werner Hegeman. See his *Das steinerne Berlin* Bauwelt Fundamente Nr. 3 (Frankfurt: Ullstein, 1963).

18. Schultze-Naumburg as quoted from 1906 in Winfried Nerdinger, *Theodor Fischer: Architekt und Städtebauer*, p. 117.

19. Letter from Schmidt to Muthesius, June 8, 1903, NMWA.

20. Letters from Schmidt to Muthesius, March 28, 1906 and March 24, 1909, NMWA.

21. Muthesius to W. H. Lever, July 26, 1902, NMWA, Letter Book II.

22. Hermann Muthesius, "Das Fabrikdorf Port Sunlight bei Liverpool," *CdB* 19 (1899): 133–36, 146–48.

23. J. Frahm, "Die Anlage von Gartenstädten in England zur Lösung der Arbeiterwohnungsfrage," *CdB* 25 (1905): 120–22; 138–39.

24. Hermann Muthesius, "England als Weltmacht und Kulturstaat," *Tägliche Rundschau*, Unterhaltungs-Beilage, September 14, 1899, p. 861.

25. Muthesius to Dönhoff, January 28, 1903, NMWA.

26. Muthesius, "England als Weltmacht und Kulturstaat," p. 867. "Aber es muss auch möglich sein, industriell gross zu werden, ohne eine Klasse von Menschen in den Boden zu treten und mit Beibehaltung der harmonischen Pflege der inneren Güter der Nation."

27. W. H. Lever, "Dwellings Erected at Port Sunlight and Thornton Hough," *The Builder* (9 March 1902): 312–18.

28. Ibid.

29. Ibid., pp. 134, 148.

30. Ibid., p. 133.

31. Walter L. Creese, *The Search for Environment*, pp. 108–43; also Stanley Buder, *Visionaries and Planners*, pp. 81–87.

32. Hartmann, *Deutsche Gartenstadtbewegung*, pp. 22–24.

33. Muthesius, *Die englische Baukunst der Gegenwart*, pp. 315–16; *Das englische Haus*, vol. 1, pp. 200–02.

34. Muthesius mentions in this connection the London County Council projects in Bethnal Green and Pimlico. See *Das englische Haus*, vol. 1, pp. 203–05. See also the discussion in Hans-Joachim Hubrich, "Das Landhaus und Kleinhaus im Kontext von Städtebau und Siedlungswesen," Akademie der Künste, *Hermann Muthesius 1861–1927*, pp. 17–21.

35. Muthesius, *Das englische Haus*, vol. 1, p. 202. See also Hubrich, *Hermann Muthesius: Die Schriften*

zu Architektur, Kunstgewerbe, Industrie in der "Neuen Bewegung," pp. 124–27.

36. See, for example, Deutsche Gartenstadt-Gesellschaft, *Die Gartenstadt im Wort und Bild*; "Die Deutsche Gartenstadtbewegung und ihr Vorstoss nach Gross-Berlin," *Baugewerks-Zeitung* 41 (1909): 915; "Aus englischen Gartenstädten," *Gartenstadt: Mitteilungen der deutschen Gartenstadtgesellschaft* 4 (1911): 8–11; "Das Englische Landhaus: Die Arbeiterhäuser der Bournville Kolonie erbaut von W.A. Harvey," *Hohe Warte* 1 (1904): 112–21.

37. Hermann Muthesius, "Wirtschaftsformen im Kunstgewerbe: Vortrag, Gehalten 30. Januar 1908 in der Volkswirtschaftlichen Gesellschaft in Berlin," in *Volkswirtschaftlichen Gesellschaft in Berlin, Volkswirtschaftliche Zeitfragen: Vorträge und Abhandlungen*, Heft 233 (Berlin: Verlag von Leonhard Simion, 1903), 23. At the same time, the company also combined forces with the Munich United Workshops for Art in Handcrafts. The two firms did not merge, but cooperated by exhibiting together and opening joint stores in Berlin, Munich, and Bremen. See Wichmann, *Aufbruch zum neuen Wohnen*, p. 20.

38. Schmidt to Muthesius, May 7, 1909, NMWA.

39. Karl Schmidt to Hermann Muthesius, March 28, 1906, NMWA.

40. Thiekötter, "Erste Kontakte," p. 25.

41. Friedrich Naumann, "Deutsche Gewerbekunst: Eine Arbeit über die Organisation des Deutschen Werkbundes," in *Werke*, Band 6, "Aesthetische Schriften," pp. 254–89.

42. Matthew Jeffries, *Politics and Culture in Wilhelmine Germany: The Case of Industrial Architecture*, pp. 164–65.

43. Schmidt to Muthesius, March 28, 1906, NMWA.

44. Ibid.

45. See Schmidt to Muthesius, June 8, 1903, NMWA, in which the entrepreneur requests that Muthesius write four one-page statements for a Schmidt exhibition in 1903 that would specifically target the public, government officials, applied-arts producers, and businesspeople about such topics as the "Applied Arts and Politics" and the "Applied Arts and the People's Economy."

46. Hermann Muthesius, "Das Maschinenmöbel," *Dresdener Hausgerät Preisbuch 1906* (Dresden 1906), as reprinted in *Hohe Warte* 2, Beilage (1905–06): 2.

47. Muthesius, "Die Bedeutung des Kunstgewerbes," p. 183. See also "Werkbundaktivitäten zur Konsumentenerziehung," in Siepmann und Thiekötter, eds., *Herman Muthesius im Werkbund-Archiv*, pp. 61–66.

48. Muthesius, "Wirtschaftsformen im Kunstgewerbe," p. 27.

49. Sonja Günther, "Richard Riemerschmid und die Dresdener Werkstätten für Handwerkskunst," in Winfried Nerdinger, ed., *Richard Riemerschmid: vom Jugendstil zum Werkbund*, p. 36.

50. Letter from Schmidt to Riemerschmid, September 17, 1906; as quoted in Hartmann, p. 142, n. 282.

51. "Dem erweiterten Vorstand gehören an," in Bernhard Kampffmeyer, *Von der Kleinstadt zur Gartenstadt*, Flugschrift 11 (Berlin-Schlachtensee: Deutsche Gartenstadt-Gesellschaft, 1907), 14.

52. Hans Kampffmeyer, "Die Gartenstadt in ihrer kulturellen und wirtschaftlichen Bedeutung," *Hohe Warte* 3 (1906–07): 106, 109.

53. Joseph Lux, "Die Gartenstadt Hellerau: Gründung der Deutschen Werkstätten für Handwerkskunst," *Hohe Warte* 3 (1906–07): 314, 316.

54. Schmidt to Riemerschmid, September 17, 1906, as reproduced in Hartmann, *Deutsche Gartenstadtbewegung*, p. 169; Hartmann also writes that Schmidt's work force grew to approximately five hundred by 1908; Hartmann, *Deutsche Gartenstadtbewegung*, p. 47.

55. Muthesius in *Hohe Warte* 3 (1906–07): 322–23. Naumann also believed in Hellerau as an important contributor to Germany's process of creating "a higher class of trained workers with special technical and artistic abilities." Naumann as quoted in *Hohe Warte* 3 (1906–07): 325.

56. Schmidt to Muthesius, May 6, 1908; Muthesius to Schmidt, May 5, 1908, NMWA.

57. The original German is important here:

> Darauf schickten Sie mir eine Ansichtsäusserung von Theodor Fischer, die ein absprechendes Urteil über Kunstgewerbeschulen enthielt und namentlich von der ungerechtfertigten Vorraussetzung ausging, dass die Schulen das niedergehende Handwerk wieder auf einen goldenen Zustand hätten bringen sollen. Es liegt auf der Hand, dass man das von der besten Schule nicht erwarten kann, denn der Niedergang des Handwerks hat wirtschaftliche und soziale Ursachen, auf die eine Schule nicht im entferntesten Einfluss haben kann.

Muthesius to Schmidt, May 5, 1908, NMWA.

58. Klaus-Peter Arnold, *Vom Sofakissen zum Städtebau: Die Geschichte der Deutschen Werkstätten und der Gartenstadt Hellerau* (Dresden, Basel: Verlag der Kunst, 1993), 335.

59. Wolf Dohrn, *Die Gartenstadt Hellerau und weitere Schriften* (Dresden: Hellerau-Verlag, 1992), 23; Hartmann, *Deutsche Gardenstadtbewegung*, pp. 49, 51.

60. "Die Gartenstadt Hellerau," typewritten manuscript alleged to be by Hermann Muthesius, Riemerschmid estate, GNM-ABK Nürnberg (1911), as cited in Hartmann, *Deutsche Gardenstadtbewegung*, p. 142, n. 284. On the fascinating case of Staaken, see Karl Kiem, *Die Gartenstadt Staaken (1914–1917):*

Typen, Gruppen, Varianten (Berlin: Gebr. Mann Verlag, 1997); Julius Posener, *Berlin auf dem Wege zu einer neuen Architektur*, pp. 275–78; Karl Kiem, "Die Gartenstadt Staaken als Prototyp der modernen deutschen Siedlung," in Vittorio Magnago Lampugnani and Romana Schneider, eds., *Moderne Architektur in Deutschland 1900 bis 1950: Reform und Tradition* (Stuttgart: Verlag Gerd Hatje, 1992), 133–50. Kiem identifies links between the building of this munitions "factory town" and the Interior Ministry of Clemens Delbrück; this rich avenue of research, however, has not yet been fully explored.

61. See Hartmann, *Deutsche Gardenstadtbewegung*, pp. 34–40; Posener, *Berlin auf dem Wege zu einer neuen Architektur*, pp. 275, 279, 556–60.

62. Hartmann, *Deutsche Gardenstadtbewegung*, pp. 68, 87–89; Nerdinger, *Richard Riemerschmid vom Jugendstil zum Werkbund*, pp. 400–06.

63. Ibid., pp. 52–82.

64. Theodor Fischer, "Gmindersdorf bei Reutlingen: Arbeiterkolonie von Ulrich Gminder GmbH in Reutlingen," in Casimar Hermann Baer, *Kleinbauten und Siedlungen* (Stuttgart: Verlag J. Hoffmann, 1919), 1–44, quotation p. 2. See also Nerdinger, *Theodor Fischer*, pp. 114–21; 211–13.

65. Direktorium der Ausstellung, *Das Deutsche Kunstgewerbe 1906*, pp. 268–79.

66. Ferdinand Tönnies, *Gemeinschaft und Gesellschaft: Grundbegriffe der reinen Soziologie* (Leipzig: 1887), translated as *Community and Society*, trans. by Charles P. Loomis (East Lansing: Michigan's State University Press, 1957). Tönnies is also discussed in Harry Liebersohn, *Fate and Utopia in German Sociology*, 1870–1923 (Cambridge, Mass.: MIT Press, 1988).

67. The original text reflects the intended mood even better:

> Wenn alles so bedacht und gemacht ist, dann müsste das Ergebnis sein, dass die Wohnstätten aussen wie innen dieselben Eigenschaften zeigen, die wir auch an den Bewohnern finden möchten: ehrlich und anständig, schlicht, genügsam und dazu stolz und ruhig, selbstbewusst, heiter und treu. Wenn man an einem Feierabend in einer solchen Gasse eine Schar gemütlich beieinander stehen sieht, nicht in Reih und Glied, nicht aufgeputzt, nicht irgendwie zur Schau sich stellend, sondern ohne strenge Ordnung, aber auch ohne dass sich einer belästigend vordrängte, in Hemdsärmeln vielleicht und die Pfeife zwischen die Zähnen, in behaglichem Gespräch, dann sollte man sich denken müssen: ja, die passen zueinander, die Häuser und die Menschen.

Richard Riemerschmid, "Das Arbeiterwohnhaus," *Hohe Warte* 3 (1906–07): 141, as cited in Harmann, *Deutsche Gardenstadtbewegung*, p. 83.

68. Hartmann, *Deutsche Gardenstadtbewegung*, p. 99.

69. Ibid., pp. 90–94.

70. Wenzel Holek, Lebensgang eines deutschtschechischen Handarbeiters, has reprinted in Julius Posener, "Die deutsche Gartenstadtbewegung – Dokumentation," in *Berlin auf dem Wege zu einer neuen Architektur*, pp. 285–87.

71. Letter from Walter Gropius to Karl Ernst Osthaus, March 23, 1912, as cited in Nerdinger, *Richard Riemerschmid: vom Jugendstil zum Werkbund*, p. 404.

72. On Behrens's AEG buildings, his German Embassy in St. Petersburg, and other works see Stanford Anderson, *Peter Behrens and a New Architecture for the Twentieth Century*.

73. Frank Jackson, *Sir Raymond Unwin: Architect, Planner and Visionary* (London: A. Zwemmer, 1985), 72–73.

74. Spiro Kostof, *The City Shaped: Urban Patterns and Meanings through History* (Boston: Bulfinch, 1991), 76.

75. Bournville and the almshouses were featured in *DK* 10 (1906–07): 316–23; Bennett and Bidwell's Rushby Mead in Mervin Miller, *Letchworth: The First Garden City*, pp. 72–73; Asmuns Hill and the English use of German precedents are discussed in Jackson, *Sir Raymond Unwin*, pp. 93–95. Numerous German townscapes, including an entire fold-out supplement map series of German cities, appear in Raymond Unwin, *Town Planning in Practice: An Introduction to the Art of Designing Cities and Suburbs*, 2nd ed. (London: T. Fischer Unwin, 1911). Additional discussion is contained in C. B. Purdom, *The Garden City: A Study in the Development of a Modern Town* (New York: Garland, 1985).

76. Muthesius, "Die Bedeutung des Kunstgewerbes," p. 183.

77. Barry Parker and Raymond Unwin, *The Art of Building a Home* (London: Longmans, Green & Co., 1901). For Unwin's book, see n. 75, this chapter.

78. This term has particular significance for the Werkbund debates, and is discussed in detail in Chapter 7, this volume.

79. Muthesius, "Wo Stehen Wir?" Vortrag auf der 4. Jahresversammlung des Deutschen Werkbundes in Dresden 1911, *Jahrbuch des Deutschen Werkbundes* (1912): 11–26; also reproduced in Julius Posener, *Anfänge des Funktionalismus*, pp. 187–205; the quotation is from Posener, *Anfänge des Funktionalismus*, p. 190.

80. Posener, *Anfänge des Funktionalismus*, p. 190.

81. Muthesius, *Landhäuser* (1912), pp. 178–85.

82. Hermann Muthesius, "Die Bedeutung der Gardenstadtbewegung," Vortrag von April 1914 abgedruckt in *Die Bedeutung der Gartenstadtbewegung: Vier Vorträge in Gegenwart der Frau Kronprinzessin* (Leipzig und Paris: Renaissance-Verlag Robert

Federn, 1914), 1–16; quote from p. 1. For a contemporary study of the garden city as a broadly interpreted approach to planning and real-estate development see F. Biel, *Wirtschaftliche und technische Gesichtspunkte zur Gartenstadtbewegung* (Leipzig: Verlag von H. A. Ludwig Degener, 1914).

83. Muthesius, "Die Bedeutung der Gartenstadt Bewegung," pp. 15–16.

84. Martin Wagner, "Gartenstadthäuser," *Neudeutsche Bauzeitung*, 6 (1910): 84.

85. See Marco De Michelis, "Gesamtkunstwerk Hellerau," in Werner Durth, ed., *Entwurf zur Moderne, Hellerau: Stand, Ort, Bestimmung* (Stuttgart: Deutsche Verlags-Anstalt, 1996), 35–56.

86. Erich Haenel, "Die Gartenstadt Hellerau," *Die Kunst*, 24 (April 1911), 327, as quoted in Hartmann, *Deutsche Gardenstadtbewegung*, p. 87.

87. On Wagner see Posener, *Berlin auf dem Wege zu einer neuen Architektur*, pp. 289–318.

88. Wagner, "Gartenstadthäuser," p. 82.

89. See Karl Lorenz's biographical essay in Wolf Dohrn, *Die Gardenstadt Hellerau und weitere Schriften*, pp. 94–109.

90. Hartmann, *Deutsche Gardenstadtbewegung*, p. 142, n. 292.

91. Schmidt's original language is important: "Wesentlich ist aber, dass vom Vorstand der Gardenstadt-Gesellschaft die netten, idealen Leute, die aber doch recht unklare Köpfe sind, nicht überwiegen. Die Herren haben z.B. auch keinerlei architektonisches Urteil. Insofern ist ganz wesentlich, dass sich der Aufsichtsrat aus den besten und fähigsten Leuten zusammensetzt, auch rein vom kaufmännischen Standpunkt." Letter from Karl Schmidt to Herr Israel, November 17, 1910, NMWA.

92. Ibid.

93. Hartmann, *Deutsche Gartenstadtbewegung*, p. 48.

SEVEN. *WERKBUNDPOLITIK* AND *WELTPOLITIK*: THE GERMAN STATE'S INTEREST IN GLOBAL COMMERCE AND "GOOD DESIGN," 1912–1914

1. Hermann Muthesius, *Die Werkbundarbeit der Zukunft und Aussprache darüber* (Jena: Eugen Diederichs, 1914); Friedrich Naumann, "Werkbund und Weltwirtschaft," in Naumann, *Werke*, 6: 331–50.

2. There is no evidence in the archives of the "Norms for German Industry" (*Deutsche Industrie-Normen*, or DIN) that Muthesius collaborated directly with various branches of industry or with the Association of German Engineers (*Verein deutscher Ingenieure*) in the development of his theses. Among the items at the DIN Archive that are helpful for

understanding the gradual development of standards, types, and norms for German industry, see "Begründung des Ausschusses für wirtschaftliche Fertigung," Versammlung im Reichswirtschaftsamt, 23. Februar 1918. In *Mitteilungen des Ausschusses für wirtschaftliche Fertigung* 1 (1918): 1–5; Karl Strecker, ed. *Verhandlungen des Ausschusses für Einheiten und Formelgrössen in den Jahren 1907 bis 1914* (Berlin: Julius Springer Verlag, 1914); W. Hellmich, "Der Normenausschuss der Deutschen Industrie," *Mitteilungen der Normenausschuss der Deutschen Industrie* 1 (January 1918): 1–2; J. Wallot, ed. *Verhandlungen des Ausschusses für Einheiten und Formelgrossen in den Jahren 1907 bis 1927* (Berlin: Verlag Julius Springer, 1928).

3. This was literally the text of Muthesius's first of ten theses distributed to his Werkbund colleagues; for the original text and a new translation of all ten theses, see Appendix B; see also the concise and insightful synopsis of the "Werkbund debate" by Stanford Anderson, "Deutscher Werkbund – the 1914 Debate: Hermann Muthesius versus Henry van de Velde," in Ben Farmer and Hentie Louw, eds., *Companion to Contemporary Architectural Thought* (London and New York: Routledge, 1993), 462–67.

4. The CDI represented heavy industry, led by coal, iron, and steel, which exerted particular influence through its control of prices and supplies of raw materials. The BDI contained industries in which textiles, foods production, light machinery and instrument-making, and wood and paper industries predominated. Since 1906, the two organizations had engaged in an extended on-again, off-again effort to function in a joint *Interessengemeinschaft* (Partnership of Interests), but such cooperation could not be achieved until the government's formation of an official War Commission (Kriegsausschuss) in 1915. The Hansa League represented more of a broad mix of *Mittelstand* trades workers and commercial and white-collar employees. It is worth noting, however, that industrialists like AEG-owner Emil Rathenau spoke at the organization's founding in 1909. See Hans-Peter Ullman, *Der Bund der Industriellen: Organisation, Einfluß und Politik klein- und mittelbetrieblicher Industrieller im Deutschen Kaiserreich 1895–1914* (Göttingen: Vandenhoeck & Ruprecht, 1976), 34–48; 184–92; 214–15; Stegmann, *Die Erben Bismarcks*, pp. 176–78; 242–44.

5. Klaus Wernecke, *Der Wille zur Weltgeltung: Außenpolitik und Öffentlichkeit im Kaiserreich am Vorabend des Ersten Weltkrieges* (Dusseldorf: Droste, 1970), 294.

6. Geoff Eley, *Reshaping the German Right*, p. 349.

7. The Werkbund contributed 1,000 Marks annually to Osthaus's Deutsches Museum. Though supportive of the need to provide superior examples of German advertising designed by artists, Muthesius

did not want to get too close to the idea. He chafed, for example, at being credited as the initiator of the Deutsches Museum's rotating exhibition of advertisements at the Berlin College of Commerce, which Muthesius facilitated. See Anna-Christa Funk, *Karl Ernst Osthaus gegen Hermann Muthesius: Der Werkbundstreit 1914 im Spiegel der im Karl Ernst Osthaus Archiv erhaltenen Briefe* (Hagen: Karl Ernst Osthaus Museum, 1978), 2. Werkbund funding for the museum is discussed further in Laurie Stein, " 'Der neue Zweck verlangte eine neue Form' " – Das Deutsche Museum für Kunst in Handel und Gewerbe im Kontext seiner Zeit," in Sabine Röder and Gerhard Storck, eds., *Deutsches Museum für Kunst in Handel und Gewerbe: Moderne Formgebung 1900–1914* (Krefeld: Kaiser Wilhelm Museum, 1997), 23.

8. Schwartz, *The Werkbund*, p. 165.

9. BArch, R901 18206 ("Förderung der deutschen Kunst im Auslande durch Ausstellungen – Deutsches Museum für Kunst in Handel und Gewerbe in Hagen, 1914").

10. See Ernst Jäckh, *Der goldene Pflug: Lebensgeschichte eines Weltbürgers* (Stuttgart: Klett Verlag, 1957); also Klaus Wernecke, *Die Wille zur Weltgeltung: Aussenpolitik und Öffentlichkeit im Kaiserreich am Vorabend des Ersten Weltkrieges* (Dusseldorf: Droste Verlag, 1970), 68, and Campbell, *The German Werkbund*, p. 95, n. 47.

11. This is the characterization of Jäckh by Wilhelm Arnhim, writing to the Pan-Germanist Heinrich Class in February 1914, as quoted in Wernecke, *Die Wille zur Weltgeltung*, p. 300.

12. Ernst Jäckh to Undersecretary of Foreign Affairs Alfred Zimmerman, May 29, 1913, as quoted in Wernecke, *Die Wille zur Weltgeltung*, p. 300. This list included the *Berliner Tageblatt, Vossische Zeitung, Berliner Börsen-Courier, Frankfurter Zeitung, Münchner Neuesten Nachrichten, Leipziger Neuesten Nachrichten*, Vienna's *Neue Freie Presse, Hilfe, Preussische Jahrbücher, Süddeutschen Monatshefte*, and others. For a sense of the background and various orientations of these newspapers, see the fascinating study by Peter de Mendelssohn, *Zeitungsstadt Berlin*, 2nd ed. (Berlin: Ullstein Verlag, 1982). I am indebted to the historian Kevin Repp for this reference.

13. Deutscher Werkbund, *Die Wiener 5. Jahresversammlung des Deutschen Werkbundes vom 6. bis 9. Juni 1912* (Berlin: Geschäftsstelle des Werkbundes [1912]), 3, 25 (cited hereafter as *5. Jahresversammlung*).

14. On Foreign Ministry and Interior Ministry support for the Werkbund see, for example, Staatssekretär des Innern (Delbrück) an Gottlieb von Jagow, Staatssekretär des Auswärtigen Amtes, February 27, 1913, in Barch, R 901/18350, 7a–8b. Also Borchard, *50 Jahre Preussisches Ministerium für Handels und Gewerbe, 1879–1929* (Berlin: Reichsver-

lag H. Kalkoff, 1929), p. 58; Thiekötter, *Hermann Muthesius im Werkbund-Archiv*, p. 67. On Delbrück's status as "most trusted" colleague of the Chancellor, see Stegmann, *Die Erben Bismarcks*, pp. 415, 420, quotation from p. 420.

15. Deutscher Werkbund, *5. Jahresversammlung*, p. 7. Dönhoff was the official to whom Muthesius most frequently reported from England, as the files of the GStA PK confirm (see Chapter 2, this volume). Muthesius, as vice chair of the Werkbund executive committee, naturally also represented the Prussian government at the Vienna meeting, but since this was considered coincidental with respect to his Werkbund duties, he was never mentioned in his capacity as a ranking government civil servant. This appears to be typical for the Wilhelmine government's behavior in forging ties with associations through overlapping memberships.

16. *5. Jahresversammlung*, pp. 10–11.

17. Ibid., p. 8.

18. Deutscher Werkbund, *5. Jahresversammlung*, p. 10. In this connection, Bruckmann reminded Werkbund architects that wealthy clients commissioning "impressive, beautiful new homes" represented ideal candidates for Werkbund membership. In a tone that drew a laugh from the membership, Bruckmann added that their evident good taste and financial resources also qualified them to make even better potential donors. Bruckmann's comment applied particularly to Muthesius. Among commissions carried out by the government architect were *Landhäuser* for Heinrich Soetbeer (1907), a Werkbund member as of 1912 and General Secretary of the Deutscher Handelstag (Association of German Chambers of Commerce); Fritz Gugenheim (1914), executive committee member of the German Industrial Exhibitions Commission; Hermann Freudenberg (1909), owner of the Hermann Gerson Fashion House and Interior Furnishings Store in Berlin and future director of the Werkbund Fashion Commission; and Alfred Mohrbutter (1913), Werkbund member and professor of decorative painting at the School of Applied Arts in Charlottenburg. For a full discussion, see Chapter 5, this volume.

19. On the work of Rehorst and other architects in Cologne, see Richard Klapheck, "Die Stadt Cöln a. Rh. in Ihrer neuen baulichen Entwickelung," *Moderne Bauformen* 13 (1914): 249–313. See also "Ausstellung 'Alt- und Neu-Cöln' 1914," *Die Woche* 16 Nr. 23 (6 June 1914): 975–76; Wolfram Hagspiel, "Die Kölner Architekten um 1914," in Wulf Herzogenrath et al., eds., *Der westdeutsche Impuls 1900–1914, Kunst und Umweltgestaltung im Industriegebiet: Die Deutsche Werkbund-Ausstellung Cöln 1914* (Köln: Kölnischer Kunstverein, 1984), 42–52.

20. Undated letter from Hermann Muthesius to Ernst Jäckh (mid-1912), as reprinted in Ernst Jäckh,

Der goldene Pflug (Stuttgart: Klett Verlag, 1957) and cited in Angelika Thiekötter, "Vorbereitung der Deutschen Werkbund-Ausstelung Köln 1914," in Siepmann and Thiekötter, eds., *Hermann Muthesius im Werkbund-Archiv*, p. 67. Just as he had written in earlier treatises such as *Style-Architecture and Building-Art*, Muthesius remained completely convinced of the state's role as a promoter of German culture. Concerning Muthesius's stated low opinion of the Werkbund's "ash heap existence," see Chapter 6, this volume.

21. Thomas Nipperdey, *Deutsche Geschichte, 1866–1918*, pp. 748–57.

22. Thomas Nipperdey, *Deutsche Geschichte, 1866–1918*, pp. 745–48; Carl Schorske, *German Social Democracy, 1905–1917: The Development of the Great Schism* (Cambridge, Mass.: Harvard University Press, 1955), 224–35. For an excellent recent analysis of electoral practices in Wilhelmine Germany, see Margaret Lavinia Anderson, *Practicing Democracy: Elections and Political Culture in Imperial Germany* (Princeton: Princeton University Press, 2000).

23. Stegmann, *Die Erben Bismarcks*, pp. 246; 269–73; 415–20.

24. Ullmann, *Der Bund der Industriellen*, pp. 27–33; also Stegmann, *Die Erben Bismarcks*, p. 33.

25. Ullmann, *Der Bund der Industriellen*, pp. 214–16; Stegmann, *Die Erben Bismarcks*, pp. 178–81.

26. Stegmann, *Die Erben Bismarcks*, pp. 136–38; 218–21. Chancellor Bülow resisted BDI attempts to enlarge its presence from the dismal proportion of five out of thirty-five members of the Wirtschaftsausschuss. Increases in 1909 and 1910 in the total number of members making up the commission also neglected to accord the BDI a significantly larger proportion of representatives.

27. Naumann, "Von wem werden wir regiert?" in *Die Neue Rundschau* 20 Nr. 2 (1909): 636, as quoted in Stegmann, *Die Erben Bismarcks*, p. 180.

28. Jäckh first met Kiderlen-Wächter in Constantinople on August 6, 1908; see Kiderlen-Wächter to his wife, Hedwig Kypke, August 7, 1908, in Ernst Jäckh, ed., *Kiderlen-Wächter, der Staatsmann und Mensch: Briefwechsel und Nachlass* (Stuttgart: Deutsche Verlags-Anstalt, 1924). Kiderlen-Wächter died of a heart attack at age forty after serving as foreign minister for two and one-half years. See also Stegmann, *Die Erben Bismarcks*, pp. 244–45; V. R. Berghahn, *Germany and the Approach to War in 1914*, pp. 105–15.

29. BArch R901/18350, replies from German Consulates in Genoa, Jassy, Beirut, Singapore, Calcutta, and Batavia to Chancellor Bethmann-Hollweg, April 10, 1913; April 8, 1913; April 16, 1913; December 24, 1913; January 24, 1914; and February 7, 1914, respectively; German Consulates in Beirut, Kristiania to Deutscher Werk-bund Geschäftsstelle, April 16, 1913; April 29, 1913; pp. 53–142. The correspondence and attached lists of German firms active on foreign soil are interspersed in this file with Werkbund documentation and a site plan by Rehorst of the Cologne Exhibition grounds. For a discussion of Krupp and other industrialists at the Werkbund Exhibition, see Jeffries, *Politics and Culture in Wilhelmine Germany*, pp. 218–19.

30. Correspondence between Imperial Foreign Office and Freiherr von Stein, German Consul of Porto Alegre; between Chancellor Bethmann-Hollweg (Im Auftrag gez. Johannes) and Freiherr von Stein; and between Bromberg & Cie.-Hamburg and Foreign Office, numerous letters all related to Carvalho's arrangements and dated between May 4, 1914, and June 30, 1914, Barch R901/18350, 147–151b.

31. Where the Werkbund would enter into a hopeful new phase by welcoming foreign dignitaries to an exhibition for the first time in 1914, the Krupp "Cannon King" (*Kanonenkönig*) was adding to a long list of foreign customers: Krupp sold armor, artillery, shells, and other materials to fifty-two foreign governments before World War I and sold 24,000 artillery pieces to the German military as well. As William Manchester notes, in Essen alone Krupp's "eighty smoke-shrouded factories . . . used more gas than the city surrounding them, more electricity than all Berlin, and constituted a huge city within a city, with its own police force, fire department, and traffic laws . . . [and] Essen was only the apex of an iceberg" of Krupp factories and foreign holdings. Because the Krupp industrial empire was a family owned business, Krupp represented, in effect, a one-man arms race, a fact that William Manchester renders effectively throughout his exhaustive study, *The Arms of Krupp: 1587–1968* (Boston: Little, Brown and Co., 1968), here 263–64, quotation from p. 253.

32. Freiherr von Stein, German Consul in Porto Alegre to Chancellor Bethmann-Hollweg, April 8, 1914, Barch R901/18350, p. 148b.

33. "Auszug aus dem Protokoll der Plenar-Vorstandssitzung der Ständige Ausstellungskommission für die Deutsche Industrie am 29 April 1913 . . . in Verbindung mit mündlichen Ausführungen des Geschäftsfuhrers Herrn Dr. Jäckh," in Barch R901/18350, pp. 59–64, quotation from p. 63.

34. Clipping from *Kölnische Volkszeitung* (n.d.), in Barch, R 3101/616, p. 35.

35. Staatssekretär des Innern (Delbrück) an Gottlieb von Jagow, Staatssekretär des Auswärtigen Amtes, February 27, 1913, in Barch, R901/18350, 7a–8b.

36. Chancellor Bethmann-Hollweg to the general consulates in Singapore, Batavia and Calcutta and Imperial consulates in Bombay and Columbo, August 14, 1913 (gez. Goetsch, im Auftrag), pp. 94–94b;

also "Das Kolonialhaus auf der Deutschen Werkbundausstellung in Coeln 1914," Sonderabdruck aus
dem *Deutschen Kolonialblatt* Nr. 14 (15 July 1913),
clipping in Barch R901/18350, p. 93. This file makes
numerous mentions of drawings of buildings submitted from German colonial outposts, and although
none were extant in this file, it does suggest an interesting avenue for further research on the design
of German colonial architecture. For a nonarchi-
tectural discussion of Wilhelmine Germany's colonial aspirations, see Woodruff D. Smith, "Colonial-
ism and Colonial Empire," in Roger Chickering,
ed., *Imperial Germany: A Historiographical Companion*,
pp. 430–53.

37. The Commerce Ministry sent only fourteen
schools as compared with seventeen in 1906; the Culture Ministry sent both Bruno Paul's Berlin School of
Applied Arts and Hans Poelzig's Breslau Academy of
Art and Applied Art, neither of which had been represented in Dresden in 1906. See Deutscher Werkbund, *Deutsche Werkbund Ausstellung Cöln 1914: Offizieller Katalog* (Cöln: Verlag von Rudolf Mosse,
1914), 37–42.

38. Sydow was to be the longest-serving Commerce Minister after Bismarck. He trained as a
lawyer and served both as a judge and as a director of
the telegraph section of the Imperial post. Borchard,
50 Jahre Handelsministerium, pp. 64–66.

39. Ibid., p. 69.

40. Ibid., p. 70.

41. Like Möller before him, Sydow faced considerable opposition from several quarters. But unlike
Möller, Sydow emerged victorious in the take-over
battle, in war circumstances of course, achieving full
recognition of the state's take-over in February 1917.
Borchard, *50 Jahre*, p. 67.

42. Stegmann, *Die Erben Bismarcks*, pp. 344–51,
quotation from p. 347.

43. Ibid., p. 347.

44. Emil Lederer, *Die wirtschaftlichen Organisatio-
nen und die Reichstagswahlen* (Tübingen: 1912), 51, as
quoted in Stegmann, *Die Erben Bismarcks*, p. 344.

45. Stresemann obtained results when he put direct pressure on Interior Minister Delbrück to back
the BDI in the context of what Stresemann called
Germany's *Weltpolitik* (global politics). In 1910,
Delbrück's ministry dropped its previous opposition
to Stresemann's call for insurance for private employees of large businesses. Stresemann had assured
Delbrück that unless the government sanctioned new
insurance programs for private employees, then the
Interior Minister would find "1.8 million private
business employees in the state of Saxony alone voting socialist" in the next election. Delbrück's ministry introduced a bill for private insurance – to the
surprise and consternation of Commerce Minister
Sydow – but this did not stop the Social Democratic
Party from winning its largest victory to date in the

elections of 1912. See Ullmann, *Der Bund der Industriellen*, pp. 215–20.

46. Stegmann, *Die Erben Bismarcks*, pp. 392–93.

47. The Saar region also saw the successful collaboration of heavy and light industries in a regional
coalition. Ibid., pp. 437–38.

48. Fachverband für die wirtschaftlichen Inter-
essen des Kunstgewerbes e.V., ed., *Der "Deutsche
Werkbund" und seine Ausstellung Koeln 1914: Eine
Sammlung von Reden und Kritiken nach der "Tat"*
(Berlin: Hermann Bergmann, 1915), 18–19.

49. Quotation from Fischer, *War of Illusions*,
p. 236. See also Campbell, *The German Werkbund*,
pp. 93–98.

50. Fischer, *War of Illusions*, p. 237.

51. See Wernecke, *Der Wille zur Weltgeltung*,
pp. 288–310.

52. In 1913 Jäckh wrote, for example: "Helgoland
and the fleet can protect Germany and hold England
at bay. Baghdad and the Railway can threaten England at its sorest spots – at the Indian and Egyptian
borders. This is what England has to fear." Ernst
Jäckh, *Deutschland im Orient nach dem Balkankrieg*
(Strassburg: Verlag Singer, 1913), as quoted in
Wernecke, *Der Wille zur Weltgeltung*, p. 292.

53. See Fritz Fischer's discussion of "Groups and
Associations aiming at Berlin-Baghdad as the 'New
German Objective,'" in *War of Illusions*, pp. 446–
58. The historian Karl Erich Born calls the Berlin-
Baghdad railway project, which was first conceived
by the Ottoman Sultan Abdul Hamid II in 1887,
"the most spectacular enterprise undertaken abroad
by German banks." See Karl Erich Born, *International Banking in the 19th and 20th Centuries*, trans. by
Volker R. Berghahn (Warwickshire: Berg Publishers,
1983), 138–46.

54. For a discussion of this competition, to which
Jäckh invited twelve Werkbund architects including Peter Behrens, Bruno Taut, and Paul Bonatz, see Wolfgang Pehnt, *Expressionist Architecture*,
pp. 71–72; Jäckh discusses the project in several
places in connection with the larger goals of the
Werkbund and German foreign policy; see *Werkbund und Mitteleuropa* (Weimar: Gustav Kiepenhauer, 1916), 16–18; *Der goldene Pflug*, p. 202;
322–34; and especially Deutscher Werkbund and
Deutsch-Türkischen Vereinigung, eds., *Das Haus
der Freundschaft in Konstantinopel, ein Wettbewerb
für deutscher Architekten* (Munich: F. Bruckmann,
1918).

55. Ernst Jäckh, *Deutschland im Orient nach
dem Balkankrieg*; Ernst Jäckh and Paul Rohrbach,
Das Grössere Deutschland, as described by Paul
Rohrbach in "Zum Weltvolk hindurch!" in *Preußis-
che Jahrbücher* (1914): 4, as cited in Fischer,
War of Illusions, pp. 448–49; 449, n. 20; Ernst
Jäckh, *Der aufsteigende Halbmond: Auf dem Weg
zum Deutsch-Türkischen Bündnis* (Stuttgart: Deutsche

Verlags-Anstalt, 1915); Ernst Jäckh, *Werkbund und Mitteleuropa*.

56. Friedrich Naumann, *Mitteleuropa*, in Naumann, *Werke*, 4: 485–835.

57. Muthesius's documents and vast correspondence were most likely housed in two locations: the State Trades Board, located in a top-floor addition to the Commerce Ministry at Leipziger Platz 2, overlooking Alfred Messel's famous Wertheim Department Store complex, or at his house in Nicolassee. In the first case, the Commerce Ministry and State Trades Board took a direct hit from an allied bomb in the late phases of World War II. In the second, Hermann Muthesius's youngest son, the architect Eckart Muthesius, reported that on returning to the Muthesius *Landhaus* in Nikolassee in 1945, Soviet soldiers were in the middle of emptying the attic of boxes of documents and burning them in the yard in order to clear more space in the house for use as a field hospital. Frantically conveying the importance of these files to the Soviet lieutenant in charge, Eckart Muthesius managed to halt the process, but not before dozens of boxes of his father's correspondence and other files had been destroyed. The remaining 7,000 letters and other documents, inherited by Hermann Muthesius's eldest son, Günther, passed on through Günther's son Wolfgang to become the heart of the collection of Muthesius papers at Berlin's Museum der Dinge-Werkbund Archiv in Berlin. I am grateful to Vera Muthesius and the late Wolfgang Muthesius for their generous cooperation in filling in gaps in the family history and for helping to trace the fate of important historical documents, both extant and missing.

58. Letter from Osthaus to Jäckh, July 14, 1914, as quoted in Thiekötter, "Vorbereitung der Deutschen Werkbund-Ausstellung Köln 1914," p. 69.

59. Osthaus got to write the article, but both he and Muthesius had to pull back from working on the yearbook any further. See the correspondence reproduced in Funk, *Karl Ernst Osthaus gegen Hermann Muthesius*, pp. 2–4. The article in question is Karl Ernst Osthaus, "Der Bahnhof," *JDWB* 1914, 33–41.

60. Jäckh, *Der goldene Pflug*, p. 196.

61. Deutscher Werkbund, *Leitsätze ausgearbeitet von dem Geschäftsführenden Ausschuss auf Grund der Gründungsversammlung des Bundes zu München am 5. Und 6. Oktober 1907*, n.p., n.d., as discussed in Campbell, *The German Werkbund*, p. 45.

62. "Von der Deutschen Werkbundausstellung in Köln," *Deutsche Bauhütte* 17, Nr. 23 (1913): 295, as quoted in Thiekötter, "Vorbereitung der Deutschen Werkbund-Ausstellung Köln 1914," p. 71.

63. Hermann Muthesius, "Der Deutsche Werkbund und die Qualitätsbestrebungen in Handel und Industrie, in *Marburgische Zeitung*, June 15, 1913, p. 19, as quoted in Thiekötter, "Vorbereitung

der Deutschen Werkbund-Ausstellung Köln 1914," p. 71.

64. 5. Jahresversammlung, pp. 16–21.

65. Letter from Behrens to Rehorst, February 21, 1913, as quoted in Thiekötter, "Vorbereitung der Deutschen Werkbund-Ausstellung Köln 1914," p. 70.

66. Letter from Osthaus to Behrens, February 27, 1913, as quoted in Thiekötter, "Vorbereitung der Deutschen Werkbund-Ausstellung Köln 1914," p. 71.

67. According to Osthaus, Muthesius apparently disapproved when a member of the board of Krupp A. G. Company, Dr. Freiherr von Bodenhausen-Degener, insisted to the Werkbund exhibition committee that both Behrens and van de Velde be commissioned to design buildings for the exhibition. Muthesius backed down only after an awkward exchange with Osthaus, who defended the artists. Osthaus-Bodenhausen correspondence quoted in Angelika Thiekötter, "Der Werkbundstreit," in Wulf Herzogenrath et al., eds., *Der westdeutsche Impuls*, p. 82.

68. Thiekötter, "Muthesius' Beiträge zum Kölner Werkbund-Ausstellung," in Siepmann and Thiekötter, eds., *Hermann Muthesius im Werkbund-Archiv*, p. 81.

69. See Dirk Kocks, "Deneken, Muthesius und die Farbenschau," in Angelika Thiekötter, ed., *Der westdeutsche Impuls*, pp. 205–11.

70. Although Van de Velde, a born Belgian, claimed he had been discriminated against on nationalist grounds, he had had the express support of Konrad Adenauer, the Cologne mayor, and Louis Hagen, a prominent Cologne banker, for his commission. It is far more likely that opposition came from Muthesius and was based on personal and aesthetic grounds, as indeed Osthaus's correspondence on the matter with Carl Rehorst indicated. See the discussion in Thiekötter, "Vorbereitung der Deutschen Werkbund-Ausstellung Köln 1914," pp. 72–73.

71. Endell to Osthaus, May 2, 1914, as quoted in Thiekötter, "Vorbereitung der Deutschen Werkbund-Ausstellung Köln 1914," in Siepmann and Thiekötter, *Hermann Muthesius im Werkbund-Archiv*, p. 75.

72. Funk, *Karl Ernst Osthaus gegen Hermann Muthesius*, p. 6.

73. Poelzig to Gropius, June 30, 1914, as reprinted in Marcel Franiscono, *Walter Gropius and the Creation of the Bauhaus in Weimar*, p. 263.

74. See the discussion of tensions between the Culture and Commerce Ministries, and particularly between Muthesius and Poelzig in 1911, in Chapter 3, this volume.

75. Gropius's exhibition architecture is analyzed insightfully in Karin Wilhelm, *Walter Gropius: Industriearchitekt* (Braunschweig/Wiesbaden: Freidr.

Vieweg & Sohn, 1983), 71–88. The historian Angelika Thiekötter has noted that it was individual exhibiting artists participating in the Cologne Werkbund Exhibition of 1914 who protested against the actions of the exhibition planning committee in Gropius's position; it was not, for example, some significant portion of the general Werkbund membership. Thiekötter sees this as symptomatic of the Werkbund's operations, highlighting the undemocratic nature of the organization, as well as the relatively subordinate position of general Werkbund members in the emerging power politics of the Werkbund. See the discussion in Thiekötter, "Der Werkbundstreit," *Der westdeutsche Impuls*, pp. 86–87.

76. Bruckmann is quoted in a letter from Gropius to Osthaus, February 26, 1914, in Funk, *Karl Ernst Osthaus gegen Hermann Muthesius*, p. 6.

77. See the discussion by Stanford Anderson of Nikolaus Pevsner's *Pioneers of Modern Design* and Reyner Banham's *Theory and Design in the First Machine Age* in *Peter Behrens and a New Architecture for the Twentieth Century* (Cambridge, Mass.: MIT Press, 2000), 216 and n. 67; also Karin Wilhelm, *Walter Gropius: Industriearchitekt*, pp. 65–88.

78. Thiekötter, "Der Werkbundstreit," *Der westdeutsche Impuls*, pp. 85–86; Angelika Thiekötter et al., eds., *Kristallisation, Splitterungen: Bruno Tauts Glashaus* (Basel: Birkhäuser Verlag, 1993); for a discussion of Taut's close connection with Scheerbart in the development of the glass pavilion, see John A. Stuart, "Introduction," *The Gray Cloth: Paul Scheerbart's Novel on Glass Architecture*, pp. xxi–xxiv.

79. Quoted in Julius Posener, "Die Ausstellung des Deutschen Werkbunds in Köln 1914," in Siepmann and Thiekötter, eds., *Hermann Muthesius im Werkbund-Archiv*, p. 84. Not all reviewers were negative toward the predominance of classicism at the exhibition, however. Eugen Kalkschmidt's review of the twenty-two schools represented at the exhibition gushed that "in (Bruno Paul's) Berlin School of Applied Arts we seem to meet the epoch of Karl Friedrich Schinkel in a new form." Quoted in Eugen Kalkschmidt, "Die Deutsche Werkbundausstellung in Köln: Die Schulen," *Frankfurter Zeitung und Handelsblatt*, June 10, 1914, p. 1.

80. Julius Posener has maintained that the exhibition buildings of the older generation can be seen as an expression of Muthesius's notion of "the type," appearing within the matrix of Wilhelmine industrial patronage and bourgeois respectability. See Julius Posener, "Die Ausstellung des Deutschen Werkbunds in Köln 1914," in Siepmann and Thiekötter, eds., *Hermann Muthesius im Werkbund-Archiv*, pp. 86–87; Stanford Anderson's interpretation is essentially in accord with that of Posener in *Peter Behrens*, pp. 216–17, and in "Deutscher Werkbund – the 1914 debate," though Anderson emphasizes that

the architecture of the 1914 Werkbund exhibition shifts the meaning of Typisierung from "standardization" to stylistic conventionalism.

81. Hermann Muthesius, "Das Formproblem im Ingenieur-Bau," *Jahrbuch des Deutschen Werkbundes* (1913): 23–32; reprinted in Posener, *Anfänge des Funktionalismus*, pp. 191–98, see especially pp. 191, 197.

82. See also Stanford Anderson's useful discussion of the nuances in Muthesius's ten theses in "Deutscher Werkbund – the 1914 debate," pp. 462–67.

83. Muthesius, "Leitsätze," in Posener, *Anfänge des Funktionalismus*, p. 205; for an English translation, see Appendix B.

84. The theses drawn on in this paragraph are numbers four, six, seven, and eight. See Muthesius, "Leitsätze," in Posener, *Anfänge des Funktionalismus*, p. 205; See also Anderson, "Deutscher Werkbund – the 1914 debate," pp. 462–67; also Appendix B, this volume.

85. These pieces are discussed in detail in Chapter 2, this volume.

86. Letter from Walter Gropius to Karl Ernst Osthaus, February 26, 1914, and letter from Osthaus to Heinersdorff, November 26, 1913, as quoted in Siepmann and Thiekötter, eds., *Hermann Muthesius im Werkbund-Archiv*, pp. 74, 76.

87. Paul Valéry, "Une conquête méthodique," quoted in Gerhard Storck, "Eine Organisation, die ihre Fäden unsichtbar spinnt. Planungsziel: Werkkunst," in Röder and Storck, eds., *Deutsches Museum für Kunst in Handel und Gewerbe*, p. 26, n. 6.

88. Henry Van de Velde, "Gegen-Leitsätze," reprinted in Posener, *Anfänge des Funktionalismus*, pp. 206–07.

89. Thiekötter, "Der Werkbundstreit," *Der westdeutsche Impuls*, p. 79.

90. Henry Van de Velde, as quoted in Franciscono, *Walter Gropius and the Creation of the Bauhaus in Weimar*, p. 35.

91. Walter Gropius, "Programm zur Gründung einer Hausbaugesellschaft auf künstlerisch einheitlicher Grundlage m.b.H.," trans. and reprinted in an article entitled "Gropius at Twenty-Six," *Architectural Review* 130 (July 1961): 49–51, as discussed in Karin Wilhelm, *Walter Gropius: Industriearchitekt*, pp. 23–26; see also Gropius's letter to Osthaus on October 31, 1911, in which he asks Osthaus to help him find partners in support of his project for prefabricated industrial housing. Gropius's letter is reproduced in Siepmann and Thiekötter, eds., *Hermann Muthesius im Werkbund-Archiv*, p. 94.

92. Hermann Muthesius, "Die Werkbundarbeit der Zukunft," in Hermann Muthesius, "Die Werkbundarbeit der Zukunft und Aussprache darüber," Sonderdruck zur 7. Jahresversammlung

des Deutschen Werkbundes vom 2. Bis 6. Juli 1914 in Köln (Jena: 1914), 33–49; reprinted in Posener, *Anfänge des Funktionalismus*, pp. 199–204, quotation from p. 199.

93. Ibid., p. 200.

94. Ibid., pp. 202–03.

95. Ibid., pp. 203–04.

96. Friedrich Naumann, "Werkbund und Weltwirtschaft," lecture on July 4, 1914, to the Werkbund Annual Meeting in the festival hall of the Werkbund Exhibition in Cologne, reprinted in Naumann, *Werke*, 6: 331–50; quotation from pp. 348–49.

97. Hermann Obrist in "Aus der Diskussion," in Posener, *Anfänge des Funktionalismus*, p. 210.

98. Bruno Taut quoted in ibid., pp. 214–15.

99. "Schlusswort von Hermann Muthesius auf der 7. Jahresversammlung des Deutschen Werkbundes, Köln 1914," in Siepmann and Thiekötter, eds., *Hermann Muthesius im Werkbund-Archiv*, p. 97 (hereafter "Schlusswort von Hermann Muthesius"); excerpts from the debates are in Posener, *Anfänge des Funktionalismus*, pp. 208–21.

100. Muthesius to Riemerschmid, December 15, 1913, GNM-ABK, Nachlass Riemerschmid, I B 146.

101. Muthesius's 1907 speech that unleashed "The Muthesius Affair," entitled "The Significance of the Werkbund" and discussed in detail in Chapter 4, this volume, had led Muthesius and Delbrück both to claim that Muthesius had been speaking purely in his capacity as a private individual, an academic in the Berlin Commercial College, and not in any way as a representative of the Prussian Commerce Ministry or its policies. Quotation from "Schlusswort von Hermann Muthesius," p. 97.

102. Historian Hans-Peter Ullmann characterizes Georg Mosse's *Berliner Tageblatt* as the "protector of the Association of German Industrialists" in Ullmann, *Bund der Industriellen*, p. 128. Dirk Stegmann shares the same view in *Die Erben Bismarcks*, p. 174. Rudolf Mosse, who came from a modest background in the province of Posen, rose quickly as an innovative businessman. Riding the heady waves of expansion during the Second Reich's post-1871 "founding years," Mosse founded a successful newspaper advertising agency in 1867, the *Berliner Tageblatt* in 1871, the *Berliner Morgen-Zeitung* in 1889, and shortly thereafter the *Berliner Volkszeitung* and the *Deutsches Reichs-Adressbuch für Industrie, Gewerbe und Handel*. In the inaugural issue of the *Berliner Tageblatt* Mosse wrote, "On Berlin's road to becoming a world city our newspaper will accompany it as a trusted companion, an advisor, and a compatriot." Rudolf Mosse, *Berliner Tageblatt*, Nr. 1 (December 1871), p. 1; see Peter de Mendelssohn, *Zeitungsstadt Berlin*, pp. 89–99; 154–55; quotation from p. 99.

103. See note 9 and the discussion, this chapter.

104. Osthaus to Jäckh, July 10, 1914, BAGP, File 7; Osthaus to Gropius and van de Velde, July 10, 1914, BAGP, File 8; the latter is also reprinted in Anna-Christa Funk, *Karl Ernst Osthaus gegen Hermann Muthesius: Der Werkbundstreit 1914 im Spiegel der im Karl Ernst Osthaus Archiv erhaltenen Briefe* (Hagen: Karl Ernst Osthaus Museum, 1978), p. 9; hereafter cited as *Osthaus gegen Muthesius*.

105. Letter from Gropius to Osthaus, July 14, 1914, in Funk, *Osthaus gegen Muthesius*, p. 13.

106. Muthesius's article is quoted in a letter from Gropius to Osthaus, July 14, 1914, in Funk, *Osthaus gegen Muthesius*, p. 13; further in Osthaus to Jäckh, July 13, 1914, copy in BAGP, file 7.

107. Osthaus to Jäckh, July 13, 1914; Osthaus to Redaktion des *Berliner Tageblatts*, July 13, 1914; Osthaus to van de Velde, July 13, 1914, all in BAGP, file 7; Gropius to Leitung des Deutschen Werkbundes, July 14, 1914, BAGP, file 8.

108. Osthaus to Gropius, July 21, 1914, in Funk, *Osthaus gegen Muthesius*, p. 18.

109. "Eine Erklärung des Deutschen Werkbundes," *Berliner Tageblatt*, July 18, 1914, reprinted in Funk, *Osthaus gegen Muthesius*, p. 17.

110. Ibid.

111. Muthesius to Osthaus, July 23, 1914, in Funk, *Osthaus gegen Muthesius*, pp. 20–21.

112. Osthaus to Gropius, July 21, 1914, in Funk, *Osthaus gegen Muthesius*, pp. 17–18.

113. "Die Deutsche Werkbundausstellung Köln," *MDWB* (1915): 1–2.

114. Van de Velde had been battling for years against mounting discrimination and xenophobia in Weimar, particularly at the hands of Grand Duke Wilhelm Ernst, Minister of State Rothe, and Academy of Art director Fritz Mackensen; see the discussion in Chapter 1, this volume.

115. See the discussion earlier as well as notes 52–53, this chapter. The Werkbund Fashion Show is discussed in "Der Ausschuß für Mode-Industrie des Deutschen Werkbundes," *MDWB* (1915): 6–8; Ola Alsen, "Erste Modeschau des Werkbundes, Unter dem Protektorat der Kronprinzessin," *Elegante Welt* 1915 (Nr. 9): 5–10; see also Adelheid Rasche, "Peter Jessen, der Berliner Verein Moden-Museum und der Verband der deutschen Mode-Industrie, 1916 bis 1925," in *Waffen- und Kostümkunde* 37 (1995): 65–92.

116. Gropius attained the rank of sergeant major. See Reginald Isaacs, *Gropius: An Illustrated Biography of the Creator of the Bauhaus* (Boston: Bulfinch Press, 1991), 38–59.

CONCLUSION

1. Representative publications in Jäckh's series, "Der Deutsche Krieg: Politische Flugschriften"

(Stuttgart, Berlin: Deutsche Verlags-Anstalt, 1915–16), include Hermann Muthesius, *Die Zukunft der Deutschen Form*, Nr. 50; Gustav Stresemann, *Englands Wirtschaftskrieg gegen Deutschland*, Nr. 36; Norbert Stern, *Die Weltpolitik der Weltmode*, Nr. 30–31; and Ernst Jäckh, *Die Deutsch-türkische Waffenbruderschaft*, Nr. 24; see also Friedrich Naumann, *Mitteleuropa* (Berlin: Verlag Georg Bremer, 1915); a reprint of *Mitteleuropa* appears in Naumann, *Werke*, 4: 485–835.

2. Hermann Muthesius, *Die Zukunft der Deutschen Form*.

3. The historian Kevin Repp, in his unpublished manuscript, "'Nicht Einmal Burgfrieden': Creativity and Conflict in Berlin's Art World during the First World War," recounts the proliferation, among other things, of enameled likenesses of field marshals on praline boxes, illustrated war albums, war-bond posters, and mass-produced statues of German heroes. I am grateful to Kevin Repp for sharing his illuminating analysis of the fine-arts and applied-arts markets during the war.

4. See Chapter 7, this volume, for a detailed assessment of the Seventh Werkbund Congress and its aftermath, along with an analysis of internal and external political pressures exerted during the planning of the First Werkbund Exhibition in Cologne of 1914.

5. Muthesius, *Die Zukunft der Deutschen Form*, p. 21. Muthesius develops this theme in greater detail in *Der Deutsche nach dem Kriege*, 2nd ed., in "Weltkultur und Weltpolitik: Deutsche und öesterreichische Schriftenfolge," series ed. Ernst Jäckh-Berlin and Institut für Kulturforschung-Wien (Munich: F. Bruckmann, 1916); the first edition appeared in 1915.

6. Ibid., p. 36.

7. See, for example, *The German Gospel of Blood and Iron. Germany's War Mania: The Teutonic Point of View as Officially Stated by Her Leaders; a Collection of Speeches and Writings*, trans. by Dudley W. Walton (London: A. W. Shaw, 1914).

8. Eugen Kalkschmidt, "Mobilmachung im Kunstgewerbe," *Die Kunst* 32 (1914–15): 11–24.

9. Paul Westheim, "Krieg und Kunstgewerbe," *Sozialistische Monatshefte* 21 (January 1915): 60–62.

10. The specific nature of Muthesius's illness is unclear. See *MDWB* 1916, Nr. 5, p. 8.

11. See Campbell, *The German Werkbund*, pp. 101–03; 139–40.

12. Wilhelm von Bode, "Aufgaben der Kunsterziehung nach dem Kriege," *Die Woche* 18 (1 April 1916): 469–71.

13. Ibid., p. 471. The schools in Breslau and Berlin are examined in the final section of Chapter 3, this volume.

14. Hermann Muthesius, "Soll die kunstgewerbliche Erziehung zukünftig den Akademien übertragen werden?" *Die Woche* (18 May 1918): 489–91; see also Karl Gross, Bernhard Pankok, Karl Hoffacker, and Richard Riemerschmid, "Die Auflösung der Kunstgewerbeschule in Düsseldorf," *MDWB* 1919, Nr. 2, pp. 9–10. There is a brief discussion of the school's fate in Moeller, *Peter Behrens in Düsseldorf*, pp. 163–64. See also the discussions in Rothkirch-Trach, *Die Unterrichtsanstalt des Kunstgewerbemuseum in Berlin zwischen 1866 und 1933*, pp. 48–64; and Hubrich, *Hermann Muthesius: Die Schriften*, pp. 210–18.

15. Muthesius, "Soll die kunstgewerbliche Erziehung zukünftig den Akademien übertragen werden?" pp. 489–91.

16. See Bruno Paul, "Unzeitgemässe Notwendigkeiten," *DKuD* 35 (1914–15): 185–88; Bruno Paul, "Künstlerlehrzeit," *Wieland* 3 (1917–18); Bruno Paul, *Erziehung der Künstler an staatlichen Schulen* (Berlin: n.p., 1919). Paul's philosophy is discussed in greater detail in Rotkirch-Trach, *Die Unterrichtsanstalt des Kunstgewerbemuseums in Berlin*, pp. 200–06.

17. See Hermann Muthesius, "Die Kunstgewerbe- und Handwerkerschulen," in Bund der Kunstgewerbeschulmänner, ed., *Kunstgewerbe: Ein Bericht über Entwicklung und Tätigkeit der Handwerker- und Kunstgewerbeschulen in Preußen* (Berlin: Ernst Wasmuth, 1922), 1–10. For other discussions see Ministerium für Wissenschaft, Kunst, und Volksbildung, "Diskussion um wichtige Kunsterziehungsfragen," typescript of meeting protocol, June 10–11, 1919, BAGP, file 2; Gruppe der Kunstgewerbeschulmänner, "21. Wanderversammlung des Deutschen Gewerbeschul-Verbandes: Ist eine einheitliche Organisation der Kunstgewerbeschulen mit Abschlussprüfungen möglich und wünschenswert?" *Zeitschrift für Gewerbliche Unterricht* 31 Nr. 33 (September 1916): 385–86, Sonderdruck in BAGP, Vorgeschichte Kunstschulreform, file 3.

18. See Richard Riemerschmid, "Künstlerische Erziehungsfragen I," in *Flugschriften des Münchener Bundes*, Nr. 1 (Munich: Münchener Bund, 1917); Riemerschmid, "Künstlerische Erziehungsfragen II," in *Flugschriften des Münchener Bundes*, Nr. 5 (Munich: Münchener Bund, 1919); see also Ekkehard Mai, "Vom Werkbund zur Kölner Werkschule: Richard Riemerschmid und die Reform der Kunsterziehung im Kunstgewerbe," in Nerdinger, ed., *Richard Riemerschmid*, pp. 39–62; Katja Schneider, *Burg Giebichenstein*, pp. 17–18. Riemerschmid directed the Munich School of Applied Arts from 1913 until 1924.

19. Katja Schneider, *Burg Giebichenstein*, p. 20; see Chapter 1, this volume, for a detailed discussion of the cultural politics of design reform in turn-of-the-century Stuttgart and Württemberg.

20. See Franciscono, *Walter Gropius*, Chapter 3; Gillian Naylor, *The Bauhaus Reassessed*; Barbara Miller Lane, *Architecture and Politics in Germany, 1918–1945*, Chapter 2.

21. Walter Gropius, "Recommendations for the Founding of an Educational Institution as an Artistic Counseling Service for Industry, the Trades, and the Crafts," reproduced in Hans M. Wingler, *The Bauhaus*, pp. 23–24.

22. Letter from Muthesius to Max Pfarrer, April 5, 1917, NMWA.

23. Walter Gropius, "Der freie Volksstaat und die Kunst," typescript in BAGP, file 6S/2B (1919); also published in *Deutscher Revolutions-Almanach für das Jahr 1919* (Hamburg and Berlin: 1919), 134–36.

24. Walter Gropius, "Address to the Students of the State Bauhaus, Held on the Occasion of the Yearly Exhibition of Student Work in July 1919," as quoted in Rainer Wick, *Teaching at the Bauhaus*, p. 32, as excerpted from Wingler, *The Bauhaus*, p. 36.

25. For a recent appraisal of the Bauhaus and its evolving organization during its formative years, see Ute Ackermann, "Einleitung: Zur Funktion und Geschichte des Meisterrates am Staatlichen Bauhaus Weimar," in Wahl and Ackermann, eds., *Die Meisterratsprotokolle des Staatlichen Bauhauses Weimar*, pp. 18–40.

26. Karl-Heinz Hüter, *Architektur in Berlin, 1900–1933* (Dresden: VEB Verlag der Kunst, 1987), 84.

27. "Muthesius' Rückzug aus dem Werkbund 1916–26," in Siepmann and Thiekötter, eds., *Hermann Muthesius im Werkbund-Archiv*, p. 99.

28. Other candidates to succeed van de Velde as director of the Weimar Applied Arts School were Heinrich Tessenow (recruited unsuccessfully by Mackensen), Rudolf Alexander Schröder, Johann Vinzenz Cissarz, Rudolf Bosselt, August Endell, and Hermann Obrist. See Ute Ackermann, "Einleitung: Zur Funktion und Geschichte des Meisterrates am Staatlichen Bauhaus Weimar, in Wahl and Ackermann, eds., *Die Meisterratsprotokolle des Staatlichen Bauhauses Weimar, 1919 bis 1925*, p. 20.

29. Otto Bartning, "Vorschläge zu einem Lehrplan für Handwerker, Architekten, und Bildende Künstler," *MDWB* 1919 (Nr. 2): 42–46; Otto Bartning, "Praktischer Vorschlag zur Lehre des Architekten," *MDWB* 1919 (Nr. 4): 148–56. See also the discussions in Hubrich, *Hermann Muthesius: Die Schriften*, pp. 213–14; Schneider, *Burg Giebichenstein*, p. 18; and Winfried Nerdinger, "Von der Stilschule zum Creative Design – Walter Gropius als Lehrer," in Rainer Wick, ed., *Ist die Bauhaus-Pädagogik aktuell?* (Köln: Verlag der Buchhandlung Walter König, 1985), 28–41; The most detailed assessment of Bartning's recommendations and Gropius's Bauhaus program remains Marcel Franciscono, *Walter Gropius and the Creation of the Bauhaus in Weimar*, pp. 127–38.

30. See Franciscono, *Walter Gropius*, pp. 130–31, n. 10; also Nerdinger, "Von der Stilschule zum Creative Design," pp. 29–31.

31. Ackermann, "Einleitung: Zur Funktion und Geschichte des Meisterrates am Staatlichen Bauhaus Weimar" pp. 36–40. Ackermann's account shows that the hierarchical structure that evolved at the Weimar Bauhaus by 1923 resembled nothing so much as the situation advocated by Muthesius in his workshop-based reforms of the Prussian applied-arts schools; see the discussion in Chapter 3, this volume.

32. Bruno Taut, *Ein Architektur-Programm*, 2nd ed., Flugschriften des Arbeitsrates für Kunst (Berlin: Stephan Geibel & Co., 1919). The first edition of Taut's program appeared in time for Christmas 1918, while the second was published in spring 1919; see the reprinted text in Ulrich Conrads, *Programs and Manifestoes on 20th-Century Architecture* (Cambridge, Mass.: MIT Press, 1970), 41–43. Also influential was Taut's "For the New Building-Art" ("Für die neue Baukunst") of January 1919, a typescript of which is at the Bauhaus Archive in Berlin. My discussion in this paragraph is indebted to Winfried Nerdinger's article, "Von der Stilschule zum Creative Design – Walter Gropius als Lehrer."

33. Gropius letter to Osthaus of February 2, 1919, is quoted in Nerdinger, "Von der Stilschule zum Creative Design," p. 30. Bartning, for his part, expressed dismay that the "graphic schemas and lapidary principles" hurriedly composed by Gropius and himself together at Bartning's desk one day had apparently led – following Bartning's return from several months of recovery from illness in Bavaria in early 1919 – to the founding of the Bauhaus by April. Bartning is quoted in Nerdinger, "Von der Stilschule zum Creative Design," p. 39, n. 24.

34. Wingler, *The Bauhaus*, p. 30.

35. Ackermann, "Einleitung," p. 25.

36. See Walter Gropius, "Program of the Staatliches Bauhaus in Weimar" (April 1919), reproduced in Hans M. Wingler, *The Bauhaus*, pp. 31–33.

37. Gropius quoted in John Willett, *Art and Politics in the Weimar Period: The New Sobriety, 1917–1933* (New York: Pantheon Books, 1978), 50.

38. Oswald Spengler, *The Decline of the West*, 2 vols., trans. by Charles Francis Atkinson (New York: Alfred A. Knopf, 1926).

39. For a detailed discussion of the Werkbund's internal struggles during World War I, see Campbell, *The German Werkbund*, pp. 98–140.

40. Walter Gropius and Otto Bartning were both born in 1883, Ludwig Mies van der Rohe in 1886, Bruno Taut in 1880, and Erich Mendelsohn in 1887.

41. Peter Behrens was born in 1868, Theodor Fischer in 1862, Richard Riemerschmid in 1868, and Hermann Muthesius in 1861.

42. Letter from Walter Gropius to Deutscher Werkbund, January 30, 1920, and Gropius to

Rudolf Bosselt, February 3, 1920, ThHStA, File 6, pp. 56 and 73, respectively.

43. For two views of the Weimar Bauhaus, see Franciscono, *Walter Gropius*, and Rainer K. Wick, *Teaching at the Bauhaus*; for texts and documents, see Wingler, *The Bauhaus*. For the latest and most detailed appraisal, see Ackermann, "Einleitung."

44. See the discussion of Weimar-era developments in Heinrich August Winkler, *Mittelstand, Demokratie und Nazionalsozialismus*.

45. Bruno Taut, *Die Neue Baukunst in Europa und Amerika* (Stuttgart: Julius Hoffmann Verlag, 1929); Gustav Adolph Platz, *Die Baukunst der Neuesten Zeit* (Berlin: Propylaen-Verlag, 1927). Platz's comprehensive, 600-page survey and catalog even omits Muthesius from its otherwise exhaustive register of major and minor architects active in Germany between 1895 and 1927.

46. For Muthesius and others, the First World War brought new relevance to the "type" in relation to mass production. See, for example, Hermann Muthesius, *Handarbeit und Massenerzeugnis*, Technische Abende im Zentralinstitut für Erziehung und Unterricht, Nr. 4 (1917); Muthesius, *Kleinhaus und Kleinsiedlung* (Munich: F. Bruckmann, 1918); Erich Leyser, *Die Typisierung im Bauwesen: Der Typengrundriss, die Normalisierung der Einzelteile im Wohnungsbau und die wissenschaftliche Betriebsführung als Mittel zur Förderung des Kleinwohnungsbaus* (Dresden: Oscar Laube Verlag, 1918).

47. On Gropius's work at Harvard, see Anthony Alofsin, *The Struggle for Modernism: Architecture, Landscape Architecture, and City Planning at Harvard* (New York: W. W. Norton and Company, 2002); Gabriele Diana Grawe, "Continuity and Transformation: Bauhaus Pedagogy in North America," in Rainer K. Wick, *Teaching at the Bauhaus*, pp. 338–65; and the contributions in Bauhaus-Archiv, gen. ed., *100 Jahre Walter Gropius/Schliessung des Bauhauses 1933*, Symposium at Harvard University, April 1983 (Berlin: Bauhaus-Archiv, 1983).

48. Werner Oechslin, "Politisches, allzu Politisches...: 'Nietzschelinge,' der 'Wille zur Kunst' und der deutsche Werkbund vor 1914," in Hermann Hipp and Ernst Seidl, eds., *Architektur als politischer Kultur: Philosphia Practica* (Berlin: Dietrich Reimer Verlag, 1996), 151–90, quotation from p. 159.

49. Jeffrey Herf, *Reactionary Modernism: Technology, Culture, and Politics in Weimar and the Third Reich* (Cambridge, UK: Cambridge University Press, 1984).

50. These terms are discussed at length in Frederic J. Schwartz, *The Werkbund*.

51. Schwartz's book does provide a characteristically insightful and original analysis of German trademark and patent law, and the impact that these early-twentieth-century laws had on artists and designers.

SELECTED BIBLIOGRAPHY ✑

PRIMARY SOURCES

Archives

1. Bauhaus Archiv, Berlin
   Archiv Walter Gropius

2. Bau- und Wohnungsaufsichtsamt Zehlendorf, Berlin-Zehlendorf
   Grundstücksakte Potsdamer Chaussee 49a, Nikolassee, Bd. I & II (I: Haus Muthesius; II: Umbau der ehemaligen Muthesius-Villa zu einem 2-Familien-Wohnhaus mit Einliegerwohnung).
   Grundstücksakte Bernadottestr. 56/58 (Haus Neuhaus), Dahlem, Bd, I & II.

3. Bundesarchiv (Federal Archives) Berlin-Lichterfelde
   R 43 Reichskanzlei
   R 1401 Reichskanzleramt
   R 1501 Reichsministerium des Innern
   R 3101 Reichswirtschaftsministerium
   R 901 Auswärtiges Amt
   R 2 Reichs Finanzministerium
   Kartenabteilung

4. DIN Deutsches Institut für Normung, Berlin
   Sammlung "Archiv der Normung"
   Normenausschuss der Deutschen Industrie
   Ausschuss für wirtschaftliche Fertigung

5. Geheimes Staatsarchiv Preussischer Kulturbesitz (Prussian State Archives, Berlin-Dahlem)
   I. Hauptabteilung Repositur 89. Königliches Geheimes Civil-Cabinett: Das Landesgewerbeamt
   I. HA. Repositur 120. Ministerium für Handel und Gewerbe
   I. HA. Repositur 169. Preussisches Abgeordnetenhaus
   Bilder Sammlung, Siegelsammlung

6. Germanisches Nationalmuseum, Nürnberg (National Archives, Nuremberg)
   Nachlass Richard Riemerschmid

7. Heimatverein Zehlendorf mit Museum und Archiv
   Nachlass Hermann von Seefeld
   Bilder- und Kartensammlung

8. Landesarchiv Berlin
   Repositur 042 Grundstücksakten
   Repositur B 210 Acc 4161 Nr. 2127 Lohengrinstr. 28 (Haus Dr. Heinrich Soetbeer)
   Grundstücksblock Gerson, Sign. A Pr. Br. Rep. 042
   Kartenabteilung

9. Thüringisches Hauptstaatsarchiv Weimar (State Archives of Thuringia, Weimar)
   Bestand Staatliches Bauhaus Weimar

10. Universität der Künste-Berlin, Archiv
    Bestand 7

11. Werkbund-Archiv Berlin
    Nachlass Muthesius (Muthesius Estate Papers)

Official Documents and Reports

Dönhoff, Friedrich, Eugen von Czihak, and Hermann Muthesius. "Das gewerbliche Unterrichtswesen in Grossbritanien, auf Grund einer Studienreise im Jahre 1903." Drucksache 70, *Sammlung der Drucksachen des Preussischen Hauses der Abgeordneten (Anlagen zu den Stenographischen Berichten)*, 20. Legislatur-periode, I. Session 1904/05, Bd. 2: 1347–80.

Handbuch über den königlich Preußischen Hof und Staat. Berlin: Decker Verlag, 1890–1918.

Handels-und Gewerbeverwaltung. "Denkschrift über die Begründung eines Landesgewerbeamts und eines ständigen Beirats." *Anlagen zum Staatshaushalts-Etat für das Etatsjahr 1905* v. 2 Nr. 16 (Beilage G) (1905): 91–95.

Handels-und Gewerbeverwaltung. "Etat der Handels- und Gewerbeverwaltung einschliesslich der Zentralverwaltung des Ministeriums für Handel und Gewerbe für das Etatsjahr 1905." *Anlagen zum Staatshaushalts-Etat für das Etatsjahr 1905* v. 2 Nr. 16 (1905): 91–95.

Königliches Preussisches Ministerium für Handel und Gewerbe. *Nachrichten über die Preussischen Kunstgewerbeschulen: Zusammengestellt gelegentlich der mit der 3. Deutschen Kunstgewerbeausstellung in Dresden 1906 Verbundenen Ausstellung Preussische Kunstgewerbeschulen.* Berlin: Julius Sittenfeld, o.J., 1906.

———. *Verwaltungsbesicht des Königlich Preussischen Landesgewerbeamtes.* Berlin: Carl Heymann Verlag, 1906–1932.

Möller, Theodor, Minister für Handel und Gewerbe. 1903. "Denkschrift über den Stand der Gewerbeförderung im Königreiche Preussen." Drucksache 92, *Sammlung der Drucksachen des Preussischen Hauses der Abgeordneten (Anlagen zu den Stenographischen Berichten).* 19. Legislatur-periode, V. Session, 1903: 1999–2016.

Muthesius, Hermann. "Heutiger Stand des kunstgewerblichen und handwerklichen Schulwesens." *I. Verwaltungs-bericht des Königlich Preussischen Landesgewerbeamts 1905.* Berlin: Carl Heymanns Verlag, 1906, 107–29.

———. "Das Kunstgewerbe, insbesondere die Wohnungskunst (auf der Weltaustellung in St. Louis)." In *Amtlicher Bericht über die Weltaustellung in St. Louis 1904,* Teil 2: 263–96. Berlin: Reichsdruckerei, 1905.

———. "Kunstgewerbliche und handwerkliche Unterrichtanstalten: Geschichtliche Entwicklung." *I. Verwaltungs-bericht des Königlich Preussischen Landesgewerbeamts 1905.* Berlin: Carl Heymanns Verlag, 1906, 88–106.

———. "Die Beteiligung der preussischen Kunstgewerbeschulen an der III. Deutschen Kunstgewerbeausstellung in Dresden 1906." *VB* (1907), p. 151.

"Rückblick auf die Entwickelung des gewerblichen Schulwesens in Preussen von 1884–1909." *Ministerial-Blatt der Handels- und Gewerbe-Verwaltung* 11 (6. Mai 1910) (Beilage): 155–164.

Seefeld, Hermann von. "Die Förderung des Kleingewerbes in Hessen, Baden, Württemberg, Elsass-Lothringen und der Schweiz, Auf Grund einer Studienreise im Jahre 1903." *Sammlung der Drucksachen des preussischen Hauses der Abgeordneten,* 20. Legislatur-periode, I. Session 1904/05, Bd.4, Drucksache 142. Berlin: W. Moeser, 1904, 2159–214.

Simon, Oskar. "Bericht des Geheimen Ober-Regierungsrats Simon über die im Mai 1903 nach Österreich unternommene Studienreise." In *Sammlung der Drucksachendes preussischen Hauses der Abgeordneten,* 20. Legislatur-periode, I. Session 1904/05, Bd. 2: 1312–46.

Verhandlungen des Preussischen Hauses der Abgeordneten, 20. Legislatur-periode, I. Session 1904/05, 136, Sitzung am 9 (Februar 1905): 9723–66.

Verhandlungen des Preussischen Hauses der Abgeordneten, 21. Legislatur-periode, I. Session 1906, 9. Sitzung am 15 (Januar 1906): 504.

Verhandlungen des Preussischen Hauses der Abgeordneten, 23. Sitzung am 3 (Februar 1908): 1527.

Interviews

Interview with Wolfgang Muthesius, June 20, 1996, Zabitz, Germany.

Interviews with Vera Muthesius, May 15, 1999; June 12, 2001; August 10, 2002.

Publications by the Deutscher Werkbund

Deutscher Werkbund. *Die Durchgeistigung der Deutschen Arbeit: Wege und Ziele in Zusammenhang von Industrie/Handwerk und Kunst. Jahrbuch des Deutschen Werkbundes* 1 (1912). Jena: Eugen Diederichs, 1912.

———. *Die Wiener 5. Jahresversammlung des Deutschen Werkbundes vom 6. bis 9. Juni 1912.* Berlin: Geschäftsstelle des Werkbundes, 1912.

———. *Die Kunst in Industrie und Handel. Jahrbuch des Deutschen Werkbundes* 2 (1913). Jena: Eugen Diederichs, 1913.

———. *Der Verkehr. Jahrbuch des Deutschen Werkbundes* 3 (1914). Jena: Eugen Diederichs, 1914.

———. *Deutsche Werkbund Austellung Cöln 1914: Offizieller Katalog.* Cöln: Verlag von Rudolf Mosse, 1914.

———. *Die Werkbund-Arbeit der Zukunft und Aussprache darüber. 7. Jahresversammlung des Deutschen Werkbundes vom 2. bis 6. Juli 1914 in Köln.* Jena: Eugen Diederichs, 1914.

———. *Deutsche Form im Kriegsjahr. Jahrbuch des Deutschen Werkbundes* 4 (1915). Jena: Eugen Diederichs, 1915.

Deutscher Werkbund, ed., *Design and Industries Association, London: Englands Kunst-industrie und der Deutsche Werkbund,* Übersetzungen von Begründungs- und Werbeschriften der englischen Gesellschaft "Design and Industries Association," 2nd ed. Munich: F. Bruckmann, 1916.

Deutscher Werkbund and Deutsch-Türkischen Vereinigung, eds. *Das Haus der Freundschaft in Konstantinopel, ein Wettbewerb für deutscher Architekten.* Munich: F. Bruckmann, 1918.

"Die Deutsche Werkbundausstellung Köln." *MDWB* (1915): 1–2.

ARTICLES AND BOOKS

Adam, Hubertus. "Zwischen Individualität und Representation: Hermann Muthesius, Haus Dryander, und der Landhaus Gedanke." Lecture at Hermann-Muthesius-Symposion, Zabitz, September 21, 1996.

Alofsin, Anthony. *Frank Lloyd Wright, The Lost Years, 1910–1922: A Study of Influence.* Chicago: University of Chicago Press, 1993.

———. *The Struggle for Modernism: Architecture, Landscape Architecture, and City Planning at Harvard.* New York: W. W. Norton and Company, 2002.

Alsen, Ola. "Erste Modeschau des Werkbundes, Unter dem Protektorat der Kronprinzessin." *Elegante Welt*, Nr. 9 (1915): 5–10.

Ältesten der Kaufmannschaft von Berlin. "Auswärtige Politik." *Berliner Jahrbuch für Handel und Industrie: Bericht der Ältesten der Kaufmannschaft von Berlin* 1 (1903): 9–21.

Ältesten der Kaufmannschaft von Berlin. "Der Charakter des deutschen Wirtschaftsjahres 1903." *Berliner Jahrbuch für Handel und Industrie: Bericht der Ältesten der Kaufmannschaft von Berlin* 1 (1903): 1–9.

Anderson, Margaret Lavinia. *Practicing Democracy: Elections and Political Culture in Imperial Germany.* Princeton: Princeton University Press, 2000.

Anderson, Stanford. "Deutscher Werkbund – The 1914 debate: Hermann Muthesius versus Henry van de Velde." In *Companion to Contemporary Architectural Thought*, edited by Ben Farmer and Hentie Louw, 462–67. London and New York: Routledge, 1993.

———. "Style-Architecture and Building-Art: Realist Architecture as the Vehicle for a Renewal of Culture." Introduction to Hermann Muthesius, *Style-Architecture and Building-Art.* Translated by Stanford Anderson. Santa Monica: Getty Center for the History of Art and the Humanities, 1994.

———. *Peter Behrens and an Architecture for the Twentieth Century.* Cambridge, Mass.: MIT Press, 2000.

Anscombe, Isabelle, and Charlotte Gere. *Arts and Crafts in Britain and America.* London: Academy Editions, 1978.

Applegate, Celia. *A Nation of Provincials: The German Idea of Heimat.* Berkeley: University of California Press, 1990.

Architecture Association. *Hermann Muthesius 1861–1927.* London: Architectural Association, 1979.

Architekten-und Ingenieur-Verein zu Berlin, gen. ed. *Berlin und seine Bauten.* Teil IV: Wohnungsbau, Band A: Die Voraussetzungen. Berlin: Ernst & Sohn, 1970.

———. *Berlin und seine Bauten.* Teil IV: Wohnungsbau, Band C: Die Wohngebäude-Einfamilienhäuser. Berlin: Ernst & Sohn, 1975.

Arnold, Klaus-Peter. *Vom Sofakissen zum Städtebau: Die Geschichte der Deutschen Werkstätten und der Gartenstadt Hellerau.* Dresden, Basel: Verlag der Kunst, 1993.

Ashbee, C. R. *An Endeavour towards the Teaching of John Ruskin and William Morris.* London: Essex House Press, 1901.

Aslin, Elizabeth. *The Aesthetic Movement: Prelude to Art Nouveau.* New York: Frederick A. Praeger, 1969.

"Ausschuß für Mode-Industrie des Deutschen Werkbundes." *MDWB* (1915): 6–8.

"Aus englischen Gartenstädten." *Gartenstadt: Mitteilungen der deutschen Gartenstadtgesellschaft* 4 (1911): 8–11.

"Ausstellung 'Alt- und Neu-Cöln' 1914." *Die Woche* 16, Nr. 23 (June 6, 1914): 975–76.

Bahr, Richard. *Clemens von Delbrück: Staatssekretaer des Innern von 1909 bis 1916.* Berlin: Reichsverlag Hermann Kalkoff, 1916.

Banham, Reyner. *Theory and Design in the First Machine Age*, 2nd ed. Cambridge, Mass.: MIT Press, 1960.

Barkin, Kenneth D. *The Controversy over German Industrialization, 1890–1902.* Chicago: University of Chicago Press, 1970.

Bartning, Otto. "Vorschläge zu einem Lehrplan für Handwerker, Architekten, und Bildende Künstler." *MDWB*, Nr. 2 (1919): 42–46.

———. "Praktischer Vorschlag zur Lehre des Architekten." *MDWB*, Nr. 4 (1919): 148–56.

Bartsch, Eva, Benno Carus, and Kurt Trumpa. "Weltgeist, wo bist du? Lebensreformer ziehen an den Schlachtensee: Die Neue Gemeinschaft, 1902–1904." *Zehlendorfer Heimatbrief: Mitteilungen und Regionalgeschichtliche Beiträge* 41 (March 1998): 3–7.

Baum, Julius, ed., *Stuttgarter Kunst der Gegenwart.* Stuttgart: Deutsche Verlags-Anstalt, 1913.

"Bautätigkeit in Berlin." *Baugewerks-Zeitung* 38 (1906): 730.

"Begründung des Ausschusses für wirtschaftliche Fertigung." Versammlung im Reichswirtschaftsamt 23. Februar 1918. *Mitteilungen des Ausschusses für wirtschaftliche Fertigung* 1 (1918): 1–5.

Behrendt, Walter Curt. *Der Kampf um den Stil im Kunstgewerbe und in der Architektur.* Stuttgart: Deutsche Verlags-Anstalt, 1920.

Behrens, Peter. "Einfluss von Zeit- und Raumausnutzung auf moderne Formentwicklung."

Jahrbuch des Deutschen Werkbundes 3 (1914): 7–10.

Bennigsen, Silvie Lampe von. *Hermann Obrist: Erinnerungen*. Munich: Verlag Herbert Post, 1970.

Bergdoll, Barry. *Karl Friedrich Schinkel: An Architecture for Prussia*. New York: Rizzoli, 1994.

Berghahn, V. R. *Germany and the Approach of War in 1914*, 2nd ed. London: Macmillan, 1993.

Berghahn, Volker R. *Imperial Germany, 1871–1914: Economy, Society, Culture and Politics*. Providence: Berghahn Books, 1994.

"Bericht über die Sitzung des Ausschusses des Deutschen Handwerks- und Gewerbekammertages." *Handwerker-Zeitung für die Provinzen Hannover und Schleswig-Holstein und die Fürstentümer Pyrmont und Schaumburg-Lippe: Amtliches Organ der Handwerkskammern zu Altona, Flensburg, Hannover, Harburg, Hildesheim, und Stadthagen*, X. Jg., Nr.14 (April 8, 1905): 59.

Berlepsch-Valendas, Hans Eduard van. "Endlich ein Umschwung!" *DKuD* 1 (1897): 1–12.

Berlepsch-Valendas, Hans Eduard van. "Kunstgewerbeschulen und Lehrwerkstätten." *Dekorative Kunst* 12 (1904): 326–28.

Betts, Paul. "The Bauhaus as Cold-War Legend: West German Modernism Revisited." *German Politics and Society* 14 (Summer 1996): 75–100.

———. *The Authority of Everyday Objects: A Cultural History of West German Industrial Design*. Berkeley: University of California Press, 2004.

Biel, F. *Wirtschaftliche und technische Gesichtspunkte zur Gartenstadtbewegung*. Leipzig: Verlag von H. A. Ludwig Degener, 1914.

Bindman, David, and Gottfried Riemann, eds., *Karl Friedrich Schinkel: "The English Journey," Journal of a Visit to France and Britain in 1826*. Translated by F. Gayna Walls. New Haven, Conn.: Yale University Press, 1993.

Blackbourn, David. "The *Mittelstand* in German Society and Politics, 1871–1914." *Social History* 4 (1977): 409–33.

Blackbourn, David, and Geoff Eley. *The Peculiarities of German History: Bourgeois Society and Politics in Nineteenth-Century Germany*. Oxford: Oxford University Press, 1984.

Blackbourn, David, and Richard J. Evans, eds. *The German Bourgeoisie: Essays on the Social History of the German Middle Class from the Late Eighteenth to the Early Twentieth Century*. New York: Routledge, 1991.

Board, H. "Die Kunstgewerbeschule zu Düsseldorf." *Dekorative Kunst* 12 (1904): 409–32.

Bode, Andreas. "Bruno Paul als Direktor der Unterrichtsanstalt des Kunstgewerbemuseums und ihrer Nachfolgeinstitutionen." *Stadt: Monatshefte für Wohnungs- und Städtebau* 29 (October 1982): 8–14, 71–72.

Bode, Wilhelm von. "Aufgaben der Kunsterziehung nach dem Kriege." *Die Woche* 18 (April 1, 1916): 469–71.

Bollé, Michael. *Die Grossfunkstation Nauen und ihre Bauten von Hermann Muthesius*. Berlin: Verlag Wilhelm Arenhövel, 1996.

Bonham, Gary. *Ideology and Interests in the German State*. New York: Garland, 1991.

Borchard, Hans-Heinrich. *50 Jahre Preussisches Ministerium für Handel und Gewerbe, 1879–1929*. Berlin: Reichsverlag H. Kalkoff, 1929.

Born, Karl Erich. *Wirtschafts- und Sozialgeschichte des Deutschen Kaiserreichs (1867/71–1914)*. Wiesbaden: Verlag Franz Steiner, 1985.

———. *International Banking in the 19th and 20th Centuries*. Translated by Volker R. Berghahn. Warwickshire: Berg Publishers, 1983.

Borst, Otto. *Württemberg und seine Herren: Landesgeschichte in Lebensbildern*. Esslingen-München: Bechtle Verlag, 1988.

Breuer, Robert. "Haus Breul von Architekt Hermann Muthesius und Haus Liebermann von Arch. Paul Baumgarten." *Deutsche Kunst und Dekoration* 29 (1911): 47–50.

Brooks, H. Allen. *Le Corbusier's Formative Years: Charles-Edouard Jeanneret at La Chaux-de-Fonds*. Chicago: University of Chicago Press, 1997.

Bruch, Rüdiger vom. *Friedrich Naumann in seiner Zeit*. Berlin: Walter de Gruyter, 2000.

Bruns, Victor, ed. *Württemberg unter der Regierung König Wilhelms II*. Stuttgart: Deutsche Verlags-Anstalt, 1916.

Buddensieg, Tilmann. *Industriekultur: Peter Behrens und die AEG 1907–1914*. Berlin: Mann Verlag, 1979.

Buddensieg, Tilmann, gen. ed. *Berlin 1900–1933: Architecture and Design*. Berlin: Gebr. Mann Verlag, 1987.

Buder, Stanley. *Visionaries and Planners: The Garden City Movement and the Modern Community*. New York: Oxford University Press, 1990.

Callen, Anthea. *Women Artists of the Arts and Crafts Movement, 1870–1914*. New York: Pantheon, 1979.

Campbell, Joan. *The German Werkbund: The Politics of Reform in the Applied Arts*. Princeton: Princeton University Press, 1978.

Carstanjen, Friedrich. "Kunstgewerbliche Erziehung." *Deutsche Kunst und Dekoration* 16 (1905): 478–80; 486–87.

Chickering, Roger, ed. *Imperial Germany: A Historiographical Companion*. Westport, Conn.: Greenwood Press, 1996.

Clark, Christopher. *Kaiser Wilhelm II, Profiles in Power*. Essex: Pearson Education Limited, 2000.

Clark, Vincent. "A Struggle for Existence: The Professionalization of German Architects." In *German*

Professions, 1800–1950, edited by Geoffrey Cocks and Konrad H. Jarausch, 143–60. New York: Oxford University Press, 1990.

Clausen, Meredith L. *Frantz Jourdain and the Samaritaine: Art Nouveau Theory and Criticism.* Leiden: E. J. Brill, 1987.

Collins, George R., and Christiane Crasermann Collins. *Camillo Sitte: The Birth of Modern City Planning.* New York: Rizzoli, 1986.

Collins, Peter. *Changing Ideals in Modern Architecture, 1750–1950.* London: Faber and Faber, 1965.

Confino, Alon. *The Nation as Local Metaphor: Württemberg, Imperial Germany, and National Memory, 1871–1918.* Chapel Hill: University of North Carolina Press, 1997.

Conrads, Ulrich, ed. *Programs and Manifestoes on 20th-Century Architecture.* Translated by Michael Bullock. Cambridge, Mass.: MIT Press, 1971.

Conze, Werner, und Jürgen Kocka, hrsgs. *Bildungsbürgertum im 19. Jahrhunder, Teil I: Bildungssystem und Professionalisierung in internationalen Vergleichen.* In Werner Conze, hrsg., Industrielle Welt, Band 38. Stuttgart: Klett-Cotta, 1985.

Craig, Gordon A. *Germany 1866–1945.* Oxford: Oxford University Press, 1978.

Crawford, Alan. *C. R. Ashbee: Architect, Designer and Romantic Socialist.* New Haven, Conn.: Yale University Press, 1985.

Creese, Walter L. *The Search for Environment, The Garden City: Before and After*, expanded ed. Baltimore, Md.: Johns Hopkins University Press, 1992.

Cumming, Elizabeth, and Wendy Kaplan. *The Arts and Crafts Movement.* London: Thomas and Hudson, 1991.

Dal Co, Francesco. *Figures of Architecture and Thought: German Architecture Culture 1880–1920.* New York: Rizzoli, 1990.

Darmstadt, Ein Dokument Deutscher Kunst 1901–1976. 5 vols. Darmstadt: Eduard Roether Verlag, 1976.

"Darmstadt, Stuttgart und München als Heim-Stätten moderner Gewerbe Kunst." *DkuD* 9 (1902): 247–50.

Davey, Peter. *Arts and Crafts Architecture.* London: Phaidon, 1995.

Delbrück, Clemens von. *Reden: 1906–1916.* Berlin: Verlag Reimar Hobbing, 1917.

Deutsche Gartenstadt-Gesellschaft. *Gartenstädte*, Flugschrift 1. Berlin: Verlag der Gartenstadt-Gesellschaft, 1903.

"Deutsche Gartenstadtbewegung und ihr Vorstoss nach Gross-Berlin, Die." *Baugewerks-Zeitung* 41 (1909): 915.

Deutsche Gartenstadt-Gesellschaft. *Der Zug der Industrie aufs Land: eine Innenkolonisation*, Flugschrift 5. Berlin: VGG, 1905.

Deutsche Gartenstadt-Gesellschaft. *Die Gartenstadt im Wort und Bild*, Flugschrift 7. Berlin: VGG, 1906.

Diez, Max. "Neuzeitliche Kunstbestrebungen in Württemberg." *Deutsche Kunst und Dekoration* 20 (1907): 117–63.

Direktorium der Ausstellung, *Das Deutsche Kunstgewerbe 1906: III. Deutsche Kunstgewerbe-Ausstellung Dresden 1906.* München: F. Bruckmann, 1906.

———. *Dritte Deutsche Kunst-Gewerbe-Ausstellung Dresden 1906, Offizieller Katalog* (12.Mai–Ende Oktober 1906), Illustrierte Ausgabe. Dresden: Wilhelm Baensch, 1906.

Dohme, Robert. *Das englische Haus: Eine Kultur- und baugeschichtliche Skizze.* Braunschweig: George Westermann, 1888.

Dohrn, Wolf. *Die Gartenstadt Hellerau und weitere Schriften.* Dresden: Hellerau-Verlag, 1992.

Dolgner, Dieter. *Henry van de Velde in Weimar, 1902–1917.* Weimar: VDG, 1996.

Dresdener Geschichtsverein, gen. ed. *Gartenstadt Hellerau: Der Alltag einer Utopie.* Dresden: Dresdener Geschichtsverein, 1997.

Dürerbund-Werkbund Genossenschaft, ed. *Deutsches Warenbuch.* Hellerau: Dürerbund-Werkbund Genossenschaft, 1915.

Durant, Stuart. *CFA Voysey, 1857–1941.* Architectural Monographs No. 19., 63–75. London: St. Martin's Press, 1992.

Durth, Werner. *Deutsche Architekten: Biographische Verflechtungen, 1900–1970.* München: DTV, 1992.

———, ed. *Entwurf zur Moderne, Hellerau: Stand, Ort, Bestimmung.* Stuttgart: Deutsche Verlags-Anstalt, 1996.

Eisold, Norbert. *Die Kunstgewerbe- und Handwerkerschule Magdeburg 1793–1963.* Magdeburg: Kloster, 1993.

Eley, Geoff. *Reshaping the German Right: Radical Nationalism and Political Change after Bismarck.* New Haven, Conn.: Yale University Press, 1980.

Eley, Geoff, ed. *Society, Culture and the State in Germany, 1870–1930.* Ann Arbor: University of Michigan Press, 1996.

Eley, Geoff, and James Retallack, eds. *Wilhelminism and Its Legacies: German Modernities, Imperialism, and the Meaninsgs of Reform, 1890–1930.* New York: Berghahn Books, 2003.

Engel, Helmut et al., eds. *Zehlendorf*, Geschichtslandschaft Berlin, Band 4. Berlin: Nicolai Verlag, 1992.

Engelhardt, Ulrich. *Bildungsbürgertum: Begriffs- und Dogmengeschichte eines Etiketts.* Stuttgart: Klett-Cotta, 1986.

"Englische Landhaus: Die Arbeiterhäuser der Bournville Kolonie erbaut von W. A. Harvey, Das." *Hohe Warte* 1 (1904): 112–21.

"Erinnerungen an Nikolassee: Aus einem Gespräch, dass Eckart Muthesius im Herbst 1977 mit Richard Friedenthal in London führte." In Sonja Günther and Julius Posener, eds. *Hermann Muthesius, 1861–1927*. Berlin: Akademie der Künste, 1978, 29–30.

Etlin, Richard A. "Turin 1902: The Search for a Modern Italian Architecture." *Journal of Decorative and Propaganda Arts* 13 (Summer 1989): 94–109.

———. *Frank Lloyd Wright and Le Corbusier: The Romantic Legacy*. Manchester: Manchester University Press, 1994.

Evans, Richard J., ed. *Society and Politics in Wilhelmine Germany*. London: Croom Helm, 1978.

Fachverband für die wirtschaftlichen Interessen des Kunstgewerbes. *Bericht über die Versammlung deutscher Kunstgewerbetreibender*, 38–48. Berlin Jägerstr. 22, 9. März 1906. Berlin: H. Bergmann, 1906.

———. *Stenographischer Bericht über den 2. Kongress deutscher Kunstgewerbetreibender*. Düsseldorf, 14. Juni 1907. Berlin: H. Bergmann, 1907.

Fachverband für die wirtschaftlichen Interessen des Kunstgewerbes e.V., ed. *Der "Deutsche Werkbund" und seine Ausstellung Koeln 1914: Eine Sammlung von Reden und Kritiken nach der "Tat."* Berlin: Hermann Bergmann, 1915.

Facius, Friedrich. *Wirtschaft und Staat: Die Entwicklung der staatlichen Wirtschaftsverwaltung in Deutschland vom 17. Jahrhundert bis 1945*. Schriften des Bundesarchivs 6. Boppard am Rhein: Harald Boldt Verlag, 1959.

Fasshauer, Michael. *Das Phänomen Hellerau: Die Geschichte der Gartenstadt*. Dresden: Hellerau-Verlag, 1997.

"Der Fall Muthesius: Ein Vortrag mit Akten und Briefen." *Hohe Warte* 3 (1907).

Fehn, Lothar et al. *Stuttgarter Architekturschule: Vielfalt als Konzept*. Stuttgart: Karl Krämer Verlag, 1992.

Feldman, Gerald D. *Hugo Stinnes: Biographie eines Industriellen, 1870–1924*. Munich: C. H. Beck.

———. *Army, Industry, and Labor in Germany, 1914–1918*. Princeton: Princeton University Press, 1966.

Fiedler, Jeannine, and Peter Feierabend, eds. *Bauhaus*. Cologne: Könemann Verlagsgessellschaft, 1999.

Fischer, Fritz. *Griff nach der Weltmacht: Die Kriegszielpolitik Kaiserlichen Deutschland 1914–1918*. Dusseldorf: Droste, 1961.

———. *War of Illusions: German Policies from 1911 to 1914*. Translated by Marian Jackson. Dusseldorf: Droste, 1975.

Fletcher, Banister. "The Smaller Houses of the English Suburbs and Provinces: Notes on Design." *Architectural Record* 5 (April–June 1896): 321–38.

———. "The Smaller Houses of the English Suburbs and Provinces: Notes on Construction." *Architectural Record* 6, 4 (1896–97): 115–25.

Forster-Hahn, Françoise, ed. *Imagining Modern German Culture: 1889–1910*. Center for the Advanced Study of the Visual Arts. Gen. Ed., Studies in the History of Art. Vol. 53. Washington, D.C.: National Gallery of Art, 1996.

Fraenke, Monika. "Schönheit und Bruttosozialprodukt: Motive der Kunstgewerbebewegung." In *Packeis und Pressglas: Von der Kunstgewerbebewegung zum Deutschen Werkbund*. Edited by Eckhard Siepmann und Angelika Thiekötter, 167–73. Werkbund-Archiv Band 16. Giessen: Anabas-Verlag, 1987.

Frahm, J. "Die Anlage von Gartenstädten in England zur Lösung der Arbeiterwohnungsfrage." *CdB* 25 (1905): 120–22; 138–39.

Franciscono, Marcel. *Walter Gropius and the Creation of the Bauhaus in Weimar: The Ideals and Artistic Theories of its Founding Years*. Urbana: University of Illinois Press, 1971.

Frank, Hartmut. "Ein Bauhaus vor dem Bauhaus." *Bauwelt* 41 (1983): 1640–58.

———, ed. *Fritz Schumacher: Reformkultur und Moderne*. Stuttgart: Hatje, 1994.

Franklin, Jill. "Edwardian Butterfly Houses." *Architectural Review* 157 (April 1975): 220–25.

Freytag, Matthias. *Theodor Fischers Stuttgarter Kunstgebäude am Schlossplatz: Entstehung und architektonische Form*. Stuttgart: Silberburg Verlag, 1989.

Fritsch, Theodor. *Die Stadt der Zukunft*. Leipzig: Hammer Verlag, 1896.

Fuhlrott, Rolf. *Deutschsprachige Architektur-Zeitschriften: Entstehung und Entwicklung der Fachzeitschriften für Architektur in der Zeit von 1789–1918*. München: Verlag Dokumentation Saur KG, 1975.

Funk, Anna-Christa. *Karl Ernst Osthaus gegen Hermann Muthesius: Der Werkbundstreit 1914 im Spiegel der im Karl Ernst Osthaus Archiv erhaltenen Briefe*. Hagen: Karl Ernst Osthaus Museum, 1978.

Fürstenberg, Hans. *Carl Fürstenberg: Die Lebensgeschichte eines deutschen Bankiers, 1870–1914*. Berlin: Ullstein, 1931.

Geelhaar, Christiane, ed. *Mathildenhöhe Darmstadt, 100 Jahre Planen und Bauen für die Stadtkrone, 1899–1999*. 2 vols. Darmstadt: J. Häusser, 2000.

Geist, Johann Friedrich, and Klaus Kurvers. *Das Berliner Mietshaus 1862–1945*. München: Prestel, 1984.

German Gospel of Blood and Iron. Germany's War Mania: The Teutonic Point of View as Officially Stated by Her Leaders; A Collection of Speeches and Writings. Translated by Dudley W. Walton. London: A. W. Shaw, 1914.

Giedion, Sigfried. *Space, Time, and Architecture: The Growth of a New Tradition*, 3rd ed. Cambridge, Mass.: Harvard University Press, 1954.

Girouard, Mark. *Sweetness and Light: The 'Queen Anne' Movement, 1860–1900*. Oxford: Oxford University Press, 1977.

Goldschmidt, Hans. *Das Reich und Preussen im Kampf um die Führung*. Berlin: Carl Heymanns Verlag, 1931.

Graubner, Gerhard, ed. *Paul Bonatz und seine Schüler*. Stuttgart: Verlag Deutsche Bauten, n.d.

Graul, Richard, ed. *Die Krisis im Kunstgewerbe: Studien über Wege und Ziele der modernen Richtung*. Leipzig: S. Hirzel, 1901.

Greenblatt, Stephen Jay. *Renaissance Self-Fashioning: From More to Shakespeare*. Chicago: University of Chicago Press, 1980.

Greenhalgh, Paul, ed. *Art Nouveau:1890–1914*. London: V&A Publications, 2000.

Greeves, T. Affleck. *Bedford Park: The First Garden Suburb*. London: Anne Bingley, 1975.

Gropius, Walter. "Der freie Volksstaat und die Kunst." *Deutscher Revolutions-Almanach für das Jahr 1919*, 134–36. Hamburg and Berlin: 1919.

Gross, Karl et al. "Die Auflösung der Kunstgewerbeschule in Düsseldorf." *MDWB*, Nr. 2 (1919): 9–10.

Grundsätze der Handwerker- und Kunstgewerbeschule Crefeld. Crefeld: Worms & Lüthgen, 1911.

Günther, Sonja. *Interieurs um 1900: Bernhard Pankok, Bruno Paul und Richard Riemerschmid als Mitarbeiter der Vereinigten Werkstätten für Kunst im Handwerk*. München: W. Fink Verlag, 1971.

Günther, Sonja, and Julius Posener, eds. *Hermann Muthesius, 1861–1927*. Ausstellung in der Akademie der Künste von 11. Dezember bis 22, Januar, 1978. Berlin: Akademie der Künste, 1978.

Gurlitt, Cornelius. *Die deutsche Kunst des Neunzehnten Jahrhunderts: Ihre Ziele und Taten*. 3. Auflage. Berlin: Georg Bondi, 1907.

Gutschow, Kai. "Schultze-Naumburg's Heimatstil: A Nationalist Conflict of Tradition and Modernity." In *Traditional Dwellings and Settlements Working Papers Series*, edited by Nezar Alsayyad, vol. 36, 1–44. Berkeley, Calif.: Center for Environmental Design Research, 1992.

Haenel, Erich, and Heinrich Tscharmann. *Das Einzelwohnhaus der Neuzeit*. Leipzig: J.J. Weber, 1910.

Hahn, Peter, and Hans M. Wingler, eds. *100 Jahre Walter Gropius: Schliessung des Bauhauses 1933*. Berlin: Bauhaus-Archiv, 1983.

Haigh, Diane. *Baillie Scott: The Artistic House*. London: Academy Editions, 1995.

Hamann, Richard, and Jost Hermand. *Stilkunst um 1900*. Epochen deutscher Kultur von 1870 bis zur Gegenwart, vol. 4, 2nd ed. Frankfurt a. M.: Fischer Taschenbuch Verlag, 1977.

Harlander, Tilman, ed. *Villa und Eigenheim: Suburbaner Städtebau in Deutschland*. Stuttgart, Munich: Deutsche Verlags-Anstalt, 2001.

Hartmann, Kristiana. *Deutsche Gartenstadtbewegung: Kultur, Politik, und Gesellschaftsreform*. München: Heinz Moos Verlag, 1976.

"Haus von Velsen." *Blätter für Architektur und Kunsthandwerk* 13 (Juli 1910): 25.

Hawkes, Dean, ed. *Modern Country Homes in England: The Arts and Crafts Architecture of Barry Parker*. Cambridge, UK: Cambridge University Press, 1986.

Haxthausen, Charles W., and Heidrun Suhr, eds. *Berlin: Culture and Metropolis*. Minneapolis: University of Minnesota Press, 1990.

Hegemann, Werner. *Das steinerne Berlin*. Bauwelt Fundamente 3. Frankfurt a. M.: Ullstein Verlag, 1963.

Heil, Bettina, and Andrea Sinzel, eds. *Briefe an Karl Ernst Osthaus*. Hagen: Karl Ernst Osthaus Museum, 2000.

Heilandt, A. "Papierformate." *Mitteilungen des Normenausschuss der Deutschen Industrie* 10 (May 1920): 295–301 (Sonderdruck).

Hellige, Hans Dieter, ed. *Walther Rathenau – Maximilian Harden: Briefwechsel, 1897–1920*. Munich: Gotthold Müller Verlag, 1983.

Hellmich, W. "Der Normenausschuss der Deutschen Industrie." *Mitteilungen der Normenausschuss der Deutschen Industrie* 1 (January 1918): 1–2.

Henderson, W. O. *The Rise of German Industrial Power, 1834–1914*. Berkeley: University of California Press, 1975.

Herf, Jeffrey. *Reactionary Modernism: Technology, Culture, and Politics in Weimar and the Third Reich*. Cambridge: Cambridge University Press, 1984.

Hermann, Jost. *Avantgarde und Regression: 200 Jahre deutsche Kunst*. Leipzig: Edition Leipzig, 1995.

Hermann, Wolfgang. *Gottfried Semper: In Search of Architecture* Cambridge, Mass.: MIT Press, 1984.

Herz, R., and B. Bruns, eds. *Hof-Atelier Elvira: 1887–1928*. Munich: Münchener Stadtmuseum, 1986.

Herzogenrath, Wulf et al., eds. *Der westdeutsche Impuls 1900–1914, Kunst und Umweltgestaltung im Industriegebiet: Die Deutsche Werkbund-Ausstellung Cöln 1914*. Köln: Kölnischer Kunstverein, 1984.

Heskett, John. *German Design 1870–1918*. New York: Taplinger Publishing Co., 1986.

Hesse-Frielinghaus, Herta, gen. ed., *Karl Ernst Osthaus: Leben und Werk*. Recklinghausen: Verlag Aurel Bongers, 1971.

Heuss, Theodor. *Friedrich Naumann: der Mann, das Werk, die Zeit*, 2nd ed. Stuttgart and Tübingen: Deutsche Verlags-Anstalt, 1949.

Hiesinger, Kathryn Bloom. *Art Nouveau in Munich: Masters of Jugendstil.* Munich: Prestel, 1988.

Hipp, Hermann, and Ernst Seidl, eds. *Architektur als politischer Kultur: Philosphia Practica.* Berlin: Dietrich Reimer Verlag, 1996.

Hitchcock, Henry Russell. *Architecture: Nineteenth and Twentieth Centuries,* 2nd ed. Baltimore, Md.: Penguin, 1967.

Hitchmough, Wendy. *The Homestead, C. F. A. Voysey.* London: Phaidon, 1994.

———. *C. F. A. Voysey.* London: Phaidon, 1995.

Hochschule für Architektur und Bauwesen Weimar, ed. *Henry van de Velde, Weimar 1902–1915: Gedächtnisausstellung zu Seinem 100. Geburtstag am 3. April 1963.* Weimar: Hochschule für Architektur und Bauwesen Weimar, 1963.

Hoh-Slodczyk, Christine et al. *Baudenkmale in Berlin: Bezirk Wilhelmsdorf, Ortsteil Grunewald.* Berlin: Senatsverwaltung für Stadtentwicklung und Umweltschutz, 1994.

Hollamby, Edward. *Red House, Philip Webb.* London: Architecture Design and Technology Press, 1991.

Howard, Ebenezer. *To-Morrow: A Peaceful Path to Real Reform.* London: 1898.

Howard, Ebenezer. *Garden Cities of Tomorrow.* London: 1902.

———. *Gartenstädte in Sicht.* Translator Unlisted. Jena: Eugen Diederichs, 1907.

Howarth, Thomas. *Charles Rennie Mackintosh and the Modern Movement,* 2nd ed. New York: Routledge, 1977.

Hubrich, Hans-Joachim. *Hermann Muthesius: Die Schriften zu Architektur, Kunstgewerbe, Industrie in der "Neuen Bewegung."* Berlin: Gebr. Mann Verlag, 1981.

Hüter, Karl-Heinz. *Henry van de Velde: Sein Werk bis zum Ende seiner Tätigkeit in Deutschland.* Berlin: Akademie Verlag, 1967.

———. *Architektur in Berlin 1900–1933.* Dresden: VEB Verlag der Kunst, 1987.

Ilkosz, Jerzy, and Beate Störtkuhl, eds. *Hans Poelzig in Breslau: Architektur und Kunst 1900–1916.* Delmenhorst: Aschenbeck und Holstein Verlag, 2000.

Isaacs, Reginald. *Gropius: An Illustrated Biography of the Creator of the Bauhaus.* Boston: Bulfinch, 1991.

Jäckh, Ernst. *Deutschland im Orient nach dem Balkankrieg.* Strassburg: Verlag Singer, 1913.

———. *Der aufsteigende Halbmond: Auf dem Weg zum Deutsch-Türkischen Bündnis.* Stuttgart: Deutsche Verlags-Anstalt, 1915.

———. *Werkbund und Mitteleuropa.* Weimar: Gustav Kiepenhauer, 1916.

———. *Die Deutsch-türkische Waffenbruderschaft.* In "Der Deutsche Krieg: Politische Flugschriften," Nr. 24, Ernst Jäckh, series ed. Stuttgart, Berlin: Deutsche Verlags-Anstalt, 1916.

———, ed. *Kiderlen-Wächter, der Staatsmann und Mensch: Briefwechsel und Nachlass.* Stuttgart: Deutsche Verlags-Anstalt, 1924.

———. *Der goldene Pflug: Lebensernte eines Weltbürgers.* Stuttgart: Deutsche Verlags-Anstalt, 1957.

Jackson, Frank. *Sir Raymond Unwin: Architect, Planner and Visionary.* London: A. Zwemmer, 1985.

James-Chakroborty, Kathleen. *German Architecture for a Mass Audience*

Jeanneret, Charles-Edouard. *Étude sur le mouvement d'art décoratif en Allemagne.* New York: Da Capo Press, 1968. (Originally published in 1912.)

Jeffries, Matthew. *Politics and Culture in Wilhelmine Germany: The Case of Industrial Architecture.* Oxford: Berg Publishers, 1995.

Jenkins, Jennifer. "The Kitsch Collections and *The Spirit in the Furniture*: Cultural Reform and National Culture in Germany." *Social History* (May 1996): 123–41.

———. *Provincial Modernity: Local Culture and Liberal Politics in Fin-de-Siècle Hamburg.* Ithaca: Cornell University Press, 2003.

Jessen, Peter. "Nachruf für Hermann Freudenberg." *Mitteilungen des Verbandes der Deutschen Moden-Industrie,* N.F., Heft 1 (1924): 3–8.

Jones, Peter Blundell. "Red House." *The Architects' Journal* 183 (1986): 36–51.

Junghanns, Kurt. *Der Deutsche Werkbund: Sein erstes Jahrzehnt.* Berlin: Henschelverlag, 1982.

Kaelble, Hartmut. *Industrielle Interessenpolitik in der Wilhelminische Gesellschaft.* Veröffentlichungen der Historischen Kommission zu Berlin, Band 27. Berlin: Walter de Gruyter & Co., 1967.

Kalkschmidt, Eugen. "Mobilmachung im Kunstgewerbe." *Die Kunst* 32 (1914–15): 11–24.

Kampffmeyer, Bernhard. *Die englische Gartenstadtbewegung. Flugschrift* 2. Berlin: VGG, 1903.

———. "Von der Kleinstadt zur Gartenstadt," *Flugschrift* 11. Berlin-Schlachtensee: Deutsche Gartenstadt-Gesellschaft, 1907.

Kampffmeyer, Hans. "Die Gartenstadt in ihrer kulturellen und wirtschaftlichen Bedeutung." *Hohe Warte* 3 (1906–07): 106, 109.

Kaplan, Wendy, ed. *"The Art that is Life": The Arts and Crafts Movement in America, 1875–1920.* Boston: Little, Brown and Company, 1987.

Kaufhold, Karl Heinrich. "Fragen der Gewerbepolitik und der Gewerbeförderung." In *Kunstpolitik und Kunstförderung im Kaiserreich: Kunst im Wandel der Sozial- und Wirtschaftsgeschichte,* edited by Ekkehard Mai et al., 95–110. Berlin: Gebr. Mann Verlag, 1982.

Kentgens-Craig, Margret. *The Bauhaus and America: First Contacts, 1919–1936.* Cambridge, Mass.: MIT Press, 1999.

Kerr, Robert. *The Gentleman's House or How to Plan English Residences, from the Parsonage to the Palace.* London: John Murray, 1865.

Kiem, Karl. *Die Gartenstadt Staaken (1914–1917): Typen, Gruppen, Varianten.* Berlin: Gebr. Mann Verlag, 1997.

Klein, Emil. "Die sociale Bedeutung des evangelischen Pfarrhauses." In *Studien der evangelisch-protestantischen Geistlichen des Grossherzogtums Baden,* edited by Emil Zettel, 20–34 (1876).

Kocka, Jürgen. "Vorindustrielle Faktoren in der deutschen Industrialisierung: Industriebürokratie und 'neuer Mittelstand.' " In *Das kaiserliche Deutschland: Politik und Gesellschaft, 1870–1918,* edited by Michael Stürmer, 276–77. Düsseldorf: Droste Verlag, 1970.

———, hrsg. *Angestellte im europäischen Vergleich: Die Herausbildung angestellter Mittelschichten seit dem späten 19. Jahrhundert.* Göttingen: Vandenhöck & Ruprecht, 1981.

Köhler, S. *Deutschlands Städtebau: Barmen,* 2nd ed. Berlin-Halensee: Deutscher Architektur- und Industrie Verlag, 1926.

Kohut, Oswald. "Aus der Geschichte der Kolonie Grunewald." *Jahrbuch für brandenburgische Landesgeschichte* 8 (1957): 70–71.

Kornwulf, James D. *M. H. Baillie Scott and the Arts and Crafts Movement.* Baltimore, Md.: Johns Hopkins University Press, 1972.

Korporation der Kaufmannschaft von Berlin. *Die Eröffnung der Handelshochschule Berlin am 27. Oktober 1906.* Berlin: Verlag von G. Reimer, 1906.

Kratzsch, Gerhard. *Kunstwart und Dürerbund: Ein Beitrag zur Geschichte der Gebildeten im Zeitalter des Imperialismus.* Göttingen: Van den Höck & Ruprecht, 1969.

Kunstreich, Jan S. "Hermann Muthesius (1861–1927) und die Reform der preussischen Kunstgewerbeschulen." *Nordelbingen: Beiträge zur Kunst- und Kulturgeschichte* 47 (1978): 128–40.

Ladd, Brian. *Urban Planning and Civic Order in Germany, 1860–1914.* Cambridge, Mass.: Harvard University Press, 1990.

Lampugnani, Vittorio Magnago, and Romana Schneider, eds. *Moderne Architektur in Deutschland 1900 bis 1950: Reform und Tradition.* Stuttgart: Verlag Gerd Hatje, 1992.

Landesdenkmalamt Berlin, ed. *Baudenkmale in Berlin: Bezirk Zehlendorf, Ortsteil Zehlendorf.* Berlin: Landesdenkmalamt Berlin, 1995.

"Landhaus Neuhaus in Dahlem." *Der Baumeister* 6 (1907): Tafel 1–2.

"Landhaus an der Rehwiese in Nikolassee bei Berlin." *Baugewerks-Zeitung* Nr. 95 (November 27, 1909): 979–80.

"Landhaus Herrmann (sic) Muthesius in Nikolassee, an der Rehwiese." *Blätter für Architektur und Kunsthandwerk* 24 (Juni 1911): 21–22.

"Landhaus Hermann Freudenberg in Nikolassee." *Blätter für Architektur und Kunsthandwerk* 23 (Februar 1910): 5–6.

"Landhaus von Velsen, Zehlendorf." *Der Baumeister* 7 (November 1908): 20–21.

"Landhausbauten in Wannsee." *CdB* 13 (1893): 69–71.

Lane, Barbara Miller. *National Romanticism and Modern Architecture in Germany and The Scandinavian Countries.* Cambridge, UK: Cambridge University Press, 2000.

Langbehn, Julius. *Rembrandt als Erzieher: Von Einem Deutschen.* Leipzig: Verlag E. L. Hirschfeld, 1893.

Lange, Konrad. *Die künstlerische Erziehung der deutschen Jugend.* Darmstadt: Verlag Arnold Bergstraesser, 1893.

Langewiesche, Dieter, ed. *Ploetz. Das deutsche Kaiserreich 1867/71 bis 1918: Bilanz einer Epoche.* Freiburg, Würzburg: Verlag Ploetz, 1984.

Lebovics, Herman. *Social Conservatism and the Middle Classes in Germany, 1914–1933.* Princeton: Princeton University Press, 1969.

Lehrplan der Königliche Kunst- und Kunstgewerbeschule zu Breslau. Breslau: A. Stenzel, 1897.

Leonhardt, Fritz. *Bridges: Aesthetics and Design.* Cambridge, Mass.: MIT Press, 1984.

Lerman, Katherine Anne. *The Chancellor as Courtier: Bernhard von Bülow and the Governance of Germany 1900–1909.* Cambridge: Cambridge University Press, 1990.

Lethaby, W. R. *Form in Civilization.* London: Oxford University Press, 1922.

———. *Philip Webb and His Work.* Oxford: Oxford University Press, 1935; reprint ed., London: Raven Oak Press, 1979.

Lever, W. H. "Dwellings Erected at Port Sunlight and Thornton Hough." *The Builder* 9 (March 1902): 312–18.

Lewis, Michael J. *The Politics of the German Gothic Revival: August Reichensperger.* Cambridge, Mass.: MIT Press, 1993.

Leyser, Erich. *Die Typisierung im Bauwesen: Der Typengrundriss, die Normalisierung der Einzelteile im Wohnungsbau und die wissenschaftliche Betriebsführung als Mittel zur Förderung des Kleinwohnungsbaus.* Dresden: Oscar Laube Verlag, 1918.

"Liberale Grundsätze bei der Handwerkerförderung." *Königsberger Hartungsche Zeitung,* April 6, 1905, p. 1.

Liebersohn, Harry. *Fate and Utopia in German Sociology, 1870–1923.* Cambridge, Mass.: MIT Press, 1988.

Löbert, Dagmar. *Fritz Schumacher, 1869–1947: Reformarchitekt zwischen Tradition und Moderne.* Bremen: Donat, 1999.

Loewenberg, Gerhard. *Parliament in the German Political System*. Ithaca: Cornell University Press, 1967.

Loos, Adolf. *Sämtliche Schriften*. Wien: Verlag Herold, 1962.

Lorenz, Karl. *Wege nach Hellerau: Auf den Spuren der Rhythmik*. Dresden: Hellerau-Verlag, 1994.

Lux, Joseph A. "Die Gartenstadt Hellerau: Gründung der Deutschen Werkstätten für Handwerkskunst." *Hohe Warte* 3 (1906–07): 314, 316.

———. "Der Deutsche Werkbund," *Fachblatt für Holzarbeiter* 7 (1907): 217–18.

Maciuika, John V. *Hermann Muthesius and the Reform of German Architecture, Arts, and Crafts*. Ph.D. dissertation, University of California Berkeley, 1998.

Madsen, S. T. *Sources of Art Nouveau*. New York: G. Wittenborn, 1956.

Mai, Ekkehard et al., eds. *Kunstpolitik und Kunstförderung im Kaiserreich: Kunst im Wandel der Sozial- und Wirtschaftsgeschichte*, Band 2. Berlin: Gebr. Mann Verlag, 1982.

Makela, Maria. *The Munich Secession: Art and Artists in Turn-of-the-Century Munich*. Princeton: Princeton University Press, 1990.

Mallgrave, Harry Francis. *Gottfried Semper: Architect of the Nineteenth Century*. New Haven, Conn.: Yale University Press, 1996.

Manchester, William. *The Arms of Krupp: 1587–1968*. Boston: Little, Brown and Company, 1968.

March, Werner, hrsg. *Otto March, 1845–1912: Ein schöpferischer Berliner Architekt an der Jahrhundertwende*. Tübingen: Wasmuth, 1972.

Masner, Karl. *Das Einfamilienhaus des Kunstgewerbevereins für Breslau und die Provinz Schlesien auf der Ausstellung für Handwerk und Kunstgewerbe in Breslau 1904*. Berlin: Ernst Wasmuth, 1905.

Matschoss, Conrad. *Preussens Gewerbefördemg und ihre Grossen Männer, dargestellt im Rahmen der Geschichte des Vereins zur Befördernng des Gewerbefleisses 1821–1921*. Berlin: Verlag des Vereines Deutscher Ingenieure, 1921.

Mebes, Paul. *Um 1800. Architektur und Handwerk im letzten Jahrhundert ihrer traditionellen Entwicklung*. 3. Auflage. München: Bruckmann, 1920.

Medalen, Charles. "State Monopoly Capitalism in Germany: The Hibernia Affair." *Past and Present* 78 (February 1978): 82–112.

Meier-Graefe, Julius. "Peter Behrens-Düsseldorf." *Dekorative Kunst* 13 (1905): 381–90; 391–413.

Meissner, Else. *Das Verhältnis des Künstlers zum Unternehmer im Bau- und Kunstgewerbe*. In *Staats- und sozialwissenschaftliche Forschungen*, edited by Gustav Schmoller und Max Sering. Heft 185. München: Verlag von Duncker und Humbolt, 1915.

Mendelssohn, Peter de. *Zeitungsstadt Berlin*, 2nd ed. Berlin: Ullstein Verlag, 1982.

Meurer, Moritz. *Pflanzenformen, vorbildliche Beispiele zur Einführung in das ornamentale Studium der Pflanze, mit erläuterndem Texte*. Dresden: Gerhard Kühtmann, 1894.

———. *Pflanzenformen. Vorbildliche Beispiele zur Einführung in das ornamentale Studium der Pflanze zum Gebrauche für Kunstgewerbe- und Bauschulen, Technische Hochschulen und Höhere Unterrichtsanstalten sowie für Architekten und Kunsthandwerker*. Dresden: Gerhard Kühtmann, 1895.

Michelis, Marco De. *Heinrich Tessenow 1876–1950: Das architektonische Gesamtwerk*. Stuttgart: Deutsche Verlags-Anstalt, 1991.

Miller, Mervyn. *Letchworth: The First Garden City*. Chichester: Phillimore, 1989.

Mislin, Miron. "Zum Verhältnis von Architektur, Kunstgewerbe und Industrie 1790–1850." In *Packeis und Pressglas: Von der Kunstgewerbebewegung zum Deutschen Werkbund*, edited by Eckhard Siepmann and Angelika Thiekötter, 41–48. Werkbund Archiv Band 16. Giessen: Anabas-Verlag, 1987.

Moeller, Gisela. "Die preussischen Kunstgewerbeschulen." In *Kunstpolitik und Kunstforderung im Kaiserreich: Kunst im Wandel der Sozial- und Wirtschaftsgeschichte*, edited by Ekkehard Mai, 113–29. Berlin: Bebr. Mann Verlag, 1981.

———. *Peter Behrens in Düsseldorf: Die Jahre von 1903 bis 1907*. Artefact Series, Tilman Buddensieg, eds. Fritz Neumeyer, and Martin Warnke. Weinheim: VCH Verlagsgesellschaft, 1991.

Mommsen, Wolfgang J. *Bürgerliche Kultur und Künstlerische Avantgarde: Kultur und Politik im deutschen Kaiserreich, 1870 bis 1918*. Frankfurt a. M.: Propyläen Verlag, 1994.

Morsey, Rudolf. *Die Oberste Reichsverwaltung Unter Bismarck, 1867–1890*. Münster: Verlag Aschendorf, 1957.

Mosse, George. *The Crisis of German Ideology: Intellectual Origins of the Third Reich*. New York: Grosset and Dunlap, 1964.

Muthesius, Anna. *Das Eigenkleid der Frau*. Krefeld: Verlag von Kramer und Baum, 1903.

———. *Gereimtes und Ungereimtes*. Privatdruck, Charlottenburg: Kunstgewerbe- und Handwerkerschule Charlottenburg, 1926.

Muthesius, Eckart. "Muthesius." In *Hermann Muthesius, 1861–1927*. Exhibition Catalog. London: Architectural Association, 1979.

Muthesius, Hermann. "Deutsche evangelische Kirche in Tokyo." *CdB* 11 (1891): 339.

———. "Die künstlerische Erziehung der deutschen Jugend." *CdB* 13 (1893): 527–28.

———. "Ist die Architektur eine Kunst oder ein Gewerbe? [A review of T. G. Jackson and Richard Norman Shaw, eds. *Architecture a Profession or an Art: Thirteen Short Essays on the Qualifications and Training of Architects*. London: John Murray, 1892].” *CdB* 13 (1893): 333–35.

———. “Deutsche Architekten.” *CdB* 14 (1894): 260.

———. “Die Ausbildung des englischen Architekten.” *CdB* 17 (1897): 446–48; 459–61.

———. “William Morris und die fünfte Ausstellung des Kunstgewerbe-Ausstellungs vereins in London.” *CdB* 17 (1897): 3–5; 29–30; 39–41.

———. “Die neuzeitliche Ziegelbauweise in England.” *CdB* 18 (1898): 581–83; 593–95; 605–07; 622–23.

———. *Italienische Reise-Eindrücke*. Berlin: Ernst & Sohn, 1898.

———. “Künstlerische Unterricht für Handwerker in England.” *Dekorative Kunst* 1 (1898): 15–20.

———. “Das Fabrikdorf Port Sunlight bei Liverpool.” *CdB* 19 (1899): 133–36, 146–48.

———. “England als Weltmacht und Kulturstaat.” *Tägliche Rundschau*, Unterhaltungs-Beilage, 14. September 1899, p. 861.

———. “Der Verein für häusliche Kunstindustrie (Home Arts and Industries Association) und der Diletantismus in den Kleinkünsten in England.” *CdB* 20 (1900): 165–67; 173–74; 197–99; 209–12.

———. “Der Zeichenunterricht in den Londoner Volksschulen.” In *Beiträge zur Lehrerbildung und Lehrerfortbildung*, edited by Karl Muthesius. Heft 16 (1900).

———. *Die englische Baukunst der Gegenwart: Beispiele neuer englischer Profanbauten*. Berlin and Leipzig: Cosmos, 1900.

———. *Die neuere kirchliche Baukunst in England: Entwicklung, Bedingungen und Grundzüge des Kirchenbaues der englischen Staatskirche und der Secten*. Berlin: Ernst & Sohn, 1901.

———. “Culturarbeiten.” *CdB* 22 (1902): 641.

———. *Der Kirchenbau der englischen Secten: von der Königlich Sächsischen Technischen Hochschule zu Dresden zur Erlangung der Würde eines Doktor-Ingenieurs Genehmigte Dissertation*. Halle: Buchdruckerei des Waisenhauses, 1902.

———. *Stilarchitektur und Baukunst: Wandlungen der Architektur im XIX. Jahrhundert und ihr heutiger Standpunkt*. Mülheim-Ruhr: Verlag von K. Schimmelpfeng, 1902.

———. “Vorwort,” *Baillie Scott, London: Haus eines Kunstfreundes*. In Meister der Innenkunst, Bd. I. Darmstadt: Alexander Koch, 1902.

———. *Stilarchitektur und Baukunst: Wandlungen der Architektur im XIX. Jahrhundert und ihr heutiger Standpunkt*. Mülheim-Ruhr: Verlag von K. Schimmelpfeng, 1903.

———. “Wirtschaftsformen im Kunstgewerbe: Vortrag, Gehalten 30. Januar 1908 in der Volkswirtschaftlichen Gesellschaft in Berlin.” In *Volkswirtschaftlichen Gesellschaft in Berlin, Volkswirtschaftliche Zeitfragen: Vorträge und Abhandlungen*, Heft 233. Berlin: Verlag von Leonhard Simion, 1908.

———. *Das moderne Landhaus und seine innere Ausstattung*. München: F. Bruckmann, 1904.

———. “Die Kunst Richard Riemerschmids.” *Dekorative Kunst* 7 (1904): 249–83.

———. *Kultur und Kunst: Gesammelte Aufsätze über künstlerische Fragen der Gegenwart*. Jena: Eugen Diederichs, 1904.

———. “Künstlerische Kulturarbeiten.” *Der Tag* (Januar 15, 1904), p. 1.

———. “Zeichenunterricht und ‘Stillehre.’” In *Kultur und Kunst: Gesammelte Aufsätze über künstlerische Fragen der Gegenwart*, 100–116. Jena/Leipzig: Eugen Diederichs, 1904.

———. *Das englische Haus: Entwicklung, Bedingungen, Anlage, Aufbau, Einrichtung und Innenraum*. Berlin: Ernst Wasmuth, 1904–05.

———. *Das moderne Landhaus und seine innere Ausstattung*, 2. verbesserte und vermehrte Auflage. München: F. Bruckmann, 1905.

———. “Die Wohnungskunst auf der Welt-Ausstellung in St. Louis.” *Deutsche Kunst und Dekoration* 15 (Okt. 1904–März.1905): 209–27.

———. “Geschichtliche Entwicklung des Kunstunterrichts im XVIII. Jahrhundert. Für Preussen Bearbeitet von Dr. Hermann Muthesius.” *Hohe Warte*, II. Jg. (1905): 159–59.

———. “Auszug aus dem Verwaltungsbericht des König. Preussischen Landesgewerbeamts 1905: Die neuere Entwicklung der Kunstgewerbeschulen.” In *Nachrichten über die Preussischen Kunstgewerbeschulen: Zusammengestellt gelegentlich der mit der 3. Deutschen Kunstgewerbeausstellung in Dresden 1906 Verbundenen Ausstellung Preussische Kunstgewerbeschulen*. Königliches Preussisches Ministerium für Handel und Gewerbe, 9–17. Berlin: Julius Sittenfeld, 1906.

———. “Das Maschinenmöbel.” *Dresdener Hausgerät Preisbuch 1906*. Dresden, 1906.

———. “Die Bedeutung der 3. Deutschen Kunstgewerbe-Ausstellung.” *Leipziger Bauzeitung* (April 19, 1906), pp. 155–56.

———. “Die Raumverteilung des Landhauses.” *Der Tag*, March 31, 1906, pp. 1–3.

———. “Heutiger Stand des kunstgewerblichen Schulwesens in Preussen.” In *Nachrichten über die Preussischen Kunstgewerbeschulen: Zusammengestellt gelegentlich der mit der 3. Deutschen Kunstgewerbeausstellung in Dresden 1906 Verbundenen Ausstellung Preussische Kunstgewerbeschulen*. Königliches Preussisches Ministerium für Handel und Gewerbe, 18–47. Berlin: Julius Sittenfeld, 1906.

———. "Die Bedeutung des Kunstgewerbes." *Dekorative Kunst* 15 (1907): 184, 190.

———. *Kunstgewerbe und Architektur*. Jena: Eugen Diederichs, 1907.

———. *Landhaus und Garten: Beispiele neuzeitlicher Landhäuser nebst Grundrissen, Innenräumen und Gärten*. München: F. Bruckmann, 1907.

———. *Die Einheit der Architektur: Betrachtungen über Baukunst, Ingenieurbau und Kunstgewerbe*. Berlin: Karl Curtius, 1908.

———. "Mein Haus in Nikolassee." *Deutsche Kunst und Dekoration* 12 (1908): 1–21.

———. "Wirtschaftsformen im Kunstgewerbe: Vortrag, Gehalten am 30. Januar 1908 in der volkswirtschaftlichen Gesellschaft in Berlin." *Volkswirtschaftlichen Zeitfragen, Vorträge, und Abhandlungen* 30, 233 (1908): 3–31.

———. "Zur architektonischen Lage." *Neudeutsche Bauzeitung* 5 (1909): 1.

———. *Dekorative Kunst* 14 (Oktober 1910): 1–24.

———. "Landhaus Herm. Freudenberg in Nikolassee, Landhaus Bloch in Nikolassee, Haus Breul in Grunewald, Haus Dr. Soetbeer in Nikolassee, Haus Neuhaus in Dahlem." *Dekorative Kunst* 14 (Sonderdruck) (1910): 1–24.

———. *Landhaus und Garten: Beispiele neuzeitlicher Landhäuser nebst Grundrissen, Innenräumen und Gärten*. 2. Auflage. München: F. Bruckmann, 1910.

———. *Landhaus und Garten: Beispiele neuzeitlicher Landhäuser nebst Grundrissen, Innenräumen und Gärten*. 4. Auflage. München: F. Bruckmann, 1910.

———. *Landhäuser von Hermann Muthesius: Abbildungen und Pläne Ausgeführter Bauten mit Erläuterungen des Architekten*. München: F. Bruckmann, 1912.

———. "Wo Stehen Wir?" Vortrag auf der 4. Jahresversammlung des Deutschen Werkbundes in Dresden 1911. *Jahrbuch des Deutschen Werkbundes* (1912): 11–26.

———. "Das Formproblem im Ingenieur-Bau." *Jahrbuch des Deutschen Werkbundes* (1913): 23–32.

———. "Die Neuere Architektonische Bewegung in Deutschland." *Dokumente des Fortschritts* (März 1913): 183–88.

———. "Die Bedeutung der Gardenstadtbewegung." In *Die Bedeutung der Gartenstadtbewegung: Vier Vorträge in Gegenwart der Frau Kronprinzessin*, 1–16. Leipzig und Paris: Renaissance-Verlag Robert Federn, 1914.

———. *Die Werkbundarbeit der Zukunft und Aussprache darüber*. Jena: Eugen Diederichs, 1914.

———. *Der Deutsche nach dem Kriege*. In "Weltkultur und Weltpolitik: Deutsche und österreichische Schriftenfolge," series ed. Ernst Jäckh-Berlin and Institut für Kulturforschung-Wien. Munich:

F. Bruckmann, 1915 (2nd ed. published 1916).

———. "Die mechanische Seidenweberei Michels & Cie. in Nowawes bei Potsdam." *DK* 19 (1916): 190–95.

———. *Die Zukunft der Deutschen Form*. In "Der Deutsche Krieg: Politische Flugschriften," Nr. 50, series ed., Ernst Jäckh. Stuttgart, Berlin: Deutsche Verlags-Anstalt, 1916.

———. *Handarbeit und Massenerzeugnis*, Technische Abende im Zentralinstitut für Erziehung und Unterricht, Nr. 4. Berlin: 1917.

———. *Wie baue ich mein Haus*. München: F. Bruckmann, 1917.

———. *Kleinhaus und Kleinsiedlung*. München: F. Bruckmann, 1918 (2nd ed. published 1920).

———. "Soll die kunstgewerbliche Erziehung zukünftig den Akademien übertragen werden?" *Die Woche* (May 18, 1918): 489–91.

———. *Kann ich auch jetzt noch mein Haus bauen?* München: F. Bruckmann, 1920.

———. "Die Kunstgewerbe- und Handwerkerschulen." In *Kunstgewerbe: Ein Bericht über Entwicklung und Tätigkeit der Handwerker- und Kunstgewerbeschulen in Preußen*, edited by Bund der Kunstgewerbeschulmänner, 1–10. Berlin: Ernst Wasmuth, 1922.

———. *Landhäuser von Hermann Muthesius: Ausgeführte Bauten mit Grundrissen, Gartenplänen und Erläuterungen*. 2. Auflage. München: F. Bruckmann, 1922.

———. "Die neue Bauweise." *Die Baugilde* 9 (1927): 1284–86.

———. "Die neuere Entwicklung des kunstgewerblichen Gedankens und ihr Einfluss auf die Schulen." *Zeitschrift für Berufs- und Fachschulwesen*, Jg. 43 (1928), pp. 1–3.

———. *The English House*. Translated by Janet Seligman. New York: Rizzoli, 1979.

———. *Style-Architecture and Building-Art: Transformations of Architecture in the Nineteenth Century and its Present Condition*. Translated by Stanford Anderson. Santa Monica, Calif.: Getty Center for Arts and Humanities, 1994.

Muthesius, Stefan. *Das englische Vorbild: Eine Studie zu den deutschen Reformbewegungen in Architektur, Wohnbau und Kunstgewerbe im späteren 19. Jahrhundert*. München: Prestel, 1974.

———. "Handwerk/Kunsthhandwerk." *Journal of Design History* 11 (1998): 85–95.

———. "The 'altdeutsche' zimmer, or Cosiness in Plain Pine: An 1870s Contribution to the Definition of Interior Design." *Journal of Design History* 16 (2003): 269–90.

Naumann, Friedrich. *Mitteleuropa*. Berlin: Verlag Georg Bremer, 1915.

———. *Neudeutsche Wirtschaftspolitik*. Berlin: Fortschritt, 1911.

———. Werke. 6 vols. Köln: Westdeutscher Verlag, 1964.

Naylor, Gillian. *The Arts and Crafts Movement: A Study of Sources, Ideals, and Influence on Design Theory*. London: Studio Vista, 1971.

———. *The Bauhaus Reassessed: Sources and Design Theory*. New York: E. P. Dutton, 1985.

Nerdinger, Winfried, ed. *Richard Riemerschmid: Vom Jugendstil zum Werkbund*. München: Prestel Verlag, 1982.

———. *Walter Gropius*. Berlin: Gebr. Mann Verlag, 1985.

———. "Theodor Fischer." *Architectural Review* 180 (November 1986): 61–65.

———. "Le Corbusier und Deutschland: Genesis und Wirkungsgeschichte eines Konflikts, 1910–1933." *Arch+* 20 (August 1987): 80–86.

———. *Theodor Fischer: Architekt und Städtebauer*. München: Ernst & Sohn, 1988.

"Neue Landesgewerbeamt, Das." *Berliner Tageblatt*, January 11, 1905, p. 27.

"Neue Landesgewerbeamt, Das." *Kölnische Zeitung*, January 12, 1905, p. 26.

"Neue Lehrwerkstätten." *Hohe Warte*, II. Jg. Nr.7 (1905): 175.

Neumeyer, Fritz. *The Artless Word: Mies van der Rohe and the Building Art*. Translated by Mark Jarzombek. Cambridge, Mass.: MIT Press, 1991.

Nichols, J. Alden. *Germany after Bismarck: The Caprivi Era, 1890–1914*. Cambridge: Harvard University Press, 1958.

Nielsen, Astrid, ed. *Jugendstil in Dresden: Aufbruch in die Moderne*. Wolfratshausen: Edition Minerva, 1999.

Niemeyer, Wilhelm. "Die Arbeiten der Kunstgewerbeschule Düsseldorf." *Dekorative Kunst*, Bd. 14 (1906): 167–76.

Niggl, Reto. *Eckart Muthesius: Der Palast des Maharadschas in Indore, Architektur und Interieur*. Stuttgart: Arnoldsche Verlag, 1996.

Nipperdey, Thomas. *Deutsche Geschichte, 1866–1918, Zweiter Band: Machtstaat vor der Demokratie*. Munich: C.H. Beck, 1992.

Nuttgers, Patrick, gen. ed. *Mackintosh & His Contemporaries in Europe and America*. London: John Murray, 1988.

Obrist, Hermann. "Die Zukunft unserer Architektur." *DK* 8 (1901): 329–49.

Oechslin, Werner. "Politisches, allzu Politisches . . .: 'Nietzschelinge,' der 'Wille zur Kunst,' und der deutsche Werkbund vor 1914." In *Architektur als politische Kultur: Philosophia Practica*, edited by Hermann Hipp und Ernst Seidl, 151–90. Berlin: Dietrich Reimer Verlag, 1996.

———. *Otto Wagner, Adolf Loos, and the Road to Modern Architecture*. Translated by Lynnette Widder. Cambridge, UK: Cambridge University Press, 2002.

Ogata, Amy F. *Art Nouveau and the Social Vision for Modern Living: Belgian Artists in a European Context*. Cambridge, UK: Cambridge University Press, 2001.

O'Neal, William Bainter, ed. *Walter Gropius*. American Association of Architectural Bibliographers papers, vol. 9 Charlottesville: The University Press of Virginia, 1972.

Osborn, Max. *Berlin 1870–1929: Der Aufstieg zur Weltstadt*. Berlin: Gebr. Mann Verlag, 1994.

Ostendorf, Friedrich. *Sechs Bücher von Bauen: Theorie des architektonischen Entwerfens*, Bd. 1–6. Berlin: 1913–1919.

Otto, Christian. "Modern Environment and Historical Continuity: The Heimatschutz Discourse in Germany." *Art Journal* 43, Nr. 2 (Summer 1983): 148–57.

Paret, Peter. *The Berlin Secession: Modernism and its Enemies in Imperial Germany*. Cambridge, Mass.: Harvard University Press, 1980.

Parker, Barry, and Raymond Unwin. *The Art of Building a Home*. London: Longmans, Green & Co., 1901.

Paul, Bruno. "Unzeitgemässe Notwendigkeiten." *DKuD* 35 (1914–15): 185–88.

———. *Erziehung der Künstler an staatlichen Schulen*. Berlin: n.p., 1919.

Pehnt, Wolfgang. *Expressionist Architecture*. Translated by J. A. Underwood and Edith Küstner. London: Thames and Hudson, 1973.

Pepper, Simon. "The Garden City Legacy." *The Architectural Review* 43 (June 1978): 321–24.

Peschken, Goerd. *Baugeschichte politisch: Schinkel, Stadt Berlin, preussische Schlösser*. Bauwelt Fundamente 96. Braunschweig, Wiesbaden: Vieweg, 1993.

Petsch-Bahr, Wiltrud. "Anmerkungen zu dem Briefwechsel von Herman Muthesius aus dem Jahren 1896 bis 1909." In *Hermann Muthesius, 1861–1927*, edited by Sonja Günther and Julius Posener. Ausstellung in der Akademie der Künste von 11. Dezember bis 22, Januar, 1978, 23–28. Berlin: Akademie der Künste, 1978.

———. "Hermann Muthesius." In *Baumeister, Architekten, Stadtplaner: Biographien zur baulichen Entwicklung Berlins*, edited by Wolfgang Ribbe and Wolfgang Schaeche, 321–40. Berlin: Stapp Verlag, 1987.

Pevsner, Nikolaus. *Pioneers of the Modern Movement from William Morris to Walter Gropius*. London: Faber and Faber, 1936.

Pfister, Rudolf. *Theodor Fischer: Leben und Wirken eines deutschen Baumeisters*. Munich: Verlag Georg D. W. Callwey, 1968.

Physick, John. *The Victoria and Albert Museum: The History of its Building*. Oxford: Phaidon, 1982.

Platz, Gustav Adolph. *Die Baukunst der Neuesten Zeit*. Berlin: Propylaen-Verlag, 1927.

Posener, Julius. "Hermann Muthesius." *Baugilde* 13, 21 (November 1931): 1639–43.

———. *Anfänge des Funktionalismus: Vom Arts and Crafts zum Deutschen Werkbund*. Bauwelt Fundamente Nr.11. Frankfurt und Berlin: Ullstein, 1964.

———. "Muthesius als Architekt." *Werkbundarchiv* I. Berlin: Werkbundarchiv, 1972.

———. "Ein Attentat: Es geht um Muthesius' Haus Freudenberg in Berlin-Nikolassee." *Bauwelt* v. 16 64 Jg. (April 30, 1973): 675–66.

———. "Vorortgründungen." *ARCH+*, 7. Jg. (1975): 1–10.

———. *Berlin auf dem Wege zu einer neuen Architektur: Das Zeitalter Wilhelms II*. München: Prestel, 1979.

———. "Vorlesungen zur Geschichte der Neuen Architektur: Das Zeitalter Wilhelms des Zweiten." *Arch+* 39 (October 1981).

———. *Hans Poelzig: Reflections on His Life and Work*. Translated by Christine Charlesworth. New York: Architectural History Foundation, 1992.

Preiss, Achim, and Klaus-Jürgen Winkler, eds. *Weimarer Konzepte: Die Kunst- und Bauhochschule 1860–1995*. Weimar: VDG, 1996.

Purdom, C. B. *The Garden City: A Study in the Development of a Modern Town*. New York: Garland, 1985.

Rach, Hans-Jürgen. *Die Dörfer in Berlin: ein Handbuch der ehemahligen Landgemeinden im Staatgebiet von Berlin*. Berlin: Verlag für Bauwesen, 1988.

Rasche, Adelheid. "Peter Jessen, der Berliner Verein Moden-Museum und der Verband der deutschen Mode-Industrie, 1916 bis 1925." *Waffen- und Kostümkunde* 37 (1995): 65–92.

Reichshandbuch der Deutschen Gesellschaft. 2 vols. Berlin: Deutscher Wirtschaftsverlag, 1930.

Repp, Kevin. *Reformers, Critics, and the Paths of German Modernity: Anti-Politics and of the Search for Alternatives, 1890–1914*. Cambridge, Mass.: Harvard University Press, 2000.

Retallack, James. *Germany in the Age of Kaiser Wilhelm II*. New York: St. Martin's Press, 1996.

Reuleaux, Franz. *Briefe aus Philadelphia*. Braunschweig: 1877.

Riemerschmid, Richard. "Das Arbeiterwohnhaus." *Hohe Warte* 3 (1906–07): 141.

———. "Künstlerische Erziehungsfragen I." In *Flugschriften des Münchener Bundes*, Nr. 1. Munich: Münchener Bund, 1917.

———. "Künstlerische Erziehungsfragen II." In *Flugschriften des Münchener Bundes*, Nr. 5. Munich: Münchener Bund, 1919.

Riley, Terence, and Barry Bergdoll, eds. *Mies in Berlin*. New York: Museum of Modern Art, 2001.

Ringer, Fritz K. *The Decline of the German Mandarins: The German Academic Community, 1890–1933*. Cambridge, Mass.: Harvard University Press, 1969.

Roberts, A. R. N., ed. *William Richard Lethaby, 1857–1931*. London: London Country Council Central School of Arts and Crafts, 1957.

Röder, Sabine, and Gerhard Storck, eds. *Deutsches Museum für Kunst in Handel und Gewerbe: Moderne Formgebung 1900–1914*. Krefeld: Kaiser Wilhelm Museum, 1997.

Röhl, John C. G. *The Kaiser and His Court: Wilhelm II and the Government of Germany*. Translated by Terence F. Cole. Cambridge, UK: Cambridge University Press, 1994.

Röhl, John C. G., and Sombart, Nicolaus, eds. *Kaiser Wilhelm II: New Interpretations*. Cambridge, UK: Cambridge University Press, 1982.

Roth, Fedor. *Hermann Muthesius und die Idee der harmonischen Kultur*. Berlin: Gebr. Mann, 2001.

Rothkirch-Trach, Johann D. A. Ferdinand Graf. *Die Unterrichtsanstalt des Kunstgewerbemuseums in Berlin zwischen 1866 und 1933: Eine Studie zur Kunstentwicklung in Deutschland*. Ph.D. dissertation, Friedrich-Wilhelm University, Bonn, 1984.

Rubens, Godfrey. *William Richard Lethaby: His Life and Work, 1857–1931*. London: The Architectural Press, 1986.

Ruskin, John. *The Stones of Venice*. London: Smith, Elder & Co., 1851–53.

———. *The Stones of Venice*. 3 vols. Boston: Dana Estes & Co., 1913.

———. *The Seven Lamps of Architecture*. New York: First Noonday Press, 1961. (Originally published in 1849.)

Saint, Andrew. *Richard Norman Shaw*. New Haven, Conn.: Yale University Press, 1976.

———. *The Image of the Architect*. New Haven, Conn.: Yale University Press, 1983.

Sarazin, Otto. "Attachirung von Bautechnikern an einzelne diplomatische Vertretungen im Auslande." *CdB* 2 (1882): 22–23.

Sarazin, Otto, and Hermann Eggert. "An unsere Leser." *CdB* (1881): 1–2.

Scheffler, Karl. *Der Architekt*. Frankfurt a. M.: Rutten & Leoning, 1907.

———. *Moderne Baukunst*. 2. Auflage. Berlin: Julius Bard, 1907.

———. "Hermann Muthesius." *Kunst und Künstler* 8 (Oktober 1909): 43–57.

―――. *Berlin: ein Stadtschicksal.* 2. Auflage. Berlin: E. Reiss, 1910.

―――. *Lesebuch aus dem Handwerk.* Berlin: P. List Verlag, 1942.

―――. *Die Fetten und die Mageren Jahre: Ein Arbeits- und Lebensbericht.* München: Paul List Verlag, 1946.

Schivelbusch, Wolfgang. *The Railway Journey: Trains and Travel in the 19th Century.* Translated by Anselm Hollo. New York: Urizen, 1979.

Schmalenbach, Fritz. *Jugendstil: Ein Beitrag zu Theorie und Geschichte der Flächenkunst.* Würzburg: Verlag Konrad Triltsch, 1935.

Schneider, Katja. *Burg Giebichenstein: Die Kunstgewerbeschule unter Leitung von Paul Thiersch und Gerhard Marcks 1915 bis 1933.* Weinheim: VCH Verlag, 1992.

Schneider, Uwe. *Hermann Muthesius und die Reformdiskussion in der Gartenarchitektur des frühen 20. Jahrhunderts.* Worms: Wernersche Verlagsgesellschaft, 2000.

Schollmeier, Axel. *Gartenstädte in Deutschland: Ihre Geschichte, städtebauliche Entwicklung und Architektur zu Beginn des 20. Jahrhunderts.* Münster: Lit Verlag 1990.

Schorske, Carl. *Germany Social Democracy, 1905–1917: The Development of the Great Schism.* Cambridge, Mass.: Harvard University Press, 1955.

Schuchard, Jutta. *Carl Schäfer, 1844–1908: Leben und Werk des Architekten der Neugotik.* München: Prestel, 1979.

Schultze, Friedrich. "Hermann Muthesius†." *CdB* 47 (November 9, 1927): 573–74.

Schultze-Naumburg, Paul. *Kulturarbeiten.* 9 vols. Munich: G. D. W. Callwey, 1902–1917.

Schumacher, Fritz. *Streifzüge eines Architekten: Gesammelte Aufsätze.* Jena: Eugen Diederichs, 1907.

―――. *Stufen des Lebens: Erinnerungen eines Baumeisters.* Stuttgart und Berlin: Deutsche Verlags-Anstalt, 1935.

Schur, Ernst. "Malerei, Plastik, Architektur auf den Grossen Berliner Kunstausstellung 1907." *Berlinerarchitekturwelt* 10 (1907): 124–28.

―――. "Drei Landhäuser von Hermann Muthesius (Haus von Velscn, Haus Stave, Haus Bernhard)." *Dekorative Kunst* 13 (1909): 1–24.

Schuster, Peter-Klaus, ed. *Peter Behrens und Nürnberg, Geschmackswandel in Deutschland: Historismus, Jugendstil und die Anfänge der Industriereform.* Munich: Prestel, 1980.

Schwartz, Frederic J. *The Werkbund: Design Theory and Mass Culture before the First World War.* New Haven, Conn.: Yale University Press, 1996.

Schwarzer, Mitchell. *German Architectural Theory and the Search for Modern Identity.* New York: Cambridge University Press, 1995.

Scully, Vincent. *The Shingle Style and the Stick Style: Architectural Theory and Design from Richardson to the Origins of Wright.* New Haven, Conn.: Yale University Press, 1971.

Seeman, Artur, ed. *Deutsche Kunstgewerbe-Zeichner: Ein Addressbuch Deutscher Künstler die sich mit Entwerfen Kunstgewerblicher Gegenstände Befassen.* Leipzig: Verlag von A. Seeman, 1893.

Sekler, Eduard F. *Josef Hoffmann: The Architectural Work.* Princeton: Princeton University Press, 1985.

Sembach, Klaus-Jürgen. *August Endell: Der Architekt des Photoateliers Elvira, 1871–1925.* Munich: Stuck Jugendstil Verein, 1977.

―――. *Henry van de Velde.* Translated by Michael Robinson. New York: Rizzoli, 1989.

Semper, Gottfried. *Style in the Technical and Tectonic Arts, or, Practical Aesthetics.* Los Angeles: Getty Research Institute, 2004.

Sharp, Dennis, ed. *Glass Architecture by Paul Scheerbart and Alpine Architecture by Bruno Taut.* New York: Praeger, 1972.

Siepmann, Eckhard, and Angelika Thiekötter, eds. *Hermann Muthesius im Werkbund-Archiv.* Katalog einer Ausstellung des Werkbund-Archivs im Martin Gropius-Bau vom 11. Oktober bis 11. November 1990. Berlin: Museumspädagogischer Dienst Berlin, 1990.

Simon, Oskar. *Die Fachausbildung des preussichen Gewerbe- und Handelsstandes im 18. und 19. Jahrhundert.* Berlin: Wasmuth, 1902.

Spengler, Oswald. *The Decline of the West.* 2 vols. Translated by Charles Francis Atkinson. New York: Alfred A. Knopf, 1926.

Sperber, Jonathan. "Bürger, Bürgertum, Bürgerlichkeit, Bürgerliche Gesellschaft: Studies of the German (Upper) Middle Class and Its Sociocultural World." *Journal of Modern History* 69 (June 1997): 271–97.

Stahl, Fritz. "Alfred Messel!" *Berliner Architekturwelt* 9 (Sonderheft, 1911).

Stalder, Laurent. "'In Wort und Bild': Bemerkungen zum Mappenwerk *Die englische Baukunst der Gegenwart* von Hermann Muthesius." *Scholion* 1 (2002): 123–32.

―――. "John Ruskin als Erzieher: Muthesius, England, und die neue nationale Tradition." In *Studien und Texte zur Geschichte der Architekturtheorie: Akten des Colloquiums "John Ruskin: Werk und Wirkung,"* edited by Werner Oechslin, 158–69. Zürich: GTA Verlag, 2002.

―――. *Wie man ein Haus baut: Hermann Muthesius (1861–1927) – Das Landhaus als*

Kulturgeschichtlicher Entwurf. Ph.D. dissertation, ETH-Zürich, 2002.

Stamp, Gavin. *The English House 1860–1914: The Flowering of English Domestic Architecture*. London: Faber & Faber, 1986.

Stansky, Peter. *William Morris, C. R. Ashbee, and the Arts and Crafts*. London: Nine Elms Press, 1984.

———. *Redesigning the World: William Morris, the 1880s, and the Arts and Crafts*. Princeton: Princeton University Press, 1985.

Stegmann, Dirk. *Die Erben Bismarcks, Parteien und Verbände in der Spätphase Wilhelminischen Deutschlands: Sammlungspolitik 1897–1918*. Köln: Kiepenheuer & Witsch, 1970.

Stern, Fritz. *The Politics of Cultural Despair: A Study in the Rise of Germanic Ideology*. Berkeley: University of California Press, 1961.

———. *Einstein's German World*. Princeton: Princeton University Press, 1999.

Stern, Norbert. *Die Weltpolitik der Weltmode*. In "Der Deutsche Krieg: Politische Flugschriften," Nr. 30–31, edited by Ernst Jäckh. Stuttgart, Berlin: Deutsche Verlags-Anstalt, 1916.

Stein, Laurie A., and Irmela Franzke. "German Design and National Identity 1890–1914." In *Designing Modernity: The Arts of Reform and Persuasion, 1885–1945*, edited by Wendy Kaplan, 49–78. New York: Thames and Hudson, 1995.

Strecker, Karl, ed. *Verhandlungen des Ausschusses für Einheiten und Formelgrössen in den Jahren 1907 bis 1914*. Berlin: Julius Springer Verlag, 1914.

Streiter, Richard. *Ausgewählte Schriften zur Aesthetik und Kunst-Geschichte*. Franz von Reber and Emil Sulger-Ebbing, ed. Munich: Delphin, 1913.

Stresemann, Gustav. *Englands Wirtschaftskrieg gegen Deutschland*. In "Der Deutsche Krieg: Politische Flugschriften," Nr. 36, edited by Ernst Jäckh. Stuttgart, Berlin: Deutsche Verlags-Anstalt, 1916.

Stuart, John A. *The Gray Cloth: Paul Scheerbart's Novel on Glass Architecture*. Translated by John A. Stuart. Cambridge, Mass.: MIT Press, 2001.

Stubmann, Peter. "Kunstgewerbepolitik." *Dekorative Kunst*, Bd. VI (1903): 214–26.

Stürmer, Michael, ed. *Das kaiserliche Deutschland: Politik und Gesellschaft, 1870–1918*. Düsseldorf: Droste Verlag, 1970.

Sutcliffe, Anthony, ed. *The Rise of Modern Urban Planning*. New York: St. Martin's Press, 1980.

———. *Towards the Planned City: Germany, Britain, the United States and France, 1780–1914*. Oxford: Basil Blackwell, 1981.

Taut, Bruno. *Alpine Architektur*. Vienna: Hagen, 1919.

———. *Ein Architektur-Programm*. Flugschriften des Arbeitsrates für Kunst, 2nd ed. Berlin: Stephan Geibel & Co., 1919.

———. *Die Neue Baukunst in Europa und Amerika*. Stuttgart: Julius Hoffmann Verlag, 1929.

Tessenow, Heinrich. *Hausbau und dergleichen*. Berlin: Cassirer, 1916.

Thiekötter, Angelika et al., eds. *Kristallisation, Splitterungen: Bruno Tauts Glashaus*. Basel: Birkhäuser Verlag, 1993.

Thiersch, Heinz, ed. *Wir Fingen Einfach An: Arbeiten und Aufsätze von Freunden und Schülern um Richard Riemerschmid*. München: Richard Pflaum Verlag, 1953.

Tipton, Frank B. Jr. *Regional Variations in the Economic Development of Germany during the Nineteenth Century*. Middletown: Weslyan University Press, 1976.

Tönnies, Ferdinand. *Gemeinschaft und Gesellschaft: Grundbegriffe der reinen Soziologie* Leipzig: 1887. Translated as *Community and Society* by Charles P. Loomis. East Lansing: Michigan State University Press, 1957.

Topp, Leslie. "An Architecture for Modern Nerves: Josef Hoffmann's Purkersdorf Sanatorium." *JSAH* 56, Nr. 4 (December 1997): 414–37.

Trommler, Frank. "The Creation of a Culture of Sachlichkeit." In *Society, Culture and the State in Germany, 1870–1930*, edited by Geoff Eley, 481–82. Ann Arbor: University of Michigan Press, 1996.

Troy, Nancy J. *Modernism and the Decorative Arts in France: Art Nouveau to Le Corbusier*. New Haven, Conn.: Yale University Press, 1991.

Trumpa, Kurt. *Zehlendorf in der Kaiserzeit: Vom Dorf zum Vorort*. Berlin: Grundkreditbank EG, 1985.

Ullman, Hans-Peter. *Der Bund der Industriellen: Organisation, Einfluß und Politik klein- und mittelbetrieblicher Industrieller im Deutschen Kaiserreich 1895–1914*. Göttingen: Vandenhoeck & Ruprecht, 1976.

"Unterricht an Kunstgewerbeschulen." *Dekorative Kunst*, Bd. XIII (1905): 379–80.

Unwin, Raymond. *Town Planning in Practice: An Introduction to the Art of Designing Cities and Suburbs*, 2nd ed. London: T. Fischer Unwin, 1911.

Vallance, Aymer. *William Morris: His Art, his Writings, and his Public Life*. London: Studio Editions, 1986.

van de Velde, Henry. *Kunstgewerbliche Laienpredigten*, 2 vols. Leipzig: Hermann Seemann Nachfolger, 1902.

———. *Vom Neuen Stil*. Leipzig: Insel, 1907.

———. *Zum Neuen Stil*. Munich: R. Piper, 1955.

Verein Deutscher Ingenieure. *Die Deutschen Industrienormen*. Berlin: Verein Deutscher Ingenieure, 1919.

Voigt, Wolfgang. "The Garden City As Eugenic Utopia." *Planning Perspectives* 4 (1989): 295–312.

Volkov, Shulamit. *The Rise of Popular Anti-Modernism in Germany: The Urban Master Artisans, 1873–1896*. Princeton: Princeton University Press, 1978.

von Pechmann, Günter. *Die Qualitätsarbeit: Ein Handbuch für Industrielle, Kaufleute, Gewerbepolitiker*. Frankfurt: Frankfurter Societäts-Druckerei, 1924.

Waentig, Heinrich. *Wirtschaft und Kunst: Eine Untersuchung über Geschichte und Theorie der Modernen Kunstgewerbebewegung*. Jena: Gustav Fischer, 1909.

Waetzoldt, Wilhelm. "Die Entwicklung des kunstgewerblichen Unterrichtswesens in Preussen." *Deutsche Rundschau* 176 (1918): 228–45; 368–80.

Wagner, Martin. "Gartenstadthäuser." *Neudeutsche Bauzeitung* 6 (1910): 84.

Wahl, Volker, and Ute Ackermann, eds. *Die Meisterratsprotokolle des Staatlichen Bauhauses Weimar, 1919 bis 1925*. Veröffentlichungen aus thüringischen Staatsarchiven Band 6. Weimar: Verlag Hermann Böhlaus Nachfolger, 2001.

Walker, Mack. *German Home Towns: Community, Estate, General Estate, 1648–1871*. Ithaca: Cornell University Press, 1971.

Walther, Heidrun. *Theodor Adolf von Möller, 1840–1925: Lebensbild eines westfälischen Industriellen*. Neustadt an der Aisch: Verlag Degener & Co., 1958.

Wallot, J., ed. *Verhandlungen des Ausschusses für Einheiten und Formelgrossen in den Jahren 1907 bis 1927*. Berlin: Verlag Julius Springer, 1928.

Ward, Janet. *Weimar Surfaces: Urban Visual Culture in 1920s Germany*. Berkeley: University of California Press, 2001.

Wehler, Hans-Ulrich. *The German Empire, 1871–1918*. Translated by Kim Traynor. Dover, NH: Berg, 1985.

———. *Deutsche Gesellschaftsgeschichte. Band 3: Von der "Deutschen Doppelrevolution" bis zum Beginn des Ersten Weltkrieges, 1849–1914*. München: C.H, Beck, 1995.

Wernecke, Klaus. *Die Wille zur Weltgeltung: Aussenpolitik und Öffentlichkeit im Kaiserreich am Vorabend des Ersten Weltkrieges*. Dusseldorf: Droste Verlag, 1970.

Westheim, Paul. "Krieg und Kunstgewerbe." *Sozialistische Monatshefte* 21 (January 1915): 60–62.

Whyte, Iain Boyd. *Bruno Taut and the Architecture of Activism*. Cambridge, UK: Cambridge University Press, 1982.

Wichmann, Hans. *Aufbruch zum neuen Wohnen: Deutsche Werkstätten und WK-Verband, Ihr Beitrag zur Kultur unseres Jahrhunderts*. Basel: Birkhäuser, 1978.

Wichmann, Siegfried. *Hermann Obrist: Wegbereiter der Moderne*. Munich: Villa Stück/Karl M. Lipp, 1968.

Wick, Rainer K., ed. *Ist die Bauhaus-Pädagogik aktuell?* Köln: Verlag der Buchhandlung Walter König, 1985.

———. *Teaching at the Bauhaus*. Ostfildern-Ruit, Germany: Hatje Cantz Verlag, 2000.

Wiener, Martin J. *English Culture and the Decline of the Industrial Spirit, 1850–1980*. Cambridge, UK: Cambridge University Press, 1981.

Wietek, Gerd, ed. *Deutsche Künstlerkolonien und Künstlerorte*. München: Verlag K. Thiemig, 1976.

Wigley, Mark. *White Walls, Designer Dresses: The Fashioning of Modern Architecture*. Cambridge, Mass.: MIT Press, 1995.

Wilhelm, Karen. *Walter Gropius: Industriearchitekt*. Braunschweig/Wiesbaden: Friedr. Veiweg & Sohn, 1983.

Willett, John. *Art and Politics in the Weimar: The New Sobriety, 1917–1933*. New York: Pantheon Books, 1978.

Willman, Anni. *Der gelernte König, Wilhelm II Von Württemberg: Ein Porträt in Geschichten*. Stuttgart DRW-Verlag, 1993.

Windsor, Alan. *Peter Behrens: Architect and Designer*. New York: Watson-Guptill, 1981.

Wingler, Hans M. *Das Bauhaus 1919–1933: Weimar, Dessau, Berlin*. Bramsche: Verlag Gebr. Rasch, 1962.

———, ed., *Kunstschulreform 1900–1933*. Berlin: Gebr. Mann, 1977.

Winkler, Heinrich A. *Mittelstand, Demokratie, und Nationalsozialismus*. Köln: Verlag Kiepenheuer & Witsch, 1972.

Wohl, Anthony S. *The Eternal Slum*. Montreal: McGill-Queen University Press, 1977.

"Wohnhaus auf dem Lande, Das." *Baugewerks-Zeitung* 41 (November 24, 1909): 971–72.

"Wohnhaus von Velsen in Zehlendorf-Beeren-strasse." *Blätter für Architektur und Kunsthandwerk* (Juli 23, 1910): 25–26.

Wright, Gwendolyn. *Moralism and the Model Home: Domestic Architecture and Cultural Conflict in Chicago, 1873–1913*. Chicago: University of Chicago Press, 1980.

Zacharias, Thomas, ed. *Tradition und Widerspruch: 175 Jahre Kunstakademie München*. München: Prestel, 1985.

INDEX ∽